Mad Scientist in the Federal Courts

edited by
Joshua Warren

DEDICATION

to my science teachers

and to
Stevenson's "clock during a thunderstorm"

ACKNOWLEDGMENT

This book would not be possible without the continuing support of my wife, dog, family, friends, and teachers.

CONTENTS

EDITOR'S NOTE

The following are nearly full federal court opinions with minimal editing. Where excerpts have been removed the symbol #***# has been added or other notation of the omitted section. All other marks are from the original opinion text. As best as possible, footnotes retain their numbering but original page numbers have been removed. In each case the phrase "mad scientist" has been bolded and made larger for easier visibility. An index of select terms of interest is also provided at the end of this book.

FOREWARD

The idea of studying law by searching for a single term would usually be considered poor legal research. This book does not attempt to provide a complete picture of the law applicable to mad scientists. It is merely a record of literal mentions of "mad scientist" in federal court opinions through the year 2012.

This is both entertaining and informative. It can be amusing or humorous to read about mad scientist references in the courts and this exposure to reading legal procedure will improve the readers' general understanding of American jurisprudence. Look up words you don't understand.

Some of these cases are old. Subsequent court action may have overruled these cases or limit their holdings. There is no guarantee that the law presented in this book is still good law. After you read a case, search the internet and find out more.

These are all serious legal texts each with a serious legal purpose about real people in real situations. These texts are also appreciable as the high art of American legal civilization. This collection is gathered with the hope of finding entertainment in the written art of jurisprudential work.

INTRODUCTION TO READING COURT OPINIONS FOR FUN (and learning)

THE ONLY RULE is PATIENCE

If you are reading this then, you already know how to read. Go somewhere with appropriate lighting and a comfortable chair and read patiently. Mark unusual words and move on, and later use a legal dictionary and internet search engines to amplify your understanding. With patience you will learn to read more.

As you begin to read a case, notice the year and notice what branch of the federal court is writing the opinion. Identify the parties, what they are seeking, what prior legal actions have occurred. Or just jump right to any paragraph you want and start reading.

This book is designed to read cases. There is no over-reaching legal thesis and the cases are not individually summarized. These real cases are simply arranged with hopes of sparking interest in reading law. The goal is merely to enjoy the reading.

Reading law will improve your ability to read law.

As you read you may consider yourself as a law clerk and try to summarize the arguments and holdings of each opinion. This is good practice and any attempt to write (and re-write) a case summary will promote your thinking. But if you prefer, just sit under a tree and enjoy the writings of the U.S. Federal Courts.

These are all serious legal texts each with a serious legal purpose but they are also appreciable as the high art of American legal civilization. This collection is gathered with the hope of finding entertainment in these works of jurisprudential art.

INTRODUCTION TO STRUCTURE
of the U.S. FEDERAL COURTS

U.S. SUPREME COURT

U.S. COURT OF APPEALS
12 Circuit Courts of Appeals
1 U.S. Court of Appeals for the Federal Circuit

U.S. DISTRICT COURTS
94 Judicial Districts
U.S Bankruptcy Courts

U.S. COURT OF INTERNATIONAL TRADE
U.S. COURT OF FEDERAL CLAIMS

OTHER FEDERAL COURTS
Military Courts (Trial and Appellate)
Court of Veteran's Appeals
U.S. Tax Court
Federal administrative agencies and boards

for much more information about the structure and jurisdiction of the US
Courts see their website at UScourts.gov
http://www.uscourts.gov/EducationalResources/FederalCourtBasics.aspx

INTRODUCTION TO
MAD SCIENTIST
IN THE FEDERAL COURT

In these court opinions, "mad scientist" is used in context with the following associated words:

"Dr." "villians" "in white lab coats" "to be locked in a corner of a castle" "full of ideas, but flighty and strong-headed" "conjure up ridiculous questions" "concocting... in his basement" "conducted a series of genetic experiments on the Island" "experiment with a deprived man from the breadlines that transformed" " constructed a time machine".

"Described himself as (a mad scientist)"

"states that he wants to grow up to be a mad scientist"

"by his mere disagreement with their position, is therefore a mad scientist"

"saving the world from a mad scientist"

CHRONOLOGICAL
TABLE OF AUTHORITY

Mad Scientist
in the
Federal Courts

1
THE SUPERMAN CONNECTION

The first usage of "mad scientist" by the Federal Courts was in a 1950 case involving the intellectual property of the comic book character Superman. Superman is a comic book character originally created by Jerome Siegel and Joseph Shuster under contract with Detective Comics. The 1950 case involved the alleged infringement by publishers of the character Captain Marvel, a similar superhero. The decision of the court is that the Superman stories were copied but that the stories had not been properly marked as copyright material (in some of the syndicated publications) and so therefore the copyright had been abandoned.

NATIONAL COMICS PUBLICATIONS, Inc.

v.

FAWCETT PUBLICATIONS, Inc., et al.

UNITED STATES DISTRICT COURT FOR THE SOUTHERN DISTRICT OF NEW YORK

93 F. Supp. 349
April 10, 1950

Opinion by Judge Coxe

OPINION

This is an action against Fawcett Publications, Inc. (hereinafter referred to as 'Fawcett') and Republic Pictures Corporation and the latter's wholly-owned subsidiary, Republic Pictures, Inc. (both hereafter referred to as 'Republic'), for copyright infringement under the 1909 Copyright Act, as amended, 17 U.S.C.A. § 1 et seq., and for unfair competition. The action was instituted on September 5, 1941, by Detective Comics, Inc. (hereafter referred to as 'Detective') and by Superman, Inc.; they were later merged into National Comics Publications, Inc., which has been substituted as sole plaintiff. An amended complaint was filed in November 1945, but the action was not brought to trial until March 1948. Damages and an injunction are sought because of alleged infringements of the copyrights upon all the issues of two comic magazines published by Detective and Superman, respectively, viz., 'Action Comics' and 'Superman'. It is asserted by plaintiff that there was published in these magazines a large amount of original matter, including 'a variety and series of original cartoons, scenes, characters, incidents and pictorial delineations revolving principally about the figure and character of 'Superman'.'

The infringements alleged in the amended complaint are:
(1) The publication by Fawcett of two magazines, entitled 'Whiz Comics' and 'Captain Marvel Adventures', which contained 'a continuity of comic strips revolving about a principal character known as 'Captain Marvel'', which strips were copied from plaintiff's copyrighted material, and the publication by

Fawcett of additional magazines, entitled 'Captain Marvel, Jr.', 'Mary Marvel Comics'. 'WOW Comics', 'America's Greatest Comics' and 'Master Comics', likewise containing the continuous strip cartoon known as 'Captain Marvel'.

(2) The production and exhibition throughout the United States during the period of 1940-1941 by Republic of a motion picture serial photoplay entitled 'The Adventures of Captain Marvel'; and

(3) The manufacture and distribution, in connection with these magazines and the motion picture, of certain articles of merchandise, upon which the figure of 'Captain Marvel' was depicted, and which constituted unfair competition.

The principal defenses are non-infringement, that the copyrights are either invalid or have been abandoned, and absence of unfair competition. Republic also asks that, if it is found liable to plaintiff, it have judgment over against Fawcett for the amount thereof under its indemnity agreement with Fawcett.

The 'Action Comics' Magazine.

Detective, which, with its affiliated companies, had been engaged in publishing comic magazines, began the publication in June 1938 of a new monthly comic magazine, entitled 'Action Comics'. Each number contained 64 pages and sold for ten cents a copy. Publication was continued until the time of the trial. Each number was copyrighted in the name of Detective. The magazine contained several comic cartoon strips featuring different characters. A strip consists of a series of panels. The panels contain scenes and incidents revolving about a principal character and, in a so-called balloon, a catch-phrase, or a remark, or a description of the incident represented. Thus the strips may be called short stories in pictorial form.

The leading feature in each number was a comic cartoon strip or story which depicted the figure and actions of an athletic human being, a new character called 'Superman', with distinctive features and a distinctive type of costume, who was portrayed in various scenes and incidents as having and exercising superhuman qualities and being a blessing to mankind as an avenger of all evil, and as being in ordinary life one Clark Kent, a meek newspaper reporter wearing eye glasses. Jerome Siegel and Joseph Shuster, the authors and artists of the strips or stories, produced them under a contract with Detective.

The 'Superman' stories in the first six numbers of 'Action Comics', published from June to November 1938, were reprinted by Detective, with a 1939 copyright date, in Numbers 1 and 3 of the 'Superman' magazine, published in the summer and winter of 1939, respectively. Fawcett insists that this resulted in loss of the copyrights upon the stories. This would be so if it were not for the fact that these two numbers of 'Superman' magazine contained substantial new and original matter, in addition to the 'Superman' stories, which made them 'new works subject to copyright' under Section 6 of the Act. This section contained no provision as to the date of the copyright notice to be used with respect to such 'new works', but it did provide that 'the publication of any such new works shall not affect the force or validity of any subsisting copyright' upon the original works or 'be construed * * * to secure or extend copyright in such original works.'

Manifestly, publication of these two numbers of the 'Superman' magazine with a 1939 copyright date did not result in loss of the copyrights upon the stories originally published in 'Action Comics' with a 1938 date. See West Publishing Co. v. Edward Thompson Co., 2 Cir., 176 F. 833, 837; Adventures in Good Eating v. Best Places to Eat, 7 Cir., 131 F.2d 809, 813; Amdur, Copyright Law & Practice, Chap. XIV, § 29, pp. 495-497; Ball, Law of Copyright and Literary Property, § 76, pp. 173-174.

I find that all the numbers of 'Action Comics' have been properly copyrighted in the name of Detective and that the copyrights upon them, and the 'Superman' stories published in them, have not been lost as the result of republication in the 'Superman' magazine.

The 'Superman' Magazine.

In the spring of 1939, Detective began to publish quarterly another comic magazine, entitled 'Superman', which also contained 64 pages and sold for ten cents a copy. Publication of the magazine was continued until the time of the trial. The magazine was devoted exclusively to 'Superman', and its contents were almost entirely either reprints of 'Superman' stories previously published in 'Action Comics' or of 'Superman' stories previously published in newspapers under an agreement between Detective and The McClure Newspaper Syndicate (hereafter referred to as 'McClure'). The first four numbers were copyrighted by Detective. All subsequent numbers were copyrighted by Superman, Inc., which was not incorporated until October 1939. Both companies had the same officers and directors. Starting with Number 6, published in the fall of 1940, the magazine was charged to a bimonthly magazine.

It is contended by plaintiff that Superman, Inc. acquired the right to copyright these later numbers in its own name by virtue of an agreement between the two companies, dated January 18, 1940. By this agreement Detective appointed Superman, Inc., for the period ending March 31, 1945, its 'exclusive agent to exploit 'Superman', the trade-marks and copyrights and/or other rights therein in any manner whatsoever', except that Superman, Inc. should not have the right 'to print, publish or distribute any pictorial or textual sequence containing the likeness of 'Superman', other than through the magazine known as 'Superman'.' The agreement further provided that 'all copyrights, trade-marks and/or other rights with respect to 'Superman' now existing' should remain in Detective and continue to be owned by it, and that 'when any further copyrights, trade-marks * * * or other similar rights are required to carry out the terms of this agreement', they should be obtained by Detective in its own name and the ownership of such rights should remain in it. The agreement contained no provision requiring or authorizing Superman, Inc. to take out copyrights in its own name. Notwithstanding this, Numbers 5 and 6, published in May and August 1940, were copyrighted in the name of Superman, Inc. It seems to have been discovered about August 1940 that this might have been an error. At any rate, Detective wrote Superman, Inc. on August 14, 1940, ratifying and confirming the copyrighting by the latter in its own name of the 'Superman' magazine since January 18, 1940, and agreeing to the amendment of the agreement, as of January 18, 1940, so as to provide that further copyrights should be obtained by Superman, Inc. in its own name and be assigned to Detective upon demand or at the termination of the agreement. This letter could not, however, operate retroactively to validate the copyrights on Numbers 5 and 6. There was some testimony as to an oral modification, made prior to May 1940, of the January 1940 agreement, to the same effect as the August 1940 letter, but I do not credit it.

'Superman' magazine No. 12 was published with the following notice: 'Sept.-Oct. 1941, No. 12. Superman is published bi-monthly by Superman, Inc.., 480 Lexington Ave., New York, N.Y. * * * Entire contents copyrighted by Superman, Inc.' Fawcett's contention that this notice was not a sufficient compliance with the statute, in that the year of publication was omitted from the sentence 'Entire contents copyrighted by Superman, Inc.', cannot be sustained. It was a substantial compliance, and that was enough. Shapiro, Bernstein & Co. v. Jerry Vogel Music Co., 2 Cir., 161 F.2d 406, 409, certiorari denied 331 U.S. 820, 67 S.Ct. 1310, 91 L.Ed. 1837; Bentley v. Tibbals, 2 Cir., 223 F. 247, 253.

Nor can Fawcett's further contention be sustained that none of the copyrights upon the 'Superman' magazine taken out in the name of Superman, Inc. is valid. It is argued that Superman, Inc. never became the proprietor of any material for which such copyrights could be taken out by it, but was merely an 'exclusive agent'. But the agreement between it and Detective, as modified on August 14, 1940, expressly authorized it to take out copyrights upon the magazine in its own name. Such an agreement is lawful, and a copyright taken out in accordance therewith is valid. In fact, that is the only way by which the rights of the publisher can be protected. Superman, Inc. holds the legal title to the copyrights as trustee, both for itself as the publisher and for Detective as the legal owner of the copyrighted material. Quinn-Brown Publishing Corp. v. Chilton Co., Inc., D.C.S.D.N.Y., 15 F.Supp. 213.

I find that all the numbers of 'Superman' magazine have been properly copyrighted, either by Detective or by Superman, Inc., except Numbers 5 and 6, published in May and August 1940, and that the copyrights on these two numbers are invalid. This finding is not to be construed as validating copyrights on such strips or stories as were reprints of those previously published without proper copyright notice.

The Fawcett Magazines.

About October 1939, Fawcett, which had previously published only detective stories, began the work of preparing for the publication of a new monthly comic magazine, to be entitled 'Whiz Comics' and to sell for the same price as 'Action Comics'. The first number appeared in January 1940. Each number contained several comic cartoon strips or stories, featuring different characters, the principal one being entitled 'Captain Marvel', who was represented as a human being possessing superhuman attributes and as 'an avenger of evil', and who had a dual personality with one Billy Batson, a radio reporter. 'Captain Marvel' closely resembled 'Superman' in his athletic figure and in his costume, as well as in the superhuman feats performed.

In June 1940 Fawcett published a 'Special Edition Comics', another new monthly comic magazine, which, in the second number in February 1941, became 'Captain Marvel Adventures'. It sold for the same price as 'Action Comics'. Its contents were almost entirely cartoon strips or stories depicting the exploits of 'Captain Marvel'.

Fawcett continued to publish both these magazines until the time of the trial, despite a demand of Detective in June 1941 that it cease. The other Fawcett magazines need not be further considered, for they were similar in every way to 'Whiz Comics' and 'Captain Marvel Adventures', and plaintiff's evidence related chiefly to the first two magazines.

The Republic Motion Picture Photoplay.

On October 9, 1940, Fawcett entered into an agreement with Republic under which it granted to Republic the right to produce and exhibit a serial photoplay and to use in its production any of the characters, incidents and other material in the comic strips theretofore or thereafter published by it and entitled 'Captain Marvel', together with the names of the characters, and the words'Captain Marvel', either alone or in conjunction with other words, as a title for the picture. Fawcett also warranted that it was the sole originator, author and owner of the characters, incidents and other material in the 'Captain Marvel' strips, and that they had been duly copyrighted.

Thereafter Republic produced a serial motion picture photoplay, using the comic strips of 'Captain Marvel' which had appeared in 'Whiz Comics'. The title, as projected on the screen, was 'Republic Pictures Presents Adventures of Captain Marvel * * * . Material from Whiz Comics, Copyright 1940 and 1941, Fawcett Publications, Inc.' The picture was completed in February 1941 and was thereafter exhibited in many theatres in the United States, despite a notice to desist given by Detective in June 1941.

Originality.

The 'Superman' character and strips are clearly original. It was so held in Detective Comics v. Bruns Publications, 2 Cir., 111 F.2d 432, 433, an action for infringement of the copyrights upon the first eleven issues of 'Action Comics', and there is no evidence in the present case to support a contrary finding. The court there said: 'So far as the pictorial representations and verbal descriptions of 'Superman' are not a mere delineation of a benevolent Hercules, but embody an arrangement of incidents and literary expressions original with the author, they are proper subjects of copyright and susceptible of infringement because of the monopoly afforded by the act. * * * the complainant is not entitled to a monopoly of the mere character of a 'Superman' who is a blessing to mankind'.

Access.

Access to the 'Action Comics' and 'Superman' magazines by those employees of Fawcett who had to do with the creation, development and portrayal of the character of 'Captain Marvel' and the cartoon strips featuring him, and with the preparation and publication of the early issues of the 'Whiz Comics' magazine, is conceded.

Copying.

The evidence as to actual copying is conflicting. Plaintiff called some of the employees of Fawcett just referred to. They testified to instructions from their superiors to imitate the 'Superman' strips and the dialogue and script as closely as possible, and that they did so. Fawcett called the superiors, who denied having given any such instructions and denied any copying. An independent artist testified to admissions by Beck, Fawcett's chief artist, who drew the first 'Captain Marvel' cartoons, as to his having copied 'Superman'. Beck, however, denied having made any such admissions. Experts were called by both parties, who contradicted each other as to the significance of claimed similarities and dissimilarities between the portrayals of the two characters, their facial appearances, costumes, etc., and the superhuman feats performed by them. It would serve no useful purpose to recite in detail the conflicting testimony, for I am satisfied from all the evidence that there was actual copying.

Both 'Captain Marvel' and 'Superman' have the same athletic physique. Both have substantially the same clean-cut faces. Both wear the conventional regalia of the gymnast or circus acrobat- skin-tight uniforms, boots and a cape which is used in flying. The only real difference is in the color of their costumes, 'Superman's' being blue and 'captain Marvel's' red. The incredible feats, performed by both, such as leaping great distances, flying through the air, exhibitions of marvelous strength and speed, and imperviousness to bullets, shells, explosions, knives and poisons, are identical, and the settings in which the feats are performed are often closely similar. Substantially all of the feats performed by 'Superman' are later duplicated by 'Captain Marvel.' Identical phrases, expressions and dialogues are frequently found in the panels.

'Superman' is represented as a normal human being, a meek newspaper reporter wearing eye glasses (Clark Kent), who, by throwing off his regular clothes, appears in his athletic costume and becomes a superhuman being and performs superhuman feats in the interests of justice and to overthrow evil. 'Captain Marvel' is likewise represented as a normal human being, a radio reporter (Billy Batson), who, by uttering the magic word 'Shazam', is transformed into a superhuman being, and, in that capacity, also performs superhuman feats in the interests of justice and to overthrow evil. There are villains in both stories, **mad scientists** who resemble each other in appearance, and who, by similar devices and methods, attempt to dispose of the hero ('Superman' or 'Captain Marvel'), so that they can execute their plans of destruction without molestation.

The stories depicted in the respective panels are much the same, as, for example, the experiences of both Clark Kent and Billy Batson in applying for jobs as reporters, being turned down, and finally being accepted as the result of having performed the same superhuman feat. In other instances they are different. For example, there is no romantic element in the 'Captain Marvel' stories, such as Lois Lane, the girl reporter, who is a permanent member of the 'Superman' cast; nor do the 'Superman' stories have an ever-present evil enemy of the hero, like Sivana.

The McClure Newspaper Syndicate Agreement

On September 22, 1938, Detective, Siegel and Shuster and McClure entered into an agreement. Briefly, it provided for the exclusive daily syndication by McClure in newspapers throughout the world of the 'Superman' strips to be supplied by the artists, copyrights thereon to be taken out by McClure in its own name but to revert to Detective at the termination of the agreement, the title 'Superman' to remain the property of Detective, McClure to return to Detective the original drawings, and Detective to have the right to use the strips, six months after newspaper release, in 'Action Comics' or any substituted magazine. McClure was to have only newspaper rights. The artists were to be paid by Detective, and McClure was to pay Detective a stipulated share of the receipts.

By a separate agreement Siegel and Shuster were employed by Detective on the same day to do the work, and they agreed that all the material should be owned by Detective and, at its option, copyrighted in its name or in the names of parties designated by it.

These newspaper strips were serialized,- i. e., the sequence of events continued on from one strip to another until the story was completed and a new one begun.

The strips were first published on January 16, 1939 in three newspapers- the Boston Transcript, the Milwaukee Journal and the San Antonio Express. The number of newspapers steadily increased and the aggregate number up to 1944 amounted to at least 160.

A very few of these strips as published in the newspapers carried the form of copyright notice required for a book. All the others carried no copyright notice whatever, or carried one of the following notices, viz.: (a) the words 'McClure Newspaper Syndicate' alone, or (b) numerals representing the year, followed by the words 'McClure Newspaper Syndicate', or (c) the letter 'C' within a circle, followed by numerals representing the year, and the words 'McClure Newspaper Syndicate' (the letter 'C' in many cases being so small, or so blurred, that it appears to be only a dot or is to be discernible only with the aid of a magnifying glass), or (d) the word 'Copyright' (sometimes spelled 'Copyrig'), followed by numerals representing the year.

None of these notices, except those few which employed the book form, was sufficient to support a valid copyright. Section 18 of the Act required that, in the case of books, the copyright notice should consist either of the word 'Copyright' or of the abbreviation 'Copr', accompanied by the name of the copyright proprietor, and, if the work was a printed literary work, the year of publication, but that, in the case of prints and pictorial illustrations, the notice might consist of the letter 'C', enclosed within a circle, accompanied by the initials, mark or symbol of the copyright proprietor. (There is no requirement in the latter case that the notice shall contain the year of publication.)

I think that Section 18 required that each 'Superman' strip, as published in the newspapers, should be copyrighted as a book. Each strip was a printed literary work, and the word 'book' is not to be limited to a bound volume but includes 'any species of publication which the author selects to embody his literary product.' Holmes v. Hurst, 174 U.S. 82, 89, 19 S.Ct. 606, 609, 43 L.Ed. 904.

It is not correct to say that these 'Superman' strips are prints or pictorial illustrations. A single panel might be called a print. But each strip consists of a number of panels, comprising a continuous sequence of events, with accompanying explanatory text. The panels are not used merely to illustrate the text, as the illustrations in a novel or other literary work do; rather, the panels themselves, together with the explanatory text, constitute the literary work- the story intended to be depicted. As the strips were not prints or pictorial illustrations, the use of the letter 'C' in a circle as the form of copyright notice did not result in obtaining valid copyrights. Advertisers Exchange v. Anderson, 8 Cir., 144 F.2d 907.

But, even if Section 18 permitted the use of a notice in the form authorized for prints, it is necessary that, in substance at least, all the requirements of the section be complied with,- that is, that the notice contain the letter 'C' in a circle, and the initials, mark or symbol of the copyright proprietor. Omission of either of these two elements is fatal. Mifflin v. R. H. White Co., 190 U.S. 260, 264, 23 S.Ct. 769, 47 L.Ed. 1040. And where the letter 'C' in a circle is used, the letter must be distinguishable by the naked eye, unaided by the use of a magnifying glass. Goes Lithographing Co. v. Apt. Lithographing Co., D.C.S.D.N.Y., 14 F.Supp. 620; Deward & Rich v. Bristol Savings & Loan Corp., D.C.W.D. Va., 34 F.Supp. 345, affirmed 4 Cir., 120 F.2d 537.

Detective, however, insists that these were errors and omissions of McClure, by which it is not bound, for McClure was merely a licensee, and a licensee cannot relinquish or abandon the rights of his licensor. I think that this contention is unsound, as the agreement with McClure was not a mere license to use the strips but an agreement of joint adventure. In Ross v. Willett, 76 Hun 211, 213, 27 N.Y.S. 785, 786, which has often been cited by the New York courts, it was said: 'A joint adventure is a limited partnership; not limited in a statutory sense as to liability, but as to its scope and duration; and under our law joint adventures and partnerships are governed by the same rules.' And in Forman v. Lumm, 214 App.Div. 579, 583, 212 N.Y.S. 487, 490, a joint adventure was defined as follows:

'A joint adventure is defined as a 'special combination of two or more persons, where combination of two or more persons, where in some specific venture a profit is jointly sought without any actual partnership or corporate designation.' Schouler, Personal Property (5th Ed.) § 167a. It is an association of two or more persons to carry out a single business enterprise for profit, for which purpose they combine their property, money, effects, skill, and knowledge. * * *

'A contract by and in pursuance of which parties engage in a joint enterprise is to be enforced, and the rights and liabilities of the parties determined, upon the same principles as are applied by courts of equity to partnership transactions.'

See also Chisholm v. Gilmer, 4 Cir., 81 F.2d 120, affirmed on other grounds 299 U.S. 99, 57 S.Ct. 65, 81 L.Ed. 63; Taylor v. Brindley, 10 Cir., 164 F.2d 235, 240-241.

The agreement with McClure contains all the elements of a joint adventure. The subject matter of the joint enterprise was the use of the 'Superman' strips for the sole purpose of newspaper syndication. The artists agreed to create and draw the strips, Detective agreed to pay them for their work and to furnish the strips to McClure, and McClure agreed to sell the strips to newspapers. Both the artists and Detective agreed to cooperate with McClure. The proceeds of the sales (there could be no losses) were to be divided between Detective and McClure. As the agreement was one of joint adventure, the errors and omissions of McClure are chargeable to Detective, for the rights and obligations of joint adventurers are substantially those of partners, and each participant in a joint adventure is an agent for the others.

Fawcett's contention that McClure was neither the author, nor the proprietor, nor the assign of the literary property in the strips, but was a mere licensee, and that it could not, therefore, take out valid copyrights upon the strips, is unsound. Section 8 of the Act limited the right to copyright a work to the author, or the proprietor, or the executors, administrators or assigns of the author or proprietor. The word 'proprietor' in this section means assign. Public Ledger v. N.Y. Times, D.C.S.D.N.Y., 275 F. 562, affirmed 279 F. 747, certiorari denied 258 U.S. 627, 42 S.Ct. 383, 66 L.Ed. 798; Egner v. E. C. Schirmer Music Co., 1 Cir., 139 F.2d 398. Although McClure was neither the author, nor the proprietor, nor an assign, it agreed with Detective that it would copyright the syndicated strips in its own name and that the copyrights would revert to Detective at the termination of the agreement. Such an agreement is lawful, and a copyright taken out in accordance therewith is valid. Quinn-Brown Publishing Corp. v. Chilton Co., D.C.S.D.N.Y., 15 F.Supp. 213.

Nor can Fawcett's further contention be sustained, that, as McClure was not the proprietor of one of the complete divisions of literary property created by the Act, it could not take out valid copyrights upon the strips. The argument is that Section 5 of the Act sets forth the divisions for which copyright may be secured, that subdivision (b) reads 'Periodicals, including newspapers', that, as the agreement with McClure gave it rights in newspapers only, less than a statutory division was transferred to it and it could not, therefore, be a proprietor entitled to take out a copyright. But subdivision (b) does not contain two separate classes- periodicals and newspapers. Like all the other subdivisions, it specifies only one class, periodicals, and it must be read as though the language were 'periodicals, which shall be construed as including newspapers'. The reason for thus mentioning newspapers by name probably was that in 1900, only a few years before the passage of the Act, it was held that newspapers could not be copyrighted. Tribune Co. of Chicago v. Associated Press, C.C.N.D. Ill., 116 F. 126.

I find that, with very few exceptions, the copyrights upon the McClure syndicated newspaper strips are invalid, and that therefore these strips have been dedicated to the public.

Abandonment.

The question remains whether the publication of this large number of syndicated newspaper strips without proper copyright notices resulted in an abandonment of the copyrights on the strips published in 'Action Comics' with proper copyright notices. (It is not necessary, in this connection, to refer to the copyrights on the 'Superman' magazine, for the strips published in that magazine were not original but merely reprints.)

There were sixty-seven different 'Superman' stories published in the monthly issues of 'Action Comics' from June 1938 to December 1943 (the only ones in evidence). During approximately the same period, i. e., from January 1939 to December 1943, there were published daily, without proper copyright notices, in many of at least 160 newspapers throughout the United States, numerous stories portraying 'Superman' and all of his superhuman feats, closely paralleling the stories published in 'Action Comics'. The number of issues of the newspapers carrying these stories literally ran into thousands.

It is quite true that the syndicated newspaper stories were not identical with the 'Action Comics' stories, but they were so nearly similar that, if they had been published by a stranger, they would clearly be held to be infringements of the copyrights on the 'Action Comics' stories. If a copyright owner authorizes or permits the republication of its copyrighted material without copyright protection, it forfeits, i.e., abandons the copyright. Dejonge & Co. v. Breuker & Kessler Co., 235 U.S. 33, 35 S.Ct. 6, 59 L.Ed. 113; Deward & Rich v. Bristol Savings & Loan Corp., 4 Cir., 120 F.2d 537; Atlantic Monthly Co. v. Post Pub. Co., D.C., Mass., 27 F.2d 556. I think the same result must certainly follow in the present case, where Detective has permitted publication in the newspapers, without copyright protection, of stories which were the same in all material respects as its own copyrighted stories.

I find, therefore, that the publication of the McClure syndicated newspaper strips without proper copyright notices resulted in the abandonment by plaintiff of the copyrights on the 'Action Comics' stories. With this disposition it is unnecessary to consider any of the other instances in which the 'Superman' stories or the 'Superman' figure were published without proper copyright notices.

Unfair Competition.

The evidence does not justify any finding of unfair competition by either Fawcett or Republic; there is no proof either of palming off or of confusion; nor is there any misrepresentation, or any misappropriation 'of what equitably belongs to a competitor'. Schechter Corp. v. United States, 295 U.S. 495, 532, 55 S.Ct. 837, 844, 79 L.Ed. 1570. I see nothing in International News Service v. Associated Press, 248 U.S. 215, 39 S.Ct. 68, 63 L.Ed. 211, to the contrary.

The amended complaint accordingly is dismissed as against defendant Fawcett, with costs; and it necessarily follows that there be a similar dismissal as against both Republic defendants.

On Motion for Retaxation.

In view of the finding already made that there was 'actual copying' by defendant Fawcett of plaintiff's cartoon strips, I am not disposed to make any allowance to Fawcett for an attorney's fee. See Advertisers Exchange v. Anderson, D.C.S.D. Iowa, 52 F.Supp. 809, affirmed 8 Cir., 144 F.2d 907;

Krafft v. Cohen, D.C.E.D. Pa., 38 F.Supp. 1022.

The situation as to the Republic defendants is different. They were charged only as contributory or secondary infringers; it was not found that they had copied plaintiff's strips. An allowance of $ 1,000 will be made to these defendants as an attorney's fee.

Plaintiff has moved to re-tax the costs of the defendants by striking from the costs as taxed by the Clerk to Fawcett the sum of $ 2132.71, and from the costs taxed to the Republic defendants the sum of $ 972.18, the amounts disbursed by them respectively for transcripts of depositions before trial of various witnesses examined by the parties. Plaintiff insists that these expenditures are not taxable unless they do more than serve the convenience of counsel in preparing the case for trial, and unless the depositions actually assist the court in deciding the case. It is customary in this District to tax such disbursements as costs where the depositions were taken in good faith, and whether or not they were actually used upon the trial. Here some of the depositions were introduced in evidence; some others were used on cross-examination. Many of them were used to develop facts which proved to be of considerable help in deciding the case. The Clerk properly included these amounts in his taxation of costs.

The Republic defendants have also moved to re-tax their costs by including the sum of $ 1017.73, the cost of a daily transcript of the trial proceedings. No direction was made by the court that any such daily transcript be furnished, and there appears to have been no necessity therefor. The motion of the Republic defendants for retaxation is accordingly denied. Stallo v. Wagner, 2 Cir., 245 F. 636.

Judgment in accordance with this memorandum has been signed.

JOANNE SIEGEL and LAURA SIEGEL LARSON, Plaintiffs,

v.

WARNER BROS. ENTERTAINMENT INC.; TIME WARNER INC.; and DC COMICS, Defendants.

CASE NO. CV-04-8400-SGL (RZx) [Consolidated for pre-trial and discovery purposes with CV-04-8776-SGL (RZx)]

UNITED STATES DISTRICT COURT
FOR THE CENTRAL DISTRICT OF CALIFORNIA

542 F. Supp. 2d 1098
March 26, 2008

STEPHEN G. LARSON, UNITED STATES DISTRICT JUDGE.

OPINION

ORDER GRANTING IN PART AND DENYING IN PART PLAINTIFFS' MOTION FOR PARTIAL SUMMARY JUDGMENT; ORDER GRANTING IN PART AND DENYING IN PART DEFENDANTS' MOTION FOR PARTIAL SUMMARY JUDGMENT

The termination provisions contained in the Copyright Act of 1976 have aptly been characterized as formalistic and complex, such that authors, or their heirs, successfully terminating the grant to the copyright in their original work of authorship is a feat accomplished "against all odds." 2 WILLIAM F. PATRY, PATRY ON COPYRIGHT § 7:52 (2007).

In the present case, Joanne Siegel and Laura Siegel Larson, the widow and the daughter of Jerome Siegel, seek a declaration from the Court that they have overcome these odds and have successfully terminated the 1938 grant by Jerome Siegel and his creative partner, Joseph Shuster, of the copyright in their creation of the iconic comic book superhero "Superman," thereby recapturing Jerome Siegel's half of the copyright in the same. No small feat indeed. It requires traversing the many impediments -- many requiring a detailed historical understanding both factually and legally of the events that occurred between the parties over the past seventy years -- to achieving that goal and, just as importantly, reckoning with the limits of what can be gained through the termination of that grant.

Any discussion about the termination of the initial grant to the copyright in a work begins, as the Court does here, with the story of the creation of the work itself.

In 1932, Jerome Siegel and Joseph Shuster were teenagers at Glenville High School in Cleveland, Ohio. Siegel was an aspiring writer and Shuster an aspiring artist; what Siegel later did with his typewriter and Shuster with his pen would transform the comic book industry. The two met while working on their high school's newspaper where they discovered their shared passion for science fiction and comics, the beginning of a remarkable and fruitful relationship.

One of their first collaborations was publishing a mail-order fanzine titled "Science Fiction: The Advance Guard of Future Civilization."[1] In the January, 1933, issue, Siegel and Shuster's first superman character appeared in the short story "The Reign of the Superman," but in the form of a villain not a hero.

The story told of a "**mad scientist's** experiment with a deprived man from the breadlines" that transformed "the man into a mental giant who then uses his new powers -- the ability to read and control minds -- to steal a fortune and attempt to dominate the world." (Decl. Michael Bergman, Ex. HH at 1126). This initial superman character in villain trappings was drawn by Shuster as a bald-headed mad man.

A couple of months later it occurred to Siegel that re-writing the character as a hero, bearing little resemblance to his villainous namesake, "might make a great comic strip character." (Decl. Michael Bergman, Ex. HH at 1126). Much of Siegel's desire to shift the role of his protagonist from villain to hero arose from Siegel's exposure to despair and hope: Despair created by the dark days of the Depression and hope through exposure to the "gallant, crusading heros" in popular literature and the movies. (Decl. Michael Bergman, Ex. HH

---

[1] A fanzine is a publication, usually distributed at no or nominal cost, produced by fans of a particular topic (such as comic books, opera, murder mystery stories, etc.) for others who share their interest.

at 1126). The theme of hope amidst despair struck the young Siegel as an apt subject for his comic strip: "Superman was the answer -- Superman aiding the downtrodden and oppressed." (Decl. Michael Bergman, Ex. HH at 1126).

Thereafter, Siegel sat down to create a comic book version of his new character. While he labored over the script, Shuster began the task of drawing the panels visualizing that script. Titling it "The Superman," "[t]heir first rendition of the man of steel was a hulking strongman who wore a T-shirt and pants rather than a cape and tights." (Decl. Michael Bergman, Ex. HH at 1129). And he was not yet able to hurdle skyscrapers, nor was he from a far away planet; instead, he was simply a strong (but not extraordinarily so) human, in the mold of Flash Gordon or Tarzan, who combated crime. Siegel and Shuster sent their material to a publisher of comic books -- Detective Dan -- and were informed that it had been accepted for publication. Their success, however, was short-lived; the publisher later rescinded its offer to publish their submission. Crestfallen, Shuster threw into the fireplace all the art for the story except the cover (reproduced below), which Siegel rescued from the flames.

[SEE EXHIBIT HH IN ORIGINAL]

Undaunted, Siegel continued to tinker with his character, but decided to try a different publication format, a newspaper comic strip. The choice of crafting the material in a newspaper comic strip format was influenced both by the failure to get their earlier incarnation of the Superman character published by Detective Dan in a comic book format, and by the fact that, at the time, black-and-white newspaper comic strips -- not comic books -- were the most popular medium for comics. As one observer of the period has commented:

It is worth noting the extent to which early comic books were conjoined with newspaper strips of the day. The earliest comic books consisted of reprints of those newspaper strips, re-pasted into a comic book page format. When original material began appearing in comic book format, it was generally because companies that wished to publish comic books were unable to procure reprint rights to existing newspaper strips. The solution to this . . . was to hire young [comic strip artists] to simulate the same kind of newspaper strip material.

(Decl. Mark Evanier, Ex. A at 5-6).

On a hot summer night in 1934, Siegel, unable to sleep, began brainstorming over plot ideas for this new feature when an idea struck him: "I was up late counting sheep and more and more ideas kept coming to me, and I wrote out several weeks of syndicate script for the proposed newspaper strip. When morning came, I dashed over to Joe [Shuster]'s place and showed it to him." (Decl. Michael Bergman, Ex. HH at 1129). Siegel re-envisioned his character in more of the mythic hero tradition of Hercules, righting wrongs in present-day society. His inspiration was to couple an exaggeration of the daring on-screen acrobatics performed by such actors as Douglas Fairbanks, Sr., with a pseudo-scientific explanation to make such fantastic abilities more plausible in the vein of Edgar Rice Burroughs' John Carter of Mars stories, and placing all of this within a storyline that was the reverse of the formula used in the Flash Gordon serials. The end product was of a character who is sent as an infant to Earth aboard a space ship from an unnamed distant planet (that had been destroyed by old age) who, upon becoming an adult, uses his superhuman powers (gained from the fact that his alien heritage made him millions of years more evolved than ordinary humans) to perform daring feats for the public good.

Siegel named his character "Superman." Unlike his previous incarnation, Siegel's new Superman character's powers and abilities were much more extraordinary and fantastic: Superhuman strength; the ability to leap 1/8th of a mile, hurdle a twenty-story building, and run faster than an express train; and nothing less than a bursting shell could penetrate his skin. Siegel placed his character in a very cosmopolitan environment that had the look and feel of mid-thirties America. He also humanized his character by giving his superhero an "ordinary person" alter ego: Mild-mannered, big-city newspaper reporter Clark Kent. Siegel developed this concept of Superman's secret identity both as a means for his superhero to maintain an inconspicuous position in everyday society and as a literary device to introduce a conflict -- and the potential for story lines centered around that conflict -- between the character's dual identities, a conflict played out no more dramatically than in the love "triangle" between the character's dual identities and another newspaper reporter, Lois Lane.

Shuster immediately turned his attention to giving life and color to Siegel's idea by drawing illustrations for the story. Shuster conceived of the costume for Siegel's Superman superhero -- a cape and tight-fitting leotard with briefs, an "S" emblazoned on an inverted triangular crest on his chest, and boots as footwear. In contrast, he costumed Clark Kent in a nondescript suit, wearing black-rimmed glasses, combed black hair, and sporting a fedora. He drew Superman and his alter ego Clark Kent with chiseled features, gave him a hairstyle with a distinctive curl over his forehead, and endowed him with a lean, muscular physique. Clark Kent hid most of these physical attributes behind his wardrobe, which he could quickly doff revealing his Superman costume underneath when he was called to action by someone in need of his superpowers. One of the earliest of Shuster's sketches of Superman and Clark Kent from this 1934 or 1935 period are depicted below:

[SEE ILLUSTRATION IN ORIGINAL]

The two then set about combining Siegel's literary material with Shuster's graphical representations. Together they crafted a comic strip consisting of several weeks' worth of material suitable for newspaper syndication. Siegel typed the dialogue and Shuster penciled in artwork, resulting in four weeks of Superman comic strips intended for newspapers. (Decl. Michael Bergman, Ex. H at 1). The art work for the first week's worth "of daily [comic] strips was completely inked" and thus ready for publication. (Decl. Michael Bergman, Ex. H at 1). The "three additional weeks of 'Superman' newspaper comic strip material" differed from the first week's material "only in that the art work, dialogue and the balloons in which the dialogue appeared had not been inked," instead consisting of no more than black-and-white pencil drawings. (Decl. Michael Bergman, Exs. G at 2 & H at 1-2).

Siegel also wrote material to which Shuster provided no illustrations: A paragraph previewing future Superman exploits, and a nine-page synopsis of the storyline appearing in the three weeks of penciled daily Superman newspaper comic strips. (Decl. James Steranko, Ex. A at 4; Decl. Michael Bergman, Ex. H at 2).

The two shopped the character for a number of years to numerous publishers but were unsuccessful. As Siegel later recalled: One publisher "expressed interest in Superman," but preferred that it be "published in comic book form where it would be seen in color" rather than "a black-and-white daily strip," a suggestion to which he and Shuster balked given their earlier experience with the comic book publisher of Detective Dan. (Decl. Michael Bergman, Ex. H at 2).

In the meantime, Siegel and Shuster penned other comic strips, most notably "Slam Bradley" and "The Spy," that were sold to Nicholson Publishing Company. When Nicholson folded shop in 1937, Detective Comics acquired some of its comic strip properties, including "Slam Bradley" and "The Spy."

On December 4, 1937, Siegel and Shuster entered into an agreement with Detective Comics whereby they agreed to furnish some of these existing comic strips for the next two years, and further agreed "that all of these products and work done by [them] for [Detective Comics] during said period of employment shall be and become the sole and exclusive property of [Detective Comics,] and [that Detective Comics] shall be deemed the sole creator thereof . . . ." (Decl. Michael Bergman, Ex. A). The agreement further provided that any new or additional features by Siegel and Shuster were to be submitted first to Detective Comics, who was given a sixty-day option to publish the material.

Soon thereafter Detective Comics decided to issue a new comic book magazine titled Action Comics and began seeking new material. Inquiry was made of many newspaper comic strip publishers, including McClure Newspaper Syndicate. Amongst the material submitted by McClure to Detective Comics was the previously rejected Siegel and Shuster Superman comic strip. Detective Comics soon became interested in publishing Siegel and Shuster's now well-traveled Superman material, but in an expanded thirteen-page comic book format, for release in its first volume of Action Comics.

On February 1, 1938, Detective Comics returned the existing Superman newspaper comic strip material to Siegel and Shuster for revision and expansion into a full-length, thirteen-page comic book production. Detective Comics' desire to place Superman in a comic book required that Siegel and Shuster reformat their existing Superman newspaper material by re-cutting the strip into separate panels and then re-pasting it into a comic book format.

An issue emerged due to Detective Comics' additional requirement that there be eight panels per page in the comic book. Siegel and Shuster's existing Superman newspaper material did not have enough drawings to meet this format. In response, portions of the thirteen-page comic went forward with fewer than eight panels per page, and in the remaining pages Shuster either trimmed or split existing panels to stay within the page size, or drew additional panels from the existing dialogue to meet the eight-panel requirement. As Shuster later recounted:

The only thing I had to do to prepare Superman for comic book publication was to ink the last three weeks of daily strips which I had previously completely penciled in detail. In addition, I inked the lettering and the dialogue and story continuity and inked in the balloons containing the dialogue. Certain panels I trimmed to conform to Detective's page size. I drew several additional pictures to illustrate the story continuity and these appear on page 1 of the first Superman release. This was done so that we would be certain of having a sufficient number of panels to make a thirteen page release. Finally, I drew the last panel appearing on the thirteenth page. Detective's only concern was that there would be panels sufficient for thirteen complete pages. Jerry told me that Detective preferred having eight panels per page but in our judgment this would hurt the property. I specifically refer to the very large panel appearing on what would be page 9 of the thirteen page release. We did not want to alter this because of its dramatic effect. Accordingly, on this page but six panels appeared.

(Decl. Michael Bergman, Ex. G at 2). Siegel similarly recollected:
Upon receiving word from Detective that we could proceed, Joe Shuster, under my supervision, inked the illustrations, lettering and dialogue balloons in the three weeks of daily strips that had been previously penciled. In addition, he trimmed certain pictures to meet Detective's panel specifications and extended others. To assure ourselves of having the proper number of panels we added several pictures to illustrate the story continuity, I had already

written. Added as well for this reason was the scientific explanation on page 1 of the release and the last panel at the foot of page 13.

(Decl. Michael Bergman, Ex. H at 5).

On or around February 16, 1938, the pair resubmitted the re-formatted Superman material to Detective Comics. Soon thereafter Detective Comics informed Siegel that, as he had earlier suggested to them, one of the panels from their Superman comic would be used as the template (albeit slightly altered from the original) for the cover of the inaugural issue of Action Comics. (Decl. Michael Bergman, Ex. I).

On March 1, 1938, prior to the printing of the first issue of Action Comics, Detective Comics wrote to Siegel, enclosing a check in the sum of $ 130, representing the per-page rate for the thirteen-page Superman comic book release and enclosing with it a written agreement for Siegel and Shuster's signatures. The agreement assigned to Detective Comics "all [the] good will attached . . . and exclusive right[s]" to Superman "to have and hold forever." (Decl. Michael Bergman, Ex. F). Siegel and Shuster executed and returned the written assignment to Detective Comics.

This world-wide grant in ownership rights was later confirmed in a September 22, 1938, employment agreement in which Siegel and Shuster acknowledged that Detective Comics was "the exclusive owner[]" of not only the other comic strips they had penned for Nicholson (and continued to pen for Detective Comics), but Superman as well; that they would continue to supply the artwork and storyline (or in the parlance of the trade, the "continuity") for these comics at varying per-page rates depending upon the comic in question for the next five years; that Detective Comics had the "right to reasonably supervise the editorial matter" of those existing comic strips; that Siegel and Shuster would not furnish "any art copy . . . containing the . . . characters or continuity thereof or in any wise similar" to these comics to a third party; and that Detective Comics would have the right of first refusal (to be exercised within a six-week period after the comic's submission) with respect to any future comic creations by Siegel or Shuster.

Detective Comics announced the debut of its Action Comics series with full page announcements in the issues of some of its existing publications. Specifically, in More Fun Comics, Vol. 31, with a cover date of May, 1938, Detective Comics placed the following black-and-white promotional advertisement on the comic's inside cover, which reproduced the cover of the soon-to-be published first issue of Action Comics, albeit in a greatly reduced size:

[SEE ILLUSTRATION IN ORIGINAL]

Similarly, Detective Comics, Vol. 15, with a cover date of May, 1938, had a full-page black-and-white promotional advertisement on the comic's inside

cover which contained within it a reproduction of the cover (again in a reduced scale) of the soon-to-be published first issue of Action Comics:
[SEE ILLUSTRATION IN ORIGINAL]
To provide some context and contrast, the cover of the first issue of Action Comics is notable for its difference from the promotional advertisements both in its scale and its colorized format.
[SEE ILLUSTRATION IN ORIGINAL]
Superman itself was published by Detective Comics on April 18, 1938, in Action Comics, Vol. 1, which had a cover date of June, 1938. A full reproduction of the original Superman comic contained in Action Comics, Vol. 1, is attached as an addendum to this Order. See Attachment A to this Order. The Superman comic became an instant success, and Superman's popularity continues to endure to this day as his depiction has been transferred to varying media formats.

The Superman character has evolved in subsequent works since his initial depiction in Action Comics, Vol. 1. These additional works have added decades of new material to further define, update, and develop the character (such as his origins, his relationships, and his powers and weaknesses) in an ongoing flow of new exploits and supporting characters, resulting in the creation of an entire fictional Superman "universe." For instance, absent from Action Comics, Vol. 1, was any reference to some of the more famous story elements now associated with Superman, such as the name of Superman's home planet "Krypton." Many of Superman's powers that are among his most famous today did not appear in Action Comics, Vol. 1, including his ability to fly (even through the vacuum of space); his super-vision, which enables him to see through walls ("x-ray" vision) and across great distances ("telescopic" vision); his super-hearing, which enables him to hear conversations at great distances; and his "heat vision," the ability to aim rays of extreme heat with his eyes. The "scientific" explanation for these powers was also altered in ensuing comics, initially as owing to differences in gravity between Earth and Superman's home planet (the latter being much larger in size than the former), and later because Krypton orbited a red sun, and his exposure to the yellow rays of Earth's sun somehow made his powers possible. In a similar Earth-Krypton connection, it was later revealed that Superman's powers could be nullified by his exposure to Kryptonite, radioactive mineral particles of his destroyed home planet.

Aside from the further delineation of Superman's powers and weaknesses, many other elements from the Superman story were developed in subsequent publications. Some of the most famous supporting characters associated with Superman, such as Jimmy Olsen and rival villains Lex Luthor, General Zod, and Brainiac, were created long after Action Comics, Vol. 1, was published. Moreover, certain elements contained in Action Comics, Vol. 1, were altered, even if slightly, in later publications, most notably Superman's crest. In Action Comics, Vol. 1, the crest emblem was a small, yellow, inverted triangle bearing the letter "S" in the middle, shown throughout the comic as solid yellow in most instances and as a red "S" in two instances. Thereafter, the emblem changed, and today is a large yellow five-sided shield, outlined in the color red, and bearing the letter "S" in the middle, also in the color red.

The acclaim to which the release of Action Comics, Vo. 1, was greeted by the viewing public quickly made Superman not only the iconic face for the comic book industry but also a powerful super-salesman for his publisher. Detective Comics oversaw the creation, development, and licensing of the Superman character in a variety of media, including but not limited to radio, novels, live action and animated motion pictures, television, live theatrical productions, merchandise and theme parks. From such promotional activity, Detective Comics came to "own[] dozens of federal trademark registrations for Superman related indicia, such as certain key symbols across a broad array of goods and services." (Decl. Paul Levitz P 10). The most notable of these marks that are placed on various items of merchandise are "Superman's characteristic outfit, comprised of a full length blue leotard with red cape, a yellow belt, the S in Shield Device, as well as certain key identifying phrases[,]" such as "'Look! . . . Up in the sky! . . . It's a bird! . . . It's a plane! . . . It's Superman!" (Decl. Paul Levitz P 10).

Meanwhile, Siegel continued to submit other comic book characters to Detective Comics that were also published. Sometimes these submissions were without Shuster serving as an illustrator and sometimes, such as in the case of Superman's youthful persona "Superboy," see Siegel v. Time Warner Inc., 496 F. Supp. 2d 1111 (C.D. Cal. 2007), without illustrations accompanying the submission. Among these subsequent creations was "The Spectre," a comic written by Siegel and illustrated by Bernard Baily, which first appeared in 1940 in Detective Comics' More Fun Comics, Vol. 52. The comic told the story about a superhero with a supernatural bent -- the character being the spirit of a police officer killed in the line of duty while investigating a gangland overlord and who, after meeting a higher force in the hereafter, is sent back to Earth with nearly limitless abilities but offered eternal rest only when he has wiped out all crime.

With Superman's growing popularity, a growing rift developed between the parties. Siegel and Shuster believed that Detective Comics' poached the artists apprenticing out of Siegel and Shuster's studio in Cleveland by moving them in-house to its New York offices, and further believed that Detective Comics had not paid them their fair share of profits generated from the exploitation of their Superman creation and from the profits generated from copycat characters that they believed had their roots in the original Superman character. As a result, in 1947, Siegel and Shuster brought an action against

Detective Comics' successor in interest in New York Supreme Court, Westchester County, seeking, among other things, to annul and rescind their previous agreements with Detective Comics assigning their ownership rights in Superman as void for lack of mutuality and consideration.

After a trial, official referee J. Addison Young issued detailed findings of fact and conclusions of law wherein he found that the March 1, 1938, assignment of the Superman copyright to Detective Comics was valid and supported by valuable consideration and that, therefore, Detective Comics was the exclusive owner of "all" the rights to Superman. The parties eventually settled the Westchester action and signed a stipulation on May 19, 1948, whereby in exchange for the payment of over $ 94,000 to Siegel and Shuster, the parties reiterated the referee's earlier finding that Detective Comics owned all rights to Superman. Two days later, the official referee entered a final consent judgment vacating his earlier findings of fact and conclusions of law, and otherwise reiterating the recitals contained in the stipulation.

The feud between the parties did not end after the Westchester action. In the mid-1960s, the simmering dispute boiled anew when the expiration of the initial copyright term for Superman led to another round of litigation over ownership to the copyright's renewal term.[2] In 1969, Siegel and Shuster filed suit in federal district court in New York seeking a declaration that they, not

---

[2] 2 Under the Copyright Act of 1909 (the "1909 Act"), which was in effect at the time of Siegel and Shuster's creation of Superman and later assignment of rights in the same to Detective Comics, an author was entitled to a copyright in his work for twenty-eight years from the date of its publication. See 17 U.S.C. § 24, repealed by Copyright Act of 1976, 17 U.S.C. § 101 et seq. Upon the expiration of this initial twenty-eight year term, the author could renew the copyright for a second twenty-eight year period (the "renewal term").

After the conclusion of the 1970s Superman litigation, the New York Times "ran a story about how the two creators of Superman were living in near destitute conditions":

Two 61-year-old men, nearly destitute and worried about how they will support themselves in their old age, are invoking the spirit of Superman for help. Joseph Shuster, who sits amidst his threadbare furniture in Queens, and Jerry Siegel, who waits in his cramped apartment in Los Angeles, share the hope that they each will get pensions from the Man of Steel.

Mary Breasted, Superman's Creators, Nearly Destitute, Invoke His Spirit, N.Y. TIMES, Nov. 22, 1975, at 62.

Detective Comics' successor (National Periodical Publications, Inc.), were the owners of the renewal rights to the Superman copyright. See Siegel v. National Periodical Publications, Inc., 364 F.Supp. 1032 (S.D.N.Y. 1973), aff'd by, 508 F.2d 909 (2nd Cir. 1974). The end result of the litigation was that, in conformity with United States Supreme Court precedent at the time, see Fred Fisher Music Co. v. M. Witmark & Sons, 318 U.S. 643, 656-59, 63 S. Ct. 773, 87 L. Ed. 1055 (1943), in transferring "all their rights" to Superman in the March 1, 1938, grant to Detective Comics (which was reconfirmed in the 1948 stipulation), Siegel and Shuster had assigned not only Superman's initial copyright term but the renewal term as well, even though those renewal rights had yet to vest when the grant (and later the stipulation) was made.

Apparently in response to the bad publicity associated with this and similar articles, the parties thereafter entered into a further agreement, dated December 23, 1975. See id. ("'There is no legal obligation,' Mr. Emmett[, executive vice-president of Warner Communications, Inc.,] said, 'but I sure feel that there is a moral obligation on our part'"). In the agreement, Siegel and Shuster re- acknowledged the Second Circuit's decision that "all right, title and interest in" Superman ("including any and all renewals and extensions of . . . such rights") resided exclusively with DC Comics and its corporate affiliates and, in return, DC Comics' now parent company, Warner Communications, Inc. ("WCI"), provided Siegel and Shuster with modest annual payments for the remainder of their lives; provided them medical insurance under the plan for its employees; and credited them as the "creators of Superman." In tendering this payment, Warner Communications, Inc. specifically stated that it had no legal obligation to do so, but that it did so solely "in consideration" of the pair's "past services . . . and in view of [their] present circumstances," emphasizing that the payments were "voluntary." The 1975 agreement also made certain provisions for Siegel's spouse Joanne, providing her with certain monthly payments "for the balance of her life if Siegel" died before December 31, 1985. Finally, Warner Communications, Inc. noted that its obligation to make such voluntary payments would cease if either Siegel or Shuster (or their representatives) sued "asserting any right, title or interest in the 'Superman' . . . copyright." As the years went by Warner Communications, Inc. increased the amount of the annual payments, and on at least two occasions paid the pair special bonuses.

As the time grew nearer to the December 31, 1985, cutoff date for surviving spouse benefits, Joanne Siegel wrote the CEO for DC Comics expressing her "terrible worry" over the company's refusal to provide Jerome Siegel life insurance in the 1975 agreement. (Decl. Michael Bergman, Ex. NN). She voiced her concern that, should anything happen to her husband after the cutoff date, she and their daughter "would be left without any measure of [financial] security." (Decl. Michael Bergman, Ex. NN). The parties thereafter agreed by letter dated March 15, 1982, that Warner would pay Joanne Siegel the same benefits it had been paying her husband if he predeceased her, regardless of the time of his death. (Decl. Michael Bergman, Ex. OO). Jerome Siegel died on January 28, 1996, and Joanne Siegel has been receiving these voluntary survival spouse benefits since that time.

In the meantime, changes in the law resurrected legal questions as to the ownership rights the parties had to the Superman copyright. With the passage of the Copyright Act of 1976 (the "1976 Act"), Congress changed the legal landscape concerning artists' transfers of the copyrights in their creations. First, the 1976 Act expanded by nineteen years the duration of the renewal period for works, like the initial release of Superman in Action Comics, Vol. 1, that were already in their renewal term at the time of the Act's passage. See 17 U.S.C. § 304(b).

Second, and importantly for this case, the 1976 Act gave artists and their heirs the ability to terminate any prior grants of the rights to their creations that were executed before January 1, 1978, regardless of the terms contained in such assignments, e.g., a contractual provision that all the rights (the initial and renewal) belonged exclusively to the publisher. Specifically, section 304(c) to the 1976 Act provides that, [i]n the case of any copyright subsisting in either its first or renewal term on January 1, 1978, other than a copyright in a work made for hire, the exclusive or nonexclusive grant of a transfer or license of the renewal copyright or any right under it, executed before January 1, 1978, ... is subject to termination ... notwithstanding any agreement to the contrary ...."

It is this right of termination that Joanne Siegel and Laura Siegel Larson now seek to vindicate in this case. [3] In pursuing such a claim, the two heirs,

---

[3] 3 Although the present case only concerns the Siegel heirs' efforts to terminate the 1938 grant, it has come to the Court's attention that the estate of Superman co-creator Joseph Shuster has recently filed termination notices to reclaim the rights to the Superman copyright. According to documents filed with the United States Copyright Office, Mark Warren Peary, the son of Shuster's sister and the court-appointed representative of the Shuster estate, has given notice of the estate's intent to terminate the 1938 grant of the Superman copyright to Detective Comics and its successors effective 2013. As executor of the Shuster estate, Peary is entitled, under changes made to the 1976 termination provisions by the 1998 Sonny Bono Copyright Term Extension Act, to make the same termination claims for the Superman copyright that Shuster or his heirs would have been entitled to bring beforehand. See 17 U.S.C. § 304(c)(2); 3 NIMMER ON COPYRIGHT § 11.03[A][2][a] at 11-40.1 (noting that when the 1976 Act was originally passed

initially sought the legal assistance of a highly regarded copyright expert, Mr. Arthur J. Levine, in compiling the information necessary to draft the termination notice itself.[4] [4]

On April 3, 1997, the two heirs served seven separate notices of termination under section 304(c) of the 1976 Act, purporting to terminate several of Siegel's potential grant(s) in the Superman copyright to defendants, including the March 1, 1938, assignment; the May 19, 1948, stipulation; and the December 23, 1975, agreement. The termination notices also specified that they covered hundreds of works, with the added proviso that the intent was for the termination notice to apply "to each and every work . . . that includes or embodies" Superman, and the failure to list any such work in the notice was "unintentional and involuntary." Each of the termination notices had an effective date of April 16, 1999. A flurry of settlement discussions between the parties quickly ensued, but just as quickly fizzled out. Nearly two years then passed without much discussion between the parties.

The day before the purported termination was to take effect, defendants sent a letter to Siegel's counsel, Mr. Levine, rejecting "the validity and scope" of the termination notices. (Decl. Marc Toberoff, Ex. Q at 171). The same day DC Comics Executive Vice President and Publisher Paul Levitz wrote to Joanne Siegel that his company would "continue to provide the income and insurance benefits you . . . have been receiving under the 1975 agreement, without prejudice to [the company's] rights under that agreement, as long as we all continue to pursue the goal of working together." (Decl. Michael Bergman, Ex. P).

Not long after the termination notices' effective date passed, the Siegel heirs retained new counsel and the parties re-entered into settlement discussions to resolve their respective claims to the Superman copyright. Towards that end, DC Comics (and its "successors, past and present subsidiaries or affiliates") and the Siegel heirs executed a tolling agreement on April 6, 2000, whereby it was agreed that neither would "assert any statute of limitations . . . defense[] relating to . . . the [Termination] Notices" based on "the passage of time

---

if an author died without leaving heirs before exercising the right to termination "the result was that no one could exercise [that] right," but this "harsh result" was "ameliorated" through the passage of the 1998 Act by providing that, "instead of lapsing," the termination right could be exercised by "the author's executor, administrator, personal representative, or trustee").

[4] [4] Before going into private practice, Mr. Levine served as General Counsel for the United States Copyright Office and also as Executive Director for the National Commission on New Technological Uses of Copyrighted Works.

during the period from the date hereof until cancellation of this Tolling Agreement pursuant to paragraph 7 hereof (the 'Tolling Period')" while the parties attempted "to find an amicable resolution in respect of the [Termination] Notices." (Reply Decl. Marc Toberoff, Ex. A at 1). The agreement further provided that the tolling period would remain in effect "until 10 business days after the earlier of: (a) one of the parties terminating negotiations, in writing, relating to the [Termination] Notices, or (b) the parties reaching an amicable resolution of the disputes between them relating to the Notices." (Reply Decl. Marc Toberoff, Ex. A at 2).

At some point the broad outline of a global settlement concerning the copyright to the Superman material, as well as to other works Siegel either authored or contributed material to Detective Comics (notably, Superboy and The Spectre properties), was reached. Specifically, on October 19, 2001, counsel for Joanne Siegel and Laura Siegel Larson sent a six-page letter to Warner Bros.' General Counsel confirming and summarizing the substance of the settlement. The letter concluded that "if there is any aspect of the above that is somehow misstated, please let me know by [October 22, 2001] at 2:00, as I will be out of the office -- and likely difficult to reach -- for the following four weeks." (Decl. Marc Toberoff, Ex. BB).

A week later, on October 26, 2001, Warner Bros.' General Counsel John Shulman responded with a letter, stating that he had "reviewed" the summary set forth in the October 19 letter, and then "enclose[d] . . . a more fulsome outline of what we believe the deal we've agreed to is"; the outline was five pages long. (Decl. Marc Toberoff, Ex. CC). The letter concluded that Warner Bros. was "working on the draft agreement" so as to "have this super-matter transaction in document form." (Decl. Marc Toberoff, Ex. CC).

A few months later, on February 1, 2002, outside counsel for Warner Bros. provided a copy of the promised draft agreement (spanning fifty-six pages), with the proviso that, "[a]s our clients have not seen this latest version of the agreement, I must reserve their right to comment." (Decl. Marc Toberoff, Ex. DD). Mention was also made in the draft agreement for the need of certain "Stand Alone Assignments" that had as yet not been finalized, something which Warner's outside counsel promised would be forthcoming. (Decl. Marc Toberoff, Ex. DD).

Three months later, on May 9, 2002, Joanne Siegel wrote a letter to Time Warner's Chief Operating Officer Richard Parsons, recounting that she and her daughter had "made painful concessions and reluctantly accepted John Shulman's last [settlement] proposal [in October, 2001]," but upon reading the proposed draft agreement learned that they had been "stabbed in the back," as it "contained new, outrageous demands that were not in the [October, 2001] proposal," such as "condition[ing] recei[pt of] financial compensation for our rights on demands which were not in the proposal we accepted." (Decl.

Michael Bergman, Ex. Z). The letter concluded that "[a]fter four years we have no deal and this contract makes an agreement impossible." (Decl. Michael Bergman, Ex. Z).

Time Warner's CEO quickly responded with a letter of his own on May 21, 2002, expressing shock and dismay as "each of the major points covered in the draft agreement . . . accurately represented the agreement previously reached" by the parties. (Decl. Michael Bergman, Ex. AA). The letter continued by acknowledging that, as with all lengthy negotiations, Time Warner "expected" that the submission of the draft agreement would result in further "comments and questions on the draft" by Siegel family's representatives that "would need to [be] resolve[d]." (Decl. Michael Bergman, Ex. AA). The letter concluded by reaffirming Time Warner's continued interest "that this agreement can be closed based upon the earlier discussions with [the Siegel family's] lawyers." (Decl. Michael Bergman, Ex. AA).

Not long thereafter, the Siegel heirs' lawyers submitted for the family's review and approval a re-draft of the February 4, 2002, agreement the lawyers had crafted. (Decl. Marc Toberoff, Ex. AA). The Siegel heirs, on September 21, 2002, rejected the redraft and fired their attorneys. (Decl. Marc Toberoff, Ex. AA). That same day Joanne Siegel and Laura Siegel Larson sent a letter to DC Comics' General Counsel Paul Levitz notifying the company that they were "stopp[ing] and end[ing] negotiations with DC Comics, Inc., its parent company AOL Time Warner and all of its representatives and associates concerning" their rights to, among other things, Superman. (Decl. Michael Bergman, Ex. DD).

Joanne Siegel and Laura Siegel Larson thereafter filed the present action, with the assistance of new counsel, Marc Toberoff, on October 8, 2004. Both sides have since filed cross-motions for partial summary judgment.

Reduced to their essentials, the legal questions at stake in the parties' cross-motions are two-fold:

(1) The validity and enforceability of the termination notices in light of (a) whether any copyrightable Superman material contained in the promotional advertisements for Action Comics, Vol. 1, lies outside the reach of the termination notice (and hence, the termination notice is not enforceable against it); (b) whether certain portions of the Superman comic in Action Comics, Vol. 1, are in the nature of a work for hire (and hence, not subject to termination); (c) whether the failure to list the 1948 consent judgment in the notices as one of the grants sought to be terminated materially affects the notices of termination; (d) whether the post-termination receipt of benefits under the 1975 agreement acts as a novation to regrant the Superman copyright; (e) whether the statute of limitations ran out before the instant action was instituted thereby forestalling this lawsuit; and (f) whether the settlement negotiations that took place between the parties resulted in an

enforceable agreement disposing of the claims asserted in the present action; and,

(2) The parameters of what was recaptured (and the rights flowing therefrom) through the termination notices, namely, (a) whether plaintiffs have a right to defendants' post-termination foreign profits from the exploitation of the Superman copyright; (b) whether plaintiffs are entitled to profits from any of the various trademarks that defendants have procured since the grant in marketing Superman; (c) whether plaintiffs are entitled to profits from the derivative works of the Superman material published by Detective Comics and its successors in interest prior to the termination notice's effective date; and (d) whether any recovery of profits extends beyond those made through DC Comics' exploitation of the Superman copyright to that of its corporate siblings and parent who are licensees to that copyright's movie and television rights, be it based on an alter-ego theory or other notion of equity.

I. Validity and Enforceability of Termination Notices

The 1976 Act created a new right allowing authors and their heirs the ability to terminate a prior grant to the copyright in their creations. See 17 U.S.C. § 304(c). The 1976 Act also set forth specific steps concerning the timing and contents of the notices that had to be served to effectuate the termination of a prior grant. One of the most important steps was placing a limit on the temporal reach such a notice could have on what was subject to being recaptured. Specifically, the "[t]ermination of the grant may be effected at any time during a period of five years beginning at the end of fifty-six years from the date copyright was originally secured." 17 U.S.C. § 304(c)(3) (emphasis added). Moreover, the notice is required to be "served not less than two or more than ten years before" its effective date.

Taken together, someone seeking to exercise the termination right must specify the effective date of the termination, and that effective date must fall within a set five-year window which is at least fifty-six years, but no more than sixty-one years, from the date the copyright sought to be recaptured was originally secured, and such termination notice must be served two to ten years before its effective date. The purpose of this time window for terminating pre-1978 grants was so that the only rights to the copyright affected thereby were those to the 19-year extension in the renewal term created by the 1976 Act, leaving undisturbed the grantee's vested interest to the original 28-year renewal term as set forth in the 1909 Act, the governing statute at the time the grant itself was made.

Additional procedures required to be followed to make the termination notice effective were specified as well: The author or his or her heirs had to serve "an advance notice in writing upon the grantee or the grantee's successor in title"; the notice had to be signed by the author or his or her heirs; the notice was required to "state the effective date of the termination"; and the notice must be "recorded in the Copyright Office before the effective date of termination." 17 U.S.C. § 304(c)(4).

Beyond these statutory requirements, the notice was also required to "comply, in form, content, and manner of service, with [the] requirements that the Register of Copyrights . . . prescribe[s] by regulation." 17 U.S.C. § 304(c)(4)(B). Toward that end, the Register promulgated regulations implementing this statutory proviso. See 37 C.F.R. § 201.10. Among those regulations was one requiring the terminating party to identify in the notice "each work as to which the notice of termination applies." 37 C.F.R. § 201.10(b)(1)(ii).

As one noted author has commented, "[i]t is difficult to overstate the intricacies of these [termination] provisions, the result of which is that they are barely used, no doubt the result desired by lobbyists for assignees." William Patry, Choice of Law and International Copyright, 48 AM. J. COMP. L. 383, 447 (2000); see also Burroughs v. Metro-Goldwyn-Mayer, Inc., 683 F.2d 610, 621 (2nd Cir. 1982) (commenting that the steps necessary to make a termination effective oftentimes create "difficult, technical questions"). Those intricate provisions oftentimes create unexpected pitfalls that thwart or blunt the effort of the terminating party to reclaim the full measure of the copyright in a work of authorship. This case is no different.

1. Promotional Announcements

Plaintiffs gave notice that the effective date of the termination notices was April 16, 1999, meaning that, backdating from that date sixty-one years, the termination notices would leave unaffected (or better said, beyond their reach) any statutory copyright that had been secured in the Superman material before April 16, 1938. Defendants contend that the promotional announcements for Action Comics, Vol. 1, featuring a graphical depiction of Superman, fall just a few days outside the five-year effective window of plaintiffs' termination notices; therefore, they argue, any copyright material contained in those promotional announcements, notably the illustration of Superman on the cover of Action Comics, Vol. 1, is unaffected by the termination notices and remains theirs to exploit exclusively. As defendants frame it, section 304(c)(3)'s five-year effective window "is tantamount to a statute of limitations[;] . . . if any work falls outside the five-year window established by the [termination] effective date, it cannot be recaptured, and the original copyright grant remains in force for that work, allowing the grantee to continue exercising the granted rights without liability." (Defs' Mot. Partial Summ. J. at 29). Thus, any work that was published with notice prior to April 16, 1938, i.e., sixty-one years before the stated effective date, remains untouched by the termination notice. [55]

Plaintiffs do not dispute the legal consequence section 304(c)'s five-year window has in this case on the effective reach of their termination notices. As drafters of the notice, Siegel's heirs were given carte blanche in identifying the termination notices' effective date. Once they chose a date, certain consequences flowed therefrom, the most important of which is to cabin the five-year window within which the notice can recapture any copyright secured in the material to which the grant was directed. A copyright in a work statutorily secured even just days outside this five year window is beyond the effective reach of the termination notice, in much the same way a tardily-filed renewal registration has been held to be ineffective. Cf. 3 NIMMER ON COPYRIGHT § 9.05[b][1] at 9-44 ("a variance of even several days is fatal and that the purported renewal is void to rescue the subject work from the public domain, whether filed after expiration of the one year or prior to its initiation"). A leading treatise supports such a calculation and the consequences flowing from it:

The appropriate dates for termination notices are measured from "the date copyright was originally secured, or beginning on January 1, 1978, whichever is later." In the case of pre-January 1, 1978 works, "secured" means the actual date the work was first published with notice (or in the case of unpublished works, the date of registration), e.g., April 15, 1970, not December 31, 1970. Failure to pay attention to the differences between the date the copyright was originally secured for purposes of section 304(c) termination of transfer and section 305 expiration of term may lead to an untimely notice of termination.

2 PATRY ON COPYRIGHT § 7:43; see also 3 NIMMER ON COPYRIGHT § 11.05[B][1] at 11-40.11 ("Suppose that statutory copyright for a song were first secured on May 21, 1925. Based on the statutory provision that termination may be effected 'beginning at the end of fifty-six years from the date copyright was originally secured,' the first effective date

---

[5] 5 Defendants also contend that the promotional advertisements are not effected by the termination notices because plaintiffs failed to list those works in their notices. As the Court finds that the promotional advertisements fall outside the five-year window during which those notices could effectively terminate the grant in the copyright contained in them, the Court will not pass on the consequences, if any, stemming from plaintiffs' additional failure to list those promotional announcements in their notices.

for termination should be May 21, 1981 "); 3 JAY DRATLER, JR. AND STEPHEN M. MCJOHN, INTELLECTUAL PROPERTY LAW: COMMERCIAL CREATIVE AND INDUSTRIAL PROPERTY § 6.04A[3][a] (2008) ("If the year in which a work was so published predates the current year by more than sixty-one years, then the termination right [to that work] under section 304(c) has expired. The statute apparently requires calculation of all these termination periods from the exact date of publication, rather than from the end of the publication year, as is appropriate for determining copyright terms under the 1976 Act").

It is in this sense that one can say whether a termination notice is timely or not, a question that does not go to the notice's validity (the notice remains valid with respect to a copyright in works that was secured during the five year window) but as to its enforceability against a copyright in a particular work pre- or post-dating that window. Thus, the key in deciding this timeliness question begins with a determination of when the copyright in the work in question was secured, and not when the work itself was created.

The determination of when the copyright in a work is secured is when the material was protected by statute, meaning when the copyright in such a work secured protection under this country's copyright laws. Under the 1909 Act, "works could have obtained statutory copyright . . ., without the necessity of registration, simply by the act of publishing copies of the work bearing a proper copyright notice. As to such works, registration did not create the copyright, but merely recorded it." 2 NIMMER ON COPYRIGHT § 7.16[A][2][b] at 7-148 (emphasis added); see also 17 U.S.C. § 10 (repealed). Thus, the initial question is whether the comic books containing the promotional announcements bore such a copyright notice upon them.

Section 19 of the 1909 Act delineated what constituted proper notice: "The notice of copyright required by section 10 of this title shall consist either of the word 'Copyright', the abbreviation 'Copr.', or the symbol (C), accompanied by the name of the copyright proprietor, and if the work be a printed literary, musical, or dramatic work, the notice shall include also the year in which the copyright was secured by publication." If the comic books in question contained such a notice, then the date of publication is also the date the copyright in the material contained therein was secured. If not, then any of the copyrightable material in the works (including the promotional announcements) was never secured (absent evidence that the material had been registered beforehand with the Copyright Office when it was in an unpublished state) but instead was injected into the public domain.

Here, the material submitted by defendants (the cover page for the magazine and the page on which the promotional announcements is displayed) does contain such a notice. At the bottom of the promotional announcement itself is the following: "Entire contents copyright 1938 by Detective Comics, Inc."

(Decl. Michael Bergman, Ex. C at 10 & Ex. D at 14). Thus, the copyright for any of the works contained in the comic books in question was secured on the date they were published.

This leads to the next question: What are the publication dates for the two comic books that contained the promotional announcements for Action Comics, Vol. 1, featuring an illustration of Superman? Defendants have submitted the initial copyright registrations for these comics, which indicate that More Fun Comics, Vol. 31, was published on April 5, 1938, eleven days before the effectiveness of the plaintiffs' termination notices, and that Detective Comics, Vol. 15, was published on April 10, 1938, six days outside the temporal reach of the termination notices. Under the 1909 Act the initial (as opposed to the renewal) copyright registration constituted prima facie evidence of the publication date for a work. [6] See 17 U.S.C. § 209 (repealed)

---

[6] 6 Defendants' suggestion that the addition of section 304(a)(4)(B) by the Copyright Amendments Act of 1992 somehow altered this rule by extending the prima facie imprimatur to renewals like those in this case is simply mistaken. (Defs' Reply at 40 & n.16). That section provides that, so long as the renewal occurred "within 1 year before [the] expiration" of the initial term, then "the certificate of such registration shall constitute prima facie evidence as to the . . . the facts stated in the certificate." However, the 1992 Act's provisions placed one very important proviso on its applicability -- its provisions applied only where a party was filing a renewal registration to the "extended term of copyright in a work." Thus, the amendments' provisions were limited to renewal claims to works that were still in their initial term when the 1976 Act became effective, January 1, 1978, meaning for copyrights whose first term of copyright was secured on or after January 1, 1950. That is to say, section 304(a)(4)(B)'s provisions only applies to works that had yet reached the time for renewal before the 1976 Act extended the term of the renewal period (unlike Superman in Action Comics, Vol. 1, or the comics containing the promotional announcements). For those works, the 1992 amendments allowed such renewal to be made at anytime, but provided incentives for prompt renewal, the most notable being the extension of the prima facie rule to such promptly filed renewal claims. See 2 PATRY ON COPYRIGHT § 7:50 ("Effective June 26, 1992, Congress abolished the requirements that works in their first term of copyright published or registered between 1964 and 1977 must be timely renewed in order to enjoy the (now) 67-year renewal term. Instead, these works are now automatically renewed for the full term of 75 years. Copyrights whose first term of copyright was secured between January 1, 1950, and December 31, 1963, still had to have been renewed according to the requirements of the 1909 Act. Failure to do so resulted in the work falling into the public domain. . Renewal

(providing that a "certificate of registration" issued by the Register of Copyrights "shall be admitted in any court as prima facie evidence of the facts stated therein"); see also Epoch Productions Corp. v. Killiam Shows, Inc., 522 F.2d 737, 745-46 (2nd Cir. 1975); 5 PATRY ON COPYRIGHT § 17:115 (observing that the reason that renewal certificates issued during the 1909 Act were not accorded prima facie status was because of the "minimal attention" the Register of Copyrights paid to the information contained therein; "[a]s long as original registration for a work has been made, the Copyright Office accept[ed] it at face value").

Plaintiffs attempt to refute this prima facie evidence through expert testimony and by legal argument.

As to the latter, plaintiffs seek to discredit the value of the initial copyright registration for More Fun Comics, Vol. 31, because Detective Comics' successor did not obtain that registration until nearly 28 years after its publication, on the eve of the expiration of the initial copyright term. The 1909 Act required that, once copyright had been secured by publication with notice, "there shall be promptly deposited" the required copies of the published work and the registration claim itself. 17 U.S.C. § 13 (repealed). Plaintiffs suggest that such a "late" initial registration raises questions as to the trustworthiness of any of the information contained in that registration. (Pls' Opp. at 48-49). Plaintiffs correctly point out that Professor Nimmer in his treatise has commented that, "where there was a failure to promptly register and deposit, under the 1909 Act, some questions as to the viability of the copyright might be raised." 2 NIMMER ON COPYRIGHT § 7.16[A][2][b] at 7-150. But Professor Nimmer's comments as to the collateral consequences flowing from such a delay were not geared toward the validity of the copyright itself, but to the existence of an impediment to bringing an action for infringement. See id. at 7-149 (noting that Supreme Court's Washingtonian decision effectively read the "words 'promptly deposited' in Section 13 . . . not . . . as a condition subsequent that, if not satisfied, would result in destruction of the copyright," but rather "[t]he deposit . . . requirement was (as it still is) clearly a condition precedent to the right to bring an infringement action").

Although the general line of reasoning plaintiffs seek to draw from such a "late-in-time" registration makes sense from a policy perspective, plaintiffs

---

claims may still be filed at any time during the renewal period, and a number of incentives have been added to encourage filing. [One such] incentive[] for renewing provided in the Copyright Act of 1992 are the prima facie status that is accorded to the validity of the work"). Given that none of the comics in question fall within the class affected by section 304(a)(4)(B), that section's expansion of the prima facie status to renewal claims does not apply here.

have cited no authority that such long delays in registration vitiates or otherwise diminishes the statutorily conferred prima facie presumption to which such registration claims (and the information contained therein) are entitled, especially once a registration has (as here) been tendered. Moreover, even were the Court to entertain plaintiffs' invitation, there remains the initial registration for the other comic book in question -- Detective Comics, Vol. 15 -- which was obtained shortly after that comic book's publication and, hence, the problem pressed by defendants with the promotional announcement contained therein falling outside the effective reach of the termination notice remains.

Plaintiffs next contend that the copies of the registration certificates submitted by defendants have not been authenticated by the declarant to whose declaration they are affixed, and hence, are not admissible as proof of the comic books' publication date. (Pls' Opp. at 48-49 ("the certificate is not properly authenticated, but is merely attached to the declaration of defendants' attorney, who appears to have no personal knowledge of it"). Such extrinsic evidence of authenticity by the declarant is unnecessary for these copyright registration certificates. Under Federal Rule of Evidence 902(1), a "document bearing a seal purporting to be that of the United States . . . or of a . . . department, officer, or agency thereof," with "a signature purporting to be an attestation or execution," is considered self-authenticated. Close inspection of the copyright registration certificates submitted by defendants clearly reveals the seal issued by the United States Copyright Office, signed by the Register of Copyrights, and bearing the following legend: "[A]ttached are additional certificates for the [comics in question] which were registered in accordance with provisions of the United States Copyright Law." (Decl. James Weinberger, Ex. B & C). The requirements of Rule 902(1) have been met, rendering the copies of the copyright registration certificates as self-authenticated and, thus, admissible.

The obscure nature of these promotional announcements does not alter this analysis. It is undoubtedly true that the existence of these announcements was not widely recognized even by comic book aficionados. That, however, does not change the effect their existence has vis-a-vis the termination notices' effective reach. Once a termination effective date is chosen and listed in the notice, the five-year time window is an unbendable rule with an inescapable effect, not subject to harmless error analysis. See 37 C.F.R. § 201.10(e) (limiting application to "[h]armless errors in a notice" that does not "materially affect the adequacy of the information") (emphasis added). That good cause may have existed for failing to structure the termination notices so as to sweep the announcements within its reach does not obviate application of the rule itself.

The importance such promotional announcements may have on the reach of a termination notice that has been tendered was not lost on plaintiffs' counsel, Mr. Levine, who drafted the termination notices in this case. He also drafted plaintiffs' termination notice with respect to The Spectre copyright, and structured it in such a way so as to include among the works affected by the notice's five-year window a promotional announcement for The Spectre contained in a comic published a month before the one containing the first comic book story of the character. (Decl. Michael Bergman, Exs. WW-YY (termination notice describing among the works affected by the notice the promotional announcement as "Spectre character appearing in costume in an ad in issue No. 51 of More Fun Comics, copyrighted November 28, 1939, as Copyright Registration No. B437786, publication date January 1940") & Decl. Paul Levitz, Ex. A (containing picture of The Spectre ad)).

Having provided prima facie evidence of the comic books' publication dates, the burden shifts to the plaintiffs to produce some evidence calling into question those dates. The burden of production is not a heavy one (in large measure owing to the fact that so little is proffered by the applicant or scrutinized by the Copyright Office in the application process to procure the registration in the first instance), but it is one that must be met nonetheless. See 3 PATRY ON COPYRIGHT § 9:14 ("the Copyright Office has no ability to verify facts stated in the certificate, and not surprisingly makes no effort to do so. . . . At the most, the Office can take notice of any inconsistent facts that appear on the deposit copy and request clarification from the claimant . . . . In any event, [the opposing party] should be required to present only a small degree of evidence calling into question the fact at issue in order to rebut the certificate's presumption").

On that point all that plaintiffs have submitted is the opinion of a comic book historian, Mark Evanier, who was retained by DC Comics in the 1970s to, among other things, assist it "in attempting to determine approximate dates of past publication" of its comics. (Decl. Mark Evaier P 12). From this particular experience, as well as his long history in the comic book industry, Mr. Evanier seeks to cast doubt on the veracity of the asserted publication dates for the comics containing the promotional announcements. The general thrust of his expert opinion is that, outside the first printing of certain famous comic superheros such as Superman in Action Comics, Vol. 1, a particular "run of the mill" comic book's exact date of publication during the 1930s and 1940s is difficult to determine, rendering the dates listed on the certificates as nothing more than "mere guesstimates" by the publisher. (Decl. Mark Evanier P 10). Furthermore, Mr. Evanier downplays the significance of the fact that the comic books in question contained promotional announcements for Action Comics, Vol. 1, as necessarily meaning that their publication must have preceded Action Comics publication. As Mr. Evanier explains, the dates provided by publishers were often the dates initially scheduled or intended for publication, but the actual dates often varied with printing, delivery, and other delays. (Decl. Mark Evanier P 11).

Mr. Evanier's expert opinion is chalk full of information on the publication of comic books in general during this time period, but is void of any specific evidence or opinion as to the publication of the particular comic books in question in this case. He offers no evidence of any specific printing, delivery, or other problems that may have affected the publication of More Fun Comics, Vol. 31, or Detective Comics, Vol. 15. His general opinion thus does not sufficiently refute the prima facie evidence set forth in the initial copyright registration certificates for these particular comic books. At most, his opinion raises some doubts as to the precision of the dates contained in initial copyright registrations for comic books in general from this period. However, those copyright notices were completed at a time which, by Mr. Evanier's own opinion, the copyright holder was attempting to be as accurate as possible in listing those dates and long before any incentive to provide inaccurate dates by virtue of contemplating this present litigation or the termination provisions of the 1976 Act existed. Plaintiffs evidence does no more than inform the Court that, despite efforts to be precise about publication dates for comic books during this particular period, mistakes could be made; it is not at all probative on the issue of whether mistakes were in fact made with respect to the information contained in the particular registration certificates at issue in this case. The Court therefore finds that the promotional announcements containing an illustration of Superman from the cover of Action Comics, Vol. 1, are outside the effective reach of the termination notices.

Perhaps anticipating this finding, plaintiffs next seek to downplay the significance of the promotional announcements themselves by arguing that, legally and factually, little, if any, copyrightable Superman material is contained in those announcements. Specifically, plaintiffs submit that Siegel and Shuster's material was an indivisible joint work, and that the advertisements were a derivative work of the authors' material. Thus, they claim that none of the Superman material contained in the promotional announcements (namely, the cover artwork from Action Comics, Vol. 1) could be copyrighted, and thus, defendants cannot continue to exploit the same, regardless of the termination notice. As framed by plaintiffs: "Defendants' entire argument is falsely premised on the erroneous assumption that they can take the cover of Action Comics, No. 1, one of many illustrated panels in Siegel and Shuster's first 'Superman' comic book story, rip it from this copyrighted joint work, and own a separate copyright in the illustration in the form of a mere 'in house announcement' depicting a reduced image of the illustration. [Moreover,] Detective's 'in-house announcements,' at best, are derivative works based on the pre-existing cover and interior panel of Siegel and Shuster's pre-existing

'Superman' story." (Pls' Opp. at 44, 46).

This emphasis on the joint nature of Siegel and Shuster's Superman material is rendered nugatory by the fact that Siegel and Shuster granted the copyright in their material to Detective Comics on March 1, 1938, well before the promotional advertisements were published by Detective Comics in April of that year. Thus, by the time the promotional announcements were published, Siegel and Shuster's Superman material was owned solely by Detective Comics to do with it as it saw fit, whether it be as a full-length comic or as artwork in its advertising. That Siegel and Shuster intended their work to be combined together and depicted as a unitary whole is a separate and distinct question from whether, in later using some of Shuster's artwork from that combined material it had acquired, Detective Comics somehow unraveled the copyrightability in that portion of the work. The manner of a work's authorship is entirely separate from the way in which an assignee may exploit that material once it has acquired exclusive ownership of the same and, correspondingly, whether there were anything copyrightable in the work the assignee subsequently published using only parts of that material.

In this respect it is important to remember that a joint work can consist of either inseparable or interdependent parts, the latter example of which include "the collaborative musical works of Gilbert and Sullivan . . . ., [t]hese works are the result of the interdependent contributions of the collaborators, i.e., one person wrote the lyrics and the other the music, either of which could on its own [stand] as an independent work, but which, when combined, form a single[, separate] 'interdependent' joint work." 2 PATRY ON COPYRIGHT § 5:6. The original Superman material was the product of the story and dialogue written by Siegel and the art work drawn by Shuster; each on its own could have been a work in its own right subject to copyright protection, but when merged together they formed a single new and unified interdependent work. See Siegel v. Time Warner, Inc., 496 F.Supp.2d 1111, 1145 (C.D. Cal. 2007) (where this Court held, in regard to Superboy, "the copyright to [the same] (if a joint work) would be considered comprised of interdependent parts -- Siegel's dialogue and storyline . . . and Shuster's artwork giving life and color to those words").

At most, Detective Comics took a part of Shuster's independently copyrightable art work out of the joint work and utilized it, in conjunction with other material (namely, the advertising slogan), in a promotional announcement. There is no rule preventing a publisher or others from publishing portions or excerpts of works, joint or otherwise, that it solely owns, and then seeking a separate copyright in the same. Indeed, the opposite is true -- the holder of a copyright is expressly entitled to prepare derivative works based upon a copyrighted work it owns or to utilize portions of that work in other materials. See 17 U.S.C. § 106(2); see generally 17 U.S.C. § 1 (repealed). Detective Comics could just as well have decided to split up the Superman material for publication into two or three installments as it could (and did) decide to publish a portion of that material in an advertisement to promote the comic.

This leads to plaintiffs' contention that the "derivative nature" of the promotional advertisement itself works to exclude any of the copyright in the pre-existing Superman material (notably, the art work for the Action Comics, Vol. 1 cover) contained therein from enuring to the benefit of the defendants to continue to exploit. Generally, if an author contributes additional original material to a pre-existing work so as to recast, transform, or adapt that work, then the copyright protection afforded to the author of that derivative work extends only to that additional material and in no way extends to the underlying, pre-existing material. See 17 U.S.C. § 103(b) (specifying that a derivative work's copyright does not extend to any part of that work using "preexisting material in which copyright subsists"); 1 NIMMER ON COPYRIGHT § 3.03, at 3-10. Thus, it is asserted that the author of the pre-existing material work (here Siegel and Shuster) would continue to retain ownership in the same despite its use in the derivative work (the promotional announcement).

Even assuming that the changes made to the cover page for Action Comics, Vol. 1, in the promotional announcements is not merely a reproduction, but sufficiently "recast, transform, or adapts" the pre-existing material so as to be considered a derivative work thereof (e.g, the cover is shown in black and white instead of color, the scale of the artwork itself is diminished, and text is placed alongside the artwork), there remains a complicating wrinkle. At the time the promotional announcements were placed in Detective Comics' existing comic book publications, the underlying pre-existing Superman material from which a portion of the announcements were derived (again the artwork for the cover) had yet to be published, and, hence, copyright in the same was protected at the time under state common law. See 17 U.S.C. § 2 (repealed).

Given that the portion of the pre-existing material at issue had yet to achieve statutory copyright protection when it was first published in More Fun Comics, Vol. 31, and Detective Comics, Vol. 15, it was injected into the public domain upon the publication of the promotional announcements themselves, absent investiture of statutory copyright protection through its publication. See 17 U.S.C. § 10 (repealed). That is to say, the copyright in the cover of Action Comics, Vol. 1, itself first achieved statutory protection, if at all, upon its publication in the announcements, not its later publication in Action Comics, Vol. 1. See 2 PATRY ON COPYRIGHT § 6:35 ("where an investitive publication occurs, the derivative work copyright covers the unpublished material").

This fact has repercussions on plaintiffs' derivative works argument, as it alters the general rule described above. Once Detective Comics published a portion of the previously unpublished pre-existing material -- as was its right as owner of the material at that time -- its continued protection resided exclusively under statutory copyright in the derivative work itself lest that portion of the pre-existing material (the art work for the cover) be injected into the public domain. See Batjac Productions Inc. v. GoodTimes Home Video Corp., 160 F.3d 1223, 1233 (9th Cir. 1998); 2 PATRY ON COPYRIGHT § 6:35 ("to the extent that previously unpublished material is included in an authorized published derivative work, the derivative work publishes the previously unpublished material"). As Professor Nimmer explains:

Because a derivative work by definition to some extent incorporates a copy of the pre-existing work, publication of the former necessarily constitutes publication of the copied portion of the latter. Of course, an article that merely describes a pre-existing work but does not incorporate any substantial portion of it is not a derivative work and hence, does not publish the pre-existing work. Unless the basic work is reproduced in the published work, it is not published. If only the broad outlines or other fragmentary portion of the pre-existing work are copied and published in the derivative work, then only to that extent is the pre-existing work published.

1 NIMMER ON COPYRIGHT § 4.12[A] at 4-59 to 4-60; see also id. § 4.13[A] at 4-73 ("any work published prior to January 1, 1978, was not only thereby divested of common law copyright; it was also injected into the public domain, unless at the moment of publication copies of the work bore a proper copyright notice"). Thus, included in defendants' right to continue to exploit the copyright in the derivative work (the promotional announcements) is the right to the copyright in that part of the pre-existing work (the illustration from the cover) that was published for the first time in that derivative work.

The cases cited by plaintiffs as standing for the contrary are all distinguishable, as either the act of publication in question fell within the "limited" publication exception because the material was distributed for promotional purposes to members in the trade and not, as here, the general public itself, see Rushton v. Vitale, 218 F.2d 434 (2nd Cir. 1955); Hub Floral Corp. v. Royal Brass Corp., 454 F.2d 1226 (2nd Cir. 1972); or because the underlying work reproduced in the derivative work was itself in the public domain (unlike here where the underlying material was in an unpublished state protected by common law copyright), thereby mooting any question about divestiture of the underlying work through publication. See Alfred Bell & Co. v. Catalda Fine Arts, 191

F.2d 99 (2nd Cir. 1951).

Here, the promotional announcements represent the first time Superman appeared to the public, and consequently, the first time any of Siegel and Shuster's Superman material was protected by statutory copyright, albeit in conjunction with the other material contained in the advertisement itself. Thus, all of the material in the promotional announcement (which included the graphic depiction of Superman later portrayed on the cover of Action Comics, Vol. 1) obtained statutory copyright protection before the earliest possible date covered by the plaintiffs' termination notices. The Court therefore finds that the publication date for at least one of the comics containing the promotional announcements falls outside the reach of the termination notice and, therefore, any copyrightable material contained therein (including that found in the cover to Action Comics, Vol. 1, as depicted in those announcements) remains for defendants to exploit.

This leads to the question of the scope of the copyrighted material remaining in defendants' possession by way of the promotional announcements, a question that defendants themselves acknowledge "is most obviously answered by [looking at] the ads which speak for themselves" and that does not require some "special 'lens'" to resolve. (Defs' Reply at 44).

The Court begins by observing what is not depicted in the announcements. Obviously, nothing concerning the Superman storyline (that is, the literary elements contained in Action Comics, Vol. 1) is on display in the ads; thus, Superman's name, his alter ego, his compatriots, his origins, his mission to serve as a champion of the oppressed, or his heroic abilities in general, do not remain within defendants sole possession to exploit. Instead the only copyrightable elements left arise from the pictorial illustration in the announcements, which is fairly limited.

The person in question has great strength (he is after all holding aloft a car). The person is wearing some type of costume, but significantly the colors, if any, for the same are not represented, as the advertisement appears only in black and white. The argument that the "S" crest is recognizable in the promotional advertisement is not persuasive. What is depicted on the chest of the costume is so small and blurred as to not be readily recognizable, at best all that can be seen is some vague marking or symbol its precise contours hard to decipher. The Court thus concludes that defendants may continue to exploit the image of a person with extraordinary strength who wears a black and white leotard and cape. What remains of the Siegel and Shuster's Superman copyright that is still subject to termination (and, of course, what defendants truly seek) is the entire storyline from Action Comics, Vol. 1, Superman's distinctive blue leotard (complete with its inverted triangular crest across the chest with a red "S" on a yellow background), a red cape and boots, and his superhuman ability to leap tall buildings, repel bullets, and run faster than a locomotive, none of which is apparent from the announcement.

2. Work Made for Hire Aspect of Portions of Action Comics, Vol. 1

Under the 1976 Act, an author's (or his or her heirs') ability to terminate a prior grant in the copyright to a creation does not apply to a "work made for hire," because the copyright in such a creation was never the artist's to grant, belonging instead to the one who employed the artist to create the work. See 17 U.S.C. § 304(c); Playboy Enterprises, Inc. v. Dumas, 53 F.3d 549, 554 (2nd Cir. 1995) ("Once it is established that a work is made for hire, the hiring party is presumed to be the author of the work"). The manner in which Siegel and Shuster's Superman material was submitted, then re-submitted in a reformatted version, and finally accepted for publication by Detective Comics raises questions about the work for hire status of the re-formatted material (but not the initial material submitted to the publisher) later published in Action Comics, Vol. 1.

Defendants argue that portions of the copyrightable material contained in Action Comics, Vol. 1, are unaffected by the termination notice because those portions belong exclusively to them as "works for hire," arguing that certain material found in the comic book was created by Detective Comics' in-house employees, or that the material was added to the underlying Superman material by Siegel and Shuster at the publisher's direction. (Defs' Opp. at 27). Specifically, the alleged "additional" material provided by Detective Comics' in-house employees is the color choices made throughout the comic, notably, the red color of the letter "S" on Superman's crest and the art work for the cover to the magazine itself (albeit modeled after a interior panel in the Superman comic illustrated by Shuster). Similarly, the additional material supplied in response to the publisher's February 1, 1938, letter is Shuster's admitted (and as acknowledged by Siegel) drawing of "several additional pictures to illustrate the story continuity" appearing "on page 1 of the first Superman release" and "the last panel appearing on the thirteenth page." (Decl. Michael Bergman Ex. G at 2 & Ex. H at 5).

The thrust of defendants' argument was made and rejected by the Second Circuit in the 1970s Superman copyright renewal litigation, and is thus precluded as a matter of collateral estoppel here. In that litigation, defendants' predecessors-in-interest presented much of the same evidence now submitted in this case to argue that this additional material transformed the entirety of Siegel and Shuster's pre-existing Superman material published in Action Comics, Vol. 1, into a work made for hire. The Second Circuit rejected this argument, elaborating: "In the case before us, Superman and his miraculous powers were completely developed long before the employment relationship was instituted. The record indicates that the revisions directed by the defendants were simply to accommodate Superman to a magazine format. We do not consider this sufficient to create the presumption that the [comic book] strip was a work for hire." Siegel, 508 F.2d at 914. This conclusion forecloses any further litigation on the point of whether Shuster's additional drawings when reformatting the underlying Superman material into a comic book format or other facts related to such a theory such as the colorization process for Action Comics, Vol. 1, or the party responsible for the illustration of the cover to the magazine, rendered all or portions of the resulting comic book a work made for hire.

Defendants seek to avoid the collateral estoppel effect of the Second Circuit's decision by arguing that the only issue concerning the work for hire status of Action Comics, Vol. 1, related to Siegel and Shuster's 1934-1935 "contributions," and not what was "added to the first Superman story by Detective's employees," amongst whom defendants count Siegel and Shuster after they executed the December, 1937, contract. (Defs' Opp. at 36). Such a reading conflicts with the record. The evidence that was proffered during the 1970s litigation in the trial court on the work for hire question included declarations from Siegel and Shuster discussing what took place during the reformatting process. This is the same evidence that defendants now seek to use in this case to argue that the reformatted material was a work made for hire.

Moreover, the circumstances surrounding the reformatting of the underlying Superman material was not only mentioned by the Second Circuit, but discounted by that court in passing on the work for hire nature of Action Comics, Vol. 1, itself, not just the initial contributions made by Siegel and Shuster back in 1934 and 1935. It would be incongruous for the Court, in respecting as it must the Second Circuit's judgment, to now hold that, while that reformatted material did not transform the entirety of the material in Action Comics, Vol. 1, into a work made for hire, some subpart thereof (and, indeed, a very limited subpart, consisting of but a few panels) was somehow excised out and should be accorded work made for hire status. The litigation of the larger question sweeps within it defendants' opportunity to litigate a subpart thereof.

A contrary holding would transgress certain core principles of collateral estoppel: "A new contention is not necessarily a new issue. If a new legal theory or factual assertion raised in the second action is relevant to the issues that were litigated and adjudicated previously, the prior determination of the issue is conclusive on the issue despite the fact that new evidence or argument relevant to the issue was not in fact expressly pleaded, introduced into evidence, or otherwise urged." 18 JAMES WM. MOORE, MOORE'S FEDERAL PRACTICE § 132.02[2][c] at 132-25 (3rd ed. 2007). Significantly, much of the evidence underlying defendants' arguments was presented in the Second Circuit litigation (notably Siegel and Shusters' declarations submitted in that litigation) or, if not, was certainly available to be used in that case (the colorization process for the initial printing of Action Comics, Vol. 1, or that in-house employees supposedly drew the cover to the magazine). "A party may be precluded from re-litigating an issue if evidence supporting the party's position on the issue could have been submitted in previous litigation but, for whatever reason, was not properly raised. Evidence that is not the result of a different factual situation or changed circumstances, but is instead historical in nature and could have been admitted at the first trial if properly submitted, cannot be introduced in subsequent litigation of the same issue." Id. § 132.02[2][d] at 132-25 to 132-26 (citing Yamaha Corp. v. United States, 295 U.S. App. D.C. 158, 961 F.2d 245, 257 (D.C. Cir. 1992)).

Nowhere have defendants explained why they did not bring up the question of the colorization process for Action Comics, Vol. 1, or the cover art work for the magazine, before the courts handling the 1970s Superman litigation. The question about the legal effect the reformatting of the underlying Superman material had on the work for hire question was litigated by the parties and resolved by the courts during the 1970s Superman matter. Similarly, the question about the colorization and cover art work (and who was responsible for the same) could have been raised in conjunction with the work for hire question, but defendants failed or decided not to do so. Having litigated the question and having the opportunity to present all the evidence that pressed on the issue, defendants are now barred from seeking to relitigate it anew even under the purported limited guise that it is now being offered.

Some noted treatise writers have commented that the Second Circuit's analysis focusing on the work for hire nature of the additional reformatted material should have been analyzed as a derivative work, that is, that the additional material was derivative of the underlying Superman material. See 1 NIMMER ON COPYRIGHT § 5.03[B] [1][b][I] at 5-33 n.92. ("The Siegel decision . . . may be understood as holding that the first expression of the Superman character was the underlying work, and the later development of the character was a derivative work. Because only the derivative work was produced in a for-hire relationship, the underlying work remains the property of the creators"). However, this analysis does not benefit defendants.

First, no additional literary material was supplied in re-formatting the underlying Superman material into a comic book format. All the dialogue and storyline contained in Action Comics, Vol. 1, was present before Detective Comics requested the pair to provide a reformatted version of the material, and that literary material remained unchanged through the reformatting process. All that is left was supplying some additional illustrations by Shuster, the precise ones specified in his declaration. From the Court's review of these additional illustrations, it appears that the material is completely derivative of other panels in the Action Comics, Vol. 1, comic, with its origins in the underlying Superman material. Thus, for instance, while the final panel on page 13 shows Superman's crest with a red "S" on a yellow background, so, too, does another panel containing the underlying, pre-existing material. Similarly, while the panels on the first page to the comic show Superman leaping skyscapers, running at high rates of speed, and demonstrating feats of great strength, so, too, do other panels containing the pre-existing material. Indeed, the earliest sketches by Shuster from 1934 and 1935 demonstrate that the graphical depiction of Superman was well on its way to being completely developed before the re-formatted material in question was created some three years later. Thus, even if the additional material in question was tendered as a derivative work that was made for hire by Shuster, all the potentially copyrightable material contained therein is completely derivative of the pre-existing material and, hence, is not subject to independent copyright protection in the first instance. This, then, lends strong support to the Second Circuit's observation: "Superman and his miraculous powers were completely developed long before the employment relationship was instituted." Siegel, 508 F.2d at 914.

Defendants also argue that the coloring for Action Comics, Vol. 1, was not created or chosen by Siegel or Shuster, but was instead the product of some of Detective Comics' in-house employees working in the printing department. Even if this argument was not otherwise precluded by collateral estoppel, the evidence produced in support is less than persuasive. According to "eye-witness" Jack Adler, the material contained in comic books "at the time" was provided by artists to the Detective Comics' production staff in black and white. (Decl. Jack Adler P 3). "Typically," members of the staff then decided upon the color that would be applied throughout the magazine, something that defendants argue is an additional element added to the underlying Superman material that is itself subject to copyright protection. (Decl. Jack Adler P 3). Defendants' argument depends entirely upon Mr. Adler's declaration, which is not as clear as they suggest.

Mr. Adler does not state that he worked on the colorizing of Action Comics, Vol. 1, itself. Instead he states that he "worked for the engraving company that made the metal plates for printing of, among other things, comic books for Detective Comics." (Decl. Jack Adler P 3). He then states that, "[a]t the time, comic book artists . . . submitted drawn and inked comic book work in black and white." (Id.). Mr. Adler further states that the black-and-white pages "were then photographed by the engraver and a photo print was hand[-]colored by staff at Detective and by the engravers." (Id.). Of course, nothing in this statement precludes the possibility that, even if the Superman material was so submitted, Siegel and Shuster may have also placed certain color directions with their material to be utilized in the engraving process. In fact, that the earlier incarnation of Superman as hulking strongman in the tradition of Tarzan was created by the pair as a comic book with color illustrations lends to the possibility that they already had pre-conceived color choices in mind for the later comic if it were later reformatted into a comic book, rather than a newspaper comic strip.

Moreover, viewed in context, Mr. Adler's declaration appears to describe procedures generally employed in the printing process, not as evidence of what actually occurred with respect to the printing of Action Comics, Vol. 1, itself. His statement (and, in fact, the entire Adler declaration) is of dubious evidentiary value in light of his candid admission that he has "no knowledge of Siegel and Shuster selecting any of the color in Action Comics, No.1." (Id. P 4). Mr. Adler attempts to temper his admission of lack of knowledge by stating, without any basis, that he is "aware that Detective staff member, Ed Eisenberg, selected the color for Superman's 'S' in Shield on his costume." (Id.) Of course, Mr. Adler's statement on this point is inadmissible as it is based on hearsay. Without any direct link between Mr. Adler's work and the printing of Action Comics, Vol. 1, in particular, there exists an insufficient evidentiary foundation for his conclusions concerning the manner in which the Superman material was supplied to the printer and the colorization of the same was handled.

Finally, defendants argue that the cover for Action Comics, Vol. 1, was drawn by Detective Comics' in-house artists. However, the scant evidentiary basis provided in support of this argument is ambiguous. In a letter sent to Jerome Siegel dated February 22, 1938, Detective Comics' editor, Vin Sullivan, enclosed "a silverprint of the cover of Action Comics," with the observation that Detective Comics "used one of those panel drawings of SUPERMAN, as you suggested in your recent letter." (Decl. Michael Bergman, Ex. I). The inference sought to be drawn by defendants is that when Mr. Sullivan stated that the publisher "used" an interior illustration from the Superman comic for the cover artwork he was stating that one of the publisher's in-house artists saw the interior panel in question and then drew the cover using the interior panel as inspiration. Of course, given the limited nature of the information contained in the passage it could also be argued that, in his earlier letter, Siegel enclosed an illustration by Shuster as a suggestion for the comic book's cover and Detective Comics decided to "use" this suggestion. This alternative reading is not implausible. As demonstrated by the pair's attempt to have their earlier incarnation of Superman published by Detective Dan, Shuster had in the past drawn exemplars for the cover illustration for his comics well before they were ever accepted for publication.

In conclusion, the Court finds that the question of the work-for-hire nature of certain portions of the Superman material published in Action Comics, Vol. 1, is precluded from further litigation by operation of the 1974 Second Circuit decision. Accordingly, the binding nature of that court's decision leads to the conclusion that all the Superman material contained in Action Comics, Vol. 1, is not a work-made-for-hire and therefore is subject to termination.

3. Failure to Include 1948 Consent Judgment

Among the regulatory requirements promulgated by the Register of Copyrights concerning the termination notice's "form, content, and manner of service," 17 U.S.C. § 304(c)(4)(B), is the requirement that the notice must "reasonably" identify "the grant" to which it applies. 37 C.F.R. § 201.10(b)(1)(iv). Thus, if the author entered into five separate grants of rights for the same work, and a notice of termination identifies only four of those grants, the fifth grant remains "intact," and the grantee's rights thereunder remain unaffected. See 3 NIMMER ON COPYRIGHT § 11.06[B] at 11-40.22(1) n.63 ("if a grant was not effectively terminated, then the rights licensed under such grant remain").

Here, defendants argue that plaintiffs' failure to identify the 1948 consent judgment from the Westchester action is fatal to their attempts to terminate their grant to the copyright in Superman, as that consent judgment was among the grants leading to the transfer of ownership from the artists to Detective Comics. Such argumentation is predicated upon the notion that, notwithstanding the plaintiffs' act of identifying the stipulation between the parties from the Westchester litigation that resulted in the consent judgment, identification of the consent judgment from the Westchester action itself as (or part of) a "grant" was necessary because it constituted the final step in "effectuat[ing] the transfer to [Detective Comics] of the sole and exclusive ownership of all rights relating to 'Superman'"; "without it the rights identified in the Stipulation would not have been transferred." (Defs' Opp. at 39). The Court disagrees.

Although the 1976 Act nowhere defines the term "grant," the central question raised is plainly one of transfer: Did Siegel and Shuster transfer any rights to Superman through or in conjunction with the 1948 consent judgment? If so, then it operated as a grant by the artists in the same.

On that point, the 1976 Act is helpful as it defines a "transfer of copyright ownership" as "an assignment, mortgage, exclusive license, or any other conveyance, alienation, or hypothecation of a copyright." 17 U.S.C. § 101; see Melville B. Nimmer, Termination of Transfers under the Copyright Act of 1976, 125 U. PA. L. REV. 947, 951-52 (1977) ("In general, the termination provisions apply to any 'transfer' of copyright and to nonexclusive licenses of copyright or of any right comprised in a copyright. [Thus, a] 'transfer' includes not only assignments (as understood under the [1909] Act), but also exclusive licenses and any other conveyance of copyright or of any exclusive right comprised in a copyright").

The consent judgment at issue did not effectuate any transfer of rights from

Siegel and Shuster to Detective Comics. If any rights were transferred as a result of the Westchester action, such a transfer was effectuated by the execution of the earlier stipulated agreement of the parties, not a document created two days later which simply memorialized the transfer that the stipulation itself had accomplished. The binding nature of the transfer contained in the stipulation was completed the moment that agreement was executed. The consent judgment was a mere formality whose execution (or lack thereof) did not detract from the otherwise binding nature of the parties' earlier agreement. It merely parroted what was already agreed to by the parties in the stipulation itself.

Finally, even if the 1948 consent judgment is a "grant" separate and apart from (or part and parcel with) the 1948 stipulation, the regulations recognize that not all errors in compliance with its terms impact the validity of the termination notice: "Harmless errors in a notice that do not materially affect the adequacy of the information required to serve the purposes of . . . section 304(c) . . . shall not render the notice invalid." 37 C.F.R. § 201.10(e)(1). Here, viewing the issue in the light most favorable to the defendants, the 1948 consent judgment simply served to culminate or otherwise finalize the transfer of the Superman copyright achieved through the stipulation the parties reached two days earlier. That plaintiffs only identified the latter rather than the former does not materially affect defendants' understanding of the "grant" sought to be affected by the notice. Indeed, courts have required much less in meeting the regulation's requirement of providing "a brief statement reasonably identifying the grant being terminated." See Music Sales Corp. v. Morris, 73 F.Supp.2d 364, 378 (S.D.N.Y. 1999) (holding that description of the grant in the termination notice as the "grant or transfer of copyright and the rights of the copyright proprietor" was sufficient as "it appears to be boilerplate on termination notices customarily accepted by the Register of Copyrights"); see also 2 PATRY ON COPYRIGHT § 7:45 (approving Music Sales). Nowhere do defendants argue why the harmless error rule should not apply in a situation such as this where one document that is a part in the process leading to the "transfer" of rights is identified, but its necessary corollary was not.

Accordingly, the Court concludes that, even if the consent judgment is viewed as integral to the transfer of rights, plaintiffs' failure to identify it as a grant subject to the termination notice was a harmless error that did not diminish the notice defendants received regarding the nature of the grant (and resulting transfer of rights) that plaintiffs intended to terminate.

4. Continued Acceptance of Benefits Under 1975 Agreement

Defendants argue that Joanne Siegel's continued acceptance of benefits under the parties' 1975 agreement constitutes, "as a matter of equity," a de facto post-termination grant of rights in the Superman copyright to defendants under the terms of that agreement (or as phrased by defendants, plaintiffs have "effectively reaccepted the terms of the grant"). (Defs' Opp. at 41). The legal premise of their argument is that the 1976 Act recognizes that, once a termination notice has been served and thereby vested, see 17 U.S.C. § 304(c)(6)(B), the terminating party is free to make "a further grant . . . of any right covered by a terminated grant" to the original grantee or its successor in title. 17 U.S.C. § 304(c)(6)(D). The Court ultimately rejects this argument as unpersuasive because it mistakenly assumes the 1975 agreement was a "grant" to the Superman copyright.

A look at the context leading up the execution of the 1975 agreement illuminates in what way the parties believed (and just as importantly did not intend) for that agreement to bind them. The 1975 agreement appears to have been drafted in response to bad publicity (apparently due to the juxtaposition of the creators' misfortune and the Superman character's commercial success), and not as a means to transfer or convey the party's rights to the Superman copyright. The agreement observed that nothing therein should be construed as undermining the rights defendants had been conferred by virtue of the March 1, 1938, assignment, rights which were later vindicated in the Westchester action and the 1970s Second Circuit litigation. Indeed, the agreement reaffirmed defendants' existing rights to Superman and provided plaintiffs with annual payments, medical insurance, and screen credits. Such conferral of benefits was identified in the agreement as a "voluntary" act by defendants in recognition of Siegel and Shuster's "past services." The 1982 codicil, in turn, removes the condition for the promised benefits to Siegel's widow on the timing of her husband's death.

This context and the language in the agreement itself demonstrate that the 1975 agreement was not a "grant." The agreement's execution did not result in the transfer or assignment of the Superman copyright. Indeed, the agreement itself expressly disavows such an interpretation by including language that the conferring of benefits by defendants to Siegel and Shuster was simply a "voluntary" act in recognition of the pair's "past services," and that nothing therein should be construed as undermining the rights defendants had been conferred in the March 1, 1938, assignment as vindicated in the Westchester action and the 1970s Second Circuit litigation. Thus, by its own terms, no rights were transferred through the execution of that agreement. A reaffirmation of existing rights without more is no more "an assignment" or "conveyance" of rights to a copyright than it would if Detective Comics had instead issued a press release declaring that previous court rulings had recognized its existing ownership rights to that copyright.

Similarly, the 1982 codicil under which Joanne Siegel continued to receive annual payments and benefits did not transfer any rights. The codicil consists of five paragraphs. The first merely notes that the letter is in response to a letter written by Joanne Siegel to the company's executive officer regarding her concern over how she would provide for herself after her husband's death. The second referenced the 1975 agreement, noted the increase in the amount of the annual payments from $ 20,000 to $ 50,000 thereunder, and the payment of an additional bonus. The third clarified a royalty policy that applied to creators other than Siegel and Shuster. The fourth set forth the agreement to continue to pay benefits to Joanne Siegel for the balance of her life in the event her husband predeceased her before 1985. The fifth and final paragraph merely wishes Joanne Siegel and her family well. Nowhere in these five humble paragraphs is a transfer of rights to be inferred, much less explicitly found.

Thus, even if Joanne Siegel's continued receipt of the benefits of the bargain contained in the 1975 agreement post-termination somehow operated as a de facto re-acceptance of the agreement itself (and the obligations flowing thereunder), nowhere among those re-accepted "obligations" or "commitments" in that agreement was there a grant to the Superman copyright. Defendants protest the Court drawing this conclusion, arguing that plaintiffs have admitted in their pleadings (their complaint, and by filing a termination notice directed at the 1975 agreement) that the 1975 agreement contained a grant to the Superman copyright. It certainly is true that "[f]actual assertions in pleadings and pre-trial orders . . . are considered judicial admissions" that bind the party who made them. American Title Ins. Co. v. Lacelaw Corp., 861 F.2d 224, 226 (9th Cir. 1988). That being said, "courts still have discretion not to apply the doctrine in particular cases." 18 JAMES WM. MOORE, MOORE'S FEDERAL PRACTICE § 134.33[6] at 134-84 (3rd. ed. 2007) (citing New Hampshire v. Maine, 532 U.S. 742, 750, 121 S. Ct. 1808, 149 L. Ed. 2d 968 (2001) ("Because the rule is intended to prevent 'improper use of judicial machinery,' judicial estoppel 'is an equitable doctrine invoked by a court at its discretion'")).

As noted at the outset, the termination provisions contained in the 1976 Act are among the most complex and technical ones in the statute. Given this complexity, it is not surprising that a party seeking to harness its machinery may, out of an abundance of caution, be more "over-inclusive" in terms of listing the possible "grants" it seeks to terminate. To penalize a party for being over-inclusive rather than under-inclusive is all the more inequitable given the high hurdles the termination provisions put in place. Here, plaintiffs were represented by highly experienced counsel who decided to list the 1975 agreement as a "grant" so as to leave no stone unturned; an approach all the more justified given the extremely technical and arcane arguments that have been advanced in this litigation concerning the efficacy and enforceability of the termination notices themselves. The Court therefore concludes that in these circumstances discretion counsels against applying the judicial estoppel doctrine in the manner advocated by defendants.

Accordingly, the Court concludes that Joanne Siegel's continued receipt of payments and benefits under the 1975 agreement and 1982 codicil thereto does not constitute a "further grant" or "an agreement to make a further grant" pursuant to 17 U.S.C. § 304(c)(6)(D).

5. Statute of Limitations

Defendants contend that the present action was filed untimely. The statute of limitations itself is clear enough. The Copyright Act of 1976 provides that "[n]o civil action shall be maintained under the provisions of this title unless it is commenced within three years after the claim accrued." 17 U.S.C. § 507(b). The issue raised by defendants implicates the latter clause and requires the Court to determine when plaintiffs' claims accrued.

At the outset, a clarification of terms is in order. The instant matter, although couched in terms of terminating the 1938 grant, is in effect one for co-ownership of the copyright in the Superman material contained in Action Comics, Vol. 1, because, if successful, plaintiffs would gain only a joint ownership interest in that material with DC Comics, owing to the fact that Shuster left no heirs who could simultaneously seek to terminate his half of the grant in the material. Claims of co-ownership accrue when there is a "plain and express repudiation of co-ownership . . . communicated to the claimant." Zuill v. Shanahan, 80 F.3d 1366, 1369 (9th Cir. 1996).

Here, defendants assert that such a repudiation was expressed by a letter submitted to plaintiffs' counsel dated December 18, 1997, during the whirlwind of negotiations that took place between the parties shortly after the submission of the termination notices. The Court finds to the contrary. As explained more fully below, although the letter stated a position that the termination notices were "defective," the letter addressed only the scope of the rights that could be recaptured by the termination notices and left unchallenged the notices' validity and enforceability, thus falling short of the required repudiation.[7] 7

---

[7] 7 One could quibble with whether any date other than the termination effective date itself can serve as the accrual date in a case involving the right to termination of a grant. Much like having to await a judicial determination whether one is a heir (as opposed to instances when an ownership claim is based on whether or not someone is a creator) has been held to be the earliest instant for an accrual date, see Stone v. Williams, 970 F.2d 1043 (2nd Cir. 1992) (Hank Williams' putative daughter's claim to be an owner had to await judicial determination that she was in fact his daughter and heir, thus accrual date was not triggered when Hank Williams' first contested her putative

Specifically, the letter upon which defendants rely notified plaintiffs' counsel, Mr. Levine, that they considered "the Superman Notices to be defective in several respects." (Defs' Opp. at 50). What is telling is that the areas of defect elaborated upon in the letter did not relate to the validity or enforceability of the termination notices themselves, but pointed to areas curtailing the scope of what could be recaptured even assuming the notice to be properly presented. These defects thus did not call into question plaintiffs asserted right to termination contained in the notices. For example, the letter remarks that defendants would still retain its rights in trademarks that it had secured over the years to certain Superman-related material, and that the termination would not give plaintiffs access to an accounting of the foreign profits defendants gained from exploiting the copyright. Far from repudiating plaintiff's co-ownership to the copyright, the letter acknowledged the validity of that ownership interest. Thus, the letter remarked that, "if the Siegels do not execute a re-grant to DC, beginning in April of 1999, DC and the Siegels will be joint owners of the United States copyright in the 'Superman' comic published in Action Comics No. 1 in June, 1938."

---

status but instead when state court made determination that she was his heir), so too a claim of ownership by way of termination of a grant cannot be realized unless and until after the termination's effective date. Stated another way, a party's status as a creator is a factual question subject to being challenged by the other putative co-owner at any time, and hence, the accrual date for the same would begin at that instant. The same, however, is not true of a putative co-owner by way of termination. Their status as co-owner is not predicated upon a pre-existing factual scenario, like whether they were involved in jointly creating the material per se. Instead, their status as a co-owner is predicated upon a legal mechanism -- the exercise of a new statutory right revoking an earlier transfer in the copyright in question, be it one they solely or jointly created -- that takes place at a certain defined point in time. Unless and until that legal triggering point is passed, there is nothing for the other co-owner to reject or challenge. This is particularly the case given that termination notices can be served up to ten years before the effective termination date. Defendants' position would, as a matter of logic, countenance scenarios where due to an early "rejection" of the termination notice, the passage of the limitations period would occur well before the termination effective date even arrived (and with it the putative co-owner's rights even vested). Nonetheless, the Court need not resolve this question as the letter in question does not constitute a plain and express repudiation of plaintiffs' termination notice (and, hence, its right to co-ownership to the copyright in the Siegel and Shuster Superman material).

(Decl. Michael Bergman, Ex. U at 2).

Even more telling was DC Comics' subsequent conduct. The parties' negotiations quickly broke down and not much of substance was communicated between the parties thereafter. Then, the day before the termination effective date, DC Comics sent a letter to plaintiffs' counsel denying the validity of the termination notice, proclaiming:

The absence of any steps towards negotiation for two years, particularly on the 'eve' of the April 16, 1999 purported 'effective' date of the termination, leaves us concerned. Thus our client has no alternative but to move to the stage of putting your clients on clear notice, as set forth below, of DC Comics' rights and of its determination, if it becomes necessary, to take all appropriate and necessary steps to protect those rights. First, your clients are hereby put on notice that DC Comics rejects both the validity and scope of the Notices . . . .

(Decl. Marc Toberoff, Ex. Q (emphasis added)).
If, as defendants contend, such notice of intent had been so clearly and unmistakably communicated over a year and half earlier, it is odd for them to have to repeat it and then state that they were "putting" plaintiffs "on notice" about it. Accordingly, the Court finds that the present action seeking declaratory relief regarding plaintiffs' termination of the 1938 grant accrued on April 16, 1999, the effective date of that termination. DC Comics' submission of the letter the day before that date denying the validity of the termination notice gave a plain and express indication to plaintiffs that a claim for declaratory relief vis-vis the validity of their termination notice was now ripe. See 28 U.S.C. § 2201 ("In a case of actual controversy within its jurisdiction, . . . any court of the United States, upon the filing of an appropriate pleading, may declare the rights and other legal relations of any interested party seeking such declaration, whether or not further relief is or could be sought.")
Applying both the date of the accrual of the claim, the parties' tolling agreement to the three-year statute of limitations, and the filing date of this action, the Court concludes that it is timely. The effective date of the termination notice, and therefore the date of accrual, is April 16, 1999. The parties entered into a tolling agreement on April 6, 2000, which amounts to nine days less than one year that the limitations clock ran before being tolled. [8]8 The tolling agreement lasted until ten business days after plaintiffs'

---

[8] 8 Defendants' argument that the tolling agreement does not apply to plaintiffs' claims against Time Warner, Inc., and Warner Bros. Entertainment, Inc., because neither was a "party to" or bound by that agreement is

September 21, 2002, letter providing written notice that they were ending settlement negotiations, that is, October 4, 2002, at which time the limitations clock started ticking once more.[9] 9 The present action was filed two years and four days later, on October 8, 2004. Adding the periods of time the limitations period was running together, it is clear that they add up to a period of time just short of the three-year period set forth in § 507(b).

Accordingly, the Court concludes that the present action is timely.

6. The 2001-2002 Settlement Negotiations
Defendants contend that plaintiffs' termination notice is no longer effective as the parties' settlement negotiations led to them entering into a binding post-termination agreement that resolved the issues presently before the Court. A brief review of the time line regarding those negotiations is helpful to the Court's analysis of the present issue:

October 19, 2001 Pursuant to the parties' negotiations, plaintiffs' counsel sent to defendants' counsel a six-page letter outlining the substance of a settlement offer from defendants that was "accepted" by the plaintiffs.
October 26, 2001 Defendants responded, noting they were working on a draft agreement and enclosing "a more fulsome outline" of "what" they "believe the deal" they have "agreed" to is.

---

disingenuous. (Defs' Opp. at 52). The tolling agreement expressly provides that its terms bound not only DC Comics but also its "past and present subsidiaries or affiliates." (Decl. Marc Toberoff, Ex. Z). Being the parent company (Time Warner, Inc.) or corporate sibling (Warner Bros. Entertainment, Inc.,) of another (DC Comics) certainly qualifies as a corporate affiliate to the same; a point defendants later admit when speaking to the alter ego question presented in the pleadings. (Defs' Mot. Summ. J. at 79 ("the following is a chart of the current corporate structure and affiliations between DC, WBEI and TWI")). Moreover, representatives for both companies were actively involved in the settlement negotiations themselves, further undermining any suggestion that they were bystanders to the process.

[9] 9 Defendants argue that the tolling period concluded much earlier based on the parties earlier having reached "an amicable resolution of the dispute." (Defs' Opp. at 51 (emphasis in original)). Given that the Court finds that no such "resolution," as opposed to a naggingly close potential for the same, occurred through the parties settlement discussion post-termination, see infra A.6, their argument is without merit.

February 1, 2002 Defendants' counsel provided a fifty-six page draft agreement that reserved the right to have their clients comment upon it and noted that certain, related "stand alone" assignments were in the process of being finalized.

May 5, 2002 Plaintiffs responded to defendants' draft by stating that the proposed agreement contained new, unacceptable terms to which they had not agreed.

May 21, 2002 Defendants sent a letter to plaintiffs stating that they believed that each of the major points in the settlement had already been agreed upon.

Sept 21, 2002 Plaintiffs rejected their counsel's proposed draft agreement and advised defendants in writing that they were ending negotiations.

The parties are in agreement that California law should be applied in deciding this question, but disagree as to its application. "California law is clear that there is no contract until there has been a meeting of the minds on all material points." Banner Entertainment v. Superior Court, 62 Cal.App.4th 348, 358, 72 Cal. Rptr. 2d 598 (1998). The failure to reach a meeting of the minds on all material points prevents the formation of a contract even if the parties have orally agreed upon some of the terms, or have taken some action related to the contract. Grove v. Grove Valve & Reg. Co., 4 Cal.App.3d 299, 311-12, 84 Cal. Rptr. 300 (1970). Similarly, the terms proposed in an offer must be met exactly, precisely, and unequivocally for its acceptance to result in the formation of a binding contract. See Panagotacos v. Bank of America, 60 Cal.App.4th 851, 855-56, 70 Cal. Rptr. 2d 595 (1998); Apablasa v. Merritt & Co., 176 Cal.App.2d 719, 726, 1 Cal. Rptr. 500 (1959). A qualified acceptance constitutes a rejection terminating the original offer and the making of a counteroffer to the original offeror, which must also be unequivocally accepted by the former offeror for a binding contract to form. See Panagotacos, 60 Cal.App.4th at 855-56; Glende Motor Co. v. Superior Court, 159 Cal.App.3d 389, 396, 205 Cal. Rptr. 682 (1984) ("California law has generally held that a qualified acceptance . . . affects the viability of the offer itself, so that 'a qualified acceptance amounts to a new proposal or counteroffer putting an end to the original offer'"); In re Pago Pago Air Crash, 637 F.2d 704, 706 (9th Cir. 1981); see also CAL. CIV. CODE § 1585 ("A qualified acceptance is a new proposal.").

The parties disagree over whether the terms contained in plaintiffs' October 19, 2001, letter differ in substance from those set forth in defendants' later letter of October 26, 2001 (and accompanying outline), such that there was no unequivocal acceptance of an offer and, thus, no agreement. As with much in both life and law, materiality is in the eye of the beholder. From the Court's reading of the parties' correspondence, it is clear that the parties went well beyond reaching a settlement in principle regarding their respective positions to the Superman property. Rather, as suggested by the time line above, the parties' correspondence, and the actions taken in response thereto, illustrates that they found themselves in the all-too-familiar situation in which verbal settlement negotiations result in what the parties believe to be an agreement on all the major points of dispute, but which, upon further discussion, falls short of the agreement needed to resolve their dispute. The devil, as it often is, was in the details.

That material details remained is evidenced by defendants' response to plaintiffs' initial letter, enclosing "a more fulsome outline" of what it "believed the deal" they had "agreed to." Moreover, defendants' February, 2002, draft agreement was not even considered final by its authors, who reserved the right for their clients to "comment" on it, and would also require the further submission of a number of "stand alone" agreements yet to be finalized. Indeed, Time Warner's CEO later commented that submission of the draft agreement was "expected" to result in further "comments and questions" from the Siegel heirs that "would need to be resolved."

This give and take reveals that the parties, while close to agreeing to a complete and comprehensive settlement of their dispute, had not passed the threshold where they had finalized and assented to all material terms of such a settlement. Rather, as they attempted to sketch in the finer details of a settlement from the broad outlines contained in the October 19 letter, more and more issues arose upon which they could not reach agreement, resulting in the negotiations falling apart. In this respect, the present case is not unlike Callie v. Near, 829 F.2d 888 (9th Cir. 1987), and Weddington Prods. v. Flick, 60 Cal.App.4th 793, 71 Cal. Rptr. 2d 265 (1998), in which the courts held that no enforceable agreement was reached when the parties had agreed to a rough outline of an agreement, but were thereafter unable to reach agreement on the finer details and the negotiations fell apart.

Defendants' argument to the contrary is premised on the notion that they can limit the scope of the legal analysis to the October 19, 2001, letter and call it a contract, regardless of their materially different October 26, 2001, letter in reply ("I enclose . . . a more fulsome outline of what we believe the deal . . . is") and their vastly different February 1, 2002, draft, which were both part and parcel of the same settlement negotiation. Ignoring these contemporaneous communications is at odds with the requirement in contract formation that courts must consider "all the surrounding circumstances." Donovan v. RRL Corp., 26 Cal.4th 261, 271, 109 Cal. Rptr. 2d 807, 27 P.3d 702 (2001). These subsequent efforts to sketch in a more fulsome outline of the parties' alleged agreement provides context and meaning as to the understanding the parties had about the effect of the October 19 letter itself.

Defendants further seek to create issues of fact through post hoc testimony and rationalizations. None of this subjective belief is sufficient to defeat the objective manifestation of the parties' intent relayed in the documents referenced above that aptly demonstrate that there was no "meeting of the minds" on all material terms. See Meyer v. Benko, 55 Cal.App.3d 937, 942-43, 127 Cal. Rptr. 846 (1976) ("The existence of mutual consent is determined by objective rather than subjective criteria, the test being what the outward manifestations of consent would lead a reasonable person to believe. Accordingly, the primary focus in determining the existence of mutual consent is upon the acts of the parties involved"); Stewart v. Preston Pipeline Inc., 134 Cal.App.4th 1565, 1587, 36 Cal. Rptr. 3d 901 (2005) ("mutual assent to a contract is based upon objective and outward manifestations of the parties"); CAL. CIV. CODE § 1639.

One need only review the language of the parties' correspondence, their conduct in reaction thereto, and the numerous material differences between the terms relayed in the October 19 and 26, 2001, letters and the February 1, 2002, draft to reach the conclusion that the parties failed to come to an agreement on all material terms. See Grove v. Grove Valve & Reg. Co., 4 Cal.App.3d 299, 311-12, 84 Cal. Rptr. 300 (1970) (failure to reach meeting of the minds on all material points prevents contract formation even though parties orally agreed on many terms, or have taken action relating to the contract). Far from signifying that the parties' "negotiations . . . result[ed] in a binding contract" leaving nothing more than the drafting of more formal documentation memorializing that agreement, see Louis Lesser Enterprises, Ltd. v. Roeder, 209 Cal.App.2d 401, 404, 25 Cal. Rptr. 917 (1962), these submissions between the parties went far beyond that by adding in or further refining areas from what was contained in the October 19 letter. That after the submission of the October 19 letter defendants began the process of creating a settlement trust account and the parties negotiated about providing Siegel and Shuster screen credits in the then upcoming movie Superman Returns could as much be seen as goodwill gestures on defendants' part while the negotiations continued as it could reflect an indication on their part that they thought they were contractually bound to do the same.

From all of this there is no document or set of documents reflecting agreement by the parties to singular, agreed terms. Defendants cannot explain to the Court what from the parties' differing exchange constitutes this purported contract; rather, it appears that defendants wish to take the plaintiffs' "acceptance" reflected in the October 19 letter and either festoon upon it all the terms contained in the February 1, 2002, draft settlement agreement (even though Joanne Siegel clearly and unequivocally rejected that latter draft agreement), or have the Court perform that task. The Court's responsibility is not to create a patch-quilt agreement by stringing together certain expressions of assent made at one point (October 19), and attaching to it material terms spelled out later in time (and to which the supposedly assenting party promptly rejected). See Industrial Indemnity v. Superior Court, 224 Cal.App.3d 828, 832, 275 Cal. Rptr. 218 (1990) ("courts will not write a new contract").

Accordingly, the Court concludes that the parties' settlement negotiations did not result in an enforceable agreement resolving the issues presently before the Court.

B. Limitations on Scope of Recaptured Rights

The principal purpose behind the creation of the termination right was to give authors (and their heirs) a chance to retain the extended renewal term in their work and then re-bargain for it when its value in the marketplace was known. See H.R. REP. NO. 1476, 94th Cong., 2d Sess. 124 (recognizing as the justification for the termination right "safeguarding authors against unremunerative transfers . . . because of the unequal bargaining position of authors, resulting in part from the impossibility of determining a work's prior value until it has been exploited").

The need for such a second bite at the apple flowed from the fact that the 1909 Act created a dual term in the copyright to a work, one realized upon the work's publication and the second occurring twenty-eight years later with the copyright's renewal. Justification for this splitting of terms was based, in part, on the understanding that an author's ability to realize the true value of his or her's work was often not apparent at its creation, but required the passage of time (and the marketing efforts by a publisher) to materialize. The renewal term in the copyright to the work thus served as a mid-course re-valuation tool allowing the author, by giving him or her the right of renewal in the work, leverage in re-negotiating a better deal with the original grantee or any other suitor who desired to continue to market the copyright. See Patry, Choice of Law, 48 Am. J. Comp. L. at 446 ("The main theory behind a dual system of term was that it gave the author or the author's heirs a 'second bite at the apple;' when the renewal term came around, the value of the copyright would be better known than at the time of initial publication. With this information, a new bargain could be struck that would more accurately reflect the market rate"). This re-valuation mechanism provided by the renewal term under the 1909 Act was largely frustrated by the Supreme Court's decision in Fred Fisher Music, 318 U.S. at 656-59, allowing authors to assign away at the outset all of their rights to both the initial and the renewal term.

Although the termination right contained in the 1976 Act sought to correct the damage done by Fred Fisher to an author's ability to renegotiate through the reversion of rights, it did not revert to the author the full panoply of rights he or she would have enjoyed upon renewal under the 1909 Act. Owing in large measure to objections by publishers seeking to minimize the disruption to "existing contracts and authorized derivative works already in distribution" that such a recapture right would engender, see 2 PATRY ON COPYRIGHT

§ 7:43, Congress placed certain limitations on what authors (or their heirs) gained from exercising the termination right. It is to these limits on the termination right that the Court now turns.

1. Foreign Profits

Section 304(c)(6)(E) to the 1976 Act provides that "[t]ermination of a grant under this subsection affects only those rights covered by the grant that arise under this title[, Title 17 of the United States Code, governing copyrights], and in no way affects rights arising under any other Federal, State, or foreign laws." Defendants read from this a statutory limitation on the scope of any accounting arising from the termination notices in this case to those profits realized by the domestic exploitation of the Superman copyright contained in Action Comics, Vol. 1, excluding those realized from foreign sources. The Court finds this argument persuasive.

Although the Court can locate no case that has specifically addressed the issue of accounting profits from the foreign exploitation of a copyright that is subject to a valid termination notice, the statutory text could not be any clearer on this subject. Through this section, Congress expressly limited the reach of what was gained by the terminating party through exercise of the termination right; specifically, the terminating party only recaptured the domestic rights (that is, the rights arising under title 17 to the United States Code) of the grant to the copyright in question. Left expressly intact and undisturbed were any of the rights the original grantee or its successors in interest had gained over the years from the copyright through other sources of law, notably the right to exploit the work abroad that would be governed by the copyright laws of foreign nations. Thus, the statute explains that termination "in no way affects rights" the grantee or its successors gained "under foreign laws."

Such a reading is supported by leading commentators, who are in agreement as to the effect of § 304(c)(6)(E) has in a case such as this. Professor Nimmer states:

A grant of copyright "throughout the world" is terminable only with respect to uses within the geographic limits of the United States. Because copyright has no extraterritorial operation, arguably American law is precluded from causing the termination of rights based upon foreign copyright laws. A response to this argument is that the nonextraterritoriality of copyright is irrelevant because the question here is one of contract law, not copyright law, in that it concerns the effect of a contract granting certain rights. The contract law of one nation may be applicable in another nation under the latter's conflict-of-laws rule. The conclusive answer to this problem lies in the text of the termination provisions of the Copyright Act, which expressly provide that

statutory termination "in no way affects rights arising under . . . foreign laws" -
- that is, under foreign copyright (not contract) laws. Thus, even if the
conflicts rule of a foreign nation were to call for application of the American
termination rule as a rule of contract law, that rule by its own terms excepts
from termination the grant of those rights arising under foreign copyright
laws.

3 NIMMER ON COPYRIGHT § 11.02[B][2] at 11-19.
Professor Patry agrees: "Accordingly, where a U.S. author conveys worldwide
rights and terminates under either section, grants in all other countries remain
valid according to their terms or provisions in other countries' laws." 7
PATRY ON COPYRIGHT § 25:74.
Plaintiffs argue, however, that the section also allows for the possibility that
the terminating party gains not only the domestic rights to the copyright in
question (the "rights covered by the grant that arise under this title"), but also
retains whatever other rights it may have under "Federal, State, or foreign
laws." From this premise, plaintiffs argue that, because an accounting between
co-owners in a copyright is governed by state law, and California state law
allows for the sharing of foreign profits between tenants in common, so, too,
should defendants be forced to account for their foreign profits. This
argument misses the fact that all plaintiffs have gained from the termination
right is a recapturing of the domestic copyright in the Superman material
published in Action Comics, Vol. 1. Defendants continue to hold, unaffected,
separate rights to that copyright arising under foreign copyright laws. This
distinction is important for two reasons.
First, such an open effort to extend the reach of U.S. copyright law overseas,
as plaintiffs' reading of the statute avows, would be in direct contradiction to
not only the plain terms of the statute (stating that termination does not affect
another parties' rights arising under the copyright laws of "foreign" nations),
but stands in stark juxtaposition to the longstanding rule "that the copyright
laws [of this country] have no application beyond the U.S. border." Los
Angeles News Serv. v. Reuters TV Intern., 340 F.3d 926, 931 (9th Cir. 2003).
If Congress contemplated the ability to attach or otherwise force the
accounting of foreign profits to which the original grantee or its successors
are legally entitled under the copyright laws of other nations through the
backdoor of applying state law tenant in common principles, one would have
expected such an intention to have been made expressly, and certainly with
some explanation given the incongruity that arises from the statutory
language's notation that termination did not affect another's rights under
"foreign laws."
Second, the cases cited by plaintiffs requiring one co-owner to account to the
other for both domestic and foreign profits involved parties who were co-

owners to the "world-wide" copyright in the work and, not as with the termination right, to only the domestic copyright. See Goodman v. Lee, 78 F.3d 1007, 1010 (5th Cir. 1996) (noting that declaratory action was filed after other co-owner obtained a "renewal of the copyright" listing himself as the sole author in the song "Let the Good Times Roll"). Plaintiffs have directed the Court to no case wherein a co-owner of the domestic copyright in a work was allowed an accounting of a co-owner's foreign profits. See 3 NIMMER ON COPYRIGHT § 11.02[B][1] at 11-17 ("Only such rights as were originally the subject of a grant will revert upon the termination of that grant. [T]o the extent that a grant includes rights based upon federal law other than the Copyright Act, state law, or foreign law, such rights are not subject to termination").

Accordingly, the Court holds that the termination notice affects only the domestic portion of Siegel's and Shuster's 1938 worldwide grant ("all rights") to Detective Comics of the copyright in the Superman material contained in Action Comics, Vol. 1. The termination notice is not effective as to the remainder of the grant, that is, defendants exploitation of the work abroad under the aegis of foreign copyright laws. Thus, although defendants retain the unfettered right to exploit the works (and retain the profits derived therefrom) in foreign nations, they may do so domestically only as a co-owner (through Shuster's share) of the works. See Oddo v. Ries, 743 F.2d 630, 632-33 (9th Cir. 1984) ("[E]ach co-owner has an independent right to use or license the use of the copyright. . . . A co-owner of a copyright must account to other co-owners for any profits he earns from licensing or use of the copyright . . . ."). As such, defendants must account to plaintiffs only for the profits from such domestic exploitation of the Superman copyright.

2. Trademark Rights and Ownership of Pre-Termination Derivative Works

As noted in the previous section, the right to termination leaves undisturbed the original grantee or its successors in interests rights arising under "federal law." 17 U.S.C. § 304(c)(6)(E). Among the rights based on federal law that defendants secured over the years were several trademarks that utilized or incorporated portions of the copyrighted material found in Action Comics, Vol. 1. Defendants seek a declaration from the Court that, even if successful in terminating the Superman copyright contained in Action Comics, Vol. 1, plaintiffs cannot share in defendants' profits "purely attributable to [Superman] trademark rights." (Defs' Reply at 11). Plaintiffs admirably concede the point in their briefs, but argue that they are "entitled to profits from mixed trademark uses to the extent such exploit recaptured copyright elements (e.g., 'Superman costume')." (Pls' Reply at 49 n.28).

Similarly, defendants seek a declaration that, to the extent plaintiffs are entitled to an accounting as a result of their successfully terminating the 1938 grant, it should not include any profits attributable to the "post-termination exploitation of derivative works [of Action Comics, Vol. 1,] prepared prior to termination." (Defs' Mot. Summ. J. at 28). Again, plaintiffs concede, as they should, this point. (Pls' Reply at 49 n.28). Section 304(c)(6)(A) provides that derivative works created during the grant (meaning up until the termination effective date) may continue to be exploited after termination. Again, however, plaintiffs hold out as a separate question the existence of pre-termination derivative works that are "altered so as to become post-termination derivative works." (Pls' Reply at 49 n.28).

Given that these contentions by plaintiffs -- the recapture or accounting from the mixed use of trademark and copyright and what to do with any alteration in pre-termination derivative works -- are not the subject of the present motion, the Court will not address them in this Order. Even though it is clear that these issues will impact the accounting of profits in some manner, they cannot be fully adjudicated based on the narrow record currently before the Court and absent a full briefing of the particular mixed uses or altered pre-termination derivative works that are specifically at issue.

Accordingly, the Court holds that the profits defendants garner from the use of Superman trademarks that "are purely attributable to [those] trademark rights," and from its use of unaltered pre-termination derivative works are not subject to accounting.

3. Accounting for Profits of Warner Bros. Entertainment, Inc., and Time Warner, Inc.

The parties are in disagreement over whether plaintiffs may directly share in the profits from the exploitation of the works by DC Comics corporate sibling, Warner Brothers Entertainment, Inc. ("WBEI"), and its corporate parent, Time Warner, Inc. ("TWI"). The genesis for this claim stems from certain inter-corporate transactions amongst these actors concerning the Superman copyright. In the same year that plaintiffs' termination notices became effective, DC Comics executed an exclusive license in favor of WBEI (and a year later a separate exclusive license with WBEI's television division) to exploit the Superman copyright for the remainder of its extended renewal term in certain media formats, notably movies, television, and home video. (Decl. Marc Toberoff, Exs. E & F). Defendants contend that, as co-owners of the joint works at issue, plaintiffs are entitled to an accounting of the profits made by DC Comics (in the form of the licensing fees it has collected), but that plaintiffs are not entitled to an accounting of the profits WBEI has made pursuant to the license. [10]10

---

[10] 10 It appears to the Court that because TWI is not a licensee of the works, it may not have any profits to account for; however, absent evidence of this

Defendants' argument is not without support. The Court starts with the general principle that "each co-owner has an independent right to use or license the use of the copyright[, but that a] co-owner of a copyright must account to other co-owners for any profits he earns from licensing or use of the copyright." Oddo, 743 F.2d at 633. Licensees, on the other hand, are accountable only to their licensors, and owe no duty of accounting to the non-licensor co-owner of a copyright the licensee exploits. See Ashton-Tate Corp. v. Ross, 916 F.2d 516, 523 (9th Cir. 1990).

Plaintiffs, however, take a different view of the licenses, arguing that "Warner has stepped exclusively into DC's shoes with respect to such motion picture and television copyrights." (Pls' Opp. at 30). In other words, the exclusive license had the net effect of substituting WBEI for DC Comics as a joint owner with plaintiffs (assuming the successful termination of the 1938 grant) insofar as the exploitation of the copyright in the mediums in which those licenses are concerned.

This theory, however, requires large legal leaps that are not countenanced by current law. To begin, in order for an exclusive license in the entirety of the interest in a joint work itself (such as Superman) to be effective, the consent of both joint owners in the copyrighted work is required. See 2 PATRY ON COPYRIGHT § 5:7 ("A joint author (or co-owner) may not, however, transfer all interest in the work without the other co-owner's express (and written) authorization, since that would result in an involuntary transfer of the other joint owner's undivided interest in the whole"). The same requirement for prior consent holds true even with respect to the wholesale transfer of exclusive licenses in subparts to a copyright, such as a license transferring all the stage rights (not just the joint owner's rights) to a novel but not the movie or literary rights. Cf. 1 NIMMER ON COPYRIGHT § 6.12[C][3] at 6-38.8 to 6-39.

Such consent simply did not occur here. DC Comics unilaterally sought to give an exclusive license to the entirety in the Superman property's movie and television rights to WBEI post-termination. As a result, the attempt to provide an exclusive license was ineffective. At best, all that was conveyed was a non-exclusive license, and, at worst, a license agreement whose terms are null and void absent ratification by plaintiffs. See 3 NIMMER ON COPYRIGHT § 10.03[A][7] at 10-51.

Applying these principles in a vacuum, the Court would readily reach the

---

fact from either side (or the representation that such is not the case), the Court cannot rule on this issue at this time.

conclusion championed by defendants: WBEI, as a licensee, is answerable only to DC Comics as its licensor; that DC Comics is the only entity that must account for profits to plaintiffs; and, absent exploitation of the works by DC Comics itself, that DC Comics' accounting to plaintiffs is limited to those profits derived from licensing the Superman copyright to WBEI.

However, the Court's analysis does not occur in vacuum; rather, it must take into account the relevant facts of this case, particularly given that the accounting sought by plaintiffs in this action is an equitable remedy, and the Court must conduct its inquiry accordingly. See Oddo, 743 F.2d at 633 ("A co-owner of a copyright must account to other co-owners for any profits he earns from licensing or use of the copyright, . . . but the duty to account does not derive from the copyright law's proscription of infringement. Rather, it comes from equitable doctrines relating to unjust enrichment and general principles of law governing the rights of co-owners.") (internal quotation marks and citations omitted).

Here, the relatedness of the transferor and the transferee entities cannot be ignored. The evidence before the Court reveals that the relevant entities are all closely related entities -- parent corporations, wholly and partially-owned subsidiaries, partners, sibling business entities (owned directly or indirectly by the same parent) -- although it is not entirely clear to the Court exactly what those relationships have been at all relevant times. This fact alone raises a specter of a "sweetheart deal" entered into by related entities in order to pay a less than market value fee for licensing valuable copyrights. If such were the case, the related entity might be able to exploit the copyrights without the responsibility of answering to the co-owner of a joint work, and the licensor co-owner would thereby be relieved of the responsibility of accounting for any profits (other than a greatly reduced licensing fee) to the non-licensor co-owner. This result would be inequitable.

This concern is bolstered by the declaration of Paul Levitz, President and Publisher for DC Comics, which states that under the post-2003 corporate restructuring of Time Warner's business, "for operating management purposes, DC reports" not to immediate corporate parent WCI, but to its sibling corporation "WBEI," the licensee of the rights at issue in this action. (Decl. Paul Levitz P 17). As Levitz explains, "I report to and obtain approvals from WBEI's President and Chief Operating Officer before making significant acquisitions or certain financial decisions or investments that are outside the scope of DC's customary acquisitions and investments; before implementing meaningful strategic changes; and before embarking on something substantially outside DC's normal course of business." (Id.). Although this is not evidence of what occurred at the time of the license, it is still probative evidence of the relatedness of the licensee and licensor that could result in an extremely favorable licensing arrangement that works to the detriment of the non-licensor co-owner. These open issues also touch upon factors to be considered in analyzing alter ego claims. See Sonora Diamond Corp. v. Superior Court, 83 Cal.App.4th 523, 99 Cal. Rptr. 2d 824 (2000); Mesler v. Bragg Management Co., 39 Cal.3d 290, 216 Cal. Rptr. 443, 702 P.2d 601 (Cal. 1985) ("The essence of the alter ego doctrine, in which it is claimed that an opposing party is using the corporate form unjustly, is that justice be done. What the formula comes down to, once shorn of verbiage about control, instrumentality, agency and corporate entity, is that liability is imposed to reach an equitable result").

Whether the license fees paid represents the fair market value therefor, or whether the license for the works between the related entities was a "sweetheart deal," are questions of fact that are not answered on summary judgment, certainly not without the benefit of expert testimony which has not been presented by either party on this topic. The Court therefore concludes that summary judgment on this issue is inappropriate at this time. [11]11

CONCLUSION

After seventy years, Jerome Siegel's heirs regain what he granted so long ago -- the copyright in the Superman material that was published in Action Comics, Vol. 1. What remains is an apportionment of profits, guided in some measure by the rulings contained in this Order, and a trial on whether to include the profits generated by DC Comics' corporate sibling's exploitation of the Superman copyright.

DATE: March 26, 2008

/s/ Stephen G. Larson

STEPHEN G. LARSON

UNITED STATES DISTRICT JUDGE

---

[11] 11 Because the Court concludes that defendants' motion for summary adjudication of this issue must be denied for the reasons stated above, the Court does not at this time resolve other arguments raised by plaintiffs regarding this issue.

2

Commercial Concoctions

Quirky advertising for two kinds of chewing gum, Snapple beverage and wine. Similar to the superhero comic book style character emerging in cross-product marketing.

JIM BOUTON CORPORATION, Plaintiff,

v.

WM. WRIGLEY JR. COMPANY and AMUROL PRODUCTS COMPANY, Defendants

No. 85 CIV. 2308 (PKL)
July 7, 1989

UNITED STATES DISTRICT COURT FOR THE SOUTHERN DISTRICT OF NEW YORK

FINDINGS OF FACT AND CONCLUSIONS OF LAW

PETER K. LEISURE, UNITED STATES DISTRICT JUDGE:
On January 25, 26, 27, 28 and 29, 1988, this case was tried to the Court without a jury. The parties submitted post-trial proposed findings of fact and conclusions of law on March 3, 1988, and thereafter submitted simultaneous reply papers. Plaintiff subsequently moved to reopen the testimony to offer additional evidence. For the reasons stated below, the Court dismisses the action as to defendant Wm. Wrigley Jr. Company, finds for plaintiff on its first claim for relief, for defendant Amurol on plaintiff's second and third claims for relief, and for plaintiff on defendant Amurol's counterclaim. The Court also denies plaintiff's motion to reopen the testimony on the present record as set forth below. The following constitutes the Court's findings of fact and conclusions of law pursuant to Rule 52(a) of the Federal Rules of Civil Procedure.
FINDINGS OF FACT
THE PARTIES
Plaintiff Jim Bouton Corporation ("JBC") is a corporation organized and existing under the laws of the State of New Jersey. The president of the corporation is Jim Bouton ("Bouton"), a former major league baseball player. The only other shareholder in the corporation is Rob Nelson ("Nelson"). The corporation was formed in 1979, with Bouton as president and Nelson as

vice-president. Each then owned and continues to own 50% of the corporation.

Bouton is a well-known sports figure and entertainment personality. He played professional baseball in the minor leagues for three years, and then was a pitcher for the New York Yankees beginning in 1962. He was subsequently sold to the Seattle pilots, and then traded to the Houston Astros. In 1970, he retired from baseball. Also in 1970, Bouton wrote the book Ball Four, which was on the best-seller list for seventeen weeks, and sold over 250,000 copies, and about three million copies in paperback.

After his retirement from baseball, he joined local network television station WABC in New York as a sportscaster on the 6:00 and 11:00 o'clock evening news. In 1973, he joined WCBS in New York as a television sportscaster, where he remained until 1976. In 1976, Bouton also created, wrote and acted in a situation comedy that aired on the CBS network in the fall of 1976. The show ran five weeks before it was canceled.

In 1977, Bouton began a comeback to the major leagues. He played in the minor leagues in Knoxville, Tennessee, Durango, Mexico and Portland, Oregon. In 1978, he played in the Atlanta Braves' organization in Savannah, Georgia. At the end of the 1978 season, he was called up to the Atlanta Braves. His return to the major leagues was short-lived. In 1979, after retiring from professional baseball permanently, Bouton formed JBC. Bouton is also engaged in other endeavors, and in 1983 he formed a company called Big League Cards, which makes personalized baseball cards. Bouton also engages in after-dinner and motivational speech-making.

Wm. Wrigley Jr. Company ("Wrigley") is a Delaware corporation having its principal place of business in Chicago, Illinois. Wrigley is a leading manufacturer and distributor of chewing gum and related goods.

Amurol Products Company ("Amurol") is an Illinois corporation with its principal place of business in Naperville, Illinois. Amurol is a wholly-owned subsidiary of Wrigley. Amurol is engaged in the manufacture, sale and distribution of candy, gum, dietetic food products and novelty products.

DEVELOPMENT OF THE PRODUCT

In 1977, while playing for the Portland, Oregon minor league baseball team, Bouton and Nelson came up with the concept that developed into the product which is the subject of this suit. One day, while Bouton was in the bullpen with Nelson, the team's pitching coach, they observed that all the other players and coaches on the team were chewing tobacco. The players did not particularly like the taste of chewing tobacco, and it made many of them sick, particularly when used over sustained periods of time, but many thought that it contributed to their maintaining "macho" images. It was then that Nelson commented that it was unfortunate that there was not something available that looked like tobacco but was good-tasting, such as gum. Bouton and Nelson laughed at the idea, and did not think any more about it at that time.

Several months later, after the season had ended, Bouton could not get the idea out of his head. He contacted Nelson and suggested that the concept might be a commercial success, and that they should try to produce and market the gum. Nelson made some gum in his kitchen, colored and flavored it with molasses, and cut it into strips with a large knife. Nelson and Bouton then contacted an advertising agency in Portland, and, with the help of the agency, developed a package design for the pouch in which the gum would be sold. Bouton and Nelson contacted an attorney in Portland to advise them about selling the product and filing for trademark application.

In 1978, Bouton contacted U.S. Licensing, a professional licensing organization, and Vincent Alati ("Alati"), President of U.S. Licensing, to license the concept of BIG LEAGUE CHEW shredded gum in a pouch. On June 15, 1979, Bouton filed an application for a trademark for BIG LEAGUE CHEW. In the meantime, U.S. Licensing contacted various gum manufacturers to see if there was any interest in manufacturing and marketing BIG LEAGUE CHEW. In November of 1979, Bouton entered into a contract with U.S. Licensing. Under that contract, Bouton was obligated to pay U.S. Licensing 35% of all royalties earned by Bouton from any license agreement for BIG LEAGUE CHEW.

In the middle of 1979, Alati contacted Amurol to determine if it would be interested in entering into a license agreement. Alati conducted negotiations on behalf of Bouton with Amurol's then vice-president and current president and chief executive officer, A.G. Atwater ("Atwater"). At the beginning of the negotiations, Amurol and Bouton exchanged product disclosure forms and other written documents.

Prior to being contacted by Alati, Amurol had dealt with the Conwood Corporation, a manufacturer of chewing tobacco, about selling shredded gum in a pouch. Accordingly, Amurol informed Alati that although it did not wish to use Bouton's concept of shredded gum because it already had the idea, it did wish to use the trademarked name BIG LEAGUE CHEW.

EARLY CONTRACTUAL RELATIONS

After further negotiations between the parties, attorneys representing U.S. Licensing prepared a licensing contract covering the BIG LEAGUE CHEW mark. The agreement ("The Original Agreement"), Defendants' Trial Exhibit[1] 1 was executed on or about December 5, 1979. The Original Agreement was for a term of three years from initial market entry of the product. Bouton was

---

[1] 1 Hereinafter, Defendants' Trial Exhibits will be abbreviated DTX   , and Plaintiff's Trial Exhibits PTX   .

to receive a 2 1/2% royalty on gross sales, as well as power to approve art work, packaging and related advertising material. The Original Agreement also gave Amurol the right to market another shredded gum product with a Western theme rather than a baseball theme. The Original Agreement further provided that it set forth the entire understanding of the parties and that it could not be modified except in writing.

In the first half of 1980, Amurol developed the packaging and graphics, with Bouton's approval, and conducted market testing. In the middle of 1980, Amurol proceeded to introduce the product. BIG LEAGUE CHEW was an immediate success and became Amurol's best-selling product. In its first six months on the market, without any advertising or promotion, sales of BIG LEAGUE CHEW totaled $ 3.4 million.

In the meantime, however, problems between the parties surfaced. Bouton's application for a trademark for BIG LEAGUE CHEW was rejected by the patent and trademark office in May of 1980. It was then arranged for Amurol's outside counsel, Jerome Gilson, Esq. ("Gilson") of Willian Olds Hofer Gilson & Lione Ltd. ("Willian Olds"), to assist Bouton in assuring that the trademark was properly registered.[2] In part as a result of the difficulties with the registration of the trademark, there was concern at Amurol that trademark litigation might ensue. Amurol therefore wished to have more substantial indemnification from Bouton in the event of litigation. Amurol also wanted to correct the representation in the Original Agreement that Bouton had registered his trademark when, in fact, he had only applied for such registration.

For his part, Bouton was dissatisfied with Amurol's handling of Bouton's own concept for a Western shredded gum, under the BUCKAROO CHEW name. It was then discovered by Amurol that the Mars Candy Company had previously registered the trademark BUCKAROO for candy, but was not actively using the mark. As previously stated, Amurol had already developed a Western theme, and was therefore reluctant to use Bouton's concept. Nevertheless, Amurol purchased the BUCKAROO trademark from the Mars Candy Company and assigned the mark to Bouton. Because both parties were dissatisfied with the state of relations between them, but optimistic about the potential of BIG LEAGUE CHEW, they negotiated over certain revisions to the Original Agreement.

These negotiations culminated in a new agreement between the parties. The new agreement was signed in November of 1980, but was dated as of December 5, 1979. In effect, then, the November 1980 agreement superceded the Original Agreement and became known as the 1979 agreement (the "1979

---

[2] 2 The registration ultimately issued in October 1983.

Agreement"). [3]

The 1979 Agreement provided that Bouton would receive a 2 1/2% royalty rate on the sales of BIG LEAGUE CHEW. The 1979 Agreement also required that Amurol receive prior written approval from Bouton for all advertising and promotions. Paragraph 20 of the 1979 Agreement provided:

The Terms of this agreement cannot be waived or modified except by an agreement in writing. There are no representations, warranties or covenants other than those set forth in this agreement which sets forth the entire understanding between us.

PTX 12. In addition to the 1979 Agreement, the parties executed a separate agreement relating to BUCKAROO CHEW, providing for royalty payments to Bouton for BUCKAROO CHEW.

The sales of BIG LEAGUE CHEW proved to be impressive; in 1981, sales of BIG LEAGUE CHEW totaled $ 18 million. When it became evident that the product would be a commercial success, the parties began to think about extending the term of the 1979 Agreement, which was originally set for a term of three years. Negotiations between Bouton, Alati, and JBC's counsel, James K. Silberman, Esq. ("Silberman") of Blum, Kaplan, Friedman, Silberman & Beran ("Blum Kaplan"), on the one side and Amurol and its counsel on the other side resulted in the signing of a letter of intent (the "Letter of Intent") in August of 1981. The Letter of Intent was prepared and executed at that time to "avoid misunderstandings" as to the terms of revised agreement. DTX RR. Both parties wanted to be bound by the new terms, and were not sure how long it would take to draw up a new agreement, so they drew up the Letter of Intent. Bouton direct, Tr. at 83.

The Letter of Intent provided for an increase in the royalty rate to be paid Bouton and an extension of the license term, among other things. Specifically, the Letter of Intent provided for a sliding scale of royalty payments by which Bouton would receive 2 1/2% on the first $ 20 million in annual sales, 3 1/2% on the second $ 20 million, 5% on sales over $ 40 million, and 5% on all sales during the option period of the contract.

Bouton understood that he would receive the 5% royalty rate in either of two ways. First, if Amurol did not advertise, he would be entitled to 5%. Second, if

---

[3] 3 Bouton did not recall that there was a signed Original Agreement in 1979 before what later came to be known as the 1981 Agreement. Bouton explained that at the time of the Original Agreement, Alati was handling the negotiations and preparation of contracts for JBC, and the Original Agreement was drafted by Franklin, Weinrib and Rudell, attorneys for U.S. Licensing. I find Bouton's explanation for his failure of recollection to be entirely credible.

Bouton did not approve advertising, he thought he was entitled under the contract to receive 5%. Bouton acknowledged, however, that the Letter of Intent nowhere explicitly provided that he would receive the full 5% under the second circumstance. Bouton cross, Tr. at 382-83.

From August 1981, when the Letter of Intent was signed, until June 1982, when the 1981 Agreement was signed, the parties operated under the terms of the Letter of Intent. Paragraph ten of the Letter of Intent provided that the royalty rate for BUCKAROO CHEW would increase from 1 1/2% to 2 1/2% and that all royalty payments for BIG LEAGUE CHEW would be made on a monthly basis. Upon signing the Letter of Intent in 1981, Amurol increased the royalty rate on BUCKAROO CHEW to 2 1/2% and started paying BIG LEAGUE CHEW royalties monthly instead of quarterly.

In June of 1982, approximately ten months after the signing of the Letter of Intent, an agreement was signed by the parties (the "1981 Agreement"). Between the signing of the Letter of Intent and execution of the 1981 Agreement, the parties continued to discuss whether certain terms would be included in the final agreement, but the 1981 Agreement as executed embodied all the elements set forth in the letter of intent. Bouton direct, Tr. 114.

The 1981 Agreement provided that Bouton retained the right to approve all advertising, and that he would have to give prior written approval of advertising. Bouton now claims that he understood he could receive a 5% royalty payment in either of the aforesaid two ways. This interpretation was based on the interaction of paragraphs 4, 5 and 16(a) of the 1981 Agreement. Paragraph 4 provided that Amurol would pay JBC a royalty rate on a sliding scale of 2 1/2% on the first $ 20 million in sales, 3 1/2% on the next $ 20 million, 5% on all sales over $ 40 million, and 5% during the option period. This was the same sliding scale that was agreed to in the Letter of Intent. Paragraph 5 provided that Amurol was not obligated to advertise, and to the extent that Amurol "does not spend the following amounts for advertising, it shall remit the difference between its actual expenditure and the following amounts to JBC . . . :" on the first $ 20 million in sales 2 1/2%, on the second $ 20 million in sales 1 1/2% Paragraph 16(a) provided that

all artwork, copy, packaging, literary text, advertisements and advertising materials, including the quality and style thereof, shall be subject to the prior written approval of JBC; provided, however, that such materials shall be deemed approved if JBC does not notify the Company in writing to the contrary within seven (7) days after receipt.

PTX 66. Once again, as with the Letter of Intent, there was no indication in the contract that Bouton could refuse to approve advertising for no reason, and thereby gain a full 5% royalty, nor did Bouton ever express to anyone at

Amurol that that was his view of the 1981 Agreement.[4]

Paragraph 29 of the 1981 Agreement provides in its entirety:

The terms of this Agreement cannot be waived or modified except by an agreement in writing. There are no representations, warranties or covenants other than those set forth in this Agreement which sets forth the entire understanding between the parties.

This paragraph does not explicitly require that any subsequent writing be formally executed or signed by both sides. It requires only that any modification be in writing.

The new agreement between the parties also contemplated the introduction of a candy product under the BIG LEAGUE trademark, identified as BIG LEAGUE PLUG. Atwater and Bouton agreed informally in a telephone conversation that the time by which Amurol had to introduce the BIG LEAGUE PLUG would be extended. That agreement was memorialized and confirmed in a handwritten letter dated September 20, 1982, PTX 70, which Atwater marked "attach to our contract." Both parties then operated on the basis of the letter, although it was never formally executed by both parties as an amendment to the contract. The parties also agreed informally to extend the BUCKAROO CHEW trademark agreement, and confirmed that understanding by a telex. Bouton direct, Tr. 219-20; Neal direct, Tr. 780-81, 788, 790; PTX 122.

ADVERTISING AND PROMOTIONS

At the outset of the relationship, Bouton wanted advertising to promote the brand. Atwater, however, was reluctant to advertise because Amurol was 160,000 cases behind in deliveries, and could not keep up with the orders coming in. Until such time as Amurol could keep current with orders, Atwater thought advertising ill-advised. Once the back orders were processed, however, Atwater felt that advertising would be a good idea, and the parties agreed to advertise. Hence, the parties included provisions relating to advertising in the Letter of Intent and in the 1981 Agreement.

The course of dealings between the parties became strained, however, because of Amurol's continual failure to consult with Bouton, much less gain his consent or approval, before embarking on an advertising campaign until

---

[4] 4 An earlier draft of the 1981 Agreement provided that "all artwork, copy, packaging, literary text, advertisements and advertising materials, including the quality and style thereof, shall at all stages of production be subject to prior written approval of JBC, which approval shall not be unreasonably withheld." PTX 54a, para. 17(a) (emphasis in original). This language was not included in the 1981 Agreement as it was finally executed.

considerable expenditures had been made. By the time he was consulted, Bouton felt compelled to go along with the advertisements because of the considerable sums of money already expended.

Bouton was concerned with the image of the product. He wanted to convey a macho sports image and felt that the product would benefit in the long run if a consistent image were built up. In order to convey that image consistently, Bouton wanted to be involved in the creative process of advertising, and the 1981 Agreement gave him that right.

Amurol used the advertising agency of Needham, Harper & Steers ("NH&S") for its advertising, as did its parent company, Wrigley. In 1981, NH&S developed and Bouton approved a commercial entitled "The Coach." This commercial was rejected by the networks, however, because it portrayed an authority figure telling children what to do. Accordingly, the commercial never aired. NH&S then developed the "Mad Professor" commercial, featuring a **mad scientist** concocting shredded bubble gum in a pouch in his basement. Bouton objected to Atwater that the commercial was juvenile, and that it did not properly reflect the image of the product that Bouton wished to convey. Bouton approved use of the commercial, but conditioned his approval on the running of modified and better commercials the following year.

NH&S then developed another commercial, "You're in the Big Leagues." Bouton did not like this commercial, and made his objections known to Amurol and NH&S. He objected that the commercial could be used to promote any product, and that it appeared to be prepared by someone who knew nothing about sports. The commercial was first shown to Bouton after the initial creative process and after the storyboard had been completed. Because of the sizable expenditure of time and money already incurred, Bouton approved the commercial, and Amurol aired the "You're in the Big Leagues" commercial in 1982.

Bouton then went to another advertising agency, Della Femina, Travisano & Partners, Inc. ("Della Femina") to try to provide Amurol with new ideas. Bouton went to the Della Femina agency on his own, but Amurol paid half the fee for consulting that agency, even though Amurol was not obligated to do so, and there was no written agreement that Amurol would do so. Della Femina suggested three different advertising themes to Amurol, but Amurol rejected all of them and continued to run the "You're in the Big Leagues" commercial.

Bouton pressed for one of the advertising themes suggested by Della Femina as an alternative to the "You're in the Big Leagues" commercial. The Della Femina advertisement that Bouton liked best was a parody of the Miller Lite Beer advertisements, in which celebrities argue whether Lite beer tastes great or is less filling. Bouton and Della Femina envisioned a commercial in which a child resembling Rodney Dangerfield would argue that BIG LEAGUE CHEW is shredded, while children resembling other celebrities in Miller Lite ads would argue that the gum came in a pouch. Bouton direct, Tr. 146. Amurol, however, did not want to engage in that type of advertising because it feared a lawsuit from the people at the Miller Brewing Company. By letter dated February 1, 1984, Amurol informed Bouton that "Amurol being a part of the Wrigley Company would not want to engage in a legal battle with the Miller Bring Company over such an issue." PTX 82. Amurol's brand manager for BIG LEAGUE CHEW wrote: "Mr. Wrigley would not allow us to proceed any further." PTX 86; see Atwater direct, Tr. at 496.

In 1983, Amurol again ran the "You're in the Big Leagues" commercial, despite the fact that Bouton protested that he did not like the commercial and had claimed to have approved it only conditionally for the 1982 advertising season. In 1983, Bouton and Atwater agreed that a new commercial would be run in 1984. This agreement was not reflected in any writing. Atwater promised Bouton that a new commercial would be prepared and aired in 1984. Bouton direct, Tr. at 149; Atwater direct, Tr. at 471-72.

In the Fall of 1983, Amurol requested Bouton's approval of a promotion called the Baseball Bonanza Instant Winner ("Baseball Bonanza"). The promotion featured a game card in each pouch of chewing gum. Each card had bases on it, and by scratching the covering off the bases, the buyer would see if he or she had won a prize. Atwater cross, Tr. 585. Bouton's creative input was not sought during the developmental and conceptual stages of the project. By letter dated February 1, 1984, PTX 82, Amurol sent Bouton the storyboard for the Baseball Bonanza commercial. Atwater and Amurol considered this to be a new commercial, but the storyboard was basically the "You're in the Big Leagues" storyboard with inserts focusing on the Baseball Bonanza. Amurol had announced the Baseball Bonanza promotion and commercial to its brokers before Bouton had been consulted for his approval of the commercial.

THE 1984 MODIFICATION

In February of 1984, Amurol wanted to run the Baseball Bonanza advertisement. NH&S had committed to the purchase of media time for the Baseball Bonanza commercials. Bouton refused, however, to give his consent. On or about February 16, 1984, at Amurol's direction, NH&S put the media network package on hold temporarily.

Atwater then went to the National Confectionery Wholesalers' Association convention in Anaheim, California, and, while there, spoke to Bouton by telephone on or about February 22, 1984. After some discussion, they came to an agreement: Bouton would relinquish all approval rights over advertising and promotions. In return for that, Bouton would receive a full 5% royalty payment on the sales of BIG LEAGUE CHEW. In addition, Atwater agreed that Amurol would not introduce a competing shredded gum product. Bouton had Atwater read the terms to him over the telephone. Atwater agreed to send a telex setting forth the terms discussed over the telephone. Atwater then instructed his secretary at Amurol headquarters to send telexes to Bouton and Silberman confirming the agreement they had reached. Atwater's secretary sent telexes, but because of a problem with the telex transmission, also sent a confirmatory mailgram. Bouton received the mailgram, and compared it to his notes of his agreement reached with Atwater on the telephone, and saw that they matched. At that point, both Bouton and Atwater testified that they had an understanding. Bouton cross, Tr. 347; Atwater direct, Tr. 506-08. Bouton then gave Atwater his verbal approval to run the Baseball Bonanza commercial.

The mailgram sent by Atwater to Bouton reads as follows:

This is the text we talked about. Will be in touch with Gilson to draw up final papers next week.

If Amurol Products Company elects to continue advertising, it will create and run advertising for BIG LEAGUE CHEW with a masculine sports theme featuring the brand in a quote macho unquote image.

If promotional advertising is run, it will make every attempt to feature the brand in the same image.

Any promotions to the consumer will continue to feature prizes which are sports-oriented and in keeping with the image of the brand.

Amurol, in consideration of Jim Bouton Corporation relinquishing all approval of advertising and promotions, will, during the life of the contract, refrain from introducing another quote shredded unquote bubble gum which would compete with BIG LEAGUE CHEW. POPEYE and BUCKAROO CHEW, already on the market can continue to be produced and sold.

PTX 92.

Atwater testified that he and Bouton had an understanding at that point. The following colloquy between plaintiff's counsel and Atwater clearly demonstrates that Atwater and Bouton had reached an agreement:

Q: Was it your understanding that this was -- do you think you had a mutual understanding as to what that clause meant, noncompete?

A: Yes. I think we had an understanding, yes.

Q: And so it would be fair to state that Mr. Bouton, as you had your discussions in Anaheim, Mr. Bouton understood that he would get a 5 percent royalty in the future?

A: An additional 2-1/2 percent which was proposed to him, yes.

Q: Which would be a total of 5 percent?

A: Yes.

Q: And, in turn, you would not compete in the future, is that correct?

A: Yes.

Q: And additionally, Mr. Bouton would agree to relinquish his approval rights over commercials?

A: Yes.

* * *

Q: . . . I am only asking you if you and Mr. Bouton, on or about the date that you sent your telex or telegram, February 22, understood each other on those points?

A: Yes. We had a good understanding. Yes.

Atwater direct, Tr. 507-09. Despite this testimony, Atwater later said that it was his firm belief that there was no contract yet between them as to this modification because the lawyers had not reviewed the document. Atwater claimed that there would be no agreement until the lawyers for both sides read and commented on and drew up the agreement, and the parties signed it. Atwater cross, Tr. 595-97. Atwater's testimony on this point was strained and contradicted his earlier testimony that he and Bouton had reached an understanding. Tr. 507-512. Atwater's testimony on this point was also undercut by his statement that he thought the telex was a sufficient basis for him to produce the Baseball Bonanza commercial, without further approval from JBC. Atwater cross, Tr. 597. It is not disputed that Atwater had authority to bind Amurol. See Atwater redirect, Tr. 676-77.

Bouton testified that he understood that the parties were bound from the moment they reached an agreement. Bouton stated that the document was to be given to the lawyers not for their review, but only to put the terms into more formal language. I find Bouton's testimony to have been credible on this point. He answered straightforwardly when asked about the lawyers' roles in drafting the final agreement, and his answers are consistent with his statement that he and Atwater had reached an agreement.

In effect, Atwater knew that he "had a gun to his head" Atwater direct, Tr. 492, and needed Bouton's approval to run the Baseball Bonanza advertisement. To get what he needed, he agreed to give Bouton the full 5% royalty and also agreed not to introduce a competing "shredded gum in a pouch" product. Bouton, however, insisted on having something in writing. Bouton direct, Tr. 181, 184. The parties did discuss having the agreement drawn up by lawyers, but did not contemplate that lawyers would review the terms of the agreement. Bouton direct, Tr. 185.

By letter dated February 28, 1984, Bouton's counsel confirmed that he no longer objected to the "Baseball Bonanza" commercial and authorized Amurol to use the commercial "based on the understandings as to modification of the Agreement which is to be reduced to writing in due course." DTX-DDD. The February 28 letter spelled out in further detail the February 22, 1984 modification. Specifically, the letter stated that Bouton relinquished all approval of advertising for BIG LEAGUE CHEW and BIG LEAGUE PLUG; that royalties would be paid at the rate of 5% from January 1, 1984 to the end of the Agreement; that relinquishment of approval over advertising and promotion did not include relinquishment of the right to approve package graphics.

At that time or shortly thereafter, Silberman requested that Amurol pay Bouton at the increased royalty rate of 5%. Atwater thereupon directed Amurol's accounting department to pay Bouton a royalty of 5% of net sales without consulting Amurol's counsel and without having any written document other than the February 22 telex and Silberman's February 28 letter. Amurol paid a 5% royalty retroactive to January 1, 1984, and throughout the remainder of calendar year 1984. Indeed, an internal Amurol memorandum dated February 24, 1984 to Atwater from the BIG LEAGUE CHEW brand manager discussed where the money for the additional 2 1/2% royalty would come from. The memorandum deals with the "Royalty Payment Increase to Jim Boutin [sic] for Big League Chew," rather than the possibility of any proposed increase. PTX 93.

Production of the Baseball Bonanza commercial then went forward and the commercial was aired starting on April 14, 1984. The commercial stopped running at the end of July 1984 or beginning of August 1984. Atwater direct, Tr. 517. Shortly after the commercial stopped running, Amurol began to press Silberman about the draft of the final agreement. Amurol did not in any way inform JBC that it felt that no binding modification had been made to the 1981 Agreement until after the commercial had stopped running and it had secured the benefit of the bargain it had obtained from Bouton, namely, being able to run advertising for which it had already blocked time.

Amurol sought and obtained Bouton's approval for package graphics in the period after the modification. Other promotions were run without seeking Bouton's approval, such as a jacket giveaway with the Atlanta Braves, and batting glove giveaways with the Louisville Redbirds and Texas Rangers. Thus, as they had operated in the past, Amurol and Bouton began performing under the February 22, 1984 telex immediately, without waiting for execution of a formal document.

As reflected in their exchange of correspondence in the week following the February 22, 1984 telex, the parties contemplated that the agreement would be reduced to writing. Bouton cross, Tr. 340-42; Atwater cross, Tr. 594-97 No letter or other document indicated that either party intended not to be bound until the finalized writing was executed, and no testimony was given to the effect that one party said to the other that final execution of the agreement was required. The parties contemplated that the final writing would not be an entirely new contract; rather, they expected it to be a letter agreement, modifying certain paragraphs of the 1981 Agreement. Gilson direct, Tr. 723.

The first mention by Atwater or anyone acting on behalf of Amurol to Bouton that an agreement had not been reached in February came after the Baseball Bonanza commercial stopped airing in late July or early August.

Shortly after the February 22 telex was sent, counsel for the parties reviewed the document. Gilson, counsel for Amurol, had a concern about the propriety of the no-compete clause under the antitrust laws. Gilson expressed his concern to Silberman, counsel to Bouton, who had the responsibility of drafting the formal agreement. Silberman did not produce a draft of the modification until June of 1984. The no-compete clause was still in this draft, and Gilson recommended to Atwater that the clause either be deleted, or that it be approved by Amurol's antitrust counsel, Gordon Lang, Jr., Esq. ("Lang"), of Gardner, Carton & Douglas. Lang and David Braun, Esq., an associate at Gardner Carton & Douglas gave an oral opinion to Susan Somers Neal, Esq. ("Neal"), then an associate at Willian Brinks, to the effect that the no-compete provision was not per se illegal, but that it would be subject to scrutiny under the rule of reason, and that any claim raised about the clause would likely survive a motion to dismiss, and thus possibly involve Bouton and Amurol in long and costly litigation.

Over the next few months, various counter-proposals to resolve the difficulty over the no-compete clause were put forward and rejected. Amurol agreed to give Bouton a 5% royalty on any competing shredded gum product that it introduced during the term of the agreement. Bouton rejected this offer, finding that it did not provide him with sufficient protection in the event Amurol manufactured and marketed a competing shredded gum product. Bouton feared that even paying him a 5% royalty on competing brands was not a sufficient disincentive to dissuade Amurol from bringing out a new product; Bouton feared that in the last years of the license agreement, Amurol would let BIG LEAGUE CHEW fall by the wayside and promote another gum in its place.

Accordingly, Bouton proposed that he be given a 5% royalty on competing brands in perpetuity. In that way, he would, in effect, own the trademarks to the competing brands. This would certainly provide a disincentive to bringing out another shredded gum product. Amurol was unwilling to assign its rights in any trademark to Bouton. Instead, Amurol proposed that Bouton be given a 5% royalty on any competing shredded gum products for the life of the license agreement between Bouton and Amurol. Bouton wanted greater assurances and also wanted any such agreement to be contained in a separate contract so that U.S. Licensing would not be entitled to receive any portion of the royalty payments. Discussions between the parties continued until mid-November of 1984.

At that time, Neal and Gilson drafted a proposal that was substantially the same as their most recent proposal detailed above. Atwater took this proposal to a November 19, 1984 meeting with Bouton at Silberman's office in New York; but only Bouton and Atwater were present at the meeting. The parties spoke for several hours, but could not reach agreement on an alternative to the no-compete language. When the meeting ended, Atwater left and took a taxi to the airport. Bouton later discussed the meeting with Silberman.

Over the 1984 Thanksgiving weekend, Silberman died. On the following Monday, November 26, 1984, Amurol's counsel informed Bouton that it intended to terminate discussions and would revert to the terms of the 1981 Agreement. Bouton then contacted another law firm, Amster, Rothstein & Engelberg and dealt with Morton Amster, Esq. ("Amster") of that firm. With Amster, Bouton drafted a letter to Amurol refusing to approve or disapprove of a storyboard for a commercial that Amurol had sent Bouton for approval.

On or about December 18, 1984, Amurol sought Bouton's approval for advertising and promotions, consistent with its position that the February modification was of no effect, and the 1981 Agreement then in force required Bouton's approval. Bouton refused to approve or disapprove the advertising, consistent with his position that under the February 1984 modification he had relinquished that right.

In January of 1985, Amurol went back to paying Bouton royalty fees at the rate of 2 1/2% as provided in the 1981 Agreement. Bouton then served a notice of breach on Amurol:

This letter is to inform you that Jim Bouton Corporation believes that Amurol Products Company has materially breached the Agreement dated July 6, 1981 as amended. This material breach relates to the failure by Amurol Products Company to remit to the Jim Bouton Corporation royalties in the full amount at the rate of five percent (5%), in accordance with the modifications to Paragraph 4 of the Agreement.

Pursuant to Paragraph 27 of the Agreement, Amurol Products Company has thirty (30) days within which to cure its breach. After the expiration of that time, Jim Bouton Corporation will have no alternative but to seek redress through the Courts, and thereby obtain a declaration of its right to obtain royalties at the rate of five percent (5%).

PTX 145. JBC did not claim a breach as to any other provision of the 1981 Agreement or February modification.[5] JBC attempted to work out its dispute with Amurol by letter dated February 19, 1985, from Amster to Amurol's

---

[5] 5 Bouton subsequently filed a second notice of breach on October 26, 1987, relating to co-packing of BIG LEAGUE CHEW with other gum products in violation of the 1981 Agreement. PTX 165. Amurol cured that breach within thirty days as provided under paragraph 27 of the 1981 Agreement, and there remains no issue as to that purported breach.

counsel, and in that letter JBC expressly elected not to seek termination of the 1981 Agreement. DTX RRRRR.

CLAIMS OF THE PARTIES

JBC then filed this action in March 1985, when Amurol refused to pay the higher royalty rate to which JBC claimed it was entitled. In its original complaint, JBC claimed only that Amurol's failure to pay the full 5% royalty rate violated the 1984 modification to the 1981 Agreement. Defendant Amurol counterclaimed for the additional 2 1/2% royalty that it had paid Bouton during 1985. In 1987, however, JBC amended its complaint to assert additional causes of action. JBC has asserted three causes of action against Amurol in its amended complaint. First, JBC maintains that the 1981 Agreement was modified by the February 22 telex, either alone or in conjunction with the February 28 letter from Bouton's counsel, and that Amurol breached the 1981 Agreement as modified. This is essentially the same claim that formed the basis of the original complaint. Second, JBC alleges that, if no modification of the 1981 Agreement is found to have taken place, Amurol breached the 1981 Agreement because Bouton withheld approval of advertising during and after 1985, and was therefore entitled to the full 5% royalty payment. Third, JBC seeks a declaratory judgment that Amurol has anticipatorily breached the terms of the 1981 Agreement by failing to work closely with Bouton, that such failure will continue to foreclose Bouton from meaningfully participating in the creation and development of advertising, and therefore warrants the equitable remedy of rescission of the 1981 Agreement.

JBC has requested the following relief: a determination that the 1981 Agreement was modified in February of 1984; an award of damages to bring JBC's royalty payments to 5% for the entire period after January 1, 1984; an injunction barring defendants from manufacturing, distributing, or selling competing shredded bubble gum products; an accounting of defendants' profits by reason of its sales of competing shredded gum products; a declaration that defendants have anticipatorily breached the 1981 Agreement; a declaration that plaintiff is entitled to elect to terminate its relationship with defendants by reason of the anticipatory breach; and the costs of the action and reasonable attorney's fees.

WRIGLEY AS A PROPER PARTY DEFENDANT

Bouton contends that Wrigley is a proper party to this suit because of its involvement with and control over Amurol. In sum, Wrigley was mentioned during the trial with regard to the no-compete provision, its shipping policies, its policies on touring manufacturing facilities and its manufacture of gum at one point for Amurol. More specifically, each of these is discussed below, as follows.

When Bouton pressed Atwater to run the Miller Lite Beer ad parody, Atwater told Bouton that Wrigley would not want to get into a legal battle with the Miller Brewing Company. Atwater direct, Tr. 496; PTX 82, 86. In the period just before the 1984 modification, Atwater contemplated that if Amurol could not use the advertising time it had reserved with NH&S to run the Baseball Bonanza commercial, Amurol would advertise another of its products or Wrigley would take over the time and use it to advertise Hubba Bubba bubble gum. Atwater direct, Tr. 504.

Wrigley also came up in connection with the no-compete provision in the February 22, 1984 telex. Bouton testified that Atwater said, "the Wrigley people were very hot under the collar" about Bouton owning the trademarks of competing brands. Bouton direct, Tr. 223; see Atwater cross, Tr. 617-18. Bouton also testified that Atwater threatened that Wrigley would come out with a competing product and let BIG LEAGUE CHEW "fall by the wayside." Bouton direct, Tr. 178. Atwater stated that he merely invoked the name of Wrigley because he was mad. Atwater direct, Tr. 494. The Court finds his testimony on this point to have been entirely credible. Atwater wanted to pressure Bouton into giving in on the no-compete, and simply used the name Wrigley because he thought it would have extra weight.

Paul Rogers, now Chairman of Amurol, was a "rotating director" of Wrigley in 1979-1980, and at the same time was a director of Amurol. Bouton never negotiated with Rogers. Bouton direct, Tr. 115-16. Martin Garrity is vice-president of production for Wrigley, and was a board member of Amurol for one year between 1980 and 1988. There is no indication that Bouton ever negotiated with Garrity. Atwater is the nephew of William Wrigley and was vice-president of advertising of Wrigley from 1974 to 1979, but was never an officer or director of both Wrigley and Amurol simultaneously. Atwater direct, Tr. 454-55. No other persons were board members of Amurol as well as Wrigley officers; nor were any Wrigley board members directors of Amurol. Atwater cross, Tr. 481.

Wrigley and Amurol both use the same law firm, Willian Brinks, and the same advertising agency, NH&S. Wrigley and Amurol have separate sales systems. Atwater direct, Tr. 538-39. Wrigley and Amurol also have separate manufacturing facilities, but when Amurol had a large backlog of orders to fill shortly after the initial marketing of BIG LEAGUE CHEW, Wrigley did manufacture gum, which was then shipped to be shredded. Atwater redirect, Tr. 658. Amurol would not let Bouton tour the manufacturing facility when he came to tour the Amurol offices because Wrigley and Amurol have a policy against allowing any non-employees into its production facilities. Atwater direct, Tr. 462.

SUBSEQUENT DEVELOPMENTS

While this action was pending, in or about June of 1987, Amurol introduced a new shredded gum product under the mark GARFIELD STRIPES. That product does not have a sports theme.

On April 18, 1988, counsel for JBC moved to reopen the testimony and offer additional evidence, claiming that Bouton has recently discovered new facts relevant and necessary to its case. The new evidence relates to the no-compete clause of the February modification of the 1981 Agreement. In short, Bouton states that while attending the National Candy Wholesalers' Association in San Antonio, Texas, on February 27-28, 1988, he visited the Amurol display booth and discovered prototypes of three net shredded gum products: KING KONG, GODZILLA and WEREWOLF shredded bubble gum in a pouch. Affidavit of Jim Bouton, sworn to on April 15, 1988, paras. 4-5. None of these products has a sports theme.

CONCLUSIONS OF LAW
THE 1984 MODIFICATION

The Second Circuit has stated that the primary question in determining whether parties have bound themselves prior to the execution of a formal contract is whether the parties intended to be so bound. Reprosystem, B.V. v. SCM Corp., 727 F.2d 257, 261 (2d Cir.), cert. denied, 469 U.S. 828 (1984). As the Second Circuit phrased the issue:

Did the parties intend not to be bound prior to execution of a formal contract? Or, did they merely contemplate that their informal agreement would be reduced to a formal writing at some later time?

Reprosystem, 727 F.2d at 261. The starting point for any discussion of the law must be the corollary general principles: (1) "if parties do not intend to be bound by an agreement until it is in writing and signed, then there is no contract until that event occurs," R.G. Group, Inc. v. Horn & Hardart Company, 751 F.2d 69, 74 (2d Cir. 1984), and (2) "the mere fact that the parties contemplate memorializing their agreement in a formal document does not prevent their informal agreement from taking effect prior to that event" Reprosystem, 727 F.2d at 261 (quoting V'Soske v. Barwick, 404 F.2d 495, 499 (2d Cir. 1968), cert. denied, 394 U.S. 454 (1969)).

Accordingly, the first question the Court must answer is whether the parties intended to be bound before the execution of a final written document. The second question, assuming that the first is answered in the affirmative, is whether the writing is sufficiently definite to bind the parties.

In determining whether the parties intended to be bound by something short of a written agreement, the courts have looked to certain factors. First among them is whether the parties explicitly stated that they intended to be bound only when a written agreement is signed. R.G. Group, 751 F.2d at 75; Reprosystem, B.V. v. SCM Corp., 727 F.2d 257, 262 (2d Cir.), cert. denied, 469 U.S. 828 (1984). A second factor is whether one party has partially performed. R.G. Group, 751 F.2d at 75-76; V'Soske v. Barwick, 404 F.2d 495 (2d Cir. 1968), cert. denied, 394 U.S. 921 (1969). A third factor is whether there was nothing left to negotiate or settle, so that signing was a mere ministerial act. R.G. Group, 751 F.2d at 76; Banking & Trading Corp. v. Floete, 257 F.2d 765, 769 (2d Cir. 1958). A fourth factor is whether the agreement concerns complex business matters where the requirement of a writing is the norm rather than the exception. R.G. Group, 751 F.2d at 76; International Telemeter v. Teleprompter Corp., 592 F.2d 49, 57-58 (2d Cir. 1979) (Friendly, J., concurring). And, as the Second Circuit has held, mere intention to commit the agreement to writing will not prevent contract formation prior to execution. Winston v. Mediafare Entertainment Corp., 777 F.2d 78, 80 (2d Cir. 1985).

Application of the four R.G. Group factors in this case leads to the conclusion that there was an effective modification of the 1981 Agreement.

The first factor is whether the parties explicitly stated that they did not intend to be bound until a written, signed agreement was effectuated. In this case, paragraph 29 of the 1981 Agreement provides:

The terms of this Agreement cannot be waived or modified except by an agreement in writing. There are no representations, warranties or covenants other than those set forth in this Agreement which sets forth the entire understanding of the parties.

The 1981 Agreement therefore contemplates modification only by written agreement. The terms of the February 22, 1984 mailgram were agreed to by both sides and, needless to say, the mailgram was in writing. It should be noted, however, that the 1981 Agreement does not explicitly require the agreement to be signed by both parties in order to be valid.

The confirming mailgram states: "This is the text we talked about. Will be in touch with Gilson to draw up final papers next week." PTX 92a. This is fully consistent with the view that the parties had reached an agreement, in writing, and contemplated that the agreement would later be formalized. At no time until after the Baseball Bonanza commercial stopped running did Amurol express to JBC its claimed view that a binding modification had not been effected. Accordingly, the first factor weighs in favor of a finding that the parties intended to be bound when they reached agreement on February 22, 1984.

The second factor is whether one party has partially performed. It is clear that the conduct of the parties, after the modification was allegedly reached, is relevant in determining whether the parties had indeed conclusively modified the agreement. See Farnsworth, Precontractual Liability and Preliminary

Agreements: Fair Dealing and Failed Negotiations, 87 Colum. L. Rev. 217, 262 (1987). The conduct of the parties both contemporaneously with the sending of the mailgram and after its mailing indicates that the parties intended to be bound by the terms of the February 22, 1984 telex. In this case, both parties partially performed. Bouton relinquished his right to disapprove of the Baseball Bonanza commercial, and Amurol began paying Bouton almost immediately at the rate of 5%. At no time did Atwater or anyone at Amurol state that the increase in royalty payments was merely an accommodation. Accordingly, the second factor weighs heavily in favor of finding that there was a binding contract.

The third factor is whether there was nothing left to negotiate or settle. In this case, the differences between the parties later emerged, but those differences were not present when Atwater and Bouton agreed to modify the 1981 Agreement. The Court is mindful of Judge Pratt's cautionary words that:

The actual drafting of a written instrument will frequently reveal points of disagreement, ambiguity, or omission which must be worked out prior to execution. Details that are unnoticed or passed by in oral discussion will be pinned down when the understanding is reduced to writing. These considerations are not minor; indeed, above a certain level of investment and complexity, requiring written contracts may be the norm in the business world rather than the exception. R.G. Group, 751 F.2d at 75.

But in this case, the parties debated over an agreement for several weeks before the February 22 agreement was reached. That modification was the product of intense negotiations between Bouton and Atwater. The parties negotiated over language, and, when they finally reached an agreement, they committed that agreement to writing. The parties reached a firm understanding, and this is not seriously disputed. See Atwater direct, Tr. 506-509.

The fourth factor is whether complex business matters are involved that would ordinarily require a writing. In this case, the course of dealings between the parties was to have important documents in writing but not necessarily formally executed by the parties. For example, Atwater and Bouton agreed over the telephone that Amurol would be granted an extension of time within which to introduce BIG LEAGUE PLUG. Bouton then confirmed that understanding in a handwritten letter. PTX 70. The parties informally agreed to extend the BUCKAROO CHEW trademark agreement, and confirmed that understanding by a telex. Bouton direct, Tr. 219-20; Neal direct, Tr. 780-81, 788, 790; PTX 122. Those matters involved significant sums of money. The amount of money at stake here was an additional 2 1/2% royalty, or an amount that would total approximately $ 200,000 per year at the rate of net sales in 1984. Surely that is no small amount. Nevertheless, Amurol's counsel testified that he expected this to be only a letter agreement, not a completely new contract. Gilson direct Tr. 723. That is precisely what the parties agreed to -- an informal agreement, in keeping with their customary way of doing business.

Application of these four factors reveals that the parties intended to be bound before execution by Amurol and JBC of a final written document.

SUFFICIENCY OF THE 1984 MODIFICATION

Section 15-301 of the General Obligations Law of New York provides in pertinent part:

1. A written agreement or other written instrument which contains a provision to the effect that it cannot be changed orally, cannot be changed by an executory agreement unless such executory agreement is in writing and signed by the party against whom enforcement of the change is sought or by his agent.

N.Y. Gen. Oblig. L. § 15-301 (McKinney's 1978). This provision is a Statute of Frauds requirement, but is more specific than the general Statute of Frauds provision under New York Law. See § 5-701. The purpose of the Statute of Frauds is to guarantee that there is some evidence of contract, and that one party does not simply claim that an oral modification was made without submitting some proof of such a claim. In this case, it is clear beyond cavil that there was a writing sufficient to satisfy section 15-301. The February 22, 1984 mailgram contained the material provisions of the agreement between Bouton and Atwater.

The only possible question as to the enforceability of the February 1984 modification is whether the terms of the February 22, 1984 mailgram are sufficiently definite and include all material terms. The Second Circuit has recently reaffirmed the well-settled principle that "[t]o be enforceable an agreement must contain, either expressly or by implication, all of the terms deemed material by the parties." Cinema North Corp. v. Plaza at Latham Associates, 867 F.2d 135, 140 (2d Cir. 1989); see Enercomp. Inc. v. McCorhill Publishing, Inc., No. 88-7323, slip op. 2649, 2669-70 (2d Cir. 1989); V'Soske v. Barwick, 404 F.2d 495, 500 (2d Cir. 1968), cert. denied, 394 U.S. 921 (1969).

WRIGLEY AS A PROPER PARTY

Plaintiff contends that Wrigley is a proper party to this suit because there exists a unity of interest between Amurol and Wrigley and because "Wrigley dominates and controls Amurol to such an extent that Amurol is a mere instrumentality." Plaintiff's Post-Trial Proposed Conclusions of Law para. 59. This contention is unfounded. The only evidence of control that plaintiff has adduced is that Paul Rogers has served on the board of directors of Wrigley and on the board of directors of Amurol and that Martin Garrity served on the Amurol board of directors and was vice-president of production for Wrigley. At several times during the negotiations, Atwater invoked the name of Wrigley. Beyond that, however, there was no indication that Wrigley had any involvement in the dealings here at issue. First, Wrigley was not a party to any agreement with Bouton. Amurol and Wrigley are separate corporate entities. Even the 1984 modification, which resulted in part because of Bouton's fear that Wrigley would introduce a direct competitor to BIG LEAGUE CHEW, did not mention Wrigley. Bouton has failed to make a showing sufficient to justify the extraordinary relief of going behind corporate formalities when they are maintained in good faith. Plaintiff has set forth the correct legal standard, however: in order to go behind corporate formalities, a party must show:

(1) chat the parent controls and dominates the subsidiary to such a degree that the subsidiary is a mere instrumentality of its parent;

(2) that through its domination and control of the subsidiary the parent is perpetrating a fraud or working an injustice . . . ; and

(3) these elements result in an unjust loss or injury to the party disavowing corporate independence, such as the insolvency of the subsidiary.

United Rubber Cork Linoleum and Plastic Workers v. Great American Industries, 479 F. Supp. 216, 242 (S.D.N.Y. 1979); see American Protein v. AB Volvo, 844 F.2d 56, 60 (2d Cir.), cert. denied, 109 S. Ct. 136 (1988). As the Second Circuit has recently noted, there is a presumption of separateness that is entitled to substantial weight, American Protein, F.2d at 60, and Bouton has failed to overcome that presumption. Accordingly, Wrigley is not a proper party to the suit and is hereby dismissed as a defendant.

JBC'S CLAIM FOR BREACH OF THE 1981 AGREEMENT

Bouton contends alternatively that Amurol breached the 1981 Agreement by its failure to obtain Bouton's approval for commercials run in 1985, 1986 and 1987. Amurol contends, however, that it ran a commercial that had been approved for 1982, and that once approval is given, such approval cannot be withdrawn. Bouton, on the other hand, contends that he made it clear to Atwater that he did not approve the running of "You're in the Big Leagues" beyond the 1983 advertising season. Bouton consented to Baseball Bonanza running in 1984 in reliance on what he bought was the binding 1984 modification. Acting under that alleged agreement, Bouton refused to approve or disapprove advertising and promotions. Because Amurol ran unauthorized advertising, Bouton claims he is entitled to an additional 2 1/2% royalty as provided in para. 5 of the 1981 Agreement.

In the event that the Court finds that there was no modification to the 1981 Agreement, JBC claims that the 1981 Agreement was breached by Amurol. In light of the Court's finding that the 1981 Agreement was effectively modified in February 1984, the Court need not reach this issue. Nevertheless, for the sake of completeness, the Court addresses plaintiff's arguments. Plaintiff has failed to show that there was a breach of the 1981 Agreement by reason of Amurol's failure to pay Bouton a royalty at the rate of 5%.

JBC relies on the interrelationship of paragraphs 4, 5 and 16(a) of the 1981 Agreement to support its position that Amurol breached the 1981 Agreement. JBC contends that it had the right to refuse to approve all advertising, for any reason or for no reason at all, and thereby to become entitled to a full 5% royalty. In effect, JBC contends that because an earlier draft of the 1981 Agreement provided that JBC "shall not unreasonably withhold" its approval, JBC had no obligation to deal fairly with Amurol in this regard. Such a contention is untenable. It is well settled that there is implicit in every contract a covenant of good faith and fair dealing. See, e.g., Durham Industries v. North River Ins. Co., 673 F.2d 37, 41 (2d Cir.) cert. denied, 459 U.S. 827 (1982). The mere fact that the 1981 Agreement did not explicitly provide that Bouton could not unreasonably withhold his approval does not in any way mean that there was no covenant of good faith and fair dealing in the contract.

Furthermore, the very terms of the contract preclude the interpretation that Bouton seeks here to establish. Paragraph 16(a) provides that materials "shall be deemed approved if JBC does not notify the Company in writing to the contrary within seven (7) days after receipt." JBC has not notified Amurol that it disapproves of advertising that Amurol has been running because JBC has been operating under the assumption that the 1981 Agreement was effectively modified in 1984. Accordingly, under the terms of the 1981 Agreement, JBC is deemed to have approved the advertising and promotions run by Amurol. JBC's claim for relief for breach of the 1981 Agreement must, for this reason alone, be denied.

JBC's CLAIM FOR TERMINATION

Plaintiff seeks a declaratory judgment that Amurol has anticipatorily breached the 1981 Agreement, and that JBC is therefore entitled to elect to terminate the 1981 Agreement. This view is unfounded in the facts and in the law. Paragraph 27 of the 1981 Agreement provides that, in the event of a material breach, the other party may terminate the agreement by giving thirty days notice. At no time did JBC give notice that Amurol's conduct in this regard constituted a material breach of the 1981 Agreement by continuing to receive the benefits of the contract after the events which would arguably be cause for termination. In such a situation, the party that chooses to accept the continued benefits under the contract cannot then terminate the agreement when it is convenient. Apex Pool Equipment v. Lee, 419 F.2d 556, 562-63 (2d Cir. 1969). As noted above, Bouton chose not to seek termination of the 1981 Agreement when it commenced this lawsuit. See supra p.26; Bouton cross, Tr. 429-30; DTX RRRRR.

Furthermore, a claim for anitcipatory breach requires unambiguous repudiation of the contract. Tenavision, Inc. v. Neuman, 45 N.Y.2d 145, 150, 408 N.Y.S.2d 36, 38 (1978); Phillips Puerto Core, Inc. v. Tradax Petroleum Ltd., 782 F.2d 314, 321-22 (2d Cir. 1985); Restatement 92d) of Contracts § 253; Farnsworth, Contracts § 8.21 at 634 (1982). Amurol has not taken any action to repudiate the 1981 Agreement. In fact, by exercising its option to entend the contract and repeatedly asserting its desire to continue as JBC's licensee, it has clearly indicated that it intends to perform fully its obligations under the contract.

Finally, Bouton has testified that Amurol has been more cooperative since the commencement of this action. Bouton direct. Tr. 288-89. Therefore, if ever there were cause for Bouton to terminate the contract, such cause, by Bouton's own admission, is not sufficiently likely to continue in the future to warrant a declaration that Amurol has anticipatorily breached the 1981 Agreement.

AMUROL'S COUNTERCLAIM

Amurol has counterclaimed for $ 301,396.50, the amount by which its payment to Bouton exceeded the 2 1/2% royalty rate it claims should have been paid. In light of the Court's ruling on Bouton's claim, it is evident that Amurol cannot succeed on its counterclaim. There was an effective modification to the 1981 Agreement, and Amurol has no claim to recover money paid to Bouton as an accommodation because Bouton was entitled to receive that money.

Moreover, even were the Court to rule in favor of Amurol on Bouton's claim, Amurol has failed to prove a claim for relief for unjust enrichment. To state a cause of action under New York law for unjust enrichment, a party must show: (1) that the defendant was enriched, (2) that such enrichment was at plaintiff's expense and consists of property rightfully belonging to the plaintiff, and (3) that the circumstances require, in equity and good conscience, that the money be returned to the plaintiff. Bank of Castle v. Salerno, 99 A.D.2d 663, 663-64, 471 N.Y.S.2d 924, 925 (4th Dep't 1984); Spallina v. Giannoccaro, 98 A.D.2d 103, 105, 469 N.Y.S.2d 824, 826 (4th Dep't 1983); Chase Manhattan Bank v. Banque Intra. S.A., 274 F. Supp. 496, 499 (S.D.N.Y. 1967); see Reprosystem, 727 F.2d at 263.

The facts are clear that JBC was enriched at Amurol's expense. There is no suggestion, however, of any unjust enrichment of plaintiff. JBC received the money in exchange for relinquishment of its advertising approval rights.

Amurol made the payments in order to get out of a difficult situation. There was never any mention by Amurol that it was paying the 5% royalty rate only on condition that an acceptable final document would be executed. Indeed, Atwater testified that it was not until after his attorneys informed him that he was entitled to get back the money he paid to Bouton that he thought he could get the money back. At no time did he suggest to Bouton that the money advanced was only an   accommodation. Atwater cross, Tr. at 519-20; see Bouton direct, Tr. 285. Under these circumstances, there is nothing unjust about plaintiff's retaining the money paid it by Amurol in 1984.

ATTORNEY'S FEES

JBC has also requested that the Court grant plaintiff 30% of its attorney's fees for two reasons. First, it claims that Amurol's counterclaim is frivolous, and sanctions should be awarded for a total of 15% of plaintiff's fees. Second, plaintiff claims that it should be awarded an additional 15% because of Amurol's change of counsel that required additional pretrial preparation and trial examination of Gilson and Neal. The Court had stated at a pretrial conference that an award of counsel fees might be appropriate if the substitution of counsel that resulted when Amurol's present counsel were substituted for Willian Brinks caused added expense to plaintiff. The Court also notes that Defendants have reserved their right to seek attorney's fees for the amendment to the complaint to add plaintiff's second and third claims for relief. Consistent with the Court's comments before trial, the Court will not preclude either party from making a formal motion for attorney's fees. Plaintiff's informal application is denied on the current record.

CONCLUSION

The parties reached an agreement, in writing, to modify the 1981 Agreement. Amurol now refuses to abide by that modification. This it cannot do.

Accordingly, it is hereby ordered that judgment be entered for the plaintiff on its first claim for relief that Amurol has breached the 1981 Agreement as modified by failing to pay JBC the full 5% royalty to which it is entitled under the 1984 modification. Plaintiff shall be entitled to an accounting of the royalties payable from January 1, 1985 to the beginning of the option period, and shall receive damages amounting to the difference between 5% and the royalty actually received for that period. Amurol shall be enjoined from producing, selling or distributing any "shredded" gum in a pouch. Amurol shall make an accounting to JBC of all profits earned as a result of the sales of competing "shredded" gum in a pouch other than POPEYE and BUCKAROO CHEW and pay to JBC a royalty of 5% on those sales. In light of this ruling, it is unnecessary to reopen the proceedings to accept further testimony, as requested by Bouton, and plaintiff's motion to reopen the trial testimony is denied on this basis.

Wrigley is hereby dismissed as an improper defendant. Judgment shall be entered for defendant on plaintiff's second and third claims for relief. Judgment shall be entered for plaintiff on defendant Amurol's counterclaim. Plaintiff's application for attorney's fees is denied on the current record.

Plaintiff is hereby ordered to submit a judgment on or before July 28, 1989.

SO ORDERED
Dated: New York, New York
July 7, 1989

THE COCA-COLA COMPANY, a corporation, Plaintiff,

v.

ALMA-LEO U.S.A., INC., Defendant

No. 89 C 6045

UNITED STATES DISTRICT COURT FOR THE NORTHERN DISTRICT OF ILLINOIS, EASTERN DIVISION

719 F. Supp. 725
August 17, 1989

MEMORANDUM AND ORDER
JAMES B. MORAN, UNITED DISTRICT JUDGE.

Plaintiff, The Coca-Cola Company (Coca-Cola), brings suit against defendant, Alma-Leo U.S.A., Inc. (Alma-Leo), alleging various claims for relief stemming from the latter's marketing and selling of a bubble gum product entitled "**Mad Scientist** Magic Powder" (Magic Powder). The gum comes in the form of a white powder and, as we describe infra, is sold in a plastic container resembling a Coca-Cola bottle. We here evaluate Coca-Cola's motion for a temporary restraining order (TRO) enjoining disposition of the current Magic Powder inventory as, inter alia, violating and diluting Coca-Cola's trademarks governing their soft drink bottles.[6][1] For the following reasons, we grant that motion.

In its six-count complaint Coca-Cola alleges violations of the Federal Trademark Act (count I), the Illinois Anti-Dilution Act (count IV), the Illinois Uniform Deceptive Trade Practices Act (count V), and the Illinois Consumer Fraud and Deceptive Business Practices Act (count VI). It further claims relief

---

[6][1] See exhibits in support of Coca-Cola Company's request for a temporary restraining order.

based on both federal and common law unfair competition grounds (counts II and III respectively). Because we find a violation of the Illinois Anti-Dilution Act so likely, we need not discuss the complaint's other counts to predict likely success on the merits.

I. TRO Standards

The motion at bar, while labeled a request for a TRO, more closely resembles a motion for a preliminary injunction. The former term usually attaches to a request for relief ex parte. In recognition thereof, Rule 65 provides explicit durational limits and various requirements respecting attorney representations. Here, however, counsel for Alma-Leo have been amply notified of this litigation and have submitted a 13-page response, supplemental pleadings and memoranda, and various supporting exhibits (some written, some edible). In such circumstances we choose to apply the traditional standards governing preliminary injunctions. See 11 Wright & Miller, Federal Practice and Procedure: Civil § 2951, at 499 (1973) ("When the opposing party actually receives notice of the application for a restraining order, the procedure that is followed does not differ functionally from that on an application for a preliminary injunction and the proceeding is not subject to any special requirements"). Nonetheless, this order will remain in effect only until a hearing can be had, and having scheduled it "at the earliest possible time," cf. Rule 65(b), we therefore limit the term of this order to twenty days.[7]

We therefore evaluate, in order, the likelihood of success on the merits, the threat of irreparable injury, the balance of harms, and the public interest at issue. We do so within the "sliding scale" framework established by Judge Posner in Roland Machinery Co. v. Dresser Industries, 749 F.2d 380 (7th Cir. 1984). That opinion noted the interrelationship between the above purportedly independent demonstrations and, in relevant part, held:

5. If the plaintiff does show some likelihood of success, the court must then determine how likely that success is, because this affects the balance of relative harms (point 3 above). The more likely the plaintiff is to win, the less likely need the balance of harms weigh in his favor, the less likely he is to win, the more need it weigh in his favor. This is a most important principle, and one well supported by cases in this and other circuits, and by scholarly commentary.

_____

[7] 2 Having neither made our decision ex parte, nor after a hearing, we adopt the term of Rule 65(b) (doubling of the ten-day period), even though that provision technically limits only the terms of TROs granted "without notice."

Id. at 387 (citations omitted). This court has wholeheartedly embraced the "sliding scale" approach elsewhere, most recently in Dobson, et al. v. Chicago and Northeast Illinois District, United Brotherhood of Carpenters, et al., 707 F. Supp. 348 (N.D. Ill. 1989), and we apply that analysis here.

II. Success on the Merits

The Illinois Anti-Dilution statute explicitly affords potential plaintiffs injunctive relief. In relevant part, that statute provides:

22. Injunction against use of same or similar trademark, trade name, label, etc.

§ 15. Every person, association, or union of working men adopting and using a mark, trade name, label or form of advertisement may proceed by suit, and the circuit court shall grant injunctions, to enjoin subsequent use by another of the same or any similar mark, trade name, label or form of advertisement. If there exists a likelihood of injury to business reputation or of dilution of the distinctive quality of the mark, trade name, label or form of advertisement of the prior user, notwithstanding the absence of competition between the parties or of confusion as to the source of goods or services.

Ill.Rev.Stat. ch. 140, para. 22. An injunction "must be granted if the prior user can show that the mark is distinctive and that the subsequent user's use dilutes that distinctiveness." Hyatt Corp. v. Hyatt Legal Services, 736 F.2d 1153, 1157 (7th Cir.), cert. denied, 469 U.S. 1019, 83 L. Ed. 2d 361, 105 S. Ct. 434 (1984) (emphasis added). The scope of that provision addresses several of Alma-Leo's objections. The prohibition extends protection respecting even non-competitors, and targets dilution of existing marks, not confusion of those marks with others. Hyatt Corp., 736 F.2d at 1157. Since Alma-Leo does not dispute Coca-Cola's prior use, we evaluate the Anti-Dilution Act's two criteria. We hold initially that the mark is distinctive. To be so considered, a mark must have come to be identified with its owner and its owner's products or services. Universal City Studios, Inc. v. Montgomery Ward & Co., Inc., 207 U.S.P.Q. (BNA) 852, 858 (N.D. Ill. 1980). Relevant factors to be evaluated include the commonness of the mark, the length of time the mark has been used, the scope of advertising and promotion, the nature and extent of the business and the scope of the first user's reputation. Hyatt Corp., 736 F.2d at 1158. Generally, "distinctiveness will only be found where the work has acquired a widespread reputation and good will through plaintiff's efforts." Ye Olde Tavern Cheese Products, Inc. v. Planters, Peanuts Division, Standard Brands, Inc., 261 F. Supp. 200, 208 (N.D. Ill. 1966), aff'd 394 F.2d 833 (7th Cir. 1967). See also Kern v. WKQX Radio, 175 Ill. App. 3d 624, 635, 529 N.E.2d 1149, 1156, 125 Ill. Dec. 73, 80 (1st Dist. 1988).

Easy application of these factors renders Coca-Cola's mark distinctive within the meaning of the Illinois Anti-Dilution law. Consumers certainly identify the Coca-Cola bottle with the company and its soft drink. The bottle mark is quite common and one which has been used for decades. Coca-Cola spends considerable sums advertising and promoting its product to further enhance its already extensive reputation. Put succinctly, Coca-Cola's bottle represents the archetypical distinctive mark.

We further believe that Alma-Leo's use dilutes the distinctiveness of the Coca-Cola bottle. The Magic Powder container closely resembles the Coca-Cola mark. The contours mirror each other: both have circular bottoms that narrow at the container's one-quarter point, then expand at the center to a circumference similar to that of the base (an hourglass configuration), maintain that shape for a time (bordered by separate indentations), and finally narrow to a cap covering the container's top. Magic Powder's plastic container even contains vertical lines covering the length of the bottle. Those physical resemblances sufficiently demonstrate the requisite dilution without ever inquiring into whether individuals might believe that Alma-Leo's product originated from or was sponsored by Coca-Cola.

Alma-Leo alleges its product also resembles other products in the existing marketplace. First, the similarity between Alma-Leo's container and Coca-Cola's mark is striking. Further, that other candies may also dilute the bottle's distinctiveness does not necessarily mean that Alma-Leo's conduct here should not be enjoined. Alma-Leo's claim merely demonstrates that Coca-Cola has grounds to bring suits it has not as yet filed.

We finally note that the sale of Magic Powder will likely injure Coca-Cola's reputation. That finding may be separately determinative as "an injunction must also be granted if the prior user shows a likelihood of injury to reputation." Hyatt Corp., 736 F.2d at 1157 n. 2. Alma-Leo markets its bubble gum as Magic Powder. While the front label reads "**Mad Scientist** Magic Powder Bubble Gum," the seal across the container's top reads only "Magic Powder." The powder not only resembles cocaine but also has a texture remarkably similar to the drug. While we cannot dispute that the powder itself may not be solely the color white, that distinction is blurred by the containers in which the powder is sold. Slightly pink powder comes in a bright pink container, leaving the definite impression that the powder inside is white. The same applies to the yellow container. And respecting the latter, the powder inside does seem to be plain white. In sum, the association with Coca-Cola through the use of a bottle with the same shape will likely injure Coca-Cola's reputation, whether or not confusion takes place. Cf. Coca-Cola Company v. Gemini Rising, Inc., 346 F. Supp. 1183, 1189 (E.D.N.Y. 1972)

("To associate such a noxious substance as cocaine with plaintiff's wholesome beverage as symbolized by its 'Coca-Cola' trademark and format would clearly have a tendency to impugn that product and injure plaintiff's business reputation"). That association "is not a flight of fancy" as Coca-Cola's name is "derived from the Andean coca leaf plant and the African cola nut, extracts of which gave the beverage its flavor. The coca leaf is the source of cocaine." Id. at 1189 n. 7.[8] Our judgment is therefore informed not by the affidavits of the participants in the Davenport incident, but also by our own assessment.

That other powdered candy has been sold by a variety of companies does not exonerate Alma-Leo here either. Those products do not proclaim themselves to be "Magic Powder." Further, association with illicit drugs, especially rock-like cocaine ("crack"), may well present uniquely severe risks to reputation in today's environment.

Having ruled that the Illinois Anti-Dilution Act alone likely ensures success on the merits, we need not evaluate Coca-Cola's federal trademark allegations, nor its other claims. We are quite aware that Alma-Leo virtually neglects to discuss the Illinois Anti-Dilution Act in its response, but that omission cannot remove the state provision from consideration. Alma-Leo can and should address the Anti-Dilution Act at the preliminary injunction stage. For now, we evaluate that provision without aid from its counsel.

III. Other Requirements

We quickly note that even though "consideration of the factors generally required to obtain a preliminary injunction may not be necessary under the Illinois Anti-Dilution Act," Ringling Bros.-Barnum & Bailey Combined Shows, Inc., v. Celozzi-Ettelson Chevrolet, Inc., 855 F.2d 480, 485 (7th Cir. 1988), prudence dictates that we do so. The Illinois statute defines the circumstances under which permanent injunctions should issue. Those limited criteria do not at all eliminate the need to make the various other demonstrations traditionally required for preliminary relief. See, e.g., Kern, 175 Ill.App.3d at 632, 529 N.E.2d at 1155, 125 Ill.Dec. at 79 (respecting claims arising out of the Illinois Anti-Dilution Act, "in order to obtain [a preliminary] injunction, a party must show an ascertained right in need of protection, a likelihood of success on the merits, an inadequate remedy at law, and irreparable injury"); see also American Snacks, Inc. v. Schaul, 132 Ill. App.

---

[8] 3 Reiterating the obvious, courts have noted the absence of cocaine in the beverage Coca-Cola. See Coca-Cola Co. v. Koke Co., 254 U.S. 143, 145-46, 65 L. Ed. 189, 41 S. Ct. 113 (1920); see also Coca-Cola Company v. Gemini Rising, Inc., 346 F. Supp. at 1189 n. 7.

2d 718, 721, 270 N.E.2d 209, 211 (1st Dist. 1971) (respecting same, "plaintiff however failed to support its petition with a showing that irreparable injury would result. . . . Moreover, the immediate harm caused the defendants by the issuance of a temporary injunction clearly outweighs whatever injury might result to plaintiff"). We therefore evaluate the relevant requirements one at a time.

A. Irreparable Injury

Even absent our delving into the federal trademark/confusion issue, the dilution claim suffices respecting irreparable injury. "It is the very nature of dilution to gnaw away insidiously at the value of a mark. " Hyatt Corp., 736 F.2d at 1158. That injury would be irreparable, not because money damages would fail to make the plaintiff whole, but rather because Coca-Cola cannot be expected to quantify the probable reduction in revenue. "There is no effective way to measure the loss of sales or potential growth -- to ascertain the people who don't knock on the door or to identify the specific persons who do not reorder because of the existence of the infringer." Instrumentalist Co. v. Marine Corps League, 509 F. Supp. 323, 333 (N.D. Ill. 1981), aff'd, 694 F.2d 145 (7th Cir. 1982). See also Ringling Brothers-Barnum & Bailey, 855 F.2d at 484 ("there is no effective way to measure the loss of audience or potential growth"). This difficulty in proving damages for the loss of corporate good will adequately demonstrates irreparable injury. See, e.g., id.; see also Omega Importing Corp. v. Petri-Kine Camera Co., 451 F.2d 1190, 1195 (2d Cir. 1971).

Coca-Cola's delay in filing its motion does not render it potential harm any less irreparable. In fact, both sides allege that settlement efforts were attempted and only recently broke down. These events do not affect our consideration of the pending motion.

B. The Balance of Harms

To reiterate, the marketing of Magic Powder risks significant injury in Coca-Cola's reputation and corporate good will. That potential harm cannot be outweighed by Alma-Leo's claims that the loss of its current inventory will be costly or that "mend[ing] its ways will be too expensive." Processed Plastic Co. v. Warner Communications, Inc., 675 F.2d 852, 859 (7th Cir. 1982). Defendants in trademark dilution cases will always be able to marshall that claim. The point remains that Alma-Leo should have taken the risk of a TRO into account ex ante. It cannot now claim issuance would be too costly. Further, its repackaging expenses will merely be incurred in the short-term, as only the current inventory is at issue here. The vast majority of Alma-Leo's manufacturing, advertising and sales apparatus will remain the same, for compliance requires only that it choose a different container in which to market Magic Powder. Contra Stokely-Van Camp Inc. v. Coca-Cola Co., 2 U.S.P.Q.2D (BNA) 1225, 1226 (N.D. Ill. 1987) (defendant "would have to rename the product as well as change the name on all existing products, advertisements, promotionals and programs"). Finally, the sliding scale approach requires that we consider the strength of Coca-Cola's claim in balancing the equities. See Hyatt Corp., 736 F.2d at 1159 ("we consider Hyatt Hotels' proof that Hyatt Legal Services is violating the Anti-Dilution Act to go substantially farther than showing a likelihood of success, and we may certainly take into account the strength of Hyatt Hotels' case in balancing the equities"). Accordingly, we have little difficulty in concluding that the balance of harms augur for issuance, and we make that call without debating whether issuance would preserve the vague notion of the "status quo."

C. The Public Interest
We finally address the rather elusive public interest element. As a general matter, "the public has an interest in the protection of trademarks," Hyatt Corp., 736 F.2d at 1159, and dilution thereof cannot help but operate to the public's detriment. That conclusion renders unnecessary any inquiry into whether the dilution at bar trivializes the nation's anti-drug campaign and/or Coca-Cola's own efforts.

The public interest in having an additional competitor in the powdered candy market does not alter our conclusion. First, even assigning full weight to Alma-Leo's claim, we cannot conclude that a single additional competitor outweighs the admittedly more general interest in trademark protection. Second, our order does not at all preclude market participation of Alma-Leo's own Magic Powder in any other container. Only the present inventory is at issue, and the public's interest in receiving solely that quantity cannot be terribly significant.

CONCLUSION
For the foregoing reasons, plaintiff's motion for a temporary restraining order is granted for twenty days. The preliminary injunction hearing is set for August 30, 1989 at 10:00 a.m.
August 17, 1989.

EVAN WEINER and TIMOTHY McCLAUSLAND, on behalf of themselves and all others similarly situated, Plaintiffs,

-v-

SNAPPLE BEVERAGE CORPORATION, Defendant.

07 Civ. 8742 (DLC)
August 3, 2010

UNITED STATES DISTRICT COURT
FOR THE SOUTHERN DISTRICT OF NEW YORK

OPINION & ORDER

DENISE COTE, District Judge:

This case concerns whether defendant's labeling of its teas and juice drinks as "All Natural," despite their inclusion of high fructose corn syrup ("HFCS"), was misleading to consumers. The plaintiffs move for class certification pursuant to Rules 23(a) and (b)(3), Fed. R. Civ. P. For the following reasons, the motion is denied.

BACKGROUND

A. Snapple Beverage Corporation

Defendant Snapple Beverage Corporation ("Snapple") was founded in New York's Greenwich Village in 1972. Snapple began selling and marketing its teas and juice drinks in the late 1980s. In marketing its beverages, Snapple focused on, among other things, flavor, innovation, and humor. Snapple became known for its quirky personality and funny advertising, as well as its colorful product labels and beverage names. For instance, Snapple's television advertisements featured, among other silly things, Snapple bottles dressed in wigs and hats, singing in a "boy-band," running with the "bulls"[1] 1 in Spain, saving the world from a **mad scientist**, being attacked by robots, and performing synchronized swimming. Snapple also built brand loyalty through promotions like the "Snaffle" and the "Snapple Yardsale."

Most relevant to this action, Snapple labeled and marketed its teas and juice drinks as being "All Natural." When Snapple entered the beverages market in the late 1980s, it avoided putting preservatives, which were then commonly found in similar beverages, in its teas and juice drinks. Snapple was able to do so by using a "hot-fill" process, which uses high-temperature heat pasteurization to preserve products immediately before bottling. Snapple also used 16-ounce glass bottles instead of aluminum cans or plastic. The glass bottles are vacuum-sealed with metal lug caps, the underside of which features "Snapple Facts" on a variety of topics.

From their inception, Snapple's beverages were sweetened with HFCS.[2] HFCS is made from corn and its primary constituents are glucose and fructose, the sugars that comprise table sugar and honey. It is undisputed that Snapple disclosed the inclusion of HFCS in the ingredient list that appears on the label of every bottle of Snapple that was labeled "All Natural."

Snapple does not sell its teas and juice drinks directly to consumers. Instead, Snapple sells to independent and company-owned distributors who sell to retailers, who in turn sell to consumers. Snapple "line prices" beverages that it sells to its distributors. Line pricing involves assigning a single, uniform price to all products sold in identical quantities. For instance, all 24-packs of 16-ounce glass Snapple products, regardless of flavor or whether they are regular or diet, are priced identically for sale to distributors. Thus, a case of 16-ounce "All Natural" lemon tea had the same wholesale list price as a case of 16-ounce diet lemon tea, which had artificial sweeteners and was not labeled "All Natural." Likewise, distributors of Snapple beverages line price when selling to retailers. Retailers set their own prices for Snapple beverages. Thus, Snapple does not have any control over the prices that consumers ultimately pay for its beverages.

B. The Plaintiffs

Plaintiffs   Evan   Weiner   ("Weiner")   and   Timothy   McCausland[3]

---

[1] 1 The "bulls" were played by hamsters with fake horns in the commercial.

[2] 2 Since early January 2009, Snapple's "All Natural" teas and fruit drinks have been sweetened with sugar, not HFCS.

[3] 3 McCausland's name is spelled "McClausland" in the complaint and caption. The correct spelling, as indicated in the transcript of his deposition, is

("McCausland," and with Weiner, the "plaintiffs") are purchasers of Snapple beverages sold in New York state. Plaintiffs allege that they paid a price premium for Snapple beverages as a result of the "All Natural" labeling. Plaintiffs contend that Snapple's "All Natural" labeling was misleading because Snapple beverages were sweetened with HFCS.[4] Plaintiffs assert claims for violation of N.Y. Gen. Bus. L. § 349, unjust enrichment, and breach of express and implied warranty. Plaintiffs seek damages on behalf of a putative class that consists of:

All persons and entities who, within the State of New York, purchased for personal consumption and not for resale or assignment, a Snapple beverage marketed, advertised and promoted as "All Natural," but that contained [HFCS], from October 10, 2001 to January 1, 2009.[5]

Based on this definition, the class is not limited to New York residents, but includes, among millions of others, commuters from neighboring states, college students studying in New York, foreign travelers passing through New York airports, and tourists who purchased a Snapple beverage while in New York. Nor is the class limited by type of retailer that sold Snapple, and thus includes consumers who purchased Snapple beverages at, among other places, grocery stores, mass merchandisers, drug stores, movie theaters, push cart vendors, and vending machines.

The potential diversity among putative class members is apparent even among the named plaintiffs. Weiner lives and works in New Jersey. He bought Snapple beverages "hundreds of times" in New York and New Jersey. For Weiner, there were "numerous reasons" why he might have purchased

---

"McCausland."

[4] 4 Plaintiffs' claims are directed only at Snapple's caloric beverages that were labeled "All Natural" and contained HFCS. Snapple's diet beverages, which were artificially sweetened and were not labeled "All Natural," are not at issue here.

[5] 5 The Second Amended Class Action Complaint, which is the operative pleading, originally defined the putative class to include "[a]ll persons residing in the United States, except in the State of New Jersey." By letter dated November 6, 2009, plaintiffs advised that they intended to seek only a New York state class. In their motion for class certification, plaintiffs again modified the class definition to presumably include non-United States residents, as well as "entities," who purchased an "All Natural" Snapple beverage within New York state during the class period. The plaintiffs have not defined "entities" or explained what that term encompasses

Snapple beverages instead of its competitors, but his primary motivation was to "find something that tasted good." Weiner also bought Snapple because of Snapple's humorous promotions, flavor offerings, and because Snapple beverages were refreshing and thirst-quenching.

Weiner bought single bottles of Snapple from pushcart vendors and convenience stores while he was in New York City at various times during the class period. For instance, Weiner recalls purchasing a Snapple juice drink in 2003 or 2004 at Penn Station. He does not know exactly what price he paid, but believes it was between $1.50 and $1.75. The prices Weiner paid for Snapple varied based on the location and type of retailer, but he thinks that he generally paid between $1.49 and $1.79 per bottle for the Snapple beverages that he bought at convenience stores in New York. Weiner last purchased a Snapple beverage that was labeled "All Natural" and that contained HFCS sometime in 2005.

The other named plaintiff, McCausland, is a lawyer and lives in rural Sullivan County, New York.[6] 6 For more than twenty years, McCausland has bought various brands of teas, including those produced by Snapple. When choosing among Snapple and its competitors, McCausland considered a "combination of things," the first of which was taste. He also prefers teas that come in glass bottles rather than plastic or aluminum cans. For McCausland, Snapple's "All Natural" label was not the "deciding factor" in his purchasing decision. In fact, he would have bought Snapple over other teas and juice drinks "regardless of whether it was labeled 'All Natural.'" McCausland chose Snapple because, among other things, he liked that it was "New York-bred," that it was a "funny" brand, and because he liked the "Snapple Facts." He acknowledges that it was "plain from the label" that Snapple's "All Natural" beverages contained HFCS.

When purchasing Snapple, McCausland mostly bought single bottles from a convenience store, occasionally bought cases, and sometimes purchased six-packs. He recalls paying $1.79 per bottle at a Rock Hill, New York, gas station on one occasion, but has no idea what price he paid for the cases of Snapple that he purchased during the class period. McCausland also believes that he bought six-packs of Snapple for between seven and nine dollars, and his wife sometimes used coupons to obtain a discount off the multi-pack price. McCausland has no way to quantify how much Snapple he purchased during the class period. He has no receipts or other records for his Snapple purchases, which were generally made with cash. McCausland last purchased a Snapple beverage that was labeled "All Natural" and that contained HFCS in

---

[6] 6 McCausland's close friend, who is a partner in the law firm that represents plaintiffs in this action, told him about this lawsuit before it was filed.

the summer of 2006 or 2007.

Putative class member Stacy Holk ("Holk")[7] lives in New Jersey and works on Wall Street.[8] She started drinking Snapple beverages when she was a child. Holk was attracted to the taste and variety of Snapple beverages, the glass bottles, the "Snapple Facts," and the humor associated with the Snapple brand. Holk did not purchase Snapple because it was labeled "All Natural." In fact, because she liked Snapple's taste, glass bottle, and brand, she would have purchased Snapple even if it were not labeled "All Natural." Holk acknowledges that Snapple's labels disclosed that HFCS was an ingredient in its "All Natural" beverages.

Holk does not recall which Snapple beverages she bought, where or when she bought them, or what prices she paid. She recalls that the prices at different retailers where she purchased Snapple varied, and sometimes were lowered due to sales or other discounts. Holk believes that the per-bottle price that she paid during the class period could have ranged anywhere between $1.00 and $2.00. Holk also bought Snapple by the case if it was on sale. Like Weiner and McCausland, Holk does not have any receipts or other records for her Snapple purchases.

C. Procedural History

On October 10, 2007, Weiner filed a class action complaint against Snapple seeking certification of a nationwide class of consumers who purchased Snapple beverages labeled "All Natural" and that contained HFCS, exclusive of consumers whose purchases were made in New Jersey. On November 7, Snapple moved to dismiss. On November 20, a first amended complaint was filed which named McCausland as an additional plaintiff.

On December 7, the action was stayed pending the outcome of an appeal of the dismissal of a nearly identical action concerning purchases of Snapple's

---

[7] 7 Holk is the named plaintiff in a nearly identical lawsuit filed against Snapple in the United States District Court for the District of New Jersey on behalf of a putative class of consumers who purchased "All Natural" Snapple beverages in New Jersey. Holk v. Snapple Beverage Corp., No. 07 Civ. 3018 (MLC) (D.N.J.) ("Holk"). Holk is represented in the New Jersey action by plaintiffs' counsel in this action. Like Weiner, Holk purchased Snapple in both New York and New Jersey, and thus she is a putative member of both the New York and New Jersey classes.

[8] 8 Holk's mother, who works as a babysitter for an attorney at the law firm that represents plaintiffs in this action, told Holk about this lawsuit before it was filed.

"All Natural" beverages in New Jersey. See Holk v. Snapple Beverage Corp., No. 07 Civ. 3018 (MLC), 574 F. Supp. 2d 447 (D.N.J. 2008). On August 12, 2009, the Court of Appeals for the Third Circuit reversed the district court's dismissal in Holk and remanded for further proceedings. See Holk v. Snapple Beverage Corp., 575 F.3d 329 (3d Cir. 2009). By letter dated September 9, Snapple advised that it would not appeal the Third Circuit's decision. On October 2, plaintiffs filed a second amended complaint and on October 15, Snapple answered.

Discovery closed on February 26, 2010. On March 12, plaintiffs moved for class certification, which became fully submitted on April 30. On April 9, Snapple moved to exclude the testimony of two of plaintiffs' expert witnesses, Dr. Alan Goedde ("Goedde") and Lauran Schultz ("Schultz"), offered in support of plaintiffs' class certification motion. On April 27, plaintiffs moved to exclude the testimony of one of Snapple's expert witnesses, Dr. Keith Ugone ("Ugone"), offered in opposition to class certification. The parties' motions to exclude expert testimony were fully submitted on May 14.[9]

DISCUSSION

A. Requirements for Class Certification

"[A] district judge may not certify a class without making a ruling that each Rule 23 requirement is met." McLaughlin v. Am. Tobacco Co., 522 F.3d 215, 221 (2d Cir. 2008) (citation omitted). Thus, the plaintiffs will be able to sue Snapple as representatives of a class only if (1) the class is so numerous that joinder of all members is impracticable, (2) there are questions of law or fact common to the class, (3) the claims or defenses of the representative parties are typical of the claims or defenses of the class, and (4) the representative parties will fairly and adequately protect the interests of the class.

Fed. R. Civ. P 23(a); see Brown v. Kelly, No. 07-3356-cv, 609 F.3d 467, 2010 U.S. App. LEXIS 12936, 2010 WL 2520040, at *5 (2d Cir. June 24, 2010).

If the Rule 23(a) criteria are satisfied, an action may be maintained as a class action only if it also qualifies under at least one of the categories provided in Rule 23(b). Brown, 2010 U.S. App. LEXIS 12936, 2010 WL 2520040, at *5. In this case, plaintiffs seek to certify a class under Rule 23(b)(3), Fed R. Civ. P. Rule 23(b)(3) permits certification "if the questions of law or fact common to class members predominate over any questions affecting only individual

---

[9] 9 Because Snapple sought to redact and file certain briefs and exhibits under seal, the parties' motion papers were filed and docketed on dates later than they were served.

members, and . . . a class litigation is superior to other available methods for fairly and efficiently adjudicating the controversy." Fed. R. Civ. P. 23(b)(3); Brown, 2010 U.S. App. LEXIS 12936, 2010 WL 2520040, at *6.

"In evaluating a motion for class certification, the district court is required to make a 'definitive assessment of Rule 23 requirements, notwithstanding their overlap with merits issues,' and must resolve material factual disputes relevant to each Rule 23 requirement." Brown, 2010 U.S. App. LEXIS 12936, 2010 WL 2520040, at *6 (quoting In re Initial Pub. Offering Sec. Litig., 471 F.3d 24, 41 (2d Cir. 2006) ("In re IPO")). "The Rule 23 requirements must be established by at least a preponderance of the evidence." Brown, 2010 U.S. App. LEXIS 12936, 2010 WL 2520040, at *6 (citing Teamsters Local 445 Freight Div. Pension Fund v. Bombardier Inc., 546 F.3d 196, 202 (2d Cir. 2008) ("Teamsters")). In other words, the district judge must "receive enough evidence, by affidavits, documents, or testimony, to be satisfied that each Rule 23 requirement has been met." Teamsters, 546 F.3d at 204. The burden of proving compliance with all of the requirements of Rule 23 rests with the party moving for certification. In re IPO, 471 F.3d at 40.

In this case, while serious doubts exist as to whether plaintiffs have carried their burden with respect to the Rule 23(a) requirements[10] 10 there is no need to reach that question given that plaintiffs have plainly not satisfied the predominance requirement of Rule 23(b)(3). E.g., McLaughlin, 522 F.3d at 222.

B. Predominance

"As a general matter, the Rule 23(b)(3) predominance inquiry tests whether proposed classes are sufficiently cohesive to warrant adjudication by representation." Brown, 2010 U.S. App. LEXIS 12936, 2010 WL 2520040, at *6 (citation omitted). The predominance requirement is met only "if the plaintiff can establish that the issues in the class action that are subject to generalized proof, and thus applicable to the class as a whole, predominate over those issues that are subject only to individualized proof." 2010 U.S. App. LEXIS 12936, [WL] at *11 (citation omitted); see also McLaughlin, 522

---

[10] 10 For instance, plaintiffs completely ignore Snapple's argument that the named plaintiffs are not typical of class members who purchased Snapple after this action was filed in October 2007. While the putative class includes persons who purchased Snapple beverages as late as January 1, 2009, Weiner decided that HFCS was not natural and stopped purchasing non-diet Snapple beverages by 2005. The same was true for McCausland by 2006 or 2007. In addition, plaintiffs do not explain how Weiner and McCausland are typical of any "entities" that may be included in the putative class.

F.3d at 222.

In making this determination, a court considers whether the putative class members "could establish each of the . . . required elements of [their] claim[s]. . . using common evidence." In re Visa Check/MasterMoney Antitrust Litig., 280 F.3d 124, 136 (2d Cir. 2001), overruled on other grounds by In re IPO, 471 F.3d 24 (2d Cir. 2006). While a plaintiff need not show the "exclusivity" of common questions, it must show their predominance. McLaughlin, 522 F.3d at 231 (citation omitted). The requirement that the court conduct a "rigorous analysis" to ensure "actual, not presumed conformance" applies with "equal force to all Rule 23 requirements, including those set forth in Rule 23(b)(3)." In re IPO, 471 F.3d at 33 n.3.

1. Section 349, N.Y. Gen. Bus. L.

Section 349, N.Y. Gen. Bus. L., provides: "Deceptive acts or practices in the conduct of any business, trade or commerce or in the furnishing of any service in this state are hereby declared unlawful." N.Y. Gen. Bus. L. § 349. "Generally, claims under [§ 349] are available to an individual consumer who falls victim to misrepresentations made by a seller of consumer goods through false or misleading advertising." Small v. Lorillard Tobacco Co., Inc., 94 N.Y.2d 43, 720 N.E.2d 892, 897, 698 N.Y.S.2d 615 (N.Y. 1999). "To state a claim under § 349, a plaintiff must allege: (1) the act or practice was consumer-oriented; (2) the act or practice was misleading in a material respect; and (3) the plaintiff was injured as a result." Spagnola v. Chubb Corp., 574 F.3d 64, 74 (2d Cir. 2009); accord Stutman v. Chem. Bank, 95 N.Y.2d 24, 731 N.E.2d 608, 611, 709 N.Y.S.2d 892 (N.Y. 2000).

"The New York Court of Appeals has adopted an objective definition of 'misleading,' under which the alleged misleading act must be 'likely to mislead a reasonable consumer acting reasonably under the circumstances.'" Cohen v. JP Morgan Chase & Co., 498 F.3d 111, 126 (2d Cir. 2007) (quoting Oswego Laborers' Local 214 Pension Fund v. Marine Midland Bank, 85 N.Y.2d 20, 647 N.E.2d 741, 745, 623 N.Y.S.2d 529 (N.Y. 1995)). "[A] private action brought under § 349 does not require proof of actual reliance." Pelman ex rel. Pelman v. McDonald's Corp., 396 F.3d 508, 511 (2d Cir. 2005) (citing Stutman, 731 N.E.2d at 612). "The plaintiff, however, must show that the defendant's 'material deceptive act' caused the injury." Stutman, 731 N.E.2d at 612. "In addition, a plaintiff must prove 'actual' injury to recover under the statute, though not necessarily pecuniary harm." Id.

As in McLaughlin, 522 F.3d 215, proof of actual injury in this case "is bound up in proof of damages, or by how much plaintiffs have been harmed." Id. at 227. Only by showing that plaintiffs in fact paid more for Snapple beverages as a result of Snapple's "All Natural" labeling can plaintiffs establish the requisite elements of causation and actual injury under § 349. At the class certification stage, plaintiffs may demonstrate that these elements are susceptible to generalized proof by disclosing a suitable methodology. [11] See, e.g., Fogarazzo v. Lehman Bros., Inc., 263 F.R.D. 90, 106-07 (S.D.N.Y. 2009); Lapin v. Goldman Sachs & Co., 254 F.R.D. 168, 186 (S.D.N.Y. 2008); In re Alstom SA Secs. Litig., 253 F.R.D. 266, 281 (S.D.N.Y. 2008). When plaintiffs attempt such a showing, however, they must demonstrate that the proposed methodology can be applied class-wide and "that they could, at trial, marshal facts sufficient to permit them to rely upon" the proposed methodology. McLaughlin, 522 F.3d at 229. Like any component of a Rule 23 requirement, the court must "assess all of the relevant evidence admitted at the class certification stage," including expert testimony, and "determine whether . . . [this] requirement has been met." oIn re IPO, 471 F.3d at 42.

Even assuming, arguendo, that the first two elements of plaintiffs' § 349 claim -- i.e., that Snapple's alleged misrepresentation was "consumer-oriented" and was "likely to mislead a reasonable consumer acting reasonably under the circumstances" -- are susceptible to class-wide proof [12] plaintiffs have not proposed a suitable methodology for establishing the critical elements of causation and injury on a class-wide basis. Without a reliable methodology, plaintiffs have not shown that they could prove at trial using common evidence that putative class members in fact paid a premium for Snapple beverages as a result of the "All Natural" labeling. And since the issue of damages is bound up with the issue of injury in this case, plaintiffs have likewise failed to show how damages could be proven class-wide.[13] 13 Because

---

[11] 11 While the disclosure of the proposed methodology may suffice when a motion to certify precedes the completion of discovery, it would be inadequate when the motion is brought after the close of expert discovery.

[12] 12 There is a serious question whether plaintiffs will be able to use generalized proof to show that Snapple's use of "All Natural" was likely to mislead a reasonable consumer. Because plaintiffs' motion for class certification must be denied in any event, it will be assumed here that evidence common to the class could be used with respect to this element of the § 349 claim.

[13] 13 "[W]hile the fact that damages may have to be ascertained on an individual basis is not, standing alone, sufficient to defeat class certification, it is nonetheless a factor that we must consider in deciding whether issues susceptible to generalized proof 'outweigh' individual issues." McLaughlin, 522 F.3d at 231 (citation omitted).

individualized inquiries as to causation, injury, and damages for each of the millions of putative class members would predominate over any issues of law or fact common to the class, plaintiffs' § 349 claim cannot be certified under Rule 23(b)(3).

a. Admissibility of Goedde's Testimony

In support of their contention that causation and injury are susceptible to generalized proof on a class-wide basis, plaintiffs rely solely on a skeletal, four-page expert report of Dr. Alan Goedde, an economist. In his report, Goedde proposes two "approaches" for determining the purported price premium attributable to Snapple's "All Natural" labeling: (1) a "yardstick" approach, which would use "class-wide economic data and standard economic methodologies" to "compare the price of products labeled 'All Natural' to similar products which do not have 'All Natural' labeling;" and (2) an "inherent value" approach, which would analyze unspecified "studies and market research" to gather "data that can be used to determine the increased value, standing alone, that a product realizes due to the perception of that product being natural." Goedde opines that both approaches could be used to develop an empirical algorithm, or formula, to prove causation and injury on a class-wide basis.

Snapple has moved, pursuant to Rule 702, Fed. R. Evid., to exclude Goedde's expert testimony. Rule 702 provides:

If scientific, technical, or other specialized knowledge will assist the trier of fact to understand the evidence or to determine a fact in issue, a witness qualified as an expert by knowledge, skill, experience, training, or education, may testify thereto in the form of an opinion or otherwise, if (1) the testimony is based upon sufficient facts or data, (2) the testimony is the product of reliable principles and methods, and (3) the witness has applied the principles and methods reliably to the facts of the case.

Fed. R. Evid. 702. "While the proponent of expert testimony has the burden of establishing by a preponderance of the evidence that the admissibility requirements of Rule 702 are satisfied, the district court is the ultimate gatekeeper." United States v. Williams, 506 F.3d 151, 160 (2d Cir. 2007) (citing Fed. R. Evid. 104(a)). "The Federal Rules of Evidence assign to [the district court] 'the task of ensuring that an expert's testimony both rests on a reliable foundation and is relevant to the task at hand.'" Williams, 506 F.3d at 160 (quoting Daubert v. Merrell Dow Pharmaceuticals, Inc., 509 U.S. 579, 597, 113 S. Ct. 2786, 125 L. Ed. 2d 469 (1993)).

"[A] trial judge should exclude expert testimony if it is speculative or conjectural or based on assumptions that are so unrealistic and contradictory as to suggest bad faith." Zerega Ave. Realty Corp. v. Hornbeck Offshore Transp., LLC, 571 F.3d 206, 213-14 (2d Cir. 2009) (citation omitted). While a district court has "broad latitude" in deciding both "how to determine reliability" and in reaching "its ultimate reliability determination," it may not abandon its "gatekeeping function." Williams, 506 F.3d at 160-61 (citation omitted). "[N]othing in either Daubert or the Federal Rules of Evidence requires a district court to admit opinion evidence that is connected to existing data only by the ipse dixit of the expert." Kumho Tire Co. v. Carmichael, 526 U.S. 137, 157, 119 S. Ct. 1167, 143 L. Ed. 2d 238 (1999) (citation omitted).

Goedde's testimony is unreliable. Goedde does not demonstrate in adequate detail how his proposed "approaches" would be used to develop an empirical algorithm to determine, on a class-wide basis, whether there was a price premium as a result of Snapple's "All Natural" labeling and, if so, how such a premium could be quantified. Goedde's bare-bones report provides no details concerning the significant conceptual, implementation, or data issues that would be encountered if his two approaches were adopted. While Goedde suggests that he "can make use of class-wide economic data and standard economic methodologies," he does not discuss whether such "class-wide economic data" is even available, or specify which "standard economic methodologies" he will use to analyze such data.

The only detail that Goedde provides with respect to his "yardstick" approach is that it will "analyze[] all aspects and attributes of a product that impact the product's value . . . [which] would include, but not be limited to, the type of tea used in the beverage, brewing process, bottling, and ingredients and marketing representations." Goedde does not identify the products to which Snapple should be compared. Goedde also does not explain how his approach would isolate the impact of the "All Natural" labeling from the other factors that purportedly affect the price of Snapple and its competitors. He readily admits that there may be additional factors that he has not yet considered. Further undermining the reliability of his opinion, Goedde fails to acknowledge that there was no uniform price for Snapple beverages during the class period, and thus does not explain how his approach would account for the various prices that putative class members actually paid in determining injury on a class-wide basis. [14]

---

[14] 14 In his report, Goedde does not specify whether his yardstick approach would rely on retail or wholesale price data. At his deposition, Goedde asserted that his approach could determine whether a premium exists "at any point in the distribution chain," but provided no support for this assertion. Given that neither the plaintiffs nor Snapple have access to wholesale price data of Snapple's competitors, and that fact discovery is closed, it is doubtful

As for his "inherent value" approach, Goedde proposes "to assess the inherent premium value placed on such claims [that a product is "All Natural"] by consumers at large." While Goedde intends to gather data for this approach from "studies and market research," he does not actually cite any specific studies or market research, much less demonstrate that such reports are relevant and reliable. The documents referenced in his report refer primarily to newspaper articles and websites concerning generalized consumer perceptions about "natural" products. Goedde concedes that he has not yet performed a review of the scientific literature[15] or designed, much less conducted, his own survey or study of consumer perceptions about "All Natural" labeling.

Goedde's testimony is also unreliable because it is based on, at most, a cursory review of the underlying record in this action. His report shows that Goedde reviewed the complaints, but no other pleadings or testimony. He did not read the plaintiffs' depositions, which describe how the plaintiffs purchased Snapple beverages at various types of retailers, in different geographic locations, at various prices and times, in bulk and in single bottles, with and without discounts. Goedde relies on two internal Snapple marketing strategy documents to support his hypothesis that Snapple's "All Natural" label allowed it to command a premium in the marketplace. Yet he did not review the deposition transcripts of Snapple's witnesses or any of the other 240 documents produced by Snapple, which would have provided critical context for these documents. [16]

Goedde himself concedes that he has done nothing to confirm that his proposed approaches would be workable in this case. For instance, Goedde

---

that Goedde could apply the yardstick approach at the wholesale level.

[15] 15 In his report, Goedde states that he "reviewed literature along with documents provided in discovery which disclosed that the use of the healthy, pure natural claims has value in the marketplace." Instead of reviewing the full text of the "literature" that purportedly informed his testimony, however, Goedde oftentimes read only summaries and abstracts of articles, brochures for certain reports, and, in one case, the table of contents of a report.

[16] 16 In any event, Snapple's internal strategies alone do not prove that class members actually paid a premium as a result of the "All Natural" labeling, much less quantify the amount of any such premium paid across the class.

admits that if he is unable to identify comparable products for Snapple's "All Natural" beverages, then his "yardstick" approach will not work. And yet, Goedde has not even attempted to identify any comparable products to be used in his analysis. Nor has Goedde attempted to use his two approaches to actually build an empirical algorithm to determine whether a price premium was paid for Snapple's beverages as a result of the "All Natural" labeling. He has stated that he will not do so until after a decision on class certification.

Given the paucity of detail in Goedde's report, particularly the absence of any indication that Goedde has considered whether, and how, his proposed methodology could account for the specific circumstances of this case, Goedde's opinion that causation and injury can be proven on a class-wide basis is speculative and, therefore, unreliable. At a minimum, Goedde would need to determine what "standard economic methodologies" he will employ, identify the relevant "class-wide economic data" and "studies and market research," and build an actual algorithm before it could be determined whether Goedde's proposed methodology can reliably prove injury and causation on a class-wide basis.

Plaintiffs attempt to defend Goedde's testimony based not on an analysis of his work, but rather by pointing to his education, knowledge, and experience. Goedde's qualifications as an expert are not at issue, but rather whether he has invested sufficient time and effort to develop a reliable methodology to support an expert opinion in this case. Although plaintiffs are correct that Goedde does not need to "implement" or "test" his methodology at the class certification stage, he must still provide sufficient detail about the proposed methodology to permit a court to determine whether the methodology is suitable to the task at hand.

While plaintiffs assert that Goedde has proposed a "suitable methodology," in reality, Goedde has done nothing more than identify two possible approaches and assert that they will work in this case. Plaintiffs essentially ask that Goedde be taken at his word. As Goedde himself concedes, however, because he has not performed any empirical analysis or identified any relevant data, he does not yet know whether his methodology will, in fact, be workable in this case. Plaintiffs have thus failed to demonstrate that the Court would not "have to engage in a series of speculative calculations to ascertain whether, and in what amount, plaintiffs suffered a loss." McLaughlin, 522 F.3d at 230.

Plaintiffs contend that it is disingenuous for Snapple to argue that Goedde's testimony is unreliable given that Snapple's own expert, Dr. Keith Ugone, opined that a "benchmark" approach -- which plaintiffs contend is identical to Goedde's "yardstick" approach -- could be used to determine whether a price premium exists for Snapple beverages. Ugone's testimony, however, is the exact opposite. At his deposition, Ugone testified that "in this case the yardstick will not yield common proof answers for an entire class, so it's inappropriate here." (Emphasis added.) Ugone's expert report also concludes that Goedde's two proposed approaches "are unreliable and would be ineffective in determining or quantifying actual harm in this case."[17] Plaintiffs' reliance on Ugone's testimony is therefore misplaced.

Ugone used average annual retail price data for the period of 2005-2008 collected by the Nielsen Company -- which Snapple contends is the only data available -- to perform a "benchmark" analysis.[18] Among other things, this data reveals, unsurprisingly, that the price any class member paid for Snapple during the class period varied depending on numerous factors, including the type of retailer, the location and date of purchase, the quantity of bottles purchased, and whether there was a sale or other discount available. Ugone also opined that aggregate data, such as average retail prices, could not be relied upon to determine class-wide injury accurately because average prices are not the prices actually paid by consumers and mask significant price variations in retail prices charged by retailers. Tellingly, Goedde does not address the serious issues raised by Ugone concerning the feasibility of proving causation and injury on a class-wide basis, much less explain how his proposed methodology would overcome them.

---

[17] 17 Plaintiffs have moved to exclude Ugone's testimony pursuant to Rule 702, Fed. R. Evid. Plaintiffs argue, inter alia, that Ugone's testimony is irrelevant and based on improper assumptions, and that his benchmark analysis is flawed. Plaintiffs provide no sound basis for excluding Ugone's testimony. At most, plaintiffs' arguments address the weight that should be accorded Ugone's testimony, not its reliability. Accordingly, plaintiffs' motion is denied.

[18] 18 While not dispositive at the class certification stage, Ugone's comparison of average retail prices of Snapple beverages to comparable competing beverages containing HFCS, but lacking an "All Natural" label, indicated that the average retail price of Snapple was not systematically higher than that of its competitors. In addition, Ugone's analysis shows that just as retail prices for Snapple beverages varied over time, geographic location, type of retailer, and availability of discounts, the differences in retail prices between Snapple and comparable competing products also varied based on these factors. Thus, even if plaintiffs could identify a premium associated with a particular Snapple purchase, the amount of this premium could not be generalized to all purchases by putative class members. Goedde does not explain how his methodology would account for this complexity.

In a not-so-veiled attempt to skirt the problems raised by Ugone's report concerning Goedde's proposed methodology, plaintiffs assert in their opposition to Snapple's motion to exclude Goedde's testimony that Goedde's report shows "that wholesale price premium can be demonstrated on a class-wide basis." (Emphasis added.) Plaintiffs' assertion that causation and injury can be proven class-wide using wholesale, rather than retail, price data is purely speculative and unsupported by Goedde's testimony. Goedde does not explain how his methodology could be applied to wholesale prices, or how he would obtain the data for such an analysis. The word "wholesale" does not even appear in Goedde's report. In addition, Goedde has not attempted to explain how an alleged wholesale price premium would translate into retail premiums across the class, or how such a retail premium could then be measured. Because Goedde has examined only two of over two hundred documents produced by Snapple, and has not read any deposition transcripts, he could not even have begun to analyze Snapple's wholesale pricing structure, much less that of Snapple's competitors. [19] As such, even if it were Goedde's opinion that wholesale price data could be used to demonstrate causation and injury on a class-wide basis, he would have no basis to render such an opinion.

Because Goedde's testimony is unreliable, Snapple's motion to exclude is granted. Without Goedde's testimony, plaintiffs offer no evidence that a suitable methodology is available to prove the elements of causation and actual injury on a class-wide basis. Individualized inquiries would therefore be required in order to determine whether class members in fact paid a premium for Snapple beverages, and whether any such premium was attributable to the "All Natural" labeling. This would require, among other things, an examination of each of the millions of class members' Snapple purchases, which the evidence shows were made in different locations, at different times, and for different prices, over the nearly eight-year class period. While Rule 23(b)(3) does not require that all issues of fact or law be common to the class,

---

[19] 19 Had Goedde examined Snapple's wholesale pricing structure, he would have observed that Snapple's wholesale list prices for its "All Natural" beverages, diet beverages with artificial sweeteners, and unsweetened iced tea drinks, are uniform. Because Snapple "line prices" its beverages, wholesale list prices are based on the size of the bottle and the number of bottles in a package, not on whether the beverage is labeled "All Natural." Consistent with this practice, Snapple's price lists to its distributors, and the distributors' price lists to retailers, indicate no price differences between Snapple's "All Natural" beverages and its diet beverages of the same size and package.

in this case, individual issues concerning causation and injury would be so substantial and burdensome that it cannot be said that common issues predominate. As such, plaintiffs have failed to establish that the Rule 23(b)(3) predominance requirement has been met with respect to their § 349 claim.[20]

2. Unjust Enrichment

"A claimant seeking relief under a theory of unjust enrichment in New York must demonstrate (1) that the defendant benefited; (2) at the plaintiff's expense; and (3) that equity and good conscience require restitution." Leibowitz v. Cornell Univ., 584 F.3d 487, 509 (2d Cir. 2009) (citation omitted). Thus, plaintiffs must show "that the benefits that the members of the plaintiffs' class received were less than what they bargained for." Vigiletti v. Sears, Roebuck & Co., 42 A.D.3d 497, 838 N.Y.S.2d 785 (2d Dep't 2007); accord In re Canon Cameras Litig., 237 F.R.D. 357, 359 (S.D.N.Y. 2006).

As with their § 349 claim, plaintiffs have not shown that they will be able to prove on a class-wide basis that class members paid a price premium for Snapple beverages as a result of the "All Natural" labeling, much less the amount of any such premium. As such, plaintiffs have not shown that they could prove with common evidence the extent to which Snapple was unjustly enriched or the amount of restitution to which class members would be entitled. Thus, plaintiffs have not carried their burden to show that common issues predominate with respect to the first two elements of their unjust enrichment claim.

In addition, plaintiffs do not address the issue of how they would prove, on a class-wide basis, whether the benefits that putative class members received were "less than what they bargained for." Individualized inquiries would be required to determine, for instance, whether class members were fully informed about the inclusion of HFCS in Snapple beverages, whether they believed HFCS to be natural, and whether they continued to purchase Snapple despite their beliefs concerning HFCS. Such individual issues would also dwarf any issues of law or fact common to the class. Thus, plaintiffs have failed to show that the Rule 23(b)(3) predominance requirement is satisfied with respect to their unjust enrichment claim.

3. Express Warranty

---

[20] 20 Snapple also argues that its defenses, including the voluntary payment doctrine, statutes of limitations, and laches, present individual questions. Because plaintiffs have plainly failed to carry their burden to satisfy the predominance requirement as to the elements of claims, there is no need to reach this additional argument.

"A prima facie claim for breach of express warranty requires the plaintiff to show that there was an affirmation of fact or promise by the seller, the natural tendency of which was to induce the buyer to purchase and that the warranty was relied upon to the plaintiffs detriment." Fendi Adele S.R.L. v. Burlington Coat Factory Warehouse Corp., 689 F. Supp. 2d 585, 604 (S.D.N.Y. 2010) (citation omitted). Although "[a] cause of action to recover damages for breach of an express warranty requires proof of reliance," J.C. Constr. Mgmt. Corp. v. Nassau-Suffolk Lumber & Supply, 15 A.D.3d 623, 789 N.Y.S.2d 903 (2d Dep't 2005), "[i]n contrast to the reliance required to make out a claim for fraud, the general rule is that a buyer may enforce an express warranty even if it had reason to know that the warranted facts were untrue." Merrill Lynch & Co. Inc. v. Allegheny Energy, Inc., 500 F.3d 171, 186 (2d Cir. 2007); see also CBS, Inc. v. Ziff-Davis Publ'g Co., 75 N.Y.2d 496, 553 N.E.2d 997, 1000-01, 554 N.Y.S.2d 449 (N.Y. 1990). In order for this rule to apply, however, "[t]he plaintiff must show that it believed that it was purchasing seller's promise regarding the truth of the warranted facts." Merrill Lynch, 500 F.3d at 186. This particular conception of reliance mandates "fine factual distinctions in [New York's] law of warranties: a court must evaluate both the extent and the source of the buyer's knowledge about the truth of what the seller is warranting." Rogath v. Siebenmann, 129 F.3d 261, 264 (2d Cir. 1997).

Given New York's "basis of the bargain" conception of reliance for express warranty claims, it is clear that plaintiffs' purported reliance on Snapple's "All Natural" label cannot be the subject of generalized proof. The record in this case, including the plaintiffs' own testimony, shows that consumers may have purchased Snapple beverages for many reasons other than the "All Natural" label, including their taste, glass bottles, quirky advertising, or even the "Snapple Facts." Individualized inquiries would therefore be required to determine whether putative class members purchased Snapple beverages in reliance upon the "All Natural" label, as opposed to other considerations. See, e.g., Klein v. Robert's Am. Gourmet Food, Inc., 28 A.D.3d 63, 808 N.Y.S.2d 766, 773-74 (2d Dep't 2006). In addition, the extent and source of each putative class members' knowledge concerning the truthfulness of Snapple's "All Natural" representation might require examination. Thus, plaintiffs have failed to show that the Rule 23(b)(3) predominance requirement is satisfied with respect to their express warranty claim.

4. Implied Warranty

Under New York law, "[a] claim based upon a breach of an implied warranty requires a showing of privity between the manufacturer and the plaintiff when there is no claim for personal injuries." Adirondack Combustion Techs., Inc. v. Unicontrol, Inc., 17 A.D.3d 825, 793 N.Y.S.2d 576, 579 (3d Dep't 2005) (citing Arthur Jaffee Assocs. v. Bilsco Auto Serv., Inc., 58 N.Y.2d 993, 448

N.E.2d 792, 461 N.Y.S.2d 1007 (N.Y. 1983)). Plaintiffs do not allege that putative class members were in privity with Snapple. Accordingly, certification of plaintiffs' implied warranty claim would be improper. See McLaughlin, 522 F.3d at 228 ("[W]hen a claim cannot succeed as a matter of law, the Court should not certify a class on that issue." (citation omitted)).

C. Manageability and Ascertainability

Given that plaintiffs have failed to satisfy the Rule 23(b)(3) predominance requirement, it is not necessary to address whether plaintiffs have satisfied the remaining requirements for class certification. It must be noted, however, that even if the plaintiffs overcome the predominance hurdle, potentially serious impediments to class certification remain.

In addition to meeting the Rule 23(a) threshold requirements, as noted above, plaintiffs would also have to satisfy the Rule 23(b)(3) superiority requirement. Factors to be considered in determining whether a class action is superior include the "difficulties likely to be encountered in the management of a class action." Fed. R. Civ. P. 23(b)(3)(D); see Seijas v. Republic of Argentina, 606 F.3d 53, 58 (2d Cir. 2010) ("[W]hether the court is likely to face difficulties managing a class action bears on whether the proposed class satisfies the predominance and superiority requirements."). "[M]anageability is an issue peculiarly within a district court's discretion." Seijas, 606 F.3d at 58.

The difficulty of managing a class of the size and scope proposed by the plaintiffs is self-evident. Based on the latest iteration of their proposed class definition, plaintiffs would include "[a]ll persons and entities who, within the State of New York, purchased . . . a Snapple beverage marketed . . . as "All Natural," but that contained [HFCS], from October 10, 2001 to January 1, 2009." It is undisputed that during the class period, several millions of bottles of Snapple were sold in the State of New York. Because the purported class is not limited to New York, or even United States, residents, it could potentially include millions of consumers from around the world. Plaintiffs have offered no explanation for how such a geographically-dispersed class of consumers who purchased Snapple beverages in different locations, at different times, and for different prices, could be effectively managed.

Related to, but distinct from, the issue of manageability, is the "implied requirement of ascertainability," which turns on the definition of the proposed class. See In re IPO, 471 F.3d at 30. "[C]lass members must be ascertainable at some point in the case, but not necessarily prior to class certification." Id. at 45 (citation omitted). "To be ascertainable, the class must be readily identifiable, such that the court can determine who is in the class and, thus, bound by the ruling." Charrons v. Pinnacle Group N.Y. LLC, No. 07 Civ. 6316(CM), 269 F.R.D. 221, 2010 U.S. Dist. LEXIS 42327, 2010 WL 1752501, at *6 (S.D.N.Y. Apr. 27, 2010) (citation omitted). "A class is ascertainable when defined by objective criteria that are administratively feasible, and when identifying its members would not require a mini-hearing on the merits of each case." Id. (citation omitted).

Plaintiffs have failed to show how the potentially millions of putative class members could be ascertained using objective criteria that are administratively feasible. Plaintiffs suggest that after certification, the Court could require that "[c]lass members produce a receipt, offer a product label, or even sign a declaration to confirm that the individual had purchased" a Snapple beverage within the class period. This suggestion, to say the least, is unrealistic. Plaintiffs offer no basis to find that putative class members will have retained a receipt, bottle label, or any other concrete documentation of their purchases of Snapple beverages bearing the "All Natural" description. Cf. In re Holocaust Victim Assets Litig., 413 F.3d 183, 186, 14 Fed. Appx. 132 (2d Cir. 2005) (per curiam) (affirming district court's approval of claims that had "the ability of being proved with concrete documentation" and denial of claims that "would have been very difficult to prove at trial"); Jermyn v. Best Buy Stores, L.P., 256 F.R.D. 418, 431 (S.D.N.Y. 2009) (plaintiff provided "documentary evidence," including a "receipt" for his purchase, to "establish[]that he falls within the definition of the class"). However beloved Snapple may be, there is no evidence to suggest that its consumers treat it like a fine wine and remove and save its labels.

Further, putative class members are unlikely to remember accurately every Snapple purchase during the class period, much less whether it was an "All Natural" or diet beverage, whether it was purchased as a single bottle or part of a six-pack or case, whether they used a coupon, or what price they paid.[21] As such, soliciting declarations from putative class members regarding their history of Snapple purchases would invite them to speculate, or worse. Moreover, the process of verifying class members' claims would be extremely burdensome for the court or any claims administrator. Plaintiffs have thus failed to prove that it would be administratively feasible to ascertain the members of the putative class using objective criteria.[22]

---

[21] 21 Notably, none of the named plaintiffs have receipts or any other records for their Snapple purchases. Nor can they recall with any degree of certainty the quantity of Snapple beverages they purchased or the prices that they paid during the class period.

[22] 22 In support of their motion for class certification, plaintiffs offer the expert testimony of Lauran Schultz, the Executive Director of Hilsoft Notifications ("Hilsoft"), a firm that specializes in legal notification. In his affidavit, Schultz estimates that in 2008 and 2009, Snapple beverages were purchased by an estimated five million adults within a six-month period in the

Snapple has moved to exclude Schultz' testimony based on plaintiffs' failure to comply with Rule 26(a)(2)(B), Fed. R. Civ. P., and Schultz's lack of qualifications. While Snapple raises serious questions about Schultz' qualifications and about plaintiffs' compliance with zRule 26, Schultz' testimony is itself irrelevant to the issue of class certification. Schultz opines only that notification would be feasible if a class were to be certified, but offers no opinion as to whether the requirements for class certification have been met. Further, plaintiffs do not rely on Schultz' testimony in support of class certification, except to demonstrate numerosity, which Snapple does not dispute, and to support their assertion that the class is ascertainable. Schultz' opinion, however, does not address ascertainability, and thus plaintiffs' reliance on his testimony to satisfy this requirement is misplaced. Accordingly, Snapple's motion to exclude Schultz' testimony is denied as moot.

CONCLUSION
For the foregoing reasons, plaintiffs' March 12, 2010 motion for class certification and April 27, 2010 motion to exclude Ugone's expert testimony are denied. Snapple's April 9, 2010 motion to exclude Goedde's expert testimony is granted and its April 9, 2010 motion to exclude Schultz' expert testimony is denied as moot. A separate scheduling order governing further proceedings in this action shall issue with this Opinion.
SO ORDERED:
Dated: New York, New York
August 3, 2010
/s/ Denise Cote
DENISE COTE
United States District Judge

State of New York. Schultz opines that he "is confident [Hilsoft] will be able to develop   and implement an effective notice program in [this case]."

CHRISTIAN STARK et al., Plaintiffs,

vs.

DIAGEO CHATEAU & ESTATE WINES CO., Defendant.

Case No.: 12-CV-4385 YGR
November 1, 2012

UNITED STATES DISTRICT COURT
FOR THE NORTHERN DISTRICT OF CALIFORNIA

YVONNE GONZALEZ ROGERS,
UNITED STATES DISTRICT COURT JUDGE.

OPINION

ORDER ON MOTION FOR PRELIMINARY INJUNCTION

Plaintiffs Christian Stark, Stark Wine LLC ("Stark Wine"), and Stay @ Home Sommelier, LLC ("S@HS") (collectively "Plaintiffs") bring this trademark infringement action against Defendant Diageo Chateau & Estate Wines Company ("Diageo"), alleging that the mark for Defendant's "Stark Raving[TM]" wine is confusingly similar to Plaintiffs' "Stark Wine®" and "Stark Thirst[TM]" marks. Plaintiffs bring seven trademark claims: (1) Federal Trademark Infringement under 15 U.S.C. § 1114; (2) Cancellation of Trademark Registration under 15 U.S.C. § 1119; (3) Federal Unfair Competition under 15 U.S.C. § 1125(a); (4) Trademark Infringement under Cal. Bus. & Prof. Code § 14335; (5) Unfair Competition under Cal. Bus. & Prof. Code §§ 17200 et seq.; (6) False or Misleading Statements under Cal. Bus. & Prof. Code §§ 17500 et seq.; and (7) Common Law Trademark Infringement.

Plaintiffs have moved for a preliminary injunction to stop the advertisement, promotion, distribution and sale of Defendant's "Stark Raving[TM]" wine on the grounds that consumers will likely and mistakenly associate Diageo's "Stark Raving[TM]" wine with Plaintiffs' wines, which will irreparably harm the Plaintiffs' businesses. The parties submitted briefs, the Court held a two-day hearing with live testimony, at the end of which counsel presented oral argument.

Having reviewed the parties' briefs, the admissible evidence offered into the record, including during the hearing, the argument of counsel following the close of evidence, and having compared the marks themselves and the context of their use in the marketplace, the Court hereby GRANTS the Motion for Preliminary Injunction only as to Sonoma County, otherwise the Motion is DENIED.

I. BACKGROUND

A. STARK WINE
Plaintiff Christian Stark is a winemaker located in Sonoma County, California. He started his business in 2003, and sold his first wines, a 2003 vintage, in 2005. Since that time he has grown the business, and now produces eight varietals, which he sells in certain parts of the United States.[1] His passion is the Rhône varietals, Syrah and Viognier. Christian Stark testified that he had earned a reputation in the industry for producing and selling ultra-premium handcrafted wines. His mission was, and still is, quality over quantity. He sells his wine with the slogan "deliciously down-to-earth."

Mr. Stark testified about his involvement in the winemaking process over which he maintains full control. He starts by selecting grapes grown by reputable farmers with proven track records for growing exceptional quality fruit. He is responsible for fruit sourcing, grower relations and wine production. The reputational evidence in the record for Stark Wine® focused on the winemaker himself, Christian Stark,[2] and the labels on his wine simply state "STARK" as shown below:
[IMAGE OMMITTED]
Def. Opp'n, Dkt. No. 37, at 1; Dkt. No. 3, Ex. C at 18.

Christian Stark sells Stark Wine® primarily direct-to-consumer in Garagiste, a

---

[1] 1 Plaintiffs' Motion lists fifteen states: California, New York, Florida, New Jersey, Connecticut, Montana, New Mexico, Maine, Rhode Island, Oregon, Colorado, Virginia, Georgia, Ohio, Minnesota, and Washington, D.C. On the advice of counsel, Plaintiff would not confirm, at deposition or at the hearing, whether he is licensed to lawfully sell his product in any of these states or the District of Columbia.

[2] 2 See Plaintiffs' Exhibits 1, 8, 17, 18, and 23. Plaintiffs' correspondence to customers connect the winemaker "Stark" to the wine. (Exs. 10, 11, 14, and 15.)

tasting room co-owned by Stark Wine LLC and located in Healdsburg, Sonoma County, California. He also sells his wine online via starkwine.com,[3] through wholesale accounts with California restaurants, wine bars and retail shops, and through the Stark Wine Club. Stark Wine® ranges in price from $28 to $44 per bottle, with an average price point of $36. Output of Stark Wine® has increased from 150 cases in 2003 to 850 cases in 2011. Christian Stark expects to produce 1000 cases of Stark Wine® in 2012.

Christian Stark individually owns the "Stark Wine®" trademark, registered in International Category 33 with a description of "Wine" with the United States Patent and Trademark Office ("PTO") since October 17, 2006, Registration No. 3,160,031. The "Stark Wine®" mark achieved "incontestability" status on or about June 2, 2012.

B. STAY @ HOME SOMMELIER[4] AND STARK THIRST[TM]
In April 2012, Stark Wine LLC and S@HS launched a new sub-brand of wine called "Stark Thirst[TM] ." Based in New York City, Kersten Krall Walz ("Krall Walz") is the founder, marketing director, and co-owner of S@HS. (Krall Walz Dec. 1.) A self-described Madison Avenue refugee, Ms. Krall Walz worked in New York City's advertising industry for fourteen years, rising from administration to account director. (Id. 3.) Ms. Krall Walz worked at two of "Madison Avenue's" flagship agencies: Young & Rubicon and Saatchi & Saatchi. (Id. 3.)
In 2010, Krall Walz left the advertising industry to start a business that would allow her to "stay at home" to raise her son and to pursue her passion for wine. Prior to leaving the advertising industry, she spent five years taking classes to obtain a diploma in Wine Studies from London's Wine & Spirit Education Trust, one of the world's most comprehensive and rigorous wine study programs. (Id. 5.) She met Christian Stark in the fall of 2010. (Id. 7.) Initially, she did brand consulting for Stark Wine, helping to develop its

---

[3] 3 Plaintiffs' moving papers and the accompanying declaration of Christian Stark stated that Stark Wine® was sold through a number of third party websites. The evidence produced during the hearing contradicted this assertion, as none of the third-parties identified sell Stark Wine® . Subsequent to the filing of his declaration and motion, Plaintiffs arranged for the website www.lot18.com to sell Stark Wine®.

[4] 4 A "sommelier" is a wine steward, the person in charge of the wines in a club or restaurant. See Merriam-Webster's Ninth New Collegiate Dictionary, p. 1124 (1988).

current strategic brand position and update the website. (Id.)

In the summer of 2011, Krall Walz formed S@HS to merge her advertising experience with her knowledge and passion for wine. At this point she had been working on several brand extensions for Stark Wine, i.e. using other words in combination with the word "stark" for purposes of selling wine. Krall Walz conceived of this idea on her own. Christian Stark never attempted brand extensions and did not assist in her work. In the summer of 2011, Krall Walz and S@HS partnered with Christian Stark to create the Stark Thirst[TM] brand extension.

Ms. Krall Walz conducted market research, including holding focus groups to decide on a brand name and a brand identity using extensions on the word "stark." Her target audience was Generation Y, defined in the alcohol industry as individuals in the 21-35 year range ("Gen Yers"). Her research revealed that (i) 24% of Gen Yers drink wine as their preferred alcoholic beverage, (ii) Gen Yers are looking for bottles priced under $15 and are socially conscious, and finally, (iii) the name "Stark Thirst" tested better than the other extensions.

Plaintiffs launched Stark Thirst[TM] as a more affordable brand, marketed towards these younger wine drinkers. It retails for approximately $16 per bottle, with 10% of profits donated to WaterAid, an international charitable organization that brings safe drinking water to those in need. The mission for Stark Thirst[TM] is to give people a charitable way to drink delicious wine. Plaintiffs have produced 216 cases of Stark Thirst[TM] .

On October 19, 2011, S@HS applied to the PTO to trademark "Stark Thirst[TM] ." In February 2012, the PTO denied the "Stark Thirst[TM]" on the basis that the dominant feature of both the "Stark Wine®" and "Stark Thirst[TM]" marks is the word "Stark," which the PTO stated is identical in sight, sound, and meaning. Subsequently, Christian Stark filed a consent agreement with the PTO noting that Stark Wine LLC and S@HS are business partners that sell wines under both the Stark Wine® and Stark Thirst[TM] marks.[5] On June 20, 2012, PTO found that the "Stark Thirst[TM]" appeared to be entitled to registration and approved the mark for publication. The trademark registration for Stark Thirst[TM] is pending with the PTO.

C. DEFENDANT DIAGEO CHATEAU & ESTATE WINES COMPANY

Diageo is a subsidiary of an international beverage conglomerate that owns such recognized brands as Smirnoff Vodka, Jose Cuervo Tequila, Guinness Beer, Tanqueray Gin, Johnnie Walker Scotch, Captain Morgan Rum, Veuve Cliquot Champagne and Dom Perignon. Diageo Chateau & Estate Wines

---

[5] 5 Separately another applicant, not a party to this lawsuit, applied for the mark "Stark Naked" and was denied for the same reasons that "Stark Thirst[TM]" initially was denied.

Company focuses exclusively on wines. Its brands include Acacia Vineyard, Beaulieu Vineyard, Chalone Vineyard, Provenance Vineyards, Sterling Vineyards, and Rosenblum Cellars. Stark Raving[TM] is a sub-brand of Rosenblum Cellars.

In November 2011, Diageo began plans for sub-brands of wine to target the millennial consumer segment of the population, defined as ages 28-38. This resulted in the "Stark Raving[TM]," "Rose-N-Blum[TM]" and "Butterfly Kisses[TM]" sub-brands. Diageo wanted to create a wine that goes against the grain and celebrates the idea of doing things differently and with great passion. The concept for "Stark Raving[TM]" was to bring to life the personality of Rosenblum Cellars' founder, Kent Rosenblum, who left a successful career as a veterinarian to pursue his passion for winemaking. (See Declaration of Mary Frances Light Dusenbury ("Light Dec."), 11 ("Our founder quit his day job to make wine in his garage. They said he was stark raving mad. Mad? We call it inspired!").) The Stark Raving[TM] sub-brand revolves around a **mad scientist** persona and uses the tag line "Crazy Good Wine" as illustrated below:

[TWO IMAGES OMMITTED]

The wine attempts to appeal to male millennials by being fruitier and juicier than other wines, and it is packaged in a screw-top bottle with a label design modeled on craft beers.

On February 13, 2012, Diageo applied to the PTO for the trademark "Stark Raving[TM]" in International Category 33 with a description of "Alcoholic beverages other than beer." Plaintiffs allege that Diageo not only knew of the "Stark Wine®" trademark in the same International Category 33, but with a description of "Wine," but in fact, knew that the "Stark Thirst[TM]" mark had been rejected days earlier for being too similar to the "Stark Wine®" mark. Plaintiffs allege that Diageo intended to mislead the PTO by using the description "Alcoholic beverages other than beer" instead of "Wine," knowing that its application likely would be rejected if Stark Raving[TM] was described as "Wine." The actual evidence produced at the hearing demonstrated that Diageo had filed over 80% of all of relevant applications in International Category 33 with the broader description "Alcoholic beverages other than beer." The PTO approved Diageo's application on June 26, 2012.

In the summer of 2012, Diageo introduced Stark Raving[TM] wine. Its suggested retail price is between $12.99 and $13.99, although approximately 75% of the wine is expected to be sold at the sale price of $10.99 primarily through mass market retailers such as Target. Diageo has produced approximately 80,000 cases of Stark Raving[TM] wine. Stark Raving[TM] wine began shipping in June 2012, and by the end of August 2012, Diageo had delivered 17,000 cases to distributors, of which 7,000 had been delivered to retailers. As of August 15, 2012, Stark Raving[TM] wine was on the shelves at over 1,500 stores across the United States. In October, Diageo started rolling out a Stark Raving[TM] food truck program, which offers wine tastings of the Stark Raving[TM] sub-brand in coordination with food truck rallies across the nation. (Light Dec. 16.)

Plaintiffs requested Diageo to cease and desist from producing and selling wine under the "Stark Raving[TM]" brand. Diageo refused and Stark brought this action to enjoin Diageo from producing, promoting, distributing and selling the "Stark Raving[TM]" wines to prevent loss of goodwill and seek compensation for any damage already inflicted.[6]

II. LEGAL STANDARD

A preliminary injunction is an extraordinary remedy, which should be granted only in limited circumstances and where the merits of the case clearly favor one party over the other. Winter v. Natural Resources Defense Council, 555 U.S. 7, 24, 129 S. Ct. 365, 172 L. Ed. 2d 249 (2008).

The Court considers four factors when deciding whether to issue a preliminary injunction: (1) whether the moving party has demonstrated that it is likely to succeed on the merits; (2) whether the moving party will suffer irreparable injury if the relief is denied; (3) whether the balance of the hardships favor the moving party; and (4) whether the public interest favors granting relief. See Miller v. California Pacific Medical Ctr., 19 F.3d 449, 456 (9th Cir. 1994) (en banc). In a trademark case, a plaintiff is entitled to a preliminary injunction if it can demonstrate either: (1) a combination of "probable success on the merits" and "the possibility of irreparable injury"; or (2) the existence of "serious questions going to the merits" and that "the balance of hardships tips sharply in his favor." Sardi's Restaurant Corp. v. Sardie, 755 F.2d 719, 723 (9th Cir. 1985) (quoted in Brookfield Communications, Inc. v. West Coast Entertainment Corp., 174 F.3d 1036, 1046 (9th Cir. 1999)). This represents two points on the sliding scale in which the required degree of irreparable harm increases as the probability of success decreases. See Oakland Tribune, Inc. v. Chronicle Publishing Co., 762 F.2d 1374, 1376 (9th Cir. 1985). The burden of showing a likelihood of success on the merits is "placed on the party seeking to demonstrate entitlement to the extraordinary remedy of a preliminary injunction at an early stage of the

---

[6] Plaintiffs initially moved for a nationwide injunction, but have since limited the requested injunction to five states: California, Florida, Illinois, New York and Texas.

litigation, before the defendant has had the opportunity to undertake extensive discovery or develop its defenses." Perfect 10, Inc. v. Amazon.com, Inc., 487 F.3d 701, 714 opinion amended on reh'g, 508 F.3d 1146 (9th Cir. 2007).

III. DISCUSSION
A. OVERVIEW OF TRADEMARK PROTECTION

The Lanham Act defines a trademark as "any word, name, symbol, or device, or any combination thereof used by a person ... to identify and distinguish his or her goods, including a unique product, from those manufactured or sold by others and to indicate the source of the goods, even if that source is unknown." 15 U.S.C. § 1127. Thus, a trademark is anything that serves to indicate the source of one company's goods and to distinguish them from the goods of others. It "is merely a convenient means for facilitating the protection of one's good-will in trade by placing a distinguishing mark or symbol--a commercial signature--upon the merchandise or the package in which it is sold." United Drug Co. v. Theodore Rectanus Co., 248 U.S. 90, 98, 39 S. Ct. 48, 63 L. Ed. 141, 1918 Dec. Comm'r Pat. 369 (1918).

The owner of a trademark has a limited property right to exclude others from using that mark. New Kids on the Block v. News America Pub., Inc., 971 F.2d 302, 306 (9th Cir. 1992). A person acquires the right by being the first to use it in the marketplace, or by using it before the alleged infringer. Unlike a copyright or a patent for an invention, a trademark is a property right only in connection with its use by an existing business. See United Drug, supra, 248 U.S. 90; Roger E. Meiners, Patents, Copyrights, and Trademarks: Property or Monopoly?, 13 HARV. J.L. & PUB. POL'Y 911, 930 (1990) ("It is property only in the sense that trade reputation or goodwill is a property right.").

Courts focus on protecting consumers in cases involving infringement of a trademark which is the reason for classifying it as a form of unfair competition. See 15 U.S.C. § 1125(a)(1); Mars Inc. v. Kabushiki-Kaisha Nippon Conlux, 24 F.3d 1368, 1373 (Fed. Cir. 1994) ("The law of unfair competition generally protects consumers and competitors from deceptive or unethical conduct in commerce .... Patent law, on the other hand, protects a patent owner from the unauthorized use by others of the patented invention, irrespective of whether deception or unfairness exists."). "The law of unfair competition has its roots in the common-law tort of deceit: its general concern is with protecting consumers from confusion as to source. While that concern may result in the creation of 'quasi-property rights' in communicative symbols, the focus is on the protection of consumers, not the protection of producers as an incentive to product innovation." Bonito Boats, Inc. v. Thunder Craft Boats, Inc., 489 U.S. 141, 158, 109 S. Ct. 971, 103 L. Ed. 2d 118 (1989).

The elements of a trademark infringement claim are: (1) a valid, protectable ownership interest in a trademark; and (2) defendant's use of a mark similar to plaintiff's trademark in a manner that is likely to cause consumer confusion. See 15 U.S.C. § 1114(1).[7] 7 Likelihood of confusion is the central inquiry in the trademark infringement analysis: whether a "reasonably prudent customer in the marketplace is likely to be confused as to the origin of the good or service bearing one of the marks" because of the similarities between the two marks. Dreamwerks Prod. Group, Inc. v. SKG Studio, 142 F.3d 1127, 1129 (9th Cir. 1998). "[B]ecause we are at the preliminary injunction stage, [Plaintiffs] must establish that it is likely to be able to show such a likelihood of confusion." See Brookfield, supra, 174 F.3d at 1052 n.15 (citing Sardi's Restaurant, supra, 755 F.2d at 723). At this time the Court is not making ultimate findings of fact after a full trial on the merits. The discussion of infringement, and factual findings in that regard, is directed only towards Plaintiffs' likelihood of success on the merits.[8]

---

[7] 7 Section 43(a)(1) of the Lanham Act itself provides that:

Any person who, on or in connection with any goods or services, ... uses in commerce any word, term, name, symbol, or device, or any combination thereof, or any false designation of origin, false or misleading description of fact, or false or misleading representation of fact, which--(A) is likely to cause confusion, or to cause mistake, or to deceive as to the affiliation, connection, or association of such person with another person, or as to the origin, sponsorship, or approval of his or her goods, services, or commercial activities by another person, ... shall be liable in a civil action by any person who believes that he or she is or is likely to be damaged by such act.

15 U.S.C. § 1125(a)(1).

[8] 8 Plaintiffs' state law and common law trademark infringement claims and claim under California's Unfair Competition Law based on infringement are subject to the same legal standards as their Lanham Act trademark claim. See Rearden LLC v. Rearden Commerce, Inc., 683 F.3d 1190, 1221 (9th Cir. 2012) (citing Jada Toys, Inc. v. Mattel, Inc., 518 F.3d 628, 632 (9th Cir. 2008). Therefore, the same findings that the Court makes with respect to Plaintiffs' entitlement to a preliminary injunction with respect to the federal trademark claim, also apply to Plaintiffs' related state trademark infringement and unfair competition claims.

B. FIRST ELEMENT: VALID, PROTECTABLE OWNERSHIP INTERESTS IN THE TRADEMARKS AT ISSUE

Rights in a trademark are obtained only through commercial use of the mark. One way to establish trademark rights is through use of a trademark in commerce and federal registration under the Lanham Act.

Registration constitutes prima facie evidence of the validity of the registered mark and of a plaintiff's exclusive right to use that mark. 15 U.S.C. § 1115(a). To acquire ownership of a trademark under the Lanham Act it is not enough to have invented the mark first or even to have registered it first; the party claiming ownership must have been the first to actually use the mark in the sale of goods or services, and, therefore, a party pursuing a trademark claim must meet a threshold "use in commerce" requirement. Id. § 1051 et seq.

Once a registered trademark has been in use for five years and if certain statutory formalities are met (e.g., timely filed affidavit of continuous use), the registration is considered "incontestable" evidence of the registrant's right to use the mark. See id. § 1065. Incontestable status provides that the "validity and legal protectability, as well as [the registrant's] ownership therein, are all conclusively presumed." Brookfield, supra, 174 F.3d at 1046-47 n.10; 15 U.S.C. § 1115(b).[9] 9 A registrant may rely upon the incontestability of the mark in an infringement action. See Park 'N Fly, Inc. v. Dollar Park & Fly, Inc., 469 U.S. 189, 204, 105 S. Ct. 658, 83 L. Ed. 2d 582 (1985).

1. Stark Wine®

Since the "Stark Wine®" mark is incontestable, it is immune from challenge on certain grounds. 15 U.S.C. § 1065; see Barentzen Dec., Ex. D at 1 (PTO's notice of acceptance of declaration of incontestable status). Diageo challenges the "Stark Wine®" mark on the grounds that it was never used in commerce, and therefore, has been abandoned.

A mark is "used in commerce" when (1) "it is placed in any manner on the goods or their containers or the displays associated therewith," and (2) "the goods are sold or transported in commerce." 15 U.S.C. § 1127.

Diageo points out that the wines are labeled "STARK," not "Stark Wine®," and that the phrase "Stark Wine®" only appears in fine print to identify the company's business name (this is both on the front and back labels of the

---

[9] 9 "Incontestable trademark" is a legal term of art which provides the owner with certain presumptions. It does not mean that a challenge can never exist. For example, contests are appropriate where the trademark has been abandoned, is being used to misrepresent the source of goods, or was obtained fraudulently. See Park 'N Fly, Inc. v. Dollar Park & Fly, Inc., 469 U.S. 189, 195, 105 S. Ct. 658, 83 L. Ed. 2d 582 (1985).

wine bottles). On that basis, Diageo challenges the use of the "Stark Wine®" mark, arguing that Plaintiffs only use the phrase "Stark Wine®" as a trade name and not a trademark.[10] 10 At the hearing Plaintiffs introduced evidence of Stark Wine's use of the trademark "Stark Wine®" on packaging and correspondence. (See Exs. 2-7, 9-10, 12-13, 16, and 18.)

For purposes of a preliminary injunction, Stark Wine is "likely" to be able to show that it has a protectable ownership interest in the registered trademark "Stark Wine®" based upon the trademark's incontestable status and evidence that it has used the mark in commerce.

2. Stark Thirst[TM]

Diageo challenges the validity of S@HS's right to use the trademark "Stark Thirst[TM]" because the "Stark Thirst[TM]" mark is not registered. Here, S@HS asserts common law trademark rights in "Stark Thirst[TM]" through its use of the mark in New York City, and in interstate commerce, beginning on April 20, 2012. On June 20, 2012, the PTO found that "Stark Thirst[TM]" appeared to be entitled to registration and approved the mark for publication. The time to oppose registration has expired. S@HS contends that its federal trademark registration is imminent.

To succeed on an infringement claim, S@HS will have to show use and geographic scope of that use. "Stark Thirst[TM]" is available for purchase at only three locations in New York City--a high end wine store in Manhattan, and a wine bar and a restaurant in Brooklyn. S@HS's use of the Stark Thirst[TM] mark has priority over Diageo's "Stark Raving[TM]" in this geographic area.

S@HS is likely to be able to show that it has common law trademark rights in "Stark Thirst[TM]" in a limited geographic area to satisfy the first element.

C. SECOND ELEMENT: LIKELIHOOD OF CONFUSION

To prevail on a claim for trademark infringement, Christian Stark, Stark Wine LLC, and S@HS must establish that Diageo is using a mark confusingly similar to their own marks. See AMF Inc. v. Sleekcraft Boats, 599 F.2d 341, 348 (9th Cir. 1979) abrogated by Mattel, Inc. v. Walking Mountain

---

[10] 10 A "trade name" is defined in the Lanham Act as "any name used by a person to identify his or her business." 15 U.S.C. § 1127. In contrast to trademarks, which refer to words or symbols used to identify and distinguish particular goods, trade names refer to the words or symbols used to identify and distinguish businesses. See SunEarth, Inc. v. Sun Earth Solar Power Co., Ltd., 846 F. Supp. 2d 1063, 1073 n.6 (N.D. Cal. 2012), appeal dismissed (Apr. 18, 2012) (citing 15 U.S.C. § 1127).

Productions, 353 F.3d 792 (9th Cir. 2003). The central issue in a trademark action is whether consumers "'are likely to assume that a product or service is associated with a source other than its actual source because of similarities between the two sources' marks or marketing techniques.'" Nutri/System, Inc. v. Con-Stan Indus., Inc., 809 F.2d 601, 604 (9th Cir. 1987) (quoting Shakey's Inc. v. Covalt, 704 F.2d 426, 431 (9th Cir. 1983)); Official Airline Guides v. Goss, 6 F.3d 1385, 1391 (9th Cir. 1993) (issue can be recast as whether "the similarity of the marks is likely to confuse customers about the source of the products.").

Courts in the Ninth Circuit use the eight Sleekcraft factors to guide the likelihood of confusion analysis: (1) the similarity of the marks; (2) the relatedness of the companies' goods; (3) the marketing channels used; (4) the strength of mark(s) of the junior holder or senior holder or both; (5) Diageo's intent in selecting its mark; (6) evidence of actual confusion; (7) the likelihood of expansion into other markets; and (8) the degree of care likely to be exercised by purchasers. E. & J. Gallo Winery v. Gallo Cattle Co., 967 F.2d 1280, 1290 (9th Cir. 1992). Courts do not mechanically apply these factors and then tally the results; some factors are considered to be more important than others and each factor is not necessarily relevant in every case. Id. Accordingly, this?list functions as guide and is "neither exhaustive nor exclusive." Id.

1. First Factor: Similarity of the Marks.
The Ninth Circuit has developed "certain detailed axioms to guide this comparison" of marks for similarity: (i) the marks must be considered in their entirety and as they appear in the marketplace; (ii) the marks should be analyzed by their sound, sight, and meaning; and (iii) similarities are weighed more heavily than differences. GoTo.com, Inc. v. Walt Disney Co., 202 F.3d 1199, 1206 (9th Cir. 2000) (citing Filipino Yellow Pages, Inc. v. Asian Journal Publications, Inc., 198 F.3d 1143, 1147-50 (9th Cir. 1999); Dreamwerks, supra, 142 F.3d at 1131; and Goss, supra, 6 F.3d at 1392).

a) Sound
Plaintiffs argue that the word "stark"--used in Diageo's "STARK RAVING[TM]," and Plaintiffs' "STARK WINE®" and "STARK THIRST[TM]"--is the dominant portion of the trademark and is identical in sound, sight and meaning in all three marks. Plaintiffs base this argument on the PTO's rejection of the "STARK THIRST[TM]" and "STARK NAKED" marks on the grounds that those marks are similar in sound, sight, and meaning to "STARK WINE®" due to the common use of the dominant word "stark." Plaintiffs argue that because "STARK RAVING[TM]," "STARK THIRST[TM]" and "STARK NAKED" all begin with the word

"stark" there is no difference between the rejected "STARK THIRST[TM]" and "STARK NAKED" marks, and the "STARK RAVING[TM]" mark. Therefore, Plaintiffs argue that these similarities in sound, sight, and meaning due to the common use of the dominant word "stark" are case dispositive. Plaintiffs rely too heavily on the PTO determinations regarding the STARK THIRST[TM] and STARK NAKED applications. The Ninth Circuit has held that a preliminary determination by a PTO administrator is entitled to consideration but should not be accorded much weight where the examiner did not have access to the all the evidence before the District Court.

Any such determination made by the Patent Office under the circumstances just noted must be regarded as inconclusive since made at its lowest administrative level ... . The determination by the Patent Office is rendered less persuasive still by the fact that the Patent Office did not have before it the great mass of evidence which the parties have since presented to both the District Court and this court in support of their claims.

Carter-Wallace, Inc. v. Procter & Gamble Co., 434 F.2d 794, 802 (9th Cir. 1970). Thus, even if the PTO rejected Diageo's trademark application for the "STARK RAVING[TM]" mark, this evidence would be entitled to minimal weight. Here, Plaintiffs did not call the PTO examiner to testify as to the basis for the PTO's rejection of the "STARK THIRST[TM]" and "STARK NAKED" marks. Nevertheless, in a vacuum while using the "sound" test, the use of the words "STARK RAVING[TM]" as compared next to "STARK THIRST[TM]" and "STARK Wine®" in the context of selling wine is likely to cause confusion. For instance, as seen[11] on a menu or wine list, little difference exists to alert the customer that the products are not related. Thus, the sound metric weighs in favor of finding similarity.

b) Sight

Diageo argues that aside from the commonality of the word "stark," the marks have nothing in common. Even if the dominant portion of the wines' names is "stark," this does not mean that the other words in the name have no significance. Alpha Indus., Inc. v. Alpha Steel Tube & Shapes, Inc., 616 F.2d 440, 444 (9th Cir. 1980) ("These other words are significant words, indicating a different origin, not merely descriptive words.").

The marks must be "[c]onsidered in their entirety and as they appear in the marketplace." Goss, supra, 6 F.3d at 1392; Kern v. Mindsource, Inc., 225 F.3d

---

[11] 11 One cannot fully separate sound from sight or meaning in this context.

663 (9th Cir. 2000) (similarity must be considered in light of the way the marks are encountered in the marketplace); First Brands Corp. v. Fred Meyer, Inc., 809 F.2d 1378, 1383-84 (9th Cir. 1987) (examining the "total effect of the defendant's product and package on the eye and mind of an ordinary purchaser."); Adidas Am., Inc. v. Payless Shoesource, Inc., 546 F. Supp. 2d 1029, 1052 (D. Or. 2007) ("similarity of design is determined by considering the overall impression created by the mark as a whole rather than simply comparing individual features"). "The proper test for likelihood of confusion is not whether consumers would be confused in a side-by-side comparison of the products, but whether confusion is likely when a consumer, familiar with the one party's mark, is presented with the other party's goods alone." E. & J. Gallo Winery v. Consortia del Gallo Nero, 782 F. Supp. 457, 466 (N.D. Cal. 1991) (quoting Elizabeth Taylor Cosmetics Co. v. Annick Goutal, S.A.R.L., 673 F. Supp. 1238, 1248 (S.D.N.Y. 1987)). Here, the marketplace is not only restaurants, which may list only the name of a wine on a wine list, but other consumer outlets where the consumer would see the labels of the wines themselves.

Here, Defendant argues that these:

[IMAGES OMMITTED]

look nothing like these:

[IMAGES OMMITTED]

Kersten Krall Walz disagreed and testified that they all appear to come from the same source.

Diageo produced examples of other wines also using the word "stark" on the wine label which are not the subject of this action and questioned Ms. Krall Walz about the possibility of confusion of Plaintiffs' Stark Wine® and Stark Thirst[TM] marks with these other wines, such as "Stark-Condé," as shown below:

[IMAGE OMMITTED]

Ms. Krall Walz testified that consumers would not confuse Stark-Condé wines with either of the Plaintiffs' wines because the Stark-Condé label used a hyphen which suggested it was derived from the name of a person.

The Court finds that in terms of the "sight" sub-factor as it relates to the Stark Wine® and Stark Raving[TM] marks, it is not likely that consumers would be confused. The Stark Wine® label is a sophisticated, traditional wine label, with block lettering, set against a linen background, and only uses the word

"STARK" suggesting the last name of the winemaker himself. The Stark Raving[TM] label is not traditional. The image of the **mad scientist**/inventor, with vibrant colored paint splatters--blue, orange, red, or green, depending on the varietal--suggests the exact opposite of a traditional, personally crafted, boutique wine affiliated with a winemaker. It is more radical in approach and does not even list the wine's vintage or vineyard, calling out the varietals in a non-traditional way--Red, White, Cab (except for the Malbec).

The call is closer with respect to whether consumers would be confused about the source of Stark Thirst[TM] and Stark Raving[TM] . The similarities between the Stark Thirst[TM] and Stark Raving[TM] labels are more pronounced and the differences are more subtle than between the Stark Wine® and Stark Raving[TM] labels. Both Stark Thirst[TM] and Stark Raving[TM] have non-traditional wine labels. The Stark Thirst[TM] label appears to be a hand drawn picture of an old bottle with simple colors--black and white, while the label for Stark Raving[TM] has a picture of a person, is more colorful--blue, orange, red, green--and does not list vintage or vineyard.

This sub-factor weighs against a finding of similarity with respect to Stark Wine®, but in favor of finding similarity with respect to Stark Thirst[TM].

c) Meaning

In this context, one cannot fully separate sight or sound from meaning. As to Stark Wine®, the most prominent feature of the label is the word "STARK." On a wine label, the use of the single word "STARK," without modifying another word, suggests solely the name of the winemaker. The Court is not persuaded by Plaintiffs' argument that their use of the word "STARK" on a wine label conveys a meaning of "to the fullest extent" separate and distinct from wine produced by Christian Stark. (Reply 8.) In this context, the word "STARK" is being used as a proper noun and not as an adverb or adjective, and it evokes the name of the winemaker himself, not the dictionary definition of the word.

On the other hand, because both Stark Thirst[TM] and Stark Raving[TM] are used as adverbs, confusion is more likely as "stark" in this context means "to an absolute or complete degree." Merriam-Webster's Ninth New Collegiate Dictionary, p. 1150 (1988). The image of a **mad scientist** on the label for Stark Raving[TM] communicates a message that the consumer is bold, young and rebellious. A picture of an old bottle with information that 10% of profits to WaterAid on the label for Stark Thirst[TM] suggests complete thirst, and the impetus to buy wine which contributes 10% of profits to WaterAid. While Stark Raving[TM] ("totally crazy," or "completely wildly insane") and Stark Thirst[TM] (totally and completely thirsty), communicate distinct meanings, both labels communicate more than just the name of a winemaker.

An analysis of the components of the similarity of the marks, in their entirety and as they appear in the marketplace, and weighing the similarities more heavily than the differences, strongly suggests a finding of no confusion between "STARK RAVING[TM]" and "STARK WINE®," but in favor of finding confusion between "STARK RAVING[TM]" and "STARK THIRST[TM] ."

2. Second Factor: Relatedness of the goods.

"Related goods are generally more likely than unrelated goods to confuse the public as to the producers of the goods." Brookfield, supra, 174 F.3d at 1055.[12] 12 Related goods are those "'which would be reasonably thought by the buying public to come from the same source if sold under the same mark.'" Sleekcraft, supra, 599 F.2d at 348 n. 10 (citations omitted).

"[W]ines of all types constitute a single class of goods." E. & J. Gallo Winery, supra, 782 F. Supp. at 464. All of the goods at issue are wine; that is enough to satisfy the relatedness element. Adidas, supra, 546 F. Supp. 2d at 1054 ("Here, the parties' products are essentially identical in use and function. Both parties sell athletic and casual footwear. Aside from arguable differences in quality, the parties' products are 'reasonably interchangeable by buyers for the same purposes,' and thus competitive.") (citing 4 McCarthy, supra, § 24:23). This factor weighs in favor of confusion.

3. Third Factor: Common marketing channels.

This factor considers how and to whom the respective parties' goods are sold. 4 McCarthy, supra, § 24:51. "Convergent marketing channels increase the likelihood of confusion." Nutri/System, supra, 809 F.2d at 606 (quoting Sleekcraft, supra, 599 F.2d at 353). If the "general class" of purchasers of the respective products of the parties is the same, confusion is more likely. Sleekcraft, supra, 599 F.2d at 353. In contrast, significant differences in the price of the products, or the type of stores (i.e., discount or specialty) at which the respective products are sold may decrease the likelihood of confusion. See

---

[12] 12 To satisfy the relatedness factor Plaintiffs do not need to establish that the parties are direct competitors, although where the goods are directly competitive, "the degree of similarity of the marks needed to cause likely confusion is less than in the case of dissimilar goods." 4 McCarthy, supra, § 24:22.

L.A. Gear, Inc. v. Thom McAn Shoe Co., 988 F.2d 1117, 1134 (Fed. Cir. 1993). In determining whether significant overlap exists between the general classes of purchasers exposed to the products, relevant considerations include whether the goods are sold under the same roof; the normal marketing channels are similar or parallel; the same sales methods are employed; and the products are advertised in the same places (internet, newspapers and classified telephone directories). Sleekcraft, supra, 599 F.2d 353.

The evidence presented suggests no overlap in the parties' channels. Mary Frances Light Dusenbury, Defendant's Senior Director of Marketing and Innovation, explained that wine is distributed through a "three-tier" system whereby producers sell their products to distributors, who in turn sell to retail accounts. (Light Dec. 18.) Consumers then can purchase wine "on premises" at restaurants and bars or "off premises" from mass merchandisers, grocery stores, liquor stores, and wine shops. (Id.)

Stark Wine® is sold in Christian Stark's tasting room in Healdsburg located in Sonoma County, California. Consumers can also purchase Stark Wine® over the telephone and on Stark Wine's website. Stark Thirst[TM] is sold off premises at one high-end wine store in Manhattan and through the internet, and is available on premises at two locations in Brooklyn, one upscale restaurant and one wine bar. Diageo estimates that approximately 90% of Stark Raving[TM] wine will be sold "off premises" through Diageo's current network of distributors, approximately 80% of whom exclusively distribute only Diageo products. According to Diageo, this means that Stark Raving[TM] wines are, and will continue to be, on the shelves at large national grocery stores and mass merchandise chains (such as Safeway, Target, and Jewel-Osco) that require a large volume supply of product, which Plaintiffs could not supply. And any on-premises sale would most likely be served at "fast casual" chain restaurants like T.G.I. Friday's.

Plaintiffs testified of future plans to sell their wines through channels similar to the channels through which Diageo sells its Stark Raving[TM] wines. Plaintiffs' expansion plans are relevant to the seventh factor, infra, but are not pertinent to the analysis of whether there is any overlap in the respective marketing channels now. Plaintiffs did not submit any evidence that the parties advertise their products in the same places.

This factor weighs against finding confusion, as it seems that there is no overlap in the parties' respective marketing channels, except, perhaps to the extent consumers in Sonoma County shop at the mass merchandise chains and boutique wine shops.

4. Fourth Factor: Strength of the mark.

The more likely a mark is to be remembered and associated in the public mind with the mark's owner, the greater the likelihood of confusion. Brookfield, supra, 174 F.3d at 1058 (citing Kenner Parker Toys Inc. v. Rose Art Indus., Inc., 963 F.2d 350, 353 (Fed. Cir. 1992)). The "strength" of a trademark is evaluated both in terms of its conceptual strength and its commercial strength. See 2 McCarthy, supra, § 11:83.

a) Conceptual Strength

Marks can be conceptually classified along a spectrum of increasing inherent distinctiveness, the weakest being generic and the strongest being fanciful:

generic -> descriptive -> suggestive -> arbitrary -> fanciful

See Brookfield, supra, 174 F.3d at 1058. A "weak trademark" is a mark that is a meaningful word in common usage or is merely suggestive or descriptive of the product or service. "A 'generic' term is one that refers, or has come to be understood as referring, to the genus of which the particular product or service is a species. It cannot become a trademark under any circumstances." Surgicenters of America, Inc. v. Medical Dental Surgeries, Co., 601 F.2d 1011, 1014 (9th Cir. 1979) (citing Abercrombie & Fitch Co. v. Hunting World, Inc., 537 F.2d 4, 9-11 (2d Cir. 1976)). A descriptive mark specifically "describes" a characteristic or ingredient of an article or service to which it refers or its purpose (e.g., "Park 'N Fly"), while a suggestive mark "suggests," rather than describes, an ingredient, quality or characteristic (e.g., Sleekcraft) and thereby moves along the spectrum to the stronger category. See Self-Realization Fellowship Church v. Ananda Church of Self-Realization, 59 F.3d 902, 910 (9th Cir. 1995).

A "strong trademark" is one used only in a fictitious, arbitrary, and fanciful manner. [13]13 Marks that are suggestive, arbitrary or fanciful "serve[ ] to identify a particular source of a product, [and] are deemed inherently distinctive." Two Pesos, supra, 505 U.S. at 768; Kendall-Jackson Winery. Ltd. v. E. & J. Gallo Winery, 150 F.3d 1042, 1046 (9th Cir. 1998). Arbitrary marks are words, symbols, pictures, etc., that may be in common linguistic use but which, when used in combination with the goods or services at issue, have no descriptive connotation with those goods or services. 2 McCarthy, supra, § 11:11. Fanciful marks are "coined" words or phrases that are either invented or selected--i.e., words that are unknown or out of common usage at the time--solely for the purpose of functioning as a trademark. Id. § 11:5.

Where a particular mark falls along this spectrum is determined by the "imagination test" and the "need test." See Earthquake Sound Corp. v.

---

[13] 13 For example, Ivory soap is not made of ivory, and a "common" word such as "apple" can be used as an arbitrary and inherently strong trademark on a product such as personal computers. 2 McCarthy, supra, § 11:11.

Bumper Indus., 352 F.3d 1210, 1221 n.4 (9th Cir. 2003) (citing Miss World (UK) Ltd. v. Mrs. Am. Pageants, Inc., 856 F.2d 1445, 1449 (9th Cir. 1988), abrogated in part on other grounds as recognized by Eclipse Assoc., Ltd. v. Data General Corp., 894 F.2d 1114, 1116 n.1 (9th Cir. 1990). The "imagination test" considers "how much imagination a consumer must use to associate a given mark with the goods or services it identifies," with greater effort on the consumer's part corresponding to a stronger mark. Id. The "need test" considers whether "a mark is actually needed by competitors to identify their goods or services." Id.

Typically, in analyzing the strength of a mark, the Court would evaluate the mark which had priority; a more well-known senior mark suggests greater likelihood of future or "forward" confusion because a junior user's mark is more likely to be associated with that established famous mark. In that case, the concern is whether the junior mark-holder is benefiting from the goodwill of the more well-known senior mark-holder.

In a reverse confusion case, as alleged here, the concern is that consumers will believe that the senior mark-holder's goods are produced by the junior mark holder or that consumers will believe that the senior mark-holder is trying to "palm off" its goods as those of the junior mark-holder. For that reason, the focus in a reverse confusion case is on the strength of the junior user's mark. Dreamwerks, supra, 142 F.3d at 1130 n.5 (issue was whether a consumer attending a Dreamwerks-sponsored science fiction convention might do so believing that it is sponsored by DreamWorks) (citing Sands, Taylor & Wood Co. v. Quaker Oats Co., 978 F.2d 947, 959 (7th Cir. 1992)). Accordingly, the Court reviews the strengths of all three marks.

i. The "Stark Raving[TM]" mark

Conceptually, the "Stark Raving[TM]" mark is arbitrary because the mark "uses common words in a fictitious and arbitrary manner to create a distinctive mark which identifies the source of the product." Dreamwerks, supra, 142 F.3d at 1131. It is neither suggestive of the goods--people do not ordinarily associate drinking wine with insanity--nor descriptive of the wine's characteristics--people will not go stark raving mad after they drink the wine.

Based on the foregoing, the Court finds that the mark "Stark Raving[TM]" is arbitrary and therefore conceptually strong.

ii. The "Stark Wine®" mark

Diageo argues that Stark Wine®, as a personal name, is a descriptive term. Under the trademark laws, a mark that is "primarily merely a surname" is considered descriptive and not protectable unless it acquires a secondary meaning. 15 U.S.C. § 1052(e)(4), (f); 2 McCarthy, supra, § 13:1 (proof of secondary meaning is required to protect a family name). Where, as here, "stark" has a non-surname meaning, the mark is not primarily a surname, and no secondary meaning is required. See Lane Capital Management, Inc. v. Lane Capital Management, Inc., 192 F.3d 337 (2d Cir. 1999) (mark Lane Capital Management is not a personal name mark requiring secondary meaning because "lane" also has a non-surname meaning, even though "Lane" was the nickname and middle name of the father of the founder of plaintiff and the middle name of the son of the founder).

Stark Wine argues that its mark is "arbitrary" because the adjective "stark" has nothing to do with wine. (See Reply 8 ("Stark is not only a surname, but also an adjective that appears in the dictionary .... When it comes to describing wine, 'Stark' is arbitrary and, therefore a strong mark.").) The PTO initially rejected Christian Stark's trademark application for the "Stark Wine®" mark on the basis that "Stark" "is primarily merely a surname." (Barentzen Dec., Ex. D at 52 ("in support of the assertion that Stark is a surname, the examining attorney points out that the applicant's surname is Stark.")). Christian Stark responded that "[t]he word 'Stark' is not primarily a surname. In many instances it is used as an adjective ... such as 'a stark white room' or a 'stark contrast.'" (Barentzen Dec., Ex. D at 44.)

Christian Stark testified at the preliminary injunction hearing that he was reluctant to use his surname for his wine but felt that the dictionary definition of the word "stark"--complete, bold, to the fullest extent--adequately captured the essence of his wines. While conceptually, stark would be an arbitrary name for a wine--as one does not normally think of wine as being "bare" or "harsh," or "utterly" and "completely" so?Christian Stark and S@HS have closely associated the Stark Wine® and Stark Thirst[TM] brands with Christian Stark as the winemaker throughout its history of use. His after-the-fact attempt to distance himself from this use is belied by his own documents:

"Krall Walz is launching her own wine brand, Stark Thirst (of course, made by Christian)" (Exh. 18)
"Stark Wine is a reflection of our passion for family." (Ex. 8.)
"The name Stark Wine derives from the owners family name ... The goal is for consumers to associate the wine and its quality with the name 'Stark.'" (Ex. 23.)
"We chose the name Stark Thirst because Christian Stark is the winemaker." (Ex. 240.)

Thus, while "stark" can be used as an adjective or an adverb, here, the evidence demonstrates that until Krall Walz partnered with Christian Stark it had only, and intentionally, been used descriptively to identify the wine with the winemaker himself.

Based on the foregoing, the Court finds that on this record the mark "Stark

Wine®" is, at best, descriptive and therefore relatively weak.

iii. The "Stark Thirst®" mark
Plaintiffs argue that the "Stark Thirst[TM]" mark is conceptually strong for the same reasons that the "Stark Wine®" mark is strong. (See Reply 8 ("When it comes to describing wine, 'Stark' is arbitrary and, therefore a strong mark").) Conceptually, the "Stark Thirst[TM]" mark can be classified as suggestive because it "suggests" that the product is a beverage that will quench the consumer's "thirst." Based on the foregoing, the Court finds that the mark "Stark Thirst[TM]" is suggestive and therefore moderately strong.

b) Commercial Strength.
None of the marks has acquired commercial strength. Plaintiffs contend that Christian Stark has "strengthened his brand to acquire commercial strength based upon the favorable reviews of his wine, and its recognition as a charitable organization." Defendant does not dispute that Christian Stark is a good winemaker, and that his wines have received numerous accolades. However, neither Christian Stark's wines nor the "STARK Wine®" trademark has commercial strength. At best, the goodwill that Christian Stark has built into his brand through favorable reviews and charity work has created recognition in Sonoma County only.
Plaintiffs' companies are struggling financially, with little to no advertising budget. Stark Wine LLC will spend approximately $1,000 out-of-pocket marketing Stark Wine® in 2012, while S@HS has not spent any money advertising Stark Thirst[TM] .[14] 14 Stark Thirst[TM] is a relatively new brand, and Stark Wine produced no wines in either 2008 or 2010--Christian Stark testified that 2008 was a bad year for grapes and that he devoted 2010 to building his tasting room. Sales outside of Christian Stark's tasting room totaled $20,000 over the past two years, $500 in 2011. Kern v. Mindsource, Inc., 225 F.3d 663 (9th Cir. 2000) (evidence did not show mark was strengthened by mark holder's activities: (1) his advertising in magazines aimed at lawyers and the purchase of a spot on a local radio show was discontinued in 1996; (2) he had used his mark less than seven years and there was at least one other federal registration for the same mark that predated his; and (3) he did not produce any financial records of his business but only estimated annual sales to be "a couple thousand dollars, maybe").

Additionally, Tony Yarborough, a private investigator with Robert & Jackson

---

[14] 14 Ms. Krall Walz has devoted a significant amount of uncompensated time marketing Stark Thirst[TM].

Associates, discussed the relative unavailability of Stark Thirst[TM] and Stark Wine® . The investigator attempted to locate the Plaintiffs' wines on the websites where Plaintiffs Krall Walz and Christian Stark stated by Declaration that Stark Wine® and Stark Thirst[TM] were available, but neither wine was available to purchase on any of the websites.

Also relevant to the analysis is the extent of any advertising or marketing campaign by Diageo that may result in "a saturation in the public awareness of the junior user's mark." Glow Indus., Inc. v. Lopez, 252 F. Supp. 2d 962, 989 (C.D. Cal. 2002). Advertising, length of time in business, and public recognition are factors taken into account when classifying the commercial strength of marks. Sleekcraft, supra, 599 F.2d at 350; Brookfield, supra, 174 F.3d at 1058 (significant advertising expenditures can transform a suggestive mark into a strong mark where that mark has achieved actual marketplace recognition). Stark Raving[TM] has been marketed and promoted, only recently, on Diageo's website and via the website www.starkravingwines.com, through YouTube videos, and through distribution of marketing materials-- including pallet wraps, playing cards, iPhone covers, bottle carriers, bar mats, and menu inserts.

With respect to Stark Raving[TM], whether Diageo will achieve commercial strength or brand awareness remains speculative. Ms. Krall Walz testified that given Diageo's resources it can promote its Stark Raving[TM] wine brand to create high brand awareness. However, she was unable to quantify the cost of creating such brand awareness in a wine label given the saturation in the market. Ms. Light testified that wines generally do not have brand awareness, with Gallo being an exception. Moreover, Ms. Light testified that the cost to gain such brand awareness would be extraordinary, many millions of dollars. Ms. Light explained that she does not expect the Stark Raving[TM] brand to gain brand awareness because it does not have a sufficiently large advertising budget. Diageo has not placed any television or radio advertisements, and its internet advertising has been to encourage web users to visit the Diageo Chateau & Estate Wines Company website, www.diageowines.com. Additionally, while Diageo has spent or committed more than one million dollars to market the Stark Raving[TM] brand, this marketing has been directed primarily towards distributors and retailers and not consumers.

c) Third party use

Finally, Diageo argues that the Stark Wine® and Stark Thirst[TM] marks are weak because many other wines also using the word "stark" on their label. "Use of similar marks by third-party companies in the relevant industry weakens the mark at issue." M2 Software, Inc. v. Madacy Entm't, 421 F.3d 1073, 1088 (9th Cir. 2005) (citing Miss World, supra, 856 F.2d at 1449); Quality Semiconductors, Inc. v. QLogic Corp., C-93-20971 JW, 1994 U.S.

Dist. LEXIS 7101, 1994 WL 409483, at *2 (N.D. Cal. May 13, 1994) ("an arbitrary mark may be classified as weak where there has been extensive third party use of similar marks on similar goods") (citing General Mills, Inc. v. Kellogg Co., 824 F.2d 622, 627 (8th Cir. 1987).

Diageo has provided evidence of the use of the word "stark" by a number of other winemakers (and potential infringers). Mr. Yarborough, Diageo's private investigator, testified about the market availability of other wines that use the word "stark" on their label: "Stark-Condé"; "Stark Wines" made by Stark Wines LLC, a Minnesota based company that has been making its Stark Wines for over a year; a dessert wine "Stark's Star"; "Starkweather Alley" Pinot Grigio; and Indian Creek Vineyard's "Stark County Red." In response, Plaintiffs contend that Stark-Condé, Stark County and Starkweather Alley relate to a name or place and therefore are not relevant; Stark Wines makes "fruit wine" and is therefore not a competitor; and Stark's Star describes a grape varietal.

After considering the relative conceptual and commercial strengths of the parties' respective marks, the Court finds that this factor weighs against a finding a likelihood of consumer confusion between Stark Wine® and Stark Raving[TM] or between Stark Thirst[TM] and Stark Raving[TM].

5. Fifth Factor: Intent of holder of alleged infringing mark in adopting mark.

If intent to deceive consumers is shown, courts will presume that the defendant will be able to accomplish its deceptive purpose. Goss, supra, 6 F.3d at 1394 (citing Gallo, supra, 967 F.2d at 1293); Network Automation, supra, 638 F.3d at 1154 (defendant's intent relevant insofar as it bolsters a finding that the public will be deceived by the junior mark-holder's use of the mark). Thus, when "an alleged infringer knowingly adopts a mark similar to another's, courts will presume an intent to deceive the public." Goss, supra, 6 F.3d at 1394; Interstellar Starship Services, Ltd. v. Epix Inc., 184 F.3d 1107, 1111 (9th Cir. 1999), superseded by statute on other grounds ("Adopting a designation with knowledge of its trademark status permits a presumption of intent to deceive"). Generally, the intent factor will be of minimal importance because intent can be hard to prove and "intent to confuse customers is not required for a finding of trademark infringement." Brookfield, supra, 174 F.3d at 1059 (citing Dreamwerks, supra, 142 F.3d at 1132 ("Absence of malice is no defense to trademark infringement.")). Further, this factor generally focuses on whether the junior holder of the mark intended to "palm off" its goods as those of the senior mark-holder, thus plays a less critical role in a reverse confusion case. Chattanoga Mfg., Inc. v. Nike, Inc., 140 F. Supp. 2d 917, 930 (N.D. Ill. 2001), aff'd as modified on other grounds, 301 F.3d 789 (7th Cir. 2002)

Here, Diageo was aware of both the Stark Wine® trademark and the Stark

Thirst[TM] trademark application at the time it sought to register its Stark Raving[TM] mark. Diane Plaut, Diageo's Director and Senior Counsel of Intellectual Property, commissioned a trademark search for the word "stark" which uncovered both the Stark Wine® trademark and the Stark Thirst[TM] application. Ms. Plaut spent a few hours reviewing the 298-page trademark search report.[15] 15 (See Ex. 29.) Even though Diageo's legal team was aware of the Plaintiffs' trademarks, Diageo chose to file an application to register the "Stark Raving[TM]" mark.

Plaintiffs contend that Diageo not only was aware of their trademarks, but that Diageo intended to mislead the PTO by describing its wine as "Alcoholic beverages other than beer" rather than "Wine." As proof, Plaintiffs argue that on April 2, 2012, which was within two months of applying for the "Stark Raving[TM]" mark, Ms. Plaut, who filed the "Stark Raving[TM]" application, filed a trademark application for another brand of wine Diageo was launching for Rosenblum Cellars called "Butterfly Kisses[TM]," but in that application, Diageo disclosed that the trademark was for the goods "Wine."

For purposes of this proceeding, the evidence provided at the hearing supports Ms. Plaut's testimony that her practice on behalf of Diageo was to apply for the broadest possible protection of its trademarks so that if the opportunity arises in the future it can expand its product line. First, she testified that Diageo has expanded wines into spirits. Second, Ms. Plaut testified that to her understanding the description "Alcoholic beverages other than beer" was an acceptable description for a wine because it includes wine. And, third, business records showed that approximately 80% of all of the trademark applications that she had filed for wines while she has worked at Diageo had been more expansively described as "Alcoholic beverages other than beer," not "wine."

Awareness of a senior mark-holder's trademark is not dispositive of a junior mark-holder's intent or bad faith in adopting its mark. Thus far, the Court is aware of no evidence to show that Diageo believed that its "Stark Raving[TM]" mark would be confusingly similar to the "Stark Wine®" or "Stark Thirst[TM]" marks when Diageo selected the "Stark Raving[TM]" mark. Likewise, there has been no showing that "despite acting innocently, the junior user 'was careless in not conducting proper research to avoid

---

[15] 15 The standard practice at Diageo is for the legal team to render its own report after conducting the trademark search. Diageo did not produce that report in discovery or testify about the contents of that report at the hearing, asserting that the information is protected by attorney-client privilege and the work product doctrine. The parties did not brief this issue nor is it ultimately material in this context.

infringement prior to development of its trademark.'" 4 McCarthy, supra, §
23:10 (quoting Mars Musical Adventures, Inc. v. Mars, Inc., 159 F. Supp. 2d
1146, 1152 (D. Minn. 2001)).

Balancing the competing considerations, the preponderance of the evidence
does not suggest that Diageo intended to deceive the public, and therefore,
this factor weighs against a finding a likelihood of confusion.

6. Sixth Factor: Evidence of actual confusion.

In the end, "consumer confusion" constitutes "the sine qua non of trademark
infringement." Network Automation, supra, 638 F.3d at 1149. Because of the
difficulty in obtaining such evidence, the failure to prove instances of actual
confusion is not dispositive. Id. at 1151 (citing Sleekcraft, supra, 599 F.2d at
352). Consequently, like the intent factor, this factor is weighed heavily only
when there is evidence of past confusion or, perhaps, when the particular
circumstances indicate such evidence should have been available but was not
provided. Sleekcraft, supra, 599 F.2d at 353. Given that there is no evidence
of actual confusion, this factor is neutral.

7. Seventh Factor: The likelihood of expansion into other markets.

"Inasmuch as a trademark owner is afforded greater protection against
competing goods, a 'strong possibility' that either party may expand its
business to compete directly with the other will weigh in favor of a finding
that the present use is infringing." Sleekcraft, supra, 599 F.2d at 354 (citing
Restatement of Torts § 731(b) & cmt. c). When goods are closely related, any
expansion is likely to result in direct competition. Id.

Stark Wine and S@HS claim that they plan to grow Stark Wine® and Stark
Thirst[TM] into nationwide brands. S@HS "is aggressively seeking a wider
distribution for [Stark] wine in various markets throughout the U.S." (Stark
Dec. 11.) Stark Wine LLC and S@HS also "plan to grow the [Stark
Thirst[TM]] brand and sell it nationally by 2015." Ms. Krall Walz testified
about Plaintiffs' five-year plan to grow Stark Thirst[TM] to a 20,000 case per
year brand and Stark Wine® to a 3,500 case per year brand. Within two years
Plaintiffs expect to be selling their wines in all of the major wine markets:
New York, California, Texas, Florida and Illinois, and nationally within five
years. Starting as early as 2014, Plaintiffs plan to introduce additional "Stark"
sub-brand extensions, including Stark Wild, Stark Naked and/or Stark Raving
Mad. When cross-examined about the likelihood of these plans materializing,
Ms. Krall Walz explained that Stark Wine and S@HS have access to capital to
implement their plans and thus far, S@HS has met every one of its growth
goals.

By contrast, Ms. Light's testimony revealed that penetration of the wine
market is incredibly difficult and expensive. Christian Stark himself is a

boutique winemaker with no experience in nationwide marketing or business. He lacks any significant third-party distribution chains even for his small enterprise and does not demonstrate a sophisticated knowledge of the challenges of the market at issue. On this record, the possibility remains speculative as to whether Plaintiffs can expand to Diageo's current market position. However, Diageo is fully capable of accessing Stark Wine's established market in Sonoma County. Accordingly, this factor weights in favor of no finding of confusion except as to Sonoma County.

8. Eighth Factor: The degree of care likely to be exercised by purchasers.
In assessing whether there is a likelihood of confusion, courts look to the reasonably prudent purchaser exercising ordinary caution. Sleekcraft, 599 F.2d at 353 ("The care exercised by the typical purchaser, though it might virtually eliminate mistaken purchases, does not guarantee that confusion as to association or sponsorship is unlikely"). "[T]he standard of care to be exercised by the reasonably prudent purchaser will be equal to that of the least sophisticated consumer." Ford Motor Co. v. Summit Motor Prods., Inc., 930 F.2d 277, 293 (3d Cir. 1991). Wine is considered a good with which the average consumer does not exercise care when purchasing. E. & J. Gallo Winery, supra, 782 F. Supp. at 465 (with respect to wine drinkers, "lack of consumer sophistication significantly enhances the likelihood of confusion between the two products"); Taylor Wine Co., Inc. v. Bully Hill Vineyards, Inc., 569 F.2d 731, 734 (2d Cir. 1978) ("the average American who drinks wine on occasion can hardly pass for a connoisseur of wines. He remains an easy mark for an infringer.").[16] This factor weighs in favor of finding consumer confusion.

---

[16] 16 Diageo attempts to distinguish purchasers of its wine from consumers of Plaintiffs' wines to suggest that the two classes of consumers are so different that no confusion can occur. Diageo argues that due to the relative unavailability of Plaintiffs' wines, consumers will need to seek them out. This niche audience is "far more likely than the average consumer to have achieved the level of connoisseurship that would allow them to distinguish between the parties' products." Sutter Home Winery, Inc. v. Madrona Vineyards, L.P., C 05-0587 MHP, 2005 U.S. Dist. LEXIS 4581, 2005 WL 701599, at *11 (N.D. Cal. Mar. 23, 2005). In contrast, Diageo characterizes consumers of Stark Raving wine as less sophisticated wine drinkers, which Diageo believes precludes them from knowing or caring about Plaintiffs' wines. It is the care exercised by this less sophisticated consumer that the Court must consider in the likelihood of confusion analysis.

9. Overall Analysis of the Sleekcraft Factors
"There are at least three types of proof of likelihood of confusion: (1) survey evidence; (2) evidence of actual confusion; and (3) an argument based on an inference arising from a judicial comparison of the conflicting marks themselves and the context of their use in the marketplace." Dr. Seuss Enterprises, L.P. v. Penguin Books USA, Inc., 109 F.3d 1394, 1404 n.14 (9th Cir. 1997). Plaintiffs did not present survey evidence or evidence of actual confusion. This leaves a judicial comparison of the marks.

As set forth above, the Court has compared the marks using the Sleekcraft factors. As to Plaintiffs' collective claims, the factors which weigh in favor of confusion focus on sound (i.e. the use of the word "stark"), the fact that all goods at issue are wine, and the presumption that wine purchases will not exercise due care. By contrast, the factors weighing against confusion include the visual comparison of the product labels, the meanings and marketplace associations connected with each of the variations (Stark Wine®, Stark Thirst[TM], and Stark Raving[TM]), the lack of both conceptual and commercial strength in Plaintiffs' marks, and the lack of any actual intent on Diageo's part to confuse consumers.

Based upon that collection of evidence, the Court concludes that Plaintiffs have not shown generally a "likelihood of success on the merits."

D. THE EQUITIES
Under the Lanham Act, a district court has the "power to grant injunctions, according to the principles of equity and upon such terms as the court may deem reasonable." 15 U.S.C. § 1116. Even if "serious questions going to the merits" existed, the balance of the hardships does not tip "sharply in favor" of granting the full scope of the requested injunction. Brookfield, supra, 174 F.3d 1046 (where there are "serious questions going to the merits," to obtain an injunction, plaintiff must show that "the balance of hardships tips sharply in his favor"). On the current record, the balance tips in Diageo's favor except as to Christian Stark and Stark Wine LLC's own market in Sonoma County.

1. Harm to Plaintiffs Absent an Injunction
Even where infringement has been proven, a plaintiff cannot be granted injunctive relief unless it can show irreparable injury absent an injunction. This requires a plaintiff to "demonstrate a likelihood of irreparable injury--not just a possibility--in order to obtain preliminary relief. " Winter, supra, 555 U.S. at 21. Irreparable injury means an injury that is imminent, and that cannot be remedied by an award of money.

Misidentification of goods poses a threat to goodwill and reputation. A trademark holder is entitled to control the reputation and goodwill associated with its mark. This potential loss of goodwill or loss of control over one's reputation cannot be measured precisely and "may constitute irreparable harm for purposes of preliminary injunctive relief." SunEarth, supra, 846 F. Supp. 2d at 1083 (quoting Mortgage Elec. Registration Sys. v. Brosnan, 2009 U.S. Dist. LEXIS 87596, 2009 WL 3647125, at *8 (N.D. Cal. 2009)).

Both Christian Stark and Ms. Krall Walz testified about a subjective fear that if Diageo floods the wine market with Stark Raving[TM] wine, it will be impossible to undo the damage to Plaintiffs' goodwill and reputation. Christian Stark testified that reputation is everything in the wine industry and that people will assume that he produced Diageo's Stark Raving[TM], which will damage his reputation. He testified that consumers will come to expect low quality "stark" wine, which will prevent him from selling his Stark Wine® at its current price point of $28 to $44 per bottle. The alleged difference in price and quality between the wines could be damaging to the Stark Wine® brand. Because there is not a likelihood of confusion generally, it is unlikely that there will be such reputational harm or loss of goodwill except in Sonoma County.

Ms. Krall Walz testified that the Stark Wine® and Stark Thirst[TM] brands would be damaged beyond repair. Ms. Krall Walz and Christian Stark testified that if an injunction does not issue, they will lose the opportunity to expand their businesses nationally, which they argue is a harm that cannot be quantified. Ms. Krall Walz testified that absent an injunction, Stark Raving[TM] wine will be on shelves in the same stores where Plaintiffs plan to sell Stark Wine® and Stark Thirst[TM].

Plaintiffs did not present credible evidence of the reputation or goodwill associated with the Stark Thirst[TM] mark. S@HS has not advertised the brand, and its wine is available at only three locations in New York City.

Plaintiffs testified that they will not be able to do their brand extensions because the Stark Raving[TM] wines will damage the reputation of the word "stark" in connection with wine. However, neither Ms. Krall Walz nor Christian Stark own the trademark rights to these brand extensions--one acquires the exclusive right to use a trademark through its actual use in commerce; expansion plans are not use in commerce.

2. Balancing the Relative and Potential Harm to Each Party

Diageo has identified concrete and particularized harm that an injunction would cause to its business. First, Diageo claims an injunction will end the Stark Raving[TM] brand. Ms. Light testified that retailers have reserved shelf space for Stark Raving[TM], which would be lost if Diageo could not ship (or had to recall) cases of Stark Raving[TM] wine.[17] Additionally, an injunction

---

[17] 17 Diageo has produced approximately 80,000 cases of Stark Raving wine, approximately 17,000 cases were delivered to distributors and in turn 7,000 of

would also harm Diageo's goodwill with these distributors and retailers who have agreed to distribute and stock the wine. Ms. Light explained that the Stark Raving[TM] sub-brand is Diageo's first foray into this wine submarket and its success impacts Diageo ability to establish itself as serious competitor in that submarket. Diageo argues that it would be cost prohibitive to do anything other than destroy the bottles if the wine cannot be sold under the Stark Raving[TM] label.

Plaintiffs argue that any hardship is of Diageo's own making. See Cadence Design Sys. v. Avant! Corp., 125 F.3d 824, 829 (9th Cir. 1997) ("a defendant who knowingly infringes another's copyright cannot complain of the harm that will befall it when properly forced to desist from its infringing activities") (internal quotations omitted). Plaintiffs also discount the potential harm to DiageoThey argue that Diageo could just re-label the bottles if enjoined.[18] According to Plaintiffs, the Stark Raving[TM] sub-brand was introduced to the market recently, with no goodwill in its trademark, and that Diageo is a large company with a large portfolio of beverages, of which the Stark Raving[TM] sub-brand is a small component.

The harm from an erroneously issued, widespread injunction far outweighs any harm should such relief be erroneously denied. By the same token, closing Sonoma County off from Diageo will have little impact and will protect Plaintiffs locally. In that county, evidence exists that Plaintiffs have built a positive reputation for Stark Wine® and there consumers are more likely to be confused thus bolstering Plaintiffs' claim of hardship and tipping the scales in their favor.

3. Public Interest.

Before issuing an injunction a court also must ensure that the "public interest would not be disserved." eBay v. MercExchange, LLC, 547 U.S. 388, 391, 126 S. Ct. 1837, 164 L. Ed. 2d 641 (2006). Preventing consumer confusion serves the public interest and there is a strong policy in favor of protecting rights to trademarks. As set forth above, the potential for confusion is local to Sonoma

---

those cases have been delivered to retailers. As of August 15, 2012, Stark Raving wine is on the shelves at over 1,500 stores across the United States. Neither party proffered evidence of the cost of relabeling or recalling the bottles already shipped.

[18] 18 The Court notes that the actual relief sought in this action includes destroying the bottles.

County. The public interest is served by an injunction in that county.

IV. CONCLUSION

For the reasons set forth above, the Court will GRANT a preliminary injunction, limited in geographic scope to Sonoma County, California, in favor of Christian Stark and Stark Wine LLC, only. Stay @ Home Sommelier, LLC's request for a preliminary injunction is DENIED.

Therefore, the Motion for Preliminary Injunction is GRANTED AS TO SONOMA COUNTY, CALIFORNIA, and otherwise DENIED.

Defendant, its officers, agents, servants, employees, and attorneys are hereby ENJOINED and RESTRAINED from directly or indirectly using the mark "Stark Raving" in connection with the advertisement, promotion, distribution, offering for sale or selling of wine or related goods or services in Sonoma County, California.

Issuance of this preliminary injunction is contingent upon Plaintiffs filing proof of issuance of a bond in the amount of $500.00 [19] by no later than 2:00 p.m. on November 30, 2012. Should Plaintiffs fail to file proof of such undertaking by that time, this injunction shall be dissolved without further Order by the Court.

This Order Terminates Docket Number 26.

IT IS SO ORDERED.

Date: November 1, 2012

/s/ Yvonne Gonzalez Rogers

YVONNE GONZALEZ ROGERS

UNITED STATES DISTRICT COURT JUDGE

---

[19] 19 Rule 65(c) of the Federal Rules of Civil Procedure requires that the party seeking an injunction must post security "in an amount that the court considers proper to pay the costs and damages sustained by any party found to have been wrongfully enjoined or restrained." Fed. R. Civ. Pro. 65(c). Defendant seeks a $5,000,000.00 bond based upon its expected harm if the Court issues a nationwide injunction. There is no showing that Diageo will suffer more than negligible harm if enjoined from Sonoma County. There is no evidence that Stark Raving[TM] wine is being sold in Sonoma County or that Diageo will be harmed if prevented from entering that market. The Court, in its discretion, will require Plaintiffs post $500.00 as security.

3

Judicial Disagreement

Supreme Court dissent evokes Gulliver's "sunbeams from cucumbers"; Scientific disagreements at the FDA; and "Back to the Future" time travel in statutory interpretation.

BAGGETT ET AL.

v.

BULLITT ET AL.

No. 220

SUPREME COURT
OF THE UNITED STATES

377 U.S. 360
June 1, 1964

Warren, Black, Douglas, Clark, Harlan, Brennan, Stewart, White, Goldberg

OPINION

MR. JUSTICE WHITE delivered the opinion of the Court.

Appellants, approximately 64 in number, are members of the faculty, staff and student body of the University of Washington who brought this class action asking for a judgment declaring unconstitutional two Washington statutes requiring the execution of two different oaths by state employees and for an injunction against the enforcement of these statutes by appellees, the President of the University, members of the Washington State Board of Regents and the State Attorney General.

The statutes under attack are Chapter 377, Laws of 1955, and Chapter 103, Laws of 1931, both of which require employees of the State of Washington to take the oaths prescribed in the statutes as a condition of their employment. The 1931 legislation applies only to teachers, who, upon applying for a license to teach or renewing an existing contract, are required to subscribe to the following:

"I solemnly swear (or affirm) that I will support the constitution and laws of the United States of America and of the State of Washington, and will by precept and example promote respect for the flag and the institutions of the United States of America and the State of Washington, reverence for law and order and undivided allegiance to the government of the United States." Wash. Laws 1931, c. 103.

The oath requirements of the 1955 Act, Wash. Laws 1955, c. 377, applicable to all state employees, incorporate various provisions of the Washington Subversive Activities Act of 1951, which provides generally that "no subversive person, as defined in this act, shall be eligible for employment in, or appointment to any office, or any position of trust or profit in the government, or in the administration of the business, of this state, or of any county, municipality, or other political subdivision of this state." Wash. Rev. Code § 9.81.060. The term "subversive person" is defined as follows:

"'Subversive person' means any person who commits, attempts to commit, or aids in the commission, or advocates, abets, advises or teaches by any means any person to commit, attempt to commit, or aid in the commission of any act intended to overthrow, destroy or alter, or to assist in the overthrow, destruction or alteration of, the constitutional form of the government of the United States, or of the state of Washington, or any political subdivision of either of them by revolution, force, or violence; or who with knowledge that the organization is an organization as described in subsections (2) and (3) hereof, becomes or remains a member of a subversive organization or a foreign subversive organization." Wash. Rev. Code § 9.81.010 (5).

The Act goes on to define at similar length and in similar terms "subversive organization" and "foreign subversive organization" and to declare the Communist Party a subversive organization and membership therein a subversive activity.[1]

---

[1] 1 " 'Subversive organization' means any organization which engages in or advocates, abets, advises, or teaches, or a purpose of which is to engage in or advocate, abet, advise, or teach activities intended to overthrow, destroy or alter, or to assist in the overthrow, destruction or alteration of, the constitutional form of the government of the United States, or of the state of Washington, or of any political subdivision of either of them, by revolution, force or violence." Wash. Rev. Code § 9.81.010 (2).

" 'Foreign subversive organization' means any organization directed, dominated or controlled directly or indirectly by a foreign government which engages in or advocates, abets, advises, or teaches, or a purpose of which is to engage in or to advocate, abet, advise, or teach, activities intended to overthrow, destroy or alter, or to assist in the overthrow, destruction or alteration of the constitutional form of the government of the United States, or of the state of Washington, or of any political subdivision of either of them, and to establish in place thereof any form of government the direction and control of which is to be vested in, or exercised by or under, the domination or control of any foreign government, organization, or individual." Wash. Rev. Code § 9.81.010 (3).

"COMMUNIST PARTY DECLARED A SUBVERSIVE

On May 28, 1962, some four months after this Court's dismissal of the appeal in Nostrand v. Little, 368 U.S. 436, also a challenge to the 1955 oath,[2] the University President, acting pursuant to directions of the Board of Regents, issued a memorandum to all University employees notifying them that they would be required to take an oath. Oath Form A[3] requires all teaching

---

ORGANIZATION.
"The communist party is a subversive organization within the purview of chapter 9.81 and membership in the communist party is a subversive activity thereunder." Wash. Rev. Code § 9.81.083.

[2] 2 Although the 1931 Act has not been the subject of previous challenge, an attack upon the 1955 loyalty statute was instituted by two of the appellants in the present case, Professors Howard Nostrand and Max Savelle, who brought a declaratory judgment action in the Superior Court of the State of Washington asking that Chapter 377, Laws of 1955, be declared unconstitutional and that its enforcement be enjoined. The Washington Supreme Court held that one section was unconstitutional but severable from the rest of the Act, whose validity was upheld. Nostrand v. Balmer, 53 Wash. 2d 460, 335 P. 2d 10. On appeal to this Court the decision of the Washington court was vacated and the case remanded for a determination of whether employees who refused to sign the oath would be afforded a hearing at which they could explain or defend the reasons for their refusal. Nostrand v. Little, 362 U.S. 474. The Washington Supreme Court held upon remand that since Professors Nostrand and Savelle were tenured professors the terms of their contracts and rules promulgated by the Board of Regents entitled them to a hearing. Nostrand v. Little, 58 Wash. 2d 111, 361 P. 2d 551. This Court dismissed a further appeal, Nostrand v. Little, 368 U.S. 436. The issue we find dispositive of the case at bar was not presented to this Court in the above proceedings.

[3] 3 "Oath Form A
"STATE OF WASHINGTON
"Statement and Oath for Teaching Faculty
of the University of Washington
"I, the undersigned, do solemnly swear (or affirm) that I will support the constitution and laws of the United States of America and of the state of Washington, and will by precept and example promote respect for the flag and the institutions of the United States of America and the state of Washington, reverence for law and order, and undivided allegiance to the government of the United States;
"I further certify that I have read the provisions of RCW 9.81.010 (2), (3), and
170

personnel to swear to the oath of allegiance set out above, to aver that they have read, are familiar with and understand the provisions defining "subversive person" in the Subversive Activities Act of 1951 and to disclaim being a subversive person and membership in the Communist Party or any other subversive or foreign subversive organization. Oath Form B[4] requires

---

(5); RCW 9.81.060; RCW 9.81.070; and RCW 9.81.083, which are printed on the reverse hereof; that I understand and am familiar with the contents thereof; that I am not a subversive person as therein defined; and
"I do solemnly swear (or affirm) that I am not a member of the Communist party or knowingly of any other subversive organization.
"I understand that this statement and oath are made subject to the penalties of perjury.
....
(SIGNATURE)
.........?........
(TITLE AND DEPARTMENT)
"Subscribed and sworn (or affirmed) to before me this .... day of ....,
19....

....
NOTARY PUBLIC IN AND FOR THE STATE OF WASHINGTON,
RESIDING AT ....
"(To be executed in duplicate, one copy to be retained by individual.)
"NOTE: Those desiring to affirm may strike the words 'swear' and 'sworn to' and substitute 'affirm' and 'affirmed,' respectively."

[4] 4 "Oath Form B
"STATE OF WASHINGTON
"Statement and Oath for Staff of the University of WashingtonOther Than Teaching Faculty
"I certify that I have read the provisions of RCW 9.81.010 (2), (3), and (5); RCW 9.81.060; RCW 9.81.070; and RCW 9.81.083 which are printed on the reverse hereof; that I understand and am familiar with the contents thereof; that I am not a subversive person as therein defined; and
"I do solemnly swear (or affirm) that I am not a member of the Communist party or knowingly of any other subversive organization.
"I understand that this statement and oath are made subject to the penalties of perjury.
....
(SIGNATURE)

....
(TITLE AND DEPARTMENT OR OFFICE)

other state employees to subscribe to all of the above provisions except the 1931 oath. Both forms provide that the oath and statements pertinent thereto are made subject to the penalties of perjury.

 Pursuant to 28 U. S. C. §§ 2281, 2284, a three-judge District Court was convened and a trial was had. That court determined that the 1955 oath and underlying statutory provisions did not infringe upon any First and Fourteenth Amendment freedoms and were not unduly vague. In respect to the claim that the 1931 oath was unconstitutionally vague on its face, the court held that although the challenge raised a substantial constitutional issue, adjudication was not proper in the absence of proceedings in the state courts which might resolve or avoid the constitutional issue. The action was dismissed. 215 F.Supp. 439. We noted probable jurisdiction because of the public importance of this type of legislation and the recurring serious constitutional questions which it presents. 375 U.S. 808. We reverse.

I.

Appellants contend in this Court that the oath requirements and the statutory provisions on which they are based are invalid on their face because their language is unduly vague, uncertain and broad. We agree with this contention and therefore, without reaching the numerous other contentions pressed upon us, confine our considerations to that particular question.[5]

"Subscribed and sworn (or affirmed) to before me this .... day of ...., 19....

....

NOTARY PUBLIC IN AND FOR THE STATE OF WASHINGTON, RESIDING AT ....

"(To be executed in duplicate, one copy to be retained by individual.)

"NOTE: Those desiring to affirm may strike the words 'swear' and 'sworn to' and substitute 'affirm' and 'affirmed,' respectively."

[5] 5 Since the ground we find dispositive immediately affects the professors and other state employees required to take the oath, and the interests of the students at the University in academic freedom are fully protected by a judgment in favor of the teaching personnel, we have no occasion to pass on the standing of the students to bring this suit.

In Cramp v. Board of Public Instruction, 368 U.S. 278, the Court invalidated an oath requiring teachers and other employees of the State to swear that they had never lent their "aid, support, advice, counsel or influence to the Communist Party" because the oath was lacking in "terms susceptible of objective measurement" and failed to inform as to what the State commanded or forbade. The statute therefore fell within the compass of those decisions of the Court holding that a law forbidding or requiring conduct in terms so vague that men of common intelligence must necessarily guess at its meaning and differ as to its application violates due process of law. Connally v. General Construction Co., 269 U.S. 385; Lanzetta v. New Jersey, 306 U.S. 451; Joseph Burstyn, Inc., v. Wilson, 343 U.S. 495; United States v. Cardiff, 344 U.S. 174;Champlin Refining Co. v. Corporation Comm'n of Oklahoma, 286 U.S. 210.

The oath required by the 1955 statute suffers from similar infirmities. A teacher must swear that he is not a subversive person: that he is not one who commits an act or who advises, teaches, abets or advocates by any means another person to commit or aid in the commission of any act intended to overthrow or alter, or to assist the overthrow or alteration, of the constitutional form of government by revolution, force or violence. A subversive organization is defined as one which engages in or assists activities intended to alter or overthrow the Government by force or violence or which has as a purpose the commission of such acts. The Communist Party is declared in the statute to be a subversive organization, that is, it is presumed that the Party does and will engage in activities intended to overthrow the Government.[6] Persons required to swear they understand this oath may quite reasonably conclude that any person who aids the Communist Party or teaches or advises known members of the Party is a subversive person because such teaching or advice may now or at some future date aid the activities of the Party. Teaching and advising are clearly acts, and one cannot confidently assert that his counsel, aid, influence or support which adds to the

---

[6] 6 The drafters of the 1951 Subversive Activities Act stated to the Washington Legislature that "the [Communist Party] dovetailed, nation-wide program is designed to . . . create unrest and civil strife, and impede the normal processes of state and national government, all to the end of weakening and ultimately destroying the United States as a constitutional republic and thereby facilitating the avowed Soviet purpose of substituting here a totalitarian dictatorship." First Report of the Joint Legislative Fact-Finding Committee on Un-American Activities in Washington State, 1948, p. IV.

resources, rights and knowledge of the Communist Party or its members does not aid the Party in its activities, activities which the statute tells us are all in furtherance of the stated purpose of overthrowing the Government by revolution, force, or violence. The questions put by the Court in Cramp may with equal force be asked here. Does the statute reach endorsement or support for Communist candidates for office? Does it reach a lawyer who represents the Communist Party or its members or a journalist who defends constitutional rights of the Communist Party or its members or anyone who supports any cause which is likewise supported by Communists or the Communist Party? The susceptibility of the statutory language to require forswearing of an undefined variety of "guiltless knowing behavior" is what the Court condemned in Cramp. This statute, like the one at issue in Cramp, is unconstitutionally vague.[7]

The Washington statute suffers from additional difficulties on vagueness grounds. A person is subversive not only if he himself commits the specified acts but if he abets or advises another in aiding a third person to commit an act which will assist yet a fourth person in the overthrow or alteration of constitutional government. The Washington Supreme Court has said that knowledge is to be read into every provision and we accept this construction. Nostrand v. Balmer, 53 Wash. 2d 460, 483-484, 335 P. 2d 10, 24; Nostrand v. Little, 58 Wash. 2d 111, 123-124, 361 P. 2d 551, 559. But what is it that the

---

[7] 7 The contention that the Court found no constitutional difficulties with identical definitions of subversive person and subversive organizations in Gerende v. Board of Supervisors, 341 U.S. 56, is without merit. It was forcefully argued in Gerende that candidates for state office in Maryland were required to take an oath incorporating a section of the Maryland statutes defining subversive person and organization in the identical terms challenged herein. But the Court rejected this interpretation of Maryland law and did not pass upon or approve the definitions of subversive person and organization contained in the Maryland statutes. Instead it made very clear that the judgment below was affirmed solely on the basis that the actual oath to be imposed under Maryland law requires one to swear that he is not a person who is engaged "'in the attempt to overthrow the government by force or violence,' and that he is not knowingly a member of an organization engaged in such an attempt." Id., at 56-57 (emphasis in original). The Court said: "At the bar of this Court the Attorney General of the State of Maryland declared that he would advise the proper authorities to accept an affidavit in these terms as satisfying in full the statutory requirement. Under these circumstances and with this understanding, the judgment of the Maryland Court of Appeals is Affirmed." Id., at 57.

Washington professor must "know"? Must he know that his aid or teaching will be used by another and that the person aided has the requisite guilty intent or is it sufficient that he know that his aid or teaching would or might be useful to others in the commission of acts intended to overthrow the Government? Is it subversive activity, for example, to attend and participate in international conventions of mathematicians and exchange views with scholars from Communist countries? What about the editor of a scholarly journal who analyzes and criticizes the manuscripts of Communist scholars submitted for publication? Is selecting outstanding scholars from Communist countries as visiting professors and advising, teaching, or consulting with them at the University of Washington a subversive activity if such scholars are known to be Communists, or regardless of their affiliations, regularly teach students who are members of the Communist Party, which by statutory definition is subversive and dedicated to the overthrow of the Government?

The Washington oath goes beyond overthrow or alteration by force or violence. It extends to alteration by "revolution" which, unless wholly redundant and its ordinary meaning distorted, includes any rapid or fundamental change. Would, therefore, any organization or any person supporting, advocating or teaching peaceful but far-reaching constitutional amendments be engaged in subversive activity? Could one support the repeal of the Twenty-second Amendment or participation by this country in a world government?[8]

---

[8] 8 It is also argued that § 2 of the Smith Act, 18 U. S. C. § 2385, upheld over a vagueness challenge in Dennis v. United States, 341 U.S. 494, proscribes the same activity in the same language as the Washington statute. This argument is founded on a misreading of § 2 and Dennis v. United States, supra.

That section provides:

"Whoever knowingly or willfully advocates, abets, advises, or teaches the duty, necessity, desirability, or propriety of overthrowing or destroying the government of the United States or the government of any State . . . by force or violence . . . ."

The convictions under this provision were sustained in Dennis, supra, on the construction that the statute means "teaching and advocacy of action for the accomplishment of [overthrowing or destroying organized government] by language reasonably and ordinarily calculated to incite persons to such action . . . as speedily as circumstances would permit." Id., at 511-512. In connection with the vagueness attack, it was noted that "this is a federal statute which we must interpret as well as judge. Herein lies the fallacy of reliance upon the manner in which this Court has treated judgments of state courts. . . ." Id., at 502.

In reversing convictions under this section in Yates v. United States, 354 U.S.

II.

We also conclude that   the 1931 oath offends due process because of vagueness. The oath exacts a promise that the affiant will, by precept and example, promote respect for the flag and the institutions of the United States and the State of Washington. The range of activities which are or might be deemed inconsistent with the required promise is very wide indeed. The teacher who refused to salute the flag or advocated refusal because of religious beliefs might well be accused of breaching his promise. Cf. West Virginia State Board of Education v. Barnette, 319 U.S. 624. Even criticism of the design or color scheme of the state flag or unfavorable comparison of it with that of a sister State or foreign country could be deemed disrespectful and therefore violative of the oath. And what are "institutions" for the purposes of this oath? Is it every "practice, law, custom, etc., which is a material and persistent element in the life or culture of an organized social group" or every "established society or corporation," every "establishment, esp[ecially] one of a public character"?[9] 9 The oath may prevent a professor from criticizing his state judicial system or the Supreme Court or the institution of judicial review. Or it might be deemed to proscribe advocating the abolition, for example, of the Civil Rights Commission, the House Committee on Un-American Activities, or foreign aid.

It is likewise difficult to ascertain what might be done without transgressing the promise to "promote . . . undivided allegiance to the government of the United States." It would not be unreasonable for the serious-minded oathtaker to conclude that he should dispense with lectures voicing far-reaching criticism of any old or new policy followed by the Government of the United States. He could find it questionable under this language to ally himself with any interest group dedicated to opposing any current public policy or law of the Federal Government, for if he did, he might well be accused of placing loyalty to the group above allegiance to the United States. Indulging every presumption of a narrow construction of the provisions of the 1931 oath, consistent, however, with a proper respect for the English language, we cannot say that this oath provides an ascertainable standard of

---

298, the Court made quite clear exactly what all the above terms do and do not proscribe: "The Smith Act reaches only advocacy of action for the overthrow of government by force and violence." Id., at 324.

[9] 9 Webster's New Int. Dictionary (2d ed.), at 1288.

conduct or that it does not require more than a State may command under the guarantees of the First and Fourteenth Amendments.

As in Cramp v. Board of Public Instruction, "the vice of unconstitutional vagueness is further aggravated where, as here, the statute in question operates to inhibit the exercise of individual freedoms affirmatively protected by the Constitution." 368 U.S. 278, 287. We are dealing with indefinite statutes whose terms, even narrowly construed, abut upon sensitive areas of basic First Amendment freedoms. The uncertain meanings of the oaths require the oath-taker -- teachers and public servants -- to "steer far wider of the unlawful zone," Speiser v. Randall, 357 U.S. 513, 526, than if the boundaries of the forbidden areas were clearly marked. Those with a conscientious regard for what they solemnly swear or affirm, sensitive to the perils posed by the oath's indefinite language, avoid the risk of loss of employment, and perhaps profession, only by restricting their conduct to that which is unquestionably safe. Free speech may not be so inhibited.[10] 10 Smith v. California, 361 U.S. 147; Stromberg v. California, 283 U.S. 359, 369. See also Herndon v. Lowry, 301 U.S. 242; Thornhill v. Alabama, 310 U.S. 88; and Winters v. New York, 333 U.S. 507.

III.

The State labels as wholly fanciful the suggested possible coverage of the two oaths. It may well be correct, but the contention only emphasizes the difficulties with the two statutes; for if the oaths do not reach some or any of the behavior suggested, what specific conduct do the oaths cover? Where does fanciful possibility end and intended coverage begin?

---

[10] 10 "The maintenance of the opportunity for free political discussion to the end that government may be responsive to the will of the people and that changes may be obtained by lawful means, an opportunity essential to the security of the Republic, is a fundamental principle of our constitutional system. A statute which upon its face . . . is so vague and indefinite as to permit the punishment of the fair use of this opportunity is repugnant to the guaranty of liberty contained in the Fourteenth Amendment." Stromberg v. California, 283 U.S. 359, 369. "Statutes restrictive of or purporting to place limits to those [First Amendment] freedoms must be narrowly drawn to meet the precise evil the legislature seeks to curb . . . and . . . the conduct proscribed must be defined specifically so that the person or persons affected remain secure and unrestrained in their rights to engage in activities not encompassed by the legislation." United States v. Congress of Industrial Organizations, 335 U.S. 106, 141-142 (Rutledge, J., concurring).

It will not do to say that a prosecutor's sense of fairness and the Constitution would prevent a successful perjury prosecution for some of the activities seemingly embraced within the sweeping statutory definitions. The hazard of being prosecuted for knowing but guiltless behavior nevertheless remains. "It would be blinking reality not to acknowledge that there are some among us always ready to affix a Communist label upon those whose ideas they violently oppose. And experience teaches us that prosecutors too are human." Cramp, supra, at 286-287. Well-intentioned prosecutors and judicial safeguards do not neutralize the vice of a vague law. Nor should we encourage the casual taking of oaths by upholding the discharge or exclusion from public employment of those with a conscientious and scrupulous regard for such undertakings.

It is further argued, however, that, notwithstanding the uncertainties of the 1931 oath and the statute on which it is based, the oath does not offend due process because the vagaries are contained in a promise of future conduct, the breach of which would not support a conviction for perjury. Without the criminal sanctions, it is said, one need not fear taking this oath, regardless of whether he understands it and can comply with its mandate, however understood. This contention ignores not only the effect of the oath on those who will not solemnly swear unless they can do so honestly and without prevarication and reservation, but also its effect on those who believe the written law means what it says. Oath Form A contains both oaths, and expressly requires that the signer "understand that this statement and oath are made subject to the penalties of perjury." Moreover, Wash. Rev. Code § 9.72.030 provides that "every person who, whether orally or in writing . . . shall knowingly swear falsely concerning any matter whatsoever" commits perjury in the second degree. Even if it can be said that a conviction for falsely taking this oath would not be sustained, the possibility of a prosecution cannot be gainsaid. The State may not require one to choose between subscribing to an unduly vague and broad oath, thereby incurring the likelihood of prosecution, and conscientiously refusing to take the oath with the consequent loss of employment, and perhaps profession, particularly where "the free dissemination of ideas may be the loser." Smith v. California, 361 U.S. 147, 151. "It is not the penalty itself that is invalid but the exaction of obedience to a rule or standard that is so vague and indefinite as to be really no rule or standard at all." Champlin Refg. Co. v. Corporation Comm'n of Oklahoma, 286 U.S. 210, 243; cf. Small Co. v. American Refg. Co., 267 U.S. 233.

IV.

We are asked not to examine the 1931 oath statute because, although on the books for over three decades, it has never been interpreted by the Washington courts. The argument is that ever since Railroad Comm'n v. Pullman Co.,

312 U.S. 496, the Court on many occasions has ordered abstention where state tribunals were thought to be more appropriate for resolution of complex or unsettled questions of local law. A. F. L. v. Watson, 327 U.S. 582; Spector Motor Service v. McLaughlin, 323 U.S. 101; Harrison v. NAACP, 360 U.S. 167. Because this Court ordinarily accepts the construction given a state statute in the local courts and also presumes that the statute will be construed in such a way as to avoid the constitutional question presented, Fox v. Washington, 236 U.S. 273; Poulos v. New Hampshire, 345 U.S. 395, an interpretation of the 1931 oath in the Washington courts in light of the vagueness attack may eliminate the necessity of deciding this issue.

We are not persuaded. The abstention doctrine is not an automatic rule applied whenever a federal court is faced with a doubtful issue of state law; it rather involves a discretionary exercise of a court's equity powers. Ascertainment of whether there exist the "special circumstances," Propper v. Clark, 337 U.S. 472, prerequisite to its application must be made on a case-by-case basis. Railroad Comm'n v. Pullman Co., 312 U.S. 496, 500; NAACP v. Bennett, 360 U.S. 471.[11] Those special circumstances are not present here. We doubt, in the first place, that a construction of the oath provisions, in light of the vagueness challenge, would avoid or fundamentally alter the constitutional issue raised in this litigation. See Chicago v. Atchison, T. & S. F. R. Co., 357 U.S. 77. In the bulk of abstention cases in this Court,[12]

---

[11] 11 "When the validity of a state statute, challenged under the United States Constitution, is properly for adjudication before a United States District Court, reference to the state courts for construction of the statute should not automatically be made." NAACP v. Bennett, 360 U.S. 471. See also United States v. Livingston, 179 F.Supp. 9, 12-13 (D. C. E. D. S. C.), aff'd, Livingston v. United States, 364 U.S. 281: "Though never interpreted by a state court, if a state statute is not fairly subject to an interpretation which will avoid or modify the federal constitutional question, it is the duty of a federal court to decide the federal question when presented to it." Shelton v. McKinley, 174 F.Supp. 351 (D. C. E. D. Ark.) (abstention inappropriate where there are no substantial problems of statutory construction and delay would prejudice constitutional rights); All American Airways v. Village of Cedarhurst, 201 F.2d 273 (C. A. 2d Cir.); Sterling Drug v. Anderson, 127 F.Supp. 511, 513 (D. C. E. D. Tenn.).

[12] 12 See, e. g., Railroad Comm'n of Texas v. Pullman Co., 312 U.S. 496; Chicago v. Fieldcrest Dairies, Inc., 316 U.S. 168; Spector Motor Service, Inc., v. McLaughlin, 323 U.S. 101; Alabama State Federation of Labor v. McAdory, 325 U.S. 450; American Federation of Labor v. Watson, 327 U.S.

including those few cases where vagueness was at issue,[13] the unsettled issue

---

582; Stainback v. Mo Hock Ke Lok Po, 336 U.S. 368; Shipman v. DuPre, 339 U.S. 321; Albertson v. Millard, 345 U.S. 242; Leiter Minerals, Inc., v. United States, 352 U.S. 220; Government & Civic Employees Organizing Committee, C. I. O., v. Windsor, 353 U.S. 364; City of Meridian v. Southern Bell Tel. & Tel. Co., 358 U.S. 639.

[13] 13 In Musser v. Utah, 333 U.S. 95, the appellants were convicted of committing "acts injurious to public morals." The vagueness challenge to the statute, either as applied or on its face, was raised for the first time in oral argument before this Court, and the Court vacated the conviction and remanded for a determination of whether the conviction for urging persons to commit polygamy rested solely on this broad-challenged provision. In Albertson v. Millard, 345 U.S. 242, the Communist Party of the State of Michigan and its secretary sought to enjoin on several constitutional grounds the application to them of a state statute, five days after its passage, requiring registration, under pain of criminal penalties, of "any organization which is substantially directed, dominated or controlled by the Union of Soviet Socialist Republics or its satellites, or which . . . acts to further, the world communist movement" and of members of such an organization. They argued that the definitions were vague and failed to inform them if a local Communist organization and its members were required to register. The lower court took judicial notice of the fact that the Communist Party of the United States, with whom the local party was associated, was a part of the world Communist movement dominated by the Soviet Union, and held the statute constitutional in all other respects. This Court vacated the judgment and declined to pass on the appellants' constitutional claims until the Michigan courts, in a suit already pending, construed the statutory terms and determined if they required the local Party and its secretary, without more, to register. The approach was that the constitutional claims, including the one founded on vagueness, would be wholly eliminated if the statute, as construed by the state court, did not require all local Communist organizations without substantial ties to a foreign country and their members to register. Stated differently, the question was whether this statute applied to these plaintiffs, a question to be authoritatively answered in the state courts.
In Harrison v. NAACP, 360 U.S. 167, the NAACP and the NAACP Legal Defense and Education Fund sought a declaratory judgment and injunction on several constitutional grounds in respect to numerous recently enacted state statutes. The lower court enjoined the implementation of three statutes, including one provision on vagueness grounds, and ordered abstention as to two others, finding them ambiguous. This Court ordered abstention as to all

of state law principally concerned the applicability of the challenged statute to a certain person or a defined course of conduct, whose resolution in a particular manner would eliminate the constitutional issue and terminate the litigation. Here the uncertain issue of state law does not turn upon a choice between one or several alternative meanings of a state statute. The challenged oath is not open to one or a few interpretations, but to an indefinite number. There is no uncertainty that the oath applies to the appellants and the issue they raise is not whether the oath permits them to engage in certain definable activities. Rather their complaint is that they, about 64 in number, cannot understand the required promise, cannot define the range of activities in which they might engage in the future, and do not want to forswear doing all that is literally or arguably within the purview of the vague terms. In these circumstances it is difficult to see how an abstract construction of the challenged terms, such as precept, example, allegiance, institutions, and the like, in a declaratory judgment action could eliminate the vagueness from these terms. It is fictional to believe that anything less than extensive adjudications, under the impact of a variety of factual situations, would bring the oath within the bounds of permissible constitutional certainty. Abstention does not require this.

Other considerations also militate against abstention here. Construction of this oath in the state court, abstractly and without reference to concrete, particularized situations so necessary to bring into focus the impact of the terms on constitutionally protected rights of speech and association, Ashwander v. Tennessee Valley Authority, 297 U.S. 288, 341 (Brandeis, J., concurring), would not only hold little hope of eliminating the issue of vagueness but also would very likely pose other constitutional issues for decision, a result not serving the abstention-justifying end of avoiding constitutional adjudication.

We also cannot ignore that abstention operates to require piecemeal

---

the statutes, finding that they were all susceptible of constructions that would limit or eliminate their effect on the litigative and legal activities of the NAACP and construction might thereby eliminate the necessity for passing on the many constitutional questions raised. The vagueness issue, for example, would not require adjudication if the state courts found that the challenged provisions did not restrict the activities of the NAACP or require the NAACP to register. Unlike the instant case, the necessity for deciding the federal constitutional issues in the above and other abstention cases turned on whether the restrictions or requirements of an uncertain or unclear state statute were imposed on the persons bringing the action or on their activities as defined in the complaint.

adjudication in many courts, England v. Louisiana State Board of Medical Examiners, 375 U.S. 411, thereby delaying ultimate adjudication on the merits for an undue length of time, England, supra; Spector, supra; Government & Civic Employees Organizing Committee v. Windsor, 353 U.S. 364, [14] a result quite costly where the vagueness of a state statute may inhibit the exercise of First Amendment freedoms. Indeed the 1955 subversive person oath has been under continuous constitutional attack since at least 1957, Nostrand v. Balmer, 53 Wash. 2d 460, 463, 335 P. 2d 10, 12, and is now before this Court for the third time. Remitting these litigants to the state courts for a construction of the 1931 oath would further protract these proceedings, already pending for almost two years, with only the likelihood that the case, perhaps years later, will return to the three-judge District Court and perhaps this Court for a decision on the identical issue herein decided. See Chicago v. Atchison, T. & S. F. R. Co., 357 U.S. 77, 84; Public Utilities Comm'n of Ohio v. United Fuel Co., 317 U.S. 456.[15] Meanwhile, where the vagueness of the statute deters constitutionally protected conduct, "the free dissemination of ideas may be the loser." Smith v. California, 361 U.S. 147, 151.

V.

As in Cramp v. Board of Public Instruction, supra, we do not question the power of a State to take proper measures safeguarding the public service from disloyal conduct. But measures which purport to define disloyalty must allow public servants to know what is and is not disloyal. "The fact . . . that a person is not compelled to hold public office cannot possibly be an excuse for barring him from office by state-imposed criteria forbidden by the Constitution." Torcaso v. Watkins, 367 U.S. 488, 495-496.
Reversed.

---

[14] 14 See Clark, Federal Procedural Reform and States' Rights, 40 Tex. L. Rev. 211 (1961); Note, 73 Harv. L. Rev. 1358, 1363 (1960).

[15] 15 "Where the disposition of a doubtful question of local law might terminate the entire controversy and thus make it unnecessary to decide a substantial constitutional question, considerations of equity justify a rule of abstention. But where, as here, no state court ruling on local law could settle the federal questions that necessarily remain, and where, as here, the litigation has already been in the federal courts an inordinately long time, considerations of equity require that the litigation be brought to an end as quickly as possible." 317 U.S. 456, at 463.

DISSENT

MR. JUSTICE CLARK, whom MR. JUSTICE HARLAN joins, dissenting.

The Court strikes down, as unconstitutionally vague, two Acts of the State of Washington. The first, the Act of 1955, requires every state employee to swear or affirm that he is not a "subversive person" as therein defined. The second, the Act of 1931, which requires that another oath be taken by teachers, is declared void without the benefit of an opinion of either a state or federal court. I dissent as to both, the first on the merits, and the latter, because the Court refuses to afford the State an opportunity to interpret its own law.

I.

The Court says that the Act of 1955 is void on its face because it is "unduly vague, uncertain and broad." The Court points out that the oath requires a teacher to "swear that he is not a subversive person: that he is not one who commits an act or who advises, teaches, abets or advocates by any means another person to commit or aid in the commission of any act intended to overthrow or alter, or to assist the overthrow or alteration, of the constitutional form of government by revolution, force or violence." The Court further finds that the Act declares the Communist Party to be a subversive organization. From these premises, the Court then reasons that under the 1955 Act "any person who aids the Communist Party or teaches or advises known members of the Party is a subversive person" because "at some future date" such teaching may aid the activities of the Party. This reasoning continues with the assertion that "one cannot confidently assert that his counsel, aid, influence or support which adds to the resources, rights and knowledge of the Communist Party or its members does not aid the Party . . . in furtherance of the stated purpose of overthrowing the Government by revolution, force, or violence." The Court then interrogates itself: Does the statute reach "endorsement or support for Communist candidates for office? . . . a lawyer who represents the Communist Party or its members? . . . [defense of the] constitutional rights of the Communist Party or its members . . . [or support of] any cause which is likewise supported by Communists or the Communist Party?" Apparently concluding that the answers to these questions are unclear, the Court then declares the Act void, citing Cramp v. Board of Public Instruction, 368 U.S. 278 (1961). Let us take up this reasoning in reverse order.

First, Cramp is not apposite. The majority has failed to recognize that the statute in Cramp required an oath of much broader scope than the one in the instant case: Cramp involved an oath "that I have not and will not lend my aid, support, advice, counsel or influence to the Communist Party . . . ." That oath was replete with defects not present in the Washington oath. As MR. JUSTICE STEWART pointed out in Cramp:

"The provision of the oath here in question, it is to be noted, says nothing of advocacy of violent overthrow of state or federal government. It says nothing of membership or affiliation with the Communist Party, past or present. The provision is completely lacking in these or any other terms susceptible of objective measurement." At 286.

These factors which caused the Court to find the Cramp oath unconstitutionally vague are clearly not present in the Washington oath. Washington's oath proscribes only the commission of an act of overthrow or alteration of the constitutional form of government by revolution, force or violence; or advising, teaching, abetting or advocating by any means another person to commit or aid in the commission of any act intended to overthrow or alter or to assist the overthrow or alteration of the constitutional form of government by revolution, force or violence. The defects noted by the Court when it passed on the Cramp oath have been cured in the Washington statute. It is strange that the Court should find the language of this statute so profoundly vague when in 1951 it had no such trouble with the identical language presented by another oath in Gerende v. Board of Supervisors of Elections, 341 U.S. 56. There, the constitutionality of Maryland's Ober Law, written in language identical to Washington's 1955 Act, was affirmed by a unanimous Court against the same attack of vagueness. It is unfortunate that Gerende is overruled so quickly.[1] Other state laws have been copied from the Maryland Act -- just as Washington's 1955 Act was -- primarily because of our approval of it, and now this Court would declare them void. Such action cannot command the dignity and respect due to the judicial process. It is, of course, absurd to say that, under the words of the Washington Act, a professor risks violation when he teaches German, English, history or any other subject included in the curriculum for a college degree, to a class in which a Communist Party member might sit. To so interpret the language of the Act is to extract more sunbeams from cucumbers than did Gulliver's

mad scientist. And to conjure up such ridiculous questions, the

---

[1] * It has been contended that the crucial section of Maryland's Ober Act, that which is identical to the Washington Act, was not before the Court in Gerende, but a review of the record in that case conclusively demonstrates to the contrary. Further, while the Gerende opinion was stated with a qualification, the fact remains that the Court approved the judgment of the Maryland court and rejected the argument that the Act was unconstitutionally vague.

answers to which we all know or should know are in the negative, is to build up a whimsical and farcical straw man which is not only grim but Grimm.

In addition to the Ober Law the Court has also found that other statutes using similar language were not vague. An unavoidable example is the Smith Act which we upheld against an attack based on vagueness in the landmark case of Dennis v. United States, 341 U.S. 494 (1951). The critical language of the Smith Act is again in the same words as the 1955 Washington Act.
"Whoever knowingly or willfully advocates, abets, advises, or teaches the duty, necessity, desirability, or propriety of overthrowing or destroying the government of the United States . . . ." 18 U. S. C. § 2385. (Emphasis supplied.)
The opinion of the Court in Dennis uses this language in discussing the vagueness claim:
"We agree that the standard as defined is not a neat, mathematical formulary. Like all verbalizations it is subject to criticism on the score of indefiniteness. . . . We think [the statute] well serves to indicate to those who would advocate constitutionally prohibited conduct that there is a line beyond which they may not go -- a line which they, in full knowledge of what they intend and the circumstances in which their activity takes place, will well appreciate and understand." At 515-516.
It appears to me from the statutory language that Washington's 1955 Act is much more clear than the Smith Act. Still the Court strikes it down. Where does this leave the constitutionality of the Smith Act?

II.
Appellants make other claims. They say that the 1955 Act violates their rights of association and free speech as guaranteed by the First and Fourteenth Amendments. But in light of Konigsberg v. State Bar of California, 366 U.S. 36 (1961); In re Anastaplo, 366 U.S. 82 (1961); Adler v. Board of Education, 342 U.S. 485 (1952); Garner v. Board of Public Works, 341 U.S. 716 (1951); and American Communications Assn. v. Douds, 339 U.S. 382 (1950), this claim is frivolous. Likewise in view of the decision of Washington's highest court that tenured employees would be entitled to a hearing, Nostrand v. Little, 58 Wash. 2d 111, 131, 361 P. 2d 551, 563, the due process claim is without foundation. This conclusion would also apply to those employees without tenure, since they would be entitled to a hearing under Washington's Civil Service Act, Rev. Code Wash. § 41.04 et seq. and its Administrative Procedure Act, Rev. Code Wash. § 34.04.010 et seq.

III.

The Supreme Court of Washington has never construed the oath of allegiance required by the 1931 Act. I agree with the District Court that Washington's highest court should be afforded an opportunity to do so. As the District Court said:

"The granting or withholding of equitable or declaratory relief in federal court suits which seek to limit or control state action is committed to the sound discretion of the court. Accordingly, in the absence of a concrete factual showing that any plaintiff or any member of the classes of state employees here represented has suffered actual injury by reason of the application of the oath of allegiance statute (Chapter 103, Laws of 1931) this court will decline to render a declaratory judgment as to the constitutionality of that statute in advance of an authoritative construction by the Washington Supreme Court." 215 F.Supp. 439, 455.

For these reasons, I dissent.

LAKESHIA DYSON, personally and as
Personal Representative for the ESTATE OF RICO MONROE, JR., Plaintiff

v.

JOSEPH K. WINFIELD, M.D.,
Defendant; LAKESHIA DYSON, personally and as Personal Representative for the ESTATE OF RICO MONROE, JR., Plaintiff v. PHARMACIA & UPJOHN, INC., Defendant

C.A. No. 97-1665 (RCL)
C.A. No. 97-1666 (RCL)

UNITED STATES DISTRICT COURT
FOR THE DISTRICT OF COLUMBIA

113 F. Supp. 2d 44
September 21, 2000

ROYCE C. LAMBERTH, UNITED STATES DISTRICT JUDGE.

OPINION

MEMORANDUM AND ORDER

On July 23, 1997, Lakeshia Dyson, the plaintiff, filed a complaint against Dr. Joseph Winfield, alleging two counts of malpractice. The defendant now moves for exclusion of the plaintiff's expert testimony and for summary judgment. He supports his motion for summary judgement with several alternative arguments: (1) plaintiff has no evidence that Provera caused her son's injuries, (2) plaintiff has no evidence that defendant departed from the standard of care in prescribing Provera or failing to warn her of its risks, and (3) plaintiff has no evidence that defendant's substandard care, if any, caused her to have her son. The Court is not persuaded by any of the defendant's arguments, and therefore DENIES his motion for exclusion as well as his motion for summary judgment.

MAD SCIENTIST IN THE FEDERAL COURT

BACKGROUND

This case arises from Lakeshia Dyson's use of Provera in September and October of 1992. Concerned that she was pregnant, Ms. Dyson went to see Dr. Joseph Winfield, her OB/GYN, on September 26, 1992. She explained to Dr. Winfield that she had had unprotected sex a week prior and that her period was now late. Dr. Winfield gave her a urine pregnancy test which he interpreted as negative. Dr. Winfield then prescribed Provera to Ms. Dyson with the goal of inducing her menstruation.

Ms. Dyson took the Provera and, not having her period, returned to Dr. Winfield's office on October 17, 1992. During the consultation, Dr. Winfield took a blood sample to make certain whether or not she was pregnant. Although Dr. Winfield denies it, Ms. Dyson and her mother, who accompanied her on this visit, assert that they were told by the doctor that Ms. Dyson was pregnant. In any event, as the blood test later revealed, Ms. Dyson was indeed pregnant. At no point during this consultation did Dr. Winfield warn the patient of the risks associated with taking Provera in the early stages of pregnancy.

After her consultation, Ms. Dyson never talked with Dr. Winfield again, choosing instead to continue her prenatal care with a different doctor. In February of 1993, when she was over five months pregnant, Ms. Dyson received a sonogram that revealed the possibility of a birth defect. After considering abortion as an option, she decided to carry her pregnancy to full term because she felt that the child was "a baby" and not "a fetus." Dyson Aff. at P 9.

On May 15, 1993, Rico Monroe Jr. was born. Sadly, the child had numerous birth defects including, but not limited to, impairments of sight, hearing, ingestion, and intellect.[1] The child required intense medical care, both in and out of the hospital, throughout his entire life. On November 24, 1996, at an age of about 3 and a half years old, the child died.

PROCEDURAL HISTORY

Basing her claims on the District of Columbia Wrongful Death statute, 16 D.C. Code § 2701, and Wrongful Survival statute, 12 D.C. Code § 101, Ms.

---

[1] 1 Specifically, the child was diagnosed with microcephalia, blindness, hearing impairedness, abnormal smallness, mental and physical developmental delays, severe muscular/skeletal anomalies, undescended testes, ambiguous genitalia, malformed cardio/pulmonary blood vessels, esophagial atresia, palate deformities, inability to ingest by mouth, simian creases, and "numerous other defects and malfuntions." See Plaintiff's compl at 3.

Dyson instituted a suit against Dr. Winfield on July 23, 1997. She alleged two counts of malpractice, one on her own behalf and one on behalf of her deceased child. On January 21, 2000, after a long period of discovery, defendant filed the motions now before this Court.

ANALYSIS

As a preliminary matter, the Court notes jurisdiction under 28 U.S.C. § 1332. All defendants are citizens of states other than the District of Columbia, where the plaintiff is a citizen. The amount in controversy exceeds $ 75,000 exclusive of interest and costs. In all matters requiring the application of substantive law, the law of the District of Columbia will govern. See Erie R.R. v. Tompkins, 304 U.S. 64, 78, 82 L. Ed. 1188, 58 S. Ct. 817 (1938).

I. Standard for Summary Judgement

Federal Rule of Civil Procedure 56(c) provides that a district court shall grant summary judgment "if the pleadings, depositions, answers to interrogatories, and admissions on file, together with the affidavits, if any, show that there is (1) no genuine issue as to any material fact and that (2) the moving party is entitled to judgment as a matter of law." See Fed. R. Civ. P. 56(c); Anderson v. Liberty Lobby, Inc., 477 U.S. 242, 248, 106 S. Ct. 2505, 91 L. Ed. 2d 202 (1986); Diamond v. Atwood, 310 U.S. App. D.C. 113, 43 F.3d 1538, 1540 (D.C.Cir.1995). To survive a motion for summary judgment, the nonmovant must make a "sufficient showing to establish the existence of an element essential to that party's case." Celotex, 477 U.S. 317, 322, 106 S. Ct. 2548, 91 L. Ed. 2d 265. A "sufficient showing" exists when the evidence is such that a reasonable jury could return a verdict for the nonmovant. Anderson, 477 U.S. at 248.

II. Defendant's Motion to Exclude Plaintiff's Expert Testimony

In alleging liability, plaintiff relies on several experts. Defendant takes issue with two of these experts: Dr. Brian L. Strom and Dr. Robert F. Smith. In making his objection, defendant relies chiefly on Daubert v. Merrell Dow Pharmaceuticals and Ambrosini v. Labarraque. Also relying on these opinions, the Court disagrees with the defendant and finds the plaintiff's expert testimony admissible.

A. The Admissibility of Expert Testimony under Rule 702, Daubert and Ambrosini

1. Rule 702

The best place to start is almost always with the rule. Rule 702 states that a "witness qualified as an expert by knowledge skill, experience, training, or education may testify" if the expert's "scientific, technical, or other specialized knowledge will assist the trier of fact to understand the evidence or to determine a fact in issue." Fed. R. Evid. 702. Although the provision is now a mainstay in determining the admissibility of expert evidence, it was not always that way. Prior to the rule's adoption, and indeed for many years afterward, the admissibility of expert testimony was determined under the Frye test. See Frye v. United States, 54 App. D.C. 46, 293 F. 1013 (D.C. Cir 1923). Frye permitted expert testimony so long as the expert's methodology "was sufficiently established to have gained general acceptance" in the relevant scientific community. 293 F. at 1014. Frye's own "general acceptance," however, was displaced in an instant by Daubert v. Merrell Dow Pharmaceuticals, 509 U.S. 579, 125 L. Ed. 2d 469, 113 S. Ct. 2786 (1993).

2. Daubert v. Merrell Dow Pharmaceuticals

In Daubert, the Supreme Court held that the "Frye test was superseded by the adoption of the Federal Rules of Evidence." Daubert, 509 U.S. at 587. "A rigid 'general acceptance' standard," the Court opined "would be at odds with the 'liberal thrust' of the Federal Rules and their general approach of relaxing the traditional barriers to opinion testimony." Id. at 587 (quoting Beech Aircraft Corp. v. Rainey, 488 U.S. 153, 169, 102 L. Ed. 2d 445, 109 S. Ct. 439 (1988)).

In interpreting the requirements of Rule 702, the Court promulgated a two-pronged approach for evaluating the admissibility of expert testimony. The first prong, the "reliability" prong, focuses on evidentiary reliability and requires the district court to perform "a preliminary assessment of whether the reasoning or methodology underlying the testimony is scientifically valid." Daubert, 509 U.S. at 592-93. In illustrating this prong, the Court went onto to suggest four factors that may be used in determining scientific validity: (1) whether the theory or technique "can be (and has been) tested," (2) whether the theory or technique has been "subjected to peer review and publication," (3) the method's "known or potential rate of error," and (4) whether the theory or technique finds "general acceptance" in the "relevant scientific community." Id. at 593-94. The Court offered these factors cautiously, emphasizing that they did not comprise a "definitive checklist" because a Rule 702 inquiry is understood to be a "flexible one."[2] Id. at 594.

---

[2] 2 In the most recent Supreme Court case dealing with Rule 702,

Kumho Tire, Co. v. Carmichael, the Court affirmed its commitment to a flexible approach:

The test of reliability is 'flexible' and Daubert's list of specific factors neither necessarily nor exclusively applies to all experts or in every case. Rather the law grants a district court the same broad latitude when it decides how to

The second prong of the Daubert approach is rather straightforward. Besides being reliable, evidence must be relevant. Basing its logic on the text of Rule 702 (evidence must "assist the trier of fact"), the Court explained that "expert testimony which . . . is not relevant [is] ergo non-helpful." 509 U.S. at 591 (quoting 3 Weinstein & Berger, paragraph 702[02], at 702-18).

3. Ambrosini v. Labarraque

Although the edicts of Daubert of course control this case, a discussion of Ambrosini v. Labarraque, 322 U.S. App. D.C. 19, 101 F.3d 129 (D.C. Cir. 1996) is especially warranted in this case. Besides being the leading case on expert testimony in this circuit, Ambrosini involved testimony by one of the same experts seeking to testify in the instant case. Further, the underlying issue in Ambrosini, whether Depo-Provera caused birth defects in the plaintiff's child, is quite similar to the underlying issue in the case at hand. Thus, a short discussion of Ambrosini is in order.

In Ambrosini, Dr. Brian L. Strom intended to testify that Depo-Provera was "capable of causing the types of defects suffered by the plaintiff." 101 F.3d at 135. The defendant moved for the exclusion of this testimony on relevance grounds, asserting that the testimony failed to show that the drug did in fact cause the plaintiff's injuries, and therefore did not "fit" the needs of the jury in deciding the issue. The circuit court disagreed. It held Dr. Strom's testimony admissible because it "related to a contested issue and could aid the jury in the resolution" of the claim. The court explicitly rejected the notion that evidence should be excluded "simply because it fails to establish the causal link to a specified degree of certainty." Id. at 135. Rather, the court found the "dispositive question" to be "whether the testimony will assist the trier of fact . . . ." Id. at 135.

The court also addressed the scientific validity of Dr. Strom's methodology. Of note here is that the court found his lack of publications to be understandable, as there would be "no reason in the world" to publish a study because "Depo-Provera is no longer prescribed during pregnancy." Id. at 136. Besides Dr. Strom, Ambrosini involved the testimony of an expert who sought to testify that Depo-Provera did in fact cause the alleged injuries. Although the expert relied on many "animal, pharmacological, and human studies," he could not cite any specific study to support his conclusion.

---

determine reliability as it enjoys in respect to the ultimate reliability determination.

Kumho Tire, Co. v. Carmichael, 526 U.S. 137, 141, 143 L. Ed. 2d 238, 119 S. Ct. 1167 (1999).

Instead, "following the traditional methodology of experts in his field," the expert concluded that "there was significant data to conclude that progestins produced a significant malformation rate." Id. at 137. Finding the testimony admissible, the circuit court stated that "a cause-effect relationship need not be clearly established by . . . studies before [an expert] can testify that, in his or her opinion, such relationship exists." Id. at 138.

B. Dr. Strom's Testimony in the Instant Case

Viewing the testimony of Dr. Strom against the above precedent, this Court finds his testimony to be both reliable and relevant, rendering it admissible in the case at hand. Each aspect of his testimony will now be considered in turn.

1. Reliability

Dr. Strom seeks to testify that Provera, the drug supposedly ingested by the plaintiff, is capable of causing a wide variety of birth defects. The defendant asserts that his scientific methodology is faulty for three main reasons: (1) his opinion was formed for the purpose of litigation, (2) his opinion has not been subjected to peer review, and (3) his opinion and the means used to form the opinion, are not generally accepted in the medical community. The Court finds none of these objections persuasive.

The first objection may be disposed of quite easily. Defendant argues that the Dr. Strom's opinion is suspect because it was formed in preparation for testimony in Ambrosini v. Labarraque. This is true. It is also true that the Ambrosini court had no objection to it at the time. Further, this Court sees no reason to question Dr. Strom's scientific integrity. Dr. Strom stated in his declaration that he has testified in over 25 matters since 1994, including "many cases where his opinion was not supportive of the party presenting the case." Declaration at 3. The context in which Dr. Strom formed his opinion may be great fodder for cross examination, but it is not that for a motion to exclude.

The defendant's second objection can also be disposed of easily. The defendant argues that Dr. Strom has failed to publish his conclusions and subject them to peer review. As mentioned above, the Ambrosini court specifically addressed this issue, finding that "some scientifically valid studies may not be published because of 'too limited interest.'" Ambrosini, 101 F.3d at 137 (quoting Daubert, 509 U.S. at 593). The limited interest in Dr. Strom's opinion in Ambrosini and this case comes from the fact that Provera "is no longer prescribed during pregnancy" due to its "known effects on offspring when exposed in utero." 101 F.3d at 136-37. Repeating the Ambrosini court's declaration, "there would be 'no reason in the world' to publish his findings." Id. at 136.

Finally, the defendant asserts that Dr. Strom's opinion and the means used to form it are not generally accepted in the scientific community. First, his opinion in this case is essentially the same as his Ambrosini opinion. In both cases, Dr. Strom is of the opinion that "the studies establish a link [between Provera and] a variety of birth defects." Declaration of Strom at 3. As should be clear by now, the Ambrosini court accepted this opinion as satisfying the reliability prong of the Daubert test. Nonetheless, the defendants make much hay out of the fact that in 1992, the FDA approved the "deletion of warnings [from progestin packaging] that progestins may cause non-genital birth defects." Brief for Defendant at 21. Such an act by the FDA would seem to imply that Dr. Strom's opinion is not "generally accepted in the relevant scientific community." Daubert, 509 U.S. at 594. While such an argument is initially appealing, a closer analysis reveals its faults. First, while the FDA's disagreement with Dr. Strom is notable, it is no more notable than it was in 1996, when the Ambrosini court accepted his testimony. And it is no more notable than it was in 1995, when a federal district court in Illinois accepted a similar opinion from Dr. Strom. See Grismer v. The Upjohn Company, 1995 U.S. Dist. LEXIS 9066, 1995 WL 390053 (N.D. Ill. 1995). Further, the FDA, the alleged bellwether of the scientific community, has itself agreed, then disagreed with the position of Dr. Strom. While the FDA is no doubt an organization rich with expertise, this is not a situation that suggests to the court that Dr. Strom, by his mere disagreement with their position, is

therefore a **mad scientist**.

Regarding the scientific methodology employed by Dr. Strom, this Court has no objections. In forming his opinion, Dr. Strom reviewed "all the human studies that have been done on the teratogenicity of sex hormones, including progestins." Declaration of Strom at 3. In his declaration, he demonstrated this by critiquing many studies, both those supporting and detracting from his opinion. Id. at 4-7. There is no reason to think that this methodology, itself found acceptable to the Ambrosini court, is so devoid of the scientific method as to render it unreliable.

2. Relevance

The defendant asserts that Dr. Strom's testimony should be excluded because his testimony only shows that "Provera may cause some birth defects different from the ones suffered by [plaintiff's son]." Brief for Defendant at 18-19. Although this is a fair characterization of Dr. Strom's testimony, it is not grounds for exclusion. As the Ambrosini court stated, "evidence does not warrant exclusion simply because it fails to establish the causal link to a specified degree of probability." Ambrosini, 101 F.3d at 135. Rather "the dispositive question is whether the testimony will assist the trier of fact to understand the evidence or to determine a fact in issue." Id. (quoting Daubert, 509 U.S. at 592, and Fed. R. Evid. 702). Here, Dr. Strom's testimony can assist the trier of fact as it relates to one of the central issues of the case, whether

Provera causes birth defects. The fact that this testimony, by itself, does not show that Provera caused the specific injuries of the plaintiff's son does not make it somehow irrelevant to the jury's consideration. To hold otherwise would be to hold that all expert testimony must be independently dispositive on the issue for which it is offered, or else be excluded. The Ambrosini court specifically rejected this proposal, finding that, just because "Dr. Strom's testimony alone may be insufficient . . . to survive summary judgment does not necessarily defeat its admissibility under the fitness prong of Daubert." Ambrosini, 101 F.3d at 136.

C. Dr. Smith's Testimony

Dr. Robert L. Smith seeks to testify that "the birth defects noted in the deceased child . . . were induced by his mother's ingestion of Provera during her very early pregnancy." Declaration of Smith at 2. The defendant opposes the admissibility of this testimony, asserting that Dr. Smith is unqualified to render a medical opinion in this case, and that his scientific methodology is unreliable. The Court disagrees on both counts.

It is true that Dr. Smith is not a physician. But that does not automatically render him ineligible to testify on scientific matters pertaining to the human body. Rather, the key to qualifying him as an expert is his knowledge, not his academic degree. See Kumho Tire, 526 U.S. at 147 (holding that non-scientifically trained witnesses, such as auto mechanics, may qualify as experts under Rule 702 and Daubert). Dr. Smith describes himself as a "neuroscientist specializing in the effects of chemical exposure during pregnancy on fetal development." Declaration of Smith at 1. His curriculum vitae confirms this assertion. He is a full professor at George Mason University and is a member of the Neurobehavioral Teratology Society.[3] Dr. Smith has published extensively on subjects similar to the one at hand in this case, and has been invited to present his findings just as often. He has received substantial funding from public and private organizations, and his work has been cited by numerous physicians and non-physicians in their own studies. In short, Dr. Smith is a firmly established member of the scientific community which studies birth defects and their causes. He is thus appropriately qualified to give testimony in this case. [4]

---

[3] 3 A substance is teratogenic if it causes "developmental malformations." Webster's Ninth New Collegiate Dictionary 1216 (1990). Teratology is commonly understood as the study of the causes and prevention of human birth defects. See Brief for Plaintiff at 26.

[4] 4 Much of the defendant's objection to Dr. Smith's qualifications is predicated on his "diagnosis" of VACTERL in the plaintiff's son.

The defendant also objects to the methodology used by Dr. Smith in forming his opinion. In forming his opinion, Dr. Smith relied on the medical records in this case, numerous studies relevant to this matter, and his many years of personal experience on the subject.[5] After this research, Dr. Smith concluded that Provera is a teratogen, that there exists a biologically plausible mechanism by which Provera could cause the birth defects alleged in this case, and that there is no specific alternative causal explanation for the alleged birth defects. In commenting on his methodology, he further stated that his "analysis in this matter is consistent with conventional scientific methodology of deriving a thesis logically from confirming evidence in the absence of evidence negating the plausibility of the thesis." Declaration of Smith at 8. Given this methodology, the Court is unable to say that Dr. Smith's conclusions are not "grounded in the methods and procedures of science." Daubert, 509 U.S. at 590. Dr. Smith draws his opinion from a comprehensive review of the applicable literature, and elaborates on each step of his analysis. He also addresses studies that might seem to contradict his conclusion, stating why he believes he is still correct. Most persuasive to this Court, the Ambrosini court approved of methods which are strikingly similar to those used by Dr. Smith. Like the physician in Ambrosini, Dr. Smith also "identified [the] animal, pharmacological, and human studies that he relied on" and "followed the

---

"VACTERL" is a term used to describe the coincidence of several specific birth defects in a patient. An infant with the requisite number and type of birth defects is considered to have VACTERL. The defendant asserts that, since Dr. Smith is not a physician, he is not qualified to diagnose someone with VACTERL. The Court disagrees with this argument. To "diagnose" an infant for VACTERL, one need only compare the physcian's diagnoses of the individual birth defects to the list of defects encompassed by VACTERL. Thus, a diagnosis of VACERTL can be made by anyone who can compare lists of medical data. Any degree of expertise needed to compare the lists is undoubtedly possessed by Dr. Smith. Further, as Dr. Smith explains in his declaration, his VACTERL-based opinion is tangential to his main opinion on the causes of the birth defects in this case. Declaration of Smith at 7-8.

[5] 5 Specifically, Dr. Smith stated: "In developing an opinion for this case, I have relied heavily upon my own background knowledge of biological signaling systems. I have also examined the medical records of [the plaintiff's son], read the opinions of several other experts testifying on this case, and conducted some specific literature searches to obtain recent articles of particular relevance. I have also drawn upon a wide variety of literature I was already aware of and materials I use in my teaching." Declaration of Smith at2.

traditional methodology of experts in his field." Ambrosini, 101 F.3d at 137. Thus, Dr. Smith's procedures are not only well grounded in the scientific method, but also accepted by this circuit as meeting the first prong of Daubert.

* * *

The opinions of Drs. Strom and Smith, viewed under Rule 702, Daubert and Ambrosini, are thus admissible. The defendant's motion to exclude is therefore denied. The Court now considers the defendant's summary judgment motion.

III. Defendant's Motion for Summary Judgment Based on Inadequate

Evidence that Provera Caused the Injuries in Question
The defendant's assertion of inadequate evidence on this ground was predicated on the plaintiff's experts being excluded. As detailed above, the defendant's motion to exclude was denied, making the disposition of this motion therefore quite clear. Nonetheless, completeness demands a short explanation of the reasoning behind the decision.
The plaintiff's experts argue that Provera is capable of causing, and did in fact cause, birth defects in the plaintiff's child. As this testimony is admissible, the Court finds that there is a "genuine issue as to . . . material fact." Fed. R. Civ. P. 56(c). Accordingly, defendant's motion for summary judgment on inadequate proof that Provera caused the birth defects in question is denied.

The plaintiff alleges that the defendant rendered substandard care to her in two ways: (1) he prescribed Provera to her while she was pregnant, and (2) he failed to inform her of the risks of prenatal exposure to Provera once he knew she was pregnant. The defendant argues that neither of these assertions are supported by evidence. The Court disagrees and denies the defendant's motion.

A. Evidence of Substandard Care in Prescribing Provera
To survive the defendant's motion, the plaintiff must offer evidence sufficient for a reasonable jury to conclude that prescribing Provera to the plaintiff was substandard care. The plaintiff, through the straightforward testimony of Dr. S. James Dispenza, has satisfied this burden. In response to a question about the appropriateness of the defendant's prescription, Dr. Dispenza stated "I think [the defendant's use of Provera] is an inappropriate use of a hormone in this patient." Deposition of S. James Dispenza at 37. Later, when probed as to why, Dr. Dispenza explained that the defendant, in using a urine pregnancy test, had failed to conclusively rule out pregnancy which would make Provera

an inappropriate prescription. The following excerpt illustrates this:

Q. Within a reasonable degree of medical certainty, . . . [is it] your opinion that [the plaintiff's condition] required another type of test [besides the urine pregnancy test]?
A. Yes
Q. What test was that?
A A blood pregnancy test.

Deposition of S. James Dispenza at 38.
It is of course likely that this testimony will be contradicted by the defendant's experts. But that is not the question for the Court. Rather, as long as the evidence is sufficient for a reasonable jury to find substandard care, summary judgment is inappropriate. Dr. Dispenza's testimony clearly meets this threshold.
B. Evidence of Substandard Care in Not Informing the Plaintiff of Provera's Risks
To survive the defendant's motion, the plaintiff must produce evidence sufficient for a reasonable jury to find the defendant deviated from the standard of care in not informing the plaintiff of Provera's risks. The plaintiff has satisfied this burden.
The defendant admits that he did not inform the plaintiff of Provera's risks, but claims that he is not at fault because she failed to return for a subsequent appointment at which he was planning to apprise her of the risks. Like the above issue, the testimony of Dr. Dispenza is dispositive on the matter. Regarding the plaintiff's October 17, 1992 visit, Dr. Dispenza was asked:

Q. Do you have an opinion one way or the other whether or not it is a deviation from the standard of care for Dr. Winfield at that October 17 visit, [to] fail[] to at least apprise [the patient] of the information contained in the [Physician's Desk Reference] warning box?
A. Yes
Q. What is that opinion?
A. That it is a deviation.

Deposition of Dr. S. James Dispenza at 61.
The defendant tries to advance his summary judgment motion by using another portion of Dr. Dispenza's testimony. Prior to the above statement, Dr. Dispenza testified that the defendant did not deviate from the standard of care in failing to warn the plaintiff when she failed to keep her appointment. Deposition of Dr. S. James Dispenza at 46-47. The defendant misapprehends Dr. Dispenza's testimony. Dr. Dispenza expressed two opinions on the

defendant's failure to warn. First, according to Dr. Dispenza, the defendant deviated from the standard of care in failing to warn the plaintiff when she was in his office. Second, the defendant did not deviate from the standard of care in failing to warn to patient after she left his office. Thus, the plaintiff does have evidence that the defendant's failure to warn was substandard care. Accordingly, the defendant's summary judgment motion is denied.

V. Defendant's Motion for Summary Judgment Based on Inadequate Evidence that the Failure to Warn Caused the Child's Birth

To survive the defendant's motion, the plaintiff must offer sufficient evidence for a reasonable jury to conclude that she would have terminated her pregnancy if informed of Provera's risks. The plaintiff has met this burden. In her affidavit, she stated, "If [the defendant] had told me that there was any possibility that I could end up with a child with any sort of birth defects because of the Provera I took, I would have wanted to terminate the pregnancy." Dyson Aff. at P 4.

The defendant rightly suggests that a pertinent issue here is whether a reasonable person would terminate a pregnancy after such a warning. See Canterbury v. Spence, 150 U.S. App. D.C. 263, 464 F.2d 772 (D.C. Cir. 1972) (applying District of Columbia law). But the defendant is incorrect in asserting that the plaintiff has not presented such evidence. As this jurisdiction's leading case on physician warnings put it,

If adequate disclosure could reasonably be expected to have caused that person to decline the treatment because of the revelation of the kind of risk or danger that resulted in harm, causation is shown. . . . The patient's testimony on that score is relevant . . . .

464 F.2d at 791. The plaintiff's affidavit supplies sufficient evidence for a jury to conclude that a reasonable person would have chosen to terminate the pregnancy when properly warned. The defendant's motion is thus denied.

IV. Defendant's Motion for Dismissal of Plaintiff's Claim for Emotional Distress and Extraordinary Child Rearing Expenses

The plaintiff seeks compensation for her emotional distress and child rearing expenses. The defendant argues that such claims are not recoverable under the District of Columbia's Wrongful Death and Survival statutes. See 12 D.C. Code § 101 (1967); 16 D.C. Code § 2701 (1967). For the following reasons, the Court grants the defendant's motion to dismiss these claims.

In the District of Columbia, "if a tort results in death, two causes of action arise, one under the Survival Statue and the other under the Wrongful Death Act." Graves v. U.S., 517 F. Supp. 95, 99 (D.D.C. 1981) (citations omitted).

"Each of these causes of action has its own elements of damages." Id. (citing Runyon v. District of Columbia, 150 U.S. App. D.C. 228, 463 F.2d 1319, 1321 (D.C. Cir. 1972)). The Survival statute permits recovery for what the "deceased would have been able to recover had he lived." Graves, 517 F. Supp. at 99. The Wrongful Death Act permits a deceased's guardian or next of kin to recover for the financial loss caused to that party by the death. The claimant may recover for personal financial losses including the "reasonable expenses of last illness and burial." § 16-2701. However, a claimant "may not be compensated for [its] grief." Runyon, 463 F.2d at 1322. See also Hughes v. Pender, 391 A.2d 259 261 n.2 (D.C. 1978).

The above law makes it clear that the plaintiff may not recover for emotional distress. A slightly more difficult issue is presented, however, by her claim for child rearing expenses. It might be argued that, since her child was born with chronic birth defects which eventually led to his death, the defects lasting his whole life would constitute his "last illness" and thus permit recovery for care during this period. The Court is not convinced that such an extended interpretation is consistent with wrongful death statutory scheme. As Washington D.C.'s highest court has recognized, the Wrongful Death Act is a "derogation[] from the common law" and therefore must be "strictly construed." Waldon v. Covington, 415 A.2d 1070, 1076 n.17 (D.C. 1980) (citing Pitts v. District of Columbia, 391 A.2d 803, 807 (D.C. 1978)). The Court thus grants the defendant's motion for dismissal of the plaintiff's claims for extraordinary child rearing expenses.

VII. Defendant's Motion for Dismissal of the Plaintiff's Punitive Damages Claim

The Court is unable to understand the defendant's motion regarding punitive damages. A careful reading of the plaintiff's complaint reveals no claim for punitive damages. Thus, the defendant's motion is denied.

VIII. Defendant's Motion for Summary Judgment based of Proximate Cause and Adequacy of Warnings

This motion for summary judgment was originally filed by Dr. Winfield's co-defendant, Pharmacia & Upjohn, Inc. Dr. Winfield joined in this motion on January 11, 2000. Similar to the defendant's motion regarding punitive damages, the Court is perplexed as to the defendant's reasoning in the instant motion. The motion submitted by Pharmacia & Upjohn argues that Provera's labeling was not inadequate, and even if it was, the inadequacy did not cause the plaintiff's damages. Defendant Winfield is being sued for prescribing Provera to a pregnant woman and failing to warn her of the drug's risks. Given these claims, Pharmacia and Upjohn's motion fails to assist defendant Winfield in any way. Accordingly, the defendant's motion is denied.

CONCLUSION

In the case of Dyson v. Winfield, Civil Action No. 97-1665, it is hereby ORDERED that the defendant's motion to exclude [35-1] be DENIED; further, it is

ORDERED that the defendant's motion for summary judgment [60-1] be DENIED; further, it is

ORDERED that the defendant's motion to dismiss the plaintiff's claim for emotional distress and extraordinary child rearing expenses [57-1] be GRANTED; further, it is

ORDERED that the defendant's motion to dismiss the plaintiff's punitive damage claim [61-1] be DENIED; further, it is

ORDERED that the defendant's motion for summary judgment based on proximate cause and adequacy of warnings [59-1] be DENIED; further, the clerk is

ORDERED to correct the docket by deleting the defendant's joinder with Pharmacia & Upjohn in Pharmacia & Upjohn's motion for summary judgment on the fraud and breach of warranty counts [58-1]; further, the clerk is

ORDERED to correct the docket by adding the defendant's joinder with Pharmacia & Upjohn in Pharmacia & Upjohn's motion to dismiss the plaintiff's claim for punitive damages [61-1]; further, the clerk is

ORDERED to correct the docket by adding the defendant's joinder with Pharmacia & Upjohn in Pharmacia & Upjohn's motion to exclude the plaintiff's expert testimony [35-1].

SO ORDERED.

Date: 9-21-00

ROYCE C. LAMBERTH

UNITED STATES DISTRICT JUDGE

RHJ MEDICAL CENTER, INC.,
Plaintiff,

v.

CITY OF DUBOIS, Defendant.

Civil Action No. 3:09-131

UNITED STATES DISTRICT COURT
FOR THE WESTERN DISTRICT OF PENNSYLVANIA

754 F. Supp. 2d 723
December 6, 2010

KIM R. GIBSON, UNITED STATES DISTRICT JUDGE.

MEMORANDUM and ORDER OF COURT

This matter comes before the Court on the Defendant's Motion for Judgment on the Pleadings and Motion for a More Definite Statement (Document No. 25). Plaintiff filed a Brief in Opposition to Defendant's Motion for Judgment on the Pleadings and Motion for a More Definite Statement (Document No. 31). Defendant, without requesting leave of court, filed a Reply in Support of Its Motion for Judgment on the Pleadings and Motion for a More Definite Statement (Document No. 32). The Court DENIES Defendant's Motion for Judgment on the Pleadings and Motion for a More Definite Statement.
* * *

"This case presents the familiar conflict between the legal principle of non-discrimination and the political principle of not-in-my-backyard." New Direction Treatment Services v. City of Reading, 490 F.3d 293, 296 (3rd Cir. 2007) (Smith, J.). When an organization submits plans to open a methadone treatment facility, the story usually unfolds as follows. First, after filing the appropriate zoning paperwork, the organization begins preparation to open the facility. Second, after concerned community leaders learn of this proposal, fears of attracting drug addicts to their town generates massive opposition to the plan.[1] Third, invariably, a town meeting of some kind is held to allow

---

[1] 1 See e.g., Discovery House, Inc. v. Consolidated City of Indianapolis, 319

representatives from the methadone clinic to address community concerns. Fourth, the discussions at the town hall meeting primarily focus on the dangers that a methadone clinic poses to the municipality. Fifth, through some zoning mechanism--whether an existing zoning ordinance, or a new one which is enacted for the instant situation-- the community finds a reason why the methadone clinic should not be opened.

Although in most cases the die is cast following step two, invariably following step five, the organization is left without redress, and is effectively banned from opening a facility in the town. Tragically, the victims of exclusionary zoning tactics--recovering opiate addicts--tend to be those least prepared to fight against such tactics. Left with no other remedy, the organization files suit in court. The facts presented in this case fall neatly into this paradigm.

FACTS

RHJ Medical Center, Inc. ("RHJ") is a Pennsylvania corporation in the business of operating methadone treatment facilities. (Compl. 15-16.) RHJ opened its first methadone treatment center in 2002 in Hunker, Pennsylvania. (Compl. 16.) RHJ has met the standards for federal certification and state licensure in outpatient treatment and methadone maintenance. (Compl. 9, 15.) In February 2006, RHJ began to search for a site on which to open a methadone treatment center in the City of DuBois. (Compl. 4.) The City of DuBois ("the City") is a Third Class City covering 3.1 square miles with a population of less than 10,000. (Compl. 20; Answer 92.) The City's population consists of 55% low to middle income persons. (Answer 92.) According to RHJ, the methadone treatment center located closest to the City is in the Borough of Clearfield, 20 miles away, and has a significant waiting list. (Compl. 24.) Plaintiff reports that as a result, many of the City's residents make a daily three-hour round trip to the methadone treatment center operated by RHJ in the Borough of Vandergrift. (Compl. 25.) The City asserts that there are private physicians and other healthcare professionals within the City to provide residents with methadone treatment. (Answer 24-25.)

F.3d 277, 278 (7th Cir. 2003) ("Most people are in favor of programs that help drug addicts shake their addictions. But a lot of people also do not want drug treatment programs operating in their neighborhoods. These programs, some fear (whether the fear is rational or not is another question), will bring hoards of drug addicts, many of whom are embroiled in the criminal justice system, to "centers" that dispense one drug, methadone for instance, to the addicts who are trying to free themselves from the grip of another, more dangerous drug, like heroin.")

RHJ chose a site at 994 Beaver Drive, DuBois, Pennsylvania, 15801 ("the site"), and signed a ten-year lease on March 31, 2006. (Compl. 4, 28.) The site was zoned in the "Transitional District" and was previously occupied by an insurance agency.[2] (Compl. 4, 26.) Adjacent to the rear of the site was a sidewalk known as Beaver Meadow Walkway ("the walkway"), which was dedicated as a public park on June 25, 1979. [3] (Compl. 27; Answer 27.) By law at the time, methadone treatment centers were forbidden to operate within 500 feet of a public park unless the municipal governing body voted to authorize such use following public notice and one or more public hearings. 53 P.S. § 10621 ("Section 621").

In late September or early October of 2006, RHJ's plans to open a methadone treatment center became public. (Compl. 30; Answer 30.) RHJ asserts that they were then subjected to a wave of negative press coverage, including a radio interview in which the mayor of DuBois stated that RHJ would likely not receive approval from the City to open such a facility and compared having a methadone treatment center in the City to "other cities dumping their garbage in DuBois." [4] (Compl. 31.)

At a work session on October 19, 2006, the DuBois City Council authorized the City Solicitor to draft a letter to RHJ "to advise them that if they still plan[ed] on opening their Center at 994 Beaver Drive, they need[ed] to follow all procedures, including Public Hearings and to remind them that they [we]re

---

[2] 2 The nature of the occupancy permit for the site is a matter of dispute between the parties. RHJ asserts that the existing permit allowed use for a medical facility and that this was confirmed by an unidentified City inspector. (Compl. 26.) The City states that a change of use would not have been permissible under the permit and cites as evidence the fact that the site is now occupied by another insurance agency. (Answer 26.)

[3] 3 RHJ states that they did not know the sidewalk was part of the public park system. (Compl. 27.) The City avers that RHJ knew or should have known that the sidewalk was a public park based on the fact that the City was using state and federal funds to maintain the sidewalk, which was in continuous use by the public. (Answer 27.) In its communications with RHJ, the City specifically cited a $51,000 grant from the Pennsylvania Department of Conservation and Natural Resources Community Conservation Partnerships Program in 2005. (Def.'s Ex. 2.)

[4] 4 The City denies that such an interview ever took place. (Answer 31.) Whether this interview took place would seem to be an important fact with respect to showing animus in the substantive due process analysis.

still too close to a recreational park (walkway)." [5] (Def.'s Ex. 1; Compl. 32; Answer 32.) A copy of this letter (Def.'s Ex. 2) was distributed at a City Council meeting on October 23, 2006, (Compl. 33) and also mailed to RHJ on that date (Answer 33). RHJ opened the methadone treatment center as planned two days later, on October 25, 2006. (Compl. 34.)

The City filed suit in the Clearfield County Court of Common Pleas on October 27, 2006, to enjoin RHJ from operating the methadone treatment facility at the site pursuant to Section 621. (Compl. 35; Answer 35.) The court granted the City a preliminary injunction with a continuance hearing scheduled for November 1, 2006. (Pl.'s Ex. 1.) The parties disagree as to whether or not the court heard oral argument from both sides before granting the injunction. RHJ says it did not (Compl. 35), while the City says that it did (Answer 35). The hearing was postponed to December 7, 2006. (Answer 35.) At that time, RHJ stipulated that the walkway was a public park within the meaning of Section 621 and that they had not obtained a certificate of use from the City before opening the clinic; and the court granted a permanent injunction until such time as the City approved RHJ's application following a public hearing and granted a certificate of use. (Def's Ex. 3; Compl. 35; Answer 35.)

In January of 2007, RHJ submitted to the City an application for a public hearing and a request for certificate of use.[6] (Compl. 36; Answer 36.) The City provided notice to surrounding property owners, and a public hearing was held on April 23, 2007. (Compl. 37; Answer 37.) At a public meeting on May 14, 2007, the City Council voted unanimously to deny RHJ's application and directed the City Solicitor to prepare a document of findings of fact and conclusions of law to support the decision. (Answer 38.) The Solicitor's document was unanimously adopted at the public City Council meeting on May 29, 2007 and was served on RHJ on June 1, 2007. (Answer 38; Def.'s Ex.

---

[5] 5 According to the City, this action was taken in response to an appearance by "agents and employees of RHJ" at the October 9, 2006, City Council meeting, at which they "refused to answer any questions concerning the proposed use of the facility." (Answer 32.) RHJ does not mention any such meeting and asserts that the letter was drafted as a result of the negative press the center was receiving. (Compl. 32.)

[6] RHJ asserts that they filed their application on January 9, 2007. (Compl. 36.) The City states that the application was first filed on January 11, 2007, but that RHJ failed to pay the necessary fee for a public hearing until January 29, 2007, at which time the application was deemed complete. (Answer 36.)

4, 5.) The finding of the City Council was that RHJ had not presented evidence sufficient to justify deviating from the restrictions of Section 621. (Def's Ex. 5 at 6.) The concerns of the Council included the methadone treatment center's lack of on-site security personnel, lack of means to transport patients to the regional medical facility if necessary, and insufficient parking for the expected number of patients and staff. (Def. Ex. 5 at 4-5.) The Council also noted that RHJ had not performed "any need assessment to determine whether its center was needed in the area and had no statistics concerning area drug use." (Def. Ex. 5 at 5.)

On June 15, 2007, the Third Circuit Court of Appeals ruled that § 621 violated the Americans With Disabilities Act ("ADA"), 42 U.S.C. §§ 12101, et seq., and the Rehabilitation Act ("RA"), 29 U.S.C. §§ 701, et seq. New Directions Treatment Services v. City of Reading, 490 F.3d 293 (3d Cir. 2007). RHJ moved to dissolve the Clearfield County Court of Common Pleas injunction in November 2007, based on New Directions. (Compl. 43.) The City opposed this motion. Id. The motion was granted and the injunction dissolved on March 6, 2008. [7] (Pl.'s Ex. 3.) According to RHJ, at that time, the City refused to reconsider the earlier decision to deny the methadone treatment center a certificate of use. (Compl. 44.) The City responded that RHJ did not make any further petition to the City for any permits. (Answer 44.)

Also following the Third Circuit decision in New Directions, at a November 21, 2007, work session, the City Council heard first reading of Ordinance Number 1720, which amended City zoning in a number of ways, including prohibiting "methadone or drug treatment clinics or centers" in the "Transitional District" and permitting medical facilities "with the exception of methadone treatment facilities and other drug treatment facilities of any kind" in the "Commercial-Highway Zoning District." (Pl.'s Ex. 4.) Ordinance Number 1720 also amended City zoning to expressly permit "drug treatment clinics or facilities including methadone treatment facilities or clinics" in the "O-1 Office District." [8] (Pl.'s Ex. 4.) The ordinance passed after a second

---

[7] 7 RHJ states that the City opposed its motion to dissolve the injunction. The City claims that it advised the court in that action that it did not oppose such a motion, but "only pointed out that a request to dissolve an injunction issued to prevent disobedience of a municipality's regulations is not a substitute for a land use appeal." (Answer 44.)

[8] 8 According to RHJ, there are no sites available in the "O-1 Office District" suitable for housing a methadone treatment center. (Compl. 45.) The City

reading at the City Council meeting on November 27, 2007.[9] (Pl.'s Ex. 4; Compl. 45; Answer 45.) In July 2008, RHJ terminated its lease on the site. (Compl. 44.)

Plaintiff filed a six-count complaint against Defendant. Count I asserts a violation of the Fourteenth Amendment's Due Process and Equal Protection Clauses for Defendant's actions under 53 P.S. § 10621. Count II asserts a claim under the Rehabilitation Act for Defendant's actions under 53 P.S. § 10621. Count III asserts a claim under Title II of the ADA for Defendant's actions under 53 P.S. § 10621. Count IV asserts a violation of the Fourteenth Amendment's Due Process and Equal Protection Clauses for Defendant's actions under its new zoning ordinance. Count V asserts a claim under the Rehabilitation Act for Defendant's actions under its new zoning ordinance. Count VI asserts a claim under Title II of the ADA for Defendant's actions under its new zoning ordinance.

Defendant makes six claims why judgment should be entered based on the pleadings. First, Plaintiff lacks standing. Second, Plaintiff is barred by res judicata from asserting Counts I-III. Third, Plaintiff is estopped from raising Counts I-III due to waiver. Fourth, Defendant is immune from actions taken in accordance with a court order. Fifth, the Court should not impose an equitable remedy--to do so would infringe on principles of federalism. Sixth, Plaintiff is barred by the statute of limitations. All six of Defendant's claims fail, and its motion is denied. Defendant's motion for a more definite statement is also denied.

STANDARD OF REVIEW

Defendant filed a motion for judgment on the pleadings. FED. R. CIV. P. 12(c) ("After the pleadings are closed but within such time as not to delay the trial, any party may move for judgment on the pleadings.") In the past, a motion for judgment on the pleadings under FED. R. CIV. P. 12(c) was

---

claims that there are such suitable sites and points out that the DuBois Regional Medical Center and many doctors offices are currently located in the "O-1 Office District." (Answer 45.) This seems to be a disputed issue of an important fact.

[9] 9 RHJ claims that the amendments were proposed in response to inquiries from RHJ as to filing an application for a Change of Use certificate to locate the methadone treatment center at an alternate site in the "Transitional District." (Compl. 45.) According to the City, no such conversations took place before or after the adoption of the ordinance. (Answer 45.)

analyzed under the same standard as a 12(b)(6) motion, wherein the Court must "accept as true all allegations in the complaint and all reasonable inferences that can be drawn therefrom, and view them in the light most favorable to the non-moving party." Mele v. Fed. Reserve Bank, 359 F.3d 251, 253 (3d Cir. 2004); Rocks v. City of Philadelphia, 868 F.2d 644, 645 (3d Cir. 1989); D.P. Enters., Inc. v. Bucks County Cmty. Coll., 725 F.2d 943 (3d Cir. 1984).

That was the standard. No longer. There is a "new sheriff in town" now policing FED. R. CIV. P. 12(c), and his name is "Twiqbal." Bell Atlantic Corporation v. Twombly, 550 U.S. 544, 127 S. Ct. 1955, 167 L. Ed. 2d 929 (2007), and Ashcroft v. Iqbal, 129 S.Ct. 1937, 173 L. Ed. 2d 868 (2009), or Twiqbal as they are commonly known, have caused a sea change in federal pleading standards.[10] In Iqbal, the Supreme Court "provide[d] the final nail-in-the-coffin for the 'no set of facts' standard"[11] derived from Conley v.

---

[10] 10 See Moss v. U.S. Secret Service, 572 F.3d 962, 972 (9th Cir. 2009) (Twombly's plausibility standard was "a significant change, with broad-reaching implications"); Phillips v. Cty. of Allegheny, 515 F.3d 224, 230 (3d Cir. 2008) ("Few issues in civil procedure jurisprudence are more significant than pleading standards, which are the key that opens access to courts."); The Evolution Of A New Pleading Standard: Ashcroft v. Iqbal, 88 OREGON. L. REV. 1053 (2009) ("Iqbal thus represents a logical progression in the march toward greater judicial scrutiny at the outset of the litigation to avoid the inefficiencies and burdens that may be imposed on defendants later in the process."); Robert G. Bone, Twombly, Pleading Rules, and the Regulation of Court Access, 94 IOWA L. REV. 873, 875 (2009) ("Many judges and academic commentators read the decision as overturning fifty years of generous notice pleading practice, and critics attack it as a sharp departure from the 'liberal ethos' of the Federal Rules, favoring decisions 'on the merits, by jury trial, after full disclosure through discovery."); Edward D. Cavanagh, Twombly, the Federal Rules of Civil Procedure and the Courts, 82 ST. JOHN'S L. REV. 877, 878-79 (2008) (arguing that Twombly changed the law "dramatically", "put[ting] an end to notice pleading as it has been understood in the seventy years since the enactment of the Federal Rules of Civil Procedure"); Robert L. Rothman, Twombly and Iqbal: A License to Dismiss, 35 No. 3 LITIGATION 1, 2 (2009) (arguing that "Iqbal drastically changed the landscape for Rule 12(b)(6) motions.").

[11] 11 Fowler v. UPMC Shadyside, 578 F.3d 203 (3rd Cir. 2009). See also, Courie v. Alcoa Wheel & Forged Prods., 577 F.3d 625, 2009 WL 2497928, at *2 (6th Cir. 2009) (the Supreme Court's decision in Iqbal "raised the bar for pleading requirements beyond the old 'no-set-of-facts' standard of Conley v.

Gibson[12]. Following Iqbal, conclusory or "bare-bones" complaints will not survive a motion to dismiss: "threadbare recitals of the elements of a cause of action, supported by mere conclusory statements, do not suffice." Iqbal, 129 S.Ct. at 1949.

Under Twombly and Iqbal, in order to survive a motion to dismiss, a plaintiff's complaint must "contain sufficient factual matter, accepted as true, to 'state a claim to relief that is plausible on its face.'" Iqbal, quoting Twombly at 570. In Iqbal, Justice Kennedy writing for the majority, concluded that a claim has "facial plausibility when the plaintiff pleads factual content that allows the court to draw the reasonable inference that the defendant is liable for the misconduct alleged." Iqbal, citing Twombly at 556. "The Supreme Court's ruling in Iqbal emphasizes that a plaintiff must show that the allegations of his or her complaints are plausible." Fowler v. UPMC Shadyside, 578 F.3d 203 (3rd Cir. 2009). Following Iqbal, the District Court must dismiss a complaint that pleads facts that are "merely consistent with" a defendant's liability, if the complaint "stops short of the line between possibility and plausibility of 'entitlement to relief.'" Iqbal, quoting Twombly, at 557.

In Fowler v. UPMC Shadyside, 578 F.3d 203 (3rd Cir. 2009), the Third Circuit provided the test district courts should apply when considering a motion to dismiss under Iqbal:

Therefore, after Iqbal, when presented with a motion to dismiss for failure to state a claim, district courts should conduct a two-part analysis. First, the factual and legal elements of a claim should be separated. The District Court must accept all of the complaint's well-pleaded facts as true, but may disregard any legal conclusions. Iqbal at 1949. Second, a District Court must then determine whether the facts alleged in the complaint are sufficient to show that the plaintiff has a "plausible claim for relief." Id. at 1950. In other words, a complaint must do more than allege the plaintiff's entitlement to relief. A complaint has to "show" such an entitlement with its facts. See Phillips, 515 F.3d at 234-35. As the Supreme Court instructed in Iqbal, "[w]here the well-pleaded facts do not permit the court to infer more than the mere possibility of misconduct, the complaint has alleged-but it has not 'show[n]'-'that the

---

Gibson, 355 U.S. 41, 78 S. Ct. 99, 2 L. Ed. 2d 80 (1957)").

[12] 12 Conley v. Gibson, 355 U.S. 41, 78 S. Ct. 99, 2 L. Ed. 2d 80 (1957) (permitting district courts to dismiss a complaint for failure to state a claim only if "it appear[ed] beyond doubt that the plaintiff can prove no set of facts in support of his claim which would entitle him to relief.").

pleader is entitled to relief.'" Iqbal, 129 S.Ct. at 1949. This "plausibility" determination will be "a context-specific task that requires the reviewing court to draw on its judicial experience and common sense." Id. Fowler, at 210-211.

While the Third Circuit has not definitively resolved this issue, a number of district courts within the Third Circuit,[13] as well as other Courts of Appeals[14] have applied the Iqbal standard to motions filed under FED. R. CIV. P. 12(c). This Court is inclined to agree, though this decision will have several consequences that may not have been discussed elsewhere. For decades, granting a motion for judgment on the pleadings was only appropriate where the movant "clearly establishes that no material issue of fact remains to be resolved and that he is entitled to judgment as a matter of law." Jablonski v. Pan Am. World Airways, Inc., 863 F.2d 289, 290 (3d Cir. 1988) (citing Society Hill Civic Assoc. v. Harris, 632 F.2d 1045, 1054 (3d Cir. 1980)). Generally, federal courts were reluctant to grant a Rule 12(c) Motion for Judgment on the Pleadings, because it provides for summary disposition of a party's claim on the merits before discovery. See Cardio-Med Assoc. v. Crozer-Chester Med. Ctr., 536 F.Supp. 1065, 1072 (E.D.Pa. 1982); Southmark Prime Plus, L.P. v. Falzone, 776 F.Supp. 888, 891 (D.Del. 1991).

These prior standards mirrored the previous notice pleading standard articulated in Conley v. Gibson, 355 U.S. 41, 78 S. Ct. 99, 2 L. Ed. 2d 80 (1957)--but Iqbal changed the game. No longer are cases dismissed only if "plaintiff can prove no set of facts in support of his claim," but rather a viable complaint must "contain sufficient factual matter, accepted as true, to 'state a claim to relief that is plausible on its face.'" Iqbal, quoting Twombly at 570. Iqbal effected not only motions to dismiss, but has also impacted motions for judgments on the pleading, and imported the higher burden of "plausibility."
Applying the Iqbal standard will likely make it tougher for complaints to survive motions under FED. R. CIV. P. 12(c). Yet, to do otherwise would frustrate Iqbal. In many cases, motions filed under FED. R. CIV. P. 12(c) and

---

[13] 13 See Gray Holdco. Inc. v. Cassady, Civil No. 09-1519, 2010 U.S. Dist. LEXIS 65055 (W.D. Pa. June 30, 2010), Onconome, Inc. v. Univ. of Pittsburgh, Civil No. 09-1195, 2010 U.S. Dist. LEXIS 27304 (W.D. Pa. Mar. 23, 2010), Boretsky v. Corzine, Civil No. 08-2265 (GEB), 2010 U.S. Dist. LEXIS 13149 (D.N.J. Feb. 16, 2010).

[14] 14 See Hayden v. Paterson, 594 F.3d 150, 160-61 (2d Cir. 2010), Johnson v. Rowley, 569 F.3d 40, 43-44 (2d Cir. 2009), Hole v. Tex. A&M Univ.,360 Fed. Appx. 571, 573 (5th Cir. 2010).

12(b)(6) are complimentary and largely interchangeable--the key difference being that the right to file motions under FED. R. CIV. P. 12(b)(6) is waived if an answer is filed. A plaintiff should not be able to benefit from a weaker standard and higher probability of success under FED. R. CIV. P. 12(c) than he would under FED. R. CIV. P. 12(b)(6). The burden of proof on the Plaintiff should increase at each stage of litigation. If the Plaintiff bears the higher "plausibility" standard to challenge a motion to dismiss, a lower standard should not apply later if a motion for judgment on the pleadings is subsequently filed.

If different standards were to apply, defendants attempting to have cases dismissed may cease to rely on the less strict standard for FED. R. CIV. P. 12(c)--which would have a lower probability of success--and proceed to file motions for summary judgment. Motions for summary judgment are significantly more time consuming and cumbersome than motions for judgment on the pleadings. This additional litigation step would in turn serve to increase costs and frustrate judicial economy in cases which could have been resolved at the motion for judgment on the pleadings stage. Imposing the "plausibility" standard for FED. R. CIV. P. 12(c) helps to maintain the status quo--as much as possible following the changes posed by Iqbal--and avoid unnecessarily nudging cases towards summary judgment when a motion for judgment on the pleadings would suffice.

Iqbal has also impacted the manner in which courts must assess subject matter jurisdiction, even when considering a motion for judgment on the pleadings. Historically, when considering whether to dismiss a case for lack of subject matter jurisdiction under FED. R. CIV. P. 12(b)(1), the Court generally "must accept the allegations in the complaint as true and determine whether they are sufficient to invoke its jurisdiction." Common Cause of Pa. v. Pennsylvania, 558 F.3d 249, 257 (3d Cir. 2009). See also, McNutt v. Gen. Motors Acceptance Corp., 298 U.S. 178, 189, 56 S. Ct. 780, 80 L. Ed. 1135 (1936); McNabb v. United States, 54 Fed.Cl. 759, 763 (2002) (If a defendant or the court challenges jurisdiction[,] . . . the plaintiff cannot rely merely on allegations in the complaint, but must instead bring forth relevant, competent proof to establish jurisdiction."). Now, the Plaintiff "has the burden of establishing that subject matter jurisdiction exists within the parameters of the 'plausibility' standard established by and when confronted with Defendant's 12(b)(1) motion to dismiss." Sanchez v. United States, 707 F. Supp. 2d 216, 2010 WL 1626118 (D.P.R. 2010). If a Defendant challenges subject matter jurisdiction in a motion to dismiss or a motion for judgment on the pleadings, or if the court raises this issue sua sponte, FED. R. CIV. P. 12(h)(3) ("If the court determines at any time that it lacks jurisdiction, the court must dismiss the action."), the Court should apply the standard recognized in Sanchez.

ANALYSIS

I. Standing

In order to obtain standing, Plaintiff must traverse a jurisdictional labyrinth that would make Daedalus envious. In this case, the Minotaur takes not the form of part-man and part-bull, but rather coalesces from an amalgam of complex jurisdictional questions--determining attenuated third party standing, finding whether an association is imminent under Article III, identifying whether prospective patients suffer from a qualified disability, and answering whether associational standing warrants equitable and compensatory relief. This chimeral conundrum is exacerbated by two decades of precedents that have not fully addressed the constitutional limitations on adjudication for associational standing. This memorandum will address how these issues have swirled together into a jurisprudential maelstrom, and perhaps, to some degree, calm the waters and provide some clarity in a confounding area of the law.

The labyrinth in this case winds as follows. First, in order to avail itself of the protections of the ADA and RA, Plaintiff must establish third party standing by showing an "association" with an individual with a disability. In this case, because no disabled persons were joined in the case or even identified in the complaint, Plaintiff can only receive standing based on a relationship or association with a patient.

Second, because Plaintiff was unable to open up the methadone clinic, it was unable to service any patients. Any patients could only be prospective. Nonetheless, our precedents have construed the ADA and RA as evincing Congress's intent to grant third party standing to entities that have a prospective association with disabled persons.

Third, Plaintiff--which never actually opened the methadone clinic due to the city's zoning decision--must show that the opening of the clinic and admittance of patients was "imminent." Associational standing notwithstanding, this court could not take cognizance of a fledgling clinic that has not taken enough steps towards establishing the requisite association, lest our jurisdiction traverse the boundaries of Article III. In this case, because Plaintiff took sufficient steps towards opening its doors for business, the opening of the clinic is considered imminent, and Article III standing is satisfied.

Fourth, even if the prospective patient suffers from a disability per se, Plaintiff must resolve a statutory Gordian knot and show that a curious "carve out" exemption--aimed at allowing employers to discharge employees with drug addictions--is inapplicable in the context of methadone clinics. Congress provided for an exemption for patients, separate from employees, engaging in drug treatment programs--even if those individuals have a current drug addiction.

Fifth, even if the requisite association is established, and the opening of the clinic is imminent, Plaintiff must prove that the prospective patients--none of whom have been ascertained--would be protected by the ADA or RA. Merely having an impairment, such as an opioid addiction is inadequate; rather, the disability must substantially impact a major life activity. The Supreme Court's precedents dictate that inquiries into a person's disabilities must be an individualized present examination. This would seem to render generalized prospective examinations--the approach several other courts have undertaken--a Sisyphean task. Yet in this case, the Court finds that a serious opioid addiction that warrants admission to a methadone clinic, with the attendant daily disruptions of life activities in order to obtain the treatment, could satisfy this test. This finding would obviate the need for an individualized, fact intensive inquiry.

Sixth, if Plaintiff shows an "association" with an individual with a disability who is protected by the ADA and RA, exemptions notwithstanding, Plaintiff must show that it, RHJ--and not any associated disabled patients--was injured in violation of the ADA and RA. How can an entity be discriminated against by a statute aimed at protecting individuals with disabilities? This counterintuitive standard seems to be in tension with the text of the statute, but comports with subsequent guidance from the DOJ and relevant precedents from some--but not all--Circuits. If Plaintiff shows that it was discriminated against, standing is established in order to bring suit.

Seventh, even if the Plaintiff shows it was injured in violation of the ADA and RA, and can bring suit, the question remains whether standing exists for equitable relief as well for compensatory damages. Associational standing exists to grant third parties the right to sue on behalf of others. The benefit of such litigation should inure to the benefit of those aggrieved. Generally speaking, the third party is not the aggrieved party. Rather, the third party is suing on behalf of wronged individuals. Thus, equitable relief--ordering a city to issue a zoning permit, for example--would seem to be an appropriate remedy. In contrast, compensatory damages--lost profits, for example--would not directly benefit wronged disabled persons. For claims of damages, the Court considers whether the third party itself--and not aggrieved individuals--was injured. In such situations, compensatory damages would be appropriate because the benefit would inure to the injured party--the entity--regardless whether any individuals are actually injured.

* * *

The Court finds that the Plaintiff meets all of these requirements, and after a journey worthy of Theseus through the heart of the labyrinth, the Minotaur is slain, and the Plaintiff remains in federal court, with standing to proceed on all of its claims.

a. ADA and RA Grant Third Party Standing

The Court starts from first principles. The objects to which "the judicial authority of the union ought to extend to" are enumerated in Article III of our Constitution. Federalist No. 80 (Hamilton). The bounds of the judicial power are limited to Article III's "cases" and "controversies." Lujan, at 560. The "cases" and "controversies" requirements "serve to identify those disputes which are appropriately resolved through the judicial process," Lujan, at 560 citing Whitmore v. Arkansas, 495 U.S. 149, 155, 110 S. Ct. 1717, 109 L. Ed. 2d 135 (1990). While some of the elements of standing "express merely prudential considerations that are part of judicial self-government, the core component of standing is an essential and unchanging part of the case-or-controversy requirement of Article III." Lujan, at 560 citing Allen v. Wright, 468 U.S. 737, 751, 104 S. Ct. 3315, 82 L. Ed. 2d 556 (1984).

Generally, a "plaintiff. . . must assert his own legal rights and interests, and cannot rest his claim to relief on the legal rights or interests of third parties." Warth v. Seldin, 422 U.S. 490, 499, 95 S. Ct. 2197, 45 L. Ed. 2d 343 (1975) (citations omitted). However, "Congress may grant an express right of action to persons who otherwise would be barred by prudential standing rules." Id. at 501. In certain cases, standing may exist because of statutorily created rights: "[T]he standing question in such cases is whether the constitutional or statutory provision on which the claim rests properly can be understood as granting persons in the plaintiff's position a right to judicial relief." Warth, at 500. Where Congress grants a right of action to an entity or association, the entity may assert standing either in its own right or on behalf of its members. Warth, at 511.

A]n association has standing to bring suit on behalf of its members when: (a) its members would otherwise have standing to sue in their own right; (b) the interests it seeks to protect are germane to the organization's purpose; and (c) neither the claim asserted nor the relief requested requires the participation of individual members in the lawsuit. Hunt v. Washington State Apple Adver. Comm'n, 432 U.S. 333, 343, 97 S. Ct. 2434, 53 L. Ed. 2d 383 (1977).

The ADA and RA are statutes in which Congress has granted third party standing. The regulation implementing Title II of the ADA provides, "A public entity shall not exclude or otherwise deny equal services, programs, or activities to an individual or entity because of the known disability of an individual with whom the individual or entity is known to have a relationship or association." 28 C.F.R. § 35.130(g) (emphasis added). This provision establishes the basis for associational standing. The "prudential limits imposed in pure associational standing cases do not apply to" statutory grants of associational standing. Addiction Specialists, 411 F.3d 399, 407 (3rd Cir.

2005). This broad conception of standing does indeed "extend standing to the full limits of Article III." Id. So "long as this requirement [of Article III] is satisfied, persons to whom Congress has granted a right of action, either expressly or by clear implication, may have standing to seek relief on the basis of the legal rights and interests of others, and indeed, may invoke the general public interest in support of their claim." Warth, 422 U.S. at 501.

In Addiction Specialists, the plaintiff was denied a permit to open a methadone clinic, and sought a declaration that the city's denial of the permit violated the ADA and RA. Addiction Specialists, Inc., v. The Township of Hamilton, El Al., 1:04-CV-696 (W.D.P.A. Sept. 8, 2004). Relying on 28 C.F.R. § 35.130(g)--which provides "A public entity shall not exclude or otherwise deny equal services, programs, or activities to an individual or entity because of the known disability of an individual with whom the individual or entity is known to have a relationship or association"--the Third Circuit held that a methadone clinic could bring suit on its own behalf. Addiction Specialists, 411 F.3d 399 (3rd Cir. 2005). The Court expressly rejected the Seventh Circuit's holding to the contrary in Discovery House, which held a methadone clinic could not sue for damages on its own behalf under the ADA and RA. Id. citing Discovery House, 319 F.3d 277 (7th Cir. 2003).

The Third Circuit found that the Seventh Circuit test "ignores that the protections of the ADA and RA have been extended to shield entities themselves from discrimination." Addiction Specialists, at 407 (emphasis added). The court noted that "[a]lthough ASI ["Addiction Specialists"] is protected by these statutes only by virtue of its association with disabled individuals, ASI's standing to sue arises from its own alleged injuries, not those of its clients." Addiction Specialists, at 407 (emphasis added). The broad remedial purposes underlying the ADA and the RA do not limit relief to "qualified individuals with disabilities." Addiction Specialists, at 405 (citing MX Group, Inc. v. City of Covington, 293 F.3d 326, 334-35 (6th Cir. 2002); Innovative Health Sys., Inc. v. City of White Plains, 117 F.3d 37, 47 (2nd Cir. 1997)). Rather, the protections of the ADA are not limited to actual persons, as "any person," has been interpreted to include "individuals as well as entities." Addiction Specialists, at 406. The Third Circuit "has conclusively settled that the proprietors of a proposed methadone clinic have standing to seek relief both on their own behalf and on behalf of their clients under the ADA and Rehabilitation Act." New Directions, at 300 citing (Addiction Specialists 411 F.3d 399, 405-408 (3rd Cir. 2005)).

The Third Circuit noted that the Discovery House court "assumes that an entity bringing suit under the ADA and RA must necessarily assert the rights of its members rather than bringing suit 'in its own right.'" Addiction Specialists, at 407 citing (Discovery House, 319 F.3d 277 (7th Cir. 2003)). This rule is premised on the questionable assumption that a methadone clinic "has a claim to standing under the ADA and RA only because it runs a business which provides services--like dispersing methadone--to persons presumably covered by those Acts." Discovery House, at 280 (emphasis added). The Seventh Circuit postulated that if the plaintiff "were running a plumbing business, it could hardly claim relief under either statute." Discovery House, at 281.

This "provide services" rationale seems to conflict with the guidance given in the Department of Justice's Technical Assistance Manual, the creation of which was mandated by an act of Congress. When drafting the ADA, Congress delegated to the Attorney General the responsibility to "render technical assistance to individuals and institutions" affected by the ADA in order to provide guidance to this, and other regulations in the ADA. 42 U.S.C. § 12206(c)(1). Under this authority, the Department of Justice issued the Title II Technical Assistance Manual, which aimed to "assist individuals and entities in understanding their rights and duties under the Act." The Americans with Disabilities Act, Title II Technical Assistance Manual, http://www.ada.gov/taman2.html.

Section II-3.9000, titled "Discrimination on the basis of association," provides an interpretation of 28 C.F.R. § 35.130(g[15])--the provision the courts interpreted in Addiction Specialists and Discovery House: "In addition to familial relationships, the prohibition covers any type of association between the individual or entity that is discriminated against and the individual or individuals with disabilities, if the discrimination is actually based on the disability." Id. As long as the discrimination is based on a disability, any type of association suffices to grant third party standing. Illustration 2 in the Manual illustrates this concept: "[a] local government could not refuse to allow a theater company to use a school auditorium on the grounds that the company has recently performed at an HIV hospice." Id. As the Sixth Circuit remarked, "the theater company would have a right of action because of the wrong done to it." MX, at 335. Simply put, as long as the theater company had an "association" with disabled HIV hospice patients, even though none of the patients were injured or discriminated against, the theater company was wronged, and had standing to sue.

Contrary to the assertions of the Discovery House court, the entity need not "provide services" to disabled persons in order to obtain standing. A

---

[15] 15 28 C.F.R. § 35.130(g) ("A public entity shall not exclude or otherwise deny equal services, programs, or activities to an individual or entity because of the known disability of an individual with whom the individual or entity is known to have a relationship or association").

plumbing business, like a theater company, would be able to receive protection under the ADA. Accordingly, the Third Circuit rejected the standard from the Seventh Circuit which held that a methadone clinic has standing "only because it provides services . . . to persons covered by those Acts." Addiction Specialists, at 407 citing Discovery House at 281 (emphasis added). If a plumbing business performed sewage work for a home of disabled persons, and a local government decided not to hire that plumbing business because of its association with disabled persons, under the Third Circuit and Technical Assistance Manual's understanding of the law, the plumbing business would have been injured by loss of profits, and have standing under the ADA. Through the ADA and RA, Congress has allowed an entity, such as a methadone clinic, to assert standing on behalf of a disabled third party.

b. An "Association" with a Prospective Patient Generates Third Party Standing

A methadone clinic has third party standing if it has an association with disabled patients. The plain text of the statute permits entities to bring suit on behalf of disabled individuals with whom they have an "association." 28 C.F.R. § 35.130(g). This much is clear. What is unclear, however, is whether a methadone clinic that never opened--and thus never treated any actual patients--can claim standing based on a prospective association. The definition of "association," and whether the association can be prospective, presents several wrinkles.

In this case Plaintiff did not join any patients in the suit, and did not name any patients-- current or prospective--in the complaint.[16] Plaintiff provided no details as to who would frequent the clinic beyond conclusory allegations that they intended to "provide comprehensive, medically supervised and licensed outpatient methadone treatment directed at rehabilitating persons living in DuBois and its surrounding community who require the treatment to alleviate their opiate dependency." Elsewhere Plaintiff noted that "RHJ targets clients with a primary dependence on opiates."

Defendant asserts that Plaintiff has not demonstrated the requisite "relationship or association" with any disabled individuals under the ADA or RA. Defendant notes that Plaintiff has not named a single patient in the

---

[16] 16 In a footnote in its reply brief, Plaintiff remarked that prior to the issuance of the temporary injunction, it had "approximately ten clients." However, this clientele was not mentioned in the Complaint, and is not considered in this opinion. (Pl.'s Repl. p. 7 n, 3.)

caption of the complaint and only refers to "prospective patients," Plaintiff counters that it has standing to assert a claim under the ADA or the RA even if the entity's relationship with the disabled individual is "purely prospective." Addiction Specialists presented a fact pattern similar to the instant case. Addiction Specialists v. Township of Hampton, 411 F.3d 399 (3rd Cir. 2005). ASI ("Addiction Specialists Incorporated") sought to open a methadone treatment facility in the Township of Hampton, Pennsylvania ("Township"). Id. at 403. ASI entered into a lease for a property in Hampton and submitted a "Change of Use Application" with the Township. While the proposed location of the clinic was zoned as "highway commercial district"--which permitted drug stores, hospitals, medical offices and clinics--at the time Pennsylvania law treated methadone clinics differently from other medical facilities. Id. at 403. The Municipalities Planning Code ("MPC") prohibited the establishment of methadone clinics--but not other types of medical clinics-- "within 500 feet of an existing school, public playground, public park, residential housing area, child-care facility, church, meetinghouse or other actual place of regularly stated religious worship . . . ." Id. citing MPC § 621 (codified at 53 P.S. § 10621) ["§621"].

At first, the Township granted ASI's permit. Id. However, one week later, the Township informed ASI that there was a "problem" involving their proposed facility. Id. After a hearing-- where a number of Township officials and residents expressed their opposition to the establishment of a methadone treatment facility in Hampton--the Township found that the subject property was within 500 feet of a school and a public park and therefore rescinded its approval of ASI's permit. Id. The Township found that a travel agency located next door to the subject property--which offered on-site training to students enrolled in a travel and tourism class at the Community College of Allegheny County--qualified as a "school" within the meaning of § 621. Id. The Township also determined that the "Depreciation Lands Museum" was a "public park" within the meaning of § 621. Id.

ASI filed an appeal from the Township's zoning decision with the Court of Common Pleas of Allegheny County, alleging that "the Township acted arbitrarily and capriciously and abused its discretion by determining that the travel agency qualified as a school and that the museum qualified as a public park" Id. at 405. Additionally, ASI alleged that the denial of access to health services that ASI would provide to disabled individuals constituted unlawful discrimination under the "Pennsylvania Human Relations Act ("PHRA"), 43 P.S. §§ 952, et seq.; the Americans With Disabilities Act ("ADA"), 42 U.S.C. §§ 12101, et seq.; and the Rehabilitation Act ("RA"), 29 U.S.C. §§ 701, et seq." Id. at 405. While the land use appeal was pending in state court, ASI filed a federal complaint in the Western District of Pennsylvania, alleging violations of the United States Constitution, the Pennsylvania Constitution, the ADA, and RA.

Even though standing was not addressed in their initial briefs to the Court, on appeal the Third Circuit noted that it was "required to raise issues of standing sua sponte if such issues exist." Addiction Specialists, at 405. The parties did not dispute "that the broad language of the ADA and RA evidences a Congressional intent to confer standing on entities like ASI to bring discrimination claims based on their association with disabled individuals." Id. at 405. Despite the fact that no patients were joined in the suit, the Third Circuit held that the clinic had standing to bring the claim.

In MX Group v. City of Covington, a case favorably cited by the Third Circuit in Addiction Specialist, MX Group attempted to open a methadone clinic in Covington, Kentucky. 293 F.3d 326, 328-29 (2002). Initially, the City awarded MX Group a zoning permit, but after "town residents expressed their displeasure regarding the proposed clinic at a City Commission meeting," the city held a hearing regarding the application. Id. at 329. Emotions at the meeting ranged "from 'proper decorum' to anger." Id. at 329.

After a tenant in the building where the clinic was to be located filed an appeal, the Covington Board of Adjustments held a hearing. Id. at 329. Witnesses testified that there was no need for a methadone clinic in Covington, for-profit methadone clinics "spawn criminal activity," methadone clinics spur "drug use and/or trafficking and drug trade, violence, shootings and death," and witnesses expressed concern "about the safety of the neighborhood children." Id. at 329. The Board of Adjustments subsequently revoked the zoning permit. Id. at 330. When MX Group attempted to locate the clinic at another site, the City informed the plaintiff that a methadone clinic "was not a permitted use in any zone in the city." Id. at 330. The City amended the zoning code, which "completely foreclosed Plaintiff's opportunity to locate in the city," Id. at 330-31.

The facts in Addiction Specialists and MX Group are quite similar to each other, and similar to the facts in the instant case. In both cases, a methadone clinic signed a lease, and submitted all of the appropriate paperwork to open a facility. Following a series of local zoning decisions, the town decided to deny the clinic the requisite permit. Relying on 28 C.F.R. § 35.130(g), both courts found that the clinic had an "association" with disabled patients, and thus had "standing to seek damages on its own behalf." Addiction Specialists, at 408; MX Group, at 335. In both cases no patients were joined in the suit, and none were identified in the complaint.[17]

_____

[17] 17 In fact, during trial in MX Group, witnesses testified about the prospective patients in purely hypothetical terms. MX Group at 331 (A witness for the plaintiff "testified that often a drug addiction affects a person's life in numerous ways, including loss of employment, spouses and children.

Yet, in neither of these opinions did the Circuit Court specifically address the issue central to the instant case--all of the patients with whom the methadone clinic associated were prospective. However, even though not specifically addressed, it is clear that because standing is a jurisdictional matter, the courts could not have proceeded unless an association with prospective patients created standing. If Article III is only satisfied by having an association with a present patient, standing could not have been found in these cases. Implicit in the courts' holdings in Addiction Specialists and MX Group is the principle that a relationship with patients, even those not yet ascertained, can be sufficient to generate standing.

An alternative holding would present somewhat of a Catch-22. Under the Defendant's understanding, a methadone clinic could only bring a claim under the ADA or RA if actual patients are identified. But how can a clinic treat actual patients--that is people with whom they "have" an actual relationship--before the clinic is allowed to open? If a town consistently denies an entity the opportunity to open a clinic, all patients, whether named in the complaint or not, must be purely prospective. Assume a plaintiff named several patients who signed up for services at the clinic prior to the issuance of a zoning decision. These patients could have never received any drug treatment services. The Defendant could argue quite convincingly that these patients are still prospective, due to the fact that they have not received any treatment, and have simply signed up on a list. Under this approach an entity will not be protected by the ADA or RA unless they provide treatment to patients in a clinic. But if the entity cannot open--perhaps due to discrimination by a municipality that violates the ADA or RA--and cannot treat any actual plaintiffs, the entity would never possess standing. That is, unless an association with prospective patients is found to satisfy Article III.

If the Court were to accept Defendant's line of reasoning, an entire class of recovering drug addicts would be excluded from the protections of the ADA and RA. This position stands in conflict with Addiction Specialists and MX Group, and more importantly, the text of the ADA and RA. While defendant emphasizes the use of the present-tense word have in the ADA,[18] this phrasing does not connote the requirement that the patient must in fact be a

---

She testified that the addiction affects a person's ability to hold a job, to engage in parenting, or to function socially.").

[18] 18 28 C.F.R. § 35.130(g) ("A public entity shall not exclude or otherwise deny equal services, programs, or activities to an individual or entity because of the known disability of an individual with whom the individual or entity is known to have a relationship or association.")(emphasis added).

current patient. Rather, the statute requires that the entity must have an association with a disabled individual-- the meaning of association, and how attenuated that relationship is with the third party entity, is the key to providing a proper construction to this statute.

At what point does a prospective relationship become relevant for purposes of constitutional standing? Because, the "broad language of the ADA and RA enforcement provisions evidences a Congressional intent to extend standing to the full limits of Article III," Addiction Specialists, at 407, in order to define the contours of an association, the Court must look to the outer bounds of all of our jurisdictional inquiries--Article III.

c. Article III Standing is Satisfied When Association with Disabled Person is "Imminent"

While questions of associational standing and "injury in fact" are generally distinct inquiries, these two concepts have blurred, especially in the context of standing based on prospective patients under the ADA and RA, In order for an entity that seeks associational standing to suffer an injury under the ADA or RA, the entity must have an "association" with a disabled person. 28 C.F.R. § 35.130(g). While Third Circuit precedents have held that an entity itself can suffer an injury--that is experiencing discrimination in violation of the ADA or RA-- an injury in the absence of an association still lacks standing. Whether an association is too attenuated to constitute standing is a question that tests the contours of Article III. In order to determine if the association remains within the confines of Article III, the court considers the Supreme Court's standing jurisprudence with a focus on "injury in fact"--more precisely, whether the injury is "actual or imminent." Lujan v. Defenders of Wildlife, 504 U.S. 555, 560, 112 S. Ct. 2130, 119 L. Ed. 2d 351 (1992) citing (Whitmore v. Arkansas, 495 U.S. 149, 155, 110 S. Ct. 1717, 109 L. Ed. 2d 135 (1990) (emphasis added)).

The Court's discussion of "injury in fact" in Lujan v. Defenders of Wildlife is instructive. Lujan involved a challenge to a rule promulgated interpreting the Endangered Species Act of 1973 (ESA), 87 Stat. 892, as amended, 16 U. S. C. § 1536, so as to render it only applicable to actions taken against endangered species within the United States or on the high seas, but not to actions taken against endangered species in foreign nations. Lujan, at 558-59. Respondent, an organization dedicated to wildlife conservation, filed suit, seeking a declaratory judgment that the new regulation was in error as to the geographical scope. Respondents claimed they were injured by this rule change, as the decrease in funding for endangered species living in foreign nations would "increase[] the rate of extinction of endangered and threatened species." Lujan, at 563. On appeal, the Supreme Court considered whether respondents had standing to bring this suit.

Writing for the majority, Justice Scalia remarked that "the irreducible constitutional minimum of standing contains three elements":

First, the plaintiff must have suffered an "injury in fact"--an invasion of a legally protected interest which is (a) concrete and particularized . . . and (b) actual or imminent, not "conjectural" or "hypothetical," Second, there must be a causal connection between the injury and the conduct complained of the injury has to be "fairly. . . trace[able] to the challenged action of the defendant, and not. . . th[e] result [of] the independent action of some third party not before the court." Third, it must be "likely," as opposed to merely "speculative," that the injury will be "redressed by a favorable decision." Id., at 38, 43. Lujan, at 560-561 (citations omitted).

First, the Court considered whether the respondents suffered an injury in fact. The Court conceded that the "the desire to use or observe an animal species, even for purely esthetic purposes, is undeniably a cognizable interest for purpose of standing." Lujan, at 562-63. "But the 'injury in fact' test requires more than an injury to a cognizable interest. It requires that the party seeking review be himself among the injured." Lujan, at 563 citing Sierra Club v. Morton, 405 U.S., 727, 734-35, 92 S. Ct. 1361, 31 L. Ed. 2d 636 (1972). The Court required respondents to show that that "one or more of respondents' members would thereby be 'directly' affected apart from their 'special interest' in th[e] subject.'" Lujan, at 563 citing Sierra Club, at 735, 739.
While two of the Respondents--Joyce Kelly and Amy Skilbred-- had previously visited the habitats of endangered species in Egypt and Sri Lanka, respectively, neither had actually seen any endangered species. Lujan, at 563-64. Ms. Skilbred expressed an intent to return to Sri Lanka, "but confessed that she had no current plans." Lujan, at 564. The Court found that these facts made no "showing how damage to the species will produce 'imminent' injury to Mses. Kelly and Skilbred." Lujan, at 564. Justice Scalia wrote that a mere "intent" to return is "simply not enough" as "'some day' intentions--without any description of concrete plans, or indeed even any specification of when the some day will be--do not support a finding of the 'actual or imminent' injury that our cases require." Lujan, at 564 (emphasis added). Because the harm was not "imminent," the Court found that the respondents did not suffer an injury in fact, and lacked standing. Lujan, at 565-67.
While the statutory regimes are quite dissimilar, the underlying jurisdictional issues of Lujan and the instant case bear many similarities. In Lujan, plaintiffs claimed standing based on injuries to prospective endangered species. In the case sub judice, Plaintiff claims standing based on injures to prospective

patients.[19] While the Supreme Court in Lujan found that the harm was not "imminent," the facts in this case dictate a different result. In contrast with the conjectural associations of Mses. Kelly and Skilbred, RHJ took numerous, specific, unambiguous, and concrete steps towards opening up a methadone clinic--and fostering an association with patients.

RHJ "signed a ten-year lease for the site at 994 Beaver Drive on March 31, 2006, and soon after commenced renovations of the space to meet the standards of the Pennsylvania Department of Health." (Compl. 28). RHJ also took the requisite steps towards obtaining the appropriate licenses, as in "September 2006, representatives from the Division of Drugs and Alcohol of the Pennsylvania Department of Health and the DEA conducted an on-site inspection of RHJ's DuBois facility." (Compl. 30). Further, prior to the scheduled opening date, "RHJ incurred expenses relating to the hiring of staff, setting up utilities, and advertising, in addition to rent and renovations." (Compl. 29).

Defendant asserts that "from a practical standpoint," granting standing based on an "anticipated relationship" would permit "entities to recover § 1983 damages" if an entity is "created under the guise that it intends' to treat disabled individuals." (Def.'s Rep, p. 6.)[20] The Court is cognizant of the perils of granting standing based on prospective associations. This was the concern that animated Justice Scalia's framework in Lujan. If a plaintiff could gain standing under the ADA or RA by merely expressing an intent to open a methadone clinic, the courts would be flooded with premature associations, and in many cases, disingenuous litigants who seek to take advantage of lax standing law. Justice Scalia's opinion, rejecting the "some day" approach to standing in Lujan, counsels against adhering to such a liberal standard. Lujan, at 564.

In a concurring opinion in Lujan, Justice Kennedy remarked that "[w]hile it may seem trivial to require that Mses. Kelly and Skilbred acquire airline tickets to the project sites or announce a date certain upon which they will return . . . this is not a case where it is reasonable to assume that the affiants will be using the sites on a regular basis," Lujan, at 579 (Kennedy, J., concurring). Similarly, while "it may seem trivial" to require an organization to sign a lease or obtain the proper licenses to open a methadone clinic, in the absence of

---

[19] 19 This injury to prospective patients is only considered for purposes of Article III standing. As discussed infra, Plaintiff itself was injured, and this provides for relief under the ADA and RA.

[20] 20 The Court notes that Defendant did not seek leave of court before filing this reply brief, as required by this Court's Practices and Procedures.

these steps, it is not reasonable to assume that a methadone clinic will in fact open. If a plaintiff takes such concrete steps, the injury should be considered imminent.

Third party standing is an essential tool for methadone clinics to enforce the rights of those with debilitating drug addictions. Drug addicts are the prototypical "discrete and insular minorities" who are the "outs" in society. See McDonald v. Chicago, 561 U.S. ___, 130 S. Ct. 3020, 177 L. Ed. 2d 894 (2010) (Stevens, J., dissenting) ("Conversely, we have long appreciated that more 'searching' judicial review may be justified when the rights of 'discrete and insular minorities'--groups that may face systematic barriers in the political system--are at stake.") citing United States v. Carolene Products Co., 304 U.S. 144, 152-53 n. 4, 58 S. Ct. 778, 82 L. Ed. 1234 (1938). See City of Cleburne v. Cleburne Living Ctr., 473 U.S. 432, 105 S. Ct. 3249, 87 L. Ed. 2d 313 (1985), JOHN HART ELY, DEMOCRACY AND DISTRUST: A THEORY OF JUDICIAL REVIEW 77-78 (1980) (arguing that the courts should ensure that all groups receive sufficient representation and access to the political and legislative processes). Allowing treatment facilities, which undoubtedly have better legal resources to bring suit on behalf of patients--to give those with disabilities equal access to the courts and ensure that their disabilities are not used to discriminate against them by improperly restricting their access to drug addiction treatment-- vindicates the protections that the ADA and RA champion. While the "broad language of the ADA and RA enforcement provisions evidences a Congressional intent to extend standing to the full limits of Article III," Addiction Specialists, at 407, the association with the patients must be imminent to fall within the ambit of Article III. Without this association, Plaintiff cannot recover for an injury under the ADA, even if the Plaintiff itself suffers the injury.

At this stage, the Court considers Iqbal's "plausibility" standard for construing a motion for a judgment on the pleadings. Ashcroft v. Iqbal, 129 S.Ct. 1937, 1959-1960, 173 L. Ed. 2d 868 (2009). Following the Third Circuit's framework in Fowler v. UPMC Shadyside, the Court first separates the "factual and legal elements of [the] claim." 578 F.3d 203, 210 (3rd Cir. 2009). Second, the Court determines "whether the facts alleged in the complaint are sufficient to show that the plaintiff has a "plausible claim for relief." Id. at 210. The legal elements to this claim are quite distinct from the factual elements. The legal elements require that an association with disabled patients needs to be "imminent" in order to satisfy the requirements of Article III. The facts show that RHJ took several concrete steps in order to open up its clinic. Combining these factual elements with the legal elements yields a "plausible" claim. The complaint alleges that RHJ took certain concrete steps towards opening of the methadone clinic and establishing a relationship with patients. This association was imminent, and not hypothetical or conjectural. The Court

finds that this claim is "plausible," and meets the requirements of Iqbal.
* * *
Even though the association was imminent, the requirements of Article III have not yet been fully addressed, and the standing inquiry continues.

d. Standing and Remedies
Standing is inextricably linked to the type of relief sought. In this case, RHJ requests both equitable relief and damages. For equitable relief, Plaintiff seeks a declaration that the Defendant's actions and inaction of failing to issue an occupancy permit violates the Constitution, the ADA, and the RA. Plaintiff also seeks an injunction enjoining Defendant from continuing to violate the Constitution, the ADA, and the RA. Finally, Plaintiff seeks an injunction forcing the City to issue Plaintiff a permit to operate a methadone treatment facility. Additionally, Plaintiff seeks "damages for the harm it experienced as a result of Defendant's discriminatory practices," as well as reasonable attorney fees and costs. Before addressing whether plaintiff has standing, the Court first separates the analysis based on the type of relief sought.
The Supreme Court held in Friends of the Earth, Inc. v. Laidlaw Environmental Services (TOC), Inc. that "a plaintiff must demonstrate standing separately for each form of relief sought." 528 U.S. 167, 185, 120 S. Ct. 693, 145 L. Ed. 2d 610 (2000). See also City of Los Angeles v. Lyons, 461 U.S. 95, 103 S. Ct. 1660, 75 L. Ed. 2d 675 (notwithstanding the fact that plaintiff had standing to pursue damages, he lacked standing to pursue injunctive relief). These considerations are especially relevant in the context of associational standing. In Warth v. Seldin, the Supreme Court commented that

whether an association has standing to invoke the court's remedial powers on behalf of its members depends in substantial measure on the nature of the relief sought. If in a proper case the association seeks a declaration, injunction, or some other form of prospective relief, it can reasonably be supposed that the remedy, if granted, will inure to the benefit of those members of the association actually injured. Indeed, in all cases in which we have expressly recognized standing in associations to represent their members, the relief sought has been of this kind. 422 U.S. 490, 515, 95 S. Ct. 2197, 45 L. Ed. 2d 343 (1975) (emphasis added).

In short, "standing is not dispensed in gross." Lewis v. Casey, 518 U.S. 343, 358, n. 6, 116 S. Ct. 2174, 135 L. Ed. 2d 606 (1996).
In Addiction Specialists, the plaintiff sought a declaration that the defendant's denial of a permit to open a methadone clinic was unconstitutional, and requested an order requiring the defendant to grant the plaintiff a permit.

Addiction Specialists, Inc. v. The Township of Hamilton, Et AL., 1:04-CV-696 (W.D.Pa. Sept. 8, 2004). The plaintiff also sought an order enjoining the defendant from engaging in further discriminatory acts. Id. Additionally, the plaintiff sought $1,000,000 for lost profits under 42 U.S.C. § 1983. Id. Due to the pendency of concurrent state court proceedings, relying on Younger abstention, Younger v. Harris, 401 U.S. 37, 91 S. Ct. 746, 27 L. Ed. 2d 669 (1971), the District Court "abstain[ed] from deciding plaintiff's claims for equitable relief," and dismissed those claims. Id. Because the claims for damages "could be adequately raised and addressed in the state proceedings" the court dismissed those claims. Id. The District Court did not address the issue of standing.

On appeal, the Third Circuit found the District Court "abused its discretion by abstaining from exercising jurisdiction" over the constitutional and statutory rights claims. Addiction Specialists, 411 F.3d 399, 411 (3rd Cir. 2005). While, the Court affirmed the "District Court's decision to abstain from [plaintiff's] claims for declaratory and injunctive relief," the Court reversed the lower court's opinion regarding damages, as Younger abstention was not proper for these claims. Id. at 414-415. In light of the posture of the case, the Third Circuit did not consider standing with respect to the equitable claims. Rather the Third Circuit's thorough and reasoned analysis on standing only focused on damages, and not the equitable claims. In the final paragraph of the standing section, the Court noted:

In recognizing that ASI has standing to assert its claims under § 1983, the ADA, and the RA, we of course pass no judgment as to the merits of those claims. Moreover, we do not reach the issue of whether ASI's lost profits would be the correct measure of damages if and when this suit reaches the damages stage. We hold only that ASI has standing to seek damages on its own behalf. We therefore will not affirm the District Court's dismissal on standing grounds, and we will go forward to determine whether the District Court properly applied the Younger abstention analysis to ASI's claims.

Addiction Specialists, at 408 (emphasis added). This rationale applies to damages only, and makes no mention of the declaratory and injunctive relief requested. Subsequent discussions in the opinion regarding the equitable claims consider Younger abstention, and not Article III standing. The standing analysis in Addiction Specialists only seems to apply to the claims of damages. The Third Circuit has not directly addressed the issue of standing for claims of equitable relief based on prospective associations. Because "a plaintiff must demonstrate standing separately for each form of relief sought, "Friends of the Earth, Inc. v. Laidlaw Environmental Services (TOC), Inc., 528 U.S. 167, 185, 120 S. Ct. 693, 145 L. Ed. 2d 610 (2000), the Court first considers standing for claims of equitable relief.

When equitable relief is awarded in cases of third party standing, the benefit will inure to the third party--in this case, the patients seeking methadone treatment--as well as to the entity--the methadone clinic--itself. For example, if the Court were to grant Plaintiff's requested equitable relief, and order the issuance of a permit, the patients of the methadone clinic, as well as the methadone clinic itself would benefit. The patients would benefit from their ability to receive services in the City of DuBois. RHJ would benefit from the ability to open up a new business and earn profits.

Such was the case in MX Group, Inc. v. City of Covington. 293 F.3d 326 (6th Cir. 2002). In this case, the 6th Circuit considered whether a methadone clinic had standing to seek injunctive relief, and obtain a permit to open a clinic. See Id. at 327 ("The district court also entered an order and injunction, which provided that Defendants' ordinance, essentially banning Plaintiff's proposed methadone clinic from operating anywhere in the City of Covington, violated the ADA."). While the remedy of damages was argued before the District Court, the issue was not resolved and was not presented on appeal. See MX Group, Inc. v. City of Covington, 106 F. Supp.2d 914, 920-21 (E.D. Ky. 2000) ("plaintiff having reserved on the issue of damages").

The Sixth Circuit found that the methadone clinic had standing, as it was "an entity suing primarily on its own behalf, because of injury it suffered as a result of its association with individuals with disabilities." MX Group, at 335 (emphasis added). The right to sue, resulting from the injury suffered, is "primarily on [the entity's] own behalf." In other words, it is not entirely on the entity's own behalf. If the right is not entirely on the entity's own behalf, on whose behalf is the residuum? The residuum logically and textually can only derive from the "individuals with disabilities" with whom the entity had an "association." In this case, when seeking equitable relief, the standing to sue was in part due to the entity's injury, and in part due to the injury of the patients.

Unlike the opinion in MX Group, in Addiction Specialists the Third Circuit considered the plaintiff's request for both equitable relief and damages under § 1983. Addiction Specialists, at 407. While the Third Circuit favorably cited MX Group, which held that an entity has standing if it is "suing primarily on its own behalf," MX Group, at 335, the Court took what could be construed as a somewhat contradictory stance on this issue. The Court remarked that "ASI has standing to seek damages on its own behalf under § 1983 . . . . As with its claims under the ADA and RA, ASI does not assert its § 1983 claims on behalf of individuals with disabilities, but rather brings these claims primarily on its own behalf." Addiction Specialists, at 407 (emphasis added). In the same paragraph the Court wrote that ASI had standing to seek damages "on its own behalf and "primarily on its own behalf--these are not the same thing. Elsewhere, the Third Circuit wrote "We hold only that ASI has standing to seek damages on its own behalf." Addiction Specialists, at 408 (emphasis added). In light of the entire opinion, it would seem that the Third Circuit endorsed the former standard, and held that ASI had standing to seek damages solely "on its own behalf"--and not merely primarily on its own behalf.

This holding--when seeking equitable relief, the standing to sue is due solely to the entity's injury--is buttressed by the Third Circuit's rejection of the Seventh Circuit's holding in Discovery House v. City of Indianapolis, 319 F.3d 277 (7th Cir. 2003). In Discovery House, a methadone clinic sued under the ADA and RA for damages, namely lost profits. Id. With respect to standing, the Seventh Circuit asked whether a methadone clinic could obtain "relief which perhaps indirectly will benefit its clients, but which primarily is designed to benefit its for-profit business." Discovery House, at 280. The recipient of the benefits in a suit for damages--just the entity--contrasts with the recipients of the benefits in a suit for equitable relief--the benefit will inure to the third party as well as to the entity. The Seventh Circuit chose to limit the scope of relief, noting that "the remedies we may find (other than those specifically set out in the statute) must, at the very least, be those which directly benefit the disabled." Discovery House, at 280 (emphasis added). In short, "the one thing that is clear, however, is that lost profits are not expressly provided," as "we see no way that either the ADA or the RA contemplates a recovery for lost profits for a business like that of the Discovery House." Discovery House, at 280-281. Because damages will only benefit the entity, and not the third party disabled patient, the Seventh Circuit did not permit this claim to proceed.

The opinion in Discovery House only considered damages as the clinic had received an award of "over a million dollars in damages for lost profits." Discovery House, at 280. In this case, the plaintiff did "not seek equitable relief," and only sought damages. Discovery House, at 280. The Seventh Circuit on appeal only considered whether the "ADA or the RA grant Discovery House standing to recover lost profits." Discovery House, at 280. The Third Circuit discussed the holding of Discovery House, in the context of its own analysis for standing for third party claims. While the Seventh Circuit rejected the plaintiff's claims for damages, the court favorably cited other precedents that "concern[ed] equitable relief to allow facilities to exist where they had been prohibited." Id. at 280. The Court noted that "for purposes of this case, we have no need to agree or disagree with those courts because the reasoning advanced in those cases does not address the problem posed by this case" where the plaintiff only seeks damages. Id. at 279-280. The analysis the Third Circuit rejected and "declined to follow," Addiction Specialists, at 407, only pertained to damages, and not to equitable relief. It seems that both the

Third and Seventh Circuit recognize this bifurcation of standing based on the relief sought.

The reasoning in Warth endorses this distinction between standing for equitable claims and standing for damages. Chief Justice Burger recognized that in all of the cases the Supreme Court had considered, the requested remedy for third party standing was equitable, and not damages. Warth, at 515 ("Indeed, in all cases in which we have expressly recognized standing in associations to represent their members, the relief sought has been of this kind [equitable]."). This makes sense in light of the fact that the equitable remedy "will inure to the benefit of those members of the association actually injured," and not purely to the benefit of the association itself. Warth, at 515. In contrast, when the association is seeking damages, the benefit will only inure to the association itself.

These precedents suggest that courts impose different standing requirements based on the remedy sought. If the remedy sought is injunctive relief, then Article III requires that the injury should be suffered by the third parties as well as the entity itself. In this case, the benefit of the injunctive relief inures to the advantage of both of the injured parties--the patients and the entity. In contrast, if the remedy sought is damages, then Article III requires that the injury need only to be suffered by the entity, and not the patients. In this ease, the advantage of the damages inures only to the injured party--the entity, and not the patients.

Assume a methadone clinic is denied a permit, cannot open, and suffers lost profits. The monetary damages could only possibly inure to the benefit of the methadone clinic itself. Other types of damages--future damages, incidental damages, punitive damages, attorney fees, and filing fees--will similarly only benefit the clinic. It could be argued that a clinic that receives compensatory damages will be better funded, and will be able to provide better services to the patients. However, the inquiry here focuses on the injury at the time of the denial of the permit, and not potential future benefits to the members. See Discovery House, at 280 (noting that damages "perhaps indirectly will benefit its clients, but. . . [they are] primarily . . . designed to benefit its for-profit business."). To paraphrase the American Humane Association's seal of approval, which is emblazoned during the end credits of all movies produced by the Screen Actors Guild, no patients were harmed during the attempted-opening of this methadone clinic. No injury, no benefit, no standing. The Plaintiff's complaint recognizes this distinction. While praying for damages, the complaint sought "damages for the harm it experienced as a result of Defendant's discriminatory practices," (Compl. p 20.) (emphasis added). That is, the damages it experienced, and not any damages to patients.

Assume a methadone clinic is denied a permit, cannot open, and as a result of this denial, disabled patients are unable to receive methadone treatment and drug counseling. The clinic, on behalf of the patients, sues for equitable relief to obtain the permit and stop the discrimination. This is a different case from the facts of Discovery House, in that patients were in fact injured. Equitable relief--such as injunctions, declarations, specific performance, and estoppel--will benefit the patients, as well as the clinic. Unlike compensatory damages, if the court orders the issuance of a permit, the clinic will open, and the injury the patients suffered--discrimination and denial of treatment--will be remedied. Now, the patients can receive treatment at the clinic. Similarly, the injury the entity suffered--the inability to open a clinic--will also be remedied. With a permit, the clinic can open and operate. There is an injury to both parties, a benefit will inure to both parties, and therefore standing exists.

In a footnote in the reply brief, Plaintiff notes: "RHJ only asserts Counts II, III, V, and VI on its own behalf and does not assert any such counts on behalf of its prospective patients." (PL's Rep., p. 5, n. 1.) Although RHJ does not assert any claims on behalf of named plaintiffs, RHJ still needs to rely on "prospective patients" with drug-addiction problems--the patients referred to in the complaint--in order to invoke the ADA or RA. To read this disclaimer any other way would amount to a waiver. Plaintiff would be effectively admitting that the ADA or RA is inapplicable, as RHJ by itself, without any associated disabled persons is unable to claim protection of these acts. The Court will not find a waiver here in the absence of clear language to that effect.

In essence, the discrimination against RHJ yielded two separate and cognizable injuries. The first injury--the lost profits by the clinic due to the denial of the permit--was only suffered by the clinic itself, and dictates a remedy of damages. The second injury--the discrimination against the patients who were unable to receive treatment from the unopened clinic--was suffered in part by the patients, and in part by the clinic. This injury dictates an equitable remedy.

Accordingly, the analysis for standing in this case is bifurcated based on the type of remedy.

e. Standing for Equitable Claims

For claims of equitable relief, the standing to sue is in part due to the entity's injury, and in part due to the injury of the third party. In this case, because no third parties were identified, Plaintiff needs to rely on prospective patients to generate standing for equitable claims. Relying on prospective patients--that is patients not yet ascertained--raises two issue. First, the ADA and RA contain nearly identical "carve-out" sections that provide that individuals "currently engaging in the illegal use of drags" will not be considered "qualified" under the statute.[21] Without naming any patients, how could the City be expected to show whether these patients are engaging in the use of drugs, and thus exempted from the protections of the ADA and RA? Second, how can the Defendant know whether a prospective patient is an individual who possesses a "known disability?" If a prospective patient does not have a disability, the ADA and RA would not apply, and plaintiff's case would fail. Both of these issues would be essential elements of the City's defense.

i. Statutory Carve-Out for Current Drug Use

Defendant notes that because no patients are named, the City would be unable to prove whether any of the patients are currently "engaging in the illegal use of drugs." Without this knowledge, Defendant cannot show if the patients would be protected by the ADA or RA, or would be exempted by the so-called "carve-out" provision. If an individual has used illegal drugs "recently enough so that continuing use is a real ongoing problem," he cannot claim the protection of the RA or ADA. Brown v. Lucky Stores, Inc., 246 F.3d 1182, 1188 (9th Cir. 2001).

This "carve-out" provision allows employers to discharge workers who engage in the illegal use of drugs, but prevents employers from discharging recovering addicts who are no longer using drugs. While this provision makes sense in the context of employment law--as most reported cases interpreting this provisions emerged from the workplace--it makes little sense as applied to methadone clinics, where the patients must be "engage[ed] in the illegal use of" opioids for at least one year in order to be admitted.[22] As the   Third

---

[21] 21 See   42 U.S.C. § 12210(a) ("For purposes of this chapter, the term "individual with a disability" does not include an individual who is currently engaging in the illegal use of drugs, when the covered entity acts on the basis of such use);   29 U.S.C.A. § 705(20)(C)(1) ("For purposes of subchapter V of this chapter [29 U.S.C.A. § 790 et seq.], the term "individual with a disability" does not include an individual who is currently engaging in the illegal use of drugs, when a covered entity acts on the basis of such use.").

[22] 22   42 C.F.R. 8.12(e) ("An OTP [Opioid Treatment Program] shall maintain current procedures designed to ensure that patients are admitted to maintenance treatment by qualified personnel who have determined, using accepted medical criteria such as those listed in the Diagnostic and Statistical Manual for Mental Disorders (DSM--IV), that the person is currently addicted to an opioid drug, and that the person became addicted at least 1 year before admission for treatment. In addition, a program physician shall ensure that each patient voluntarily chooses maintenance treatment and that all relevant facts concerning the use of the opioid drug are clearly and adequately

Circuit noted in New Directions, this statutory carve-out is "an odd fit for" cases involving methadone clinics. New Directions Treatment Services v. City of Reading, 490 F.3d 293, 309 (3d Cir. 2007).

The carve-out was intended to ensure that employers could discharge employees who were actually under the influence while at work and that employers could not discharge employees who were recovering addicts but were, at the time of any personnel action, drug free. See id. (quoting H.R.Rep. No. 101-596, at 62 (1990), U.S. Code Cong. & Admin.News 1990, pp. 565, 570-571 (Conf.Rep.)). This provision makes its first appearance at 42 U.S.C. § 12114(a). The carve out provision is repeated nearly verbatim--not verbatim as the Third Circuit suggested in New Directions, as there are several slight changes--in two portions of the ADA, Subchapter I and Subchapter IV. Subchapter I, which only pertains to employment matters, provides "[f]or purposes of this subchapter, a qualified individual with a disability shall not include any employee or applicant who is currently engaging in the illegal use of drugs, when the covered entity acts on the basis of such use," 42 U.S.C. § 12114 (emphasis added). Subchapter IV governs Miscellaneous Provisions, and applies to all cases governed by the ADA, and not just employment situations--including discrimination of patients attending a methadone clinic. This provision provides "[f]or purposes of this chapter, the term 'individual with a disability' does not include an individual who is currently engaging in the illegal use of drugs, when the covered entity acts on the basis of such use," 42 U.S.C. § 12210 (emphasis added).

The language in Subchapter I refers to "employees or applicants" while the language in Subchapter IV uses the broader term of "individual." While the carve out's inclusion in Subchapter I makes sense, as this provision fits neatly into employment paradigms, its inclusion in Subchapter IV fits poorly into situations dealing with methadone clinics. The broader provision in Subchapter IV appears to consume the provision in Subchapter I. However, Congress made several important changes to distinguish the provision affecting employment and the provision affecting all of the ADA. The most significant distinction is section (c), which provides:

(c) Health and other services. Notwithstanding subsection (a) of this section and section 12211(b)(3) of this title, an individual shall not be denied health services, or services provided in connection with drug rehabilitation, on the basis of the current illegal use of drugs if the individual is otherwise entitled to such services. 42, U.S.C. 12210(c) (emphasis added).

---

explained to the patient, and that each patient provides informed written consent to treatment.") (emphasis added).

The RA contains a nearly identical provision.[23] This clause, which is not included in Subchapter I, speaks directly to the matter before the Court, Even if an individual is "currently engaging in the illegal use of drugs," 42 U.S.C. 12210(a), if that person is receiving "services provided in connection with drug rehabilitation," that person "shall not be denied health services" on the "basis of current illegal drug use if the individual is otherwise entitled to such services." 42 U.S.C. § 12210(c). In other words, even assuming that RHJ's prospective patients were currently engaging in the illegal use of drugs, if they would be otherwise entitled to such drug counseling services, they would still be eligible for protection under the ADA or RA. It would seem that this provision was drafted specifically to remedy situations wherein individuals who currently engage in drug use seek the services of a methadone clinic.

This provision so understood recognizes the broad remedial purposes of the ADA and RA with respect to individuals recovering from a drug addiction. Invariably, the people who sign up for drug rehabilitation programs are either "currently engaging in the illegal use of drugs," 42 U.S.C. 12210(a), or have used illegal drugs "recently enough so that continuing use is a real ongoing problem." Brown, 246 F.3d at 1188. In fact, in order to be admitted to a methadone clinic under federal law, a person needs to have had an opioid addiction for at least one year.[24]

People who abstain from drug use have little need for methadone clinics. If

---

[23] 23 29 U.S.C. § 705(20)(c)(iii)("Notwithstanding clause (i), for purposes of programs and activities providing health services and services provided under subchapters I, II, and III of this chapter [29 U.S.C.A. §§ 720 et seq., 760 et seq., and 771 et seq.], an individual shall not be excluded from the benefits of such programs or activities on the basis of his or her current illegal use of drugs if he or she is otherwise entitled to such services.") (emphasis added).

[24] 24 42 C.F.R. 8.12 ("An OTP [Opioid Treatment Program] shall maintain current procedures designed to ensure that patients are admitted to maintenance treatment by qualified personnel who have determined, using accepted medical criteria such as those listed in the Diagnostic and Statistical Manual for Mental Disorders (DSM-IV), that the person is currently addicted to an opioid drug and that the person became addicted at least 1 year before admission for treatment. In addition, a program physician shall ensure that each patient voluntarily chooses maintenance treatment and that all relevant facts concerning the use of the opioid drug are clearly and adequately explained to the patient, and that each patient provides informed written consent to treatment.") (emphasis added).

the ADA and RA were interpreted to exempt from its protections individuals with drug addictions seeking help--the argument the Defendant makes--section (c) would be reduced to a nullity and mere surplusage. Some of the very people the acts seek to protect would not be protected. Whether any of the prospective patients were engaging in the use of illegal drags is orthogonal to the question of whether the ADA or RA provides protection for them. Contrary to Defendant's assertions, this question has no bearing on the resolution of this case. In a sense, any patients that would receive treatment at the clinic could be considered per se exempted from the "carve out" provision.

ii. "Back to the Future" of Disability

Reliance on an association with prospective patients for equitable claims raises another curious issue. The ADA provides "[a] public entity shall not exclude or otherwise deny equal services, programs, or activities to an individual or entity because of the known disability of an individual with whom the individual or entity is known to have a relationship or association." 28 C.F.R. § 35.130(g) (emphasis added). Our precedents, namely MX Group and Addiction Specialists, have found, or perhaps merely assumed, that prospective patients affiliated with an unopened methadone clinic would be disabled, without engaging in the fact-intensive, case-by-case analysis that Supreme Court disability jurisprudence requires. In this case, Plaintiff remarks that "[l]ogically, RHJ's prospective clientele would consist of individuals with opiate addictions." (Pl.'s Rep. p. 7). That is not necessarily the case in all situations.

Associating with conjectural patients is permissible for purposes of ascertaining standing, as Article III grants standing if the injury is "actual or imminent" Lujan, at 560 citing Whitmore, at 155 (emphasis added). However, the ADA does not countenance assuming individuals are disabled without conducting an individualized, fact-intensive inquiry. Even if Plaintiff can establish the requisite association under Article III, that association must in fact be with an individual with a disability. A plaintiff cannot merely speculate that a prospective patient in the future may be disabled. Rather, the burden of proof is placed on the plaintiff to show that a disability exists. Section 12102 of the ADA provides three means by which a person can have a disability:

The term "disability" means, with respect to an individual- (A) a physical or mental impairment that substantially limits one or more of the major life activities of such individual; (B) a record of such an impairment; or (C) being regarded as having such an impairment. 42 U.S.C. § 12102

Not one of these three subsections can possibly apply to prospective patients-

-that is, without encountering certain paradoxes generally reserved to science fiction.

1. Impairment That Substantially Limits Major Life Activity

To determine whether an individual is disabled under subsection A of Section 12102, the courts must determine whether an individual has a mental or physical impairment that substantially limits a major life activity. Bragdon v. Abbott, 524 U.S. 624, 632, 118 S. Ct. 2196, 141 L. Ed. 2d 540 (1998). Drug abuse can constitute such impairment. Id. at 632-33 (explaining that commentary accompanying the Department of Health, Education and Welfare's regulations interpreting the Rehabilitation Act includes drug addiction and alcoholism as a physical impairment); 28 C.F.R. § 35.104 ("The phrase physical or mental impairment includes, but is not limited to, such contagious and noncontagious diseases and conditions as . . . drug addiction."). However, merely identifying an impairment does not qualify one as a disabled individual. The plaintiff has the all-important burden of showing that this impairment "substantially limits one or more . . . major life activities." Toyota Motor Manuf., Kentucky, Inc. v. Williams, 534 U.S. 184, 122 S.Ct. 681, 689, 151 L. Ed. 2d 615 (2002).

This inquiry must be made on a case-by-case basis. Williams, at 691-92. In Williams, the Supreme Court stated that it is not enough that someone presents evidence of a medical diagnosis of an impairment. Id. at 691. The ADA requires those "claiming the Act's protection . . . to prove a disability by offering evidence that the extent of the limitation [caused by their impairment] in terms of their own experience . . . is substantial." Id. at 691-92 (citation and internal quotation marks omitted). In light of the fact that "the Act defines 'disability' 'with respect to an individual,' . . . Congress intended the existence of a disability to be determined in such a case-by-case manner." Id. (citations omitted)(emphasis added).

In Sutton v. United States Air Lines, Inc., the Supreme Court held that "because the phrase 'substantially limits' is presented in the present tense, it must be read as requiring a person to be presently--not potentially or hypothetically--substantially limited in order to demonstrate disability." 527 U.S. 471, 482, 119 S. Ct. 2139, 144 L. Ed. 2d 450 (1999) (emphasis added). In addition, "[t]he definition of disability also requires that disabilities be evaluated with respect to an individual." Id. at 483, Accordingly, "whether a person has a disability under the ADA is an individualized inquiry," Id. at 483, not a hypothetical inquiry.

In Addiction Specialists, the defendant "did not dispute that ASI's clients [were] disabled within the meaning of the ADA and RA." Addiction Specialists, at 406. However, the Defendant in this case does contest whether RHJ's prospective clients should receive protections under the ADA and RA.

Considering the existence of a disability of future patients necessitates judging the physical or mental states of people in the future. A "case-by-case" investigation for facts that have not happened yet is not only impractical--it is impossible.

How can the Court possibly conduct a thorough, fact intensive discourse on the life activities, and how substantially they are impaired, for unidentified patients? Perhaps a prospective patient has an impairment, but the impairment does not substantially impact a major life activity. If a patient's impairment substantially affects a life activity, how can the court determine if that life activity is major? If an impairment impacts a major life activity, how can the court determine if the impairment is substantial? These are all questions without possible answers, questions that do not seem to have been addressed in our precedents, and questions that this Court is not prepared to answer. While Cosmologist Stephen Hawking concedes that time travel is theoretically possible,[25] the Court is not prepared to engage in jurisprudential speculation along the spacetime continuum.

2. Record of Impairment

To determine whether an individual is disabled under subsection B of Section 12102, the courts must determine whether an individual has a record of impairment. 42 U.S.C. § 12102. A record of an impairment signifies that an individual has "a history of, or has been misclassified as having, a mental or physical impairment that substantially limits one or more major life activities." 28 C.F.R. § 35.104(3) (emphasis added). In order to combat the effects of erroneous but nevertheless prevalent perceptions about the handicapped, Congress expanded the definition of "handicapped individual" so as to preclude discrimination against "[a] person who has a record of, or is regarded as having, an impairment [but who] may at present have no actual incapacity at all." School Board of Nassau County, Florida v. Arline, 480 U.S. 273, 279, 107 S. Ct. 1123, 94 L. Ed. 2d 307 (1987) quoting (Southeastern Community College v. Davis, 442 U.S. 397, 405-406, n. 6, 99 S. Ct. 2361, 60 L. Ed. 2d 980 (1979)).

This inquiry must be precise, as a record that identifies a person as disabled for some other purpose which does not meet the ADA's definition of "disability"--such as receipt of Social Security disability benefits--will not necessarily establish the fact that the person has a record of being disabled

---

[25] 25 Scott Warren, Stephen Hawking backs possibility for humans to travel millions of years into the future, UK DAILY MAIL ONLINE (May 4, 2010, 8:49 AM), http://www.dailymail.co.uk/sciencetech/article-1270531/Stephen-Hawking-backs-possibility-time-travel-millions-years-future.html.

under the ADA. 29 C.F.R. Part 1630, Appendix, § 1630.2(k). In Arline, the Supreme Court considered the plaintiff's detailed medical record in order to establish that her "hospitalization for tuberculosis in 1957 suffices to establish that she has a 'record of . . . impairment.'" Arline, at 281.

How could a hypothetical patient have any history, let alone a record of impairment? Any record could only be conjectural. However, the Sixth Circuit seems to have accepted such paradoxical reasoning. In MX Group, the plaintiff showed that in order to be admitted into the methadone clinic--which had not yet opened or admitted any patients--a "person must have a history of one year of opiate or narcotic addiction, including physical dependence" and show "proof of an addiction that has lasted for at least one year is required." MX Group, at 339.

The Court noted that "to succeed under this prong, Plaintiff must show that its potential clients have a record of 'an impairment that would substantially limit one or more of the individual's major life activities.' MX Group, at 339 citing (Hilburn v. Murata Electronics North America, Inc., 181 F.3d 1220, 1229 (11th Cir.1999) (emphasis added)(. The citation to Hilburn is inapposite. Hilburn considered the case of Linda Hilburn, the named plaintiff-appellant, who sued under the ADA alleging she was discriminated against based on a record of impairment. Id. Hilburn is not a "potential" client of the future. While Hilburn can have a record, "potential patients" of the future cannot.

In MX Group the Court relied on the "record of" test to find that "potential clients" of a methadone clinic have a record of an impairment. MX Group, at 339. Judge Clay, seemingly aware of the tenuousness of this holding, remarked "that to overturn the district court's disposition in plaintiff's favor on the basis that an individualized inquiry of a client is needed would defy reason as plaintiff has presented evidence that it was altogether foreclosed from opening its clinic." MX Group, at 336. Additionally, the Court noted that "Plaintiff has submitted sufficient proof that its potential clients qualify as disabled under the ADA." Id. at 336. While the former rationale shows deference to the finding of the lower court, and recognizes the untenable position of the methadone clinic that was never allowed to open, the latter rationale simply cannot be reconciled with the fact that any proof submitted was purely conjectural.

The conflicting tenses used by the MX Group court shed some light on this issue: "Plaintiff nevertheless would prevail inasmuch as it has shown that its potential clients[--as in patients of the future (future tense)--] have [--at the current moment (present tense)--] a record of a disability." MX Group, at 340. The Sixth Circuit noted that proof for these matters "can come from letters from other treatment facilities or social service agencies or probation/parole officers, jails, courts, and/or parents." Id. Additionally, at trial, testimony indicated that "the types of individuals [who would be] admitted into

Plaintiff's programs would include persons who are unable to work and 'function' because of their addiction, and who, according to documentary evidence, may not have been able to do so for at least a year." Id. at 339-340. The Court inserted "who would be" into the previous quotation because it stresses the fact that no patients had actually been admitted--largely because the clinic had never been allowed opened. Any proof, whether in the form of letters or testimony, would by necessity be purely conjectural and premature. Potential clients of the future cannot have a record of disability. To paraphrase a quote from the movie trilogy "Back to the Future," no one's future is ever written.[26]

---

[26] See Back to the Future, IMDB, http://www.imdb.com/title/tt0088763/; Back to the Future Part II, IMDB, http://www.imdb.com/title/tt0096874/; Back to the Future Part III, IMDB, http://www.imdb.com/title/tt0099088/.

In the Back to the Future Trilogy, which began in the year 1985, the protagonist Marty McFly agreed to participate in a risky drag race, unable to back down after being called a "chicken". Tragically, Marty's car was hit by a Rolls Royce. With his hand injured, Marty could not play the guitar professionally, effectively halting his music career before it started. As the story goes, Marty's girlfriend Jennifer marries him because she felt sorry for him, Marty's future was forever changed--or was it? Marty's friend Dr. Emmet Brown, a **mad scientist**, constructed a time machine out of a plutonium-powered DeLorean. In the second installment of the trilogy, Dr. Brown travels from the year 1985--prior to the injurious drag race--to the year 2015, along with Marty and Jennifer. While in 2015, Jennifer witnesses the Marty of 2015--whose hubris seems to have only grown since 1985--goaded into an illegal business transaction, after his colleague calls him a "chicken." Immediately following the completion of this deal, Marty's boss calls, tells him that he was monitoring the transaction, and notifies him that he is fired. Fax machines all over the house immediately receive faxes--I suppose e-mail is not popular in that version of the future--reading "YOU'RE FIRED!" Jennifer kept a copy of that fax. After a roaring time-traveling journey through the years 2015, 1955, and 1885, the time travelers return home to good old 1985. Marty, now a changed man refuses to participate in the drag race. At that moment, Jennifer's fax that read "YOU'RE FIRED!" was erased. Jennifer asks Dr. Brown about why the note was erased. Brown replies, "It means that your future hasn't been written yet. No one's has. Your future is whatever you make it." Unlike the drivers of the time-travelling DeLorean in Back to the Future, people of the future cannot have histories. When a court relies on the record of a patient from the future, they may as well be relying on the fax

3. Regarded as Having an Impairment

For an individual to be regarded as having an impairment under subsection C, he must be "treated by a public entity" as having a substantial impairment of a major life activity, or have an impairment "only as a result of the attitudes of others toward such an impairment," or be "treated by a public entity" as if he had an impairment. 28 C.F.R. § 35.104(4). Following the Court's holding in Sutton, 527 U.S. at 489, the Supreme Court has held that "a person is 'regarded as' [being] disabled within the meaning of the ADA if a covered entity mistakenly believes that the person's actual, nonlimiting impairment substantially limits one or more major life activities." Murphy v. United States Parcel Service, Inc., 527 U.S. 516, 521-22, 119 S. Ct. 2133, 144 L. Ed. 2d 484 (1999).

To resolve this inquiry in Murphy, the Court conducted a detailed inquiry as to whether the plaintiff was in fact regarded as unable to obtain a Department of Transportation certification. Similar to the analysis in Sutton, the Court treated the question of whether a person is regarded as having a disability "as an individualized inquiry," Sutton, at 483, and not a hypothetical inquiry. Murphy, at 523 ("The evidence that petitioner is regarded as unable to meet the DOT regulations is not sufficient to create a genuine issue of material fact as to whether petitioner is regarded as unable to perform a class of jobs utilizing his skills.").

The objections that apply to subsections A and B apply equally to Subsection C. How can a person not yet ascertained be regarded as having any impairment? A person may be regarded or perceived as being impaired in the present moment. However, at the present moment, the entity has no association with that person. Thus, any perceptions of a disabled person would have to take place after the entity opens for business--namely, in the future.[27] With the three provisions of the ADA relegated to the realm of H.G. Wells and Dr. Emmet Brown, the Court turns to alternative approaches.

iii. Per Se Disability

There are several fundamental problems inherent in relying on prospective patients to establish the requisite association for purposes of the ADA and

---

Jennifer brought back from 2015. If it is not adequate proof for science fiction movies, then it is certainly not adequate proof for the Court to consider.

[27] 27 To use an example from Back to the Future, even if Marty's boss in 2015 regarded Marty as having a disability in his hand, due to the notorious car accident, that perception would be irrelevant for a suit brought in 1985.

RA. Any inquiry that is fact-intensive and individualized--the required test for all disability inquiries--is impossible for future patients. But what if an intensive and individualized test was unnecessary--that is, what if a patient had a disability per se? If a certain type of disability renders a person disabled per se, then the "case-by-case" examination would be unnecessary--a person would be disabled simply by the terms of the impairment. When dealing with future, prospective patients, a per se disability is the only type that withstands the exacting "case-by-case" scrutiny of the ADA and RA. If an entity can show that any patient who would be admitted to its methadone clinic is disabled per se, then that entity would automatically and by necessity have an association with an individual known to have a disability. While courts in other Circuits have held that drug addiction is not a per se disability,[28] the Third Circuit has not settled this matter.

Per se is defined as "[o]f, in, or by itself; standing alone, without reference to additional facts," or simply "as a matter of law."[29] In the context of torts, libel per se is a type of libel "that is actionable in itself, requiring no proof of special damages."[30] Relatedly, words that are actionable per se "are inherently libelous or slanderous."[31] In the context of antitrust, a per se rule is a "judicial principle that a trade practice violates the Sherman Act simply if the practice is a restraint of trade, regardless of whether it actually harms anyone."[32] In short, the Latin per se connotes that in certain circumstances, a conclusion--which generally requires that specific premises be established--can be proven without establishing these premises. A disability per se connotes that in certain circumstances, an impairment--which usually must substantially impair a major life activity--can constitute a disability without the need to prove a substantial impairment of a major life activity. In such a case, an individualized inquiry--such as whether the impairment is substantial, or whether a major life activity is implicated--is not required. The notion of "per se" disabilities under

---

[28] 28 See Burch v. Coca-Cola Co., 119 F.3d 305, 316-17 (5th Cir. 1997) (holding that alcoholism is not a per se disability under the ADA and evidence that alcoholics, in general, are impaired is inadequate to show the substantial limitation of one or more major life activities), cert. denied, 522 U.S. 1084, 118 S. Ct. 871, 139 L. Ed. 2d 768 (1998).

[29] 29 Black's Law Dictionary 1257 (9th ed. 2009).

[30] 30 Id.

[31] 31 Id.

[32] 32 Id.

the ADA and RA in the context of drug addiction is a developing doctrine that sheds some light on this issue.

1. Disability Per Se Precedents

The Supreme Court addressed the issue of disability per se in a single sentence, and provided no meaningful resolution to this evolving area of law. In Bragdon v. Abbott, the Supreme Court considered whether asymptomatic HIV can constitute a disability under the Americans with Disabilities Act. 524 U.S. 624, 628, 118 S. Ct. 2196, 141 L. Ed. 2d 540 (1998). The Court answered this question affirmatively, noting that "[r]espondent's HIV infection is a physical impairment which substantially limits a major life activity, as the ADA defines it." Bragdon, at 642."[33] In light of the Court's holding, Justice Kennedy did not see the "need . . . [to] address the second question presented, i.e., whether HIV infection is a per se disability under the ADA." Id. In her concurring opinion, however, Justice Ginsburg observed that "HIV infection is 'a physical ... impairment that substantially limits . . . major life activities,' or is so perceived, including the afflicted individual's family relations, employment potential, and ability to care for herself...." Bragdon, 524 U.S. at 656 (Ginsburg, J., concurring) (citations omitted). In the subsequent decision of Albertson's, Inc. v. Kirkingburg, 527 U.S. 555, 119 S. Ct. 2162, 144 L. Ed. 2d 518 (1999), the Supreme Court noted that "some impairments may invariably cause a substantial limitation of a major life activity...." Id. at 56 (citing Bragdon).

In addition to HIV, several courts have considered whether alcoholism can constitute a disability per se. Many courts have found that alcoholism is not a disability per se.[34] 34 The Third Circuit has mentioned in a dictum in an

---

[33] 33 This holding comports, but does not concur with guidance issued by the EEOC and DOJ, which finds that HIV is a per se disability. See 28 C.F.R. pt. 36, app. A at 610 (noting that "symptomatic HIV disease is an impairment that substantially limits a major life activity" tic HIV disease is an impairment that substantially limits a major life activity, either because of its actual effect on the individual with HIV disease or because the reactions of other people to individuals with HIV disease cause such individuals to be treated as though they are disabled"); 29 C.F.R. pt. 1630, app. 1630.2(j) at 350 (1998) (noting that "impairments ... such as HIV infection, are inherently substantially limiting").

[34] 34 See Burch v. Coca-Cola Co., 119 F.3d 305, 316-17 (5th Cir. 1997) (holding that alcoholism is not a per se disability under the ADA and evidence that alcoholics, in general, are impaired is inadequate to show the substantial

unpublished opinion that "alcoholism is not a per se disability under our extant jurisprudence." Szczesny v. General Elec. Co., 66 Fed. Appx. 388 (3d Cir. 2003). District Courts in the Third Circuit have taken varying approaches towards disability per se, though no consensus has emerged. Compare Hinnershitz v. Ortep of Pennsylvania, Inc., 1998 U.S. Dist. LEXIS 20264, 1998 WL 962096 (E.D. Pa. 1998) ("Though the ADA does not designate any impairment as a disability per se, alcoholism is a condition which can rise to the level of a disability") with Maull v. Div. of State Police, 141 F. Supp. 2d 463 (D. Del. 2001) (holding that "Plaintiff, in accordance with the express language of the ADA, [would need] to establish that his alcoholism substantially limits a major life activity"). In Lopez v. Correctional Medical Services, a recovering heroin addict alleged that his impairment constituted a disability per se. Lopez v. Correctional Medical Services, 2009 U.S. Dist. LEXIS 55386 (D.N.J. June 30, 2009). The Court declined to rule on the disability per se issue, as the plaintiff had failed to allege any facts showing discrimination based on his addiction.[35]

The Federal Circuit in Office of Senate Sergeant at Arms v. Office of Senate Fair Employment Practices, a pre-Bragdon case, seems to have held that alcoholism is a disability per se, holding "it is well-established that alcoholism meets the definition of a disability." 95 F.3d 1102, 1105 (Fed.Cir. 1996). That is, alcoholism is a disability by itself, and not simply an impairment that must

---

limitation of one or more major life activities), cert. denied, 522 U.S. 1084, 118 S. Ct. 871, 139 L. Ed. 2d 768 (1998); see also Wallin v. Minnesota Dep't of Corrections, 153 F.3d 681, 686 n. 4 (8th Cir. 1998) (citing Burch and requiring that a plaintiff show impairment of a major life activity), cert. denied, 526 U.S. 1004, 119 S. Ct. 1141, 143 L. Ed. 2d 209 (1999); Buckley, 127 F.3d at 274 (citing Burch and requiring the plaintiff to demonstrate both "that he was actually addicted and that this addiction substantially limited one or more of his major life activities").

[35] 35 Id. The Lopez Court misstates a holding from New Directions, noting that "[i]n New Directions Treatment Servs. v. City of Reading, 490 F.3d 293, 308 (3d Cir. 2007), the Third Circuit stated that 'recovering heroin addicts are presumptively 'qualified' persons under the ADA and Rehabilitation Act.'" The Third Circuit did not make this holding. Rather, the Third Circuit in New Directions wrote "The parties do not dispute that recovering heroin addicts are presumptively 'qualified' persons under the ADA and Rehabilitation Act." New Directions, at 308 (emphasis added). The Third Circuit merely noted that the parties did not contest this fact. This was not the holding of the Court.

substantially impact a major life activity in order to constitute a disability. But it is not clear if the Federal Circuit was referring to a disability, or a mere impairment.

Miners v. Cargill Commc'ns. could be read to support the proposition that alcoholism is a disability per se, but the Court's opinion is not clear. 113 F.3d 820 (8th Cir. 1997). The Court found that the plaintiff had "made a prima facie case of discrimination under ADA." Id. at 823. With respect to proving a disability, the plaintiff "introduced evidence sufficient to establish that Cargill regarded her as being an alcoholic, thus making her disabled within the meaning of the ADA." Id. This would seem to indicate that merely introducing evidence of alcoholism constitutes a disability. Yet, in a footnote following this sentence, the Court remarked:

The ADA defines a disability as "a physical or mental impairment that substantially limits one or more major life activities ... or being regarded as having such an impairment." 42 U.S.C. § 12102(2). Although alcoholism qualifies as a disability for the purposes of the ADA, Crewe v. United States Office of Personnel Management, 834 F.2d 140, 141 (8th Cir. 1987), employers need not tolerate employees under the influence of alcohol in the workplace, 42 U.S.C. § 12114(c)(1),(2), and may hold an employee who is an alcoholic to the same standards of performance and behavior as non-alcoholics. 42 U.S.C. § 12114(c)(4). Id. at 824 fn. 5.

Did the Eighth Circuit hold that "introduc[ing] evidence sufficient to establish" that the Plaintiff was an "alcoholic" is adequate to show that she was "disabled within the meaning of the ADA"? Id. at 823. Or did the sufficient evidence adduced show that the "physical or mental impairment . . . substantially limit[ed] one or more major life activity." Id. at 824 fn. 5, The District Court of Delaware noted that this case "suggested that alcoholism is per se a disability." Maull v. Division of State Police, 141 F. Supp. 2d 463, 473 (D. Del. 2001).

None of these cases have invoked the talismanic incantation of "disability per se" This omission is even more unfortunate in light of the fact that several courts seem to conflate the notion of an impairment with the notion of a disability. A disability is defined as an impairment that substantially impairs a major life activity. An impairment, if it substantially impairs a major life activity, becomes a disability. The two concepts are not equivalent. Merely identifying an impairment, such as alcoholism, is inadequate to show a disability. Yet many courts use the terms impairment and disability interchangeably, and this generates some confusion. When a court labels an impairment like alcoholism a disability, they seem to indicate that it is a disability per se. But closer readings of these opinions show that when these courts used the term disability with regard to these conditions they appear to mean impairment. See e.g., Bryant v. Madigan, 84 F.3d 246 (7th Cir. 1996) ("alcoholism and other forms of addiction are disabilities within the meaning of the Act"). What constitutes a disability per se is far from clear.

In Regional Economic Community Action Program, Inc. v. City of Middletown, plaintiff sought a special-use permit for the construction of a halfway house for recovering alcoholics. 294 F.3d 35, 42 (2nd Cir. 2002). After several "contentious" hearings the City's planning board denied plaintiff RECAP's application, and plaintiff bought suit alleging that the City had violated the Fair Housing Act, the ADA, and the RA. Id. at 43. Defendants argued that RECAP's clients were not disabled within the meaning of the ADA and RA. Id. at 46. The District Court merely "assumed that the prospective residents of the halfway house me[t] the statutory definition of 'individual with a disability,'" and the Second Circuit "agreed." [36]

After noting that "[a]lcoholism, like drug addiction, is an 'impairment'" under the ADA and RA, the Court remarked that "mere status as an alcoholic or substance abuser does not necessarily imply a 'limitation'" Id. at 46-47, citing Burch v. Coca-Cola Co., 119 F.3d 305, 316-17 (5th Cir. 1997) (holding that alcoholism is not a per se disability under the ADA and evidence that alcoholics, in general, are impaired is inadequate to show the substantial limitation of one or more major life activities) cert. denied, 522 U.S. 1084, 118 S. Ct. 871, 139 L. Ed. 2d 768 (1998).

In order to show that plaintiff RECAP's clients were disabled--that is they have a major life activity that is substantially impaired by their alcoholism--the Court observed that New York State regulations limit admission to the Halfway House only to "persons who are unable to maintain abstinence and continued recovery in an available independent living situation." Id. at 47 citing N.Y. Comp.Codes R. & Regs. tit. 14, § 375.1. RECAP could only have admitted patients "who, inter alia, (1) had been 'diagnosed as suffering from alcohol dependence'; (2) had 'completed a course of alcoholism treatment' in an inpatient or outpatient setting; (3) were 'determined to be unable to abstain without continued care in a structured supportive setting'; and (4) were 'in need of alcoholism services on an outpatient basis in addition to the supportive counseling available in the halfway house.' Id. citing N.Y. Comp.Codes R. & Regs. tit. 14, § 375.8(c). Additionally, residents were not able to remain in the halfway house once they had "attained the skills and ability necessary to maintain abstinence and continue recovery in . . . suitable independent living." Id. citing N.Y. Comp.Codes R. & Regs. tit. 14, § 375.1(g). Based on these facts alone, and without considering an individualized inquiry,

---

[36] 36 Id. at 46.

the court found that RECAP's clients' "addictions substantially limit their ability to live independently and to live with their families"; that they are "entitled thereby to the protections of [the FHA, ADA, and RA]"; and that their "inability to live independently constitutes a substantial limitation on their ability to 'care for themselves.'" Id. at 47 citing United States v. Borough of Audubon, 797 F.Supp. 353, 359 (D.N.J. 1991), aff'd, 968 F.2d 14 (3d Cir. 1992).

The Second Circuit relied heavily on the fact that inhabitants in the halfway house would be unable to take care of themselves; "the inability to live independently without suffering a relapse--a baseline prerequisite for admittance to the RECAP facility--limits the major life activity of "caring for one's self.'" Id. As a result of this "baseline prerequisite" which correlated with their inability to take care of themselves, the "residents of the proposed halfway houses" would suffer from an impairment that affects a major life activity. Id. (emphasis added). Considering whether the impairment was substantial, rather than temporary, under New York Law, a halfway house only admits patients that will be discharged R. & Regs. tit. 14, § 375.8(g)", thus making the impairment "long-term." Regional Economic, at 47.

The Court did not conduct the specialized inquiry required by Sutton v. United States Air Lines, Inc. 527 U.S. 471, 482, 119 S. Ct. 2139, 144 L. Ed. 2d 450 (1999) (holding that "because the phrase 'substantially limits' is presented in the present tense, it must be read as requiring a person to be presently-not potentially or hypothetically-substantially limited in order to demonstrate disability."). The Second Circuit concluded that the "plaintiffs' clients would have been deemed substantially limited because they are unable to abstain from alcohol abuse without continued care; absent assistance, they cannot adequately care for themselves." Id. (emphasis added). In short, alcoholism was an impairment that substantially impaired the major life activity of taking care of oneself--the very definition of a disability under the ADA A. 42 U.S.C. § 12102. The court held that alcoholism, in and of itself, was a disability. In other words, alcoholism in this context was a disability per se.

In order to substantiate this disability per se, the Second Circuit relied on the regulated criteria governing the admission to a halfway house in order to discern whether a prospective patient is disabled. In other words, the Second Circuit held that any patient that could be admitted to a halfway house under New York law must be disabled under the definitions of the ADA. Although the Court seemed to rely on Burch--which rejected alcoholism as a per se disability--the Second Circuit's disability analysis takes the form of a per se inquiry, even if that term is not used. A disability per se by any other name would smell just as sweet.[37] A statutory grounding to ascertain a disability per

---

[37] 37 See WILLIAM SHAKESPEARE, ROMEO AND JULIET, act 2, sc. 1

se is the key to the case sub judice.

2. Analysis

Eliminating the need for an individualized inquiry is not to be undertaken lightly. In fact, very few impairments could rise to the level of qualifying as a disability per se. In order to establish that a person suffers from a disability per se, there must be a "baseline prerequisite." See Regional Economic Community Action Program, Inc. v. City of Middle town, 294 F.3d 35, 47 (2nd Cir. 2002) ("the inability to live independently without suffering a relapse--a baseline prerequisite for admittance to the RECAP facility--limits the major life activity of "caring for one's self") (emphasis added). This baseline prerequisite establishes a person's impairment by virtue of its necessary impact on his existence.

The baseline prerequisite must show that several conditions exist-these elements largely track the Supreme Court's analysis from Sutton. 527 U.S. 471, 482, 119 S. Ct. 2139, 144 L. Ed. 2d 450 (1999). First, the person must be afflicted by a physical or mental impairment covered by the ADA and RA. Second, by virtue of the nature of the impairment, a major life activity must be implicated. Third, to show that the impairment is substantial, it must be verifiable to a high degree of certainty that the impact on the major life activity must be significant. A person with an opioid addiction who meets the criteria for admission to a federally regulated methadone clinic is a strong candidate for suffering from a disability per se--the exact prospective patient under consideration in this case.

3. Impairment

Any person who seeks admission to a federally regulated methadone clinic must suffer from an opioid addiction for at least one year.[38] Under the ADA, a drug addiction is a "physical or mental impairment" that may qualify an individual as a "handicapped person." See 28 C.F.R. § 41.31(b)(1)(i), cited in Bragdon v. Abbott, 524 U.S. 624, 632, 118 S. Ct. 2196, 141 L. Ed. 2d 540 (1998). Thus, any patient afflicted by an opioid addiction suffers from an impairment covered by the ADA.

4. Major Life Activity

Opioid addictions are a crippling impairment. By the very nature of this tragic

---

("What's in a name? that which we call a rose By any other name would smell as sweet").

[38] 38 See supra note 22 and accompanying text.

condition, a person's existence is greatly affected. The addicts who are eligible for admission to a methadone clinic, as proscribed by the federal regulatory regime, must suffer from a state of inability wherein they are no longer able to help themselves. The Center for Substance Abuse Treatment (CSAT) of the Substance Abuse and Mental Health Services Administration (SAMHSA), within the U.S. Department of Health and Human Services published a manual providing guidance for accrediting opioid treatment programs. Guidelines for the Accreditation of Opioid Treatment Programs, available at http://www.dpt.samhsa.gov/pdf/OTPAccredGuidelines-2007.pdf. Relying on the Diagnostic and Statistical Manual of Mental Disorders, the Guidelines find that "behavior supportive of a diagnosis of opioid dependence includes ... [s]uch regular patterns of compulsive drug use that daily activities are typically planned around obtaining and administering opioid." Id. at 10. Additionally "[b]ehavior indicative of opioid addiction includes . . . [c]ontinuing use of the opiate despite known adverse consequences to self, family, or society." Id. at 11. RHJ is "fully certified by both the CSAT and DEA and licensed by the Commonwealth to operate a methadone clinic." (Compl. 9.) Any patient admitted to a clinic operated by RHJ would have to be treated under the auspices of these regulations.

Major life activities constitute tasks central to most people's daily lives. Major life activities include "functions such as caring for oneself, performing manual tasks, walking, seeing, hearing, speaking, breathing, learning, and working." See Sulima v. Tobyhanna Army Depot, 602 F.3d 177 (3rd Cir. 2010) citing 29 C.F.R. § 1630.2(i). This list is merely illustrative and not exhaustive. Bragdon, 524 U.S. at 639. The Third Circuit has also considered tasks such as thinking and interacting with others as examples of a major life activity. See Andreoli v. Gates, 482 F.3d 641, 651-52 (3d Cir. 2007); see also McAlindin v. County of San Diego, 192 F.3d 1226, 1233 (9th Cir. 1999) (holding that "interacting with others" constitutes a major life activity).

Opioid addicts are unable to maintain a normal lifestyle, and the dependency on drugs disrupts their lives. Such compulsive dependencies force a person to constantly think about feeding his addiction, often at any cost. An addict's schedule revolves around obtaining his next dose of drugs. If admitted to a methadone clinic, treatments are mandatory daily (and for addicts in the City of DuBois, this regimen includes a three-hour daily commute to the closest methadone treatment facility). This rigorous schedule will inhibit an addict's ability to maintain a job, interact with friends and family, and be a productive member of society--and perhaps more importantly, impact major life activities. If an opioid addiction disrupts a person's ability to live, work, and engage with members of society in order to secure his next fix, a patient admitted to a methadone clinic with an opioid addiction would almost certainly have a major life activity affected by his impairment.

5. Substantial Impairment

While opioid addictions can impact major life activities, when an addict is eligible for admission into a methadone clinic, the impairment may rise to the level of substantiality. Though the word "[s]ubstantially in the phrase 'substantially limits' suggests considerable or . . . a large degree [of limitation]," Williams, 534 U.S. at 197 (2002) (emphasis added), the Supreme Court has made clear that "[t]he Act addresses substantial limitations on major life activities, not utter inabilities," Bragdon, 524 U.S. at 641 (emphasis added). See also Fiscus v. Wal-Mart Stores, Inc., 385 F.3d 378 (3d Cir. 2004) ("We also read the Supreme Court to hold that a substantial limitation of a major life activity does not mean impossibility or even great physical difficulty; rather, substantial limitation is weighed in a broad, practical sense."). When evaluating substantial limitation, the courts must consider a plaintiffs ability to compensate for a disability through mitigating measures, Albertson's, Inc. v. Kirkingburg, 527 U.S. 555, 565-67, 119 S. Ct. 2162, 144 L. Ed. 2d 518 (1999), but the essence of the inquiry regards comparing the conditions, manner, or duration under which the average person in the general population can perform the major life activity at issue with those under which an impaired plaintiff must perform. Taylor v. Phoenixville Sch. Dist., 184 F.3d 296, 307 (3d Cir. 1999) (emphasis added). The EEOC guidelines counsel that the following factors should be considered in determining whether an individual is substantially limited:

(i) The nature and severity of the impairment;

(ii) The duration or expected duration of the impairment; and

(iii) The permanent or long term impact, or the expected permanent or long term impact of or resulting from the impairment. 29 C.F.R. § 1630.2(j)(2) (emphasis added).

In many respects, the baseline prerequisite for opioid addicts gaining admission to a methadone clinic demands satisfaction of these requirements. First, the "nature and severity" of opioid addictions are quite significant. The "behavior supportive of a diagnosis of opioid dependence includes ... [s]uch regular patterns of compulsive drug use that daily activities are typically planned around obtaining and administering opioid." Guidelines for the Accreditation of Opioid Treatment Programs, available at http://www.dpt.samhsa.gov/pdf/OTPAccredGuidelines-2007.pdf at 10. Second, in order to qualify for admission to a methadone clinic, federal regulations require an impairment of at least one year.[39] Second, this duration of impairment is quite long, and in many cases, a patient requires methadone

---

[39] 39 See supra note 22 and accompanying text.

treatment indefinitely in order to stay clean from opiates. A study of 105 patients who left methadone treatment showed that 82.1% returned to intravenous drug use within ten to twelve months without treatment. JOHN C. BALL & ALAN ROSS, THE EFFECTIVENESS OF METHADONE MAINTENANCE TREATMENT 182-85 (1991). Third, the long term impact of this impairment, in the absence of methadone treatment, is often permanent. Id. In light of these facts, life activities impaired by an opioid addiction would almost certainly be substantial.

The Court need not find that an opioid addiction must be a disability per se. The "plausibility" determination is "a context-specific task that requires the reviewing court to draw on its judicial experience and common sense." Fowler, at 210-211. At this stage of the litigation, in light of the lengthy analysis supra, and considering the standard of review for a motion for a judgment on the pleadings, the Court finds that an opioid addiction constituting a disability per se is "plausible." Ashcroft v. Iqbal, 129 S.Ct. 1937,1959-1960, 173 L. Ed. 2d 868 (2009).

* * *

Based on the pleadings, because Plaintiff has shown that any patient who would be admitted to its methadone clinic would by necessity have an impairment that substantially impairs a major life activity, RHJ automatically has an association with an individual known to have a disability. Thus, standing for equitable relief would be proper.

f. Standing for Damage Claims
In light of the standing analysis discussed supra, the resolution of the standing inquiry for damages is relatively straightforward, and easily satisfies the Iqbal requirements. Ashcroft v. Iqbal, 129 S.Ct. 1937, 1959-1960, 173 L. Ed. 2d 868 (2009). This injury the lost profits by the clinic due to the denial of the permit--was only suffered by the clinic itself, and dictates a remedy of damages. Plaintiff does not need to rely on any injuries to third parties. While praying for damages, the complaint sought "damages for the harm it experienced as a result of Defendant's discriminatory practices," Complaint. p.19 (emphasis added). That is, the damages it experienced, and not any damages suffered by patients. Because Plaintiff's association with patients afflicted with opioid addicts is "imminent," Article III is satisfied, and the ADA and RA require no further of proof. The injury suffered here creates standing for the claims of damages.

II. Res Judicata
Defendant claims that Plaintiff is barred by the doctrine of res judicata from asserting Counts I, II, and III. Defendant bases this assertion on the consent decree the parties entered into on December 7, 2006. The City claims that

RHJ "stood silently before the Pennsylvania Court of Common Pleas and affirmatively chose not to challenge the constitutionality of § 621." The City also claims that RHJ "accepted the validity of ... § 621 and stipulated from its applicability." This is a mischaracterization of the nature of the stipulation and consent decree. In the decree, RHJ merely acknowledged that the "Beaver Meadow Walkway is a public park within the meaning of Section 621 ... and as a result, that the methadone clinic opened by [RHJ] ... is in violation of the terms of Section 621 because the site at 994 Beaver Drive is within 500 feet of the aforementioned park and RHJ ... did fail to obtain either an occupancy permit or certificate of use from the City of DuBois." (Doc. No 38-2.) RHJ only conceded that its facility was near a public park, and that it was in violation of § 621 for failing to obtain the requisite permits. The Court's order established a temporary arrangement in order for RHJ to seek the necessary permits. RHJ never actually contested the validity of § 621.

The facts in this case are quite similar to those in Sullivan v. City of Pittsburgh, 811 F.2d 171 (3rd Cir. 1987). In Sullivan, the City of Pittsburgh denied use permits for alcoholic treatment facilities, and recovering alcoholics sought declaratory and injunctive relief. Id. The parties entered into a consent decree in the Allegheny County Court of Common Pleas to cease operation of the alcohol treatment facility, but did not litigate the constitutionality of the City's decisions. Id. at 180. After the resolution of the matter in state court, the treatment center brought suit in the Western District of Pennsylvania, alleging violation of the Constitution and federal statutes. Id. The City of Pittsburgh appealed the District Court's order that the use permit shall issue, arguing that the District Court failed to accord full faith and credit to the judgment of the Court of Common Pleas. Id. at 180-81. On appeal, the Third Circuit held that in consideration of the principles of res judicata, "[i]n Pennsylvania, a consent decree is a judgment only as to matters actually litigated and cannot preclude claims which were not raised before and resolved by the approving court." Id. at 181 citing Keystone Bldg. Corp. v. Lincoln Sav. and Loan Ass'n, 468 Pa. 85, 360 A.2d 191 (1976). Because the constitutional and statutory claims were never raised before the Court of Common Pleas, the alcohol treatment center was "not afforded the full and fair opportunity to litigate those claims, which is a prerequisite for preclusive effect under Pennsylvania law." Id. at 181 citing Safeguard Mut. Ins. Co. v. Williams, 463 Pa. 567, 345 A.2d 664 (1975). Thus, it was appropriate for the parties to litigate this issue, and res judicata was not a bar.

Sullivan would seem to control the instant matter. In both cases, the consent decree precluded the opportunity for the parties to have a "full and fair opportunity to litigate those claims" before the state court. Id. at 181. Accordingly, the consent decree issued by the Court of Common Pleas has no preclusive effect under Pennsylvania laws to matters not litigated, and the doctrine of res judicata does not apply to bar claims I, II, and III.

III. Waiver & Estoppel

Defendant also claims that Plaintiff should be estopped from raising Counts I, II, and III because it previously waived these issues by failing to contest the constitutionality of § 621 before the Court of Common Pleas. This argument is not supported by the consensual agreements the parties entered into. On December 7, 2006, RHJ and the City mutually agreed that the state court should issue an injunction, and stipulated that RHJ was in violation of § 621 because it attempted to place a methadone clinic within 500 feet of a public park. That was the extent of the stipulation. In fact, the stipulation expressly noted that RHJ did not waive any of its claims regarding § 621, stating that RHJ's "defenses thereto are not waived by the issuance of this permanent injunction by consent of the parties." This stipulation is dispositive to this issue. The defenses were not waived.

Furthermore, in light of this stipulation, RHJ was not afforded a full and fair opportunity to assert its constitutional and statutory rights before the Court of Common Pleas. Where "[th]e conduct of the parties and the court, and the language of the [consent] decree itself, indicates that they did not intend that decree to act as an adjudication of the underlying statutory and constitutional issues, the "issue was not addressed and was reserved for future determination." See Keystone Bldg. Corp. v. Lincoln Sav. and Loan Ass'n, 468 Pa. 85, 360 A.2d 191, 195 (1976). In light of this stipulation, the Court will not exercise the broad equitable remedy of estoppel to find that Plaintiff waived the right to contest these issues.

IV. Immunity

Defendant claims that since its actions were authorized by a duly enacted state law, and following a Court's order, it is immune from damages for Counts I, II, and III under 42 U.S.C. § 1983, the ADA, and the RA respectively. For three decades, the Supreme Court has held that municipalities do not have immunity for suits stemming from 42 U.S.C. § 1983. See Owen v. City of Independence, Missouri, 445 U.S. 622, 657, 100 S. Ct. 1398, 63 L. Ed. 2d 673 (1980) ("municipalities have no immunity from damages liability flowing from their constitutional violations"). The ADA specifically protects disabled persons from discrimination by a "public entity," 42 U.S.C. § 12132, which would include the City of DuBois. See New Directions Treatment Services v. City of Reading, 490 F.3d 293, 301 n.7 (2007). Similarly, the RA protects disabled persons from discrimination by "any program or activity receiving Federal financial assistance," 29 U.S.C. § 794, which would include the City of

DuBois.[40] Congress specifically created causes of action against cities like DuBois, so immunity would not attach for suits under the ADA or RA.

Defendant concedes that "while general immunities may not apply to municipalities in a typical civil rights case, this case is vastly different." Defendant argues that the City was simply enforcing a state law--a valid law at the time of the enforcement. Specifically, the city merely "applied [§621] only after a state court ordered that § 621 applied to RHJ's permit application." The Defendant argues that when "the local government acted at the direction of its sovereign, the State [sic] of Pennsylvania," and the City "played no role in the development or promulgation of the state statute," this Court "must extend immunity to the City for those claims that arise from actions the City took pursuant to the direction of the state." The Defendant dubs Plaintiff's suit as amounting to "shooting the messenger." Simply put, DuBois is not liable for enforcing an unconstitutional law from the Commonwealth of Pennsylvania.

Though the notion of "shooting the messenger" dates back to Sophocles[41] and Shakespeare,[42] it finds no refuge in our jurisprudence of municipal liability. Defendant provides no citations to substantiate the "shoot the messenger" theory of liability, other than several cases that deal with immunity for individuals, rather than immunity for a municipality. These precedents are inapposite. Beyond the lack of support, the implications of this theory are troubling. The Defendant seems to assert that it is the sovereign state, and not the municipality, that should be held liable for enacting unconstitutional laws which are applied by the municipality. This cannot be correct. According to the Supreme Court's interpretation of the 11th Amendment, a state as sovereign cannot be sued in federal court by a citizen. Hans v. Louisiana, 134 U.S. 1, 10 S. Ct. 504, 33 L. Ed. 842 (1890). Citizens can only sue state officials under the Ex parte Young fiction for injunctive relief if the state official was

---

[40] 40 See e.g., TRACK THE MONEY, http://www.recovery.gov (last visited September 24, 2010) (noting that City of DuBois received numerous grants and loans from the Federal Government as a result of the American Recovery and Reinvestment Act of 2009, Public Law 111-5).

[41] 41 SOPHOCLES, SOPHOCLES, VOLUME II. ANTIGONE. THE WOMEN OF TRACHIS. PHILOCTETES. OEDPIUS AT COLONUS (Hugh Lloyd-Jones trans., Loeb Classical Library 1994) (442 B.C.) ("No one loves the messenger who brings bad news.").

[42] 42 WILLIAM SHAKESPEARE, ANTHONY AND CLEOPATRA, act 1, sc. 2. ("The nature of bad news infects the teller.").

prosecuting the citizen for violation of a state law. 209 U.S. 123, 28 S. Ct. 441, 52 L. Ed. 714 (1908).

Ex parte Young would not apply in this case, as the actor seeking to enforce the state law was the City of DuBois, not an official of the Commonwealth. A suit could not proceed against any state official under Ex parte Young. According to the Defendant's theory, a suit could not lie against the City, because it was simply enforcing a state law. If the Court were to adopt the Defendant's theory, Plaintiff would be unable to sue the municipality, and would be unable to sue the state--there would be a clear violation of rights, without a remedy. This inappropriate and unacceptable conclusion would stand in the face of the bedrock principles upon which our Republic was founded. See Marbury v. Madison, 5 U.S. 137, 2 L. Ed. 60 (1803)(Marshall, C.J.) ("The very essence of civil liberty certainly consists in the right of every individual to claim the protection of the laws, whenever he receives an injury.").

This holding also conflicts with the responsibility of government officials to comport their actions with our Constitution. Indeed, our Constitution requires that all "Members of the several State Legislatures" and executive officers "of the Several states, shall be bound by Oath or Affirmation, to support this Constitution." U.S. CONST. art. VI. See also Socialist Workers Party v. Martin, 345 F.Supp. 1132, 1134 (S.D. Tex. 1972) (finding that Article VI of the Constitution provides for affirmation of support of the Constitution from candidates for municipal offices). As the Supreme Court stated, "a decisionmaker would be derelict in his duties if, at some point, he did not consider whether his decision comports with constitutional mandates." Owen v. City of Independence, 445 U.S. 622, 656, 100 S. Ct. 1398, 63 L. Ed. 2d 673 (1980). Municipalities cannot shirk their responsibility to follow this oath, and do not receive immunity for blindly following laws passed by a state. See Owen, at 651-52 ("The knowledge that a municipality will be liable for all of its injurious conduct, whether committed in good faith or not, should create an incentive for officials who may harbor doubts about the lawfulness of their intended actions to err on the side of protecting citizens' constitutional rights."). Defendant is not immune from liability under Counts I, II, and III.

V. Federalism

Defendant argues that this Court cannot "consistent with precepts of federalism, enter the sphere of local governance and order the City to grant RHJ" a permit, as this would "impermissibly interfere in the local governance of the City." Then-Justice Rehnquist wrote in Rizzo v. Goode in 1976, long before the so-called "Federalism Revolution" of the Rehnquist Court, that "where injunctive relief is sought, not against the judicial branch of the state government, but against those in charge of an executive branch of an agency of state or local governments" the "principles of federalism which play such an important part" must be considered. 423 U.S. 362, 380, 96 S. Ct. 598, 46 L. Ed. 2d 561 (1976). In these situations, there are "delicate issues of federal-state relationships." Id. citing Mayor v. Educational Equality League, 415 U.S. 605, 615, 94 S. Ct. 1323, 39 L. Ed. 2d 630 (1974) (Powell, J.).

This Court is not prepared to sit as a "zoning court of appeals," Chesterfield Development Corp. v. City of Chesterfield, 963 F.2d 1102, 1104 (8th Cir. 1992), and does not seek to "transform[] run-of-the-mill zoning cases into cases of constitutional right," Village of Willowbrook v. Olech, 528 U.S. 562, 566, 120 S. Ct. 1073, 145 L. Ed. 2d 1060 (2000) (Breyer, J., concurring). In this case, the Court will approach the issuance of any injunctions with the proper respect for principles of federalism. Pennhurst State School & Hospital v. Halderman, 465 U.S. 89, 104 n. 13, 104 S. Ct. 900, 79 L. Ed. 2d 67 (1984) citing Rizzo v. Goode, 423 U.S. 362, 378, 96 S. Ct. 598, 46 L. Ed. 2d 561 (1976) ("Where, as here, the exercise of authority by state officials is attacked, federal courts must be constantly mindful of the 'special delicacy of the adjustment to be preserved between federal equitable power and State administration of its own law.'"). However, this challenge is somewhat premature. The Court is not awarding injunctive relief at this stage. The Court is only considering the Motion for Judgment on the Pleadings. What relief, if any, is awarded at a later stage is not before the Court at this time.

VI. Statute of Limitations

Both parties agree that claims brought under 42 U.S.C. § 1983, §504 of the Rehabilitation Act, and Title II of the Americans with Disabilities Act, apply the forum state's statute of limitations for personal injury claims. Wilson v. Garcia, 471 U.S. 261, 105 S. Ct. 1938, 85 L. Ed. 2d 254 (1985); Disabled in Action of Pennsylvania v. Southeastern Pa. Transp., 539 F.3d 199, 208 (3d Cir. 2008). Both parties agree that the Commonwealth of Pennsylvania applies a two-year statute of limitations to personal injury claims. 42 Pa. Const. Stat. § 5524. The complaint was filed on May 14, 2009. Both parties agree that Plaintiff can rely on any claims that accrued after May 14, 2007. Plaintiff asserts that "Plaintiff can only rely on events and transactions that took place on or after May 14, 2007." This is not correct, and misstates the operation of the statute of limitations. Plaintiff can only raise claims that accrued following May 14, 2007, but is in no way barred from relying on evidence that came into existence prior to that date.

Plaintiff relies on two primary events to establish its case. First, the City's denial of the zoning application on May 14, 2007, and second, the enactment of the new zoning ordinance on November 27, 2007. Both of these events occurred within the statute of limitations. Plaintiff does discuss certain facts in its pleadings, which occurred in the time period beginning in October of 2006 when the City attempted to enjoin the opening of the clinic. Plaintiff could not--and did not--assert a claim based events that occurred before May 14, 2007. Rather, Plaintiff simply relies on these events, including the actions of the City of DuBois in 2006 with respect to the enforcement of § 621, to establish the factual record. This is permissible, to the extent that Plaintiff is not attempting to litigate claims based on events that occurred before May 14, 2007. All of Plaintiff's claims are timely filed and not barred by the statute of limitations.

VII. Ripeness

Defendant claims that RHJ's attempt to raise an as-applied challenge to the new ordinance is not ripe. The Third Circuit has held that in as-applied challenges "in cases involving land-use decisions, a property owner does not have a ripe constitutional claim until the zoning authorities have had an opportunity to arrive at a final, definitive position regarding how they will apply the regulations at issue to the particular land in question." Sameric Corp. of DE v. City of Philadelphia, 142 F.3d 582 (3d Cir. 1998). See also Acierno v. Mitchell, 6 F.3d 970, 974-75 (3d Cir. 1993); Taylor Investment, Ltd v. Upper Darby Twp., 983 F.2d 1285 (3d Cir. 1993). Under the "finality rule," a plaintiff property owner must prove that a "final decision has been reached by the agency before it may seek compensatory or injunctive relief in federal court on federal constitutional grounds." Acierno, 6 F.3d at 975. It is undisputed that Plaintiff has not applied for a permit or variance under the New Ordinance. Defendant claims that the failure to seek a final decision from the Council renders this challenge unripe.

However, Plaintiffs do not challenge the constitutionality of the New Ordinance under the 14th Amendment as-applied. Rather, they challenge it on its face. (Compl. 71.) ("A city zoning ordinance that bars the establishment or operation of drug treatment clinic in districts where other medical treatment clinics are permitted to operate is discriminatory on its face against persons with disabilities ...")(emphasis added). The finality rule does not apply "to facial attacks on a zoning ordinance, i.e., a claim that the mere enactment of a regulation either constitutes a taking without just compensation, or a substantive violation of due process or equal protection." County Concrete Corp. v. Town of Roxbury, 442 F.3d 159, 164 (3rd Cir. 2006). "A 'final decision' is not necessary in that context because 'when a landowner makes a facial challenge, he or she argues that any application of the regulation is unconstitutional; for an as-applied challenge, the landowner is only attacking the decision that applied the regulation to his or her property, not the regulation in general.'" Id. citing (Eide v. Sarasota County, 908 F.2d 716, 724 n. 14 (11th Cir. 1990)). Notwithstanding the lack of a "final decision," this matter is ripe for adjudication because, as demonstrated infra, Plaintiff states a plausible claim that the mere enactment of this ordinance violates substantive due process and equal protection.

VIII. Fourteenth Amendment Claims
Plaintiff brings claims alleging a violation of substantive due process and the equal protection clauses of the Fourteenth Amendment. All of these claims survive Defendant's Motions.

a. Procedural Due Process
Defendant claims that RHJ cannot assert a procedural due process claim because it failed to rely on the Pennsylvania court system to review any alleged constitutional deprivation of rights stemming from the zoning dispute. Plaintiff replied that it "did not assert a procedural due process claim in the Complaint." Because Plaintiff expressly waived this issue, Defendant's challenge under procedural due process is moot.

b. Substantive Due Process
Substantive due process "is an area of law 'famous for controversy, and not known for its simplicity.'" DeBlasio v. Zoning Bd. of Adjustment, 53 F.3d 592, 598 (3d Cir.1995) (quoting Schaper v. City of Huntsville, 813 F.2d 709, 715 (5th Cir.1987)). The "fabric of substantive due process, as woven by our courts, encompasses at least two very different threads" pertinent to this case. Nicholas v. Pennsylvania State University, 227 F.3d 133, 139 (3rd Cir. 2000) (Alito, J.). The first strand of substantive due process claims "applies when a plaintiff challenges the validity of a legislative act." Id. The second strand "protects against certain types of non-legislative state" or executive acts. Id. As then-Judge Alito instructed "[i]t is crucial to keep in mind the distinction between legislative acts and non-legislative or executive acts." Id. at 139 n1.
Non-legislative, or executive acts, are government actions, "such as employment decisions [which] typically apply to one person or to a limited number of persons." Id. at 139 n1. citing (Homar v. Gilbert, 89 F.3d 1009, 1027 (3d Cir. 1996)(Alito, J., concurring in part and dissenting in part)). See also, McKinney v. Pate, 20 F.3d 1550, 1557 n. 9 (11th Cir. 1994) ("Executive acts characteristically apply to a limited number of persons (and often to only one person); executive acts typically arise from the ministerial or administrative activities of members of the executive branch. The most common examples are employment terminations.") (citations omitted). In contrast, legislative acts are defined as "laws and broad executive regulations, [which] apply to large segments of society." Nicholas, at 139 n. 1. See also, McKinney v. Pate, 20 F.3d 1550, 1557 n. 9 (11th Cir. 1994) ("Legislative acts, on the other hand, generally apply to a larger segment of-if not all of-society; laws and broad-ranging executive regulations are the most common

examples.").

This distinction is significant because it determines the appropriate standard for substantive due process challenges. As Judge Alito explained in Nicholas v. Pennsylvania State Univ., "typically, a legislative act will withstand substantive due process challenge if the government 'identifies the legitimate state interest that the legislature could rationally conclude was served by the statute.'" 227 F.3d 133, 139 (3d Cir.2000) (citation omitted). In contrast, non-legislative state action violates substantive due process if it is "arbitrary, irrational, or tainted by improper motive," or if it is "so egregious that it 'shocks the conscience.'" Id. (citations omitted). See also, United Artists Theatre Circuit, Inc. v. Township of Warrington, 316 F.3d 392, 399-400 (2003) ("executive action violates substantive due process only when it shocks the conscience")(emphasis added).

The new ordinance as well as § 621 clearly appear to be legislative acts. Both were implemented under the authority of the Pennsylvania Municipal Planning Code, which provides "The governing body of each municipality, in accordance with the conditions and procedures set forth in this act, may enact, amend and repeal zoning ordinances to implement comprehensive plans and to accomplish any of the purposes of this act." 53 P.S. § 10601. Pennsylvania courts have construed this provision such that the governing body of each municipality "is acting in a legislative capacity when considering an amendment to land use ordinances" and "the consideration and adoption of zoning amendments is a purely legislative act." Springwood Development Partners, 985 A.2d 298, 304 (Pa.Cmwlth. 2009). Furthermore, Pennsylvania courts typically characterize the duties of zoning boards as "legislative acts"[43] or "legislative functions."[44] Using Judge Alito's definition of "legislative act," the relevant zoning statutes in this case are "broad executive regulations, [and] apply to large segments of society," rather than "apply[ing] to one person or to a limited number of persons." Nicholas, at 139 n. 1. Facially, the zoning

---

[43] 43 See e.g., Ludwig v. Zoning Hearing Bd. of Earl Tp, 658 A.2d 836, 838 (Pa.Cmwlth 1995) ("Without question, the promulgation of a zoning ordinance is a legislative act.") (emphasis added).

[44] 44 See e.g., Ethan-Michael, Inc. v. Board of Supervisors of Union Tp., 918 A.2d 203, 210 (Pa.Cmwlth. 2007) (noting that the Court cannot become involved with challenges to the "designation of zoning boundaries" without "improperly assuming almost the entire legislative function.")(emphasis added); In re Long Lane Acres Appeal, 11 Pa. D. & C.4th 336, 1991 WL 356111 *3 (Pa.Com.Pl 1991) ("Rezoning is a purely legislative function reserved to the governing body")(emphasis added).

ordinances applied to all methadone clinics, and not just RHJ.[45] Additionally, this case bears similarities to Concrete Corp. v. Town of Roxbury, where the Third Circuit found that a zoning ordinance should be treated as a legislative act. 442 F.3d 159, 169 (3rd Cir. 2006). The Court finds that the statutes challenged in Counts I and IV are "legislative acts."

Because the statutes are legislative, and not executive acts, Plaintiff does not need to meet the "shocks the conscience test." See County Concrete Corp. v. Town of Roxbury, 442 F.3d 159, 169 (2006) ("But United Artists did not apply the 'shocks the conscience' standard to legislative action; rather, we clearly held in United Artists that 'executive action violates substantive due process only when it shocks the conscience.'") citing (United Artists Theatre Circuit, Inc. v. Twp. of Warrington, PA., 316 F.3d 392, 400 (3d Cir. 2003)). Defendant incorrectly asserts that Plaintiff needs to identify a property interest for a due process challenge. Plaintiff does not need to establish a "protected property interest to which the Fourteenth Amendment's due process protection applies' as this standard only applies in a 'non-legislative substantive due process claim.'" Nicholas, at 139-40 citing (Woodwind Estates v. Gretkowski, 205 F.3d 118, 123 (3rd Cir. 2000)). For Plaintiff's "facial substantive due process challenge to the Ordinance to be successful, [it] must 'allege facts that would support a finding of arbitrary or irrational legislative action by the'" City of DuBois. County Concrete Corp. at 169, citing Pace Resources, Inc., v. Shrewsbury Twp., 808 F.2d 1023, 1034 (3d Cir. 1987).

In County Concrete Corp., the Third Circuit found that the appellants alleged "facts that indicate irrationality and arbitrariness, and 'present a case involving actions aimed at [appellants] for reasons unrelated to land use planning.'" 442 F.3d at 170 citing Pace, at 1035. The "complaint charges appellees with attempting to impede appellants' sand and gravel extraction operations on one tract, and their attempts to expand to another tract, through false accusations, verbal disparagement and the imposition of illegal conditions and restrictions on their business in violation a 1993 agreement." Id. Following this alleged animus, the municipality "enacted the Ordinance, which rezoned appellants' land from Industrial to either Rural Residential or Open Space. While the land in question is of an industrial nature and has been zoned for industrial uses for close to fifty years, the new designations only permit single-family detached dwellings and a minimum lot size of three acres." Id. The Court concluded that "[t]here is nothing in the complaint that would indicate any possible motivation for the enactment of the Ordinance other than a desire to

---

[45] 45 However, as discussed infra, for purposes of the equal protection analysis it seems that Plaintiff may in fact have been singled out for different treatment.

prevent appellants from continuing to operate and expand their extraction business." Id. This type of "animus is not a legitimate reason for enacting a zoning ordinance, see Brady v. Town of Colchester, 863 F.2d 205, 216 (2d Cir. 1988), and is unrelated to land use planning, see Pace, 808 F.2d at 1035." Id.

The facts alleged in the complaint plausibly show that the actions of the City of DuBois were based on an animus toward Plaintiff, and the patients its clinic intended to serve, rather than concerns about land use planning. In this case, Plaintiff signed a lease at a site on March 31, 2006. Plaintiff claims that the property was zoned as a "Transitional District," which permitted a medical facility to open. In late September or early October of 2006, nearly six months after RHJ signed the lease, the plans to open the clinic became public. Almost immediately, Plaintiff claims they were subjected to a massive wave of negative press coverage. Plaintiff claims, and Defendant disputes, that the mayor of DuBois stated in a radio interview that RHJ would likely not receive approval from the city to open such a facility and compared having a methadone treatment center in the City to "other cities dumping their garbage in DuBois."

Following a City Council meeting on October 9, 2006, on October 19, 2006, the City Council notified Plaintiff that the location was too close to a recreational park--which was in fact a sidewalk--and could not open at that location. Notwithstanding this letter, Plaintiff opened the clinic as planned on October 25, 2006. Defendant filed for an injunction the very next day on Friday, October 27, 2006, arguing that Plaintiff was opening the clinic in violation of § 621. The Court granted the preliminary injunction on Wednesday, November 1, 2006. Plaintiff claims that the Court did not hear oral arguments from both sides before issuing the injunction. Defendant claims arguments were heard. After the parties stipulated that the sidewalk constituted a public park for purposes of § 621, the Court entered a permanent injunction.

On June 16, 2007, the Third Circuit ruled that § 621 violated the ADA and RA. New Directions Treatment Services v. City of Reading, 490 F.3d 293 (3d Cir. 2007). Relying on this opinion, in November of 2007, RHJ filed a motion to dissolve the injunction. The City opposed RHJ's motion, despite the fact that the Third Circuit had recently held the law on which the injunction was based violated the ADA and RA. That month, RHJ discussed with the City of DuBois the possibility of filing a change of use application to locate the clinic in an alternative site. On November 22, 2007, the DuBois City Council proposed an ordinance that prohibited "methadone or drug treatment clinics or centers," and not other types of medical facilities, in the Transition District. RHJ had signed a lease for a property sited in the Transition District. The ordinance also permitted medical facilities "with the exception of methadone treatment facilities and other drug treatment facilities of any kind" in the "Commercial-Highway Zoning District." Methadone clinics could only be opened in an "0-1 Office District." Plaintiff claims that there are no suitable sites for a methadone treatment facility located within the "0-1 Office District." Defendant disputes this assertion, but this issue presents a significant issue of fact that is unclear based on the pleadings. The ordinance was passed on November 27, 2007, and Plaintiff was again prevented from opening the methadone clinic. On March 7, 2008, nearly nine months after New Directions was decided, the Court dissolved the injunction. RHJ terminated its lease in July of 2008.

These alleged facts--which are all-too-common in situations where a municipality uses zoning practices to prevent the opening of a methadone clinic it opposes[46] -- suggest that the actions of the City of DuBois were based on an improper animus that was "unrelated to land use planning." Pace, 808 F.2d at 1035. "This case presents the familiar conflict between the legal principle of non-discrimination and the political principle of not-in-my-backyard." New Direction Treatment Services v. City of Reading, 490 F.3d 293, 296 (3rd Cir. 2007) (Smith, J.). If the City of DuBois were to have merely enforced § 621, and subsequently agreed to dissolve the injunction following New Directions, the City could claim to be simply adhering to § 621. This was not the case. When RHJ moved to dissolve the injunction, which was

---

[46] 46 See e.g, A Helping Hand, LLC v. Baltimore County. MD, 355 Fed.Appx. 773 (4th Cir. 2009) ("Despite significant opposition from the local community, the Clinic, a for-profit methadone clinic, opened at its current site .... At that time, in response to the public mood, the County enacted an ordinance restricting the location of all 'state-licensed medical clinics,' including the Clinic.); MX Group, Inc. v. City of Covington, 293 F.3d 326 (6th Cir. 2002) ("After the zoning permit [for the methadone clinic] was issued, town residents expressed their displeasure regarding the proposed clinic at a City Commission meeting. The Board adopted [an amendment] ... that completely foreclosed Plaintiff's opportunity to locate [a methadone clinic anywhere] in the city."); Bay Area Addiction Research and Treatment. Inc. v. City of Antioch, 179 F.3d 725, 727-729 (9th Cir. 1999) ("In 1998, Bay Area Addiction Research and Treatment, Inc ... tried to relocate their methadone clinic to the City of Antioch, California ... Antioch residents had learned of BAARTs plans for the Sunset Lane site and began to express their concern that the methadone clinic would result in an increase in crime .... On June 9, 1998, the city council approved ... another urgency ordinance ... [that] amended the first ordinance so as to prohibit only methadone clinics from operating within 500 feet of any residential property.").

premised on an invalid statute, the City actively opposed the motion. This fact suggests that DuBois wanted to prevent the clinic from opening, notwithstanding the validity of the law. With lightning speed after RHJ moved to dissolve the injunction, the City enacted a new ordinance that was much like § 621. The purpose of this statute, it would seem, was to single out methadone clinics from other medical facilities, and greatly restrict where they could be located. Taking all of these allegations, the Court finds that Plaintiff states a plausible claim for a substantive due process violations. While Plaintiff's claim "may be ultimately unsuccessful if the [City] is able to demonstrate a legitimate reason" for its actions, there is no basis for a dismissal on the pleadings. See County Concrete Corp. v. Town of Roxbury, 442 F.3d 159, 170 (3rd Cir. 2006).

c. Equal Protection
Defendant claims that Plaintiff failed to state a claim for an equal protection violation. "Unlike a substantive due process challenge, where the question is whether it was irrational for a [municipality] to have passed a zoning law at all, in an equal protection challenge the question is whether 'the [City] has irrationally distinguished between similarly situated classes." County Concrete Corp. v. Town of Roxbury, 442 F.3d 159, 171 (3rd Cir. 2006) quoting Rogin v. Bensalem Twp., 616 F.2d 680, 689 (3d Cir. 1980). Traditionally, the equal protection analysis was two-fold. First, the Court must inquire "whether the complaining party is similarly situated to other uses that are either permitted as of right, or by special permit, in a certain zone." Congregation Kol Ami v. Abington Twp., 309 F.3d 120, 137 (3d Cir. 2002). If "the entities are similarly situated, then the [City] must justify its different treatment of the two," id., by demonstrating that the ordinance is rationally related to a legitimate government purpose. Rogin, 616 F.2d at 688.
Following the Supreme Court's 2000 case of Village of Willowbrook v. Olech, 528 U.S. 562, 120 S. Ct. 1073, 145 L. Ed. 2d 1060 (2000), litigants are presented with an alternative method to state a claim under the equal protection clause of the Fourteenth Amendment for land use and zoning challenges. In Discovery House, the 7th Circuit found that "a[n Olech] 'class of one' [claim] is viable under the Equal Protection Clause" for a methadone clinic to challenge the denial of a zoning permit. Discovery House, Inc. v. Consolidated City of Indianapolis, 319 F.3d 277, 282 (7th Cir. 2003) citing Village of Willowbrook v. Olech, 528 U.S. 562, 120 S. Ct. 1073, 145 L. Ed. 2d 1060 (2000).
Under the class of one approach, a single plaintiff[47] can present himself (or

---

[47] 47 Corporations are considered persons for purposes of the Fourteenth Amendment, and their "rights are protected by 42 U.S.C. § 1983." See

itself in this case) as a class irrespective of innate characteristics. Olech, at 564 ("Historically, equal protection suits required that the plaintiff define a class based on certain inherent conditions, such as race, nationality, or gender. Under the class of one approach, a single person can present himself as a class irrespective of these characteristics.") Now, classes can be broadly defined. After Olech, a circuit split emerged as to whether a plaintiff needs to show malice, in addition to the factors the Supreme Court identified, in order to establish a claim under Olech.[48] In the Third Circuit, no malice finding is required, and "under ... [Olech], a plaintiff must allege that (1) the defendant treated him differently from others similarly situated, (2) the defendant did so intentionally, and (3) there was no rational basis for the difference in treatment." Hill v. Borough of Kutztown, 455 F.3d 225, 239 (3rd Cir. 2006).[49] Considering Olech, Plaintiff states a plausible claim under the equal protection clause. Plaintiffs complaint states "DuBois applied a different standard to RHJ than other medical facilities." (Compl. 42.) (emphasis added). The class, as

---

Safeguard Mut. Ins. Co. v. Miller, 472 F.2d 732, 733 (3rd Cir. 1973) citing Pierce v. Society of Sisters, 268 U.S. 510, 535, 45 S. Ct. 571, 69 L. Ed. 1070 (1925).

[48] 48 Compare Hilton v. City of Wheeling, 209 F.3d 1005, 1008 (7th Cir. 2000) (Posner, J.) (requiring that a plaintiff show a "vindictive action" which requires proof of a "totally illegitimate animus") with Costello v. Mitchell Pub. Sch. Dist. 79,266 F.3d 916, 921-22 (8th Cir. 2001) (malice not required element to state a claim under Olech). In the Third Circuit, malice is not a necessary element to state a claim under Olech. Hill v. Borough of Kutztown, 455 F.3d 225, 239 (3rd Cir. 2006).

[49] 49 While the Supreme Court rejected the application of the class of one claim in public employment decisions, see Engquist v. Oregon Dept. of Agriculture, 553 U.S. 591, 128 S. Ct. 2146, 170 L. Ed. 2d 975 (2008), its vitality remains in zoning and land use planning challenges, as Chief Justice Roberts went to great lengths to distinguish the case where the government acts as employer and employs a worker, as opposed to where the government acts as a sovereign and creates zoning and land use planning rules. See id. at 2151 ("[O]ur traditional view of the core concern of the Equal Protection Clause as a shield against arbitrary classifications, combined with unique considerations applicable when the government acts as employer as opposed to sovereign, lead us to conclude that the class-of one theory of equal protection does not apply in the public employment context.")(emphasis added).

stated, was RHJ as a medical facility. Under § 621, methadone clinics were not permitted within 500 feet of a park, while other similar medical facilities were allowed to operate in those areas. Under the new ordinance, methadone clinics were still treated differently, and were not allowed to open in zones where other similar medical facilities were allowed to open. Plaintiff alleges that the City intentionally treated RHJ's medical facility--a methadone clinic that treated recovering opioid addicts--differently from other similarly situated medical facilities. These alleged facts satisfy the first prong of Hill, 455 F.3d 225, 239 (3rd Cir. 2006).

The second element of intent, Hill, at 239, shares much in common with the showing of animus, and is addressed supra in the discussion of substantive due process. The Court's finding that the facts alleged in the complaint plausibly show that the actions of the City of DuBois were based on an animus towards Plaintiff, and the patients its clinic intended to serve, is a sufficient allegation that the actions of the City were intentional.

The third element of Hill, asks whether "there was ... [a] rational basis for the difference in treatment." Hill, at 239. While traditional forms of rational basis review are quite deferential, in two landmark cases, the Supreme Court has articulated a heightened, more searching form of rational basis review, dubbed by some commentators as "rational basis with bite." Maldonado v. Houstoun, 157 F.3d 179, 185 n.7 (3rd Cir. 1998) citing Gayle Lynn Pettinga, Rational Basis with Bite: Intermediate Scrutiny by Any Other Name, 62 IND. L.J. 779, 787-92 (1987).

In City of Cleburne v. Cleburne Living Center, the Court considered the city's denial of a special use permit for the operation of a home for mentally disabled patients. 473 U.S. 432, 435, 105 S. Ct. 3249, 87 L. Ed. 2d 313 (1985). Although this group of patients was not a suspect class, the Cleburne Court actively scrutinized the City's proffered reason for treating the home differently than other similarly situated institutions within the zoned area. Id. at 458 (Marshall, J., concurring in part and dissenting in part). After engaging in a "searching inquiry" into the reasons why the City denied the permit-- notwithstanding the fact that rational basis review applied--the Court found that the City lacked a rational basis, and its actions were based on "irrational prejudice against the mentally retarded." Id. at 459-60 (Marshall, J., concurring in part and dissenting in part).

In Romer v. Evans, the Court applied a similar form of heightened rational basis scrutiny. Romer v. Evans, 517 U.S. 620, 116 S. Ct. 1620, 134 L. Ed. 2d 855 (1996). In this case, Colorado passed an amendment to its constitution that prevented government action to protect gays and lesbians against discrimination. Id. at 635-636. Despite the fact that sexual orientation is traditionally considered a non-suspect class,[50] the Court engaged in heightened scrutiny, observing that "'[d]iscriminations of an unusual character especially suggest careful consideration to determine whether they are obnoxious to the constitutional provision.'" Id. at 633 quoting Louisville Gas & Elec. Co. v. Coleman, 277 U.S. 32, 37-38, 48 S. Ct. 423, 72 L. Ed. 770 (1928). Because the amendment focused solely on gays and lesbians, the Court discerned an "inevitable inference" that the law was motivated by an impermissible animus, and the amendment was struck for violating the equal protection clause. Romer, at 634.

In Cleburne and Romer, when the government discriminated against "discrete and insular minorities," United States v. Carolene Products Co., 304 U.S. 144, 152-53 n. 4, 58 S. Ct. 778, 82 L. Ed. 1234, (1938), those without access to the political process, JOHN HART ELY, DEMOCRACY AND DISTRUST: A THEORY OF JUDICIAL REVIEW 77-78 (1980), the Court employed a more thorough version of rational basis review that inquired into the government's motivation and animus. It is worthwhile to reflect on the alleged victims of the City's actions in this case--the prospective patients of the clinic that could never open. Accepting "all of the complaint's well-pleaded facts as true," Fowler, at 210, these patients are recovering opioid addicts who are attempting to get clean, and are unable to avail themselves of the proposed methadone clinic as a result of the City using zoning laws to treat methadone clinics differently than other medical facilities. RHJ alleges that the City, including the Mayor, was hostile and antagonistic to the clinic, and took numerous steps to prevent the clinic from opening. While the Court does not opine about the appropriate standard, the question remains whether they would qualify as "discrete and insular." Considering all of these facts, the Court finds that Plaintiff states a plausible claim for an equal protection violation.

IX. More Definite Statement

Finally, Defendant filed a motion for a more definite statement under FED. R. CIV. P. 12(e), alleging that "Counts I and IV are littered with conclusory allegations and conflated causes of action." The Court finds that the Plaintiffs claims under the Fourteenth Amendment were clearly separated into claims

---

[50] 50 Contra Perry v. Schwarzenegger, 704 F. Supp. 2d 921, 997 (N.D.Cal. 2010) ("The trial record shows that strict scrutiny is the appropriate standard of review to apply to legislative classifications based on sexual orientation. All classifications based on sexual orientation appear suspect, as the evidence shows that California would rarely, if ever, have a reason to categorize individuals based on their sexual orientation.").

based on Due Process and Equal Protection. The Court also finds that Plaintiff distinguished between facial and as-applied challenges.

Judging by the length and specificity of this memorandum, it seems fairly obvious to the Court that the complaint was sufficiently definite. This claim fails.

And now, this 6th day of December, 2010, the Court DENIES Defendant's Motion for Judgment on the Pleadings and Motion for a More Definite Statement (Document No. 25).

BY THE COURT:

/s/ Kim R. Gibson

KIM R. GIBSON,

UNITED STATES DISTRICT JUDGE

4
Real People described

Persons described as mad scientists include a flighty employee, an ADHD boy seeking disability, a failed inventor seeking tax exemptions, and contractually silenced software developers.

Robert P. KOEHLER et al.

v.

Thomas L. CUMMINGS, Jr., et al.

Civ. A. No. 4525

UNITED STATES DISTRICT COURT
FOR THE MIDDLE DISTRICT
OF TENNESSEE, NASHVILLE DIVISION

380 F. Supp. 1294
June 11, 1971

MEMORANDUM

MORTON, District Judge.

This is an action in two counts: one alleging conspiracy to deprive the plaintiffs of their property and property rights, and the second alleging the inducement of a key employee to breach his employment contract with plaintiff S.O.S. International. Plaintiff Robert P. Koehler is now president and majority shareholder of S.O.S. International. The suit was authorized on behalf of plaintiff S.O.S. International, Inc. by its Board of Directors. Suit is also brought by Sentry Products Corporation.

This is a suit based on diversity jurisdiction. Plaintiff Robert P. Koehler is a citizen of Florida. Plaintiffs S.O.S. International, Inc. (hereinafter referred to as S.O.S.) and Sentry Products Corporation (hereinafter referred to as Sentry), are corporations incorporated under the laws of Florida with their principal places of business in Florida. Defendants Thomas L. Cummings, Jr., Newburn K. Hayes, and George T. Roberts are citizens of Tennessee. Defendants George Thomas and E. L. Schneider are citizens of New York. Defendant Herbert Jamul was a citizen of Tennessee at the time the suit was filed, and now is a citizen of Connecticut. Defendants Cummings & Co., Inc. and Jamul Safety Products, Inc. are corporations incorporated under the laws of Tennessee with their principal places of business in Tennessee.

Plaintiff Robert P. Koehler and defendant George Thomas first met Herbert Jamul, the employee whose services are the subject matter of this suit, in late July, 1963. Jamul approached them to obtain capital in the amount of $ 2,000 to develop safety garments and products made from a combination of reflective, phosphorescent and fluorescent materials. The individual materials were not new, but the idea of applying the reflective to the fluorescent materials (producing high visibility day or night) was novel. About August, 1963, plaintiff Koehler and defendants Thomas and Jamul, along with others not parties to this lawsuit, made plans to form a corporation, S.O.S. The purpose of the corporation was to develop and exploit the ideas and abilities of the defendant, Herbert Jamul. On August 20, 1963, the corporation papers, including a shareholders' agreement and an employment agreement with Jamul, were drawn up by Richard Hunt, a Miami attorney. A loan of $ 5,000, secured by shares of S.O.S. stock pledged by Jamul, was made by Koehler, Thomas, and Streeter, shareholders of S.O.S. The employment agreement between S.O.S. and Jamul, effective August 30, 1963, was to expire August 30, 1965. One of its covenants is germane:

"7. For a period of two (2) years after the EMPLOYEE ceases to be employed by the EMPLOYER, the EMPLOYEE will not enter the employ of, or become an associate, partner, advisor or other agent, or shareholder, of any firm, association, corporation, or any other organization which manufactures or sells, as agent or principal, within any of the states listed below, the same fabricated reflective safety items (including but not limited to vests, gloves, and other garments, as well as flags, banners, and advertising displays) produced or sold by the EMPLOYER: [A list of 31 states, including the District of Columbia and Tennessee, follows.]" Employment Agreement, Plaintiffs' Exhibit 2, pp. 2-3.

An office and small plant was established at Hialeah, Florida; products and market interest developed. In October, 1963, there was good response to a booth at the Chicago Safety Show. More capital was needed so Koehler "decided to go all out" and deposited enough securities at the First National Bank of Hialeah, Florida, to make about $ 100,000 of credit available. From September, 1963, to April, 1964, the new corporation had the normal problems of a new business. Its volume of sales, although mostly samples, was only about $ 4,000, but its prospects appeared bright. An order for safety vests for the Miami Herald in the amount of $ 250 had been completed by December, 1963. In February, 1964, S.O.S. received its largest purchase order, from Tri-tix, Inc., for $ 50,000. Unfortunately, one of the conditions of the order was that the fluorescent material be guaranteed to last for a period of two years. A laboratory report from Chicago was not completed until early April and the order was cancelled in the meantime. Another of S.O.S.'s purchase orders was for $ 8,000 from L. P. Harless. This order was subsequently cancelled before the factory was able to produce, allegedly because the order had been held by Richard Hunt, the corporation's attorney. Koehler testified that about the first of April, 1964, the prospects for S.O.S. still appeared good and he consequently made another loan of $ 5,000 at this time. Koehler maintains he made a minimum amount of loans of $ 30,000 to S.O.S. A letter from Jamul to Angus Stevens, his attorney, states Koehler's loans to be about $ 35,000. Because of the lapse of time, and either failure to keep good records or loss thereof, this Court can find documentary evidence only for $ 22,946.19, exclusive of interest thereon, in loans contributed by Koehler and Sentry Products, a corporation owned by Koehler and his wife. Statement Supplementing Testimony of Robert P. Koehler, Record, at 4. Koehler testified, and his testimony was corroborated, that his bank, the First National Bank of Hialeah, had advised him not to make more loans. Nor would the bank make further personal loans to Koehler for the company, regardless of the amount of collateral, until the company was reorganized and Jamul, who was then president, was placed in charge of research only. Meanwhile, when Koehler was seeking additional investors and a reorganization of S.O.S., the defendants Thomas L. Cummings, Jr. and Newburn Hayes were introduced to S.O.S. by Richard Hunt, whom they consulted on their own legal matters. Negotiations began for an interest in S.O.S., culminating at the "marathon meeting" on April 14, 1964, in an option agreement between Thomas, Koehler, Streeter, and Jamul, shareholders of S.O.S., and Cummings & Co. or its nominees. At this point Jamul had already resigned as president of S.O.S., and pursuant to a shareholders' meeting shortly before, had been made a vice-president in charge of research and development. Koehler was having difficulty controlling Jamul at this time.

Jamul was aptly described as a **"mad scientist**," full of ideas, but flighty and strong-headed. Jamul and Hunt had met with the Cummings group prior to this marathon meeting. Jamul was highly desirous of having these parties in the corporation. The major asset of S.O.S., all parties agree, was the man Jamul and his ideas. This essentially constituted the basis for investment by all the parties. The Cummings group at the close of the marathon meeting was given an option to purchase S.O.S., and $ 1,650 was placed in escrow in case the option was exercised. On April 21, 1964, Koehler and Streeter sent a telegram cancelling the option. Exhibit 11. This was done following a telephone call from Richard Hunt informing Koehler that the terms of the agreement were going to have to be changed. Short of negotiations being resumed, further discussions ensued. Jamul, on learning of Koehler's cancellation of the option agreement, was extremely upset. There was an unsuccessful attempt on April 30, 1964, to see if any of the difficulties between Jamul and Koehler could be resolved. Finally, on May 4 and 5, 1964, there was a safety show at the Everglades Hotel in Miami, where Jamul at his own expense exhibited S.O.S. products. Jamul and Ruby Maxey, now Ruby Judkins, an employee of S.O.S. in charge of the sewing operations, met Hayes at this meeting. Hayes stated he dropped by the Everglades show on behalf of Koehler, who had asked Hayes to see if he might get the two men back together again. Koehler's testimony corroborates this. Mrs. Judkins stated it was at this time that Hayes gave Jamul some help in composing a letter to Jamul's attorney, Angus Stevens, concerning anticipated litigation seeking to avoid his employment contract with S.O.S. Hayes meanwhile wrote to Koehler that Jamul had something going on but that Jamul would not tell Hayes. Hayes states in his letter to Koehler, dated May 6, 1964:

"Sorry I didn't have time to get back with you yesterday but as you requested, I went by to chat with Herb Jamul at the Safety Engineers Show. You realize of course that I could not lead Mr. Jamul into expanding his inter-thoughts [sic] but could only be a 'good listener. ' Mr. Jamul was non-communicative and frankly I strongly suspect some deep seeded discension [sic]. He apparently has something in mind which he wouldn't elaborate on to me. Maybe you know what it is.
"In view of this I would like to emphasize again that we would not be interested in renegotiating in any way. I think you will agree that we cannot afford to get in the middle on this situation." Exhibit 17, Letter from Newburn K. Hayes, Controller-Treasurer of Cummings & Co. to Robert P. Koehler, dated May 6, 1964.

Hayes failed to reveal his helping Jamul draft his letter regarding litigation. Hayes professed to be finding out how the strain between Koehler and Jamul might be relieved, and instead was furthering only the interests of the defendants in obvious conflict with Koehler's interests.
Finally, at the end of April, Jamul was no longer regularly working at the S.O.S. plant. Koehler discovered samples, dies, equipment, and rolls of material missing, although there was no evidence of break-in. An independent inventory was taken, and it was discovered that materials valued at $ 9,124, including dies worth $ 2,100, were missing. Mrs. Judkins, who testified that she helped Jamul remove the items, said they moved these samples, materials, and dies to American Arts Advertising. She noted that Jamul claimed these were his property. Apparently these items remained at American Arts about five or six months (including the summer months of 1964). Mrs. Judkins testified these were used at American Arts by its manager, Bob Lipps, in connection with silk screening for a catalogue for use in the "future" at Nashville. She testified that she discussed with Hayes what they were doing at American Arts. Defendant Hayes testified he paid in full more than $ 2,000 to American Arts for the catalogue. His first contact with American Arts was

sometime in the summer of 1964. Later these materials were shipped in twelve or thirteen large cartons, each about three feet square, to Jamul Safety Products in Nashville. Mrs. Judkins stated that not only did Hayes see them, but that the dies and materials were used at Jamul Safety Products. The use of the items at Jamul Safety Products was disputed by defendants Hayes and Cummings. Mrs. Judkins further testified that one of the cartons was lost en route and Jamul Safety Products collected for the loss of the carton, about $ 100; Hayes kept the check. The Court believes the testimony of Mrs. Judkins.

The next event in the sequence occurred on or about May 22, 1964, when an action was filed by Jamul in the Circuit Court of Dade County, Florida, to avoid the employment contract. Releases of the employment agreement between S.O.S. and Jamul were proposed by Mr. Perse, an associate of Angus Stevens, and sent to Koehler's Florida attorney, Mr. Robert Lane, on July 2, 1964. Defendant Thomas had signed a release of Jamul. On July 9, 1964, at the Kings Bay Yacht Club in Miami, a meeting between Lane, Koehler, Jamul, Cummings, Stevens, and Perse was held. According to Koehler, the purpose of the meeting was to revive the option or renegotiate. Cummings, however, stated the purpose of the meeting was to discuss a release of Jamul. The meeting ended in a deadlock and was terminated by the Cummings group after one hour.

Meanwhile, there is unrefuted evidence in the record that, in the summer of 1964, defendant Newburn Hayes would arrange periodically to leave cash at the Miami International Airport hotel, where he testified a high school friend of his was the night manager. Jamul, on several occasions accompanied by Ruby Judkins, picked up the money that was left at the hotel. Defendants explained the exchange of the cash was an advance on the money they paid Jamul for the future use of his name in Jamul Safety Products, Inc. The total paid for the use of Jamul's name was $ 2,500. Defendants also stated these amounts were loaned Jamul to keep his spirits up, as the man had become dejected working for Koehler. At any rate, Jamul Safety Products was finally incorporated July 30, 1964, with the following officers: Newburn K. Hayes, President; Herbert Jamul, Vice-President; Thomas L. Cummings, Jr., Secretary; Don Lyda, Treasurer. The directors were: Newburn K. Hayes, Herbert Jamul, Thomas L. Cummings, Jr., Chairman of the Board. Minutes of the First Meeting of Stockholders of Jamul Safety Products, Inc., August 19, 1964, Exhibit 41. The investors were: Thomas L. Cummings, Jr., George Roberts, E. L. Schneider, and Newburn K. Hayes for $ 2,500 each. Testimony of Newburn K. Hayes.

On March 2, 1965, at the stockholders' meeting of Jamul Safety Products, Inc., the following were elected to serve as directors of Jamul Safety Products, Inc.: Thomas L. Cummings, Jr., Newburn K. Hayes, George T. Roberts, George Thomas, E. L. Schneider.

On March 2, 1965, the Board of Directors of Jamul Safety Products, Inc. met, and the following officers were elected: Thomas L. Cummings, Jr., Chairman of the Board; Newburn K. Hayes, President; Don Lyda, Treasurer; and George A. Sloan, Secretary.

A catalogue of Jamul Safety Products was introduced into evidence with a number of products which plaintiff Koehler testified were the same, or of the same design and almost identical fabric, as those of S.O.S. Essentially the catalogue represented products available in two different base materials of fluorescent fabric, one of which was used by S.O.S. The other represented a later development by the Minnesota Mining and Manufacturing Company. Hayes also testified that a newly developed 3M product of self-cleaning reflective tape was used. Koehler testified that several items in the catalogue were also made at S.O.S., and that several items were new. One item, previously mentioned above, was a coin jacket #A-401, which had been made by S.O.S. for the Miami Herald paper boys. The picture in the catalogue bears the words across it, "Miami Herald."

On February 11, 1965, the Florida Circuit Court of Dade County handed down a decree holding the covenant not to compete (paragraph 7 of the employment agreement) in Jamul's employment contract with S.O.S. was reasonable. This decree was subsequently upheld on appeal. By September 15, 1965, Hayes cancelled all agreements with Jamul except the agreement to use his name and the one concerning the assignment of patents. Jamul was also at this time given an option to purchase Jamul Safety Products for $ 150,000. If he chose not to or was unable to purchase the corporation, he would receive $ 1,000 cash consideration for his common stock and rights in Jamul Safety Products and a royalty of one percent on the sale of materials. Plaintiffs' Exhibit 29. The following cover letter, dated September 15, 1965, appears with the option:

"TO WHOM IT MAY CONCERN:

"On September 3, 1965, Thomas L. Cummings, Jr., George T. Roberts, Emanuel L. Schneider and I, Newburn K. Hayes, as majority stockholders in Jamul Safety Products, Inc., agreed in writing to grant Herbert Jamul a 90 day option for the purpose of finding other investors in Jamul Safety Products, Inc., since we do not propose, at this time, to spend further money on product and/or market research nor to operate a separate corporation if the option is not exercised. We further agreed that our interest in Jamul Safety Products, Inc. was worth $ 150,000, representing essentially our investment in this venture.

"It is our intention to concentrate on developing our sign business, which is now expanding far beyond original expectations, and to employ all our efforts and managerial talents toward this end.

"We continue to believe there is a terrific potential in the products developed by Jamul Safety Products, Inc. In fact, if Mr. Jamul does not exercise the above option we intend to operate a separate division of Cummings & Co., Inc. under the name of Cummings & Co., Inc. - Safety Materials Division. The products developed and patented will be sold through this division as another product line of our sign business. Mr. Jamul will be paid a royalty on the products he developed prior to September 3, 1965

"At this time we are no less convinced than we were one year ago that Mr. Jamul has some terrific ideas and that with full time management, the existing corporation has unlimited potential.

"Any further bona fide inquiries will be answered.

"Sincerely yours,

"Newburn K. Hayes President Jamul Safety Products, Inc. and Controller-Treasurer Cummings & Co., Inc. 615-254-7717"

Finally, on January 1, 1966, an agreement was made between Jamul Safety Products and Cummings & Co. whereby Jamul Safety Products transferred all rights, patents and royalties for its safety products to Cummings & Co. "for and in consideration of one-half (1/2) of the pre-tax profits up to a total of Sixty Thousand ($ 60,000.00) Dollars made by the division of Cummings & Co., Inc. to be set up to pursue the general field of safety items and other accessories for safety and the sign business which may use the processes and developments heretofore owned by Jamul Safety Products, Inc." Memorandum of Agreement, Defendants' Exhibit C.

It is one of defendants' theories that they dealt with Herbert Jamul only after he wrote defendant Newburn Hayes during June or July, 1964, about the possibilities of employment. Defendants maintain they made inquiries of Angus Stevens' firm concerning Jamul's ability to hold other employment. They also note that their Nashville attorney, Henry Hooker, informed them that they might be subject to only "slight exposure" in hiring Jamul. Defendants contend that Stevens represented to them that the employment contract was void under Florida law. Plaintiff Koehler, on the other hand, contends that defendants' connection with Angus Stevens was not merely to determine Jamul's ability to hold other employment, but that defendants and their attorneys in Nashville were in constant touch with the Stevens firm concerning the declaratory judgment, and that Thomas Cummings, Jr. guaranteed Stevens' fee. This is corroborated by Stevens' deposition. The record does contain a number of letters between Stevens' firm and the defendant. Plaintiffs' Exhibits 24, 34 and 35.

Defendants contend that, if any inducement was made, it "flowed the wrong way," from Jamul to defendants, not vice versa; in short, defendants contend that Jamul induced them.

Defendants further contend that at the time Jamul contacted defendants "they had good cause to believe that Herbert Jamul had been effectively discharged by S.O.S. and that the corporation was no longer a functioning business." Pre-trial Order, at 5.

Defendants also contend that the Tennessee inducement to breach a contract statute is not applicable where the corporation concerned is outside the state of Tennessee and the act allegedly transpired outside Tennessee. This statute, to-wit, T.C.A. § 47-15-113, reads as follows:

"47-15-113. Procurement of breach of contracts unlawful -- Treble damages. -- It shall be unlawful for any person, by inducement, persuasion, misrepresentation, or other means, to induce or procure the breach or violation, refusal or failure to perform any lawful contract by any party thereto; and, in every case where a breach or violation of such contract is so procured, the person so procuring or inducing the same shall be liable in treble the amount of damages resulting from or incident to the breach of said contract; and the party injured by such breach may bring his suit for said breach and for such damages."

The jurisdiction of this Court, as noted above, is based on diversity of citizenship. Therefore, the controlling law is that of the forum, Tennessee. Erie v. Tompkins, 304 U.S. 64, 58 S. Ct. 817, 82 L. Ed. 1188 (1938); Guaranty Trust Co. v. York, 326 U.S. 99, 65 S. Ct. 1464, 89 L. Ed. 2079 (1945).

The lawsuit ultimately rests on the determination of the validity of the employment contract, which was made and executed in Florida. It was entered into by plaintiff S.O.S., a Florida corporation, and defendant Jamul, a Florida resident at that time. This Court must apply not only the substantive law of the state in which it sits, but also must resolve the conflicts of law according to the conflicts rules of this state. Klaxon Company v. Stentor Electric Manufacturing Company, Inc., 313 U.S. 487, 61 S. Ct. 1020, 85 L. Ed. 1477 (1941); Griffin v. McCoach, 313 U.S. 498, 61 S. Ct. 1023, 85 L. Ed. 1481 (1941). Under the Tennessee conflict of laws rules, Florida law applies concerning the validity and enforceability of the Florida contract with the restrictive covenant not to compete. The Tennessee conflicts rule is that the validity and enforceability of a contract is governed by the law of the place where the contract is made, in the absence of any manifestation of contrary intention of the parties. Sloan v. Jones, 192 Tenn. 400, 241 S.W.2d 506 (1951); Moody v. Kirkpatrick, 234 F. Supp. 537 (M.D.Tenn.1964). Indeed, Moak v. Continental Casualty Co., 4 Tenn.App. 287, 292 (1927) states, "The lex loci contractus becomes as much a part of the contract as if specifically incorporated therein, and, in the absence of evidence of contrary intention, the parties must be held to have contemplated the application of that law to the terms of their agreement."

In the case before the Court, the validity of the restrictive covenant has already been tested in the Florida courts by Jamul, and the Florida Appellate Court rendered a final declaratory judgment on November 23, 1965, upholding the restrictive covenant. The determination of the Florida court is binding on defendant Jamul, and constitutes evidence of Florida law as to the other defendants. Since the other defendants were not parties to the Florida decree, it is not binding upon them under the principles of res judicata or collateral estoppel. Under the applicable Florida statute, F.S.A. § 542.12, the following appears:

"(1) Every contract by which anyone is restrained from exercising a lawful profession, trade or business of any kind, otherwise than is provided by subsections (2) and (3) hereof, is to that extent void.

"(2) One who . . . is employed as an agent or employee may agree with his employer, to refrain from carrying on or engaging in a similar business and from soliciting old customers of such employer within a reasonably limited time and area, so long as the buyer or any person deriving title to the good will from him, and so long as such employer continues to carry on a like business therein."

The Florida Circuit Court, apparently interpreting the above statute, found that the covenant not to compete in the employment agreement between Jamul and S.O.S.:

". . . is valid and enforceable insofar as it provides that for a period of two years after the plaintiff HERBERT JAMUL ceased to be employed by the defendant S.O.S. INTERNATIONAL, INC., i.e., on August 6, 1964, the plaintiff will not enter the employ of or become an associate, partner, advisor or other agent, or shareholder, of any firm, association, corporation or any other organization which manufactures or sells, as agent or principal, within the geographical area specified, the same fabricated reflective safety items, including but not limited to vests, gloves, and other garments as well as flags, banners and advertising displays produced or sold by the defendant." Amended Final Declaratory Decree, Circuit Court of Dade County, Florida, February 11, 1965. Plaintiffs' Exhibit 28.

The Court had found that the covenant not to compete in the employment agreement "is reasonable, with regard to time and area . . . ." Since the Florida court, interpreting a Florida statute found the covenant reasonable as to time and area, and since this Court finds no contrary authority interpreting a similar covenant under Florida law, this Court finds the Florida decree persuasive on the issue of the reasonableness of the covenant not to compete. This Court has examined the relevant Florida cases, and has considered anew the covenant not to compete, and its reasonableness as to time and place on the issue of its validity and enforceability in Florida. This Court is persuaded that the Florida Circuit Court for Dade County made the proper determination under Florida law. Defendants contend that "it is clear that Herbert Jamul breached the first of his covenants long before he knew any of the defendants and that the plaintiffs had likewise failed to perform the contract prior to the arrival of any of the defendants on the scene." Defendants' Memorandum Brief of Law and Facts, at 2. Defendants point to Jamul's alleged failure to develop and produce new safety products, and to plaintiffs' failure to continue Jamul as president, or pay him the weekly salary of $ 150 provided for in the contract, after April 4, 1964. In examining the employment contract between S.O.S. and Jamul, the Court finds that Jamul's employment was terminable for cause at any time during the two-year period that the employment agreement was effective, and would "terminate on August 30, 1965 . . . ." Employment Agreement, Plaintiffs' Exhibit 2. At the first meeting of the Board of Directors of S.O.S., the officers, including Jamul as president, were elected "to serve for one year and until their successors are elected and qualified." Minutes of First Meeting of Board of Directors, S.O.S. International, Inc., Plaintiffs' Exhibit 3. It is sufficient to point out that even if Jamul's employment with S.O.S. terminated on April 4, 1964, the contract still required that he not compete for a period of two years thereafter, which would be at least until April 4, 1966.

There is sufficient evidence in the record to establish the fact that Jamul had become uncooperative with Koehler, who was then president of S.O.S., and that some time later Jamul's salary was stopped. This constituted termination of his employment and it constituted termination for cause. Following his termination, there was a duty on Jamul to refrain from entering the employ of "any organization which manufactures or sells . . . the same fabricated reflective safety items," and a duty on all other individuals with knowledge of his employment contract, and the restrictive covenant contained therein, not to induce him to breach this covenant. The Court finds that defendants did not sustain their burden of proof at trial for their contention that the contract was breached by plaintiffs.

All that remains for consideration on the choice of law issue regarding the validity of the employment contract is to examine the Tennessee decisions to insure that the application of the Florida law does not violate the public policy of Tennessee. It is a well-established conflicts rule that the law of the place where the contract was made applies unless it is contrary to the strong public policy of the forum. "The public policy of a State, established either by express legislative enactment, or by the decisions of its courts, is supreme, and when once established will not, as a rule, be relaxed even on the ground of comity to enforce contracts, which, though valid where made, contravene such policy." Moak v. Continental Casualty Company, 4 Tenn.App. 287, 292-293 (1927).

The public policy of Tennessee is violated, and Tennessee will not enforce the restrictive covenant in a contract where there is a general or unlimited restraint of trade.

"The general rule on this subject, deducible from the authorities, is that a contract in general restraint of trade, that is, not to engage in one's trade or profession at any place in the realm, is void as being contrary to public policy; but a contract not to engage in one's business or profession, at a particular place, or for a period of time, is not invalid as being contrary to public policy, but such contracts will be upheld and enforced. 2 Parsons on Contracts, 748 et seq., note Z; 2 Pomeroy, Eq. Jur. § 934; 3 Pomeroy, Eq. Jur. § 1344, and note." Turner v. Abbott, 116 Tenn. 718, 94 S.W. 64, 66 (1906); also quoted in Ramsey v. Mutual Supply Company, 58 Tenn.App. 164, 427 S.W.2d 849 (1968).

Thus, the restraint of trade under the covenant not to compete does not violate the public policy of Tennessee unless the restraint is unreasonable. Baird v. Smith, 128 Tenn. 410, 161 S.W. 492 (1913); Herbert v. W. G. Bush & Company, 42 Tenn.App. 1, 298 S.W.2d 747 (1956); T.C.A. § 69-101 and the cases decided under it; 31 Tenn.L.Rev. 450, 454 (1964). This Court finds that while the Florida contract is broad, it is duly limited as to time and area and is not invalid or violative of Tennessee public policy. Discussion of the same legal principles is involved under both the issue of Tennessee public policy on restrictive covenants, and the issue of the validity of such a restrictive covenant under a cause of action for inducement to breach. Therefore, for the purpose of greater clarity, the Court's discussion of the reasonableness of the restrictive covenant will be reserved until the inducement to breach discussion.

INDUCEMENT TO BREACH EMPLOYMENT CONTRACT

Inducement to breach a contract, while it must be based upon a valid contract, is an action sounding in tort. Finchum Steel Erection Corp. v. Local Union 384, 202 Tenn. 580, 308 S.W.2d 381 (1957); Prosser, The Law of Torts, § 123 (3rd ed. 1964). The applicable Tennessee statute, T.C.A. § 47-15-113, is but a statutory enactment of the common law tort action, expressly setting treble damages in lieu of punitive damages. Swift v. Beaty, 39 Tenn. App. 292, 282 S.W.2d 655 (1954). Tennessee follows the traditional conflicts of law rule, the law of the place of the wrong governs an injury sounding in tort, lex loci delicti. Kennard v. Illinois Central R.R. Co., 177 Tenn. 311, 148 S.W.2d

1017 (1941); Franklin v. Wills, 217 F.2d 899 (6th Cir. 1954); Restatement, Conflict of Laws, § 378. Where there is a multi-state tort, the place of the wrong is "the state where the last event necessary to make an actor liable for an alleged tort takes place." Restatement, Conflict of Laws, § 377. In the present case, the last event necessary to establish the liability of the defendants was at that time and place where the defendants formed Jamul Safety Products, Inc., and employed Herbert Jamul. The inducement to breach the covenant of his employment contract was complete where Jamul was employed by defendants, resulting in the breach of his covenant with S.O.S. Jamul sought employment with defendants in a non-restricted area. The Court finds that he was employed within the prohibited area. The Court further finds that the last act establishing the cause of action for inducement to breach was Jamul's employment in violation of the restrictive covenant. As Jamul Safety Products was incorporated under the laws of the state of Tennessee with its principal place of business in Nashville, Tennessee, Tennessee law governs the tort of inducement to breach a contract, and also the tort of conspiracy to deprive plaintiffs of their rights under the contract. The applicable Tennessee statute on inducement to breach a contract is § 47-15-113 T.C.A., as cited above.

Plaintiffs' cause of action owes its existence in great part to the landmark case, Lumley v. Gye, 2 El. & Bl. 216, 118 Eng.Rep. 749, 1 Eng.Rul.Cas. 707 (1853). Prosser notes the following concerning the underlying contract in this cause of action:

"Lumley v. Gye and the succeeding cases laid emphasis upon the existence of the contract, as something in the nature of a property interest in the plaintiff, or a right in rem good against the world. . . . The addition of the element of a definite contract has its importance, since the person induced to break it is then under a legal duty, and the plaintiff has furnished a consideration for the expectancy with which the defendant interferes. It may therefore curtail the defendant's privilege to pursue his own ends at the expense of the plaintiff." (Footnotes omitted.) Prosser, The Law of Torts, § 123 at 954-55. (3rd ed. 1964).

Then, the first element necessary to establish a cause of action for inducement to breach a contract is the existence of a valid and enforceable contract. Turner v. Abbott, 116 Tenn. 718, 94 S.W. 64 (1906). The rationale for the Court's decision that the contract does not violate the public policy of Tennessee, and the issue of whether the restrictive covenant is reasonable in light of the Tennessee decisions will now be considered. At the outset it must be noted that the covenant is reasonable if it is sufficiently limited in time and place. Kaset v. Combs, 58 Tenn.App. 559, 434 S.W.2d 838 (1968); Allright

MAD SCIENTIST IN THE FEDERAL COURT

Auto Parks, Inc. v. Berry, 219 Tenn. 280, 409 S.W.2d 361 (1966).

"There is no inflexible formula for deciding the ubiquitous question of reasonableness, insofar as noncompetitive covenants are concerned. Each case must stand or fall on its own facts. However, there are certain elements which should always be considered in ascertaining the reasonableness of such agreements. Among these are: the consideration supporting the agreements; the threatened danger to the employer in the absence of such an agreement; the economic hardship imposed on the employee by such a covenant; and whether or not such a covenant should be inimical to public interest." Allright Auto Parks, Inc. v. Berry, 219 Tenn. 280, 409 S.W.2d 361, 363 (1966).

The controlling considerations, however, are the limitations imposed on the time and the area encompassed by the agreement.

The consideration supporting the employment agreement was the employment of Jamul as an officer of S.O.S., with a salary approved by the Board of Directors at $ 150 per week. In addition, Herbert Jamul was receiving an opportunity to have capital available to develop his ideas.

Employment, even for an indefinite period, has been held sufficient consideration in Tennessee to support a covenant against competition. Di-Deeland, Inc. v. Colvin, 208 Tenn. 551, 347 S.W.2d 483 (1961); Ramsey v. Mutual Supply Company, supra

The danger to the employer, S.O.S., has already been seen. S.O.S. had one valuable asset, the ideas of the man Jamul. About $ 30,000 was allegedly invested by Koehler to develop these ideas. When defendants formed Jamul Safety Products, Inc. and until it was sold to Cummings & Co., another $ 150,000 was invested in Jamul's ideas. Since these men were certainly not inexperienced in business ventures, it can only be concluded that at the time the loans and profit investments were made, these ideas were believed to have great potential. The key to this potential was Jamul. When plaintiff Koehler loaned this amount of money, he did so because of Jamul's ideas. When the defendants, other than Jamul, were interested in acquiring S.O.S., and entered into the option to purchase S.O.S., there was no contention that they were bargaining for the rented buildings or rented sewing machines of S.O.S. What they were clearly bargaining for and considered valuable were the abilities and ideas of Herbert Jamul.

"Q Then you were aware that Mr. Herbert Jamul did have an employment agreement with S.O.S. International, and a restrictive covenant with regard to engaging in virtually any capacity for anyone else along the same lines, and in certain states?

"A Of course we did, that was part of the - brought out clearly in the purchase

negotiations. That was one of the things that they had to sell, supposedly.
"Q Exclusive rights to his ideas and services?
"A Right.
"Q You understood that, at least at that time, when you negotiated in April?
"A Of course I did."
Deposition of Thomas L. Cummings, Jr., taken on April 6, 1967, at 27.

Defendants now say that Jamul cost them money, that others had his ideas, and that they made a mistake. Whether this is true or not, at the time they were negotiating with S.O.S. they were willing to bargain because of Jamul's covenant with S.O.S.; and by inducing a breach of Jamul's covenant with S.O.S., they were at the very least responsible for depriving S.O.S. of the opportunity to negotiate with other organizations that might also have been interested in investing in Jamul's ideas. They ended up with the one valuable asset of S.O.S. The threatened danger to the employer, S.O.S., lay in experiencing competition from its own former idea man, against which the covenant protected it.

The economic hardship imposed on Jamul was stressed by the defendants Hayes, Cummings and Thomas. Jamul, on the stand, testified to a number of past occupations. He now does independent consulting work in Connecticut. He was not deprived of his only opportunity of employment by the two-year restrictive covenant. The argument of economic hardship to Jamul does not persuade this Court that the defendants' sole motivation for employing Jamul was their underlying humanity, because of the hardship suffered by Jamul. If motivated solely by humanitarian reasons, defendants might have employed Jamul with Cummings & Co. in a position unrelated to the safety products business. Indeed, when Jamul wrote Hayes on May 14, 1964, concerning his employment, after negotiations were unsuccessful between Koehler and the defendants, he said:

"Finally, after 2 long weeks I received a letter from my attorney Mr. Stephens, copy of which I am enclosing to you and which is self explanatory. As you can well see, I cannot do business with anyone, till the declaratory degree [sic] has been granted by the Dade County Circuit Court, which will take at least another week . . . . However, it can be possible that it will take longer than a week . . . . As you can see that I have not been paid any salary by the Corporation and that I have no income of any kind and that I have spent all my savings on behalf of S.O.S. Corp. I am writing to you now as a friend and ask your advice as to what can I do in the interim time, while I waite for the 'decree.' It occured [sic] to me, perhaps I could be a consultant to one of the companies, you have connections with or in which you may have interest. It can be in any field, as you know I have at least 20 years of experience in consulting field and creating new products and ideas. And I don't think that there is any conflict of interest involved either." (Emphasis supplied.) Defendants' Exhibit B.

Clearly, Jamul was asking for a job as a consulting engineer or as a developer of new products with Cummings & Co. or one of the companies Hayes had "connections with." Jamul stated he did not wish to work in the area governed by the employment agreement until the decree was entered in the Florida court. Yet defendants employed Jamul, with knowledge of the litigation, to work with the same or similar products with which he worked at S.O.S. The economic hardship argument is not persuasive.

Finally, in considering the limitations as to time and area on the restraint of trade, several Tennessee cases have held that a covenant not to compete for as much as five years after the termination of employment is not unreasonable. Matthews v. Barnes, 155 Tenn. 110, 293 S.W. 993 (1926); Ramsey v. Mutual Supply Company, supra. The are limitation, however, is rather broad as Jamul agreed not to compete in thirty states plus the District of Columbia. In Allright Auto Parks, Inc. v. Berry, supra, the contract sought to limit competition in 46 cities, from coast to coast and from the Gulf of Mexico into Canada. The defendant there had only been required under the contract to work in three cities so the contract was held to be unreasonable and therefore unenforceable. In another case, the agreement of noncompetition included twelve hundred cities. The Fourth Circuit Court of Appeals held the territory included was so vast as to render the contract void. Welcome Wagon, Inc. v. Morris, 224 F.2d 693 (4th Cir. 1955), also noted in Ramsey v. Mutual Supply Company, supra. The criterion here is whether or not the territorial limits are greater than is necessary to protect the employer's business. See Allright Auto Parks, Inc. v. Berry, supra, citing Matthews v. Barnes, supra; Arkansas Dailies, Inc. v. Dan, 36 Tenn.App. 663, 260 S.W.2d 200 (1953); Federated Mutual Implement and Hardware Ins. Co. v. Anderson, 49 Tenn.App. 124, 351 S.W.2d 411 (1961); 17 C.J.S. Contracts §§ 238-258 (1963); and Restatement Contracts § 515. In addition, some cases state that "noncompetition covenants, which embrace territory in which the employee never performed services for his employer, are unreasonable and unenforceable." Allright Auto Parks, Inc. v. Berry, supra 409 S.W.2d at 36; 43 A.L.R.2d 175, § 66. Finally, the Supreme Court of Tennessee in the Allright case cites 17 C.J.S. Contracts § 254 (1963):

"Area limitations are reasonable if restricted to the area in which the employee was engaged in the course of his employment; but, unless trade secrets are involved, a covenant restricting an employee beyond the area of his former operations is invalid, even though the employer's business extends throughout the area designated."

In the Ramsey case two years later, a restrictive covenant including an area never previously worked by the employee was held valid. Without nothing the language quoted in Allright from C.J.S. concerning the presence of trade secrets, the court in the Ramsey case found that the area not yet covered by the covenanting salesman might have later been assigned him if the present salesman in that area were ill or temporarily absent. Also, "in addition to this fact, the frequent meetings at which both Billingsley [present salesman] and Ramsey [former employee against whom covenant is sought to be enforced] discussed customers and mutual problems would result in the appellant gaining some information, by virtue of his employment, which could be used by him as a competitor after termination of such employment." Ramsey v. Mutual Supply Company, supra, 427 S.W.2d at 853. The Ramsey opinion further cites the rule that a restrictive covenant is not invalid although it covers an area in which the employee had not yet established a business contact, where it was reasonable to anticipate that such territory might be covered by him at some future time during his employment. In light of the above, the Ramsey court notes that the territorial limitations of the contract should be determined by the situation existing at the date of the contract; it held that the covenant restricting competition was valid.

In Allright Auto Parks, Inc. v. Berry, supra, the court noted:

"Numerous cases could be cited where covenants have been declared unreasonable because of their excessive territorial limits; however, these provide little direction since the question of reasonableness must be decided on an ad hoc basis. As is stated by Professor Williston in his learned treatise on contracts, the ultimate question in each case should be 'what is necessary for the protection of the promisee's rights and is not injurious to the public.' Williston on Contracts, Vol. 5, § 1643, pp. 4606, 4608." Allright Auto Parks, Inc. v. Berry, supra, 409 S.W.2d at 364.

In the present case, Jamul traveled in many states visiting numerous customers. He exhibited S.O.S. products at safety shows in a number of cities across the country. He was far more than a salesman, however; he was the market researcher and inventor for the company. The advantage to S.O.S. at the time of the making of the contract with Jamul was the novelty of Jamul's ideas in the safety area. Testimony and exhibits demonstrated that various concerns in cities from Florida to Texas, Canada, Illinois, and New Jersey were considering the products of S.O.S. Since the market place is large in area, it appears to this Court that the agreement not to compete made by Jamul was not unreasonable in order to protect S.O.S.'s business interests in the specialized safety field. Where a covenant not to compete was entered into by an idea man, the principal asset of a corporation in a highly technical and specialized field, it seems inescapable that, in an effort to protect the investments by the corporation and by the plaintiff Koehler, the covenant was not unreasonable, though broad in its territorial limitation.

Finally, the defendants offered no proof that the restrictive covenant was unreasonable, especially in light of the specialized field involved and in light of Jamul's abilities. Plaintiff has the burden of proof to establish a cause of action for inducing a breach of contract. Once plaintiff carries the burden, as here, the burden of going forward shifts to defendants to prove the contract was unreasonable. Prosser, supra; Aikens v. Wisconsin, 195 U.S. 194, 25 S. Ct. 3, 49 L. Ed. 154 (1904). This the defendants did not do.

Another element of plaintiff's action is that the defendants must have caused the interference with Jamul's contractual relationship with S.O.S.

"It is not enough that he [defendant] merely has reaped the advantages of the broken contract after the contracting party has withdrawn from it of his own motion. Thus acceptance of an offered bargain is not in itself inducement or the breach of a prior inconsistent contract, and it is not enough that the defendant has done no more than enter into one with the knowledge of the other, although he may be liable if he has taken an active part in holding forth an incentive, such as the offer of a better price or better terms . . . .

"Some of the earlier decisions denying liability argued that the defendant's conduct can never be a proximate cause of the breach. Since there is an intervening voluntary act of the third party promisor; but where that act is intentionally brought about by the defendant's inducement, or is even a part of the foreseeable risk which he has created, it seems clear that the result is well within the limits of the 'proximate.' It is a question of fact, and so normally for the jury, whether the defendant has played a material and substantial part in causing the plaintiff's loss of the benefits of the contract." (Footnotes omitted.)

Prosser, The Law of Torts, supra, at 958-59.

It will be recalled that Herbert Jamul wrote defendant Hayes concerning any type of consulting position, but not for a position in violation of his covenant with S.O.S. Jamul stated at trial that he asked defendant Cummings "sometime later" than the May 4 and 5 safety show at the Everglades Hotel if he could work as a consultant for Cummings & Co. Cummings' reply, according to Jamul, was for Jamul to write Cummings a letter and also to get legal advice regarding his employment, and Cummings would consider it. Finally, however, on direct examination Jamul stated that he asked for a job with Cummings & Co. ("if I have a job or don't have a job"), and he stated that defendants did not solicit him. The Court finds that the more credible evidence on this last point shows defendant was solicited by the defendants as evidenced by the cash payments made to Jamul over the summer months of 1964, and Jamul's eventual employment in the prohibited area. Defendants also considered the amount of "exposure" to which this subjected them. Defendants induced Jamul to work in the area he expressly told them he could not work. Jamul apparently had little choice; he could work for the defendants in the safety products area or not at all. Therefore, the Court finds that while Jamul may have contacted the defendants, not vice versa, he came to the defendants for a very different position and not a position in violation of his employment agreement.

An evaluation of all of the evidence at trial indicates that after the May 5th show at the Everglades Hotel, the defendants were committed to Jamul's ideas on the application of reflective tape to fluorescent and phosphorescent materials in the safety field and continued to try to negotiate with Koehler for S.O.S. (July 8, 1964 meeting at the Kings Bay Yacht Club). When they could not obtain a release of Jamul or could not revive the option or renegotiate further, defendants supported Jamul, intending to use his name in their future company, Jamul Safety Products, which was incorporated July 30, 1964. This Court agrees with plaintiffs that there is ample evidence in the record that the defendants intentionally induced Jamul to work with them in the safety products area, utilizing his ideas in those areas in which he had covenanted not to compete with S.O.S.

It is useless to speculate whether Jamul might have continued employment with S.O.S. if he had not been prevented by defendants' wrongful acts. It seems clear from the proof that Jamul was desirous of working on the development of the fluorescent and reflective tape in the safety products field. It is also clear that he did not wish to do this for S.O.S. as it was then composed. However, the Court cannot speculate that Jamul would not have worked for a newly reorganized or newly managed S.O.S. after the Florida courts decided against him, and had defendants not presented Jamul with a lucrative alternative. The Court cannot then decide whether Jamul might or might not have continued to work for S.O.S.; but it is clear to this Court that Jamul's failure to return to work for S.O.S. was directly caused by defendants' wrongful inducement. Defendants did then "play a material and substantial part in causing the [plaintiffs'] loss of the benefits of the contract." Prosser, supra, at 959.

Much proof was introduced at trial on behalf of the defendants to attempt to establish that Jamul never worked on products that were the "same" as those produced by S.O.S. Defendants maintain that while some of the garments advertised in a catalogue, Exhibit 27, under the name Jamul Safety Products, were the same style as those made by S.O.S. (e.g. the vest with "Miami

Herald" on it), these garments were made out of a new orange fluorescent base fabric not in existence at the time Jamul was with S.O.S. They also contend that the use of a new reflective tape was different. Defendants contend that at most these items were "similar" to those made by S.O.S., but that the items were not the "same," as the prohibition was described in the employment agreement at paragraph seven. The intention of the parties and the language in the agreement controls the interpretation of the words of a contract. Harper v. Lindsey, 19 Tenn. 310 (1938); A. J. Armstrong Co. v. Knox County, 291 F. Supp. 1008 (E.D.Tenn.1968). The parties obviously, even in the language used, did not mean "same" to have the restrictive interpretation of "exactly the same." There is ambiguity in whether "same" modifies "items" or refers to "fabricated." The intent of the parties by the phrase "the same fabricated reflective safety items" was to prevent competition where items were produced that were fabricated "the same." In other words, "same" appears to refer to "fabricated" rather than "items." Jamul was prohibited from employment in a company which sold safety items that were made the same as those of S.O.S.; this would include items that were made exactly the same but with a new base fabric or with a new reflective tape[1]. To follow defendants' contention would be to totally emasculate the contract.

In this connection, there was also considerable testimony on behalf of the defendants that the directors of Jamul Safety Products repeatedly cautioned Jamul against using any materials or products he had developed at S.O.S.

"The desire of the defendants to avoid any conflict with the plaintiffs' interests was so strong that they abandoned the safety garment field after a protest from Mr. Koehler . . . . This was done despite the fact that new and different reflective materials were being used to make the garments. For the remainder of the time Herbert Jamul was employed by the defendants he did no work on products that were the 'same,' or even similar to those produced or sold by S.O.S. International." (Emphasis supplied.) Defendants' Memorandum Brief of Law and Facts, at 3, 4.

On the other hand, however, defendants paid for the shipment of the boxes of materials and dies of S.O.S. from American Arts Advertising to Nashville. While Jamul and the other defendants maintained that these boxes were the personal property of Jamul, when one box was lost, defendant Hayes claimed the loss on behalf of Jamul Safety Products, not on behalf of Herbert Jamul.

---

[1] 1 See Addendum to Memorandum attached hereto.

The contents of the boxes paralleled the missing items inventoried at S.O.S. The catalogue of Jamul Safety Products was made from samples, such as the Miami Herald vest, which were the property of S.O.S., and were produced by S.O.S. These facts definitely raise a question as to the desire of the defendants to avoid any conflict with the products of the plaintiffs.

A further contention of the defendants is that there are no ascertainable damages, and that at most plaintiffs are entitled to merely nominal damages. Defendants maintain that plaintiffs' damages are speculative, and that plaintiffs have failed to provide the Court with any basis upon which to assess those damages which were proximately caused by the defendants' wrongful acts. The Tennessee statute sets the damages recoverable as those "resulting from or incident to the breach of said contract . . . ." T.C.A. § 47-15-113. This language clearly includes lost profits if they are capable of ascertainment with some degree of certainty. An exact, fixed amount as the damages sustained is often difficult to establish and remains a controversial figure. See 25 C.J.S. Damages §§ 80-81. Regarding the issue of the certainty of the damages, the following language is helpful:

"'Compensation may be for a pecuniary injury which has resulted as the natural or probable result of a wrong, although the extent of the injury is not capable of precise proof.' 15 Am. Juris., page 797, sec. 356.

"'There is a clear distinction between the measure of proof necessary to establish the fact that the plaintiff has sustained some damage and the measure of proof necessary to enable the jury to fix the amount. Formerly, the tendency was to restrict the recovery to such matters as were susceptible of having attached to them an exact pecuniary value, but it is now generally held that the uncertainty which prevents a recovery is uncertainty as to the fact of the damage and not as to its amount and that where it is certain that damage has resulted, mere uncertainty as to the amount will not preclude the right of recovery. This view has been sustained where, from the nature of the case, the extent of the injury and the amount of damage are not capable of exact and accurate proof. Under such circumstances all that can be required is that the evidence, with such certainty as the nature of the particular case may permit, lay a foundation which will enable the trier of facts to make a fair and reasonable estimate, and the plaintiff will not be denied a substantial recovery if he has produced the best evidence available and it is sufficient to afford a reasonable basis for estimating his loss.' 15 Am.Juris., pages 414, 415, sec. 23." (Emphasis supplied.) Stevens v. Moore, 24 Tenn.App. 61, 139 S.W.2d 710, 719 (Tenn.Ct. of Appeals, 1940).

In Tennessee it is established then that the prohibition against assessing speculative damages applies only where the fact of damage is uncertain, but not where the amount alone is uncertain. Coverdell v. Mid-South Farm Equipment Ass'n., 335 F.2d 9 (6th Cir. 1964); Acuff v. Vinsant, 59 Tenn.App. 727, 443 S.W.2d 669 (1969).

The Tennessee treble damage statute is but a declaration of the common law, except as to the amount of damages recoverable. Emmco Insurance Co. v. Beacon Mutual Indemnity Co., 204 Tenn. 540, 322 S.W.2d 226 (1959). Determining the standard for the assessment of damages provides the Court with its greatest problem. A number of Tennessee cases have recognized that lost profits may be assessed. Inland Equipment Co. v. Tennessee Foundry and Machine Co., 192 Tenn. 548, 241 S.W.2d 564 (1951); Gardner v. Deeds and Hirsig, 116 Tenn. 128, 92 S.W. 518 (1905); Lee Shops, Inc. v. Schatten-Cypress Co., 350 F.2d 12 (6 Cir. 1965). However, here we have a new business which never was permitted to achieve its profit potential. Defendants contend that Jamul Safety Products never did either, and that it was Jamul's fate never to realize profits for anyone. However, the business for which he worked, Jamul Safety Products, eventually sold its assets to Cummings Allied Products, a division of Cummings & Co. The new division, Allied Products, also entered into the sign barrier and safety products of asbestos areas where S.O.S. never had products. Even if the Court could separate the asbestos and the sign barrier business of Allied Products from the area of the safety business in which S.O.S. was involved, lost profits as a standard of damages would prove too speculative and uncertain. Plaintiffs have cited Lee Shops, Inc. v. Schatten-Cypress Company, supra, for the principle that lost profits may be assessed even where the company never was able to do business because of a breach of contract. However, this case is obviously distinguishable from the present case since in Lee Shops the new business was one discount store of an entire corporation of similar enterprises. For this reason, by a comparison with similar operations then in existence, there were some bases for estimating profit potential. Here, we have a new corporation with a bright idea in a developing area of the safety field. Clearly lost profits as a basis of damages could only be speculative. Finally, the general rule is that no recovery for lost profits is allowed for injury to a new business with no previous history of profits. 22 Am.Jur.2d Damages § 173; Burge Ice Machine Co. v. Strother, 197 Tenn. 391, 273 S.W.2d 479 (1954).

The Court finds the proof in the record sufficient to establish that plaintiff S.O.S. has actually been damaged. However, the proof was not sufficient to ascertain the exact amount owing plaintiffs. Therefore, in accordance with plaintiffs' request, a master is hereby appointed to establish the exact amount of damages suffered by plaintiff S.O.S.

CONSPIRACY

In order to establish an action for civil conspiracy, there must be "a combination between two or more persons to accomplish by concert an unlawful purpose, or to accomplish a purpose not in itself unlawful by unlawful means." Brumley v. Chattanooga Speedway & Motordrome Co., 138 Tenn. 534, 198 S.W. 775, 776 (1917); Dale v. Thomas H. Temple Co., 186 Tenn. 69, 208 S.W.2d 344 (1948); Hux v. Butler, 220 F. Supp. 35 (W.D.Tenn.1963), reversed on other grounds, 339 F.2d 696 (6 Cir. 1964.)

In connection with the concerted action, it is not "essential that each conspirator have knowledge of the details of the conspiracy, but a common purpose is essential and that each has the understanding that the other has the purpose and such purpose must be supported by concerted action." Hux v. Butler, 220 F. Supp. 35, 41 (W.D.Tenn. 1963). The requisite elements of the cause of action are common design, concert of action, and an overt act. Brumley v. Chattanooga Speedway & Motordrome Co., supra; Hux v. Butler, supra.

Furthermore, without injury to person or property, resulting in attendant damage, a cause of action for civil conspiracy is not established. Tennessee Publishing Co. v. Fitzhugh, 165 Tenn. 1, 52 S.W.2d 157 (1932); Donnelly v. Jackson Brothers, 2 Tenn. CCA (Higgins) 408 (1911); Hutton v. Waters, 4 Tenn. CCA (Higgins) 582 (1914); Smoky Mountains Beverage Co. v. Anheuser-Busch, Inc., 182 F. Supp. 326 (E.D.Tenn.1960).

The majority rule recognizes the existence of a cause of action for conspiracy to procure or induce a breach of a contract on the part of a party who is injured thereby. 15A C.J.S. Conspiracy § 13 (1961). Indeed, the Missouri Supreme Court noted, "A person who by conspiring with another or by collusive agreement with him assists him to violate his contract with a third person and to obtain the benefit of that contract for himself commits an actionable wrong." Anheuser-Busch, Inc. v. Weber, 364 Mo. 573, 265 S.W.2d 325, 364, reversed on other grounds, 348 U.S. 468, 75 S. Ct. 480, 99 L. Ed. 546 (1955).

Where the defendants employed Jamul in breach of his employment contract, knowing of the existence of such contract, an action for conspiracy is established. The common purpose of the conspiracy was to deprive S.O.S. of its key employee Jamul, and further, to secure this employee for the defendants' future business. To accomplish this purpose, defendants "loaned" cash amounts to Jamul over the summer until they could incorporate Jamul Safety Products. The cash payments constitute an overt act done in furtherance of the common unlawful purpose.

The damage to plaintiff S.O.S. is evident. It was deprived of the very basis of its existence, a fact that is conceded by defendants. Consequently, it is the finding of this Court that defendants Hayes, Cummings and Thomas knowingly conspired to deprive plaintiff S.O.S. of its employee and induced Jamul to breach his contract.

The damages, when the exact amount is ascertained by the master, will be assessed.

Because Jamul under Tennessee law cannot be liable for inducing his own breach of contract, the cause of action for inducing a breach of contract against defendant Jamul is hereby dismissed. There appears to be some question as to whether Jamul can also be liable for conspiracy where the alleged wrongful act was the inducement of a breach of contract. 15A C.J.S. Conspiracy § 13 (1961). This Court finds the better approach in theory is to dismiss the conspiracy cause of action also as to Jamul. If a party cannot be liable for inducing the breach of his own contract, it is similarly difficult to understand how he might be liable for participating in a conspiracy to induce the breach of his own contract. Plaintiffs assert a cause of action for conspiracy to deprive them of their property or property rights against the defendants, including Jamul. In the conspiracy action considered above by the Court, the claim for so conspiring cannot include the property taken by Jamul as one of the co-conspirators since the only conspiracy in which defendants were involved was that of inducing a breach of the covenant not to compete. The proper allegations against Herbert Jamul might be a breach of his employment contract, conversion of property and so forth, but not a conspiracy to deprive plaintiffs of their property or property rights. Accordingly, the claims against defendant Herbert Jamul are hereby dismissed. There is little or no proof as to the liability of defendants Roberts and Schneider and their role either in the conspiracy claim or in the inducement to breach cause of action. Therefore, the claims of the plaintiffs as to these defendants are hereby dismissed.

The causes of action for inducing the breach of a contract right of S.O.S. International, Inc. and for conspiracy to induce breach of contract are rights which are enforceable only by plaintiff S.O.S. Where the cause of action is being prosecuted on behalf of S.O.S. as a legal entity, plaintiff Robert P. Koehler, while the principal shareholder and creditor of S.O.S., does not have standing to bring suit as an individual or a shareholder. T.C.A. § 48-718. Also, this Court finds that plaintiff Sentry Products as a mere creditor does not have standing to assert a claim for inducement to breach a contract, which right is owing solely to S.O.S. Accordingly, this action is dismissed as to plaintiffs Robert P. Koehler and Sentry Products Corporation.

While the defendants Hayes, Cummings, and Thomas, in accordance with the reasons set forth above, have been found liable to plaintiff S.O.S. under both the claim of inducing the breach of the contract and the conspiracy claim, the Court finds the damage to plaintiff S.O.S. is the same under each claim.

Therefore, the Court holds the damage to plaintiff S.O.S. under both claims to be concurrent. Proof will be submitted by the plaintiff S.O.S. to the master appointed to ascertain the amount of damages.

ADDENDUM TO MEMORANDUM

Consistent with such intent is the "Shareholders Agreement" which predated the Employment Agreement (both being signed by Jamul) which provided in Amendment IX (15):

"(b) Jamul shall not at any time establish any other business in competition with, or selling the same products or services as the Corporation."

John A. Cupler II and Margaret D. Cupler, Petitioners

v.

Commissioner of Internal Revenue, Respondent

Docket No. 4743-73

UNITED STATES TAX COURT

64 T.C. 946

August 26, 1975, Filed

OPINION

Judge Tannenwald

Respondent determined the following deficiencies in petitioners' Federal income taxes:

Year	Deficiency
1965	$ 53,487.95
1966	66,853.00
1967	47,837.17
1968	$ 105,248.90
1969	49,920.08
1970	66,128.92

Several issues have been disposed of by stipulation. Those remaining are:

(1) Did petitioner make a charitable contribution of medical equipment to the University of Maryland in 1967, and if so, what was its value?

(2) Did petitioner make a charitable contribution of medical equipment to St. Barnabas Hospital in 1969 and, if so, what was its value?

(3) What was the value of the building stone which petitioner contributed to Emanuel Episcopal Church in 1965?

FINDINGS OF FACT

Some of the facts have been stipulated and are found accordingly.

Petitioners are husband and wife. Their returns were filed with the District Director of Internal Revenue, Baltimore, Md. On the date the petition was filed, petitioners resided in La Vale, Md. Mrs. Cupler is a petitioner only because she filed joint Federal income tax returns with her husband for the years 1965 through 1970. Mr. Cupler is referred to herein as petitioner.

1. Medical Equipment

Petitioner is a highly successful engineer and inventor in the field of precision drilling equipment. He is the president of the National Jet Cos., which manufacture and market small and microscopic precision drills and related equipment, primarily for the diesel engine industry. Petitioner has produced at least 50 patents on inventions in this field since he entered the business in 1937. He is not, however, in the business of inventing or manufacturing medical equipment of any kind.

Cataract Machine

At some time during 1965 or early 1966, petitioner's father was hospitalized at the University of Maryland Hospital with an eye ailment. At that time, petitioner met Dr. Alfred A. Meisels, an ophthalmologist who was treating his father and was on the staff of the hospital. Dr. Meisels discussed with petitioner the former's dissatisfaction with the prevailing surgical method of removing cataracts. That method required a 180 o incision around the iris of the eye and the removal of the diseased lens. Dr. Meisels wanted to develop a procedure whereby the sheath of the lens would be penetrated, its cataractous contents removed, and the sheath refilled with pure silicone. Ideally, such a procedure, besides minimizing the risks of the operation itself, would result in the restoration of normal vision by avoiding the impairment necessarily resulting from the complete removal of the lens. At the time petitioner was first contacted, he was informed that the University could not afford to pay for the development of the machine which would enable this procedure to be performed. Petitioner replied that payment would not be necessary.

Petitioner decided to try to develop such a machine. Several problems had to be solved in the design of the machine. Necessary operations included penetration of the eye without damage; mastication and removal of the gelatinous and fibrous contents of the lens; flushing out the lens sheath; and injection of silicone. It was necessary for petitioner to spend considerable time acquiring the background knowledge essential to the project.

Petitioner experimented with attempting to extract the contents of gelatine capsules. In the summer of 1966, Dr. Meisels and a colleague from the hospital staff, Dr. Stanley Schocket, visited petitioner and discussed the development of the device with him.

An early version of the machine proved unsuccessful in penetrating the eye of a rabbit without damage. Petitioner solved this problem by cutting the bevel off a hypodermic needle and tapering the tip of the needle down from the outside to the inside. This "cookie cutter" effect, in connection with a low-speed drill passed down the center of the needle, permitted the operator to augur a hole through the tissue of the eyeball without damage, creating a wound so small that it was self-closing. Two needles could be inserted in the lens in this manner facilitating the replacement of the lens material with silicone.

Petitioner delivered the machine to Drs. Meisels and Schocket in February 1967. At that time, he had not satisfactorily solved the problem of removing the gelatinous and fibrous materials from within the lens sheath. This difficulty was subsequently resolved by the development of a "tricep" tool, consisting of three wires with grasping feet. The tricep tool was inserted into the lens through the hollow needle and rotated, chopping the lens contents which were then removed by suction. Its grasping feet helped to withdraw lens fibers when the tool was retracted through the needle.

Petitioner spent a substantial number of hours preparing himself and developing the cataract machine prior to February 1967. It has been returned to him on occasion for reworking since that time. The machine has never been used clinically for its intended purpose. It has been used in repairing an obstructed tearduct and in research. Another machine of the same design was later donated to the Washington Hospital Center, where it has had some clinical use in removing substances imbedded in the vitreous of the eye.

Petitioner incurred out-of-pocket expenses of at least $ 7,158.53 in developing the cataract machine, which respondent has allowed as a charitable deduction.

Petitioner first applied for a patent in his name on the cataract machine in 1972. No patent has been issued. No rights in the invention, other than ownership of the particular machine donated in 1967, have ever been transferred to the University of Maryland, although petitioner intended to transfer the patent rights to the University of Maryland when the patent issued.

In 1967, the machine was unique in the sense that no other device had been developed for the same purpose. The cataract machine is similar to a device known as the roto-extractor, also referred to as the Kemp or Douvas machine. This machine required 5 years and over $ 100,000 to develop, and was first marketed in 1972 at a price of $ 7,000. It sold for $ 9,000 in 1974. About 45 roto-extractors were in use in the United States at the time of the trial of this case, and have been used to remove cataracts as well as to remove blood from the vitreous cavity. The principal differences between the two machines are in the size of the tip of the instrument -- the roto-extractor, which requires an incision in the eye, has a tip approximately 3 times as large as that of petitioner's machine -- and in petitioner's use of millisecond timers to control pressure and suction. The millisecond timers were not a part of the machine donated to the University in 1967.

Petitioner did not deal with any representative of the University other than Drs. Meisels and Schocket regarding this machine. On occasion, Raymond W. Colton, petitioner's patent attorney, acted as intermediary between him and the doctors.

On February 13, 1967, the doctors wrote petitioner a letter of thanks for his contribution, on University stationery. Drs. Meisels and Schocket believed they were acting on behalf of the University in soliciting and accepting the gift. They did not know that University policy required formal administration acceptance. During the time period in question, it occasionally happened that persons accepted gifts on behalf of the University without such formal acceptance.

The cataract machine was not listed on the cumulative property inventory maintained by the University's Department of Ophthalmology, where it was physically located at all times after its donation. That inventory was prepared by the University on the basis of documents rather than physical inspection.

Dr. Meisels left the University's employ some time prior to the trial of this case. The cataract machine remained at the University.

One of petitioner's expert witnesses based his valuation of the cataract machine on the cost of several projects claimed to be comparable, allegedly ranging from $ 100,000-plus to $ 1 million-plus. Petitioner's other expert witness valued the machine in terms of similar costs, ranging from $ 70,000 to $ 250,000, and in terms of his estimate of what it would cost for development of such a machine as follows:

(1) Preprototype stage $ 62,000
(2) Development of a prototype   54,500
(3) Production of working model 28,000

Total   144,500

Heart-Lung Machine

From 1963 to 1970, Dr. Jacob Zimmerman was a member of the medical staff of St. Barnabas Hospital for Chronic Diseases, New York, N.Y. During that time (and thereafter), he conducted research in cardiac anatomy under various Government grants. His research included investigation of the relationship between the heart and lungs in the development of the embryo. He wanted to develop a tool for use in his research that could remove and transplant the developing lung buds of 3-day-old chicken embryos.

In 1966, Dr. Zimmerman consulted petitioner, who had been recommended as a person who might be able to assist in the development of such a machine. It was necessary for petitioner to spend considerable time acquiring the background knowledge essential for the project. Petitioner spent a substantial number of hours over a period of 3 years in so preparing himself and in developing a tool that would perform the necessary operations. By 1969, he had invented a machine using the "cookie cutter" concept with a low RPM drill of absolute measurable concentricity, capable of penetrating the egg albumin without curdling it or causing the displacement of the embryo, passing without damage between blood vessels with a clearance of two-and-one-half thousandths of an inch at an angle varying within a range of 180 o in the horizontal and 190 degrees in the vertical directions, and excising the lung bud by means of suction and slow rotation of the cookie-cutter needle. Besides developing the actual tool -- referred to herein as a heart-lung machine -- he devised delicate control mechanisms and a system of micromanipulators for holding the embryo in place while the operation was performed. The optics for the heart-lung machine were those designed for use generally on microdrilling equipment. The machine was delivered to Dr. Zimmerman in 1969.

Before receiving the heart-lung machine, Dr. Zimmerman working alone had succeeded in this operation at most once out of 500 trials. Using petitioner's machine, he or a technician assistant could accomplish the operation in one out of every two attempts.

Petitioner incurred out-of-pocket expenses of at least $ 4,479.84 in developing the heart-lung machine.[1]

No patent application has ever been filed with respect to the machine.

Petitioner did not deal with any representative of St. Barnabas other than Dr. Zimmerman regarding this machine. A version of the machine was used by Dr. Zimmerman at the hospital as early as 1966, but this was not the machine which petitioner claims to have donated in 1969.

Dr. Zimmerman was referred to petitioner by an employee of the Hirschmann Corp., who indicated to petitioner that it was the hospital which sought to acquire the machine. Dr. Zimmerman wrote letters to petitioner and to Hirschmann Corp. on hospital stationery.

The hospital administration was not officially informed of the donation of the machine in 1969. Dr. Zimmerman's superiors knew of the machine and considered it hospital property.

Dr. Zimmerman began his research under a grant from the National Institutes of Health. In 1968, that grant terminated and he was transferred to the hospital payroll. He sought renewal of his grant, which was denied for the last time in 1970. In 1970, Dr. Zimmerman moved to Israel, where he joined the

---

[1] 1 Although many of these expenses were incurred prior to 1969, respondent concedes that such amount is allowable as a charitable deduction in 1969 if the Court finds that a gift of the machine was made to the hospital in 1969.

staff of the University of Tel Aviv. Before leaving St. Barnabas, he asked and received the permission of the hospital administration to take the heart-lung machine with him.

Dr. Zimmerman was the only person doing the sort of research for which the machine was designed. Only he and a technician at St. Barnabas were trained to operate it. Since 1970, the machine has remained in Israel.

On November 29, 1972, at the request of petitioner's counsel, St. Barnabas wrote petitioner a letter acknowledging that the heart-lung machine was received in 1969 and that Dr. Zimmerman was permitted to take it with him to Israel in 1970. Dr. Zimmerman wrote a similar letter to petitioner on March 31, 1970. During 1969, no official record of the donation was made in the hospital files.

Petitioner's expert witness valued the heart-lung machine in terms of his estimate of what it would cost for development of such a machine, as follows:
(1) Preprototype stage $ 80,640
(2) Development of a prototype   36,350
(3) Production of working model 33,000

Total   149,990

2. Building Stone

In May 1965, petitioner purchased a quantity of building stone for $ 646. The stone was being removed from a 19th century mansion in Cumberland, Md. It had originally been cut from local quarries which were no longer in operation in 1965. Because of its origin, the stone was of particular value for the repair or enlargement of buildings in Cumberland constructed of stone from the same quarries. It consisted of several types of individual stones, which varied in value according to their size, the manner in which they were cut and shaped, and their condition.

The Emanuel Episcopal Church in Cumberland sought to acquire the stone from the contractor responsible for razing the mansion but learned that it had already been sold to petitioner. The church wanted the stone for the construction of an addition to its existing structure, which had been built with the same type of local material. On request, petitioner agreed to donate the stone to the church and did so in June 1965.

After acquiring the stone and up to the time of trial, the church stored it for future use. Some of it was kept in the parking lot of a local brewery, where it was eventually covered with cinders to reduce danger of pilferage and damage. In addition to the purchase price, petitioner incurred out-of-pocket expenses of $ 2,525.51 in implementing his donation to the church through the removal and transportation of the stone.

ULTIMATE FINDINGS OF FACT

Petitioner donated a cataract machine to the University of Maryland in 1967 having a fair market value of $ 10,000 at that time.

Petitioner donated a heart-lung machine to St. Barnabas Hospital in 1969 having a fair market value of $ 15,000 at that time.

Petitioner donated stone to the Emanuel Episcopal Church in 1965 having a fair market value of $ 12,000 at that time and incurred $ 2,525.51 out-of-pocket expenses in implementing that donation.

OPINION

Before proceeding to the principal problem in this case -- namely, valuation of two pieces of specialized medical equipment -- we will dispose of some subsidiary matters. At the trial, respondent raised, by way of amended answer, the issues whether petitioner made a donation of the cataract machine to the University of Maryland and a gift of the heart-lung machine to St. Barnabas Hospital.[2] Under such circumstances, the burden of proof was on the respondent. Estate of Floyd Falese, 58 T.C. 895, 899 (1972). At the conclusion of the trial, the Court ruled that respondent had not carried his burden and that consequently petitioner had donated the cataract machine to the University in 1967 and the heart-lung machine to St. Barnabas in 1969. We have carefully reviewed the record herein and find no reason to change that ruling. Our findings of fact reflect our adherence to our prior ruling.

The Court also ruled at the trial that the value of the stone donated to the Emanuel Episcopal Church in 1965 was $ 12,000. Here, too, we have carefully reviewed the record and, as our findings of fact show, we have concluded that we should adhere to that ruling. Accordingly, petitioner is entitled to a deduction in that amount for the taxable year 1965 plus out-of-pocket expenses related to the making of that donation in the amount of $ 2,525.51. [3]

The testimony of several witnesses and the nature of his achievements demonstrate that petitioner is an extraordinarily gifted and dedicated

---

[2] 2 Respondent concedes that the University and St. Barnabas are qualified charitable organizations. See sec. 170(c)(1) and (2). All references herein are to the Internal Revenue Code of 1954, as amended and in effect during the years in issue.

[3] 3 Respondent concedes that the out-of-pocket expenses are allowable as a deduction in addition to the value of the stone. Petitioners' and respondent's experts testified that the stone was worth $ 26,334 and $ 8,468, respectively.

engineer.[4]   There is no doubt that, in designing, building, and giving away the two pieces of equipment, he has made a significant contribution to medical knowledge.   Our function, however, is to make a determination within a narrower frame of reference, namely, the "fair market value" of the contributed property.

As a threshold question to that determination, we will dispose of respondent's contention that, beyond his out-of-pocket expenses, petitioner's contributions consisted only of services for which, according to respondent's regulations (see sec. 1.170-2(a)(2), Income Tax Regs.), a deduction is not allowable. Compare John R. Holmes, 57 T.C. 430 (1971). Whatever may be the merit of respondent's contention in another context (see Rudick & Gray, "Bounty Twice Blessed: Tax Consequences of Gifts of Property or in Trust for Charity," 16 Tax L. Rev. 273, 287 (1961)), we think it has no application in this case.   We are satisfied that, although there may have been an understanding that the tangible fruits of petitioner's efforts would be given to the charitable donees, neither of such donees at any time had any kind of enforceable rights in respect thereof. Cf. John R. Holmes, 57 T.C. at 437 n.6. Compare Roland Chilton, 40 T.C. 552 (1963). We think it clear that the services which petitioner performed coalesced in the resultant property interests. Cf. William H. Mauldin, 60 T.C. 749 (1973); Bernard Goss, 59 T.C. 594 (1973); John R. Holmes, supra, and cases collected therein at 57 T.C. 437 n.5. [5] As our subsequent analysis will show, however (see pp. 957-958 infra), a substantial portion of such services should not be taken into account in determining the amount of the contributions which petitioner is entitled to deduct.

The value of a charitable contribution is a question of fact. Maurice Jarre, 64 T.C. 183 (1975). The legal standard defining fair market value is "the price at which the property would change hands between a willing buyer and a willing seller, neither being under any compulsion to buy or sell and both having reasonable knowledge of relevant facts." See William H. Mauldin, 60 T.C. at 758; sec. 1.170-1(c)(1), Income Tax Regs. That standard is singularly unhelpful here.   Indeed, the parties themselves recognized this in that they produced no evidence of "fair market value" as articulated by the foregoing definition.

---

[4] 4 Petitioner described himself as a "**mad scientist**."

[5] 5 See also Robert H. Orchard, T.C. Memo. 1975-31. Compare also Maurice Jarre, 64 T.C. 183 (1975). We also reject, as without merit, respondent's attempt to limit the "coalescence cases" to those donors who are engaged in a trade or business of producing the donated property.

Nevertheless, we recognize that "absence of market price is no barrier to valuation."[6] 6 See Guggenheim v. Rasquin, 312 U.S. 254, 258 (1941). Nor does uniqueness constitute a barrier. See Publicker v. Commissioner, 206 F. 2d 250, 253 (3d Cir. 1953). Indeed, the use to which donated property will be put is an element in determining value. See Guggenheim v. Rasquin, 312 U.S. at 257. This would appear especially to be the case where medical research equipment is involved. Cost has been accepted as an element of value (see Guggenheim v. Rasquin, 312 U.S. at 258; Publicker v. Commissioner, 206 F. 2d at 254), including cost of reproduction. See Clinton Cotton Mills v. Commissioner, 78 F. 2d 292, 295 (4th Cir. 1935), reversing and remanding 28 B.T.A. 1312 (1933). In short, "All relevant facts and elements of value * * * shall be considered." See sec. 25.2512-1, Gift Tax Regs.; Publicker v. Commissioner, 206 F. 2d at 254.[7]

Preliminary to our analysis of the evidence as to value, we address ourselves to petitioners' contention that, since they produced testimony of two experts and respondent produced none, they have made a prima facie case in respect of the value of the two machines, which respondent has not rebutted, and consequently are entitled to a decision in their favor. We reject this position. Clearly, we are not required to accept expert opinion testimony as gospel. See Dayton Power & Light Co. v. Public Utilities Commission, 292 U.S. 290, 298-300 (1934); Williams' Estate v. Commissioner, 256 F. 2d 217, 219 (9th Cir. 1958); Clinton Cotton Mills v. Commissioner, supra; Wyoming Investment Co. v. Commissioner, 70 F. 2d 191, 193 (10th Cir. 1934), remanding on other grounds a Memorandum Opinion of the Board of Tax Appeals; Gloyd v. Commissioner, 63 F. 2d 649, 650 (8th Cir. 1933); Keystone Wood Products Co., 19 B.T.A. 1116, 1121 (1930), affd. 66 F. 2d 258 (2d Cir. 1933).[8] We are entitled to evaluate their testimony in light of the entire record and use our

---

[6] 6 Nor is the presence of a limited market. Publicker v. Commissioner, 206 F. 2d 250, 254 (3d Cir. 1953); Maurice Jarre, supra; Estate of David Smith, 57 T.C. 650 (1972), affd. 510 F. 2d 479 (2d Cir. 1975); Brandon Barringer, T.C. Memo. 1972-234.

[7] 7 We recognize that sec. 1.170-1(c), Income Tax Regs., does not contain this language, but it is obviously implicit in the definition of fair market value.

[8] 8 Charles J. Kuderna, T.C. Memo. 1965-143, relied upon by petitioners, is not in point. While we stated that, under circumstances comparable to those herein, the taxpayer had established a prima facie case through his expert witnesses, our decision was based on the conclusion that the fair market value of the property had been "established to our satisfaction."

own judgment. This is precisely what we will now do and, as our analysis will reveal, serious doubts exist as to the efficacy of the expert testimony herein.

All of petitioners' experts provided 6-figure estimates of value; but, in each case, the valuation was based largely on the estimated cost of researching and developing machines, like the ones donated and bringing them to market. Put another way, they estimated the cost of retracing petitioner's steps to produce the machines. Petitioners then sought to corroborate the testimony of their experts by evidence of the time and effort spent by Mr. Cupler and a monetary evaluation thereof in developing the donated machines. There are several gaps in this approach.

First, adopting such an approach would require us to conclude that petitioner actually donated all he acquired by the development process to which those costs are ascribed. There is testimony that the market values of medical inventions depend largely on development cost; but the "invention" which can be sold for a figure adequate to recoup that entire cost has both tangible and intangible elements. The most valuable features of an invention are the rights acquired by the inventor -- usually embodied in a patent -- to control the use of the knowledge he has produced. A single instance of that invention, such as the prototypes developed by petitioner, may derive its value from those intangibles but ordinarily will be worth less than they are. Although petitioner has applied for a patent on the cataract machine,[9] his testimony shows that his main purposes were two: to solve challenging technical problems and to contribute to the advance of medical science. Such a contribution, while laudable, is not the sort for which Congress has seen fit to allow a charitable deduction; section 170 applies only to gifts made in property to qualified organizations.[10] The record simply does not support petitioners' argument that all of the rights in the inventions represented by the machines were vested in the donees. At most, the record indicates what petitioner intended to do in the future; there is no evidence of any present transfer of such rights by way of an assignment or otherwise. Compare Roland Chilton, supra. Even if this intention could somehow be enforced by the donee, it does not satisfy the statutory requirement that payment be made "within the taxable year." Sec. 170(a). See Lewis C. Christensen, 40 T.C. 563, 574 (1963). Furthermore, the failure to take steps at the time to patent the rights in the inventions casts considerable doubt on the relevance of petitioners' evidence as to the value of the physical equipment actually contributed. Even a patentable invention is of considerably diminished value

---

[9] 9 No patent has been applied for in respect of the heart-lung machine.

[10] 10 See William Fox, T.C. Memo. 1965-195.

without the legal protection which a patent affords the inventor's rights. Wagner v. Commissioner, 63 F. 2d 859 (9th Cir. 1933).

Second, we note that, in respect of both machines, petitioner spent a considerable amount of time preparing himself by way of background study and in a trial-and-error process of development. Clearly, such elements should not be included in determining the value of the machines themselves. Preliminary sketches or discarded paintings do not affect the value of the painting finally produced by an artist; nor do earlier rewritten materials become part of the value of the final manuscript of an author.[11] In light of the foregoing, we think that much, if not all, of the value in the appraisals of the experts relating to the preprototype and development of prototype stages should not be taken into account.

Third, there is a question as to the value placed by petitioner on his own time. The number of hours spent in developing the machines is based upon pure estimates and constitutes, even if petitioner's prodigious capacity to work is taken into account, a large portion of his time in light of the fact that he was heavily engaged as a business executive. Moreover, the $ 500-per-day value placed on petitioner's time is dubious. Cf. Bernard Goss, 59 T.C. at 597. Petitioner testified that this was what he asked for as compensation as a consultant when he was away from the plant; in respect of the machines involved herein, he did much of his work at the plant and at his nearby home.[12]

Fourth, the testimony of both of petitioners' experts was based almost entirely upon reproduction costs; we do not consider their general statements that a prospective purchaser would pay the equivalent of such cost to acquire the machines in and of itself determinative of value. Moreover, it is of some significance that one of petitioners' experts never saw the machines for which he furnished appraisals.

Fifth, in respect of the cataract machine, we have evidence of the price at

---

[11] 11 Indeed, such sketches and rewritten material may have an independent value.

[12] 12 The $ 500-per-day value is to be contrasted with the testimony of one expert that a full-time director of a project to produce a heart-lung machine would be paid $ 36,350 a year, and that the time of other personnel would cost $ 32 per day.

which the comparable Douvas machine sold in later years. Petitioners' own witness, Dr. Schocket, testified that the two machines were "quite similar." It is true that petitioner's invention preceded the appearance of the Douvas device by a few years, but that does not mean that we should ignore such evidence. See Estate of David Smith, 57 T.C. 650, 659 n. 8 (1972), affd. 510 F. 2d 479 (2d Cir. 1975). While petitioner stresses the alleged technical superiority of his invention, Dr. Schocket was unable to say it was better than Douvas'. The Douvas machine has achieved widespread clinical use, while petitioner's has been applied to its intended purpose for the most part only in research. Moreover, it appears that the amount spent in developing the Douvas machine is comparable to the hypothetical cost derived by petitioners' experts. Further, we note that there were many difficulties attendant on the use of the machine at the time of the donation and that neither the tricep tool, an important part of the machine, nor the millisecond timers were included.[13]

There is less concrete evidence of value regarding the heart-lung machine. It was suitable only for use in Dr. Zimmerman's research on chick embryos; no comparable device existed and no one else was engaged in similar research. The fact that Dr. Zimmerman solicited the development of, and was satisfied with, the machine is evidence of value. Maurice Jarre, supra; William H. Mauldin, supra; Estate of David Smith, supra.[14] Furthermore, the heart-lung machine was considerably more complex than the cataract machine and required correspondingly more effort (and hypothetical cost) to produce. We also find it significant that this machine was by far the more successful of the two in terms of application to its intended use.

Based upon the foregoing considerations, as well as our evaluation of the testimony and the record as a whole, we have concluded, as our ultimate findings of fact show, that the fair market value of the cataract machine at the time it was donated to the University of Maryland Hospital in 1967 was $ 10,000 and of the heart-lung machine at the time it was donated to St. Barnabas Hospital in 1969 was $ 15,000, both amounts inclusive of petitioner's out-of-pocket expenses.
Decision will be entered under Rule 155.

---

[13] 13 The evidence merely shows that the tricep tool was delivered to petitioner's patent attorney in 1967.

[14] 14 See also Brandon Barringer, supra.

SKK, INC., and BARRY SCHRAGER, Plaintiffs,

vs.

CAMBRIDGE SYSTEMS GROUP, INC., CSG LIMITED, and WILLIAM J. McLAREN and MARJORIE WANG-McLAREN, individually and d/b/a CAMBRIDGE SYSTEMS GROUP, Defendants.

No. 81 C 2557

IN THE UNITED STATES DISTRICT COURT FOR THE NORTHERN DISTRICT OF ILLINOIS EASTERN DIVISION

MEMORANDUM AND ORDER

Prior to 1978 three young faculty members at the University of Illinois, Chicago Circle campus, developed a data access security computer program package which, in its present form, is denominated as ACF2. The University was not interested in itself marketing the program, which was perfected outside University facilities, and none of the three, Barry Schrager, Scott Krueger and Eberhard Klemens ("the developers"), had anything beyond the most rudimentary experience in marketing.

In 1975 Shawn McLaren had developed a computer package known as ASM2 and had formed his own small company, Cambridge Systems Group, Inc. ("Cambridge"), initially consisting of himself and his wife, to market that product. He found that his strong technical background meshed well with a new-found proclivity for marketing, and the company, while remaining small, prospered.

In late 1977 the developers, while still maintaining their positions at the University of Illinois, were looking toward the marketing of the product. That required a product, and by October, 1977, Barry Schrager was spending his

302

free time writing code. In February, 1978, Barry Schrager and Klemens spent considerable time in London, Ontario, for development test-site work.

Marketing also required a marketer, and the developers had little interest in transferring their rights to IBM and having their product become another IBM product. At that time, in view of their limited business experience, they turned to Barry Schrager's brother, Leonard, for assistance. Leonard was a name partner in the firm which thereafter represented them and had extensive experience in business-oriented law, although he had no background in computers or computer technology.

The initial contacts between the developers and Cambridge came in late 1977. Cambridge was then, as now, represented by William Fenwick and the law firm of which he was a partner. Mr. Fenwick had extensive experience in computer-related legal issues and relationships. Shawn McLaren recognized the potentialities of ACF2 and the possible marketing compatibility of ACF2 with ACM2 [sic i.e., ASM2]. The developers recognized the desirability of marketing through another small company which had considerable technical capability and a technically-oriented marketing approach -- a marketing arrangement which would also permit them to remain with considerable control over the future of the product. This led, on March 5, 1978, to an agreement between the developers' new company, Schrager, Klemens & Krueger, Inc. ("SKK") and Cambridge. That agreement gave Cambridge marketing rights, and it is the nature of those rights and SKK's retained rights which is the subject of the present dispute. That agreement will be discussed more fully hereafter. The arrangement was enormously successful, and ACF2 became the major competitor to RCAF, the IBM access security product. That led, in February, 1980, to another agreement conveying to Cambridge marketing and servicing rights in Europe. Thereafter, over a period of time the relationship among the developers deteriorated, with disputes arising between Barry Schrager and Krueger on the one hand and Klemens on the other, resulting, eventually, in the ouster of Klemens from SKK. In the meantime, Schrager and Krueger had become dissatisfied with the progress of marketing in Europe, and the personal relationship between Schrager and Krueger on the one hand and Shawn McLaren and his wife on the other had also begun to deteriorate.

Shortly after Klemens' ouster SKK, now controlled by Schrager and Krueger, in April, 1981, purported to terminate the European agreement for various claimed breaches of that agreement, while leaving open the possible continuation of the United States agreement (which could be terminated if the European agreement was terminated for cause) if various changes were made. The immediate result was a highly litigious relationship between SKK and CSG which has continued ever since.

SKK in this lawsuit sued Cambridge, which counterclaimed. Klemens sought unsuccessfully to intervene and brought an action against his former compatriots in state court. The federal claims were heard, in the summer of 1981, upon cross-motions for preliminary relief. After what was supposed to be a relatively short hearing but what turned out to be a lengthy trial after very intensive and extensive discovery, this court concluded, as a preliminary matter, that SKK lacked cause for termination and ordered on September 24, 1981, that Cambridge (which had temporarily transferred European marketing to SKK) resume European marketing and that Cambridge retain its North American marketing rights. Within the month it came to light that SKK, despite the highly contentious dispute between SKK and Cambridge then in court had, without advising Cambridge (or the court), embarked upon an extensive advertising campaign in national United States publications which ignored Cambridge's marketing rights. After several pleadings, conferences and orders, this court issued its order of October 30, 1981, sharply restricting promotional activities by SKK. The court had also appointed a special master to administer the preliminary injunction.

Thereafter that later order became the primary battleground, with Cambridge complaining on several occasions that SKK was violating the October 30, 1981 order by violating, in one fashion or another, the marketing restrictions. Those led to a series of hearings before the special master (some of them extensive), full briefing, subsequent recommendations by him to this court and, almost invariably, objections to the recommendation and more briefing. Interspersed were various telephonic conferences, emergency motions and conferences. In the meantime, Klemens had composed his differences with Schrager and Krueger, which resulted in his permanent withdrawal, in return for various considerations, from the affairs of SKK, and both the 1981 orders were on appeal. In the meantime, also, SKK had invoked the quota provisions of the European agreement over the protests of Cambridge and, thereafter, in 1982, in a second federal action before this court, 82 C 1621, sought to oust Cambridge from marketing ACF2 in Europe on the ground that it had failed (or would fail) to meet the European quota.

In what was again supposed to be a relatively short trial, the parties squared off again in January of this year. After two weeks of testimony, with considerably more to come, this court again urged the parties to attempt to resolve all their differences. By then this essentially commercial dispute between two small companies had generated more paper than, or at least as much as, any case this court has had, and had occupied a considerable proportion of the time over an extended period which this court had to devote to civil trials.

Over the following two weeks this court was almost entirely engaged in the settlement discussions between the parties. The result was an extensive and detailed agreement which, in its essential respects, resolved all outstanding disputes by SKK taking over marketing in Europe, Cambridge retaining marketing rights in North America, the parties adjusting their relationship in North America in a number of respects, and SKK paying certain compensation to Cambridge. The 1982 case was dismissed, the appeal of the 1981 case was dismissed except the issues now before the court.

The issues now before the court largely stem from the October 30, 1981 order and were the substance of the continuing disputes before the special master. SKK contends that the March 5, 1978 agreement permits it to engage in whatever ACF2 marketing activities it believes appropriate. Alternatively, it contends that even if there are restrictions they are far less than those which Cambridge, largely successfully, urged before the special master. Cambridge, conversely, contends that its marketing rights permit it to control marketing entirely, and that means largely divorcing SKK from any contact with prospective customers. After the parties agreed on the basic settlement terms the court conducted yet another hearing, this one blissfully short, and the matter is before the court for decision.

Throughout all this enormous legal effort and acrimony ACF2 has continued to enjoy great commercial success in the United States and, to a considerably lesser extent, in Europe. Indeed, one wonders how these litigations could have been pressed were it otherwise. The nature of these litigations has, however, given the court extensive contact with the principals both in court and in conferences and has provided a background context far greater than is normally the case in litigated actions. In the court's view the remaining issues, while of course having significant economic implications, are greatly influenced by the progress of the litigations, with the principals of SKK firmly believing that Cambridge has unfairly sought to deprive them of the opportunity for public dialogue about their own unique product and Cambridge firmly believing that SKK's efforts to participate in any public dialogue about ACF2 or access security programs is part of a larger effort to destroy Cambridge's marketing rights. We turn then to the specific issues which are before the court.

SKK contends that it has a right to market ACF2 in the United States and Canada, a right which is coextensive to the rights of Cambridge. It recognizes that, during happier days, it consistently described ACF2 in its technical publications as exclusively marketed by Cambridge and, indeed, has continued to do so on occasion in its pleadings in these litigations, but it contends that the rights granted to Cambridge restrict any grant of marketing rights to another, but not its marketing efforts as owner. It also recognizes that, until the aborted advertising campaign in the fall of 1981, it did not engage in any prior sustained or systematic marketing efforts but it argues that this was a matter of choice -- it did not do so during that period because of limited resources and other responsibilities. Cambridge points to the contract language and past practices, contending that SKK's present assertion is clearly an afterthought.

The agreement is not self-defining, primarily because of the right accorded SKK in par. 1(b) "to solicit prospective customers of ACF2". Indeed, Shawn McLaren in an answer to one question during the 1981 hearing conceded that SKK had marketing rights, based on the "solicit" language. This court does not view that answer to a question arising in a different context and focused solely on the one clause, as providing the answer to the dispute here. Indeed, it was not uncommon in the various hearings, in which strong feelings were involved, to have recollections and responses vary somewhat by the context of the questioning. That answer does, however, illustrate as well as anything that SKK's contentions cannot be summarily dismissed. We turn then to the course of negotiations, the language of the agreement, the subsequent practices of the parties, and the commercial context in which these all occurred.

Cambridge originally would have preferred to have acquired ownership of ACF2, with the developers receiving royalties. That preference was abandoned by the middle of January, 1978. The basic structure of the agreement was established by a draft contract prepared by Leonard Schrager, with perhaps some reliance upon an earlier rough outline from Fenwick. In any event, that draft was the subject of discussions in Chicago in February, 1978. Although various proposals were considered by the parties at that meeting, the participants, both Schragers, McLaren and Fenwick -- Krueger may also have attended but he does not recall it -- agree on one thing, that the references to the "solicit" language were limited. Barry Schrager believes he referred to the SKK position in a telephone conversation and that Leonard Schrager explained at his office that it was a protection to SKK, which could sell if necessary although Cambridge would receive its 50 per cent share. Leonard Schrager's recollection was substantially similar. Shawn McLaren testified that Barry Schrager expressed a concern in a telephone call about approaching old friends and that his brother and Fenwick discussed, at the meeting, that talking to old friends would or could be a technical violation without the solicitation language. Fenwick testified that the Chicago meeting was in the context of prior discussions about purchasing marketing rights rather than ACF2 itself -- an unusual arrangement. His recollection of the events in Chicago was similar to that of McLaren. Everyone agrees that there was no extended conversation on the subject and that no one specifically referred to co-marketing, parallel advertising and the like.

After this court's extensive involvement with the parties over the past two years it cannot conclude that the parties expressly agreed that the "solicit" clause would allow SKK to have full marketing rights. McLaren might have so agreed eventually, after protest, believing that Cambridge's performance would make any resort to such an option unlikely. But this court considers it highly improbable that McLaren (and Fenwick) would have without objection consented to a parallel marketing effort. His own perception of Cambridge as an established company with a unique approach to marketing and as the dominant force in a partnership of technical and marketing capabilities argues powerfully against any other conclusion.

The then circumstances and the structure of the agreement also militate against SKK's position. In February, 1978, Cambridge was small but it was established. SKK was newly formed, a corporate vessel for ACF2 which was transferred to it by the developers coincidentally with the agreement between SKK and Cambridge, and its start-up funds would come, in large measure, from loans by Cambridge. The developers had virtually no business or marketing experience, and SKK had "developed trust and faith" in McLaren.

The agreement obligated Cambridge to exercise "best efforts" and to pay in excess of $300,000 to SKK each year -- a quota which was to prove but a small fraction of the revenues actually generated. SKK agreed to provide to Cambridge, and be reimbursed for, such selling assistance as Cambridge "shall reasonably request". Cambridge had "marketing obligations" to undertake reasonable advertising, sales promotion and "other customer solicitation," with advertisements subject to SKK's "[reasonable]" approval. SKK was to provide the technical support. The parties agreed to a cooperative effort because the "marketing" and the "operation" both required "great expertise." SKK agreed not to offer, in the United States and Canada, any data security control-related program without first giving Cambridge a right to distribute it. SKK did preserve "the right to solicit prospective customers of ACF2" (although, literally, not prospective customers of other data security control programs of SKK thereafter distributed by Cambridge).

SKK contends that it did not grant marketing rights in ACF2 and, conditioned by contact [sic] terms, related products, but did not foreclose its own efforts if it paid Cambridge its share; agreed to provide marketing assistance upon request, but that was only when it expected to be reimbursed; and that it did not expressly agree not to advertise or promote. The contract terms are capable of bearing SKK's interpretation, but that interpretation presupposes that the developers (or rather Barry Schrager and Krueger because that certainly was not Klemens' professed understanding), contemplated, while their new company was seeking a marketing "partner," a possible future major parallel marketing effort by a new company with considerable technical capabilities but no marketing capability. The court is persuaded that SKK did hope and expect to solicit those contacts with which it had or developed relationships because of its technical activities (and not just "old friends") and not be foreclosed from approaching those prospects, which was naturally the garden which it could be expected to cultivate with some success. But that is less than the expansive rights SKK now advocates and which the Schragers suggest were discussed in February, 1978. That is, this court concludes, an occasion in which a wish has fathered a recollection.

If, as this court believes, Cambridge has marketing rights exclusive of others, including SKK, what does that mean? When the agreement was executed SKK was well aware that Cambridge had considerable technical capability and emphasized technical aspects in marketing. Cambridge was well aware that SKK's developers were involved in the technical community, had hopes of developing other products and would have significant continuing technical responsibilities. In the aftermath of the contested business divorce this court heard in 1981, SKK insisted there were no restraints on its marketing. Cambridge contended, generally successfully, that any conduct by SKK which impinged upon Cambridge's then concept of marketing was a violation of the agreement or at least the October 30, 1981 order. And Cambridge's concept was, in substance, that any public exposure of SKK related to ACF2 undercut Cambridge's marketing efforts.

That concept goes too far. SKK's principals are not some **mad scientists** to be locked in a corner of the castle while they tinker with new inventions. SKK is a development company in a dynamic industry. Interaction with colleagues is necessary for professional development; participation in industry affairs is necessary for professional satisfaction and to employ and retain key employees. A feel for what is happening and how ACF2 and other products are perceived is necessary for a full understanding of where SKK should go in developing ACF2 and related products. SKK is not a shadow but a going concern which seeks to establish its own identity. ACF2 is its development, not that of Cambridge. Cambridge has exclusive marketing rights in the United States and Canada, but SKK at all times has had the marketing rights other than there and Europe, and it now has those rights in Europe.

One matter agreed upon by the parties, in the event this court determines, as it has, that SKK's rights are restricted, is that this court should state with some precision what SKK can and cannot do. SKK has, with considerable reluctance, recognized that a mandatory order is part of the overall settlement. The purpose of the post-settlement hearing was to provide a basis for some bright lines for conduct during the post-divorce era.

SKK has urged that its activities before the blowup were less than necessary for attaining non-marketing objectives and were restricted only because of limited resources. Cambridge insists that those activities were, in large part, marketing permitted by Cambridge as a matter of its marketing discretion. The court concludes that the relationship of the parties prior to their dispute is the best indication of what each considered appropriate in light of their differing functions and needs. What is now appropriate must also be considered in light of SKK's assuming marketing responsibilities in Europe.

The evidence of past practices establishes that SKK personnel did participate, from time to time, in SHARE, Guide and auditing conferences, all of which discourage efforts at marketing presentations. While it is not a certainty that a non-user might sit in at a user conference, that is not the objective of such conferences and the format is not directed toward marketing. In those instances where a user or another did indicate some interest in installations or additional installations, SKK referred them to CSG.

The evidence also indicates that SKK personnel from time to time made presentations to other conferences at which the attendance included persons who reasonably could be described as potential prospects. This did not occasion any great outcry from Cambridge because, this court finds, the level of activity of that nature prior to the litigation was not such so as to constitute marketing in any meaningful way. Indeed, Cambridge was well aware that Linda Vedder was making some presentations and was technically competent to do so. Given her background, this court concludes that it would be unreasonable both to her and to SKK's abilities to employ and retain persons of that experience if they were foreclosed from any public involvement at conferences. Further, SKK did from time to time talk to prospects, generally at the request or with the knowledge of Cambridge because of the particular needs of a pending matter.

Past practices provide much less guidance, however, when the disagreements are over matters which were not even considered, much less discussed, prior to April 1981 or involve practices which were not followed in any meaningful way. An example of the former is contacts with multi-national corporations regarding foreign sites; an example of the latter is a non-user conference sponsored by SKK, such as Operation Safeguard. Subsequent practices, such as newsletters, advertisements and listings, are also impacted by SKK's assumption of marketing responsibilities in Europe. It is reasonably clear that the primary focus of computer technology remains in the United States, with Europeans looking to the United States for information. It is also reasonably clear that publication in this country reaches far more persons here than it normally reaches elsewhere in the world. The nature of the publication, of course, makes a difference.

Further, post-dispute practices by SKK evidence its concern about a difference in marketing philosophy, with SKK being interested in visibility wherever possible and Cambridge being far more selective. To the extent that a marketing philosophy should govern, obviously that marketing philosophy should be that of Cambridge, as it has the marketing responsibility. Finally, post-dispute practices also evidence the dynamics of the dispute. Perhaps the best example is "Operation Safeguard," where SKK reasonably was interested in promoting public understanding and awareness of data security problems and also used the occasion for touting ACF2 as the solution to the problem.

The court has considered the above, as well as the specific submissions of the parties. It considers its task, pursuant to the settlement negotiations and settlement agreement, to establish "do's" and "don'ts" which properly recognize the differing functions created by the March 5, 1978 agreement as modified by the settlement agreement. It approaches that task with a recognition that European marketing by SKK increases the problem presented because of SKK's need for exposure there and, to some extent, decreases it because Europe provides a previously unavailable forum for the exchange of ideas and information. It also recognizes that restrictions on contacts must be reasonably viewed in light of the infinitely varied circumstances in which contacts occur, and that limitations in practice require good faith and common sense. A possible prospect may be easily referred to Cambridge in some circumstances; in others, some responses may be necessary to persistent requests for information in order to avoid appearing abrupt or unconcerned. Finally, it should be noted that the order defines what SKK may do, respecting various matters, which necessarily defines the limit which it cannot transgress without violating the order.

For the foregoing reasons, the court orders SKK, Barry Schrager, Scott Krueger, and each of them, and their officers, agents, employees, representatives, attorneys, and all persons acting in concert or participating with them (hereinafter collectively referred to as "SKK"), as follows:

1. Conferences in the United States and Canada

SKK may attend any conference in the United States or Canada; it may not engage in marketing activities at those conferences. Because of the nature of such conferences, it may well receive informal inquiries relating to marketing, maintenance and technical matters. With respect to marketing inquiries, SKK must refer the inquirer to Cambridge, limit its response to the least response which the circumstances reasonably permit, and promptly advise Cambridge of the inquiry (hereinafter "a limited response").

SKK may make presentations at user conferences, auditor conferences, SHARE, GUIDE and similar meetings at which presentations are, and are expected to be, non-marketing oriented. SKK may participate in and co-sponsor conferences devoted to problems of computer privacy and security and it may issue press releases for such conferences. For and at such conferences, SKK shall limit its identification to ACF2 to a description of itself as the developer and maintainer of ACF2. SKK may make presentations at not more than two conferences per year of the kind now referred to as an IDOS conference. It shall at such conferences expressly advise the audience orally and, if it presents written or visual material, in that material, that

Cambridge is the exclusive marketer in the United States and Canada. SKK shall advise Cambridge reasonably in advance of any presentation at any conference of its intention to do so in order that it can consider any timely marketing objections raised by Cambridge respecting the particular conference. It shall make a limited response to marketing inquiries at any conference.

2. Contacts with United States and Canadian users

SKK is not limited in its contact with users, and it may discuss competitive products with users. However, it shall make a limited response to any marketing inquiries.

3. Contacts with United States and Canadian non-users

SKK may contact users of competitive products which have installed a competitive product within the previous twelve months to discuss the technical considerations which led to that decision. Since there is, as Shawn McLaren testified, a considerable inertia militating against change once a decision has been made, there appears little reason for concluding that such a non-user can reasonably be viewed as a prospect during that period. Once that twelve-month period has passed, however, SKK should not contact that non-user. It shall give a limited response to any marketing inquiry.

SKK may employ consultants respecting technical and business matters, it may respond to specific technical inquiries from consultants, and it may initiate discussions of technical subjects with technical experts who are not understood to be consultants for particular non-users who are evaluating data security programs. It may contact consultants to non-users who have purchased a competing product within the previous twelve months, if it reasonably believes that the consultant participated in that decision, to discuss the technical considerations for that decision. SKK may contact persons who have been reported in the media as making technical evaluations of data security products which are favorable to a specific product, including ACF2, but only after determining from Cambridge whether there are marketing reasons why such a contact is inadvisable. In all the above contacts SKK shall make a limited response to any marketing inquiries. SKK shall consult with Cambridge in the event a prospective customer has requested a presentation by SKK or SKK's other involvement in the marketing decision and shall be bound by Cambridge's determination respecting SKK's involvement.

4. Advertisements and listings in United States and Canada

SKK may place advertisements in United States publications which are corporate-image advertisements, so long as it confines its references to ACF2 to a description of SKK as the developer and maintainer of ACF2. SKK may advertise in international publications, even though there may be some readers or subscribers in the United States. The court's understanding is that the only publication with a significant readership both in the United States and Europe is Datamation, although the court is unclear as to whether there is a sharp differentiation between a United States and international edition. Assuming that the court is correct in understanding that the Datamation circulated in the United States also is circulated to a reasonably wide readership in Europe, SKK may advertise in Datamation so long as it provides Cambridge with a copy of the proposed advertisement reasonably in advance of publication deadline and, if requested to do so by Cambridge, specifies in the advertisement that ACF2 is exclusively marketed in the United States and Canada by Cambridge. SKK may have listings in directories originating in the United States only if they are circulated in significant volume and relied upon for information outside the United States and Canada, and then only if SKK provides Cambridge with a copy of the proposed listing reasonably in advance of the publication deadline and specifies, upon Cambridge's request, that ACF2 is marketed in the United States and Canada exclusively by Cambridge. The court suggests that a joint listing specifically designating marketing areas should be discussed by Cambridge and SKK for such publications. SKK may list in international listings even though there may be some incidental distribution in the United States. SKK shall not advertise or list except as above described.

5. Newsletters

SKK shall not distribute newsletters with marketing information to non-users in the United States, except such incidental distribution to persons such as suppliers, consultants employed by SKK and similar persons who cannot reasonably be considered as prospects or in the decision-making process for prospects.

6. Multi-national organizations

SKK to the extent commercially feasible shall market outside the United States and Canada to multi-national companies at foreign sites or headquarters. In the event that commercial feasibility requires that SKK contact a United States office of a multi-national company respecting foreign sites, it shall advise Cambridge of its intention to do so prior to making such contact, shall consider any marketing objections by Cambridge and any alternatives suggested by it, shall, if it does contact the United States headquarters, keep Cambridge advised of the extent of those contacts, and shall, with respect to any marketing inquiries relating to the United States and Canada, make a limited response.

7. Interviews by United States and Canadian media

SKK may respond to unsolicited requests for interviews respecting data security, privacy and technical subjects.

Finally, it is not a violation of this order for a person at SKK to discuss ACF2 with persons with whom that person has an ongoing personal or professional relationship so long as Cambridge is promptly advised of any market-oriented interest expressed by that person and all matters respecting price and licenses are referred to Cambridge.

Except as stated above, SKK is permanently enjoined from, in the United States and Canada, marketing ACF2 or engaging in activities which may reasonably be perceived as marketing. "ACF2", for the purposes of this order, includes SKK data security-related programs or products hereafter marketed in the United States and Canada by Cambridge.

/s/ James B. Moran
JAMES B. MORAN
Judge, United States District Court
March 28, 1983

LAMEKA D. BROWN O/B/O N.B., III, a minor child, Plaintiff,

v.

MICHAEL J. ASTRUE, Commissioner of Social Security, Defendant.

Case No. 07-00377-CV-W-NKL-SSA

UNITED STATES DISTRICT COURT FOR THE WESTERN DISTRICT OF MISSOURI, WESTERN DIVISION

131 Soc. Sec. Rep. Service 418
May 30, 2008

NANETTE K. LAUGHREY, United States District Judge.

ORDER

Plaintiff Lameka D. Brown, on behalf of her minor child, Norman, challenges the Social Security Commissioner's denial of Supplemental Security Income under Title XVI of the Social Security Act, 42 U.S.C. §§ 1381, et seq. Specifically, Lameka D. Brown asserts that the record does not support the Administrative Law Judge's ("ALJ") finding that Norman Brown was not under a disability. [Doc. # 5]. Having jurisdiction under 42 U.S.C. § 405(g), this Court finds that the Commissioner's decision is supported by substantial evidence.

I. Factual Background
The complete facts and arguments are presented in the parties' briefs and will be duplicated here only to the extent necessary.[1] On August 15, 2002, Lameka D. Brown filed an application for Supplemental Security Income benefits on behalf of her son, Norman Brown, III ("Norman"), date of birth,

---

[1] 1 Portions of the parties' briefs are adopted without quotation designated

June 20, 1991, alleging an onset date of disability of March 27, 2001. (Tr. 88-92). She alleged disability due to a speech and language disorder. (Tr. 117). At the time Lameka Brown filed her application, Norman was 13 years of age and was in the 8th grade, attending special education classes for speech and language therapy. (Tr. 381-382).

On August 29, 2002, the state agency psychologist specifically found that Norman had a marked limitation in the domain of acquiring and using information. (Tr. 281). In 2003, intelligence tests showed Norman had a verbal IQ of 81, a performance IQ of 81 and a full scale IQ of 79. (Tr. 17).

Norman has been treated at Swope Health Services for ADHD and generalized anxiety disorder since June 2004. (Tr. 17). Norman "has a counselor that works on him or with him on a frequent basis. He sees a therapist twice a week. He does have a case manager, but as far as therapy, he goes to therapy and sees another lady probably like biweekly." (Tr. 333-334). Norman's social worker indicated that he had difficulty sustaining attention, focusing on direct instructions, organizing tasks and managing his worry. (Tr. 17).

On July 9, 2004, James True, M.D., noted that Norman showed "strange and bizarre behaviors including injuring himself and animals, and starting fires."[2] True diagnosed Norman with schizoaffective disorder and assessed a Global Assessment of Functioning of 41. " (Tr. 18). His mood appeared eurythmic and somewhat anxious. Dr. True noted that Norman's academic records "indicated Norman has significant problems recalling facts and comprehending what he has read. He has problems using punctuation, capitalization and grammatical construction correctly . . . . [Norman's] communication indicated the student did not pass the District's Speech and Language Screening and additional evaluation was determined to be needed. Language skills are not functional as compared to peers in the same age group. Speech/Language skills are not adequate for academic needs. Diagnostic Conclusion indicates initial evidence of Language Disorder as the primary handicapping condition. The student's language disorder adversely affects his/her school functioning." (Tr. 149-156). True then recommended immediate attention to Norman's "psychosis." Id. at 17-18.

The ALJ first held hearings on Lameka Brown's application on August 24, 2004. At that hearing, when asked by the ALJ why she thought her son was

---

[2] 2 [Norman] needs assistance with retention of word concepts, reading comprehension and written language. (Tr. 305). He stored manure in his room and added garbage to it to see it ferment. He talks about building a microwave car. He states that he wants to grow up to be a **mad scientist**. Id.

disabled, Lameka Brown likened the severity of her son's impairments to autism because of how often Norman saw medical professionals and underperformed in everyday tasks. (Tr. 385). According to Lameka Brown, Norman is forgetful and unable to "stick to, you know, a certain task that [Mrs. Brown] ask[s] him to perform." (Tr. 386). Norman has friends slightly younger than he is. He likes science but admits that he needs a lot of help with homework. (Tr. 397). According to Lameka Brown, Norman gets D's and F's in all his classes.

At the original hearing, the ALJ took testimony of the court's medical expert, Richard Kaspar, Ph.D. ("Kaspar"), by telephone. (Tr. 398). Dr. Kaspar is a clinical psychologist. Id. Kaspar testified that Norman had impairments of, "history of ADHD, Attention Deficit Hyperactive Disorder. Under children's mental category 112.06, he's got an overanxious disorder of childhood, an anxiety related disorder. Under children's mental category 112.02, he has a learning disorder, a learning disorder, NOS, not otherwise specified. Other - - at, at least history of other language delays, developmental disorders, some suggestion also of borderline intellectual functioning. And in - - under mental category 112.03, a recent diagnosis of a [schizo] affective disorder." (Tr. 18, 399-400).

After reviewing True's diagnosis, Kaspar recommended updating treatment records and obtaining a psychological consultative examination which was performed on September 23, 2004, by Jamie Prestage, M.D. ("Prestage"). (Tr. 18, 327, 403-407). Prestage is a licensed psychologist. During his evaluation of Norman, he found Norman somewhat anxious but he quickly settled down. "He was well oriented and there was no evidence of thought disorder, affective disorder or behavior disorder . . . . Within the school setting Norman reportedly functioned well, but exhibits learning deficits in reading, math and written expression." (Tr. 320). Psychologist Prestage's diagnostic impression was Attention Deficit Hyperactivity Disorder (By History), Generalized Anxiety Disorder (By History), and Learning Disorder NOS. (Tr. 320).

While Norman's school records show significant problems with acquiring and using information, they do not indicate a significant problem with concentration. (Tr. 148-256). For example, when Swope Parkway Health Center sent out questionnaires to Norman's teachers, his teachers identified "just a little" problem with distractability. (Tr. 242-256). He consistently was described as a compliant child who was able to interact appropriately with his teachers and classmates.

At a subsequent hearing, after Prestage's report was received by the ALJ and reviewed by Kaspar, Kaspar testified that the True report and the Prestage report were in conflict. The reports "didn't sound like the same young man " which was surprising given that they were based on observations two months apart. (Tr. 328).

The last hearing regarding Norman's application was held on June 6, 2005. (Tr. 350-361). Although the ALJ noted that "the law absolutely requires that we give greater weight to treatment records than we do on time consultative evaluations," the ALJ accorded greater weight to Prestage's diagnosis because there were few treatment notes from True; Norman was not taking anti-psychotic medications; and Norman's school records showed that he did not have behavioral problems. (Tr. 18).

Based on diagnoses of borderline intellectual functioning and ADHD, Kaspar concluded that Norman did not meet the requirements for a listed impairment. (Tr. 356). The ALJ also concluded that Norman's impairments are not of a severity which medically meet or equal the severity of any impairment listed in Part B of Appendix 1 to Subpart P, 20 CFR Part 404 ("Listing of Impairments"). "Neither are claimant's impairments functionally equivalent in severity to any listed impairment . . . [Norman] does not have "extreme" or "marked" limitations in any functional domains." (Tr. 21).

On June 21, 2006, the Administrative Law Judge issued an Unfavorable Decision on Lameka Brown's claim. (Tr. 13-22). Lameka Brown filed a timely Request with the Appeals Council of the Social Security Administration to review the decision of the Administrative Law Judge. On May 14, 2007, the Appeals Council denied her appeal. (Tr. 8-10).

II. Discussion

In reviewing the Commissioner's denial of benefits, this Court considers whether the ALJ's decision is supported by substantial evidence on the record as a whole. See Travis v. Astrue, 477 F.3d 1037, 1040 (8th Cir. 2007). "Substantial evidence is evidence that a reasonable mind would find adequate to support the ALJ's conclusion." Nicola v. Astrue, 480 F.3d 885, 886 (8th Cir. 2007). The Court will uphold the denial of benefits so long as the ALJ's decision falls within the available "zone of choices." See Casey v. Astrue, 503 F.3d 687, 2007 WL 2873647, at *1 (8th Cir. 2007). "An ALJ's decision is not outside the 'zone of choice' simply because we might have reached a different conclusion had we been the initial finder of fact." Id. (quoting Nicola, 480 F.3d at 886).

An individual under age eighteen will be considered disabled if he has a "medically determinable physical or mental impairment, which results in marked and severe functional limitations." 42 U.S.C. § 1382c(a)(3)(C)(I). The ALJ must apply the following sequential evaluation to determine whether an individual not yet 18 has a disability (or combination of disabilities) thereby entitling the individual to SSI benefits:

1. Whether or not the claimant is engaged in substantial gainful activity;
2. Whether or not a claimant has a severe impairment within the meaning of

the Social Security Act-that is whether or not the impairment "causes more than a minimal limitation in one's ability to function in an age appropriate manner";

3. Whether or not the severity of a claimant's impairment(s) meet or medically or functionally equals the requirements listed in the Listing of Impairments in Appendix 1, Subpart P of the Social Security Act;

4. And finally, pursuant to the following four-step analysis, whether an impairment of a combination of impairments is functionally equivalent to a listed impairment. See 20 CFR 416.926a (d) ("Whether there are disabling limitations in broad areas of functioning, such as social functioning, motor functioning, and personal functioning.").

The ALJ must consider not only what a child cannot do, but also what a child has difficulty doing, needs help doing, or is restricted from doing because of the impairments. 65 Fed Reg. 54, 756. The ALJ must consider all the limitations of a child, "even when the child has some ability to do an activity." 65 Fed. Reg. 54, 756.

There are six domains the ALJ must assess for a child's limitation. 20 CFR 926a (b)(1). If a child suffers from an "extreme" limitation under one domain, or a "marked" limitation under two domains, the child has a combination of impairments functionally equivalent to a listed impairment. The domains are:

(i) Acquiring and using information;
(ii) Attending and completing tasks;
(iii) Interacting and relating with others;
(iv) Moving about and manipulating objects;
(v) Caring for yourself; and
(vi) Health and physical well being. Id.

A. Norman's Ability to Acquire and Use Information

Lameka Brown claims that the ALJ erred by finding that Norman did not have a marked limitation in domain (i) acquiring and using information; and domain (ii) attending and completing tasks. (Tr. 19-21).[3] The State Agency Psychologist, Janet L. Raps, found that Norman's limitation as to acquiring and using information was "Marked" based upon the fact that "[Norman] has a language disorder" and "has difficulty with verbal and written instructions." (Tr. 281). A finding made by a State agency psychologist is "expert opinion

---

[3] 3 The ALJ found no impairment in any of the other domains and Lameka Brown does not challenge those findings.

evidence" which the ALJ may not ignore; the ALJ must also explain the weight given to the State agency psychologist's opinion. SSR 96-6p, 1996 SSR LEXIS 3.

The ALJ accorded Raps' evaluation "some weight" because the opinions were generally consistent with other medical evidence. (Tr. 18). However, the ALJ rejected her finding that Norman had a marked limitation in acquiring and using information. Instead, he relied on Prestage's report which stated that Norman's speech "was intelligible, although some articulation errors were noted." The ALJ also noted that Norman's speech therapy was proving "somewhat effective." (Tr. 20). Finally, Kaspar, the ALJ's consulting psychologist, concluded that Norman "has less than marked limitation in acquiring and using information." Id.

Considering the evidence in the record as a whole, the ALJ erred in rejecting the conclusion by Raps that Norman had a marked limitation in acquiring and using information. Virtually every teacher indicated that Norman was below his peers academically and that he had consistent problems with remembering information and instructions. While he was motivated to learn, he often could not perform adequately. Because Kaspar had never examined Norman, the ALJ could not reasonably rely on his opinion in the face of the overwhelming evidence which contradicted it. While Prestage's report indicated that Norman's speech was intelligible, Prestage also diagnosed Norman with Learning Disability NOS. The substantial weight of the evidence, therefore, cannot support the ALJ's conclusion that Norman did not have a marked limitation in the domain of acquiring and using information.

B. Norman's Ability to Attend and Complete Tasks

The regulations provide six nonexclusive examples of limited functioning in this domain. 20 CFR 416.926a(h)(3). These examples contain a disclaimer that these examples do not necessarily describe a "marked" or "extreme" limitation. A child may have a limitation in the domain of "attending and completing tasks" if he: (1) is easily startled, distracted, or over reactive to sounds, sights, movements, or touch; (2) is slow to focus on, or fails to complete activities of interest; (3) repeatedly becomes sidetracked from activities and frequently interrupts others; (4) is easily frustrated and gives up on tasks; (5) requires extra supervision to stay engaged in an activity. 20 CFR 416.926a(h)(3).

There is substantial evidence to support the ALJ's finding that Norman's limitation in attending and completing tasks is "less than marked." While all examining physicians agreed with Norman's diagnosis of ADHD, the ALJ noted that Norman had responded well to Lexapro for anxiety and depression and that he had recently started Adderall treatment for his ADHD. (Tr. 20, 319). More importantly, Norman's school records do not show a consistent problem with concentration and distractability. (Tr. 242-256). Thus, substantial evidence supports the ALJ's finding that Norman had a "less than marked" limitation in his ability to attend and complete tasks.

Because Norman does not have a marked limitation in two domains, he does not qualify for disability. Nor is there substantial evidence that Norman suffers an "extreme" limitation in any domain within the meaning of § 416.926a(e)(3)(i).

C. Norman's Treating Psychiatrist

Lameka Brown argues that the ALJ failed to completely develop the record regarding Brown's potential psychological impairments. Specifically, Lameka Brown argues that the ALJ did not properly defer to True's opinions as the treating psychiatrist. The record does not support Lameka Brown's allegation. The ALJ delayed administrative hearings on Lameka Brown's application to obtain greater detail as to Norman's psychological history.

The ALJ properly gave greater weight to the medical expert and examining source opinions of Kaspar and Prestage, rather than to True's assessments. A treating physician's opinion does not automatically control because the record must be evaluated as a whole. See Pirtle v. Astrue, 479 F.3d 931, 933 (8th Cir. 2007). The fact that True assigned a GAF score of 41, indicating serious symptoms (Tr. 309), does not warrant rejecting the ALJ's findings. A GAF score is a snapshot of a person's functioning at a particular point in time, and is not a longitudinal indicator of the person's functioning. Diagnostic & Statistical Manual of Mental Disorders-Text Revision (DSM-IV-TR) (2000). Questionnaires completed by Plaintiff's teachers did not indicate severe limitations on Norman's functioning in the classroom. (Tr. 245-47, 249-50, 253-56). The July 9, 2004 Assessment signed by True asserted that "Norman appears motivated to succeed academically and gets along well with his peers and teachers," that "Norman is able to make friends" and has "positive relationships," and is "creative and he plays well with his friends." (Tr. 309-310). "When a treating physician's opinions are inconsistent or contrary to evidence as a whole, they are entitled to less weight." Krogmeier v. Barnhart, 294 F.3d 1019, 1023 (8th Cir. 2002).

The ALJ properly relied on Kaspar for the medical determinable impairments: ADHD, learning disorder, with probable borderline intellectual functioning, in conjunction with Prestage's examining source opinion. The ALJ noted that while Ms. Brown reported unusual behaviors, Prestage opined that this behavior was not unusual when put in the context of being interested in science and experiments. (Tr. 18). The ALJ noted that there were virtually no treatment notes by True, and that, while True suggested unusual behavior, this behavior was not placed in the context of Norman's academic interests. (Tr. 18). In addition, while True noted that Plaintiff's psychosis and thought disorder needed primary attention, he was not treating Plaintiff for any psychotic symptoms. See Dolph v. Barnhart, 308 F.3d 876, 878-79 (8th Cir. 2002). True's diagnosis of psychosis is an aberration in this record and was not entitled to any weight.

II. Conclusion
Accordingly, it is hereby
ORDERED that Lameka Brown's petition [Doc. # 5] is DENIED. The decision of the ALJ is AFFIRMED.
/s/ Nanette K. Laughrey
NANETTE K. LAUGHREY
United States District Judge
Dated: May 30, 2008
Jefferson City, Missouri

5
Religion and Science

This is a poorly named section heading for two cases one about religious practice in the prison and the other about the use of scientific evidence in court. These are two new and exciting and frontiers of modern jurisprudence and it is appropriate for the mad scientist to have found itself in these predicaments; a villain for prison religion, and the strawman fear of evidentiary anarchy.

ABDUL-SHAHID FARRAKHAN MUHAMMAD, DARRELL X. McKINNEY, VICTOR SANTOS, CURTIS McDOWELL, URIAH WEBB, HORACE BETARD, LASHANGO LeGRAND, and KENNETH HAMMONDS, Plaintiffs,

-against-

CITY OF NEW YORK DEPARTMENT OF CORRECTIONS, ANTHONY SCHEMBRI, Commissioner, City of New York Department of Correction; ALLYN R. SIELAFF, former Commissioner, City of New York Department of Correction; and CATHERINE M. ABATE, former Commissioner, City of New York Department of Correction, Defendants.

91 Civ. 6333 (LAP)

UNITED STATES DISTRICT COURT FOR THE SOUTHERN DISTRICT OF NEW YORK

904 F. Supp. 161
October 16, 1995

LORETTA A. PRESKA, United States District Judge

OPINION

Plaintiff Abdul-Shahid Farrakhan Muhammad ("Muhammad") seeks (i) a declaratory judgment that defendants have unlawfully deprived him of his rights under the federal and state law to practice his religion, that of the Nation of Islam ("NOI"); (ii) a permanent injunction requiring the City of New York Department of Correction ("DOC") to take a variety of actions concerning the exercise of his religion in DOC facilities; (iii) compensatory damages; and (iv) costs and attorneys' fees. For the reasons stated below which largely relate to the unique characteristics of the DOC system, I find that plaintiff is not entitled to the relief he seeks.

PROCEDURAL BACKGROUND
Plaintiff Muhammad commenced a pro se action, pursuant to 42 U.S.C. § 1983, alleging that DOC staff prevented him from freely exercising his religion as a member of the NOI. On or about June 17, 1993, I appointed Gibson, Dunn & Crutcher to represent Muhammad. By an amended complaint dated February 18, 1994, joining as plaintiff Darrell X. McKinney and as defendants, along with DOC Staff (or the "City defendants"), the State of New York Department of Correctional Services ("DOCS") and Thomas Coughlin (collectively, the "State defendants"), plaintiffs alleged that DOC and DOCS had violated their rights to practice their religion under the Religious Freedom Restoration Act ("RFRA"), 42 U.S.C. § 2000bb et seq., the First Amendment to the Constitution of the United States and the Constitution and laws of the State of New York. By a second amended complaint dated July 8, 1994 (the "Second Amended Complaint"), plaintiffs sought a permanent injunction requiring defendants to take the following actions:

(i) to recognize the Nation of Islam faith as a religion within the meaning of defendants' policies and practices;
(ii) to make available to plaintiff class members free and adequate access to Nation of Islam ministers for spiritual guidance and support;
(iii) to make available to plaintiff class members free and adequate access to religious services conducted by a Nation of Islam minister or inmate follower of the Nation of Islam;
(iv) to promulgate directives recognizing the holy days of the members of the Nation of Islam and permitting daylight fasting on the holy days requiring it;
(v) to allow plaintiff class members to possess religious literature of the Nation of Islam that does not present a clear and present danger to the institution as determined by an impartial board employing specific criteria;
(vi) to refrain from any conduct that substantially burdens the right of members of the class to exercise their religion if that conduct is not the least restrictive alternative of furthering a compelling state interest; and
(vii) to refrain from making any distinction among religions based on defendants' assessment of the content of the tenets of any religion.

(Second Am. Compl. at 17.) Plaintiffs also sought compensatory damages, attorneys' fees and certification of a class of followers of NOI who are or will be incarcerated in the City and State correctional systems.

In response to plaintiffs' application to move to certify a class, the State and City defendants stipulated that any injunctive relief awarded to the individual plaintiffs would be implemented on a system-wide basis, thus obviating the need to litigate the class certification issue.

On or about July 25, 1994, the City and State defendants filed a motion to dismiss the RFRA claims on the ground that RFRA is unconstitutional. The State defendants, but not the City defendants, subsequently withdrew their constitutional challenge. The City defendants' motion is still pending before the Court.[1]

On November 8, 1994, the parties entered into a stipulation permitting six additional plaintiffs to intervene in the action.

A bench trial was conducted on December 8, 9, 12 and 13, 1994, and January 17, 18 and 30, 1995. Numerous witnesses testified, including the plaintiffs, all of whom are NOI followers; Robert Green, an NOI minister known as "Minister 9X"; four orthodox Muslim imams,[2] two of whom formerly belonged to the NOI and all of whom are employed by either DOCS or DOC;[3] one professor, Dr. C. Eric Lincoln ("Professor Lincoln"), who has written extensively about NOI for over thirty years; and Antonio McCloud, DOC's Director of Volunteer Services, who frequently attends NOI religious services in New York and New Jersey. In addition, on December 9, 1994, a site visit was conducted to the Anna M. Kross Center ("AMKC"), a DOC correctional facility on Rikers Island. During the trial, the plaintiffs and the State defendants reached a settlement, and I subsequently approved a consent decree. No settlement was reached between the plaintiffs and the City defendants. Of the eight plaintiffs, only Muhammad has asserted claims against the City defendants.[4]

---

[1] 1 As explained infra, the City defendants' conduct is not prohibited by RFRA. Accordingly, I do not address the constitutional challenge.

[2] 2 "Imam" is a Muslim religious title equivalent to "Rabbi" or "Reverend". (Trial Transcript ("Tr.") 504, 691.) "Imam" means "the leader of prayer." (Tr. 504.)

[3] 3 The imams who testified are Imam Warithu-Deen Umar, Imam Sabur Abdur Salaam, Imam Askia Muhammad and Imam Abdush Shahid Luqman.
Imam Umar, a chaplain with the Albany County Jail and a ministerial program coordinator for DOCS, was a member of the NOI. (Tr. 502-03.) Imam Askia Muhammad, a DOC chaplain, is also a former NOI member. (Tr. 667-68, 675.)

[4] 4 Although plaintiff Muhammad is the only plaintiff who has asserted claims

FINDINGS OF FACT

I. The Nation of Islam

There are dozens of Islamic sects, each sharing certain fundamental tenets, but also having distinctive beliefs, practices and spiritual leaders. (Tr. 97-101, 555-57.) The prophet Muhammad is said to have predicted that there would ultimately be seventy-two Muslim sects. (Tr. 556.) Imam Umar testified that he could currently name twenty to twenty-six such Muslim sects, and Professor Lincoln testified to fourteen splinter groups that came out of the NOI alone. (Tr. 49-50, 101, 557.)[5]

Turning to the NOI in particular, the NOI was founded in 1930 by Fard Muhammad, also known as W.D. Farad or Fard. After Fard's unexplained disappearance in 1934, his assistant, Elijah Muhammad, assumed leadership of the movement until his death in 1975. (Pl. Ex. 55 at 12, 15-16, 267.) According to Professor Lincoln, NOI leaders developed a theology aimed specifically at addressing the unique situation and need of African-Americans, including perceived needs for dignity, economic security and security from the police. (Tr. 41-42, 53.) Only African-Americans were permitted to join the NOI and to attend NOI services.[6] NOI doctrine exhorted members to use religion to do something for themselves, thereby bettering their existence. (Tr. 42-43.)

After Elijah Muhammad's death in 1975, his son, Wallace Deen Muhammad, also called Warith Deen, was designated to succeed his father as the leader of the NOI. (Tr. 47; Pl. Ex. 55 at 263-64.) Over the next decade, Wallace Deen Muhammad led the NOI into orthodox Islam. (Tr. 49; Pl. Ex. 55 at 264-65.) However, some NOI followers dropped out of the movement, while others

---

against the City, general reference is made to "plaintiffs." Where reference is intended specifically to plaintiff Muhammad, reference is made to "plaintiff" or "plaintiff Muhammad."

[5] 5 By way of comparison, while Protestant sects share the Bible, they also have traditions and supporting literature that are distinctive. (Tr. 101-02.) Individual sects have their own spiritual leaders, and members of one Protestant sect would not normally attend the services of another sect. (Tr. 102.) Similarly, there are many different sects within Judaism that have different services and religious leaders. (Tr. 102-03.)

[6] 6 Professor Lincoln could not say whether attendance at services was still limited to African-Americans exclusively. (Tr. 60.)

formed splinter groups. (Tr. 49-50; Pl. Ex. 55 at 267.) Professor Lincoln testified that fourteen such groups were formed after Elijah Muhammad's death. (Tr. 49-50, 101.) In 1977, Louis Farrakhan left Wallace Deen Muhammad's community and resurrected the original NOI as it had been under Elijah Muhammad. (Tr. 50-51; Pl. Ex. 55 at 268.) NOI currently has members throughout the country, and its principal mosque is headquartered in Chicago. There are several mosques in the New York City metropolitan area. (Tr. 850; Pl. Ex. 55 at 267.)

All NOI members are of African descent. (Tr. 218; Pl. Ex. 55 at 20.) Most NOI followers convert during adulthood to NOI from the faith, often Christianity, followed in their childhood homes. (Pl. Ex. 55 at 25-26.) Many of the men who convert to NOI, including some of the plaintiffs, do so while incarcerated. (Tr. 74, 148, 255, 847, 849.) One reason why the prisons are a rich source of recruits for the NOI is that prisoners are among the most disaffected members of society. (Tr. 74-75.) There is frequently a racial component to this disaffection; that is, some black prisoners feel that they are the victims of a world controlled by whites. (Tr. 75.) In addition, prisoners also have considerable amounts of time to reflect on their lives. (Tr. 75.) Because many of the men who convert do so while incarcerated, the NOI has made efforts to be as active as possible in prison systems throughout the United States. (Pl. Ex. 55 at 77-78, 106-10; Tr. 849.) During the trial of the instant action, at least three witnesses -- Imam Umar, Minister 9X and Antonio McCloud -- testified about the NOI's activities in the prisons in the United States. (Tr. 503, 805, 808-09, 811, 816, 848-50, 874-76, 882-83.)

While members of the NOI have some distinctive beliefs and practices not shared by other Muslim groups, followers of the NOI and orthodox Muslims[7] share some common beliefs. For example, all Muslims, including members of the NOI, believe that Islam is based on the "five pillars", i.e., shahada (declaration of the faith), salat (prayer), zakat (charity), sawam (fasting), and hajj, (pilgrimage to Mecca). (Tr. 93-94, 553-54.) Muslims throughout the world, including members of the NOI, affirm their faith in the shahada -- "there is no God but Allah and Muhammad is the seal of the prophets" -- and all Muslims believe Muhammad is the last "prophet." (Tr. 22, 33, 553-54.)

Unlike orthodox Muslims, NOI members believe that Allah came to the United States in 1930 in the person of Fard. (Tr. 32-33, 527, 688-89; Pl. Ex. 1 at 27-28, 145-46, Pl. Ex. 6 at 14.) They also believe that Fard is the great Mahdi, who is, according to Islamic tradition, the greatest teacher who comes at the end of time. (Tr. 32, 34, 52-53.) Also, unlike orthodox Muslims, NOI

---

[7] 7 Among the "orthodox Muslim" religions are Sunni Muslims, Shiites, Ah-Mahidiyas, Sufi and Alislam. (Tr. 97-98; Pl. Ex. 3 at 9.)

members believe that Elijah Muhammad is the "messenger of God." (Tr. 33, 53.) NOI followers do not recognize "imams" as religious leaders; NOI clergymen are referred to as "ministers." (Tr. 151-52, 887.) Members of the NOI do not believe in life after death. (Pl. Ex. 1 at 31-32; Pl. Ex. 6 at 14.)

NOI followers also have a distinctive creation story. They believe that trillions of years ago, a great explosion separated the earth and the moon. Once the earth cooled, there was Allah, who was black, and a world populated only by

black people. However, the devil, "Yakub," along with twenty-four **mad scientists**, conducted a series of genetic experiments on the Island of Patmos. Over time, they produced non-black genes from which the different races resulted -- brown, red, yellow and white -- each progressively less pure and less black. (Tr. 39-40; Pl. Ex. 1 at 28, Pl. Ex. 55 at 71-73.) Professor Lincoln has called this belief "the central myth of the Black Muslim movement." (Pl. Ex. 55 at 72.) Followers of the NOI believe that all blacks are divine and thus have a special relationship with Allah; they believe whites are ungodly and devils by nature. (Tr. 556; Pl. Ex. 55 at 63, 69-72, 104.) Followers of the NOI also believe that black people in America are part of the "lost and found nation." (Pl. Ex. 1 at 28; Pl. Ex. 55 at 71.)

Like all Muslims, members of the NOI follow the Holy Quran. (Tr. 23-24, 554; Pl. Ex. 55 at 118.) However, according to Professor Lincoln, the writings that are "critical" to NOI believers are those of their leaders, i.e., Elijah Muhammad and Louis Farrakhan. (Tr. 24, 76-77, 92.) The Final Call newspaper, the book Message to the Black Man in America by Elijah Muhammad and various study guides and lessons are among the publications read by followers of the NOI. (Tr. 77-78, 228-30, Pl. Ex. 55 at 124-29, 269.)

NOI members, like other Muslims, observe Ramadan. (Tr. 563-64.) NOI members also celebrate several holidays not observed by other Muslim sects. Among them are Savior's Day on February 26 (to honor Fard), Founder's Day on October 7 (to honor Elijah Muhammad) and a daylight fast similar to Ramadan during the month of December. (Tr. 33-35.) The December Fast was instituted in opposition to the Christmas holiday and to focus the attention of followers away from what Elijah Muhammad believed to be the temptations during December of irreligious excesses -- in particular, Santa Claus, commercialization of the holiday and celebratory overeating. (Tr. 35-36.)

Followers of the NOI typically attend congregational meetings, including a religious service that is commonly held on Sundays; in addition, NOI temples hold frequent meetings, and NOI members are required to attend two or more meetings a week. (Tr. 57-58, 291, 850-51; Pl. Ex. 55 at 18.) NOI services typically begin with a Muslim prayer, the introduction of some Arabic phrases and a short lecture by a minister-in-training. (Tr. 60-63.) The "main event" of an NOI service is the ceremony by the minister, which is basically a lecture on a theme such as the accomplishments and heritage of black people or black economic security. (Tr. 65-66.) The texts relied upon are often historical or anthropological. (Tr. 65-66; Pl. Ex. 55 at 113-14.) Professor Lincoln testified that the lectures are designed to foster self-esteem, empowerment and the members' reflection on their black identity. (Tr. 66.) At the end of the service, there is an opportunity for members of the audience to come forward and join the movement. (Tr. 68-69.)

Followers of the NOI follow a variety of restrictions in their day-to-day lives. For example, they are not to eat pork or cornbread, gamble, smoke, drink liquor, use drugs, overeat or buy on credit. They are taught to be clean-shaven and do not wear beards or moustaches. (Tr. 36, 150-51; Pl. Ex. 55 at 18, 76-77.) They are supposed to pray five times a day facing east. (Tr. 151.) They believe premarital and extramarital sex is immoral. (Tr. 36; Pl. Ex. 55 at 76.)

The evidence offered at trial concerning whether the NOI should be considered a "Muslim" religion and by whom it is so considered was varied. For example, certain of Professor Lincoln's writings suggest the NOI is a sect of Islam:

The Muslim dream is to have a solid Black Muslim community in the United States, recognized and supported by Moslems throughout the world as an accepted part of Islam. This is not sheer expediency: from the earliest days of the movement, the Black Muslims have considered themselves devout adherents of the Moslem faith. They recognize Allah as the one true God (though they see Him not as a unique deity but as the Supreme Black Man among Black Men, all of whom are divine). They base their services on both the Quran and the Bible, and they are learning Arabic so as to be able to rely entirely on the original Quran. They observe the classic Moslem prayer ritual and dietary laws, and they hold in high esteem the traditional pilgrimage to Mecca.

(Pl. Ex. 55 at 220.) On the other hand, Professor Lincoln also has written that: On certain fundamental points of doctrine, however, the Black Muslims have departed widely from the orthodox Muslim tradition. Partly for this reason, and partly from an instinctive militancy toward newcomers, the official representatives of orthodox Islam in the United States have refused any recognition of the Black Muslims.

(Pl. Ex. 55 at 220.) According to Professor Lincoln, two NOI doctrines are "at the heart of the controversy: their insistence that blacks must separate themselves from the abhorrent and doomed white race and their belief that it is the manifest destiny of the Black Nation to inherit the earth." (Pl. Ex. 55 at 221.) Professor Lincoln, noting "the orthodox Moslem ideal of an all-embracing unity of humankind", has questioned whether these two doctrinal differences are "so extreme that the Black Muslims must be said to have excluded themselves from Islam." (Pl. Ex. 55 at 221.) Professor Lincoln's conclusion was that the NOI appears to be a Muslim sect:

The question will have to be answered by Moslem theologians, but it seems likely that they will find the Black Muslims to be within the pale -- a legitimate if somewhat heretical Moslem sect. Every faith has its deviates, and every international faith makes broad allowances for interpretations of doctrine to fit local conditions. The fact that orthodox Moslems in America reject the movement has no real significance; most Christian sects and denominations were likewise spurned by the orthodox in their founding years. And a clear precedent exists in Islam itself for the ultimate recognition of heretics in sects despite major doctrinal differences.

(Pl. Ex. 55 at 221.) Similarly, at trial, there was other evidence and testimony indicating that some orthodox Muslims might not consider followers of the NOI to be "Muslims" (e.g., Tr. 88, 157, 191, 473, 482, 546-47; Pl. Ex. 15), but there also was testimony indicating that NOI followers would be considered "Muslims." (E.g., Tr. 88, 94, 686.) According to an article written by Imam Umar, an orthodox Muslim imam employed by the state DOCS, Louis Farrakhan, the current leader of the NOI, is not an orthodox Muslim, refuses to "accept the truth of the Holy Quran" and "teaches religious falsehood." (Pl. Ex. 60.) In this article, Imam Umar wrote:

If [Louis Farrakhan] changes and accepts to evolve and draw closer to a genuine practice of Islam, as did his leader the Honorable Elijah Muhammad and those who followed him, he will have to accept Islam the religion, admit and condemn his past teaching of religious falsehood, become Muslim[,] indeed, become an Imam and conduct himself somewhat like Imam W. Deen Mohammed [a former leader of the Nation of Islam, who has since become an orthodox Muslim) has done, as a Muslim. If he does, the Nation of Islam will be no more.

(Pl. Ex. 60.) Imam Umar's article focuses on differences between the tenets of the NOI and mainstream Muslims, in particular the NOI's beliefs already described that the black man is God and the white man is the devil. (Pl. Ex. 60.)

II. Plaintiff Muhammad's Allegations

Plaintiff Muhammad joined the NOI in the mid-1980's, prior to his incarceration. (Tr. 287.) From 1989 to 1991, Muhammad was incarcerated in the Bronx House of Detention for Men and various jails on Rikers Island while awaiting trial. (Tr. 286.) Following his conviction, he was transferred to the custody of DOCS until his parole in January 1994. (Tr. 287.) Muhammad is currently a ministerial representative under the auspices of Minister Conrad Muhammad of Mosque No. 7 in Harlem, New York. (Tr. 289.)

While on Rikers Island, Muhammad maintained a cordial relationship with Imam Luqman, currently the DOC Director of Ministerial Services, and, at least initially, with most of the individual DOC Muslim chaplains, many of whom he knew personally prior to his incarceration. (Tr. 414-15.)

While on Rikers Island, Muhammad was permitted to wear attire that identified him as an NOI member, specifically, a suit, white shirt, bow tie and crescent pin.[8] (Tr. 415.) As a result, many inmates approached Muhammad with questions about NOI and Minister Louis Farrakhan. (Tr. 415-16.) Muhammad testified he was mindful of a DOC prescription against proselytizing,[9] had no dispute with the necessity for the regulation and thus discussed NOI matters in a neutral manner, "without, of course, causing any security ruckus." (Tr. 293, 415-16.)

Muhammad explained his role as a member of the NOI to educate prospective followers. He testified that:

Our job is, as I said to you previously, we are like bait to fish. Fish that swim up against the stream or against the sea generally die, because they're going against the grain of their own nature.

Eventually, when they smell food in the atmosphere, they go after food. We become the food. Or as the bible may put it, the bread of life. And they take part of that bread of life and they become living beings again or what you and I both know as the being reborn.

(Tr. 416-17.) In fact, Muhammad testified that he provided ample bait to the fish, recalling that he "fed" approximately ninety-five young black men at three Rikers Island facilities alone. (Tr. 417-18.) Muhammad did not receive

---

[8] 8 Inmates who are awaiting trial while in DOC custody wear civilian clothes. (Tr. 644.)

[9] 9 Muhammad stated at his deposition, however, that he "recruited" several individuals while he was incarcerated at a facility on Rikers Island. A few moments later, he clarified that by "several" he meant fifteen. (Declaration of Martha A. Calhoun in Opposition to Plaintiffs' Motion to Reopen the Record dated June 26, 1995 ("Calhoun Decl."), Ex. B. at 29-31.)

an infraction from DOC staff for proselytizing. (Tr. 416.)

While at Rikers Island, Muhammad studied to become a ministerial representative. In the course of his studies, many "courtesies" were extended to him by DOC officers and officials, some of whom were themselves NOI members. (Tr. 419-20.) These officers, including one captain, personally delivered study materials to Muhammad.[10] (Tr. 419-20.) Some material was sent to him by Minister Nelson Muhammad, who was then the minister of Temple No. 7. (Tr. 420.) Muhammad also met with Minister Nelson Muhammad in a personal visit at Rikers Island and spoke on the telephone with Minister Nelson Muhammad and Minister Louis Farrakhan while at Rikers Island. (Tr. 420-421.)

Although he was an NOI member, Muhammad never requested an opportunity to observe the December Fast while incarcerated in DOC facilities because, at that time, he had not acquired sufficient knowledge of its significance to his faith. (Tr. 320.) Muhammad attended the regular Friday service for Muslims and Muslim classes. (Tr. 670.) Although Muhammad testified to a dispute between him and some Muslim inmates who once barred his access to Jumu'ah service, he does not allege that DOC personnel prevented him from attending the Muslim service. (Tr. 425-27.) He believes Imam Askia Muhammad, a DOC Muslim chaplain, played some role in this incident. (Tr. 427.)

III. Testimony of Imam Askia Muhammad

Imam Askia Muhammad ("Imam Askia") has been a chaplain for DOC for the past four and a half years. (Tr. 668.) He is currently assigned to the Queens House of Detention and the James A. Thomas Center ("JATC"), a correctional facility on Rikers Island. (Tr. 669.) At the Queens House of Detention, which houses some 500 inmates, approximately thirty inmates identify themselves as Muslim. At JATC, which houses some 1200 inmates, approximately 150 identify themselves as Muslim. (Tr. 669.) Imam Askia is currently unaware of any inmates, in either of these facilities, who identify themselves as members of the NOI (Tr. 669.) During the four and a half years

---

[10] 10 Muhammad testified in a conclusory manner that religious literature was taken away from him while he was in DOC custody. (Tr. 314.) However, he never gave any other information about the circumstances surrounding this incident. I do not credit that testimony in light of plaintiff's more detailed testimony that correction officers brought him NOI materials. In addition, I credit the testimony that NOI literature was given to inmates during workshops conducted in DOC facilities. (Tr. 810.) Even if such a confiscation occurred, it is contrary to DOC policy.

Imam Askia has been a DOC facility chaplain, he can recall only three inmates who were members of the Nation of Islam. (Tr. 677.)

Imam Askia was previously assigned to the George R. Vierno Center ("GRVC") on Rikers Island, where he knew one inmate who identified himself as a member of the NOI -- plaintiff Muhammad. (Tr. 669.) Imam Askia and plaintiff had a friendly relationship. (Tr. 671.) Plaintiff regularly attended Imam Askia's Muslim classes which were typically held three times a week, as well as the weekly congregate prayer services. (Tr. 670.) In addition, Imam Askia and plaintiff had frequent private conversations in the Imam's office, in the mosque and in the hall. (Tr. 670.) They discussed a variety of topics, including conditions in the facility, food and religious matters. (Tr. 670-71.)

While DOC does not officially recognize the position of "Muslim inmate representative," it is the practice of Imam Askia to elect or select an inmate representative to assist him in order to create a sense of community among the Muslim inmates and to teach the inmates to accept leadership from one of their own. (Tr. 671-72.) Where Imam Askia believes that the inmates are mature and knowledgeable about the principles of Islam, he presides over a process in which the inmates elect their own representative. (Tr. 672-73.) Imam Askia always supervises the process to ensure that it is conducted in a peaceful and fair manner and does not compromise the security of the facility. (Tr. 673.) While plaintiff was incarcerated at GRVC, he was selected Muslim inmate representative in an election conducted without the knowledge, consent or supervision of Imam Askia. (Tr. 673.) Imam Askia and plaintiff subsequently discussed the election, and Imam Askia explained that he was troubled because the process had taken place in his absence. (Tr. 674.) Imam Askia also explained that he did not believe that plaintiff possessed the requisite qualities for inmate representative. (Tr. 674.) Imam Askia explained that while he considered plaintiff a "good brother" and that he loved him, he did not feel that plaintiff could establish the necessary rapport with inmates and the administration required of the inmate representative. (Tr. 674.)

There was differing testimony concerning whether the discussion concerning plaintiff's suitability to serve as the Muslim inmate representative touched on plaintiff's beliefs as a member of the NOI. (Tr. 674.) Plaintiff testified that Imam Askia asked him to repudiate his beliefs, became hostile and used derogatory language. (Tr. 317-18.) However, based on the testimony and demeanor of the witnesses, I find the testimony of Imam Askia to be credible. Imam Askia testified that he did not ask plaintiff to abandon his beliefs as a member of the NOI. (Tr. 674.) I also find that Imam Askia did not raise his voice, jump out of his chair or use profanity in his discussion, as alleged by plaintiff. (Tr. 677-78.) Imam Askia noted that plaintiff was visibly disappointed that Imam Askia did not choose him as inmate representative.

(Tr. 676.)

Contrary to plaintiff's suggestions, I find that Imam Askia was not hostile or suspicious of the NOI. For most of his early life, Imam Askia was a member of the NOI. (Tr. 675.) When he was sixteen years old, his parents followed Imam W. D. Muhammad, the son of Elijah Muhammad, in a transition made by a large number of members of the NOI to what is commonly called orthodox Islam. (Tr. 675.) Imam Askia made this transition with his parents. (Tr. 675.)

Imam Askia frequently discusses his background and experiences with inmates as a way of encouraging them to get out of jail and to improve their lives. (Tr. 675-76.) In particular, he has discussed his experiences in the NOI with the plaintiff. (Tr. 675.) These discussions with the plaintiff focused on the benefits Imam Askia felt he had received from his upbringing in the NOI, such as discipline and a sense of responsibility. (Tr. 676.)

After he was told that he would not be chosen to serve as Muslim inmate representative, plaintiff made a request to Imam Askia for separate Muslim services. (Tr. 678, 679, 681.) Imam Askia responded to his request by asking why, if plaintiff considered himself a Muslim, he wanted separate Muslim services and what specific needs were not being met by the Muslim services already provided. (Tr. 679.) Plaintiff expressed his desire that certain topics -- specifically, African-American self-reliance and African-American problems -- be discussed more directly and forcefully. (Tr. 679.) Imam Askia recalled telling plaintiff that he believed these topics were already being addressed but could incorporate them to a greater degree into the classes already being offered. (Tr. 679-80.) Plaintiff apparently did not follow up on this response. (Tr. 682.)

Plaintiff testified that he was prevented from attending congregate services by a group of inmates assigned to ensure the security of the facility Mosque. (Tr. 319.) However, I find the testimony of Imam Askia to be credible. First, Imam Askia testified that plaintiff attended his Muslim services "regularly." (Tr. 670.) Second, Imam Askia testified that, just as there is a correction officer present to provide security for every inmate group activity, correction officers, and only corrections officers, are assigned to provide security for all religious services, such as Jumu'ah prayer or classes. (Tr. 677.) Imam Askia also testified that inmates do not have the authority to prevent another inmate from attending religious services. (Tr. 677.) If an inmate, for whatever reason, would have to be excluded from religious services, it would be the responsibility of the chaplain, not the inmates, to deal with the matter. (Tr. 678.) In his four and a half years as a facility chaplain, Imam Askia has never prevented any inmate from attending religious services, including the plaintiff. (Tr. 678.) Imam Askia never "directed" that plaintiff be prevented from attending services. (Tr. 678.)

Contrary to plaintiff's allegation, Imam Askia does not find NOI beliefs to be offensive. (Tr. 680.) Imam Askia is well acquainted with Minister Louis Farrakhan and agrees with many of his teachings. (Tr. 687-88.) In addition, as a chaplain in a jail, Imam Askia expects to encounter inmates with many different views about religion, including Islam. (Tr. 678-79.) Imam Askia testified that, "My basic function is to deal with differences and if I were to get offended I don't think that I could do that job successfully." (Tr. 680.)

IV. DOC Religious Accommodation Policy
The DOC religious accommodation policy is set forth in Directive 3252, "Congregate Religious Services." (Pl. Ex. 30.) This directive is based on section 8 of the New York City Board of Correction Minimum Standards (Pl. Ex. 58), as well as underlying federal consent decrees. (Tr. 744-46, 752.) Among its provisions, Directive 3252 provides as follows:

All inmates shall be permitted to congregate for the purpose of religious worship including, religious instruction such as, scriptural study, and shall also be permitted to congregate for the purpose of participating in spiritual retreats.

(Pl. Ex. 30 at III.B.)
Inmates shall have the unrestricted right to hold any religious belief and to be a member of any religious group or organization, as well as the right to disaffiliate with any religious group or organization.

(Pl. Ex. 30 at III.C.)
Inmates shall be permitted to exercise their religious beliefs in any manner, provided that the exercising of such religious beliefs does not present a clear and present danger to the safety and security of the institution or would disrupt the orderly administration of the institution.

(Pl. Ex. 30 at III.D.) In addition, Directive 3252 permits inmates to celebrate recognized religious holidays on an individual or congregate basis, observe dietary laws and to wear and possess religious articles and clothing. (Pl. Ex. 30 at III.G-H.) All persons, including inmates, are forbidden to proselytize, to compel an inmate to become part of a religious organization or to dissuade an inmate from exercising his religious beliefs. (Pl. Ex. 30 at III.E.) Under Board of Correction Minimum Standards, members of the NOI are entitled to receive, without restriction, publications from any source, including family, friends and publishers. (Pl. Ex. 58, Title 40, § 1-14(a).) Incoming publications may not be censored or delayed unless they contain specific instructions on the manufacture or use of dangerous weapons or explosives or plans for

335

escape. (Pl. Ex. 58, Title 40, § 1-14(c)(3).)

V. The Testimony of Imam Luqman

Imam Abdush Shah id Luqman ("Imam Luqman"), the DOC Director of Ministerial Services, testified about the DOC religious accommodation policies and about his personal relationship with the plaintiff. As Director of Ministerial Services, Imam Luqman is responsible for the supervision and administration of the DOC religious programs. (Tr. 691-92; Pl. Ex. 31 at 1.) Prior to assuming his current position, Imam Luqman worked as a DOC chaplain in various correctional facilities and as a religious volunteer for fifteen years. (Tr. 692-93.)

DOC currently employs forty-four salaried chaplains, eleven of whom are Muslim.[11] (Tr. 774; Pl. Ex. 1 at 32.) The remaining chaplains are either Catholic, Protestant or Jewish. (Pl. Ex. 57.) Although none is currently an NOI member, at least one chaplain, Imam Askia, is a former member. (Tr. 675, 697.)

Chaplains are hired after their credentials have been screened by various ecclesiastical organizations, including the Board of Rabbis (for Jewish rabbis), the Archdiocese of Brooklyn (for Catholic clergy), the Council of Churches for the City of New York (for Protestant ministers) and the World Community of Islam (for Muslim imams). (Tr. 695; Pl. Ex. 31 at 1.) After their credentials have been confirmed by the ecclesiastical organizations, Imam Luqman and his staff interview candidates to determine their suitability for working in a jail setting. (Tr. 695-96.) DOC interviews any candidates sent to it, and would consider for employment an NOI candidate should one be approved by the ecclesiastical organization. (Tr. 697.)

Imam Luqman testified on cross-examination that a Protestant chaplain would provide services to all Protestants, even if the chaplain were himself a Baptist and the congregation included Episcopalians. (Tr. 725-26.) However, a Protestant chaplain would not provide services to Catholic inmates. (Tr. 726.)

DOC also utilizes the services of approximately 750-800 volunteers, seventy-five percent of whom are religious volunteers.[12] Approximately twenty to twenty-five percent of the religious volunteers are of the Muslim faith. (Tr. 698-99.) NOI members have been among this pool of volunteers, although they have not historically comprised a substantial percentage. (Tr. 699.)

---

[11] 11 But see Pl. Ex. 57 (listing forty-five chaplains).

[12] 12 Antonio McCloud, the DOC Director of Volunteer Services, estimated that there were 750 volunteers, of whom approximately sixty percent were religious volunteers. (Tr. 804-05.)

DOC provides generic congregate religious services for the four major faith groups, i.e., Catholic, Jewish, Protestant and Muslim. (Tr. 699-700.) The purpose of generic services is twofold: (i) to reach effectively as many inmates as possible, in light of their large number and rapid turnover and (ii) to be tolerant and thus avoid offending members of other faiths, who may have somewhat different practices or nuances to their own form of worship. (Tr. 699-700.) Thus, for example, a generic Protestant service attempts to reflect the basic practices and beliefs of all Protestants, so that Episcopalian or Pentecostal inmates will be able to derive some benefit and solace from the generic service. (Tr. 699-700.)

In a typical generic Muslim service, a facility imam performs the ceremony, known as the "khutbah." (Tr. 700-01.) In the course of the khutbah, the imam may utilize the services of an outside religious volunteer or a member of the inmate population. (Tr. 701.) At the larger jails on Rikers Island, approximately 100-300 inmates may attend a Muslim service, with a lesser number attending at the borough correctional facilities. (Tr. 701-02.) The inmates who have attended these generic services have been members of various Muslim sects including the NOI, Sunni, Shiite, Ansarullah and Sikh. (Tr. 701.)

DOC also provides Quranic, Bible and Torah study classes. (Tr. 702-03.) In the Quranic class, a facility imam or a qualified inmate teaches the Quran to both new converts to Islam and more advanced students. (Tr. 703.) Recent converts learn the fundamentals of Islam, known as "mubadi," while advanced students study the Quran in more depth, as well as study Arabic. (Tr. 703) Attendance varies from five to seventy-five inmates, depending on the size of the facility and the season. (Tr. 703-04.)

Inmates may also meet with individual spiritual advisors of their choice in a "clergy/counsel visit." (Tr. 704.) At an inmate's request, the facility chaplain contacts the spiritual leader of a particular congregation or parish and arranges the necessary security clearances for the chosen spiritual advisor. (Tr. 704-05.) Also, clergy/counsel visits frequently are initiated in the first instance by spiritual advisors rather than by inmates. (Tr. 704-05.) These individual counsel visits are frequently utilized by inmates, and the number of visits is unlimited. (Tr. 705.) They are designed to accommodate specific or individual needs that cannot be provided on a group basis. (Tr. 714-17.)

Muslim inmates receive Halal meals while in DOC custody. (Tr. 705.) Upon their initial entry into the DOC system, they may register as members of the Muslim faith,[13] which allows them to receive Halal meals. (Tr. 705.)

---

[13] 13 Entering inmates are given the opportunity to identify their religious affiliation. DOC's current compilations of the intake data identify forty percent of arriving inmates as Catholic, twenty-five percent as Muslim, ten

DOC recognizes various religious holidays, including Ramadan. (Tr. 640, 705.) At the beginning of each fiscal year, the Director of Ministerial Services reviews the proposed holidays and submits appropriate directives about holiday celebrations to pertinent DOC officials, including facility wardens, the DOC Deputy Commissioner of Strategic Planning and Programs and food services personnel. (Tr. 706.) In the event an inmate requests to celebrate a religious holiday not on the list of approved holidays, DOC attempts to accommodate that inmate in a spirit of tolerance, unusually through a clergy/counsel-type visit. (Tr. 706-08.)

DOC maintains a procedure that allows inmates to request religious accommodations. (Pl. Ex. 30;[14] Tr. 711.) This procedure was previously utilized by a group of approximately twenty-five inmates of Chinese descent, housed on a DOC prison barge. (Tr. 707-08, 711.) The group requested that a congregate religious service be conducted by a Buddhist monk. Imam Luqman, with the assistance of the DOC Jade Society, an Asian-American fraternal organization of civilian and uniformed staff, located a Buddhist monk to provide a Buddhist service on the prison barge forthe group. (Tr.

---

percent as Protestant, three percent as Jewish, ten percent as "other" and ten percent as having no religion. (Tr. 758-60, 762-63, 774-75, 778-79.) These numbers are approximate because inmates tend to underrepresent themselves on arrival or change their religious affiliation after arrival. (Tr. 776.) Commissioner Robert Daly testified that he believed the percentage of Muslim inmates may be higher than twenty-five percent because thirty-five percent of inmates avail themselves of Halal meals. (Tr. 762.) Commissioner Daly also noted that five percent of inmates took kosher meals. (Tr. 762-63.) Commissioner Daly also testified that the number of Muslim inmates is increasing. (Tr. 774-75.)

[14] 14 Directive 3252 states in part that:

Inmates may request to exercise the beliefs and practices of a religious group not previously recognized by the Department [of Correction]. The request shall be submitted in writing, to the head of the institution, through the Deputy Warden for Programs.

(Pl. Ex. 30 at IV.A.) Directive 3252 also sets forth the various steps to be followed and the criteria to be considered. (Id.)

707-08.) Aside from this request, no other group has requested a particular religious accommodation. (Tr. 708.) There have been requests made by individual inmates either directly or indirectly, i.e., through other DOC employees to Imam Luqman. (Tr. 709.) For example, in response to individual requests, DOC has arranged for a minister of the Ansarullah community to visit a member of that sect and for a Greek Orthodox priest to visit with two Greek Orthodox inmates. (Tr. 709.)

Imam Luqman also testified about his encounters with plaintiff Muhammad. Imam Luqman's relationship with plaintiff was a cordial one, both before and after plaintiff's conversion to the NOI. (Tr. 712-13.) Originally a Sunni Muslim, plaintiff attended several congregate Muslim services conducted by Imam Luqman and sought individual counselling from the Imam on several occasions. (Tr. 712-13.) Following his conversion to the NOI, plaintiff attended a religious ceremony conducted by Imam Luqman at the GRVC on Rikers Island. (Tr. 713.)

In the course of his twenty-year career with DOC, Imam Luqman has made the acquaintance of perhaps ten inmates who identified themselves as NOI members. (Tr. 713-14.) Plaintiff was the only member of that group who made particular requests for a religious accommodation, albeit in an indirect manner. (Tr. 714-15). Although Imam Luqman understood plaintiff to have requested a collective December Fast (Tr. 714-15), he is apparently mistaken, as plaintiff himself testified that he never made such a request. (Cf. Tr. 320.) Imam Luqman may have construed the complaint or amended complaints in this action to constitute the purported "request" -- as well as a purported request for an NOI minister to teach a class, which plaintiff himself did not testify he requested.[15] In any event, Imam Luqman testified that DOC attempts to accommodate individual requests on an individual basis, typically through a clergy/counsel visit. Imam Luqman testified repeatedly that an inmate's individual request, such as one for a December Fast, would be considered.[16] (Tr. 729, 732-33.)

---

[15] 15 Plaintiff testified that he asked for religious services to be conducted for members of the NOI. He did not say he asked for classes. (Tr. 314-15.)

[16] 16 For example, Imam Luqman testified as follows:
Q. Was Mr. Muhammad accommodated for the December fast by providing him meals at any special times?
A. I'm saying that we are tolerant and that we can do that. The specifics of the situation with Mr. Muhammad I'm not fully aware of.
(Tr. 729.)

As an example of DOC's willingness to accommodate individual religious requests, Imam Luqman noted that one of DOC's current inmates is a well-known Lubavitch rabbi held at the facility known as North Infirmary Command ("NIC"). (Tr. 715-16.) Because the kosher food provided by DOC apparently did not meet that sect's standard, Imam Luqman's office arranged for members of the rabbi's Lubavitch community to be permitted to bring appropriate food directly to the jail for the rabbi. (Tr. 715-16, 729-31.)

According to Imam Luqman, the distinction between the request of the Chinese Buddhists (which was granted) and what Imam Luqman understood plaintiff to be seeking, was twofold: (i) there was no underlying generic congregate service available for Buddhist inmates in the first instance, as opposed to an NOI inmate, who can derive at least some benefit and solace from a generic Muslim service and (ii) plaintiff was an individual whom Imam Luqman believed was acting on his own behalf in seeking apparently collective accommodations -- as opposed to representing an actual group -- and honoring the request thus would be an imposition of religious services on a group of inmates without their consent. (Tr. 716-17.)

Plaintiff alleged that he was denied a position as an inmate representative by a facility chaplain at GRVC, Imam Askia. (See Second Am. Compl. PP 40-42.) According to Imam Luqman, a facility chaplain may exercise his discretion and allow an inmate to assist him in the conducting of services. (Tr. 717-18.) A person who assists a Muslim chaplain (or assists a sheykh in a Muslim mosque) is known as a "naib." (Tr. 718.) The manner, in which the person is chosen is determined by the individual chaplain, and the selection is within the chaplain's discretion. (Tr. 718-19.)

VI. NOI Volunteers in DOC Facilities: The Testimony of Antonio McCloud
Antonio McCloud ("McCloud") has been Director of Volunteer Services of DOC since 1992. (Tr. 801.) As such, he acts as a liaison between DOC and the civilian community, soliciting volunteers to provide a variety of services to inmates in DOC facilities. (Tr. 804.) The mission of the volunteer program is to solicit and use community volunteers to assist in providing inmate services and to help inmates make the transition back to the community. (Tr. 804.)

Volunteers provide a number of important services, including counseling, literacy assistance, law library assistance, general library assistance, drug and alcohol counseling, self-development and empowerment workshops, job readiness training, AIDS education, case management and, in the nursery at the women's facility, child care aid. (Tr. 805.)

Although there was no testimony that McCloud was himself an NOI member, it is undoubtedly fair to say that McCloud has been involved in a number of NOI activities. For example, he has visited NOI mosques in Harlem and New Jersey approximately four times a year for the past fifteen years. (Tr. 811.) In addition, McCloud has participated in self-development training conducted by NOI's paramilitary arm, the Fruit of Islam ("FOI"), prior to his employment with DOC. (Tr. 812.)

NOI volunteers serve the DOC inmate population in two capacities, i.e., as guest speakers and by conducting personal development workshops. (Tr. 806, 810.) For example, Minister Conrad Muhammad, a prominent NOI figure, has spoken at two Rikers Island facilities: the George Mochen Detention Center ("GMDC") and the Otis Bantum Correction Center ("OBCC"). (Tr. 811.)

NOI volunteers, under the direction of Minister 9X, the NOI Director of Prison Ministries, have been conducting self-development workshops at GRVC on Rikers Island. (Tr. 806.) These workshops stress such themes as self-esteem, responsibility, respect and empowerment. (Tr. 806, 850.) The sessions are held once a week for two hours and are open to all inmates in the facility who wish to participate, regardless of religious affiliation. (Tr. 806-07.) Generally, twenty to thirty inmates attend each session. (Tr. 807.) The volunteers bring in written materials prepared for the workshop, as well as the publication, the Final Call, to utilize as part of the discussion. (Tr. 810.) The Final Call is left for the inmates to read after the workshop is over. (Tr. 810.)

DOC began to offer these workshops after Minister 9X approached McCloud about providing NOI volunteers to become involved in New York City jails. (Tr. 808.) McCloud was "very excited about the opportunity" to have NOI volunteers serving inmates in DOC facilities. (Tr. 808.) Their self-development program, he felt, had a proven track record of helping inmates make a successful transition back into civilian life. (Tr. 808-09.) Since assisting inmates in making a successful transition back to civilian life is a major focus of the Volunteer Services program, McCloud began to work with Minister 9X and other NOI members to set up a program of self-development workshops in a DOC facility. (Tr. 809.)

At the time of trial, these self-development workshops had not been offered for two months because of scheduling difficulties with NOI volunteers. (Tr. 807-08.) However, McCloud testified that he planned to resume the program by the end of January. (Tr. 808.) In addition, McCloud plans to expand the program to other facilities. (Tr. 807.) According to McCloud, if Minister 9X and his colleagues are unavailable, McCloud will look for someone else in the NOI community to provide these workshops. (Tr. 815.)

VII. Testimony of Robert Daly and Robert Wangenstein Concerning DOC's Operations and Allocation of Resources

Robert Daly ("Daly") is the DOC First Deputy Commissioner and is responsible for the implementation of DOC policy. (Tr. 737.) He reports directly to the Commissioner. (Tr. 737.) Daly has held a variety of positions in his twenty-two-year career with DOC, including General Counsel and Special Counsel to the Commissioner. (Tr. 738.) Daly testified about the factors considered by DOC in allocating its resources and operating the correction system in New York City.

Robert Wangenstein ("Wangenstein") is the Warden of the Brooklyn House of Detention for Men. (Tr. 617.) In his twenty-three-year tenure with DOC, he has held a variety of positions, including DOC Deputy Commissioner of Security in the period 1990-1994. (Tr. 617-20.) Wangenstein testified about the logistical and security concerns inherent in the operation of DOC facilities, using the Brooklyn House of Detention as a representative facility.

A. Overview of the relevant DOC operations

DOC presently operates sixteen jails, of which ten are located on Rikers Island and the remainder in the boroughs; three hospital prison wards; and seventeen holding facilities in the city courts, known as "court pens." (Tr. 621; Joint Pretrial Order, Ex. C P 2.) About half of the DOC facilities provide cell block housing, with the other half providing dormitory housing. (Tr. 764.) These facilities hold inmates of various classifications, including detainees awaiting trial, City-sentenced inmates serving one year or less, State-sentenced inmates who are temporarily in the DOC system for a trial or appeal, State-sentenced inmates who have been paroled and have been rearrested on parole violations, Immigration and Naturalization inmates and, on occasion, federal inmates held by agreement or contract. (Tr. 622; Def. Ex. E).

At the time of trial, of the 19,000 inmates in DOC custody, about 3500 have been convicted of crimes and are serving sentences of one year or less in DOC custody. (Tr. 763, 780-81.) About 1600 inmates are paroled state inmates who have been rearrested on parole violations and are in DOC custody awaiting a hearing or remand to DOCS. (Tr. 783.) Approximately 200 inmates are sentenced inmates serving their sentences at state correctional facilities who are in temporary DOC custody for various other reasons, such as awaiting trial. (Tr. 782-83.) The balance and great majority, some 13,700 out of 19,000, are pretrial detainees who are either being held without bail or have been unable to make bail. (Tr. 785.) In short, there are significantly more pre-trial detainees than there are sentenced inmates in DOC custody. (Def. Ex. E-4.)

Unlike DOCS, which holds sentenced inmates for set periods of time, DOC's system is primarily a detention system, where inmates are held to await trial, as described above. (Tr. 750.) The inmate turnover time is brief. In fiscal year

1994, 111,072 inmates entered DOC custody. (Def. Ex. E-4.[17]) Although forty percent of these entering inmates remained in DOC custody after thirty days, forty-two percent were discharged from the system within a mere six days. (Def. Ex. E-4.) More than three-quarters of the entering inmates were discharged within sixty to eighty-nine days. (Def. Ex. E-4.)

DOC expects that 130,000 inmates will enter DOC custody this year. (Tr. 750.) Of that number, DOC expects fifty percent to leave the system in about six days and the other fifty percent to depart approximately 50 days later. (Tr. 750.)

On a typical day, 300-350 persons enter the DOC system, and approximately the same number are discharged. (Tr. 750.) On a typical day, approximately 2000 inmates are transported to the five boroughs for court appearances. (Tr. 751.) Many of those inmates do not return because they receive time-served sentences, have their cases dismissed or make bail. (Tr. 751.) About 100 sentenced inmates are transferred daily to DOCS custody, for a total of 500 transfers per week. (Tr. 751.) On a typical day, about 1200 inmates on Rikers Is land are moved to different DOC facilities on Rikers Island pursuant to the ongoing process of classifying and reclassifying inmates based upon changes

---

[17] 17 Defendants' exhibit E-4 states: FY [Fiscal Year] '94 Discharges:

Average Length of Stay Days	Number Leaving	% Leaving	Cumulative % Leaving
0 - 1	17,749	16.0%	16%
2	5,539	5.0%	21%
3	4,702	4.2%	25%
4	7,136	6.4%	32%
5	8,490	7.6%	39%
6	2,696	2.4%	42%
7	2,329	2.1%	44%
8 - 14	6,412	5.8%	50%
15 - 29	11,113	10.0%	60%
30 - 59	12,016	10.8%	70%
60 - 89	7,161	6.4%	77%
90 - 179	13,399	12.1%	89%
180 +	12,330	11.1%	100%

111,072

(Def. Ex. E-4.)

in their inmate profile. (Tr. 751.) For example, special housing may be required for medical reasons or where an inmate is deemed a suicide or escape risk. (Tr. 751.)

In sum, I find on essentially uncontroverted evidence that the DOC prison population is exceptionally dynamic; it suffers from a relatively high number of inmates as well as an exceedingly high inmate turnover rate. The dynamic nature of DOC's population distinguishes it from other systems as to which evidence was offered, making comparisons to those systems inapposite.

DOC's current operating budget for fiscal year 1995 is $ 746 million.[18] (Tr. 738, 767, 769.) The operating budget comprises staff salaries, overhead, food for inmates and the cost of services. DOC's capital budget for fiscal year 1995 is $ 45 million.[19] (Tr. 767-68.) The capital budget covers expenses such as the construction of new or additional jail space, adding new beds and fire safety. (Tr. 739.)

DOC has been reducing its operating budget. (Tr. 740.) Reductions are continuing into the immediate future; DOC, along with other City agencies, has been ordered to reduce its budget due to a $ 500 million gap in the City budget in the current fiscal year and the anticipated $ 2 billion gap in fiscal year 1996. (Tr. 740.) Specifically, at the time of trial, DOC had been directed to reduce its operations by $ 18 million by July 1, 1995, and by an additional $ 18 million six months after that. (Tr. 740, 764-65.)

Although DOC's budget has, of necessity, been reduced, its inmate population has been increasing. (Tr. 741.) At the time of trial, there were approximately 19,000 inmates in DOC custody. (Tr. 763.) Based upon the growth rate for the inmate population, DOC anticipates holding approximately 20,200 inmates in June 1995; 20,900 inmates by November 1995; and over 21,000 inmates by 1996. (Tr. 763.) In addition, in fiscal year 1994, approximately 110,000 inmates entered into DOC custody; by the end of fiscal year 1995, DOC anticipates its entering population to reach 130,000 inmates. (Tr. 741.)

Although the number of inmates is increasing, DOC has been forced to reduce its staff. For example, in calendar year 1994, 1600 additional inmates entered the system but during that same year, DOC lost 400 correction

---

[18] 18 DOC's operating budget in fiscal year 1994 was $ 763 million; in 1993, $ 760 million; in 1992, $ 762 million. (Tr. 769.)

[19] 19 During cross-examination, Daly conceded that DOC's total budget, i.e., the operating budget plus the capital budget, had increased from 1994 to 1995. (Tr. 770-71.) Daly explained that the increase in the capital budget was due to court-ordered projects. (Tr. 770-71.)

officers and 400 civilian workers. (Tr. 740.) At its high point, in 1992, DOC employed about 11,950 correction officers. (Tr. 743, 786.) The number was about 10,600 officers at the time of trial. (Tr. 786.)[20] In addition, DOC has not been able to hire any correction officers since December 1991, and so DOC has been forced to rely upon increasing amounts of overtime to operate its facilities, which strains the assigned staff. (Tr. 742.)

Furthermore, attrition has taken its toll on DOC, with 1200 additional people retiring or leaving voluntarily within the last three years. (Tr. 742.) Moreover, as a result of two recent City severance programs, 400 civilians out of a total civilian staff of 2100, have left DOC. (Tr. 742-43.) DOC also anticipates losing several hundred more civilians under the current City severance program. (Tr. 743.)

As a result of the loss of staff positions, DOC recently has been forced to close a number of correctional facilities including the Brooklyn Correctional Facility ("BCF" or the "Brig"), which formerly housed 1,350 inmates; the south wing of the Manhattan Detention Complex ("MDC" or "the Tombs"), which formerly housed 388 inmates; and a converted Staten Island ferry boat berthed at Rikers Island, which formerly housed 162 inmates. (Tr. 741-42.) Other correctional facilities closed in recent years due to budgetary concerns include the Forebell Facility, a sentenced women's facility in Brooklyn, and two prison barges. (Tr. 621-22.)

Another result of the staff cutbacks and budgetary concerns is the reduction or elimination of numerous inmate programs deemed valuable and successful by DOC. For example, a 900-bed drug program has been reduced to 200 beds. (Tr. 744.) All the correction officers assigned to the inmate grievance program have been reassigned. (Tr. 744.) DOC anticipates eliminating the inmate indoor recreation program by the end of January 1995 in order to utilize the 170 uniformed correction officers in other areas. (Tr. 744.) DOC also anticipates eliminating all its civilian counselors, who help inmates secure employment, housing and various social services, following their release from custody. (Tr. 748.)

DOC's overall aim has been to reduce discretionary programs, leaving only those programs required by consent decrees or the minimum standards of two independent oversight agencies, the New York City Board of Correction (see New York City Charter § 626) and the New York State Commission of Correction (see Correction Law, Article III, §§ 40-48). (Tr. 744-45; Pl. Ex. 58.) Currently, virtually all, if not all, of the inmate programs offered by DOC

---

[20] 20 By contrast, twenty-two years ago, when Daly first began his DOC employment, less than 3,000 officers supervised less than 8,000 inmates. (Tr. 743, 786, 795.)

provide services required by consent decrees or the minimum standards. (Tr. 752.) These programs include recreation, law library, visits, religious services and educational programs. (Tr. 752; Pl. Ex. 58.)

However, mandated programs will be affected by the current downsizing. For example, as a result of a federal consent decree, inmates cannot be "locked-in" their cells or dormitory until 11:00 p.m., which allows them to congregate in housing area "day rooms." DOC plans to move to modify the consent decree to change the lock-in time to 9:00 p.m., thereby reducing the number of correction officers needed to monitor the congregating inmates and saving 350 correction officers' posts. (Tr. 749.)

Another factor DOC considers in allocating its resources is the likely effect on the inmate population. For example, a newspaper article about the proposed early lock-in time led to a hunger strike among inmates on Rikers Island. (Tr. 757.) This required DOC immediately to meet with members of the various Inmate Councils to educate them about the process that would have to be undertaken before the change could be effected. (Tr. 757.)

Currently, the DOC programs budget comprises about 1.7% of the current operating budget ($ 12 million) and is expected to be reduced to slightly under 1% ($ 6 million). (Tr. 753.) Of this amount, the amount allocated for religious programs is $ 900,000 to $ 1 million, an amount that has been relatively stable for the past few years and which is not expected to change. (Tr. 753, 772-73.) This amount reflects a recent increase in which DOC upgraded several temporary chaplain positions to full-time permanent positions, in response to an increase in the inmate population. (Tr. 753, 773-74.) As stated supra, DOC currently employs forty-four chaplains and has no plans to reduce this number. (Tr. 773-4; Pl. Ex. 57.)

B. The Rationale of Generic Services

In determining what programs will be preserved and what programs will be reduced or eliminated, DOC considers the security implications, the program's efficiency and its cost. (Tr. 758.) As a result, DOC has developed a policy of providing programs in a generic manner.[21] (Tr. 758.) For example, generic religious services allow DOC to service large numbers of inmates in a single space within a facility at a minimal cost. (Tr. 758-59.)

---

[21] 21 Daly explained that, "We try to do things generically. We do things generically because it is much more efficient to do things generically, and it saves me money generally to do things generically." (Tr. 758.)

There are numerous factors that DOC cites in favor of its policy of generic services. Among them is the reality that space is at a premium in DOC facilities. DOC jails were built to house a far smaller inmate population than they currently do. (Tr. 759.) As the inmate population grew, DOC added housing areas to the core facilities but did not add concomitant program areas. For example, the Adolescent Reception and Detention Center on Rikers Island ("ARDC"), built for 1200 inmates, now holds almost 3,000 inmates. (Tr. 759.) As a result, there is a greater demand for program services in disproportionately smaller program areas. (Tr. 759.)

Another concern is staffing. With generic services, DOC requires fewer clergy, escort and security staff. (Tr. 759.) This also furthers security concerns, because a detention correctional system is designed to minimize inmate movement within a facility in order to lessen the chances of inmate altercations -- either with escorting officers or passing inmates -- or the exchange of contraband among inmates. (Tr. 759-60.) By minimizing different available services, DOC can reduce the movement taking place outside the housing areas, when escort officers would be needed. (Tr. 760.)

Generic services also have an impact on DOC's ability to classify and house inmates efficiently. (Tr. 760.) For example, since forty percent of inmates identify themselves as Catholic, DOC does not have to set aside a particular space for those inmates. There are enough Catholics so that they can be dispersed throughout the correction system according to their security classification, and whatever jail they are placed in will have enough other Catholic inmates to participate in a Catholic service. (Tr. 760.) If, however, inmates were classified by individual religious sects, DOC would have to consider religious affiliation in classifying and housing inmates. If such were the case, and if, for example, there were not enough Baptist inmates to be spread throughout the system, the Baptist inmates would have to be congregated in one jail in order to receive a Baptist service. This would adversely affect the security classification system in that high security Baptist inmates would be commingled with low security Baptist inmates. As a result, the jail would have to be operated at the highest security level, which is more expensive. (Tr. 760-61.) DOC is able to avoid this problem by offering generic services which gives it greater flexibility in housing inmates.[22] (Tr. 760-61.)

---

[22] 22 Once a year, at the request of DOC's rabbis, DOC gathers Jewish inmates from various facilities so that on a particular holy day there are sufficient Jewish inmates to form the "minyan" required in Jewish law for prayer. (Tr. 796-97.)

I find that it would be impossible for DOC to provide a separate congregate service for an individual sect or group such as the NOI consistent with the facts and operating principles discussed above. (See Tr. 761.)

C. Operations at the Brooklyn House of Detention

DOC offered additional evidence about the implementation of DOC policy described supra in the context of testimony concerning the daily operations of one representative facility, the Brooklyn House of Detention. A borough facility such as this one is basically a new admission facility, where arrestees are sent following their arrest and arraignment. (Tr. 623.) Following inmates' remand to DOC custody, facility personnel review the history of newly-admitted inmates to determine their security classification, which in turn determines where they are housed.[23] (Tr. 673.) These inmates must be processed and assigned to a housing unit within twenty-four hours pursuant to a court mandate. (Tr. 623, 632-33.) The intake procedure includes a review of each inmate's history and a medical examination. (Tr. 623-24, 627.) Inmates frequently are transferred to different DOC facilities -- in particular, to a Rikers Island facility -- within seventy-two hours of their admission. They generally are returned later to the borough facility for trial or are transferred to court from Rikers Island on a daily basis. (Tr. 624, 646.)

Borough correctional facilities, such as the Brooklyn House of Detention, are high-rise structures comprised of cell blocks and dormitory housing. (Tr. 625.) For example, the Brooklyn House of Detention is twenty-two stories high and is comprised of cell-block housing only. (Tr. 625.) Cell blocks in the Brooklyn House of Detention are "H"-shaped, with each section housing thirty inmates for a total of 120 inmates per block. (Tr. 625-26.) Two correction officers are assigned to supervise a cell block of 120 inmates. (Tr. 625-26.) The Queens House of Detention For Men, by contrast, consists of dormitories, each of which typically houses fifty inmates. (Tr. 625.)

At the Brooklyn House of Detention, 325 correction officers and seventy-one civilians are assigned to the facility, which houses 815 inmates. (Tr. 626-27, 630.) In the months prior to trial, the Brooklyn House of Detention's uniformed staff has been reduced by eighteen correction officer "posts" due to budget cuts. (Tr. 629.)

---

[23] 23 High security inmates are typically housed in an individual cell rather than in an open dormitory. Such inmates are also typically housed in a Rikers Island facility because in the event of an escape from the facility, the inmate still faces other obstacles before being on the street, i.e., the inmate is still trapped on Rikers Island itself. (Tr. 764.)

Approximately 785 inmates at the Brooklyn House of Detention are detainees awaiting trial, while approximately thirty inmates have been convicted and sentenced. (Tr. 644.) About half of the inmate population at the Brooklyn House of Detention is relatively stable, i.e., they will be housed there for a period of time, as opposed to the remaining half, which leaves the facility within seventy-two hours to be housed at Rikers Island. (Tr. 646-47.) The stable population consists of inmates under mental observation, in protective custody or maximum security and a portion of the general jail population. (Tr. 646-47.) The other half, which is a transient population, generally spends its short period of time in the Brooklyn House of Detention either in the law library or on the telephones trying to arrange bail. (Tr. 646-67.)

In the course of a typical weekday, approximately 200 inmates are transported from the Brooklyn House of Detention to court for trial, while approximately forty-five new admission inmates will enter the facility for the first time. (Tr. 631.) Inmates who are moved from a housing area to the Receiving Room to be transported to court must first be strip searched before leaving the facility, a process which requires approximately twelve to sixteen correction officers. (Tr. 632.) In addition, facility escort officers accompany inmates when they travel outside the jail, such as to Rikers Island for x-rays or to a City hospital for treatment. (Tr. 634-35.)

Operations at the Brooklyn House of Detention are considerably reduced on weekends, with no sanitation posts and reduced clerical functions. (Tr. 650-51.) On the busiest weekend tour of duty (8:00 a.m. to 4:00 p.m.), only forty-five officers are an duty, as opposed to eighty officers on a weekday. (Tr. 651.) The Brooklyn House of Detention provides various religious accommodations, such as Muslim, Catholic and Protestant congregate services[24] 24 and Bible and Muslim study classes. Chaplains of the Protestant, Catholic, Muslim and Jewish faiths are assigned to the facility on varying schedules, and Catholic religious volunteers conduct a weekly service. (Tr. 634-35.) Inmates are also permitted to have visits with religious or spiritual advisers. (Tr. 645.)

The Muslim congregate service at the Brooklyn House of Detention is held on Friday. (Tr. 635.) Approximately ten to fifteen inmates attend the service there. (Tr. 635.) To be transported to the chapel area -- which is not on the floor containing the housing areas -- inmates gather in each housing area,

---

[24] 24 Although Wangenstein testified to a Seventh Day Adventist service on his facility schedule, the DOC Director of Ministerial Services, Imam Luqman, testified that there are no such separate services for this Protestant sect. (Tr. 659-61, 719-21.) I credit the testimony of Iman Luqman, who I find most knowledgeable about the types of religious services offered by DOC.

where the post officer pat frisks them in order to prevent the transfer of contraband within the facility. (Tr. 636-37.) Although approximately thirty-five percent of the uniformed staff at the Brooklyn House of Detention is female, the Muslim inmates are searched only by male officers. (Tr. 637-38.) Qurans are searched by a correction officer using a hand transfixer. (Tr. 637.) A recreation post officer picks up the inmates on each housing floor on the elevator. (Tr. 636.) The inmates are then taken to the chapel area, where, prior to entry, they pass through a magnetometer and are searched once again. (Tr. 638.) During the service, an officer assigned to the chapel monitors the inmates. (Tr. 639.) At the conclusion of the service, the inmates are again frisked and escorted back to the housing areas in similar fashion. (Tr. 639-40.) The Ramadan holiday is celebrated at the Brooklyn House of Detention. (Tr. 640.) Participating inmates are awakened before sunrise and given a bagged breakfast.[25] (Tr. 640.) At the conclusion of their daylight fast, the Muslim inmates are escorted to the chapel for prayers, where they are also provided Halal meals. (Tr. 640-42.) Visitors are allowed to meet with inmates at the end of the holiday celebration. (Tr. 641.) In recent years, Muslim inmates have been transported to a Rikers Island facility to celebrate as a larger assemblage. (Tr. 641, 657-58.)

Wangenstein also indicated that he would defer to the recommendation of the DOC chaplain when confronted with an individual request such as a Ramadan fast. (Tr. 643-44.) He testified as follows:

Q. If an inmate came to you -- assuming he went through channels -- and said he wanted to celebrate a fast on a particular day in December, how would you respond to that?

A. I would probably tell him that he would have to put in an interview slip to speak to his religious adviser. And they would probably discuss it with the deputy warden of programs and bring it to me. And if it was out of my jurisdiction, then I would speak to the deputy commander for programs.

Q. Has anyone ever asked for that, in your experience?

A. I haven't had any of that, no.

(Tr. 643-44.)

Wangenstein testified that he had only one experience with a group of inmates requesting special services. (Tr. 651-52.) When Wangenstein was DOC

---

[25] 25 Breakfast for all inmates is served on a daily basis at 6:00 a.m. in order to accommodate the large number of inmates who have to be sent to court each day. (Tr. 643.) Thus, an inmate seeking to celebrate another fast, such as the NOI December Fast, would necessarily be accommodated through the normal practice.

Deputy Chief of Security, a group of inmates known as the "Latin Kings" presented a petition seeking a special meeting place to conduct services and prayers. While noting that the Latin Kings was not a recognized religion, the request was denied by DOC on the logistical grounds of limited staff and space. (Tr. 651-52, 663.) Wangenstein did not indicate that a group of NOI inmates requested special services; in fact, he stated that he was not aware of any of his inmates even being NOI members. (Tr. 650.)

D. Analogous Procedures On Rikers Island

Wangenstein also testified to the differences in operating a jail on Rikers Island. Unlike the vertical high-rise jails in the boroughs, the ten facilities on Rikers Island are flat structures. On December 9, 1994, the Court conducted a site visit at the AMKC, a correctional facility on Rikers Island. AMKC houses approximately 2800 inmates and is broken down into seventy-three housing areas. (Tr. 649.) Modular housing area annexes have been added to the core facility to hold additional inmates. Wangenstein explained that it takes more time to get inmates to services because of the physical layout of the facilities, i.e., the long hallways laid out in a "T" shape. (Tr. 649.) It takes approximately fifteen to twenty minutes to walk from one end of AMKC to the other. During the site visit, I observed a number of program activities taking place off the main corridor, such as a law library, various clinics and a barbershop. In addition, I observed individual correction officers escorting apparently newly-admitted inmates, inmates cleaning the corridor floors and inmates delivering food carts.

The AMKC mosque is on the ground floor of AMKC. To attend a service at the mosque, groups of approximately ten to twenty inmates leave their housing areas and travel down the long expansive corridors at one time, under the supervision of correction officers stationed at fixed posts. (See also Tr. 401, 656.) Prior to entering the mosque, inmates are pat frisked or directed to step through a magnetometer. During the service, one or two correction officers observe the inmates from the back of the relatively spacious mosque. There appeared to be approximately forty-five to sixty inmates attending this particular service. After the service concluded, the inmates returned to their housing units in groups. Although the inmates were mostly unescorted by corrections officers, they were observed by stationary corrections officers.[26]

---

[26] 26 Colonel Lucien LeClaire, the Director of Corrections Emergency Response Team Operations for DOCS, testified about the supervision of inmate movement. (Tr. 352, 400.) He explained that security coverage is provided both by officers who observe inmate movement and by officers who physically escort inmates. (Tr. 400.) He explained as follows:

When inmates reached their housing unit, they were checked in by a correction officer. (See Tr. 657.)

E. Evidence Concerning the Number of NOI Inmates

There was conflicting evidence concerning the number of NOI inmates incarcerated in DOC facilities. As stated supra, the evidence offered by defendants indicated that there were relatively few NOI inmates in their custody. For example, Imam Askia testified that he encountered only three inmates who belonged to the NOI during his four and a half years as a DOC facility chaplain. (Tr. 677.) Imam Luqman testified that he has encountered approximately ten inmates who belonged to the NOI during his twenty-year DOC career. (Tr. 713-14.) Imam Luqman also testified that plaintiff Muhammad was the only member of the NOI who requested special services. (Tr. 714.)

For the most part, evidence offered by the plaintiffs tended to indicate there were more, albeit an unknown number, of NOI inmates. Minister 9X was, at the time of trial, a minister of the prisons for the NOI.[27] (Tr. 848.) As such, he said, his role was to go into the prisons and offer instruction concerning NOI beliefs and that he had visited Rikers Island approximately seven times in the last nine months. (Tr. 848-50.) He testified that "many" inmates on Rikers Island had identified themselves to him as members of the NOI and that he was in written contact with NOI members. (Tr. 851-52.) Minister 9X also testified that he spoke to fifty inmates at one seminar and that, of those inmates, about twenty-five were "believers of Elijah Muhammad's teachings." (Tr. 862.) Minister 9X stated that he received about thirty or forty letters from inmates in the span of "a few months, every six months." (Tr. 866.)

However, I do not find that the evidence plaintiffs offered to be credible on the issue of the number of members of the NOI in DOC's custody. For example, Minister 9X identified only one inmate by name, a Norbert X, who

---

In a medium security facility, there may be officers stationed, as your Honor observed during the tour of Rikers Island, officers were stationed in a stationary position in a corridor and watched the inmates walk by them. . . . In a maximum security facility where inmates are escorted through long corridors where possibly visibility wouldn't be possible, by stationing an officer in a given spot, officers would escort groups of inmates up through those corridors.

(Tr. 401.)

[27] 27 Minister 9X testified that he was in the process of being hired by DOCS. (Tr. 848-49.)

was, according to Minister 9X, housed on Rikers Island.[28] (Tr. 852.) Minister 9X also offered what he described as a list from Norbert X of approximately twenty inmates housed on Rikers Island who identified themselves as members of the NOI. (Pl. Ex. 59; Tr. 854-66.) However, there was no credible evidence indicating that the list was used by Minister 9X in such a way as properly to ensure its reliability.[29] Little, if any evidence, was offered

---

[28] 28 This is despite Minister 9X's assertion that a majority of the inmates he met on Rikers Island were NOI members.

Q. Were there other instances in which you met inmates who were members of the Nation of Islam?
A. I've been on it [Rikers Island], approximately, several times. And every time I've been on it, the majority of inmates that I met were believers in the teaching of Elijah Muhammad.

(Tr. 862.) Perhaps Minister 9X simply did not encounter a random sampling of inmates, i.e., he testified that he went to Rikers Island to provide seminars concerning NOI teachings, or perhaps the inmates who met with him expressed their interest -- albeit not their membership -- in the NOI. Regardless, I find it difficult to believe that the "majority of inmates" on Rikers Island belong to the NOI, particularly in light of the other evidence and my own observations.

[29] 29 For example, Minister 9X testified as follows:

Q. What is it that you do when you receive the list of identification of inmates who are members of the Nation of Islam?
A. I compile it for my evidence, for my documents.

* * *

Q. Can you tell me, does the Nation of Islam use the list of their members to provide documents, materials and information for various purposes.
A. Yes, we do.

(Tr. 854-55.) Minister 9X believes "99 percent" of the names on NOI mailing lists were those of NOI members because the names had "X"'s on the end. (Tr. 866.) Nonetheless, the reliability of this list is not ensured by its use for the purposes stated by Minister 9X. For example, one can easily imagine that an inmate whose name appears on the list was interested in receiving and perusing NOI materials without actually belonging to the NOI.

concerning the circumstances surrounding the compilation of the list; we do not know what the inmates were told in order to induce them to put their names on the list, and the cover letter from Norbert X that accompanied the list does not assuage such concerns.[30] Also, nothing in the list or the cover letter indicates the inmates actually knew that putting their names on the list would be interpreted as meaning they belonged to the NOI. For example, there is no statement such as "I belong to the Nation of Islam" on the page with the list of names; indeed, on that page with the names, there was nothing except those names, the inmates' identification numbers and their housing area. In short, I do not find that this evidence is entitled to much weight.

The other evidence offered by plaintiffs appears to be affirmations executed by other inmates that plaintiff Muhammad obtained during his incarceration on Rikers Island after trial.[31] (Declaration of Colleen D. Duffy in Support of Motion to Reopen the Record to Admit New Evidence dated May 31, 1995 ("Duffy Decl.") P 3, Ex. B.) Each affirmation consists of a form containing three statements to which an inmate may respond and five other statements to which no response is required. The statements to which an inmate may respond are as follows:

1) IAM A MEMBER OF THE NATION OF ISLAM []
2) IAM INTERESTED AND WANT A NATION OF ISLAM SERVICE []
3) I WANT TO CHANGE MY RELIGION TO THE NATION OF ISLAM []

---

[30] 30 For example, the cover letter states in part that:

I just received your letter and I was glad and most honored to hear from you. . . I did the best that I could with the shortness of time that I had to honor your request. Allah knows that if I had more time, I could have gotten more signatures but, nevertheless, I hope this will suffice. Bro. Rob, I going through some problems with this letter & flyer you've sent. As you know, alot of brothers are believers in Al-Islam (which I explained to you in my last letter). . . . Anyway, I wish I had more time to get more signatures. So, for now, this will have to suffice.

(Pl. Ex. 59.)

[31] 31 By a Memorandum and Order dated April 25, 1995, I denied plaintiffs' request to reopen the record to admit this evidence. Upon reconsideration, I have decided to admit the evidence.

(Duffy Decl., Ex. B (capitalization and spacing in original).)[32] Plaintiffs offered approximately fifty affirmations and/or letters stating much the same as the forms. I find this evidence unreliable and, accordingly, entitled to little weight.

First, the affirmations are unreliable on their face. Some inmates have checked only that they are "interested" in NOI services. Some checked the boxes indicating that they are members of NOI and want services. Others checked all three boxes, prompting the question how an inmate could simultaneously belong to the NOI and yet desire to join the NOI. In short, it is impossible to discern whether this material is anything other than a testament to the persuasive powers of plaintiff Muhammad.[33]

---

[32] 32 The statements to which no response is required are:

4) I BELIEVE THAT ALLAH CAME IN THE PERSON OF MASTER W. FARD MUHAMMAD
5) I BELIEVE THAT THE HONORABLE ELIJAH MUHAMMAD IS THE MESSENGER OF OF [sic] ALLAH IN THE NATION OF ISLAM
6) I BELIEVE IN THE DIVINE LEADERSHIP OF MINISTER LOUIS FARRAKHAN
7) I SUPPORT MINISTER ABDUL-SHAHID FARRAKHAN-MUHAMMAD AND WANT HIM AND MINISTER ROBERT 9X AND ALL OTHER AVAILABLE MINISTERS TO COUNSEL ME AND SERVICE MY RELIGIOUS NEEDS.
8) I WANT A SEPARATE SERVICE AND CLASSES TO BE ASSISTED BY MINISTER ABDUL-SHAHID FARRAKHAN-MUHAMMAD, MINISTER ROBERT 9X AND ANY ALL REPRESENTATIVE [sic] FROM THE NATION OF ISLAM EXCLUSIVELY, AT LEAST THREE TIMES A WEEK.

(Duffy Decl., Ex. B (capitalization in original).)

[33] 33 Defendants point out that the affirmations are a response to plaintiff Muhammad's solicitation. Defendants also note that when the affirmations were originally proposed, the package forwarded to the defendants from plaintiffs' counsel included a notice from plaintiff Muhammad purportedly describing the instant lawsuit and exhorting his fellows to come forward. (Calhoun Decl. P 5 & Ex. D.) The solicitation is not presently included in the proffered package of documents. (See Duffy Decl. & Exs.) The text of the letter reads as follows:

Second, the reliability of the affirmations is called into question in light of plaintiff Muhammad's testimony. At trial, he testified about his role in educating inmates who expressed interest in learning about NOI, describing his role as "bait to fish." (Tr. 415-18.) He did not, however, testify that there were actual members of the NOI to be found in the kinds of numbers that the affirmations seem to suggest. (Tr. 415-18; Calhoun Decl., Ex. B at 29-30). In addition, plaintiff testified during his deposition that, while he was at GRVC on Rikers Island, there were "several individuals, some of whom I had recruited" who belonged to NOI, "a brother who was already a member of the Nation of Islam," and "one other individual who had been a member previously." (Calhoun Decl., Ex. B.) He also stated that he "recruited" fifteen inmates in all. (Id.) Thus, it appears plaintiff encountered rather different numbers of NOI inmates during different periods of incarceration in DOC

MY DEAR BROTHERS:
MOST RECENTLY, THE NATION OF ISLAM WON ITS LAWSUIT AGAINST CORRECTIONS FOR THE STATE AND AWAITS A FINAL DECISION AGAINST THE CITY DEPT. OF CORRECTIONS FOR A PROGRAM ENVISIONED BY THE HONORABLE ELIJAH MUHAMMAD. IT IS THE CONTENTIONS OF THE CITY TO APPEAL BASED ON THE ASSUMPTION THAT THERE IS NO ONE ON RIKER'S ISLAND WHO ARE MEMBERS OF THE NATION OF ISLAM, OR ARE INTERESTED IN LEARNING ABOUT THE NATION OF ISLAM, OR WANT TO BECOME MEMBERS OF THE NATION OF ISLAM.

WITH THE WILL OF GOD AND IN BACKING THE HONORABLE MINISTER LOUIS FARRAKHAN AND THE WORK OF THE NATION OF ISLAM, WE KNOW THAT THEIR SO-CALLED ASSESSMENT IS WITHOUT MERIT. THUS, I ASK OF YOU AS A MINISTER IN THIS DIVINE WORK, TO STAND UP AND BE COUNTED. PLEASE SIGN THE LIST THAT APPLIES TO YOU AND HAVE YOUR ILC REPRESENTATIVE OR ONE RESPONSIBLE, TO DELIVER THE FULL COMPLETION OF THE LIST TO BROTHER BROWN X WHO IS A CLERK AT THE LAW LIBRARY. IF YOU ARE UNDER STATE JURISDICTION, YOUR NAME CARRIES MORE WEIGHT. IF YOU HAVE ANY QUESTIONS, PLEASE CALL ON ME AT THE LAW LIBRARY. THANK YOU AND MAY ALLAH BLESS YOU.

(Calhoun Decl., Ex. D (capitalization and grammar in original).)

facilities. This discrepancy either diminishes the weight of plaintiffs' evidence and/or supports the defendants' point that DOC's prison population is constantly in flux.

Plaintiffs have stated that, to the extent that I deem these fifty or so affirmations unreliable, they seek to supplement the record to allow deposition or live testimony from each inmate identified in the documents about his membership in the NOI and desire to participate in NOI religious services and classes. (Plaintiffs' Memorandum of Law in Support of Motion to Reopen the Record to Admit Newly Discovered Evidence ("Pl. Mot. to Reopen") at 8-9.) Deeming plaintiffs' statement as a request to reopen the record yet again, the request is hereby denied. Plaintiff Muhammad could have given a more carefully worded form to the inmates, and plaintiffs could have offered, at the time of their motion to reopen, a more complete evidentiary background detailing the' circumstances of the completion of the forms. Their failure to do these things is hardly the fault of the defendants; it was no surprise to plaintiffs that the question of the number of inmates who belong to the NOI would be an issue in the case. In short, plaintiffs have had ample opportunity to litigate this case, i.e., first, at the time of trial and second, at the time they moved to reopen the record. They shall not have a third opportunity. To rule otherwise would result in flagrant disregard for the principles of finality and judicial economy.

In sum, considering all of the evidence and the circumstances under which testimony was given, I credit the testimony of Imam Askia and Imam Luqman and find that over the last twenty years and continuing to the time of trial, there have been no more than a handful of members of the NOI in the DOC system at any time, and, of those, only plaintiff Muhammad has made a request for additional accommodations.

F. Federal Bureau of Prisons' Religious Accommodations

Evidence was offered at trial concerning the religious accommodation policies and practices of the Federal Bureau of Prisons (the "Bureau"). (E.g., Pl. Exs. 3, 7, 11, 12.) The Bureau formally recognizes the NOI as a distinct Muslim organization (Pl. Ex. 3 at 12-13), and there can be no question that the Bureau provides greater institutional opportunity for observing NOI religious practices on a group basis.

However, the evidence indicates that DOC attempts to offer to NOI inmates as individuals opportunities similar to those provided institutionally on a group basis by the Bureau. For example, the Bureau has contracted with NOI representatives to enable knowledgeable, NOI-certified persons to speak to inmates. (Pl. Ex. 3 at 15-16; Pl. Ex. 7.) The Bureau compensates the NOI representatives who come to Bureau facilities. (Pl. Ex. 3 at 17.) There are, however, only "a few" NOI representatives with such Bureau contracts. (Pl.

Ex. 3 at 15-16.) I find this practice to be comparable to the DOC practice of inviting NOI representatives to meet with inmates for various activities other than group religious services. (Tr. 630, 805-06, 811, 849-850.)

Both the Bureau and DOC allow inmates to have access to NOI literature. For example, the Bureau permits and supports the Final Call newspaper. (Pl. Ex. 3 at 20-24; Pl. Ex. 7.) The Bureau also purchases literature pertaining to the NOI to be read by inmates. (Pl. Ex. 3 at 20-23.) DOC also allows religious literature to be disseminated freely among its inmates. (Pl. Ex. 58, Title 40, § 1-14(a).) Plaintiff himself testified that during his incarceration on Rikers Island, he received literature not only from NOI representatives, but also from DOC employees, who encouraged him in his studies. (Tr. 419-420.) Indeed, the assistance rendered by DOC employees was ample enough to allow plaintiff to train to become an NOI ministerial representative while in DOC custody. (Tr. 419-21.)

The Bureau recognizes Savior's Day and Founder's Day as NOI religious holidays. (Pl. Ex. 3 at 25-27; Pl. Ex. 12 at 3.) The Bureau also makes accommodations to allow NOI inmates to observe the December Fast. (Pl. Ex. 3 at 25, 27, 29-30; Pl. Ex. 11; Pl. Ex. 12 at 3.) The Bureau does not formally celebrate all religious holidays, however, due to the enormous number of holidays. For example, although the Jewish faith recognizes thirteen major holidays, inmates may celebrate only one holiday while in Bureau custody, which is usually Passover. (Pl. Ex. 3 at 27.) DOC, as described supra, does not recognize the December Fast formally, but has a liberal policy of accommodating individual requests. (Tr. 704-17.)

In short, there are differences between the religious accommodations available in Bureau and DOC facilities. However, I find that the differences in accommodations are only marginal when compared to the enormous differences in the characteristics of the Bureau and the DOC systems. For example, as described supra, DOC operates an essentially transitional facility that houses pre-trial detainees awaiting trial. I find that a system as dynamic as the City system -- in which over 110,000 inmates pass through yearly after relatively short periods of time in custody (Def. Ex. E) -- cannot provide its religious services in the same manner as the Bureau.[34]

---

[34] 34 Plaintiffs previously have recognized that "this Court can ascertain whether any alleged differences in size or budget bear upon conclusions plaintiffs might ask the Court to draw from the evidence," and that such differences affect "only the weight this Court should afford the evidence, not its admissibility." (Plaintiffs' Memorandum of Law in Opposition to Motion in Limine to Exclude Plaintiffs' Evidence ("Pl. Opp. to in Limine Motion") at 4-5 (emphasis in original).) Plaintiffs have not offered any evidence that persuades me that the Bureau and DOC are sufficiently similar such that the

CONCLUSIONS OF LAW
This Court has subject matter jurisdiction over this action, and venue in this district is proper pursuant to federal law. This Court has personal jurisdiction over the City defendants pursuant to federal and state law.

I. The Religious Freedom Restoration Act
Plaintiffs' first cause of action alleges that defendants' conduct violated the Religious Freedom Restoration Act of 1993 ("RFRA"). (Second Am. Compl. PP 52-58.) RFRA provides that governmental action should not substantially burden the free exercise of religion unless it advances a compelling governmental interest. Specifically, RFRA provides in pertinent part that:

(a) In general
Government shall not substantially burden a person's exercise of religion even if the burden results from a rule of general applicability, except as provided in subsection (b) of this section.
(b) Exception
Government may substantially burden a person's exercise of religion only if it demonstrates that application of the burden to the person --
(1) is in furtherance of a compelling governmental interest; and
(2) is the least restrictive means of furthering that compelling interest.

42 U.S.C. § 2000bb-1. RFRA applies to both the federal and state governments as well as subdivisions of the state government. 42 U.S.C. §§ 2000bb-2(1), 2000bb-3. RFRA applies retroactively. 42 U.S.C. § 2000bb-3(a). RFRA purports to restore the "compelling interest" test of Sherbert v. Verner, 374 U.S. 398, 10 L. Ed. 2d 965, 83 S. Ct. 1790 (1963) and Wisconsin v. Yoder, 406 U.S. 205, 32 L. Ed. 2d 15, 92 S. Ct. 1526 (1972), which had been abandoned in Employment Division v. Smith, 494 U.S. 872, 108 L. Ed. 2d 876, 110 S. Ct. 1595 (1990). 42 U.S.C. § 2000bb(b)(1); see, e.g., Alameen v. Coughlin, 892 F. Supp. 440, 446-47 (E.D.N.Y. 1995); Francis v. Keane, 888 F. Supp. 568, 572-73 (S.D.N.Y. 1995); Campos v. Coughlin, 854 F. Supp. 194, 204-07 (S.D.N.Y. 1994). In Congress's view, Smith "virtually eliminated the requirement that the government justify burdens on religious exercise

---

two corrections systems can be required to provide the same religious accommodations to NOI inmates. Indeed, as noted above, the totality of the evidence indicates that, inter alia, the smaller size and exceedingly dynamic nature of the DOC system make any comparison to the Bureau system, or, indeed, to the DOCS system, wholly inapposite.

imposed by laws neutral toward religion." 42 U.S.C. § 2000bb(a)(4); see, e.g., Alameen, 892 F. Supp. at 446.

RFRA applies to the claims of prisoners.[35] Werner v. McCotter, 49 F.3d 1476, 1479 (10th Cir.), cert. denied, 132 L. Ed. 2d 866, 115 S. Ct. 2625 (1995); Bryant v. Gomez, 46 F.3d 948, 948 (9th Cir. 1995); Brown-El v. Harris, 26 F.3d 68, 69 (8th Cir. 1994); Alameen, 892 F. Supp. at 447 (collecting cases); Francis, 888 F. Supp. at 574; Campos, 854 F. Supp. at 204-07. However, in enacting RFRA, Congress did not intend that courts would no longer extend the deference traditionally accorded prison administrators:

The committee does not intend the act to impose a standard that would exacerbate the difficult and complex challenges of operating the Nation's prisons and jails in a safe and secure manner. Accordingly, the committee expects that the courts will continue the tradition of giving due deference to the experience and expertise of prison and jail administrators in establishing necessary regulations and procedures to maintain good order, security and discipline, consistent with consideration of costs and limited resources. At the same time, however, inadequately formulated prison regulations and policies grounded on mere speculation, exaggerated fears, or post-hoc rationalizations will not suffice to meet the act's requirements.

Alameen, 892 F. Supp. at 447 (quoting S. Rep. No. 111, 103rd Cong., 1st Sess., reprinted in 1993 U.S.S.C.A.N 1892, 1899-90 (footnote omitted)); see also Werner, 49 F.3d at 1479-80; Francis, 888 F. Supp. at 574.

Under RFRA, "the threshold issue . . . is whether the plaintiff's exercise of religion has been laden with a 'substantial burden.'" Prins v. Coughlin, No. 94 Civ. 2053 (MBM), 1994 U.S. Dist. LEXIS 10564, *3, 1994 WL 411016 at *1 (S.D.N.Y. Aug. 3, 1994); see also Francis, 888 F. Supp. at 573 n.6 (stating that "a plaintiff asserting a claim under RFRA must make a threshold showing that his or her religious exercise has been substantially burdened before requiring the government to meet its burden of production and persuasion with respect

---

[35] 35 In O'Lone v. Estate of Shabazz, 482 U.S. 342, 96 L. Ed. 2d 282, 107 S. Ct. 2400 (1987), the Supreme Court stated that prison regulations affecting prisoners' right to free exercise of religion will be upheld if the regulations are reasonably related to a legitimate penological interest. However, courts since have found that RFRA overrules O'Lone. E.g., Werner v. McCotter, 49 F.3d 1476, 1479 (10th Cir.), cert. denied, 132 L. Ed. 2d 866, 115 S. Ct. 2625 (1995); Brown-El v. Harris, 26 F.3d 68, 69 (8th Cir. 1994); Campos v. Coughlin, 854 F. Supp. 194, 206 (S.D.N.Y. 1994).

to proving a compelling governmental interest and the use of the least restrictive means"). In order to establish that a plaintiff's exercise was substantially burdened, a plaintiff must "demonstrate that the government's action pressures him to commit an act forbidden by his religion or prevents him from engaging in conduct or having a religious experience mandated by his faith." Davidson v. Davis, No. 92 Civ. 4040 (SWK), 1995 U.S. Dist. LEXIS 1696, *15, 1995 WL 60732 at *5 (S.D.N.Y. Feb. 14, 1995) (citing Graham v. Commissioner, 822 F.2d 844, 850-51 (9th Cir. 1987), aff'd sub nom., Hernandez v. Commissioner, 490 U.S. 680, 104 L. Ed. 2d 766, 109 S. Ct. 2136 (1989)). In addition, "this interference must be more than an inconvenience; the burden must be substantial and an interference with a tenet or belief that is central to religious doctrine." Davidson, 1995 U.S. Dist. LEXIS 1696, *15, 1995 WL 60732 at *5 (quoting Graham, 822 F.2d at 851). See also Bryant v. Gomez, 46 F.3d 948, 949 (9th Cir. 1995); Vernon v. City of Los Angeles, 27 F.3d 1385, 1393-94 (9th Cir.), cert. denied, 130 L. Ed. 2d 417, 115 S. Ct. 510 (1994); Alameen, 892 F. Supp. 440, 448 (E.D.N.Y. 1995) (stating that "to impose a substantial burden, government interference must be more than an inconvenience. The interference must burden a belief central to a plaintiff's religious doctrine."); but see Muslim v. Frame, 897 F. Supp. 215, 1995 U.S. Dist. LEXIS 12866, *8-*9, 1995 WL 505072 at *3 (E.D. Pa. 1995) (stating that "it is unnecessary under RFRA for a prisoner to demonstrate that the religious practice at issue is mandated by his religion" but noting that "to be sure, a number of other courts have reached a different conclusion"). The Court of Appeals for the Tenth Circuit has recently explained that:

To exceed the "substantial burden" threshold, government regulation must significantly inhibit or constrain conduct or expression that manifests some central tenet of a prisoner's individual beliefs; must meaningfully curtail a prisoner's ability to express adherence to his or her faith; or must deny a prisoner reasonable opportunities to engage in those activities that are fundamental to a prisoner's religion.

Werner, 49 F.3d at 1480 (citations omitted).
Once a plaintiff has demonstrated the existence of a substantial burden on his or her exercise of religion, the burden then shifts to the government to establish that the challenged action or policy furthers a compelling state interest in the least restrictive manner. 42 U.S.C. § 2000bb-1(b); Werner, 49 F.3d at 1480 n.2; Francis, 888 F. Supp. at 572 n.6; Davidson, 1995 U.S. Dist. LEXIS 1696, at *14, 1995 WL 60732 at *5. Prison security and penological institutional safety goals are unquestionably compelling governmental

interests.[36] Woods v. Evatt, 876 F. Supp. 756, 769 (D.S.C. 1995); Campos, 854 F. Supp. at 207. Of course, "merely brandishing the words 'security' and 'safety'" does not result in a defendant's conduct "automatically being deemed constitutionally permissible." Campos, 854 F. Supp. at 207.

A. Substantial Burden

In the instant case, plaintiff Muhammad contends that DOC has substantially burdened his free exercise of religion by refusing to (i) hire any NOI ministers as chaplains, (ii) provide congregate NOI religious services, (iii) provide NOI religious texts to NOI members on the same basis as DOC provides religious texts to followers of other religions and (iv) accommodate observance of NOI holidays, i.e., Savior's Day, Founder's Day and the December Fast. I do not agree.

1. Ministers

DOC's failure to employ an NOI minister does not substantially burden Muhammad's free exercise of his religion. The Court of Appeals for the Tenth Circuit has stated recently that:

[RFRA] need not drive a prison to employ clergy from every sect or creed found within its walls; however, the failure to provide or allow reasonably sufficient alternative methods of worship would, in the absence of a compelling state interest, run afoul of [RFRA].

Werner, 49 F.3d at 1480. In Werner, plaintiff, an inmate in the Utah prison system, contended that the Utah prison system unconstitutionally interfered with the free exercise of his religion, i.e., Native American shamanism. Plaintiff challenged, inter alia, the prison's failure to provide him with access to a Cherokee Native American spiritual advisor. The Court found that this claim was without merit because the prison in which plaintiff was incarcerated employed six part-time chaplains who provided nondenominational religious

---

[36] 36 Plaintiffs contend that any additional cost to DOC of accommodating plaintiffs' religious needs as NOI members as described by the plaintiffs is not a compelling interest as a matter of law. (Plaintiffs' Proposed Findings of Fact and Conclusions of Law ("Pl. Proposed Findings") at 43.) However, the cases cited by plaintiff are inapposite inasmuch as they pertain neither to RFRA nor to prisoners. In addition, plaintiffs' argument is refuted by the language of legislative history quoted supra, in which Congress specifically approved "consideration of costs and limited resources." S. Rep. No. 111, 103rd Cong., 1st Sess., reprinted in 1993 U.S.S.C.A.N 1892, 1890.

support to the prisoners. Id. at 1481. Although none of these chaplains was a Native American, there were two Native American spiritual advisors who provided services on a volunteer basis. Id. Thus, the Court held RFRA was not violated.[37]

The need for religious services and counseling of a particular frequency and character necessarily depends on the character of the prison population and, unlike the need for kosher food, cannot be met practically on an individual basis. It is practical to require that meals meeting the standard of [Kahane v. Carlson, 527 F.2d 492 (2d Cir. 1975)) be provided daily even if only one person needs them; it is not practical to require that a clergyman be provided daily simply because one person needs him. . . . Plaintiff has made no allegation that the services and counseling provided at Clinton are inadequate to the population at that facility, but only that they do not serve his particular orientation. Thus, there is no suggestion that he has been transferred from an institution that meets the religious needs of its population to an institution that does not.

Id. at *5 (emphasis added).
Similarly, in Davidson v. Davis, No. 92 Civ. 4040 (SWK), 1995 U.S. Dist. LEXIS 1696, 1995 WL 60732 (S.D.N.Y. Feb. 14, 1995), plaintiff alleged that his rights were violated while he was incarcerated at the Metropolitan Correctional Center because, inter alia, he was denied access to the facility's Jewish chaplain. Judge Kram, concluding plaintiff's exercise was not substantially burdened and dismissing his claim, acknowledged plaintiff's

---

[37] 37 Other recent decisions, while not as focused on the issue of the availability of clergy of a particular sect or denomination, are certainly consistent with the reasoning of Werner. For example, in Prins v. Coughlin, No. 94 Civ. 2053 (MBM), 1995 U.S. Dist. LEXIS 8673, 1995 WL 378526 (S.D.N.Y. June 26, 1995), plaintiff, a prisoner, claimed that his transfer from Green Haven Correctional Facility ("Green Haven") to Clinton Correctional Facility ("Clinton") substantially burdened his free exercise in violation of RFRA. Judge Mukasey denied his motion to amend his complaint because the proposed amendment would have been subject to dismissal for insufficiency pursuant to Rule 12(b)(6) of the Federal Rules of Civil Procedure. Id. at *4. The plaintiff apparently sought to allege that there were fewer Jewish services at Clinton than at Green Haven and that there were no Orthodox services provided there. Judge Mukasey distinguished between the importance of providing kosher food and offering religious services to plaintiff's liking as follows:

constitutional right to practice his religion but found that the prison staff was "not under an affirmative duty to provide each inmate with the spiritual counselor of his choice." Id. at *15 (citations omitted). I note that, although the cases relied upon by the Court in Davidson were not RFRA cases, Judge Kram still found them worthy of reference. See also Weir v. Nix, 890 F. Supp. 769 (S.D. Iowa 1995) (finding no free exercise, RFRA or equal protection violation where plaintiff prisoner, a Christian fundamentalist, was provided with access to a minister who was also a Christian fundamentalist but with beliefs that differed concerning the religious doctrine of "separatism" and stating that a prisoner "is not entitled to insist on a religious adviser whose beliefs are completely congruent with his").

In the instant case, it is undisputed that DOC does not employ an NOI minister. However, there are numerous imams who are orthodox Muslims, and DOC offers numerous religious services and accommodations for Muslim inmates, including (i) a generic congregate Muslim prayer service (Jumu'ah) offered every Friday and (ii) religious study groups.

If an inmate who belongs to the NOI prefers spiritual guidance from an NOI minister, that inmate has that opportunity. As discussed supra, DOC has a flexible and tolerant policy of permitting inmates to have unlimited personal clergy/counsel visits with any spiritual leader, including NOI ministers. McCloud has worked with Minister 9X to have NOI volunteers provide personal development workshops.[38] The workshops focus on the themes stressed in NOI religious services, among them, African-American empowerment, self-reliance and responsibility. DOC has stated its

---

[38] 38 There was testimony at trial indicating that there had been some difficulties due to the schedules of the NOI volunteers. In a case where a prisoner sought to practice his Native American religion, the Court of Appeals for the Sixth Circuit recently noted that:

To the extent that some of the cancelled [religious] meetings involve the failure of a volunteer practitioner of Native American rituals to appear at the prison, the plaintiff offers no reason why this failure to appear should be held against the prison authorities.

Allard v. Abramajtys, 54 F.3d 776, n.1 (6th Cir. May 12, 1995) (unpublished disposition; text available in Westlaw, No. 94-2161). I merely note and do not rely upon this case inasmuch as Sixth Circuit Rule 24(c) states that citation of unpublished dispositions is disfavored except for establishing res judicata, estoppel or the law of the case.

commitment to expand this program. In addition, prominent NOI members, including Minister Muhammad of Temple No. 7 in Harlem, have visited DOC facilities as guest speakers. These activities not only contribute to meet the specific needs of NOI inmates, but also refute plaintiff's contention that DOC is hostile to NOI principles. In short, although plaintiff may not have had access to an NOI minister employed by DOC, it cannot be fairly said, and I do not find, that plaintiff's free exercise has been substantially burdened.

2. Congregate Services

I find that plaintiff's free exercise was not substantially burdened by DOC's failure to offer a congregate NOI religious service. Plaintiff has not shown that the absence of a congregate NOI service is "more than an inconvenience" and that its absence is "substantial" and an "interference with a tenet or belief that is central to religious doctrine." Bryant v. Gomez, 46 F.3d 948, 949 (9th Cir. 1995) (quoting Graham v. Commissioner, 822 F.2d 844, 851 (9th Cir. 1987), aff'd sub nom. Hernandez v. Commissioner, 490 U.S. 680, 699, 104 L. Ed. 2d 766, 109 S. Ct. 2136 (1988)). In Bryant, a Pentecostal prisoner claimed that the defendants' refusal to hold full Pentecostal services violated his religious rights under RFRA. The prisoner alleged he was precluded from "participating in the practices and using the 'traditional instruments' which are specific to his faith and distinct from other Protestant faiths." Id. The Court of Appeals for the Ninth Circuit rejected his claims. First, the Court found that the mere fact that certain practices and instruments were "unique" to the Pentecostal faith did not make them "mandated" by that faith, and plaintiff did not argue or offer evidence indicating that they were mandated. Id. Second, the Court of Appeals pointed out that:

[Plaintiff] has not given this court any basis for concluding that he cannot accomplish the mandates of his religion through the means that the defendants do provide in his prison. These include 1) "inter-faith" Christian services that are designed to accommodate the needs of various Christian denominations, 2) Pentecostal literature in the prison library, and 3) a Pentecostal volunteer who is available to attend Bible study classes and focus more specifically on the beliefs of the Pentecostal faith.

46 F.3d at 949-50.[39]

---

[39] 39 Weir v. Nix, 890 F. Supp. 769 (S.D. Iowa 1995) is not dissimilar. In that case, a fundamentalist prisoner claimed, inter alia, that the prison should provide him and other Christian fundamentalists with a spiritual adviser who could conduct services consistent with his beliefs. The court stated:

In the instant case, plaintiff has demonstrated with ample evidence many of the ways in which his beliefs differ from beliefs associated with orthodox Islam. However, he has not demonstrated that the generic Muslim service offends or ignores particular practices or beliefs that are mandated by NOI teachings.[40] Indeed, given the undisputed similarities in beliefs between orthodox Muslims and NOI members, see Findings of Fact Supra part I, I find that the generic Muslim services provide comfort and solace to NOI members without pressuring such members to commit acts forbidden by their religion or preventing them from engaging in conduct or having a religious experience mandated by their faith. Moreover, the aspect of the Muslim generic service that plaintiff told Imam Askia that was lacking -- emphasis on African-American themes such as empowerment, responsibility and self-

---

When the only option available for a prisoner is under the guidance of someone whose beliefs are significantly different from or obnoxious to his, the prisoner has been effectively denied the opportunity for group worship and the result may amount to a substantial burden on the exercise of his religion. A prisoner, however, is not entitled to insist on a religious adviser whose beliefs are completely congruent with his. As the Court has found, the present Protestant chaplain is a fundamentalist Christian whose beliefs vary from Weir's only with respect to the doctrine of separatism. [The chaplain] understands and preaches the basic tenets of fundamentalist faith. He is capable of ministering to fundamentalist inmates and he has done so to the apparent satisfaction of those who testified. Weir therefore has the opportunity to attend group worship led by a capable, willing religious leader whose beliefs are not significantly different from his own. Accordingly, there is no free exercise, RFRA, or equal protection violation here.

Id. at 788 (citations omitted). The point that a prison is not required by RFRA to provide congregate services led by a chaplain whose beliefs are completely congruent with those of any particular inmate/plaintiff is well-taken.

[40] 40 By means of comparison, in Campos v. Coughlin, 854 F. Supp. 194 (S.D.N.Y. 1994), members of the Santeria faith alleged that they "must wear sacred [Santeria] beads of certain color combinations" because the beads, "when worn, protect [them] from danger and from evil to which [they] might otherwise be vulnerable" and that the beads "when worn, will briny [them] good fortune, peace, purity and good health." Id. at 200 (alterations in original) (emphasis added).

reliance -- was, according to Imam Askia, addressed already. To the extent such topics were not addressed, Imam Askia was willing to incorporate those themes to a greater extent in the generic Muslim service. In addition, the NOI self-development workshops already available focus on these very themes. Prominent NOI figures have spoken in DOC facilities. Inmates have the opportunity for unlimited clergy/counsel visits with spiritual advisors, including NOI volunteers. In short, plaintiff has not shown that he "cannot accomplish the mandates of his faith through the means that the defendants do provide in his prison," Bryant, 46 F.3d at 949, or that the absence of an NOI congregate religious service has substantially burdened the exercise of his religious rights.[41]

The Court of Appeals, citing Bryant, explained that:

We first note that this case differs from those involving the prohibition of some specific practice of a person's religion, such as the smoking of peyote or the sacrifice of live animals. [Plaintiff] has no proscriptions placed on his beliefs or the practices of his religion, but is simply deprived of a special time and place to observe his beliefs exclusively with others who profess the same faith. We emphasize "exclusively" because all of those who claim to be Nation of Islam Muslims may attend together the regular Islamic service. . . .

The record reflects two categorical differences between the Nation of Islam Muslim and other Islamic practitioners. In the first category are those differences that do not affect the religious service itself but relate to personal beliefs. For example, Nation of Islam Muslims do not believe in reincarnation. There is no showing, however, that [plaintiff] cannot meaningfully participate in an Islamic religious service simply because he may be in the present of others who do believe in reincarnation.

---

[41] 41 In addition, I note, but do not rely upon, a recently rendered unpublished decision by the Court of Appeals for the Sixth Circuit, Johnson v. Baker,   F.3d   , No. 94-3828, 1995 U.S. App. LEXIS 32117, 1995 WL 570913 (6th Cir. Sept. 27, 1995). In Johnson, the plaintiff, a state prisoner who belonged to the NOI, brought suit under RFRA and claimed that his faith was sufficiently different from that of orthodox Islam such that he must be afforded a separate religious service. Id. at *3. The Court noted that several religious groups including Islamic, Jehovah Witness, Jewish, Protestant and Catholic were provided a time and place for meeting at the plaintiff's prison. Id. Inmates were also free to "supplement these activities with individual pursuits." Id. The plaintiff contended that what the prison offered was inadequate because, while plaintiff believed in "some of the basic tenets of the Islamic religion," he also had certain unique beliefs as a member of the NOI. Id. at *5.

The second category involves specific practices involved with the service itself. The principal, if not only, difference referenced in the record involves the body position during prayers. . . . Here again, if there is any real strength of belief, it would not seem to destroy the value or meaning of the service if people assume somewhat different postures during prayer. . . . In the prison context, actions taken for one inmate may legitimately be viewed in the context of its ripple effect on the entire prison population. What is done for one will have to be done for others.

Id. at *13 (footnotes omitted). The Johnson court concluded that plaintiff's beliefs had not been substantially burdened and declined to reach the compelling government interest issue. Id. at *16.

The Johnson court also found that "the number of persons within the prison professing belief in a specific religion or sect is also a factor properly considered in deciding an issue of this nature," id. at *14 n.6, while noting that Johnson was the only plaintiff before it and that the case was not a class action. Id.

3. Literature

I find that plaintiff's free exercise has not been substantially burdened with respect to literature. DOC's liberal policy concerning literature has been discussed at length. Inmates can and do receive and retain religious literature, including the Final Call. In addition, plaintiff himself testified that he received NOI literature during the time of his incarceration in DOC facilities.

4. Holidays

I find that plaintiff's free exercise has not been substantially burdened with respect to celebration of NOI holidays. All Muslim inmates are allowed to observe Ramadan, the month-long daylight fast observed by all Muslims, including members of the NOI. In addition, there is no prohibition on NOI members' observing their unique December Fast; during December, breakfast is served before sunrise and dinner is served after sunset in DOC facilities for all inmates. Plaintiff himself concedes that he never asked to celebrate the December Fast while he was in DOC custody.

5. Other

As discussed supra, NOI members may observe their faith in a variety of ways while in DOC custody, including provision of Halal meals and wearing Muslim attire, be it the kuffi traditionally worn by many orthodox Muslims or the white shirt, bow tie and star and crescent pin worn by NOI members, including plaintiff, during his period in DOC custody. In addition, male Muslim inmates are searched only by male correction officers.

While plaintiff was incarcerated on Rikers Island, he was able to study to become an NOI ministerial representative. He received the necessary literature from various sources, and DOC staff members, including one captain, who personally delivered literature to plaintiff from Minister Muhammad of Temple No. 7 in Harlem. These events indicate that plaintiff was not substantially burdened in the exercise of his religion.

Plaintiff's sole dissatisfaction with the religious accommodations he received while in DOC custody appears to center on a dispute he claims to have had with Imam Askia concerning his supposed election as Muslim inmate representative. Plaintiff claims that he was elected, and that, in response to his "election," Imam Askia became extremely hostile to him, refusing to allow plaintiff to serve unless he repudiated his beliefs. Even assuming I found plaintiff's testimony credible as it relates to this issue, I would find, based upon the body of evidence offered at trial, that such a dispute would be an isolated incident and not symptomatic of hostility or suspicion by DOC towards the NOI.

Based upon Imam Askia's testimony and my observations of both witnesses' demeanor at trial, however, I credit Imam Askia's testimony concerning the inmate representative election. As a former NOI member himself, Imam Askia remains tolerant of all Muslim faiths, including the NOI. Imam Askia testified that an important part of his role as a prison chaplain is to "deal with differences" without getting offended by different beliefs. I do not credit plaintiff's account of their encounter, which described Imam Askia as intolerant and disrespectful. I find that plaintiff's obvious disappointment at not being chosen to serve as inmate representative may have contributed to his somewhat harsh account of their encounter.

Plaintiff also claims that after his dispute with Imam Askia, a group of inmates assigned to security duty in the mosque kept him from attending a Friday Jumu'ah service, an act plaintiff believes to have been taken under orders from Imam Askia. Again, I credit the testimony of Imam Askia who testified that in his four-and-a-half years as a facility chaplain, he has never kept anyone from attending Muslim services. Imam Askia also testified that if he had a security problem in the mosque, he would turn for assistance to the correction officers who are always assigned to provide security during religious services. I find it improbable that a group of inmates would provide organized security at a DOC facility to keep another inmate from attending services as plaintiff claims -- particularly in light of the security regularly provided by correct ions officers which I observed during a Jumu'ah service at a Rikers Island facility.

In sum, because the numerous accommodations and activities offered by DOC did not coerce or pressure plaintiff into committing acts forbidden by his religion or prevent him from engaging in conduct that is mandated by his faith, plaintiff has failed to demonstrate that his exercise of religion has been substantially burdened under RFRA.[42]

B. Compelling Interest and Least Restrictive Means

Even if plaintiff were able to demonstrate that his exercise of religion had been substantially burdened, however, plaintiff would not prevail because DOC has demonstrated that any burden plaintiff might have suffered was in furtherance of a compelling governmental interest and was the least restrictive means of furthering that compelling interest. It is, of course, well established that correction officials have a compelling interest in maintaining internal order in penological institutions, see Bell v. Wolfish, 441 U.S. 520, 60 L. Ed. 2d 447, 99 S. Ct. 1861 (1979); Campos v. Coughlin, 854 F. Supp. 194, 207 (S.D.N.Y. 1994), and DOC has demonstrated (i) the existence of legitimate and compelling logistical, administrative and security concerns underlying its inability to provide the relief sought by plaintiff to the extent not already provided; and (ii) that the current combination of accommodations and programs is the least restrictive means of furthering those concerns. These concerns are interrelated and fundamentally affect the manner in which a dynamic and sprawling correctional system -- one that consists mainly of pre-trial detainees, most of whom typically remain in the system for less than two weeks -- can be efficiently and safely managed.

---

[42] 42 Much evidence was devoted to the question of whether the NOI is a "Muslim" sect. There was a great deal of evidence concerning the beliefs and practices of the NOI and, to a slightly lesser extent, those of "mainstream" or orthodox Muslims.

Plaintiffs urge me to find that the difference in the beliefs held by the NOI and orthodox Islam concerning the divine nature of Fard Muhammad and the role of Elijah Muhammad is analogous "in every relevant respect" to the difference in beliefs (i) held by Catholics and Jews as to the divine nature of Jesus Christ and (ii) held by Protestants and Catholics as to the status of the Pope. (Plaintiffs' Proposed Findings of Fact and Conclusions of Law ("Pl. Proposed Findings") at P 41.) I decline to adopt these propositions and find that any conclusions on such points are entirely unnecessary.

First, even if I were to adopt plaintiffs' proposed findings, the vast difference in numbers of Catholics, Protestants or Jews and the number of NOI members together with the attendant security and cost concerns discussed above might well mandate the same result I reach today. Second, and more importantly, I have found that plaintiff Muhammad was not substantially burdened in the exercise of his religion while in DOC custody. Under the statute, that is the relevant inquiry, not the inquiry plaintiffs propose into the technical issues of comparative religion.

As described supra, efficient and safe management of a correctional system is a particularly daunting task in New York City because of the increasing number of inmates and the rapid turnover of the inmate population. DOC'S mission is made more difficult by its decreasing budget and the resulting reduction in the number of facilities, correction officers and programs. At the same time, DOC is obligated to provide mandated services to its inmate population. The unique situation facing DOC -- i.e., a constantly changing and rapidly increasing inmate population yet substantially decreased resources -- has a significant bearing on DOC's ability to provide separate religious services for the NOI or any other specific sect or group.

The provision of religious services requires correction officers to search and escort the inmates to services. Many DOC facilities on Rikers Island are flat, one or two story structures requiring inmates to travel along wide, long corridors where they pass other groups of escorted inmates. This requires careful supervision since contraband can be exchanged or altercations can occur when inmates are moving. The congregate services themselves provide additional opportunities for the exchange of contraband among inmates, and thus require additional officers to monitor and search the inmates. In addition, security must be provided in the chapel or mosque area during services. It cannot be reasonably disputed that separate congregate services led by NOI ministers for NOI inmates, as well as any other group activities and/or accommodations, would require additional correction officers.

Finding space and a time slot to offer separate NOI services also poses significant hurdles. The DOC jail system was built for a much smaller inmate population. The evidence indicates there is simply insufficient space and time available for the provision of separate religious services for individual sects or groups in a system already straining to provide the required array of services to an expanding population in disproportionately smaller program areas.

An additional logistical problem is that male Muslim inmates may only be searched by male correction officers. The provision of a second weekly Muslim service where female officers are precluded from conducting searches would cause significant logistical and staffing problems.[43]

---

[43] 43 But see Rivera v. Smith, 63 N.Y.2d 501, 483 N.Y.S.2d 187, 193-94, 472 N.E.2d 1015 (N.Y. Ct. of App. 1984) (holding that under New York law, intrusion on right of Muslim inmate to free exercise of his religious beliefs by subjecting him to random pat frisk performed by correction officer of opposite sex could not be justified by states in maintaining prison security or in providing equal opportunity for women to serve as prison guards.)

In addition to large numbers of inmates who must be gathered and escorted to various activities within each facility, significant numbers of inmates are also moved throughout the system each day due to, for example, changing security classifications, medical reasons and perceived suicide or escape risk. On any given day, numerous inmates are transported to court for appearance, to hospital appointments or specialty clinics located at other facilities.

Finally, there are inherent logistical difficulties arising out of the rapid turnover of inmates. Because of the rapid turnover rate, it would be enormously difficult not only to track the relatively small number of members of the various sects or groups, but also to determine their long-term length of stay. Without being able to predict how long members of particular religious sects or smaller groups will remain in the system, there is no reasonable way to determine whether or not a particular chaplain should be added to service that sect or group or whether additional accommodations should be made. While there might be a significant number of NOI inmates one month, statistically most of them will be out of the system the next month. Even assuming that it would be possible to track the number of NOI inmates and their average length of stay, there is no way to predict where those inmates will be housed within the DOC system consistent with DOC's security classifications.

Furthermore, there has been no credible evidence that there have been more than a few NOI inmates in DOC facilities in the last decade. By contrast, twenty-five percent of DOC inmates identify themselves as Muslim on entry into the system and ten percent identify themselves as "other", that is, not Catholic, Protestant, Jewish or Muslim. (Tr. 758, 762, 778-79).[44] See Werner v. McCotter, 49 F.3d 1476, 1481 (10th Cir.) (noting that Native Americans comprise a small percentage of the Utah prison system), cert. denied, 132 L. Ed. 2d 866, 115 S. Ct. 2625 (1995). Thus, given the small number of NOI members in DOC's population at present and the dynamic nature of the entire population, there is no reasonable way to track the NOI population, just as with any other small sect or group.[45] DOC's response to its particular

---

[44] 44 Even plaintiff himself did not represent that he was one of many members of the Nation of Islam at GRVC. He testified that a number of inmates were curious about the Nation of Islam and that he responded to their questions, not that they were members. His request for separate services was an individual request.

[45] 45 DOC does modify its practices based on its observation of the inmate population. For example, in 1977, DOC added a congregate generic Muslim service because its population had significantly changed and DOC found itself

situation has been to offer generic Catholic, Protestant, Jewish and Muslim congregate services. The individual needs of particular inmates are addressed through private clergy/counsel visits, where an inmate may visit with any member of the clergy willing to visit a DOC facility. Generic services permit DOC to service large groups of inmates in a single space within a facility at a minimal cost, since they require fewer clergy staff and escort and security staff. Generic services also address security concerns by minimizing inmate movement, thus lessening the chances of altercations and exchange of contraband.

Generic services also permit DOC to classify and house inmates based on their security classification rather than their religious affiliation. If inmates were classified by individual religious sects, DOC would have to consider religious affiliation in classifying and housing inmates. This would result in facilities being operated at the highest security level, which is more expensive. DOC is able to avoid this problem by offering generic services.

I find that, given DOC's unique situation, there is no less restrictive alternative DOC could offer in the way of congregate services or classes or congregate holiday services for NOI inmates. Indeed, by accommodating the NOI with separate congregate services, DOC would likely have to accommodate similar sects, such as Shiite, Ah-Mahidiya, Greek Orthodox, Baptist, Orthodox Judaism and so on, thereby exacerbating the difficulties described above. Providing separate services and the various other accommodations sought which are not already available for even a fraction of these individual groups is clearly impossible for a detention system such as DOC for the reasons set forth above.

II. First Amendment Claims

Plaintiffs' second and third causes of action allege, pursuant to 42 U.S.C. § 1983, that the defendants' challenged policy also violates plaintiffs; First Amendment rights to the free exercise of their religion and to be free from any law establishing religion. (Second Am. Compl. PP 59-63.)

A. Free Exercise

Under pre-RFRA First Amendment analysis, regulations alleged to infringe the constitutional rights of inmates are judged under a "reasonableness" test less restrictive than that ordinarily applied to alleged infringements of fundamental constitutional rights. O'Lone v. Estate of Shabazz, 482 U.S. 342,

---

with a large enough pool of inmates to make these services feasible. (Tr. 761-62.)

349, 96 L. Ed. 2d 282, 107 S. Ct. 2400 (1987). "When a prison regulation impinges on inmates' constitutional rights, the regulation is valid if it is reasonably related to legitimate penological interests." Id. (quoting Turner v. Safley, 482 U.S. 78, 89, 96 L. Ed. 2d 64, 107 S. Ct. 2254 (1987)). The Supreme Court has explained that:

> In our view, such a standard is necessary if prison administrators . . ., and not the courts, [are] to make the difficult judgments concerning institutional operations. Subjecting the day-to-day judgments of prison officials to an inflexible strict scrutiny analysis would seriously hamper their ability to anticipate security problems and to adopt innovative solutions to the intractable problems of prison administration. The rule would also distort the decisionmaking process, for every administrative judgment would be subject to the possibility that some court somewhere would conclude that it had a less restrictive way of solving the problem at hand. Courts inevitably would become the primary arbiters of what constitutes the best solution to every administrative problem, thereby unnecessarily perpetuating the involvement of the federal courts in affairs of prison administration.

Turner, 482 U.S. at 89 (internal citations and quotations omitted) (other alterations in original).

The vitality of Turner and O'Lone continues in non-RFRA cases. E.g., Giano v. Senkowski, 54 F.3d 1050 (2d Cir. 1995) (applying standard to a prisoner's First Amendment challenge to prison policy allowing inmates to possess commercially produced erotic literature but prohibiting possession of nude or semi-nude photographs of spouses or girlfriends). However, there does not appear to be a clear consensus in the courts as to whether RFRA's heightened standard is limited in application to statutory claims brought pursuant to RFRA itself or whether it also applies to constitutional claims brought under the First Amendment. See Francis v. Keane, 888 F. Supp. 568, 572 n.5 (S.D.N.Y. 1995) (collecting cases and analyzing RFRA and constitutional claims separately, applying RFRA compelling interest standard to the former and lower First Amendment reasonableness standard to the latter); see also Alameen v. Coughlin, 892 F. Supp. 440 (E.D.N.Y. 1995) (applying higher standard to RFRA claims and lower standard to First Amendment and Equal Protection claims). Although I find the reasoning of Judge Koeltl in Francis persuasive, I need not decide this question. As determined supra, plaintiffs' statutory RFRA claims fail. Accordingly, even if the RFRA "compelling interest" standard governs plaintiffs' First Amendment claims, plaintiffs' constitutional claims fail for precisely the same reasons.

If, however, the Turner and O'Lone standard governs plaintiffs' First Amendment claims, plaintiffs' First Amendment claims fail a fortiori. As a preliminary matter, I note that the Supreme Court has stated that:

We do not suggest, of course, that every religious sect or group within a prison -- however few in number -- must have identical facilities or personnel. A special chapel or place of worship need not be provided for every faith regardless of size; nor must a chaplain, priest, or minister be provided without regard to the extent of the demand. But reasonable opportunities must be afforded to all prisoners to exercise the religious freedom guaranteed by the First and Fourteenth Amendments without fear of penalty.

Cruz v. Beto, 405 U.S. 319, 322 n.2, 31 L. Ed. 2d 263, 92 S. Ct. 1079 (1972). See also Woods v. Evatt, 876 F. Supp. 756, 766 (D.S.C. 1995).
When applying the Turner standard, a court must consider four factors, i.e.:

1) whether there is a rational relationship between the regulation and the legitimate government interests asserted; 2) whether the inmates have alternative means to exercise the right; 3) the impact that accommodation of the right will have on the prison system; and 4) whether ready alternatives exist which accommodate the right and satisfy the governmental interest.

Benjamin v. Coughlin, 905 F.2d 571, 574 (2d Cir.) (citing Turner, 482 U.S. at 89-90)), cert. denied, 498 U.S. 951, 112 L. Ed. 2d 335, 111 S. Ct. 372 (1990); see also Fromer v. Scully, 874 F.2d 69, 72 (2d Cir. 1989). The Court of Appeals for the Seventh Circuit has explained that:
The prison must afford all inmates a reasonable opportunity to practice their religion. In providing this opportunity, the efforts of prison administrators, when assessed in their totality, must be evenhanded. Prisons cannot discriminate against a particular religion. The rights of inmates belonging to minority or non-traditional religions must be respected to the same degree as the rights of those belonging to larger and more traditional denominations. Of course, economic and, at time, security constraints may require that the needs of inmates adhering to one faith be accommodated differently from those adhering to another. Nevertheless, the treatment of all inmates must be qualitatively comparable.

Al-Alamin v. Gramley, 926 F.2d 680, 686 (7th Cir. 1991) (citations omitted).
As extensively discussed supra, there can be no question that DOC's policies are rationally related to DOC's legitimate interest in running DOC facilities safely and efficiently. That is, DOC's policies are reasonably related to DOC's concerns that non-generic services and individual group accommodations will undermine DOC's ability to run a complex jail housing some 19,500 highly transitory inmates. Further accommodations -- in particular, separate

congregate services for NOI inmates -- would significantly affect DOC's ability to provide the current level of mandated services to its inmate population. Moreover, if I were to find that DOC must provide separate congregate services for NOI inmates, little, if anything, would preclude numerous other faith groups from seeking their own separate congregate services. The First Amendment surely does not require such an outcome. Also, as explained above, plaintiff as well as any other NOI inmates -- to the extent there are such inmates in DOC custody -- have adequate opportunity to practice their religion, including access to NOI clergy/volunteers.

B. Establishment Clause

In order to satisfy the Establishment Clause, "a governmental practice must (1) reflect a clearly secular purpose; (2) have a primary effect that neither advances nor inhibits religion; and (3) avoid excessive government entanglement with religion." Lee v. Weisman, 505 U.S. 577, 112 S. Ct. 2649, 2654, 120 L. Ed. 2d 467 (1992) (referring to the test set forth in Lemon v. Kurtzman, 403 U.S. 602, 29 L. Ed. 2d 745, 91 S. Ct. 2105 (1971)). The Establishment Clause guarantees at a minimum that the government may not "coerce anyone to support or participate in religion or its exercise, or otherwise act in a way which 'establishes a [state] religion or religious faith, or tends to do so.'" 112 S. Ct. at 2655 (quoting Lynch v. Donnelly, 465 U.S. 668, 678, 79 L. Ed. 2d 604, 104 S. Ct. 1355 (1984)). The Establishment Clause requires that government programs remain neutral toward religion. Rosenberger v. Rector and Visitors of the Univ. of Va., 132 L. Ed. 2d 700, 115 S. Ct. 2510, 2521-22 (1995). Furthermore, the "First Amendment forbids an official purpose to disapprove of a particular religion or of religion in general." Church of the Lukumi Babalu Aye, Inc. v. City of Hialeah, 508 U.S. 520, 124 L. Ed. 2d 472, 113 S. Ct. 2217, 2226 (1993). The government may neither encourage nor discourage religious practice. For example, the Court of Appeals has upheld a program providing military chaplains where participation was entirely voluntary and soldiers were permitted to choose whether to worship or not without fearing discipline or stigma. Katcoff v. Marsh, 755 F.2d 223, 232-33 (2d Cir. 1985).

It has long been recognized that providing chaplains in the military and in penal institutions presents a tension between the Establishment Clause and the Free Exercise Clause. School Dist. of Abington Township v. Schempp, 374 U.S. 203, 10 L. Ed. 2d 844, 83 S. Ct. 1560 (1963) ("Abington"); Theriault v. A Religious Office in the Structure of the Gov't Requiring a Religious Test as a Qualification, 895 F.2d 104, 105 (2d Cir. 1990); Monmouth County Correctional Inst'l Inmates v. Lanzaro, 834 F.2d 326, 341 (3d Cir. 1987), cert. denied, 486 U.S. 1006, 100 L. Ed. 2d 195, 108 S. Ct. 1731 (1988); Theriault v. Silber, 547 F.2d 1279, 1280 (5th Cir. 1977). In Abington, the Supreme Court noted that, although provisions for chaplains in the military or in penal institutions might contravene the Establishment Clause, they would be sustained as necessary to secure the right to worship guaranteed by the Free Exercise Clause. 374 U.S. at 296-98 (Brennan, J., concurring). In prisons, where the government has significant control over inmates' lives, "a niche has necessarily been carved into the establishment clause to require the government to afford opportunities for worship." United States v. Kahane, 396 F. Supp. 687, 698 (E.D.N.Y.), ordered modified by 527 F.2d 492 (2d Cir. 1975). Thus, in the prison context, "the establishment clause has been interpreted in the light of the affirmative demands of the free exercise clause." Kahane, 396 F. Supp. at 698.

The majority of cases dealing with the First Amendment rights of prisoners appear to be Free Exercise, not Establishment, cases. However, at least one court has held that "'the mere fact that a prison chaplain is of one particular faith' does not constitute an Establishment Clause violation." Ingram v. Ault, 50 F.3d 898, 900 (11th Cir. 1995) (quoting the decision of the district court below). See also Johnson-Bey v. Lane, 863 F.2d 1308, 1312 (7th Cir. 1988) (stating that "prisons are entitled to employ chaplains and need not employ chaplains of each and every faith to which prisoners might happen to subscribe, but may not discriminate against minority faiths except to the extent required by the exigencies of prison administration").[46]

In the instant action, plaintiffs argue that the City defendants' conduct (i) in deciding to which religions they will provide religious services and accommodations and to which they will not and (ii) in denying religious services and accommodations to followers of the NOI while allowing the same rights to inmates who adhere to other religions does not reflect a clearly secular purpose. First, I do not agree with plaintiffs' characterization of the facts. That is, I have already found that DOCS did not substantially burden

---

[46] 46 But cf. Thompson v. Commonwealth of Ky., 712 F.2d 1078 (6th Cir. 1983). In Thompson, the Court of Appeals for the Sixth Circuit noted that the question whether the state of Kentucky had "imposed the Baptist denomination of the Christian religion on the inmates at the LaGrange Reformatory by hiring only Baptist ministers and [had] thereby violated the Establishment Clause" was one which leads "into a difficult area" and explicitly declined to address it. Id. at 1080. However, Judge Jones, in his dissent, argued that "when a state prison institution allocates religious facilities in an unevenhanded manner, a threshold establishment problem is presented" and that "the mere fact that the Muslim inmates have not been denied the opportunity to practice their religion does not mean that no First Amendment violation has occurred." Id. at 1083 (Jones, J., dissenting).

plaintiff Muhammad's free exercise, and plaintiffs' blanket assertion that religious services and accommodations have been "denied" to NOI inmates is simply wrong and wholly without support in the record. Second, I find that DOC's policies do reflect a permissible purpose, i.e., providing religious accommodations to the inmates in its custody while operating within the difficult constraints of the economic and security concerns described supra.

Plaintiffs also argue that the City defendants' conduct has a primary effect that advances certain religions and inhibits the NOI religion. I disagree. First, I find that plaintiffs have not demonstrated that NOI inmates are inhibited in the practice of their religion. Second, the primary effect is to allocate DOC's limited resources equitably in order to provide spiritual guidance for all DOC inmates, not to advance any one or more religious groups.

Finally, I reject plaintiffs' argument that the City defendants' conduct entangles government excessively with religion. In order to permit inmates to freely exercise their religion, some entanglement is necessary. Kahane, 396 F. Supp. at 698. I find that DOC's activities in accommodating inmates' free exercise rights do not result in an excessive entanglement with religion. I note, for example, that as to clergy/counsel visits and literature, DOC's only inquiry is based on its security concerns. As to congregate services, DOC's only concerns are those governed by inmate numbers, security and funding -- all of which are legitimate, indeed, compelling concerns and none of which result in excessive entanglement with religion.

In sum, I find that DOC has allocated its resources among the various religious groups in an even-handed manner that does not contravene the Establishment Clause.

III. Equal Protection

In their fourth cause of action, plaintiffs allege, pursuant to 42 U.S.C. § 1983, that DOC's religious accommodation policies violate their right to equal protection. (Second Am. Compl. PP 64-65.) Prior to the enactment of RFRA, the Court of Appeals applied the Turner and O'Lone standard to equal protection claims of prisoners. The Court stated that, with respect to such claims, "the reasonableness of the prison rules and policies must be examined to determine whether distinctions made between religious groups in prison are reasonably related to legitimate penological interests." Benjamin v. Coughlin, 905 F.2d 571, 575 (2d Cir.), cert. denied, 498 U.S. 951, 112 L. Ed. 2d 335, 111 S. Ct. 372 (1990). See also Weir v. Nix, 890 F. Supp. 769, 785 (S.D. Iowa 1995) (stating that, to the extent a prisoner's equal protection claims are based on religious classification, the compelling interest governs his claims, and the reasonableness test applies to his remaining claims); Alameen v. Coughlin, 892 F. Supp. 440, 451 (E.D.N.Y. 1995) (applying reasonableness test); Campos v. Coughlin, 854 F. Supp. 194, 213 (S.D.N.Y. 1994) (declining to decide whether the Turner/O'Lone standard survives the enactment of RFRA in equal protection claims because plaintiffs were able to satisfy the less rigorous reasonableness test); Griffin v. Coughlin, 743 F. Supp. 1006, 1010-11 (N.D.N.Y. 1990). I need not determine whether the O'Lone/Turner standard applies to equal protection claims because defendants prevail regardless of whether the compelling interest standard set forth in RFRA discussed supra or the O'Lone/Turner standard applies.

As to the latter standard, as described supra, DOC's policies are reasonably related to legitimate penological interests in being able to manage effectively the large number of rapidly changing inmates in the DOC system and in maintaining security and good order. In addition, all faith groups receive generic religious services, with unlimited individual clergy/counsel visits and a flexible individual accommodation policy. I find that NOI inmates are not being treated differently from other inmates and, to the extent they might be, such differences are rationally related to legitimate penological interests.

IV. New York Law

A. State law

Plaintiffs allege in their fifth cause of action that the City defendants' religious accommodation policies violate the Constitution and laws of New York. (Second Am. Compl. PP 66-68, 71.) The New York Constitution provides in pertinent part that:

The free exercise and enjoyment of religious profession and worship, without discrimination or preference, shall forever be allowed in this state to all mankind; and no person shall be rendered incompetent to be a witness on account of his opinions on matters of religious belief; but the liberty of conscience hereby secured shall not be so construed as to excuse acts of licentiousness, or justify practices inconsistent with the peace or safety of this state.

N.Y. Const., art. 1, § 3. This free exercise right has been extended to inmates in New York correctional facilities by New York Correction Law § 610.[47]

---

[47] 47 Correction Law § 610 states in pertinent part that:

1. All persons who may have been or may hereafter be committed to or taken charge of by any of the institutions mentioned in this section, are hereby declared to be and entitled to the free exercise and enjoyment of religious profession and worship, without discrimination or preference.

2. This section shall be deemed to apply to every incorporated or unincorporated society for the reformation of its inmates, as well as houses of refuge, penitentiaries, protectories, reformatories or other correctional

Rivera v. Smith, 63 N.Y.2d 501, 483 N.Y.S.2d 187, 191-92, 472 N.E.2d 1015 (N.Y. Ct. of App. 1984). The New York Court of Appeals has held that:

The standard for assessing the validity of prison regulations that infringe on inmates' constitutional rights has been articulated by the Supreme Court as follows: "when a prison regulation impinges on inmates' constitutional rights, the regulation is valid if it is reasonably related to legitimate penological interests." . . . Similarly, a State constitutional challenge to prison regulations requires a balancing of the competing interests at stake: the importance of the right asserted and the extent of the infringement are weighed against the institutional needs and objectives being promoted. Finally, in reaching the appropriate balance of factors under either the Federal or State approach, a measure of judicial deference is to be accorded the judgment of correction officials.

Lucas v. Scully, 71 N.Y.2d 399, 526 N.Y.S.2d 927, 930, 521 N.E.2d 1070 (N.Y. Ct. of App. 1988) (quoting Turner v. Safley, 482 U.S. 78, 89, 96 L. Ed. 2d 64, 107 S. Ct. 2254 (1987)) (other citations omitted). See also Jackson v. Coughlin, 204 A.D.2d 939, 612 N.Y.S.2d 89, 90 (3d Dep't 1994); Bunny v. Coughlin, 187 A.D.2d 119, 593 N.Y.S.2d 354, 356-57 (3d Dep't 1993).

Under New York law, "freedom of exercise of religious worship is not an absolute but rather a preferred right; it 'cannot interfere with the laws which the State enacts for its preservation, safety or welfare.'" Brown v. McGinnis, 10 N.Y.2d 531, 225 N.Y.S.2d 497, 500, 180 N.E.2d 791 (N.Y. Ct. of App.

---

institutions . . . .

3. The rules and regulations established for the government of the institutions mentioned in this section shall recognize the right of the inmates to the free exercise of their religious belief, and to worship God according to the dictates of their consciences . . . in such manner as may best carry into effect the spirit and intent of this section and be consistent with the proper discipline and management of the institution; and the inmates of such institutions shall be allowed such religious services and spiritual advice and spiritual ministration from some recognized clergyman of the denomination or church which said inmates may respectively prefer or to which they may have belonged prior to their being confined in such institutions; . . . such services to be held and such advice and ministration to be given within the building or grounds, whenever possible, where the inmates are required by law to be confined, in such manner and at such hours as will be in harmony, as aforesaid, with the discipline and the rules and regulations of the institution and secure to such inmates free exercise of their religious beliefs in accordance with the provisions of this section.

N.Y. Correct. Law § 610 (McKinney 1987).

1962) (citing People ex rel. Fish v. Sandstrom, 279 N.Y. 523, 530, 18 N.E.2d 840 (1939)). That is, New York law "confers upon prison inmates the right to religious services, spiritual advice and ministration from some recognized clergyman"; however, § 610 also "expressly authorizes the reasonable curtailment of such rights if such is necessary for the 'proper discipline and management of the institution.'" Id. (citing § 610). The New York Court of Appeals more recently has stated that "notwithstanding the importance of this right, it does not prevent the imposition of reasonable restrictions by prison officials, but rather such restrictions must be weighed against the institutional needs and objectives being promoted." Rivera, 483 N.Y.S.2d at 192 (citations omitted). Prisoners do not have the free exercise rights they might outside the prison walls. Id. (stating that "the nature of a correctional facility, where confinement and order are necessary, is such that inmates cannot be afforded free exercise rights as broad as those enjoyed outside the prison setting"). Budgetary and administrative concerns may outweigh a desired religious accommodation. Bunny, 593 N.Y.S.2d at 357-58 (affirming decision that Rastafarian inmate's right to consume a particular diet was outweighed by legitimate penological interest of the Department of Corrections, i.e., budgetary and administrative concerns).

As discussed above, DOC's religious accommodation policies are based on legitimate institutional needs and objectives. The religious rights the plaintiff seeks to exercise are important; nonetheless, his rights are infringed upon, if at all, only slightly, and DOC's institutional needs and objectives are significant, as described supra. Accordingly, DOC's conduct is proper under the Constitution and laws of New York.

B. City Regulations

Plaintiffs allege that defendants' conduct violates the Rules of the City of New York. (Second Am. Compl. PP 69-71.) The New York City Board of Corrections is an independent City agency, created pursuant to Section 626 of the City Charter, whose purpose is, among other things to "establish minimum standards for the care, custody, correction, treatment, supervision, and discipline" of persons in city custody. See N.Y. City Charter § 626(e). The Board of Corrections has promulgated Minimum Standards for correctional facilities, which are codified in Title 40, Rules of the City of New York, Chapter 1.[48] These regulations have been incorporated into DOC's operating

---

[48] 48 These rules provide in pertinent part that:

§ 1-08 Religion. (a) Policy. Prisoners have an unrestricted right to hold any religious belief, and to be a member of any religious group or organization, as well as refrain from the exercise of any religious beliefs. A prisoner may change his or her religious affiliation.

procedures, in Directive 3252, "Congregate Religious Services." (Pl. Ex. 30; Tr. 746.)

The Minimum Standards require only that inmates "be permitted" to congregate for the purpose of religious activities. It does not mandate a policy

---

(b) Exercise of religious beliefs. (1) Prisoners are entitled to exercise their religious beliefs in any manner that does not constitute a clear and present danger to the safety or security of an institution.

(2) No employee or agent of the Department or of any voluntary program shall be permitted to proselytize or seek to convert any prisoner, nor shall any prisoner be compelled to exercise or dissuaded from exercising any religious belief.

(3) Equal status and protection shall be afforded all prisoners in the exercise of their religious beliefs except when such exercise is unduly disruptive of institutional routine.

(c) Congregate religious activities. (1) Consistent with the requirements of § 1-08(a), all prisoners shall be permitted to congregate for the purpose of religious worship and other religious activities.

(2) Each institution shall provide all prisoners access to an appropriate area for congregate religious worship and other religious activities. Consistent with the requirements of § 1-08(b)(1), this area shall be made available to prisoners in accordance with the practice of their religion.

(d) Religious advisors. (1) As used in this Section the term "religious advisor" shall mean a person who has received ecclesiastical endorsement from the relevant religious authority.

(2) Religious advisors shall be permitted to conduct congregate religious activities permitted pursuant to § 1-08(c). When no religious advisor is available, a member of a prisoner religious group may be permitted to conduct congregate religious activities.

* * *

(e) Celebration of religious holidays or festivals. Consistent with the requirements of § 1-08(b)(1), prisoners shall be permitted to celebrate religious holidays or festivals on an individual or congregate basis.

(f) Religious dietary laws. Prisoners are entitled to the reasonable observance of dietary laws or fasts established by their religion. Each institution shall provide prisoners with food items sufficient to meet such religious dietary laws.

(g) Religious articles. Consistent with the requirements of § 1-08(b)(1), prisoners shall be entitled to wear and to possess religious medals or other religious articles, including clothing and hats.

(Rules of the City of New York, Title 40, Ch. 1, § 1-08.)

institutionalizing congregate activities if there is no institutional demand for those activities. The evidence adduced at trial demonstrates no systematic demand for NOI congregate activities. Indeed, plaintiff Muhammad, the only plaintiff asserting claims against DOC, did not testify that he requested such institution-wide activities. When requested to provide congregate religious activities in the past, DOC has accommodated inmates, as in the case with the Buddhist inmates. This was the only group request made to the DOC Director of Ministerial Services during his tenure.

In short, the evidence at trial did not indicate that DOC has violated city regulations.

V. Qualified Immunity

Defendants Anthony Schembri, Allyn Sielaff and Catherine Abate (the "individual City defendants") are former DOC commissioners. Plaintiffs assert that each of the individual City defendants held the position of Commissioner at times relevant to the allegations made in the Second Amended Complaint. The individual City defendant assert that (i) they are not sued in their individual capacities, and thus face no personal liability and (ii) even were they sued in their individual capacities, they would be protected by the doctrine of qualified immunity.

In Harlow v. Fitzgerald, the Supreme Court described the application of summary judgment in a § 1983 action as follows:

Government officials performing discretionary functions generally are shielded from liability for civil damages insofar as their conduct does not violate clearly established statutory or constitutional rights of which a reasonable person would have known. . . . On summary judgment, the judge appropriately may determine, not only the currently applicable law, but whether that law was clearly established at the time an action occurred. If the law at that time was not clearly established, an official could not reasonably be expected to anticipate subsequent legal developments, nor could he fairly be said to "know" that the law forbade conduct not previously identified as unlawful. . . . If the law was clearly established, the immunity defense ordinarily should fail, since a reasonably competent public official should know the law governing his conduct.

457 U.S. 800, 818-19, 99 L. Ed. 2d 421, 108 S. Ct. 1220 (1982) (footnotes and citations omitted). See, e.g., Rivera v. Senkowski, 62 F.3d 80, 83 (2d Cir. 1995); Piesco v. City of New York, Dep't of Personnel, 933 F.2d 1149, 1160 (2d Cir.), cert. denied, 502 U.S. 921, 116 L. Ed. 2d 272, 112 S. Ct. 331 (1991); Kaminsky v. Rosenblum, 737 F. Supp. 1309, 1318 (S.D.N.Y. 1990).

In this case, plaintiffs primarily rely on RFRA, a statute passed in 1993, which has retroactive application. Plaintiff Muhammad, the only plaintiff asserting claims against the City, was held in City custody in the period 1989-1991. (Tr.

286.) Since the case law on RFRA only began to develop after plaintiff Muhammad's incarceration -- and since the original complaint was filed about a year prior to the passage of RFRA -- the individual defendants could not reasonably have been expected to surmise that their alleged conduct violated this new statute. This is particularly so since the legislative history specifically eschews imposing a standard that would "exacerbate the difficult and complex challenges of operating the Nation's prisons and jails in a safe manner." S. Rep. No. 103-111, 103rd Cong., 1st Sess., reprinted in 1993 U.S.S.C.A.N. 1892, 1899-90.

In Woods v. Evatt, the District Court found that prison officials were entitled to qualified immunity for acts taken prior to the passage of RFRA:

The RFRA was clearly a change in the law and was a clear and determined break from the interpretation of that law by the Supreme Court and the appellate courts. As its legislative history makes clear, the law was intended to change the standard under which claims of religious freedoms and/or discrimination were considered. 42 U.S.C. § 2000bb(b)(1) stated that the law was intended "to restore the compelling interest test" set forth in cases decided by the U.S. Supreme Court in 1963 and 1972. At the time of most of the actions taken in this case, the defendants were all acting under the former "standard" of O'Lone v. Estate of Shabazz and other related cases. Their conduct could not have violated "clearly established statutory or constitutional right" since the RFRA had not yet been passed. They would, therefore, be entitled to qualified immunity for any actions they took or decisions they made prior to the enactment of the RFRA.

876 F. Supp. 756, 771-72 (D.S.C. 1995). The Court in Woods also noted that immunity would extend only to actions taken prior to the effective date of RFRA. Id. at 772 n.18. Other courts have recognized qualified immunity as a defense to RFRA actions brought by prisoners. E.g., Werner v. McCotter, 49 F.3d 1476, 1481 (10th Cir.), cert. denied, 132 L. Ed. 2d 866, 115 S. Ct. 2625 (1995); Abordo v. Hawaii, 902 F. Supp. 1220, 1995 U.S. Dist. LEXIS 13755, *22, 1995 WL 555375 at *8-9 (D. Haw. 1995); Muslim v. Frame, 897 F. Supp. 215, 1995 U.S. Dist. LEXIS 12866, *18, 1995 WL 505072 at *6-7 (E.D. Pa. Aug. 23, 1995); Hall v. Griego, 896 F. Supp. 1043, 1995 U.S. Dist. LEXIS 11651, *14-*15, 1995 WL 476147 at *6 (D. Colo. 1995); Rust v. Clarke, 851 F. Supp. 377, 381 (D. Neb. 1994).

Moreover, even had plaintiff Muhammad been in City custody following the passage of RFRA, the individual defendants would still be entitled to qualified immunity. Up until the time of trial, the Court of Appeals for the Second Circuit had not had occasion to construe the statute, and only a handful of district court judges in the Southern and Eastern Districts had issued RFRA opinions. See Hall, 896 F. Supp. 1043, 1995 U.S. Dist. LEXIS 11651, at *14, 1995 WL 476147 at *6 (finding that defendants were entitled to qualified immunity for transfer and reclassification of a prisoner that occurred after enactment of RFRA because, at the time, there were no Supreme Court or Tenth Circuit decisions "defining the contours of prisoners' rights under the RFRA, nor was there clearly established weight of authority from other courts that could be said to have put defendants on notice regarding the wrongfulness of their conduct"). Indeed, a number of other courts had cast doubts on the constitutionality of the statute. E.g., Canedy v. Boardman, 16 F.3d 183, 186 n.2 (7th Cir 1994). Therefore, the law cannot be said to have been clearly established at the time of the incidents underlying this action, and thus the former commissioners would be protected under the doctrine of qualified immunity.

CONCLUSION
The above constitutes my findings of fact and conclusions of law pursuant to Rule 52(a) of the Federal Rules of Civil Procedure. In sum, I find that the plaintiffs have not demonstrated any violation of their constitutional and statutory rights by the City defendants. Even if such a violation occurred, the individual City defendants would be entitled to the defense of qualified immunity. Judgment shall be entered accordingly.
Dated: New York, New York
October 16, 1995
LORETTA A. PRESKA, U.S.D.J.

UNITED STATES

v.

ERIC D. HORN

CRIMINAL ACTION NO. 00-946-PWG

UNITED STATES
DISTRICT COURT
FOR THE DISTRICT OF MARYLAND

185 F. Supp. 2d 530
January 31, 2002

Paul W. Grimm, United States Magistrate Judge.

MEMORANDUM AND ORDER

At approximately 10:35 p.m. on June 28, 2000, Sergeant Eric D. Horn attempted to enter the Harford Road gate of the Army facility located at Aberdeen Proving Ground, Maryland. Officer Daniel L. Jarrell stopped Horn's vehicle for an identification check. As a result of his observations of Horn, Jarrell suspected that Horn was driving under the influence of alcohol, and he was detained and questioned. Three standard field sobriety tests ("SFSTs") were administered: the "walk and turn" test, the "one leg stand" test and the "horizontal gaze nystagmus" test.[1] As a result of his performance on these tests, Horn was charged with driving while intoxicated under Md. Code Ann., Transp. II § 21-902 (1999 Repl. Vol.),[2] as assimilated by 18 U.S.C. §§ 7,

---

[1] 1 Horn was given the opportunity to take a Breathalyzer test but refused, as he is entitled to do under Maryland law. Md. Code Ann., Cts & Jud. Proc. § 10-309 (1998 Repl. Vol. & 2001 Supp.).

[2] 2 At the time of Horn's arrest, Md. Code Ann., Transp. II § 21-902 stated in pertinent part:
(a) Driving while intoxicated or intoxicated per se. -- (1) A person may not drive or attempt to drive any vehicle while intoxicated.
(2) A person may not drive or attempt to drive any vehicle while the person is intoxicated per se.
(b) Driving while under the influence of alcohol. -- A person may not drive or

13, the Assimilative Crimes Act, a Class A misdemeanor.

Horn has filed a motion in limine to exclude the evidence of his performance on the field sobriety tests, asserting that it is inadmissible under newly revised Fed. R. Evid. 702 and the Daubert/Kumho Tire decisions.[3] The Government has filed an opposition, and Horn has filed a reply. In addition, a two day evidentiary hearing was held, pursuant to Fed. R. Evid. 104(a), on November 19 and 20, 2001, and additional testimonial and documentary evidence was received, which is discussed in detail below. At the conclusion of this hearing, the following ruling was made from the bench, the Court also announcing its intention subsequently to issue a written opinion on this case of first impression:[4]

---

attempt to drive any vehicle while under the influence of alcohol.
Effective September 30, 2001, § 21-902 was amended; a person is now charged with either (a) driving under the influence of alcohol or under the influence of alcohol per se or (b) driving while impaired by alcohol. Md. Code Ann., Transp. II § 21-902 (2001 Supp.). Subsection(a), driving under the influence, is now the most serious charge. The change in lexicon is a result partly because of the change in the level of proof, in the form of blood alcohol content results obtained from Breathalyzer tests, needed to convict under each subsection. For purposes of this opinion, this Court will continue to employ the driving while intoxicated and driving while under the influence language prevalent in most state court opinions.

[3] 3 Daubert v. Merrell Dow Pharms., Inc., 509 U.S. 579, 125 L. Ed. 2d 469, 113 S. Ct. 2786 (1993); Kumho Tire Co. v. Carmichael, 526 U.S. 137, 143 L. Ed. 2d 238, 119 S. Ct. 1167 (1999).

[4] 4 Research has not revealed any other federal case on this subject applying newly revised Rule 702 and the Daubert/Kumho Tire tests. There have been a few prior federal cases to consider the admissibility of horizontal gaze nystagmus evidence but never with the factual record of this case or a challenge to this evidence such as rendered here. See, e.g., United States v. Daras, 1998 U.S. App. LEXIS 26552, 1998 WL 726748 (4th Cir. 1998)(unpublished opinion) (court discussed in passing the SFSTs but did not analyze their admissibility as scientific or technical evidence because the evidence exclusive of the tests was sufficient to establish the defendant's guilt); United States v. Ross, CR No. 97-972M (D. Md. February 9, 2000)(unpublished memorandum order, in which Judge Connelly of this Court commented with his characteristic thoroughness and thoughtfulness on the state court decisions and narrowly held that SFST evidence is sufficient to establish probable cause to administer a breathalyzer test); United States v.

(1) The results of properly conducted SFSTs may be considered to determine whether probable cause exists to charge a driver with driving while intoxicated ("DWI") or under the influence of alcohol ("DUI");[5]

(2) The results of the SFSTs, either individually or collectively, are not admissible for the purpose of proving the specific blood alcohol content ("BAC") of a driver charged with DWI/DUI;[6]

(3) There is a well-recognized, but by no means exclusive, causal connection between the ingestion of alcohol and the detectable presence of exaggerated horizontal gaze nystagmus in a person's eyes,[7] which may be judicially noticed by the Court pursuant to Fed. R. Evid. 201, proved by expert testimony or otherwise;

(4) A police officer trained and qualified to perform SFSTs may testify with respect to his or her observations of a subject's performance of these tests, if properly administered, to include the observation of nystagmus, and these

---

Everett, 972 F. Supp. 1313 (D. Nev. 1997) (holding that "drug recognition examiner" testimony was governed by Rule 702 but not by Daubert on the basis that the testimony was not scientific in nature but utilizing the Daubert factors in analyzing the evidence).

[5] 5 Horn did not contest the Government's entitlement to rely on the results of properly conducted SFSTs for probable cause determinations related to DWI/DUI charges. To establish probable cause to arrest a suspect all that is required is reasonably trustworthy information that would support a reasonable belief that the suspect committed an offense. Beck v. Ohio, 379 U.S. 89, 91, 13 L. Ed. 2d 142, 85 S. Ct. 223 (1964). Probable cause determinations turn on practical, nontechnical determinations. Id. Thus, regardless of whether SFSTs are admissible as evidence, they may establish probable cause to arrest a motorist for DWI/DUI.

[6] 6 The Government acknowledged during the Rule 104(a) hearing that it was not seeking to admit the results of the SFSTs to prove Horn's specific BAC. Nonetheless, this opinion must discuss the admissibility of the SFSTs for this purpose to fully explain the ruling made regarding their use as circumstantial evidence of intoxication or impairment.

[7] 7 As will be discussed below, nystagmus always is present in the human eye but certain conditions, including alcohol ingestion, can cause an exaggeration of the nystagmus such that it is more readily observable. In this opinion, use of the phrase "nystagmus" or "horizontal gaze nystagmus" being "caused" by alcohol refers to the exaggeration of this natural condition and does not suggest, absent any alcohol, there would not be any nystagmus at all.

observations are admissible as circumstantial evidence that the defendant was driving while intoxicated or under the influence. In so doing, however, the officer may not use value-added descriptive language to characterize the subject's performance of the SFSTs, such as saying that the subject "failed the test" or "exhibited" a certain number of "standardized clues" during the test;

(5) If the Government introduces evidence that a defendant exhibited nystagmus when the officer performed the horizontal gaze nystagmus test, the defendant may bring out either during cross examination of the prosecution witnesses or by asking the Court to take judicial notice of the fact that there are many causes of nystagmus other than alcohol ingestion; and

(6) If otherwise admissible under Fed. R. Evid. 701, a police officer may give lay opinion testimony that a defendant was driving while intoxicated or under the influence of alcohol. In doing so, however, the officer may not bolster the lay opinion testimony by reference to any scientific, technical or specialized information learned from law enforcement or traffic safety instruction, but must confine his or her testimony to helpful firsthand observations of the defendant.

The issues addressed in this case likely will recur, given the large number of Class A and B misdemeanors prosecuted in this district under the Assimilative Crimes Act. Moreover, the admissibility of SFSTs implicates recent changes to the federal rules of evidence, as well as a large body of state cases on this topic, primarily decided under a different evidentiary standard than that governing the admissibility of the results of SFSTs in federal court.[8] Accordingly, this opinion will discuss the basis for the above rulings in more detail below.

1. Applicable Rules of Evidence

Fed. R. of Evid. 104(a) requires the Court to make preliminary determinations regarding the admissibility of evidence, the qualifications of witnesses and the existence of privileges, and Rule 104(a) now permits the Court to make definitive pretrial evidentiary rulings in limine. During Rule 104(a) hearings the rules of evidence, except those dealing with privileges, are inapplicable, permitting the Court greater latitude to consider affidavits such as those filed by Horn and the Government. Fed. Rules of Evid. 104(a), 1101(d)(1).

Whether the results of SFSTs are admissible depends first on the purpose for which they are offered. Fed. Rule of Evid. 105. Second, the SFSTS must be

---

[8] 8 See, e.g., Kay v. United States, 255 F.2d 476 (4th Cir. 1958) (The Assimilative Crimes Act "does not generally adopt state procedures . . . and federal, rather than state, rules of evidence are applicable under the Act."); U.S. v. Sauls, 981 F. Supp. 909, 915 (D. Md. 1997).

relevant and not excessively prejudicial for the purposes offered. Fed. Rules of Evid. 401, 403. Third, if the SFSTs are introduced by the testimony of a sponsoring witness who is testifying as to scientific, technical or specialized matters, the admissibility of the SFSTS is dependent on whether the witness's testimony meets the requirements of newly revised Fed. Rule of Evid. 702 and the Daubert/Kumho Tire standards. Finally, Fed. Rule of Evid. 102 emphasizes that interpretations of the rules of evidence should be made with an eye towards promptly, fairly, efficiently and inexpensively adjudicating cases.

In this case, the results of SFSTs potentially could be offered for the following purposes: (1) to establish probable cause to arrest and charge a defendant with DWI/DUI, (2) as direct evidence of the specific BAC of a defendant who performed the SFSTs or (3) as circumstantial proof that a defendant was driving while intoxicated or under the influence of alcohol. Horn has acknowledged that the tests may be used to determine probable cause, as the overwhelming majority of cases have held,[9] and the Government acknowledges that they are not admissible to prove the defendant's specific BAC, a conclusion almost universally reached by state courts, including Maryland.[10] Accordingly, the task at hand is to determine to what extent the results of SFSTs are admissible as circumstantial proof that a driver has consumed alcohol and was driving while intoxicated or under its influence. Because the results of the SFSTs invariably are introduced by the testimony of an arresting police officer, and, as will be seen, may involve application of scientific, technical or other specialized information, the requirements of Rule 702, as recently revised, are of paramount importance.

Rule 702 permits testimony in the form of an opinion or otherwise regarding scientific, technical or specialized matters from a qualified expert, provided the testimony is based on (a) sufficient facts or data, (b) is the result of methods or principles that are reliable and (c) is the result of reliable application of the methods or principles to the facts of the particular case. These three requirements, added in December 2000, are complimentary to, but not identical with, the four non-exclusive evaluative factors identified by the Supreme Court in the Daubert/Kumho Tire cases: (a) whether the opinions offered are testable; (b) whether the methods or principles used to

---

[9] 9 See, e.g., Ballard v. State, 955 P.2d 931 (Alaska Ct. App. 1998); State v. Superior Court, 149 Ariz. 269, 718 P.2d 171, 176-78 (Ariz. 1986); State v. Ito, 90 Haw. 225, 978 P.2d 191 (Haw. Ct. App. 1999); State v. Baue, 258 Neb. 968, 607 N.W.2d 191, 197 (Neb. 2000) and Appendix.

[10] 10 See cases cited infra at p. 44 and Appendix.

reach the opinions have been subject to peer review evaluation; (c) whether a known error rate can be identified with respect to the methods or principles underlying the opinion, and, finally, (d) whether the opinion rests on methodology that is generally accepted within the relevant scientific or technical community.[11]

As further will be seen, almost the entire universe of published case law regarding the admissibility of SFST evidence comes from the state courts, as would be expected, given the fact that there is no uniform federal traffic code, and DWI/DUI cases in federal court usually come about as a result of assimilating state drunk driving laws under 18 U.S.C. §§ 7 and 13. This is significant because the vast majority of the state cases that have analyzed this issue have done so under the Frye[12] standard for admitting scientific or technical evidence: whether the methods or principles have gained general acceptance within the relevant scientific or technical community.[13] While this test has continued vitality as one of the four Daubert/Kumho Tire factors, a federal court must do more in determining the admissibility of scientific, technical or specialized evidence than focus on general acceptance.

The starting point for this analysis is the SFSTs themselves, followed by a discussion of the evidence produced by the parties in this case regarding their reliability and then a consideration of the state cases that have focused on this issue.

2. The SFSTs

The three SFSTs that are the subject of this case were developed on behalf of the National Highway Traffic Safety Administration ("NHTSA") beginning in the 1970's. They are discussed in detail by a series of NHTSA publications, including:

* a student manual for DWI detection and standardized field sobriety testing;
* a June 1977 final report prepared for NHTSA by Marcelline Burns, Ph.D.[14]

---

[11] 11 Daubert, 509 U.S. at 593-94; Kumho Tire, 526 U.S. at 141.

[12] 12 Frye v. United States, 54 App. D.C. 46, 293 F. 1013 (D.C. Cir. 1923).

[13] 13 See state cases cited infra at pp. 44-45 and Appendix.

[14] 14 Dr. Burns is perhaps the most ardent advocate of the SFSTs at issue in this case, having participated in the original NHTSA studies that developed them, and thereafter as an ubiquitous--and peripatetic--prosecution expert witness testifying in favor of their accuracy and reliability in a host of state cases, over a course of many years. See cases cited infra at pp. 46-47. Despite her enthusiasm for the tests that she helped to develop, few, if any, courts have agreed with her that the SFSTs, taken alone or collectively, are

and Herbert Moskowitz, Ph.D. of the Southern California Research Institute ("SCRI") titled "Psychophysical Tests for DWI Arrests" (the "1977 Report");
* a March 1981 final report prepared for NHTSA by Dr. Burns and the SCRI titled "Development and Field Test of Psychophysical Tests for DWI Arrest" (the "1981 Final Report");
* a September 1983 NHTSA Technical Report, authored by Theodore E. Anderson, Robert M. Schweitz and Monroe B. Snyder, titled "Field Evaluation Of A Behavioral Test Battery For DWI" (the "1983 Field Evaluation");
* a November 1995 study of the SFSTs funded by NHTSA and conducted by Dr. Burns and the Pitkin County Sheriff's Office, Colorado, titled "A Colorado Validation Study of the Standardized Field Sobriety Test (SFST) Battery" (the "1995 Colorado Validation Study"); and
*an undated study, authored by Dr. Burns and a sergeant of the Pinellas County Sheriff's Office, Florida, titled "A Florida Validation Study of the Standardized Field Sobriety Test (S.F.S.T.) Battery (the "Florida Validation Study").
(Gov't. Opposition Memo. Exhs. 2-7).

These studies are very significant, as they have been cited repeatedly by the state courts in their opinions regarding the admissibility of SFSTs in connection with assessment of the reliability of the SFSTs and their general acceptance within the law enforcement and traffic safety communities. They also are important in this case because they have been the subject of critical analysis by Horn's experts, who provided detailed testimony regarding the limitations of these studies and the extent to which the SFSTs are reliable and valid tests for driver intoxication or alcohol impairment.[15]

---

sufficiently reliable to be used as direct evidence of specific BAC, as a review of the state cases listed in the Appendix to this opinion readily demonstrates. Dr. Burns has achieved, however, nearly universal success in persuading state courts that the SFSTs developed by SCRI, if properly administered, are admissible as circumstantial evidence of alcohol ingestion.

[15] 15 This underscores an important point. When analyzing the many state decisions regarding the admissibility of SFST evidence, care must be taken to focus on the factual basis supporting the rulings made. In many instances, the primary evidence that the court had before it regarding the reliability of SFSTs was Dr. Burns' testimony and the above described NHTSA, Colorado and Florida studies, as well as testimony from law enforcement officers with a vested interest in the use of the SFSTs. In most, but not all, instances, the defendant in the state cases simply did not mount a challenge to the "science" underlying the SFSTs. This is not the case here, where Horn has provided a

The three SFSTs developed by the research sponsored by NHTSA are summarized in the NHTSA student manual. (Gov't. Opposition Memo., Ex.2). The manual describes the tests and evaluations conducted to develop the SFSTs, then provides detailed instruction on how to administer and score each of the three tests.

The most "scientific" or "technical" of the three is the Horizontal Gaze Nystagmus Test ("HGN Test"). Nystagmus is "the involuntary jerking of the eyes, occurring as the eyes gaze toward the side. Also, nystagmus is a natural, normal phenomenon. Alcohol and certain other drugs do not cause this phenomenon, they merely exaggerate it or magnify it." Id. at VIII-12. Horizontal gaze nystagmus "occurs as the eyes move to the side." Id. at VIII-13. The HGN SFST requires the investigating officer to look for three "clues": (1) the inability of the suspect to follow a slowly moving stimulus smoothly with his or her eyes, (2) the presence of "distinct" nystagmus when the suspect has moved his or her eyes as far to the left or right as possible (referred to as holding the eyes at "maximum deviation") and held them in this position for approximately four seconds and (3) the presence of nystagmus before the eyes have moved 45 degrees to the left or right (which, the manual states, usually means that the subject has a BAC above 0.10). Id. at VIII-14-15. The officer is trained to look for each of the above three "clues" for each of the suspect's eyes, meaning there are six possible "clues." If the officer observes four or more clues the manual asserts that "it is likely that the suspect's BAC is above 0.10 [and] using this criterion [one] will be able to classify correctly about 77% of [one's] suspects with respect to whether they are above 0.10." Id. at VIII-17. If the results of the HGN test are offered to

---

spirited and detailed attack on the tests' reliability. This highlights an inherent limitation in the process of judicial evaluation of the reliability and validity of any scientific or technical evidence: the court must, under Rule 104(a), act as the "gatekeeper" to decide whether the evidence is reliable and admissible. The court, however, is limited in its ability to do so by the quantitative and qualitative nature of the evidence produced by the parties, whatever research the court itself may do, and any help it may derive from courts that have addressed the issue before it. This process unavoidably takes place on a continuum, and a court faced with the present task of deciding the admissibility of scientific evidence must exercise care to consider whether new developments or evidence require a reevaluation of the conclusions previously reached by courts that did not have the benefit of the more recent information. In short, neither science and technology may rest on past accomplishments--nor may the courts.

establish that the suspect's BAC is above 0.10,[16] it is readily apparent that much depends on the investigating officer properly performing the HGN test procedures and on his or her subjective evaluation of the presence of the "standardized clues." Indeed, the manual itself cautions with respect to each of the SFSTs:

[the tests are valid] only when . . . administered in the prescribed, standardized manner; and only when the standardized clues are used to assess the suspect's performance; and, only when the standardized criteria are employed to interpret that performance. If any one of the standardized field sobriety test elements is changed, the validity is compromised.

Id. at VIII-12 (emphasis in original).

The Walk and Turn ("WAT") test requires the suspect to place his feet in the heel-to-toe stance on a straight line. The subject then is instructed to place his right foot on the line ahead of the left foot, with the heel of the right foot against the toe of the left. The suspect also is told to keep his arms down at his side and to maintain this position until the officer instructs him to begin the test. Id. at VIII-18. Once told to start, the suspect is to take nine heel-to-toe steps down the line, then to turn around in a prescribed manner, and take nine heel-to-toe steps back up the line. Id. While walking, the suspect is to keep his hands at his side, watch his feet, and count his steps out loud. Id. at VIII-19. Also, the suspect is told not to stop the test until completed, once told to start. Id.
As with the HGN test, the Manual asserts that there are standardized clues, eight in all,[17] that "research . . . has demonstrated are the most likely to be

---

[16] 16 At the time of Horn's arrest, Maryland law stated that, "if at the time of [taking the breathalyzer test], a person has an alcohol concentration of at least .07 but less than .10" such results would be "prima facie evidence that the defendant was driving with alcohol in the defendant's blood." Md. Code Ann., Cts. & Jud. Proc. § 10-307 (1998 Repl. Vol.). Effective September 30, 2001, a blood alcohol concentration between 0.07 and 0.08 will be prima facie evidence that the person was driving while impaired by alcohol. If the person's BAC is .08 or higher, the defendant shall be considered under the influence of alcohol per se. Md. Code Ann., Cts. & Jud. Proc. § 10-307 (d), (g) (2001 Supp.).

[17] 17 The eight clues are the inability to keep balance while listening to instructions, starting the test before the instructions are finished, stopping to steady one's self, failure to touch heel-to-toe, stepping off the line, using arms for balance, improper turning, and taking an incorrect number of steps. Id. at

observed in someone with a BAC above 0.10." Id. at VIII-19. Further, it states "if the suspect exhibits two or more distinct clues on this test or fails to complete it, classify the suspect's BAC as above 0.10. Using this criterion, you will be able to correctly classify about 68% of your suspects." Id. at VIII-21. Once again, it is the officer's subjective evaluation of the suspect that results in the determination of whether a "clue" is present or not, and, if only two of the eight "standardized clues" are detected, NHTSA asserts that the suspect's BAC is 0.10 or more.

The third SFST is the One Leg Stand ("OLS") test. In this test the suspect is told to stand with her feet together, arms at her sides. She then is told not to start the test until told to do so. To perform the OLS test, the suspect must raise whichever leg she chooses, approximately six inches from the ground, toes pointed out. Id. at VIII-23. While holding this position, the suspect then must count out loud for thirty seconds, by saying "one-one thousand, two-one thousand," etc. Id. The NHTSA manual identifies four "standardized clues" for the OLS test[18] and instructs law enforcement officers that "if an individual shows two or more clues or fails to complete the [test] . . . there is a good chance the BAC is above 0.10. Using that criterion, [one] will correctly classify about 65% of the people [one] test[s] as to whether their BACs are above or below 0.10." Id. at VIII-24.

The NHTSA Manual advises that when the WAT and HGN tests are combined, using a decision matrix developed for NHTSA, an officer can "achieve 80% accuracy" in differentiating suspects with BACs in excess of 0.10. Id. at VIII-5. These conclusions are supported, it is claimed, by the results of research and testing done by Dr. Burns and her company that was reported in the 1981 Final Report, the 1983 Field Evaluation, the 1995 Colorado Validation Study and the Florida Validation Study.[19] Id. at Exs. 4-8. As next will be seen, Horn's experts have challenged the reliability, validity and relevance of the SFSTs to prove driver intoxication and are sharply

---

VIII-20.

[18] 18 The four clues are swaying while balancing, using arms for balance, hopping, and putting a foot down. Id. at VIII-24.

[19] 19 The Florida Validation Study is undated. During the Rule 104(a) hearing, there was testimony from Surgeon Cole, Ph.D., one of Horn's witnesses, that a third validation test had been done in San Diego, but it was not offered as an exhibit. Dr. Cole did testify, however, as to its conclusions and the defects in its design.

critical of the claims of accuracy advanced in the NHTSA publications and the so-called validation studies. They have framed these objections in terms of the factors discussed in the Daubert/Kumho Tire decisions, as amplified by this Court in Samuel v. Ford Motor Co., 96 F. Supp. 2d 491 (D. Md. 2000).

3. Horn's Challenges to the Reliability/Validity of SFST Evidence

Rule 702 prohibits expert testimony if it is not the product of reliable methods or principles that reliably have been applied to the facts of the particular case. In the context of scientific or technical testing, such as may be the case with SFSTs, reliability means the ability of a test to be duplicated, producing the same or substantially same results when successively performed under the same conditions. Daubert, 509 U.S. at 595; Samuel, 96 F. Supp. 2d at 494. Thus, for the SFSTs, if reliable, it would be expected that different officers, viewing the same suspect performing the SFSTs, would reach the same conclusion regarding the level of the suspect's impairment or intoxication. Alternatively, the same officer retesting the same suspect with the same BAC as when first tested would reach the same conclusion.

A related, though distinct concept, deals with the validity of a test. A test is valid if it has a logical nexus with the issue to be determined in a case. Daubert, 509 U.S. at 591; Samuel, 96 F. Supp. 2d at 494. In the context of SFSTs, they are valid if there is a logical nexus between what the tests measure and the true ability of a driver safely to operate a motor vehicle. Thus, for example, does the fact that a suspect missed two "cues" in the WAT test mean that the driver cannot safely drive a car, or does it simply mean that the driver has some inability to perform the test that is unrelated to his or her ability to drive? Horn has challenged both the reliability and validity of the SFSTs.

During the Rule 104(a) proceedings, Horn produced four experts, three of whom submitted affidavits, and two of whom also testified: Yale Caplan, Ph.D. (former chief toxicologist for the State of Maryland and former scientific director of the Maryland Alcohol Testing Program); Spurgeon Cole, Ph.D. (Professor of Psychology, Clemson University and author of a series of articles critical of the SFSTs); Harold P. Brull (a licensed psychologist and consultant specializing in industrial/organizational psychology, particularly the definition and measurement of human attributes in employment and related settings); and Joel Wiesen, Ph.D. (an industrial psychologist with special expertise in experimental psychology, psychometrics and statistics. Dr. Wiesen worked for more than ten years for the Massachusetts Division of Personnel Administration, developing and validating civil service examinations and is an independent consultant in the field of development and validation of human performance tests).

In his testimony and published writings, Dr. Cole was highly critical of the reliability of the SFSTs if used to prove the precise level of a suspect's alcohol intoxication or impairment. His 1994 article "Field Sobriety Tests: Are They Designed for Failure?," published in the journal Perceptual and Motor Skills, analyzed the 1977 Report, the 1981 Final Report, and the 1983 Field Evaluation report published by NHTSA regarding the SFSTs. (Def's. Memo, Ex. C.).

Dr. Cole observed the following:

(1) 47% of the subjects tested in the 1977 NHTSA laboratory study who would have been arrested by the testing officers for driving while intoxicated (BAC of 0.10 or greater) actually had BACs below 0.10;

(2) in the 1981 Final Report, 32% of the participants in the lab study were incorrectly judged by the testing officers as having BACs of 0.10 or greater; and

(3) the accepted reliability coefficient for standardized clinical tests is .85 or higher, yet the reliability coefficients for the SFSTs, as reported in the NHTSA studies, ranged from .61 to .72 for the individual tests and .77 for individuals that were tested on two different occasions while dosed to the exact same BAC. More alarmingly, inter-rater reliability rates (where different officers score each subject) ranged from .34 to .60, with an over-all rate of .57. Id. at 100.

Dr. Cole theorized that the SFSTs, particularly the WAT and OLS tests, required subjects to perform unfamiliar, unpracticed motions and noted that a very few miscues result in a conclusion that the subject failed and had a BAC in excess of 0.10. Id. His hypothesis was that individuals could be classified as intoxicated/impaired as a result of unfamiliarity with the test, rather than actual BAC. Id. He tested this hypothesis by videotaping twenty-one completely sober individuals performing either "normal-abilities tests" (such as reciting their addresses or phone numbers or walking in a normal manner) or the WAT and OLS tests. Id. at 99-102. The results of the study were that 46% of the officers that viewed the videotape of the sober individuals performing the SFSTs rated the subjects as having had too much to drink, as compared to only 15% reaching this decision after seeing the videotape of the subjects performing the normal-abilities tests. Id. at 102. Dr. Cole concluded:

[The SFSTs] must be held to the same standards the scientific community would expect of any reliable and valid test of behavior. This study brings the validity of field sobriety tests into question. If law enforcement officials and the courts wish to continue to use field sobriety tests as evidence of driving impairment, then further study needs to be conducted addressing the direct relationship of performance on these and other tests with driving. To date, research has concentrated on the relationship between test performance and BAC and officers' perception of impairment. This study indicates that these perceptions may be faulty.

Id. at 103.

During his testimony at the Rule 104(a) hearing, Dr. Cole repeated his criticism of the reliability of the 1977, 1981 and 1983 studies but also testified about the Colorado, Florida and San Diego studies performed by Dr. Burns, styled as "field validation studies." This testimony echoed Dr. Cole's written criticisms about the SFSTs' reliability as precise predictors of the level of alcohol intoxication and the SFST's validity as a measure of driver impairment in his 1994 article, co-authored with Ronald H. Nowaczyk, titled "Separating Myth from Fact: A Review of Research on the Field Sobriety Tests" and published in the Champion journal of the South Carolina Bar Association. Def's. Reply Memo, Exh. 1.

Dr. Cole's primary criticisms, as discussed in his 1994 article, include, first, that the 1981 Final Report published by NHTSA claims an 80% accuracy rate for users of the SFSTs. This is misleading because when the actual data is examined with respect to the success rate of using the SFSTs to differentiate between drivers with BACs above 0.10 and those without, the critical population, the officers had "a 50/50 chance of being correct just on the basis of guessing." Id. at 539.

Second, the SFSTs have a combined test-retest reliability rates of .77, while the scientific community "expects reliability coefficients to be in the upper .80s or .90 for a test to be scientifically reliable." Id. at 540. When different officers tested the same subjects at the same BAC dose level on different days the reliability was only .59--a 41% error rate. Dr. Cole contrasted these substandard reliability coefficients with that of the BAC machine, which is .96 or 96% reliable. Id. at 540-41.

Third, Dr. Cole argued that in order for the SFSTs to be valid predictors of BAC they must "not only identify individuals above a BAC level of 0.10 as 'failing', but also identify individuals below .10 as 'passing'." Id. at 541. The data from the NHTSA 1977 Report, however, shows that the validity of the HGN, OLS and WAT SFSTs was ".67, .48, and .55, respectively, with a combined validity coefficient of .67." Id. This means that use of the SFSTs results in an unacceptably high erroneous arrest rate, if the tests are used by the officer to make arrest decisions based on BAC levels being in excess of .10.

Fourth, Dr. Cole was particularly critical of claims that the NHTSA SFSTs have been "validated" in a "field setting." In this regard, he stated that the 1977 and 1981 NHTSA studies were done in a laboratory setting, and the difference in conditions in a controlled lab are dramatically dissimilar from field conditions that can be expected when officers employ SFSTs at all times of day and night in widely disparate weather and traffic conditions and where issues of officer safety may influence how the test is performed.[20] Id. at 542.

---

[20] 20 This criticism is especially significant in light of the third evaluative factor in Rule 702. This factor requires that the expert's opinion testimony be based

Dr. Cole stated that the NHTSA 1983 Field Evaluation purported to be a field validation study, but it failed to meet the recommendations of the authors of the NHTSA 1981 Final Report that the SFSTs be validated in the field for eighteen months in locations across the country. Id. Dr. Cole also stated that Dr. Burns herself has testified that the SFSTs adequately have not been field tested.[21] Id.

Finally, Dr. Cole disputed the claims of proponents of the SFSTs that the studies regarding them have been published in peer review journals. The 1977 and 1981 field studies were published in technical reports by NHTSA, but those reports excluded the "methods and results" sections because they were thought to be too lengthy. Id. at 543. Cole concluded "it is difficult to see how the NHTSA could claim that the FST is accepted in the scientific community, when results of studies on the validation of the FST have never appeared in a scientific peer reviewed journal, which is a basic requirement for acceptance by the scientific community." Id. Cole concluded:

Because of its widespread use, the FST battery has been assumed to be a reliable and valid predictor of driving impairment. NHTSA has done little to dispel that assumption. Law enforcement cannot be blamed for its use of the FST battery. Training documents refer to NHTSA reports and provide what appears to be supporting evidence for the validity of the FST battery. In addition, there is little doubt that individuals who have high BAC levels will have difficulty in performing the FST battery. However, what the law

---

on the use of principles/methods themselves reliable but that also reliably have been applied to the facts of the particular case. Thus, even if the SFSTs are determined to be reliable measures of driver intoxication, an officer's testimony about their use in a particular case could not be allowed absent a showing that the officer properly had administered the tests.

[21] 21 During his testimony, Dr. Cole stated that the Colorado, Florida and San Diego "validation" studies performed by Dr. Burns with various sheriff's departments do not cure the defects contained in the original reports. The three studies involved officers that made stops of drivers that were driving unsafely, and the officers evaluated them using the SFSTs, but also had the benefit of preliminary breath analysis tests, in many instances, and the studies do not permit a critical reviewer to determine whether the officer's arrest decision was based on the SFSTs alone, or on the totality of the information available to the officer, including the results of the breath test. Thus, the studies were not controlled, and there were multiple variables that affected the ultimate decision. He concluded, therefore, that these "validation" studies were scientifically unacceptable.

enforcement community and the courts fail to realize is that the FST battery may mislead the officer on the road to incorrectly judge individuals who are not impaired. The FST battery to be valid must discriminate accurately between the impaired and non-impaired driver. NHTSA's own research on that issue . . . has not been subjected to peer review by the scientific community. In addition, a careful reading of the reports themselves provides support for the inadequacy of the FST battery. The reports include low reliability estimates for the tests, false arrest rates between 32 and 46.5 percent, and a field test of the FST that was flawed because the officers in many cases had breathalyzer results at the time of the arrest. NHTSA clearly ignored the printed recommendations of its own researchers in conducting that field study.
Id. at 546. (Emphasis in original).

Horn also introduced the affidavit of Joel P. Wiesen, Ph.D. Dr. Wiesen is an industrial psychologist with special expertise in experimental psychology, psychometrics and statistics. His experience includes more than ten years working with the Commonwealth of Massachusetts developing civil service examinations and an equal number of years as an independent consultant in the area of test development and validation. In addition, he is a published author of a mechanical aptitude test used nationwide. Although he is most familiar with written tests, he does have experience in the development of human performance tests. Def's. Reply Memo, Exh.6 at 1.
Dr. Wiesen reviewed the NHTSA 1977 Report, the 1981 Final Report, the 1983 Field Evaluation, the 1995 Colorado Validation Study, the undated Florida Validation Study, and the NHTSA student manual for the SFSTs. He was highly critical of these studies, as the following summary illustrates:

[Summary omitted][22]

Dr. Wiesen concluded his evaluation of the SFST reports with the following observation:
the studies give only a general indication of the level of potential validity of the tests as described in the NHTSA manual . . . . Rather than the five studies supporting each other, they evaluate somewhat different combinations of test content and test scoring. The differences are large enough to change the validity and accuracy of the tests. The older studies are probably less germane, due to the changes in test content and scoring over time. The reports for the newer studies are grossly inadequate. Given this, and in light of the specific

---

[22] 22 The information reported in the chart is found in Def's Reply Memo, Ex.6 at 1-13.

critiques above (which are not exhaustive), I can only conclude that the field sobriety tests do not meet reasonable professional and scientific standards. Id. at 12-13.

Harold P. Brull testified on behalf of Horn and supplied an affidavit as well. Mr. Brull is a licensed psychologist with many years experience consulting in connection with the design and implementation of procedures to measure human attributes, especially in employment settings. He has designed and evaluated tests and procedures measuring human characteristics for over twenty years. Def's. Reply Memo, Exh. 5 at 2.

Mr. Brull reviewed the NHTSA 1977 Report, the 1981 Final Report, the 1983 Field Evaluation, the 1995 Colorado Validation Study, the Florida Validation Study, and the NHTSA officer training manual. Among his general observations of these materials was the opinion that there was a complete absence of evidence "which would allow one to predict a known error rate in the field," where there is no ability to control the performance of the SFSTs like there is in a laboratory setting. Def's. Reply Memo, Exh. 4 at 6. He was especially critical of the assertions in the Florida and Colorado studies regarding the reliability of the SFSTs, primarily because of their use of lower BAC thresholds (0.05 and above instead of 0.10), the fact that the population of drivers evaluated were those stopped because of unsafe driving and the complete absence of any data in the reports to enable meaningful evaluation. Id. at 6-7. He further expressed the opinion that none of the reports was published in peer review literature. While Brull was not critical of the methodology used in the 1977 and 1981 laboratory studies, he stated that the results from these studies were inconclusive, and the subsequent field tests "simply do not contain sufficient detail or rigor to support any hypothesis that field sobriety studies, as conducted by police officers in the field, are valid and reliable." Id. at 7.

Brull's evaluation of the data contained in the 1977 and 1981 reports was consistent with that of Dr. Cole and Dr. Wiesen. Regarding the 1981 Final Report, he observed that "the degree of predictive error in the field appeared to be substantially larger than in the laboratory," and that "while training clearly brought about improvement, it does not compare favorably to the laboratory condition and is [sic] a margin of error substantially higher than one would find acceptable for predicting with any degree of certainty." Id. at 11.

Brull was most critical of the Colorado and Florida "validation" studies. He noted that they "are merely summary reports, without foundation, of findings," and suffered from a "serious methodological flaw," in that the tests were done on actual motorists stopped by officers because their driving was unsafe, leading the officers automatically to suspect that they were intoxicated. Id. Use of this population likely will produce results that Brull characterized as "highly inflated." Id. He further noted that these field studies predicted 90% accuracy in identifying drivers with BAC's above 0.05, a level only one half that used in the earlier tests and below the level of legal intoxication. While the validation studies provided no data to assess the accuracy of the SFSTs in identifying drivers with BACs of 0.10 or higher, Brull suspected that the accuracy rate would be far lower than 90%. Id. at 12.

Brull's final conclusions were summarized as follows:

(1) the laboratory studies that form the foundation of the SFSTs (the 1977 and 1981 studies) were well designed;

(2) the accuracy of the SFSTs, even under laboratory conditions, is less than desired and below the level expected for tests of human performance;

(3) the field studies were not well documented, produced unknown error rates, but which, if known, likely would have been unacceptable in real world situations;[23]

(4) the error rate of SFSTs as actually performed by officers in the field is unknown;

(5) the only peer review article analyzing the SFST's was written by Dr. Cole and is highly critical of the accuracy of the SFSTs.

Id. at 14.

Finally, Horn offered the affidavit of Yale H. Caplan, Ph.D., Defs.' Motion, Ex. E. Dr. Caplan has more than thirty years experience in the field of forensic toxicology and alcohol and drug testing. He served for many years as

---

[23] 23 The concern about the reliability of SFSTs performed by officers in the field under actual stop and detain conditions is not fanciful, given the fact that the NHTSA officer training manual itself cautions that the reliability of the SFSTs depends on strict compliance with the standardized procedures. Gov't. Opposition Memo, Exh. 2 at VIII-12. Further, there is clear evidence that given the conditions under which SFSTs actually are performed in real life situations, officers often do not follow the prescribed methodology. See Def's. Reply Memo, Exh.8 at 116 ("End-position nystagmus as an indicator of ethanol intoxication," Science and Justice Journal 2001) (author studied videotapes of actual traffic stops where HGN test was administered. Over 98% of the roadside HGN tests were improperly conducted); 1981 Final Report at 18-19 (stating that officers did not necessarily follow the standardized decision criteria used with the SFSTs). The fact that officers may not perform the SFSTs properly in the field has special significance when evaluated under Rule 702, as the third factor in that rule requires the court to find that the opinion testimony is based on reliable methods or principles that reliably were applied to the facts of the particular case. Thus, if reliable methods exist, but are not used in a particular instance, the results of the misapplication of the methodology are not admissible.

the chief toxicologist for the Maryland Medical Examiner's office and now is a consultant in the field of toxicology. Id. Dr. Caplan stated that a determination that a person is impaired by alcohol consumption may be made in one of two fashions: by direct evidence of impairment derived from the chemical analysis of a breath or blood specimen; or indirectly by assessing performance indicators of the subject through field sobriety tests. Id. With respect to the latter, Dr. Caplan stated:

Although physiological assessments (e.g. standardized field sobriety tests) when coupled with the odor of alcohol on breath and alcohol's relatively high epidemiological prevalence in drivers may suggest alcohol as the causative agent, the use of drugs or the concomitant use of alcohol and drugs or other medical conditions must be considered as causes for the impairment. In fact, field sobriety tests alone were never designed for or demonstrated to be unequivocally capable of indicating alcohol impairment.

Id. He expressed the following opinions: (1) that field sobriety tests can be used to define impairment but that a specific blood/breath alcohol test is needed to confirm that the cause of the impairment is alcohol ingestion; (2) that an alcohol test of a suspect's breath or blood can alone be used to establish impairment, but field sobriety tests alone cannot establish alcohol impairment "with absolute certainty." Id.

4. The Government's Evidence

In response to the evidence submitted by Horn, the Government introduced the affidavit of Officer Jarrell, the arresting officer, describing the stop, detention and arrest of Horn and the SFSTs administered to him. The Government also introduced the 1977, 1981, and 1983 NHTSA reports, the California and Florida "validation studies," the NHTSA student manual regarding the SFSTs, and an article titled "Horizontal Gaze Nystagmus: The Science & the Law," published by the American Prosecutors Research Institute's National Traffic Law Center ("NTLC").[24] Govt's. Opposition Memo, Exhs. 1-7. Additionally, the Government introduced the affidavit of Lieutenant Colonel Jeff C. Rabin, O.D., Ph.D., a licensed optometrist on active duty in the Army, assigned as the Director of Refractive Research at the Walter Reed Army Institute for Research, Walter Reed Army Medical

---

[24] 24 The NTLC was "created in cooperation with . . . (NHTSA) and works closely with NHTSA and the National Association of Prosecutor Coordinators to develop training programs." The NTLC is a program of the American Prosecutors Research Institute, the principal function of which "is to enhance prosecution in America." Gov't. Opposition Memo, Exh. 1 at 2. The foreword to this publication was written by Dr. Marcelline Burns.

Center.[25] Id. Exh. 8. Colonel Rabin, who also testified at the Rule 104(a) hearing, has testified as an expert witness on the effects of alcohol and drugs on eye movements, given presentations to Army doctors and optometrists on this subject and reviewed the NHTSA publications regarding the HGN and other SFSTs. Id. Exhs. 8, 9. His affidavit and trial testimony confirmed the fact that alcohol ingestion can enhance the presence of nystagmus in the human eye at BAC levels as low as .04. He expressed the opinion that "there is a very good correlation between the results of the . . . [HGN] test and breath analysis for intoxication." Id. He also stated that the three "clues" that officers are taught to look for in connection with the HGN SFST "are indicative of alcohol consumption with possible intoxication." Id. Colonel Rabin expressed his belief that police officers could be trained adequately to administer the HGN test and interpret its results.

Colonel Rabin's testimony was consistent with his affidavit. He did acknowledge, however, that he acquired his knowledge of, and formed his opinions about, the SFSTs in connection with performing duties as an expert witness for Army prosecutors in two courts martial, not as a result of any independent research that he had done as an optometrist. It further was acknowledged that Colonel Rubin was not asked to analyze in any detail the reliability and validity of the NHTSA SFST studies, and he had no opinion on this subject. Further, the references to the HGN SFST that he read in peer review literature published by the American Journal of Optometry was based primarily on the NHTSA studies, rather than any independent research by that organization. He also acknowledged, in response to questions from the Court, that there are many causes of exaggerated nystagmus in the human eye that are unrelated to the ingestion of alcohol.

DISCUSSION

A. The State Case Law

State courts have wrestled with the admissibility of SFST results in drunk driving cases since 1986, when the Supreme Court of Arizona decided State v. Superior Court, 149 Ariz. 269, 718 P.2d 171 (Ariz. 1986). In that decision, based on the testimony before the trial court by Dr. Burns and three police officers, and using the Frye[26] test, the court held that the results of a HGN test were sufficiently reliable to be used to establish probable cause to arrest a

---

[25] 25 The Government also had intended to introduce the affidavit of Sergeant Thomas Woodward of the Maryland State Police but ultimately was unable to do so.

[26] 26 Frye v. United States, 54 App. D.C. 46, 293 F. 1013 (D.C. Cir. 1923).

motorist for DWI/DUI, and that it had achieved general acceptance among behavioral psychologists, highway safety experts, neurologists and law enforcement personnel. 718 P.2d at 180. The court therefore held that HGN evidence was admissible to prove driver intoxication/impairment.[27] 718 P.2d at 181.

Since the 1986 Arizona decision, a majority of the states have ruled on the admissibility of HGN and SFST evidence. A reading of these cases reveals that there are a core of decisions that have attempted to undertake a thorough review of the facts relating to admissibility of SFST evidence. Other state courts have relied more on the rulings of courts that previously had addressed the issue than on their own independent evaluation. It would unnecessarily lengthen this opinion to discuss all the state cases in detail. Thus, the Appendix attached to this opinion includes a chart that identifies the majority of state cases and briefly summarizes their holdings.[28] I will, however, discuss certain of the state cases in this opinion, as they are essential to understanding the rulings reached herein.

Maryland's appellate cases discussing the admissibility of HGN and other SFST evidence fall into the category of state court cases that have undertaken a comprehensive evaluation of the admissibility of this evidence. The principal case, Schultz v. State, 106 Md. App. 145, 664 A.2d 60 (Md. App. 1995), has

---

[27] 27 The court cautioned that it was not ruling that HGN test results were admissible to prove that a driver had a BAC in excess of 0.10 "in the absence of a laboratory chemical analysis." 718 P.2d at 181. In State v. City Court of the City of Mesa, 165 Ariz. 514, 799 P.2d 855 (Ariz. 1990), the Arizona Supreme Court clarified that in cases where no independently admissible chemical test of a driver's BAC had been performed, HGN evidence was admissible only as circumstantial evidence that the driver had consumed alcohol and not to prove a specific BAC. 799 P.2d at 860.

[28] 28 The Appendix is intended to aid future courts called upon to research the issues presented in this case. The Court gratefully acknowledges the assistance of Ms. Jennifer Warfield, Mr. Kevin Cross, Ms. Jennifer Thomas, and Mr. Rodney Butler, interns who worked tirelessly on the Appendix. If the future of the legal profession may be predicted by these law students' work, it is a bright one. It also should be noted that, in addition to appointed counsel, Horn was also represented by Mr. Ryan Potter, a law student in the University of Maryland's much respected clinical law program. Admitted to practice under Local Rule 702, and under the skillful supervision of Professor Jerry Deise, these clinical law students offer significant assistance to their clients while concomitantly gaining invaluable trial experience. Ms. Claudia Diamond, my law clerk, also was instrumental in helping to revise and edit this opinion for which I am also very thankful.

been cited repeatedly by other state courts in support of their own rulings on the admissibility of SFST evidence.

The defendant in Schultz was convicted of DUI. At the trial in the circuit court, the state's only evidence that the driver was driving under the influence of alcohol came from the arresting officer. Accordingly, the Court of Special Appeals was deprived of any evidence of record regarding the reliability of the HGN test. Its decision in Schultz was based on the court's own evaluation of other cases and the published literature regarding the HGN test from which the court took judicial notice of its reliability and general acceptance. 664 A.2d at 69-74. In doing so, the court observed that under Rule 5-702[29] of the Maryland Rules of Evidence, it was required to apply the Frye test, adopted in Maryland in Reed v. State, 283 Md. 374, 391 A.2d 364 (Md. 1978).[30] In doing so, the court used a three prong test to determine whether HGN evidence satisfied the Frye/Reed test: (1) whether the scientific theory underlying the HGN test was reliable; (2) whether the methods used in connection with the HGN test had been accepted by scientists familiar with the test and its use; and (3) whether the police officer in the case at bar properly had been trained

---

[29] 29 The Maryland rules of evidence were adopted in 1994 after the Daubert decision had been rendered by the United States Supreme Court. In the commentary to Rule 5-702, which is the state equivalent to Fed. R. Evid. 702, the drafters, however, noted that it was not their intent to adopt the Daubert test, then widely viewed as applicable only to issues regarding the admissibility of scientific evidence. Instead, the Maryland rule was intended to maintain the Frye test, which had been adopted by the state in the case of Reed v. State, 283 Md. 374, 391 A.2d 364 (Md. 1978). To this day, Maryland has declined to adopt the Daubert test. Burral v. State, 352 Md. 707, 724 A.2d 65, 80 (Md. 1999)("We have not abandoned Frye or Reed."); Clark v. State, 140 Md. App. 540, 781 A.2d 913, 935 & n.13 (Md. Ct. Spec. App. 2001); State v. Gross, 134 Md. App. 528, 760 A.2d 725, 757 (Md. App. 2000); Schultz, 664 A.2d at 64 n.3. Thus, in federal court, under the most recent version of Rule 702 and the Daubert/Kumho Tire decisions, the proponent of any expert testimony, whether scientific, technical or the product of some specialized knowledge, must undertake an analysis of reliability of the methods/principles underlying the opinion, as well as the reliability of the application of the methodology used by the expert to the particular facts of the case. Under Maryland evidence law, the Frye/Reed test applies only to introduction of scientific evidence, and Rule 5-702 alone covers all other types of expert opinion testimony.

[30] 30 Maryland cases routinely refer to the Frye test as the "Frye/Reed" test. This opinion will as well.

to administer the test and administered it properly.[31] 664 A.2d at 64. The Schultz court based its findings regarding the HGN test on the Arizona Court's decision in State v. Superior Court, the decisions of other state courts, as well as its reading of various studies and articles. 664 A.2d at 72-73. Its consideration regarding the reliability of the HGN test, however, is most significant with respect to the ruling made in this decision. Because it lacked the robust evidentiary record available to this court regarding the reliability of the HGN, OLS, WAT tests, the Court of Special Appeals was required to look at case law and published materials to determine whether the HGN test was reliable and generally accepted. The primary bases for its conclusion that it was, and that it therefore could take judicial notice of this fact, were a decision by the Texas Supreme Court in Emerson v. State, 880 S.W.2d 759 (Tex. Crim. App. 1994), a 1986 article authored by Edward B. Tenney and published in the New Hampshire Bar Journal,[32] and the NHTSA 1983 Field Evaluation. 664 A.2d at 73 and n. 12.

In Emerson, the Texas court based its conclusions regarding the reliability of the HGN test on the NHTSA studies. Emerson, 880 S.W.2d at 766-67. The Tenney article cited only the NHTSA studies regarding the scientific basis for the HGN test and reached the conclusion that "if the State of New Hampshire is still a true Frye jurisdiction, then the likelihood that results from horizontal gaze nystagmus testing will be admitted into evidence in this state is extremely thin,"[33] making it a questionable source to cite for the reliability of

---

[31] 31 As noted at pp. 7-8, in December 2000 the Federal Rules of Evidence were amended. Among the rules that were changed was Rule 702, the expert opinion rule. The amendment added three additional foundational requirements before expert testimony in any subject, whether scientific, technical or other specialized knowledge, is admissible: the opinion must be based on sufficient facts or data; it must be the product of methods and principles shown to be reliable, and the proponent must show that the methods/principles reliably had been applied to the facts of the case at hand. These factors are required by the rule itself and are independent from the factors identified by the Supreme Court in the Daubert/Kumho Tire decisions. The Maryland Rules of Evidence did not adopt the 2000 changes to the federal rules, and the Maryland expert opinion rule, Rule 5-702, does not contain the three additional foundational requirements as does Rule 702.

[32] 32 Edward B. Tenney, The Horizontal Gaze Nystagmus Test and the Admissibility of Scientific Evidence, 27 New Hampshire Bar Journal 179 (1986) (hereinafter "Tenney article").

[33] 33 Tenney article at 187.

HGN testing. Finally, the conclusions of the NHTSA 1983 Field Evaluation have been aggressively challenged by Horn's experts in this case. In short, the foundation of the Court of Special Appeals' decision that the HGN test was sufficiently reliable and generally accepted rests on taking judicial notice of studies and articles that, at the time of their publication, had not been subject to the type of critical evaluation presented in this case.

The doctrine of judicial notice is predicated upon the assumption that the source materials from which the court takes judicial notice are reliable.[34] Where, as here, that reliability has been challenged, the court cannot disregard the challenge, simply because a legion of earlier court decisions reached conclusions based on reference to the same then-unchallenged authority. For

---

[34] 34 Indeed, in this regard, the Maryland and Federal Rules of Evidence are substantially identical. Rule 5-201 and Fed. R. Evid. 201 permit the taking of judicial notice of adjudicative facts if: (a) the facts are generally known within the territorial jurisdiction of the court or (b) capable of accurate and ready determination by resort to sources whose accuracy cannot reasonably be questioned. Obviously, the scientific basis underlying HGN tests is not a matter generally known within the state; so, if judicial notice is to be taken, it must be by reference to sources whose accuracy cannot reasonably be questioned. While the sources relied on in the Schultz case may not have been subject to reasonable question at the time that court considered them, given the lack of any evidentiary facts in the record regarding the reliability of the HGN test, and the fact that judicial notice was taken on appeal-not at the trial level where the parties might have had an opportunity to develop a factual basis to challenge the propriety of judicial notice-- the same cannot be said given the record in this case. Further, Rule 201(e) and 5-201(e) permit a party to be heard on the propriety of taking judicial notice, which did not occur in the Schultz case because judicial notice was taken on appeal. As one commentator has noted "where judicial notice of an adjudicative fact is taken by an appellate court on its own motion, an issue arises as to whether the provisions of Rule 201(e) concerning an opportunity to be heard are to be applied. At the moment, the question is unresolved." Graham, Handbook of Federal Evidence § 201.07 (5th ed. 2001). In any event, Rule 201(g) provides that in criminal cases, the court must instruct the jury that "it may, but is not required to, accept as conclusive any fact judicially noted." Implicitly, the rule would permit a defendant in a criminal case to offer evidence to rebut any adjudicative fact noticed by the Court. Thus, if a Court took judicial notice of the reliability and general acceptance of the HGN test, the defendant initially could object to it doing so under Rule 201(e). Then, if unsuccessful in preventing the court from taking judicial notice, the defendant could introduce evidence contesting the fact judicially noted.

the reasons that will be explained below, on the record before me, I cannot agree that the HGN, WAT and OLS tests, singly or in combination, have been shown to be as reliable as asserted by Dr. Burns, the NHTSA publications, and the publications of the communities of law enforcement officers and state prosecutors. While I ultimately agree, in large part, with the conclusions reached by the vast majority of state courts that the results of the HGN tests are admissible as circumstantial evidence of alcohol consumption, I must do so by recognizing their limited reliability and with substantial doubts about the degree of their general acceptance within an unbiased scientific or technical community.

This is not to say that I am critical of the decisions in Schultz or the other state courts. To the contrary, they are, for the most part, well-reasoned and written, based on the information then available to the deciding courts and the inherent limitations of the process by which courts receive proof--either from evidence introduced by the parties themselves or by the taking of judicial notice from decisions of other courts or published materials. The Court of Special Appeals itself noted the danger inherent in such a process:

We note with some caution the dissent in Emerson, supra, which initially noted that, by taking judicial notice of the reliability of HGN testing and technique, the appellate court had relieved the State of its burden of establishing the reliability of the test at trial. We acknowledge that we, in taking judicial notice of the reliability of the test . . . are likewise relieving the State of that burden. We shall, nevertheless, take judicial notice that HGN testing, a scientific test, is sufficiently reliable and generally accepted in the relevant scientific community. . . . To do otherwise at this stage in the development of the science would leave to individual courts within the twenty-three jurisdictions of this State (and the various courts and judges within each jurisdiction) to determine, on a case-by-case basis, the scientific reliability of the test. In each of the various jurisdictions, the determination of the reliability and acceptability of such evidence would depend upon the competence, energy, and schedules (and even budgets) of the various prosecutors throughout the State in obtaining, and producing the attendance of experts at the thousands of trials involving alcohol related offenses in which HGN testing is sought to be admitted. Disparate results and decisions might result in many instances, not from the actual scientific reliability of the tests themselves, but from the differing abilities and resources of prosecutors and the availability of witnesses from the scientific community.
Schultz, 664 A.2d at 74.

The practical truth of the above reasoning cannot be denied. None today can doubt the serious public safety concerns related to driving by intoxicated or impaired motorists or the magnitude of this problem.[35] Neither can it be disputed that, given the volume of DWI/DUI cases, the press of other criminal cases, and the limited resources and time of prosecutors to prepare them for trial, it is highly desirable to have available a simple, inexpensive, and reliable test that can be administered by police officers on the road, which would facilitate a prompt and inexpensive trial. Indeed, Rule 102 would militate in favor of interpreting the rules of evidence in such a fashion as to accomplish this end, if fairly possible. What cannot be lost in the process, however, is the requirement that the trial be a fair one and that the sum of the evidence introduced against the defendant must be sufficiently probative to prove guilt beyond a reasonable doubt.[36] Expedient as it may be for courts to take judicial notice of scientific or technical matters to resolve the crush of DWI/DUI cases, this cannot be done in the face of legitimate challenges to the reliability and accuracy of the tests sought to be judicially noticed. As will be seen, there is a place in the prosecutor's arsenal for SFST evidence, but it must not be cloaked in an aura of false reliability, lest the fact finder, like the protagonist in the Thomas Dolby song, be "blinded by science" or "hit by technology."[37]

---

[35] 35 In FY 2000/2001, 35,962 DWI/DUI cases were filed in Maryland. Administrative Office of the Maryland Courts Judicial Information System, Maryland District Court Traffic System Citation Statistics, Report No. A70TM214, Run Date July 15, 2001.

[36] 36 In addition, if local prosecutors may lack sufficient resources to prove the reliability and general acceptance of the SFSTs, which it is their burden to do in the first instance, it can be expected, a fortiori, that individual defendants charged with DWI and DUI will have even fewer resources to challenge the science and technology underlying these tests. If, once accepted by the application of the judicial notice rule, SFSTs are ever after immune from reconsideration, even in the face of new evidence challenging their reliability, then the burden will have been shifted from the state or government to establish the admissibility of the SFSTs to the defendant to disprove their admissibility. This is a high price to pay in the interest of conserving limited prosecutorial resources.

[37] 37 "She blinded me with science!
And hit me with technology."
Thomas Dolby, "She Blinded Me With Science,"
 http://www.prebble.com/sheblinded.htm. See also State v. Ferrer, 95 Haw. 409, 23 P.3d 744, 765 n.6 (Haw. Ct. App. 2001)(quoting State v. O'Key, 321 Ore. 285, 899 P.2d 663, 672 n.6) (jurors may be "overly impressed with the aura of reliability surrounding scientific evidence").

From a review of the state court decisions regarding the admissibility of HGN evidence in particular, and SFST evidence in general, a number of observations may be made. First, most of the states that have ruled that HGN evidence is admissible have not allowed it to be used to prove specific BAC but instead only as circumstantial proof of intoxication or impairment. See, e.g., Ballard v. State, 955 P.2d 931 (Alaska Ct. App. 1998); State v. City Court of the City of Mesa, 799 P.2d 855 (Ariz. 1990); State v. Ruthardt, 680 A.2d 349 (Del. Super. Ct. 1996); State v. Garrett, 119 Idaho 878, 811 P.2d 488 (Idaho 1991); State v. Buening, 229 Ill. App. 3d 538, 592 N.E.2d 1222, 170 Ill. Dec. 542 (Ill. App. Ct. 1992); State v. Taylor, 1997 ME 81, 694 A.2d 907 (Md. 1997); Wilson v. State, 124 Md. App. 543, 723 A.2d 494 (Md. App. 1999); State v. Baue, 258 Neb. 968, 607 N.W.2d 191 (Neb. 2000); City of Fargo v. McLaughlin, 512 N.W.2d 700 (N.D. 1994); State v. Bresson, 51 Ohio St. 3d 123, 554 N.E.2d 1330 (Ohio 1990); State v. O'Key, 321 Ore. 285, 899 P.2d 663 (Or. 1995); State v. Sullivan, 310 S.C. 311, 426 S.E.2d 766 (S.C. 1993); State v. Emerson, 880 S.W.2d 759 (Tex. Crim. App. 1994).

Second, most of the states that have ruled that HGN evidence is admissible have employed the Frye standard requiring general acceptance of the test within the relevant scientific or technical community. See, e.g., Malone v. City of Silverhill, 575 So. 2d 101 (Ala. Crim. App. 1989); State v. Superior Court, 149 Ariz. 269, 718 P.2d 171 (Ariz. 1986); People v. Leahy, 8 Cal. 4th 587, 882 P.2d 321 (Cal. 1994); Williams v. State, 710 So. 2d 24 (Fla. Dist. Ct. App. 1998); Hawkins v. State, 223 Ga. App. 34, 476 S.E.2d 803 (Ga. Ct. App. 1996); Garrett, 119 Idaho 878, 811 P.2d 488 (Idaho 1991); State v. Buening, 229 Ill. App. 3d 538, 592 N.E.2d 1222, 170 Ill. Dec. 542 (Ill. Ct. App. 1992); State v. Witte, 251 Kan. 313, 836 P.2d 1110 (Kan. 1992); State v. Armstrong, 561 So. 2d 883 (La. Ct. App. 1990); Schultz, 106 Md. App. 145, 664 A.2d 60 (Md. App. 1995); People v. Berger, 217 Mich. App. 213, 551 N.W.2d 421 (Mich. Ct. App. 1991); State v. Klawitter, 518 N.W.2d 577 (Minn. 1994); State v. Baue, 258 Neb. 968, 607 N.W.2d 191 (Neb. 2000); State v. Cissne, 72 Wn. App. 677, 865 P.2d 564 (Wash. Ct. App. 1994). Some courts, however, have used other evidentiary standards. See, e.g., Connecticut v. Russo, 62 Conn. App. 129, 773 A.2d 965 (Conn. App. Ct. 2001) (remanding case to trial court to evaluate admissibility of HGN evidence under Daubert standard adopted by the Connecticut Supreme Court in 1997); State v. Ito, 90 Haw. 225, 978 P.2d 191 (Haw. Ct. App. 1999); Hulse v. State, 1998 MT 108, 961 P.2d 75, 289 Mont. 1 (Mont. 1998);[38] New Hampshire v. Duffy, 146 N.H. 648, 778

---

[38] 38 The Hulse court held that neither the Frye nor Daubert tests were applicable to admissibility of HGN evidence because those tests were restricted to admissibility of "novel" scientific evidence and HGN test was not "novel" science. 961 P.2d at 91. Instead, the court applied Montana Evidence

A.2d 415 (N.H. 2001) (using state evidence Rule 702 that requires showing of reliability before HGN evidence can be admitted; remanding to trial court to hold a hearing on the test's reliability); State v. Torres,[39] 1999 NMSC 10, 976 P.2d 20, 127 N.M. 20 (N.M. 1999) (reversing trial court's ruling that HGN evidence was admissible, remanding for hearing using Daubert test).[40]

Rule 702, which was identical to the then current version of Fed. R. Evid. 702. The court did not rule on the admissibility of HGN evidence in a DWI/DUI criminal trial, as the appeal arose from a trial court decision denying Hulse's petition to reinstate driving privileges after they were suspended because Hulse refused to take a breathalyzer, and the only legal issues presented were the existence of probable cause to arrest for DWI/DUI, and the driver's refusal to take a breath test. Id. at 91-92.

[39] 39 In Torres, the court made several significant rulings. First, it held that police officers are not qualified to testify about the scientific bases underlying the HGN test and are not competent to establish that the test is reliable. 976 P.2d at 32. It further held that it "is improper to look for scientific acceptance only from reported case law," and it declined to take judicial notice of the reliability of the HGN test because "we are not persuaded that HGN testing is 'a subject of common and general knowledge,' or a matter 'well established and authoritatively settled.'" Id. at 33. Finally, the court held that, although a qualified expert was needed to testify about the reliability of the HGN test and its results, a properly trained police officer could testify about the administration of the test "after an appropriate foundation regarding such [scientific] knowledge has been laid by another, scientific expert." Id. at 34. The care taken by the Torres court illustrates the difference in application of the Daubert test from the Frye test. Daubert requires analysis of the methodology used, its reliability and validity. Frye, on the other hand, may tempt a court faced with determining the admissibility simply to see what other courts have done in the past, as well as review publications supplied by the parties, or found by the court's own efforts, without engaging in the sometimes difficult analysis of the reliability of the science or technology underlying those sources.

[40] 40 Ito used Hawaii Evidence Rule 702, which, in addition to the requirements of the then current version of Fed. R. Evid. 702, added the provision that the court "may consider the trustworthiness and validity of the scientific technique or mode of analysis employed by the proffered expert." 978 P.2d at 200. The court held that judicial notice of the reliability of HGN evidence was not proper under Hawaii Evidence Rule 201 but that judicial notice of its reliability was proper under Hawaii common law which permits a trial court to take judicial notice of facts judicially noticed in case law from

Third, of the state cases where the courts undertook the task of evaluating the admissibility of HGN evidence, the NHTSA studies and, in many instances, the testimony of Dr. Burns, figured prominently in their conclusions that the HGN tests were admissible as evidence of intoxication or impairment. See, e.g., Ballard v. State, 955 P.2d 931 (Alaska Ct. App. 1998) (court relied on trial testimony of Dr. Burns, NHTSA training video and testimony of state trooper. Defendant called a psychology professor and neuro-ophthalmologist); State v. Superior Court, 149 Ariz. 269, 718 P.2d 171 (Ariz. 1986) (court considered trial court testimony of Dr. Burns, two police officers, NHTSA studies, and published articles on HGN test); People v. Joehnk, 35 Cal. App. 4th 1488, 42 Cal. Rptr. 2d 6 (Ca. Ct. App. 1995)(court considered trial testimony of Dr. Burns, NHTSA studies, testimony of a "criminalist" and a toxicologist. Defendant called an emergency room doctor to testify); State v. Ruthardt, 680 A.2d 349 (Del. Super. Ct. 1996) (court considered trial testimony of Dr. Burns, NHTSA studies, testimony of police officer, behavioral optometrist and neuro-ophthalmologist, defense introduced testimony of Dr. Cole, one of the defense witnesses in the pending case); Williams v. State, 710 So. 2d 24 (Fla. Ct. App. 1998) (Dr. Burns, a neurologist and three state doctors called as witnesses by the state); Hawkins v. State, 223 Ga. App. 34, 476 S.E.2d 803 (Ga. Ct. App. 1996) (court relied on NHTSA studies, other state court rulings and articles); State v. Hill, 865 S.W.2d 702 (Mo. Ct. App. 1993) (Dr. Burns only witness called at trial on HGN test); State v. O'Key, 321 Ore. 285, 899 P.2d 663 (Or. 1995)(court considered testimony of Dr. Burns, an optometrist, police officer and NHTSA studies).

Finally, those courts that did not undertake an independent evaluation of the admissibility of HGN evidence tended simply to cite to the decisions of other state courts. See, e.g., Malone v. City of Silverhill, 575 So. 2d 101 (Ala. Crim. App. 1989); Hawkins v. State, 223 Ga. App. 34, 476 S.E.2d 803 (Ga. Ct. App. 1996); State v. Garrett, 119 Idaho 878, 811 P.2d 488 (Idaho 1991); State v. Buening, 229 Ill. App. 3d 538, 592 N.E.2d 1222, 170 Ill. Dec. 542 (Ill. App. Ct. 1992); State v. Murphy, 451 N.W.2d 154 (Iowa 1990); State v. Breitung, 623 So. 2d 23 (La. Ct. App. 1993); State v. Bresson, 51 Ohio St. 3d 123, 554 N.E.2d 1330 (Ohio 1990); State v. Cissne, 72 Wn. App. 677, 865 P.2d 564 (Wash. Ct. App. 1994); State v. Zivcic, 229 Wis. 2d 119, 598 N.W.2d 565 (Wis. Ct. App. 1999).

B. Difference between Daubert/Kumho Tire/New Rule 702 and Frye.

---

other jurisdictions. Id. at 208-09. In doing so, the court relied heavily on the Maryland Schultz opinion.

The difference in approach between the Daubert/Kumho Tire/New Rule 702 and the Frye tests reveals an unmistakable irony. The Frye approach to admissibility of scientific evidence was criticized widely as being too "rigid" because it would deny admissibility to evidence that was the result of new scientific discovery that, while factually sound and methodologically reliable, had not yet gained general acceptance. Christopher Mueller & Laird Kirkpatrick, Evidence § 7.8 (4th ed. 1995); 29 Charles Alan Wright & Victor James Gold, Federal Practice and Procedure § 6266 (1997). Under the Daubert test, however, general acceptance was but one of the evaluative factors and, provided the evidence at issue was subject to being tested, did not suffer from an unacceptably high error rate and favorably had been peer reviewed, the evidence would be admitted because it was reliable. Under Daubert, therefore, it was expected that it would be easier to admit evidence that was the product of new science or technology.

In practice, however, it often seems as though the opposite has occurred-- application of Daubert/Kumho Tire analysis results in the exclusion of evidence that might otherwise have been admitted under Frye. Although this may have been an unexpected outcome, it can be explained by the difference in methodology undertaken by the trial courts when measuring proffered evidence under Daubert/Kumho Tire, as opposed to Frye. Under Daubert, the parties and the trial court are forced to reckon with the factors that really do determine whether the evidence is reliable, relevant and "fits" the case at issue. Focusing on the tests used to develop the evidence, the error rates involved, what the learned publications in the field have said when evaluating it critically, and then, finally, whether it has come be generally accepted, is a difficult task. But, if undertaken as intended, it does expose evidentiary weaknesses that otherwise would be overlooked if, following the dictates of Frye, all that is needed to admit the evidence is the testimony of one or more experts in the field that the evidence at issue derives from methods or procedures that have become generally accepted. Wright & Gold, 29 Federal Practice and Procedures § 6266 ("Daubert's focus upon multiple criteria for scientific validity compels the lower courts to abandon long existing per se rules of admissibility or inadmissibility grounded upon the Frye standard.").

Daubert's challenge is unmistakable. While courts may be skilled at research and analysis, the task of deciding the admissibility of new or difficult scientific or technical evidence involves subject matters that are highly specialized, and there is a risk that the court, forced to resolve an issue without the luxury of unlimited time to reflect on it, will get it wrong. This is especially true because judges do not determine the reliability of scientific or technical issues in the abstract but rather in the context of deciding a specific dispute.[41]

---

[41] 41 Justice Stephen Breyer, all too aware of this problem, wrote in the introduction to the Reference Manual on Scientific Evidence 4 (2d ed. 2000):

The principle shortcoming of Frye was that it excused the court from even having to try to understand the evidence at issue. 4 Jack B. Weinstein & Margaret A. Berger, Weinstein's Federal Evidence, § 702.05[1] (2d ed. 1997) (Under Frye "the court itself did not have to comprehend the science involved . . . [it] only had to assure itself that among the people involved in the field, the technique was acceptable as reliable."). Further, given the impact of the stare decisis doctrine, once a court, relying on Frye, had ruled that a doctrine or principle had attained general acceptance, it was all to easy for subsequent courts simply to follow suit. Before long, a body of case law could develop stating that a methodology had achieved general acceptance without there ever having been a contested, detailed examination of the underpinnings of that methodology. The admissibility of SFST evidence illustrates this hazard, as a review of the state cases reveals that, despite more than sixteen years of case law relating to this evidence, the number of instances where there have been factually well-developed and detailed challenges to the reliability and validity of the tests is extremely small.

Following the Kumho Tire decision and the December 2000 changes to Rule 702, a detailed analysis of the factual sufficiency and reliability of the methodology underlying expert testimony is required for all scientific, technical or specialized evidence, not just "novel scientific" evidence. This has required, at times, a reexamination of the admissibility of evidence that long has been admitted under the Frye test, which may result in exclusion of evidence that for years routinely has been admitted. See, e.g., United States v. Llera Plaza, 179 F. Supp. 2d 523, 2002 WL 32697 (E.D. Pa. 2002) (excluding aspects of evidence of latent fingerprint identification evidence on the basis of Daubert/Kumho Tire and Rule 702 analysis). As lawyers and courts become

---

Most judges lack the scientific training that might facilitate the evaluation of scientific claims or the evaluation of expert witnesses who make such claims. Judges are typically generalists, dealing with cases that can vary widely in subject matter. Our primary objective is usually process-related: seeing that a decision is reached in a timely way. And the decision of a law court typically . . . focuses on a particular event and specific individualized evidence.

See also Mueller & Kirkpatrick, Evidence § 7.8 (4th ed. 1995) ("The main difficulty [with the Daubert case] is that courts are ill equipped to make independent judgments on the validity of science. Most judges are not scientists, and they do not have the time to spend at trial or beforehand to make fully considered decisions on validity.").

fully aware of the relatively recent additional requirements of Kumho Tire and revised Rule 702, this process of reexamination can be expected to continue. It may mean, in a very real sense, that "everything old is new again" with respect to some scientific and technical evidentiary matters long considered settled. Alarmists may see this as undesirable, envisioning courtrooms populated by **mad scientists** in white lab coats and overzealous judges in black robes, busily undoing established precedent. The more probable outcome is that judges, lawyers and expert witnesses will have to learn to be comfortable refocusing their thinking about the building blocks of what truly makes evidence that is beyond the knowledge and experience of lay persons useful to them in resolving disputes. The beneficiaries of this new approach will be the jurors that have to decide increasingly complex cases. Daubert, Kumho Tire, and now Rule 702 have given us our marching orders, and it is up to the participants in the litigation process to get in step.

C. Applying Daubert/Kumho Tire and Rule 702 in this Case

Many of the state cases debate whether SFST evidence is "scientific" or "novel science," and therefore subject to Frye analysis in the first instance.[42] Under the Federal Rules of Evidence, this debate is irrelevant, as newly revised Rule 702 and the Daubert/Kumho Tire cases require the same analysis for any evidence that is to be offered under Rule 702. Thus, if the SFSTs in this case are being offered as direct evidence of intoxication or impairment, they then become cloaked in a scientific or technical aura, and the factors articulated in Daubert/Kumho Tire and Rule 702 must be evaluated by the district court under Rule 104(a) before such evidence may be admitted.[43]

With regards to the HGN test, from the testimony before me, the materials submitted for my review by counsel, my review of all of the state cases decided to date, and many of the articles cited in those cases, it cannot be disputed that there is a sufficient factual basis to support the causal connection between observable exaggerated horizontal gaze nystagmus in a suspect's eye and the ingestion of alcohol by that person. This connection is

---

[42] 42 See, e.g., Schultz v. State, 106 Md. App. 145, 664 A.2d 60 (Md. App. 1995) (discussing whether HGN and other SFSTs are "scientific evidence"); Hulse v. State, 1998 MT 108, 961 P.2d 75, 289 Mont. 1(Mont. 1998).

[43] 43If offered only as circumstantial evidence of intoxication/impairment, the HGN test still clearly invokes scientific and technical underpinnings. The WAT and OLS SFSTs, however, involve only observations of the suspect's performance, and therefore, it may be argued that they are not couched in science and technology if used for that purpose.

so well established that it is appropriate to be judicially noted under Rule 201.[44] That being said, however, it must quickly be added that there also are many other causes of nystagmus that are unrelated to alcohol consumption. The Schultz court identified thirty-eight possible causes of nystagmus,[45] and,

---

[44] 44 The existence of a causal connection between alcohol ingestion and observable horizontal gaze nystagmus is the type of discrete adjudicative fact that properly may be judicially noticed under Rule 201 because it is a fact that can be accurately and readily determined by resort to sources whose accuracy cannot reasonably be questioned. This use of judicial notice is far more narrow than attempting to take judicial notice, as did the Court of Special Appeals in Schultz, that the SFSTs have attained general acceptance within the relevant scientific or technical community. Alternatively, the government may prove the causal relationship between alcohol consumption and exaggerated nystagmus by expert testimony, but in this regard I agree with the New Mexico Supreme Court's decision in State v. Torres, which held that a police officer is unlikely to have the qualifications needed to testify under Rule 702 as to the scientific principles underlying the HGN test or as to whether there is a causal link between alcohol use and exaggerated nystagmus. 976 P.2d at 32, 34. Accordingly, asking the court to take judicial notice of this causal connection likely will be the most frequent method used by the government to prove this essential fact. An alternative would be to use learned treatises, under Rule 803(18), if a proper foundation first is established. The police officer will, of course, be qualified to testify as to the training received in how to administer the HGN test, and to demonstrate his or her qualifications properly to administer it. Because Officer Jarrell did not testify at the Rule 104(a) hearing, there is no factual basis before me at this time to permit me to make findings regarding the final factor under Rule 702, i.e., whether Jarrell properly administered and interpreted the SFSTs given to Horn.

[45] 45 The court recognized the following causes or possible causes of nystagmus: problems with the inner ear labyrinth; irrigating the ears with warm or cold water; influenza; streptococcus infection; vertigo; measles; syphilis; arteriosclerosis; Korchaff's syndrome; brain hemorrhage; epilepsy; hypertension; motion sickness; sunstroke; eye strain; eye muscle fatigue; glaucoma; changes in atmospheric pressure; consumption of excessive amounts of caffeine; excessive exposure to nicotine; aspirin; circadian rhythms; acute head trauma; chronic head trauma; some prescription drugs; tranquilizers, pain medication, and anti-convulsant medicine; barbiturates; disorders of the vestibular apparatus and brain stem; cerebellum dysfunction; heredity; diet; toxins; exposure to solvents; extreme chilling; eye muscle imbalance; lesions; continuous movement of the visual field past the eyes; and antihistamine use. 664 A.2d at 77. The fact that there are many other causes

in his testimony, Colonel Rabin agreed that most of the Schultz factors did, or possibly could, cause nystagmus in humans. Thus, the detectable presence of exaggerated HGN in a driver clearly is circumstantial, not direct, evidence of alcohol consumption.

As for the sufficiency of the facts and data underlying the assertions in the NHTSA articles that SFSTs are reliable in predicting specific BAC, the testimony of Horn's experts, as well as the literature that is critical of these studies, establishes that presently there is insufficient data to support these claims of accuracy. The early NHTSA laboratory tests were too limited to support the claims of accuracy, and the subsequent field and validation testing insufficient to establish the reliability and validity of the tests if used to establish specific BAC. Indeed, the great weight of the state authority, including that in Maryland, agrees that BAC levels may not be proved by SFST test results alone, and I adopt that holding here.

The conclusion I have reached regarding the reliability of the methods and principles underlying the SFSTs takes into account the evidence introduced by Horn about the methods used to develop these tests, and the error rates associated therewith-- the first two Daubert/Kumho Tire factors. This alone precludes their admissibility to prove specific BAC, and it therefore is not necessary to discuss in detail whether the many articles written about these tests constitute peer review analysis or something else, and whether they generally have been accepted in a relevant, unbiased scientific or technical community, the third and fourth Daubert/Kumho Tire factors. I do note, however, the testimony of Horn's experts that the NHTSA publications regarding the SFSTs do not constitute peer review publications, a conclusion that seems correct. As Dr. Cole testified, peer review as contemplated by Daubert and Kumho Tire must involve critical analysis that can expose any weaknesses in the methodology or principles underlying the conclusions being reviewed.

Further, as testified to by Horn's experts, the process of selection of articles for publication in a peer review journal involves an evaluation by one or more experts in the field, to insure that the article meets the rigors of that field.

---

of nystagmus in the human eye also is the type of adjudicative fact that may be judicially noticed under Rule 201. Thus, the defendant in a DWI/DUI case may ask the court to judicially notice this fact, once the government has proved the causal connection between alcohol ingestion and exaggerated nystagmus. Alternatively, the defendant may seek to prove the non-alcohol related causes of nystagmus by other means, such as the testimony of an expert witness, cross examination of any such witness called by the government or through a properly admitted learned treatise. (Fed. Rule of Evid. Rule 803(18)).

Under this standard, most of the publications regarding the SFST tests, including the publications in bar journals, likely do not meet this criteria.

Similarly, despite the conclusion of many state courts that the SFSTs have received general acceptance among criminologists, law enforcement personnel, highway safety experts and prosecutors I remain skeptical whether this is sufficient for purposes of Daubert and Kumho Tire. Acceptance by a relevant scientific or technical community implies that community has the expertise critically to evaluate the methods and principles that underlie the test or opinion in question. However skilled law enforcement officials, highway safety specialists, prosecutors and criminologists may be in their fields, the record before me provides scant comfort that these communities have the expertise needed to evaluate the methods and procedures underlying human performance tests such as the SFSTs. Some might say the same about judges, without fear of too much disagreement, but judges are the ones obligated to do so by Rule 104(a) when the admissibility of evidence is challenged. As to the conclusion of the state courts, more often than not expressed in passing and without analysis, that the SFSTs generally are accepted among psychologists like Dr. Burns, the evidence presented to me by the three psychologists called by Horn leads me, respectfully, to beg to differ. Thus, based on the foregoing, I conclude that the SFST evidence in this case does not, at this time, meet the requirements of Daubert/Kumho Tire and Rule 702 as to be admissible as direct evidence of intoxication or impairment.

A more difficult question, however, is whether the SFSTs may be used as circumstantial evidence of alcohol consumption and, if so, just how. The state courts overwhelmingly have concluded that the results of SFSTs are admissible as circumstantial evidence of alcohol consumption but have offered little guidance about what exactly the testifying officer may tell the fact finder about the SFSTs, their administration, and the performance of the suspect when doing them. The possibilities range from simply describing the tests--without explaining the scientific or technical bases underlying them or their claimed accuracy rates and describing only what the officer observed when they were performed, absent any opinions regarding whether the suspect "passed" or "failed" or assessment of the degree of intoxication or impairment--to a full explanation of the tests, their claimed accuracy, the number of "standardized clues" the suspect missed, and an opinion that the suspect "failed" the test--in short everything up to testimony about the specific BAC of the driver.

On the record before me there are not sufficient facts or data about the OLS and WAT SFSTs to support the conclusion that, if a suspect exhibits two out of eight possible clues on the WAT test or two out of four clues on the OLS, he has "failed" the tests. To the contrary, Horn introduced Dr. Cole's study that showed an alarmingly high error rate when police officers were asked to evaluate completely sober subjects performing the WAT and OLS.[46] Def's. Motion Exh. C. To permit a police officer to testify about each of the SFSTs in detail, their claimed accuracy rates, the number of standardized clues applicable to each, the number of clues exhibited by the suspect, and then offer an opinion about whether he or she passed or failed, stopping just short of expressing an opinion as to specific BAC, invites the risk of allowing through the back door of circumstantial   proof evidence that is not reliable enough to enter through the front door of direct proof of intoxication or impairment. Such testimony clearly is technical, if not scientific, and may not be admitted unless shown to be reliable under the standards imposed by Rule 702 and Daubert/Kumho Tire, which has not been done in this case.

There is no factual basis before me to support the NHTSA claims of accuracy for the WAT and OLS tests or to support the conclusions about the total number of standardized clues that should be looked for or that missing a stated number means the subject failed the test. There is very little before me that suggests that the WAT and OLS tests are anything more than standardized procedures police officers use to enable them to observe a suspect's coordination, balance, concentration, speech, ability to follow instructions, mood and general physical condition--all of which are visual cues that laypersons, using ordinary experience, associate with reaching opinions about whether someone has been drinking.

Indeed, in Crampton v. State, 71 Md. App. 375, 525 A.2d 1087 (Md. App. 1987) the Maryland Court of Special Appeals described field sobriety tests--other than the HGN test--administered by police to motorists as follows:

field sobriety tests are essentially personal observations of a police officer which determine a suspect's balance and ability to speak with recollection. There is nothing 'new' or perhaps even 'scientific' about the exercises that an officer requests a suspect to perform. Those sobriety tests have been approved by the National Highway Traffic Safety Administration and are simply guidelines for police officers to utilize in order to observe more precisely a suspect's coordination. It requires no particular scientific skill or training for a police officer, or any other competent person, to ascertain whether someone performing simple tasks is to a degree affected by alcohol. The field sobriety tests are designed to reveal objective information about a driver's coordination. . . . The Frye-Reed test does not apply to those field sobriety tests because the latter are essentially empirical observations, involving no controversial, new or 'scientific' technique. Their use is guided by practical experience, not theory.

---

[46] 46 See supra at pp. 17-18. Cole reported that 46% of the officers that observed videotaped subjects with BAC levels of .0% performing the WAT and OLS tests reported that the subjects had too much to drink to be driving.

525 A.2d at 1093-94. The same conclusion has been reached by many other state courts that have considered this issue. For example, in State v. Ferrer, 95 Haw. 409, 23 P.3d 744 (Haw. Ct. App. 2001), the court stated:

It is generally recognized, however, that the foundational requirements for admission of psychomotor FST evidence differ from the foundational requirements for admission of HGN evidence. Psychomotor FSTs test balance and divided attention, or the ability to perform multiple tasks simultaneously. While balancing is not necessarily a factor in driving, the lack of balance is an indicator that there may be other problems. Poor divided attention skills relate directly to a driver's exercise of judgment and ability to respond to the numerous stimuli presented during driving. The tests involving coordination (including the walk-and-turn and the one-leg-stand) are probative of the ability to drive, as they examine control over the subject's own movements. Because evidence procured by administration of psychomotor FSTs is within the common experience of the ordinary citizen, the majority of courts that have addressed the issue generally consider psychomotor FSTs to be nonscientific evidence.

23 P.3d at 760-62 (citations omitted).[47] As the Florida District Court of Appeals said in State v. Meador, 674 So. 2d 826 (Fla. App. 1996):

While the psychomotor FSTs are admissible, we agree with defendants that any attempt to attach significance to defendants' performance on these exercises is beyond that attributable to any of the other observations of a defendant's conduct at the time of the arrest could be misleading to the jury and thus tip the scales so that the danger of unfair prejudice would outweigh its probative value. The likelihood of unfair prejudice does not outweigh the probative value as long as the witness simply describe their observations. Reference to the exercises by using terms such as 'test,' 'fail' or 'points,' however, creates a potential for enhancing the significance of the observations in relationship to the ultimate determination of impairment, as such terms give these layperson observations an aura of scientific validity. Therefore, such terms should be avoided to minimize the danger that the jury will attach greater significance to the results of the field sobriety exercises than to other lay observations of impairment.

Id. at 832.

I agree with this reasoning. If offered as circumstantial evidence of alcohol intoxication or impairment, the probative value of the SFSTs derives from

---

[47] 47 The court cites to decisions from Alabama, Arizona, California, Georgia, Illinois, Maryland, Massachusetts, New York, Pennsylvania, Florida and Oregon that have reached the same conclusion about the nature of psychomotor FSTs like the WAT and OLS tests. 23 P.3d at 760-62.

their basic nature as observations of human behavior, which is not scientific, technical or specialized knowledge. To interject into this essentially descriptive process technical terminology regarding the number of "standardized clues" that should be looked for or opinions of the officer that the subject "failed" the "test," especially when such testimony cannot be shown to have resulted from reliable methodology, unfairly cloaks it with unearned credibility. Any probative value these terms may have is substantially outweighed by the danger of unfair prejudice resulting from words that imply reliability. I therefore hold that when testifying about the SFSTs a police officer must be limited to describing the procedure administered and the observations of how the defendant performed it, without resort to terms such as "test,"[48] "standardized clues," "pass" or "fail," unless the government first has established a foundation that satisfies Rule 702 and the Daubert/Kumho Tire factors regarding the reliability and validity of the scientific or technical underpinnings of the NHTSA assertions that there are a stated number of clues that support an opinion that the suspect has "failed" the test.

This is not to say that a police officer may not express an opinion as a lay witness that the defendant was intoxicated or impaired, if otherwise admissible under Rule 701. As recently amended, Rule 701 permits lay opinion testimony if: (a) rationally based upon the perception of the witness, (b) helpful to the fact finder and (c) if the opinion does not involve scientific, technical or specialized information.[49] There is near universal agreement that lay opinion testimony about whether someone was intoxicated is admissible if it meets the above criteria. See, e.g., Singletary v. Secretary of Health, 623 F.2d 217, 219 (2d Cir. 1980) ("The testimony of lay witnesses has always been admissible with regard to drunkenness."); United States v. Mastberg, 503 F.2d 465 (9th Cir. 1974); Malone v. City of Silverhill, 575 So. 2d 101 (Ala. Crim.

---

[48] 48 It would be preferable to refer to the standardized field sobriety tests as "procedures," rather than tests, as the use of the word test implies that there is an accepted method of determining whether the person performing it passed or failed, and this has not been shown in this case. I recognize, however, that the HGN, WAT and OLS procedures have been referred to as field sobriety "tests" for so many years, that it is likely that it will be impossible to stop using this terminology altogether. Occasional reference to the HGN, WAT and OLS procedures as "tests" should not alone be grounds for a mistrial in a jury case. However, repeated use of the word "test" to describe these procedures, particularly when testifying as to how the defendant actually performed them, would be improper.

[49] 49 Maryland's equivalent evidence rule, 5-701, does not contain the third requirement imposed by the federal rule.

App. 1990); State v. Lummus, 190 Ariz. 569, 950 P.2d 1190 (Ariz. App. 1997); Wrigley v. State, 248 Ga. App. 387, 546 S.E.2d 794, 798 (Ga. App. 2001) ("A police officer may give opinion testimony as to the state of sobriety of a DUI suspect and whether appellant was under the influence."); State v. Ferrer, 95 Haw. 409, 23 P.3d 744 (Hawaii Ct. App. 2001); Com. v. Bowen, 52 Mass. App. Ct. 1110, 754 N.E.2d 1083 (Ma. App. 2001); State v. Hall, 353 N.W.2d 37, 43 (S.D. 1984); Beats v. State, 2000 Tex. App. LEXIS 4542, 2000 WL 921684 (Tex. Crim. App. 2000) ("A lay witness, including a police officer, may express an opinion about a person's intoxication."). See also John W. Strong, McCormick on Evidence § 11 (5th ed. 1999) ("The so-called 'collective fact' or 'short-hand rendition rule' [permits] opinions on such subjects as. . . a person's intoxication."); Graham, Handbook of Federal Evidence § 701.1 (5th ed. 2001)(lay witness permitted to offer opinion testimony that a person was intoxicated); Mueller and Kirkpatrick, Evidence § 7.4 (4th ed. 1995) ("One common example [of the collective facts doctrine] is lay testimony that someone was intoxicated, and here the witness is not confined to descriptions of glazed eyes, problems in speech or motor coordination, changes in behavior or mood or affect, but may say directly (assuming adequate observation and common experience) that the person seemed drunk or under the influence").

In DWI/DUI cases, however, the third requirement of Rule 701, that the lay opinion is "not based on scientific, technical, or other specialized knowledge," will take on great importance. A police officer certainly may testify about his or her observations of a defendant's appearance, coordination, mood, ability to follow instructions, balance, the presence of the smell of an alcoholic beverage, as well as the presence of exaggerated HGN, and the observations of the defendant's performance of the SFSTs-- consistent with the limitations discussed above. The officer should not, however, be permitted to interject technical or specialized comments to embellish the opinion based on any special training or experience he or she has in investigating DWI/DUI cases. Just where the line should be drawn must be left to the discretion of the trial judge, but the officer's testimony under Rule 701 must not be allowed to creep from that of a layperson to that of an expert--and the line of demarcation is crossed if the opinion ceases to be based on observation and becomes one founded on scientific, specialized or technological knowledge.

CONCLUSION

To summarize, the Court holds that the following rulings apply to the case at bar:

(1) The results of properly administered WAT, OLS and HGN SFSTs may be admitted into evidence in a DWI/DUI case only as circumstantial evidence of intoxication or impairment but not as direct evidence of specific BAC. Recognizing that Officer Jarrell, the arresting police officer in this case, may

be the sponsor for this evidence, he must first establish his qualifications to administer the test. Unless qualified as an expert witness under Rule 702 to express scientific or technical opinions regarding the reliability of the methods and principles underlying the SFSTs, Officer Jarrell's foundational testimony will be limited to the instruction and training received and experience he has in administering the tests and may not include opinions about the tests' accuracy rates. If Officer Jarrell testifies about the results of the HGN test, he may testify as to his qualifications to detect exaggerated HGN, and his observations of exaggerated HGN in the Horn, but may not, absent being qualified under Rule 702 to do so, testify as to the causal nexus between alcohol consumption and exaggerated HGN. When testifying about Horn's performance of the SFSTs, Officer Jarrell may describe the SFSTs he required Horn to perform and describe Horn's performance, but Officer Jarrell may not use language such as "test," "standardized clues" or express the opinion that Horn "passed" or "failed," because the government has not shown, under Rule 702 and the Daubert/Kumho Tire decisions, that these conclusions are based on sufficient facts or data and are derived from reliable methods or principles.

(2) The government may prove the causal connection between exaggerated HGN in Horn's eyes and alcohol consumption by one of the following means: asking the court to take judicial notice of it under Rule 201; the testimony of an expert qualified under Rule 702; or through learned treatises, introduced in accordance with Rule 803(18). In response to proof of the causal connection between alcohol consumption and exaggerated HGN, Horn may prove that there are other causes of HGN than alcohol by one of the following methods: asking the court to take judicial notice of this fact under Rule 201; cross-examining any expert called by the government; by calling a defense expert witness, qualified under Rule 702, or through leaned treatises, introduced in accordance with Rule 803(18).

(3) Assuming the government can establish the elements of Rule 701, Officer Jarrell may give lay opinion testimony that Horn was intoxicated or impaired by alcohol. Such testimony must be based on Officer Jarrell's observations of Horn and may not include scientific, technical or specialized information.

Date 1-31-02
Paul W. Grimm
United States Magistrate Judge

[Appendix summary of State case holdings ommitted]

CONCLUSION

The "mad scientist" is a character taken from comic books into Federal Court opinions.

The mad scientist made superman but it becomes a villainous force and goes on to become an argument warning about supposed dangers of tinkering.

This villian character is occasionally of potential valuable - to be kept apart from the rational discourse but remembered as a sort of fictional limit on scientific possibility; a rhetorical limit used to maintain the illusion of rational order.

INDEX

"LAW OF THE HORSE PUBLICATIONS"

This book is part of a larger project tentatively titled "Law of the Horse" studying a variety of creature-character words in the U.S. Federal Courts.

COMING SOON

Mad Scientist in the Federal Courts
Ninja in the Federal Courts
Sea Monster in the Federal Courts
Vampire in the Federal Courts
Werewolf in the Federal Courts
Zombie in the Federal Courts

AND MANY MORE TO COME

ABOUT THE EDITOR

Joshua Warren is a dreamer, artist, educator, scientist, and advocate

For updates on these projects and more artwork available at
warrbo.com

www.ingramcontent.com/pod-product-compliance
Lightning Source LLC
Chambersburg PA
CBHW020721180526
45163CB00001B/60